MOUNT OLIVE COLLEGE LIBRARY

Economic Theory and Econometrics

LAWRENCE KLEIN
Economic Theory and Econometrics

Edited by
Jaime Marquez

UNIVERSITY OF PENNSYLVANIA PRESS
PHILADELPHIA

First published 1985 in the United States by the University of Pennsylvania Press.

First published 1985 in Great Britain by Basil Blackwell Limited

Copyright © 1985 by Lawrence Klein

All rights reserved. Except for the quotation of short passages for the purpose of criticism and review, no part of this publication may be reproduced, stored in a retrieval system, or transmitted, in any form or by any means, electronic, mechanical, photocopying, recording or otherwise, without the prior permission of the publisher.

Library of Congress Cataloging in Publication Data

Klein, Lawrence Robert.
  Economic theory and econometrics.

  Includes bibliographical references.
  1. Economics—Mathematical models—Addresses, essays lectures. 2. Econometrics—Addresses, essays, lectures. 3. Economics—Addresses, essays, lectures. I. Title.
  HB141.K52925 1984   330'.028   84-13142
  ISBN 0-8122-7937-9

Typeset by Bell and Bain Ltd., Glasgow
Printed in Great Britain by Bell and Bain Ltd., Glasgow

Contents

Forty years of 'rigorous observational positivism' Jaime Marquez, Federal Reserve Board	1
An autobiographical research commentary Lawrence R. Klein	5

PART I ECONOMETRIC METHODOLOGY

1	Pitfalls in the statistical determination of the investment schedule	25
2	The efficiency of estimation in econometric models	39
3	The estimation of distributed lags	54
4	Singularity in the equation systems of econometrics: some aspects of the problem of multicollinearity	68
5	On the interpretation of Theil's method of estimating economic relationships	95
6	Dynamic properties of nonlinear econometric models	103
7	Dynamic analysis of economic systems	125
8	Comments on Sargent and Sims' 'Business cycle modeling without pretending to have too much *a priori* economic theory'	150
9	Estimation of distributed lags	156

PART II ECONOMIC THEORY

10	Macroeconomics and the theory of rational behavior	179
11	Remarks on the theory of aggregation	195
12	Theories of effective demand and employment	206
13	Stock and flow analysis in economics	239
14	The use of econometric models as a guide to economic policy	246
15	A constant-utility index of the cost of living	274
16	On the interpretation of Professor Leontief's system	280
17	Some econometrics of growth: great ratios of economics	288

PART III APPLIED ECONOMETRICS

18 Some econometrics of the determination of absolute prices and wages — 317
19 Some new results in the measurement of capacity utilization — 339
20 Nonlinear estimation of aggregate production functions — 365
21 Whither econometrics? — 396
22 Notes on testing the predictive performance of econometric models — 411
23 Money in the Wharton Quarterly Model — 433
24 Money in a general equilibrium system: empirical aspects of the quantity theory — 459
25 Direct estimates of unemployment rate and capacity utilization in macroeconometric models — 468
26 The supply side — 487
27 Stochastic nonlinear models — 497

PART IV PUBLIC POLICY

28 A post mortem on transition predictions of national product — 513
29 Supply constraints in demand-oriented systems: an interpretation of the oil crisis — 541
30 Five-year experience of linking national econometric models and of forecasting international trade — 554

Index — 579

Acknowledgements

The editor and publisher gratefully acknowledge the helpful collaboration of the following journals and publishing houses:

American Economic Review
Cambridge University Press
Econometrica
Economie Appliquee
Federal Reserve Bank of Minneapolis
International Economic Review
International Journal of Mathematical Education in Science and Technology
Journal of the American Statistical Association
Journal of Money, Credit, and Banking
Journal of Political Economy
Metroeconomica
North-Holland Publishing Company
Review of Economics and Statistics
Review of Economic Studies
Quarterly Journal of Economics
Festschrift für Nationalökonomie

Forty Years of 'Rigorous Observational Positivism'

JAIME MARQUEZ
Federal Reserve Board

An econometrician wears two hats. In formulating behavioral relations, we wear a theorist's hat since we assume the parameters of the behavioral relations to be known. In estimating the parameters, we wear a statistician's hat since we take the behavioral relations as given.

This is – more or less – the way that Lawrence Klein introduced his econometrics lectures at the University of Pennsylvania in the fall of 1980, the first year I was his student. I was impressed with his work long before I met him, and I am honored to be able to assemble a (small) collection of his papers. My purpose in this brief introduction is to outline what I think has been the unifying theme of Professor Klein's academic career.[1]

As I see it, Klein's research program has addressed – over the last forty years – the following question: is it possible to develop a theory of policy stabilization which, while firmly grounded on individual's rational behavior, can be both refuted by the data and passed from one generation to another? Two key dimensions must be considered in developing such a theory. First, from a theoretical viewpoint, one needs an understanding of the functioning of the economy as a whole, and how it relates to the behavior of individual agents (domestically and abroad). Second, from a statistical viewpoint, we need to determine the existence of stable relations among the different variables of interest, the different estimation procedures, and how they can be applied. Klein knew that consideration of either economic theory or econometrics exclusively would not lead to a satisfactory theory of policy stabiliz-

---

[1] The title is not original. It is inspired by a recent article by Paul Samuelson, 'Rigorous observational positivism: Klein's envelope aggregation; thermodynamics and economic isomorphisms', (eds) F. Gerard Adams and Bert G. Hickman, *Global Econometrics: Essays in Honor of Lawrence R. Klein*, MIT Press, Cambridge: (1983). I have benefited from comments from Lawrence Klein, Paul Samuelson, and Janice Shack-Marquez. This paper represents the views of the author and should not be interpreted as reflecting the views of the Board of Governors of the Federal Reserve or other members of its staff.

ation. As an economist and statistician he was aware that a (convex) combination of the two would yield a more useful theory.

I have grouped the present collection of articles into four parts. The classification is somewhat arbitrary given Klein's combination of both econometric theory and econometrics in economic analyses.

It is hard to exaggerate the importance that Klein gives to the idea that the data must support the particular theory being advanced. Naturally, this is closely related to estimation methods and the associated statistical properties of the parameter estimates. I include in part I a few of Klein's most important contributions in econometric methodology. Klein's first paper addressed one of the oldest statistical challenges in econometrics, namely, the identification problem. Indeed, by drawing on the parallel case of demand–supply behavior, Klein finds that similar problems exist in the analysis of investment–savings behavior. A second – and frequently encountered – econometric problem is the existence of multicollinearity. Given the desirable statistical properties of system estimators, one may ask what is the effect of multicollinearity on these estimators. Klein finds that two-stage least squares are more sensitive to multicollinearity than ordinary least squares, and that both limited and full information maximum likelihood techniques are more sensitive to multicollinearity than two-stage least squares. If expectations variables are estimated using two-stage least squares, then hypothesis testing will surely be affected by the existence of multicollinearity.

More recently, econometric models have become increasingly polarized into two classes: structural models and vector autoregressive models. The first class of models is characterized by the use of economic theory in specifying the behavioral relations and accounting identities. Naturally, the specification takes the form of identifying restrictions. Some economists believe these restrictions are either too 'strong' or 'incredible', leading to the development of the second class of models.

Vector autoregressive models do not impose parameter restrictions. In other words, it is fair to say that they constitute a sophisticated version of 'measuring without theory'. Given that these models do not have any theoretical content, their usefulness lies primarily in forecasting. However, by applying the Le Chatelier principle to parameter estimation, Klein shows that the precision of parameter estimates increases as correct identifying restrictions are added to the estimation problem. Therefore, for a given degree of uncertainty in the exogenous variables, it seems clear that the model with greater parameter estimate precision (the structural model) may prove more useful in forecasting.

Part II contains a sampling of Klein's contributions to economic theory. One of his first propositions is that the design of stabilization policies is greatly improved from having forecasts of the behavior of the economy as a whole. There are many alternative approaches to forecasting: with and without economic theory, judgementally, mathematical-statistically, etc. Klein opts for the development of mathematical models of the economy as a whole, but he adds the prerequisites that the macromodels be based on individuals' rational behavior and be refutable by the data.

In explaining consumer and firm's behavior, Klein introduces the linear expenditure system and reinterprets Leontieff's input–output system in a way more suitable for practical applications. These two contributions have not only stimulated substantial research, but have also laid the foundations of both the Keynesian system and the development of the supply side of modern econometric models. Once a useful representation of individuals' rational behavior is obtained, the next question is how to aggregate the micro relations to obtain a macromodel. I will venture to say that the aggregation procedure developed by Klein is one of his greatest contributions. His approach – denoted recently by Samuelson as Envelope Aggregation – consists of taking the existing macro and micro theories as given and then measuring the economic variables in a way that aims to insure consistency between both sets of theories. Other aggregation procedures start with the micro theory and then, by applying an aggregation rule, a particular macro theory is derived. The distinguishing feature of Klein's approach to aggregation is that the measuring of variables is what is endogenous rather than theory itself.

In his contributions to economic theory, Klein also anticipated some of today's criticisms of econometric models, most notably parameter instability and supply-side considerations. Indeed, as early as 1943, Klein addressed the possibility of an unstable marginal propensity to consume as a result of changes from wartime to peacetime and of the inception of the Social Security System. With respect to the existence of supply-side considerations, it is somewhat disappointing that, after more than 30 years, the Keynesian models are thought of as having no supply elements. Indeed, the aggregate production function was *explicitly* included in Klein's system of equations representing the Keynesian model. This single aggregate production function was later replaced with an input–output system fully interacting with the rest of the model.

We wear two hats in part III, where I include papers in which economic theory and econometrics are combined in analyzing economic questions. The existence and regularity of business cycles is closely related to stabilization policies and it is one of the questions that has certainly received Klein's attention. In studying this issue, he analyzes several interrelated aspects including wage and price determination, measurement of capacity utilization, and estimation of production functions, which are different components of an economy wide model. The interesting question is whether the dynamic adjustments embodied in the estimated macromodel are capable of reproducing the observed business cycles. The dynamic process of most linear models are characterized by damped oscillations, which can be kept alive only by random shocks. There are dynamic linear models without damped oscillations, but they are characterized by endogenous variables with unbounded variances. Given that dynamic responses are crucial to the design of stabilization policies, Klein has devoted a significant amount of research to the development of nonlinear models embodying dynamic responses capable of reproducing the business cycle without having the infinite variance property.

This collection would be incomplete if we were to exclude Klein's use of econometric models as a guide to policy-making. His interest in stabilization policies started very early in his career, as it is clearly reflected in the analysis of the anticipated effects of the demobilization following the end of World War II. More recently, Klein has applied the world model developed in Project LINK to the analysis of alternative policy responses to the commodity price shocks of the seventies, the effects and the determinants of exchange rate fluctuations, the potential gains from international policy coordination, and the dimensions of the international debt problem.

After a number of years experimenting with econometric models, it seems clear now that their usefulness lies not only in the generation of forecasts for policy analysis but also as a vehicle to make explicit the assumptions about the behavior of the economy, to insure internal consistency through the use of identities and constraints, and finally as a way of accumulating knowledge. It is hard to exaggerate the importance of the role played by Professor Klein in developing a scientific approach to the understanding of economics.

So far I have described what I think are Professor Klein's main contributions as an economist, and I want to conclude with a word about him as a person. Nearly everybody who knows him is impressed by his humbleness and kindness. What has impressed me the most is his boundless energy to work, never abandoning unsolved problems. I have learned much from him, but the most important lesson is that the pursuit of excellence is an objective in itself.

An Autobiographical Research Commentary

LAWRENCE R. KLEIN

Jaime Marquez' assembling of selected papers gives me an opportunity and stimulus for looking back on some 40 years of research to see how it came about, where it led me, and where it is going in this final leg. On the occasion of the publication of the annual volume *Les Prix Nobel*, each laureate is asked to write an autobiographical sketch of his or her professional career. We do this in varying degrees of detail and style. For my own part, I noted various landmarks in my own tour over the topography of econometrics, but only cited each stage or major event. Now, with more pages and leisure, I shall try to explain some of the details associated with each landmark in relation to the evolution of my own bibliography. I shall try to explain why I did what I did and leave it to Jaime Marquez as an objective observer to appraise the entire effort.

ECONOMETRIC METHOD

My graduate teacher, Paul Samuelson, was not the first person to make a significant impression on my intellectual and professional development, but he undoubtedly made the biggest and deepest impression. When I arrived at MIT, I was (luckily for me) assigned as a research assistant to him. Paul Samuelson promptly put me to work on a problem that derived from a provocative article by Mordecai Ezekiel, whose book on *Methods of Correlation Analysis* I had just been using during my undergraduate days at Berkeley.[1] I was not given this research assignment in order to assist Paul Samuelson in his own program; I was assigned a problem as a challenge, to resolve for my own benefit, and as an extra curricular test of research ability.

Paul Samuelson had the clever idea that the problem of estimating the Keynesian macromodel for savings and investment, as functions of aggregate income was the same problem from the point of view of econometric analysis as the time-honored problem of estimating the market model for supply and demand, as functions of price. Early discussion of the problem of identification centered around the question

---

[1] 'Pitfalls in the statistical determination of the investment schedule,' *Econometrica*, **11**, July–October (1943), 246–58.

of the possibility of estimating the supply and demand functions of a given commodity when they both depend on price. Paul Samuelson saw immediately that this was the same problem for the estimation of savings and investment functions, and its resolution depended on the criteria for identification. The understanding of the identification problem had been advanced by such researchers as Working, Marschak, Leontief, Frisch, Staehle, and others. Entirely new ideas were being introduced by Haavelmo and Wald just prior to my first encounter with my graduate teacher, who saw great promise in their approach. He introduced me to this literature through the set up of the problem:

$$S_t = S(Y_t) + e_t \tag{1}$$

$$I_t = I(Y_t) + u_t \tag{2}$$

$$S_t = I_t \tag{3}$$

where

S = savings

I = investment

Y = income

e, u = random errors.

It is evident that this is the same econometric problem as:

$$S_t = S(P_t) + e_t \tag{4}$$

$$D_t = D(P_t) + u_t \tag{5}$$

$$S_t = D_t \tag{6}$$

where

S = supply

D = demand

P = price

e, u = random errors.

Through the use of lags, exogenous variables and specific equation restrictions, the supply-demand model can be identified and estimated. Mordecai Ezekiel specified the savings-investment model mainly by disaggregation into types of savings-investment flows, and it was Samuelson's hunch that he had not done enough to achieve identification; this was the issue that I set out to investigate.

Later, developments at the Cowles Commission for Research in Economics (University of Chicago) by Haavelmo, Wald, Marschak, Koopmans, Anderson, Hurwicz, Rubin, and others clarified and extended the concepts of identification, especially in linear systems. The earlier work based on supply-demand analysis remained apart, as a separate and revealing way to approach the whole subject. I was able to use the supply-demand approach to good advantage in my *Introduction to Econometrics* and was helped a great deal by discussions along these lines with Marschak at the Cowles Commission during the late 1940s.

At the Cowles Commission, attention was paid to various single equation estimators that had consistency properties in simultaneous equation systems. Instrumental variable estimators, and limited information maximum likelihood estimators were much discussed. In fact, the instrumental variable interpretation of various estimators was developed in many special cases. At the same time Henri Theil had developed his two-stage least squares and k-class estimators as an alternative group of single equation estimators. A discussion paper was distributed to staff members and associates of the Cowles Commission on the occasion of a visit by Theil in the mid 1950s when I was at Oxford.

I was fascinated by Theil's TSLS approach but found it difficult to give it a clear interpretation. I set to work on the problem and found that it was easily interpreted as an instrumental variable estimator, in which the least-squares regression values of endogenous variables, determined from reduced forms, served as instruments.

In the equation to be estimated

$$Y_t = \sum_{i=1}^{n} \alpha_i Y_{it} + \sum_{i=1}^{m} \beta_i X_{it} + e_t \tag{7}$$

reduced form regression values

$$Y_{it} = \sum_{j=1}^{k} \hat{\Pi}_{ij} X_{jt} \tag{8}$$

where

$i = 1, 2, \ldots, n$

are used together with X_{it} ($i = 1, 2, \ldots, m$) for estimation of (7).

Y_t and Y_{it} are endogenous variables in (7).
X_{it} are exogenous variables in (7).
e_t are random errors.
$\hat{\Pi}_{ij}$ are least squares estimates of reduced form coefficients.

In discussions with Hans Theil at an international conference, I asked him whether he was aware of the instrumental variable interpretation of TSLS, and he indicated that he was not. I later sent him a draft of my paper on this matter to confirm this view and then published the results in *Metroeconomica*.[2]

Soon after I worked out the instrumental variable interpretation of TSLS, I took up another issue that had intrigued me during my days at the Cowles Commission, namely, a formal interpretation of the way that *a priori* information helps to improve econometric estimation. The intuitive idea is sound; the more that relevant information is used, the better are estimates that make use of it. In looking for a formal explanation for this intuitively appealing concept I came upon the idea of using Samuelson's principle of Le Chatelier. He first introduced me to this principle in studying the economic effects of rationing, when I was a student at MIT during World War II. Samuelson showed that the equilibrium values of the diagonal elements of a certain matrix of bordered second-order derivatives of a consumer's utility function become smaller and smaller as more restrictions are placed on the maximization of the utility function. In rationing theory, each restriction corresponds to a form or phase of rationing. These diagonal elements are terms in an expression for own-price elasticity. He showed in effect that price sensitivity (elasticity) is reduced as additional restrictions are imposed. This takes the form of additional bordering, one border row and column for each restriction.

I noted that there was an analogy between the matrices of second-order derivatives in utility theory and in maximum likelihood theory for econometric estimation. The elements of the inverse matrix of second derivatives of the likelihood function determine the sampling variance of estimators. As these elements get larger (reciprocals get smaller) under the imposition of successive constraints, estimates become more efficient, in a statistical sense. Additional restrictions on specification of an econometric model lead to more bordering of the corresponding matrix of second derivatives of the likelihood functions. As *a priori* information is added, the bordering increases and the estimation-efficiency measures improve.[3]

Of all the developments in statistical methods that lead to improvements in econometric estimation and application, none is more import-

---

[2] 'On the interpretation of Theil's method of estimating economic relationships,' *Metroeconomica*, VII, December (1955), 147–53.

[3] 'The efficiency of estimation in econometric models,' in *Essays in Economics and Econometrics* (ed. R. W. Pfouts) University of North Carolina Press, Chapel Hill (1960), pp. 216–32.

ant than the estimation of lags. At the time that new developments were being introduced at the Cowles Commission for the treatment of simultaneous equations in econometric systems, we introduced time lags in our models but did not make unusual progress in their statistical handling.

Having been given the assignment of reviewing L. M. Koyck's book on distributed lags and investment behavior I became independently interested in the problem. In the Cowles Commission models that I built in the 1940s, I frequently used a lagged dependent variable in single equations. After having reviewed Koyck's book, I saw more clearly the relationship between equations with geometric lag distributions and lagged dependent variables.

$$Y_t = \alpha \sum_{i=0}^{\infty} \lambda^i X_{t-i} + e_t \qquad (9)$$

$$Y_t = \alpha X_t + \lambda Y_{t-1} + e_t - \lambda e_{t-1} \qquad (10)$$

One of Koyck's major contributions was to show how the error structures in (9) and (10) are related. He developed consistent estimates for (10) when e_t is serially uncorrelated. This prompted me to investigate the problem of obtaining maximum likelihood estimates for α and λ.[4] When I visited the Cowles Foundation (formerly the Cowles Commission at Chicago) at Yale in summer 1957, I profited greatly in discussions with Roy Radner in understanding and working out a solution to this problem. This was done before the large-scale introduction of the computer for the calculation of econometric estimates. In later work with Phoebus Dhrymes at Pennsylvania it became evident how computer search techniques could be efficiently adapted to the implementation of maximum likelihood estimation for this kind of lag.

In connection with a series of (visiting) lectures that I gave at Princeton in 1966, one of my students, J. L. Morrison, prepared a research paper on the treatment of distributed lags in the engineering literature, as a direct analog of distributed lag formulation in econometrics. His interest brought together K. Steiglitz of the Department of Electrical Engineering, Princeton, with Phoebus Dhrymes and me at Pennsylvania.[5] In a joint paper we worked out generalized procedures for estimating lags in the equation.

$$\sum_{i=1}^{n} \alpha_i(L) Y_{it} + \sum_{i=1}^{m} \beta_i(L) X_{it} = e_t \qquad (11)$$

[4] 'The estimation of distribution lags,' *Econometrica* **26**, October (1958), 553–65.
[5] 'Estimation of distributed lags,' *International Economic Review*, XI, June (1970), 235–50.

where $\alpha_i(L)$ and $\beta_i(L)$ are polynominals in the lag displacement operator $L^i z_t = z_{t-i}$. A principal econometric problem that we were trying to handle at that time was the problem of estimating different distributed lags separately for the individual variables in a multivariate relationship. This is an expression that frequently arises in econometric specifications. It is routinely handled today, given enormous advances in computer technology, but it was a formidable problem before the late 1970s.

Lag distributions were originally introduced in econometric systems because multicollinearity would be likely to stand in the way of econometric estimation of fairly general lag specifications for one or more variables in economic models. Other multivariate specifications of economic systems are also plagued by the presence of multicollinearity. It is one of the most difficult and frequent problems confronting econometricians. A major attack on the problem was made by Ragnar Frisch. He contributed much to the understanding of the problems involved, but his suggested statistical treatment did not find its way into the established tool kits of econometricians. The highly interrelated nature of variables used in simultaneous equation systems of economics came up against multicollinearity in many ways. This prompted me, together with Mitsugu Nakamura, a visiting research scholar at Pennsylvania, to investigate the way in which multicollinearity, or more generally singularity, enters the equation systems of economic models, especially from the point of view of estimation.[6] We were able to show how the presence of multicollinearity is associated with different estimation methods – usually the more interdependent the method of estimation, the more serious is the problem of multicollinearity.

The dynamic structure of econometric systems is of obvious importance for estimation of the time shape of response. But, having estimates of the parameters that determine the time shape of response, how do we use it in the analysis of properties of econometric systems? Ever since Irma and Frank Adelman studied the cyclical properties of a dynamic macromodel under the influence of stochastic disturbance, that subject has fascinated me. Building on the theoretical insights of Slutsky, Yule and Frisch, I have been interested in trying to explain and isolate the stochastic component of the business cycle. E. Philip Howrey expressed the solution of the linear dynamic stochastic model in closed mathematical form and investigated the cyclical properties by means of spectral analysis. Howrey and I extended some of his results

---

[6]'Singularity in the equation systems of econometrics: Some aspects of the problem of multicollinearity,' *International Economic Review*, **3**, September (1962), 274–99.

to nonlinear systems by means of simulation analysis.[7] This provided empirical insight, but I was long interested in a theoretical explanation of Irma Adelman's stochastic cycles, and M. Ostuki, a visiting scholar at Pennsylvania, finally provided me with a limit theorem showing why solutions to econometric systems tend to exhibit the kinds of cycles that Slutsky generated, by iterating moving averages of random numbers. Ostuki also showed how analysis of fluctuations in the time domain could be used to measure business cycles.[8]

ECONOMIC THEORY

A feature of macromodel building at the Cowles Commission was the association of statistics with economics. The specification and application of economic models had to be firmly grounded in received (or newly developed) economic analysis. It was indelibly impressed on me, in my first professional position, right out of graduate school, that this was the proper way to proceed. A great deal of economic structure has always been built into the models that I have built and used. The most frequent and important application of econometric models has proved to be alternative simulation analysis to study policies, scenarios, and multiplier responses. It is important, in this respect, for econometricians to work with structural models so that they will know where to introduce changes, in creating the alternative simulations. This approach is epitomized in Tjalling Koopmans' provocative review of Arthur Burns' and Wesley Mitchell's book on *Measuring Business Cycles*. He contrasted the approach of the Cowles Commission with that of the National Bureau of Economic Research by means of the title of his review *Measurement Without Theory*. That is precisely the way that I looked upon the attempt of Thomas Sargent and Christopher Sims to build time series models of macroeconomic fluctuations with little or no theory. I found it useful to appraise their work in the light of Koopmans' contrast between pure empirical statistical research and empirical research that is closely guided by economic theory.[9]

---

[7] 'Dynamic properties of nonlinear econometric models,' *International Economic Review*, **13,** October (1972), 599–618.

[8] 'Dynamic analysis of economic systems,' *International Journal of Mathematical Education in Science and Technology*, **4,** July–September (1973), 341–59.

[9] 'Comments on Sargent and Sims' "Business cycle modeling without pretending to have too much *a priori* economic theory",' *New Methods in Business Cycle Research, Proceedings from a Conference* (ed. C. A. Sims), Federal Reserve Bank of Minneapolis, Minneapolis (1977), pp. 203–8.

In many cases, economic theory was being developed for the specification of econometric models and in other cases, in its own right. Of course, the two streams of thought are intertwined. The Cowles Commission environment generated a great deal of theoretical analysis, much of it related to macroeconomics. But we realized that in the final analysis economic decision-making occurs at the micro level, in the firm and in the household.

Jacob Marschak always pushed me into justifying my macroeconomic relationships and models from fundamental behavior. We had extensive discussions about the aggregation problem – how to move from micro- to macroeconomic relationships. In these discussions, I fell back on the work of my first undergraduate teacher in mathematical economics at Berkeley. Francis Dresch, who developed index-number theory to show how his teacher's research (Griffith C. Evans, a founding member of the Econometric Society) macromodel, could be aggregated from the theory in Evans' work. This anticipated much modern work with Divisia Indices.

I was not entirely satisfied with Dresch's solution to the aggregation problem; so I proposed an alternative approach that exploited many properties of Cobb-Douglas production functions.[10] I was able to show that if index numbers were properly constructed, the aggregates satisfied relations that were formal analogs of the standard equations of the individual firm – production functions and first-order conditions for profit maximization. In a later publication, A. Nataf showed that my formulas were practically the only case that satisfied various restrictions that I placed on the aggregates and their interrelationships. Shou Shan Pu and Kenneth May argued that my restrictions were too severe (that the macro indicator for a given magnitude depends only on the micro components for that same variable). They argued that my index formulas lacked an intuitive base. I replied to their criticism, trying to elaborate why I structured the micro–macro correspondence as I did.[11]

At the time that the discussion about aggregation was taking place, I was preparing the manuscript of *The Keynesian Revolution* for publication. The manuscript was fundamentally my doctoral dissertation (MIT), completed in 1943, and I reworked it, with some extensions, at the Cowles Commission. In that environment, I felt challenged by my colleagues to produce an interpretation of Keynes' macro theory that stemmed from accepted micro foundations. I was trying to answer the

[10] 'Macroeconomics and the theory of rational behavior,' *Econometrica*, **14,** April (1946), 93–108.
[11] 'Remarks on the theory of aggregation,' *Econometrica*, **14,** October (1946), 303–12.

question, does a theoretically based macromodel exist? That is why I paid attention to the problem of aggregation at that time.

The core of the theoretical analysis of the Keynesian system, particularly the display of its essential differences from other systems, was examined through the medium of mathematical models in an article that summarized the argument of *The Keynesian Revolution*.[12] Some attention was paid in that article to modeling, for comparative purposes, the Marxian system. A second feature of that article was the construction of the labor-market sector in such a way that classical equations for supply and demand for labor in terms of the real wage rate were combined with a dynamic adjustment equation for the nominal wage rate as a function of imbalance in the labor market, indicated by unemployment. This was a macrotheoretical exposition of what much later came to be known as the Phillips Curve. At the same time, empirical estimates of labor market adjustment equations that expressed the change in the nominal wage rate as a function of unemployment and the price level change were being prepared at the Cowles Commission for inclusion in *Economic Fluctuations in the United States, 1921–1941* which was not published until 1950.

My work on the formal properties of the Keynesian system originated with the research on *The Keynesian Revolution*, under the critical eye of Paul Samuelson, with some indirect influence from my studies with Francis Dresch, at Berkeley, on the aggregation problem. But very intensive discussions were held at the Cowles Commission, 1944–7, with Trygve Haavelmo, Leonid Hurwicz, Jacob Marschak, Don Patinkin and others. Much of this discussion was reflected in the revision of the manuscript for publication of *The Keynesian Revolution*, but one further excursion was made on the route for constructing the underlying macromodel in a paper that tried to separate some simple, but formal, mathematics on the uses of stock or flow analysis in specifying the system, particularly the part of the system dealing with the money market and interest rate determination.[13] In a sense, flow variables can be transformed into stock variables and vice versa by simple accounting identities, but complete specifications of equations and models, especially if stochastic specification is to be taken into account, do matter. This is particularly true in market adjustment equations, and this was the point that this article tried to clarify.

Work on construction of econometric models was mainly oriented toward applications in forecasting and policy analysis, but a formal link

[12] 'Theories of effective demand and employment,' *Journal of Political Economy*, **55**, April (1947), 108–31.

[13] 'Stock and flow analysis in economics,' *Econometrica*, **18**, July (1950), 236–41, 246.

to the theory of economic policy had yet to be made. In an early application of models that were being developed at the Cowles Commission, I tried to show how they could be used in policy analysis, the main theoretical point being an appropriate allowance for error in decision-making at various levels of exogenous inputs. Policy and forecast analyses are commonly made as though the systems are deterministic and correct. There should be an allowance, at the very beginning, for uncertainty. This is what I tried to do in a paper on macro policy formation from econometric models.[14]

In Keynesian models of the macroeconomy, it was usual to consider production to consist of a single good. The Evans model with producer and consumer goods was an exception. Also, the early attempts to forecast for postwar planning, in the middle 1940s, made distinctions between durables, nondurables, and services. I noted at an early stage that the Keynesian models had to be extended to allow for relative price effects once the range of consideration was broadened to encompass two or more kinds of goods, especially within consumer goods. I, accordingly, was searching for an expression for demand functions that incorporated relative prices in a simple way and, particularly, helped overcome problems of multicollinearity in statistical analysis of demand systems.

At the same time, I had an enduring interest in the economic theory of cost-of-living index numbers, having been involved, while at MIT, in the dispute about formulas for wage indexation under wartime conditions of rationing. I was much impressed by work of N. Kaldor and J. L. Nicholson in Great Britain on the theory of measurement of the cost of living in such circumstances. I brought these two ideas together in formulating the linear expenditure system. I wrote down the marginal conditions for optimization of a consumer budget, where the demand functions were assumed to be linear in relative prices and real income. In discussions with Herman Rubin, encouraged by the collegial atmosphere of the Cowles Commission, where we regularly gathered in small groups in front of a blackboard to discuss common problems, I posed the problem of integrating the underlying differential equations. Herman, in a characteristic way, immediately saw the mathematical solution and we jointly had two formulas, the parametric expressions for the demand equations in the linear expenditure system and the expression for the 'true' cost-of-living index associated with this demand system.[15]

---

[14] 'The use of econometric models as a guide to economic policy,' *Econometrica*, **15**, April (1947), 108–31.

[15] 'A constant-utility index of the cost of living,' *Review of Economic Studies*, **15** (1947–8), 84–7.

Paul Samuelson, who refereed our paper for publication, and R. C. Geary both saw the utility function that would produce the linear expenditure system, according to the economic theory of the consumer. This system was later discovered, independently, by Richard Stone. This work has proved to be one of the more enduring developments that came out of my period at the Cowles Commission.

A related idea grew out of my fascination with Wassily Leontief's input–output system. The linear expenditure system was associated with the use of relative prices in the study of demand and was shown to be derived from a form (displaced) of Cobb-Douglas utility function. Correspondingly, a Cobb-Douglas interpretation of a production function based on intermediate input flows, made input–output coefficients depend on relative prices too. In discussing the Leontief approach with my old teacher, Francis Dresch, one day at an annual meeting of the American Economic Association, from a remark that he made I saw immediately that an extended Cobb-Douglas production function produced, by means of the theory of the firm, an input–output table in value, rather than volume, coefficients. I spelled out this analysis in a research paper, and it was later discussed by Michio Morishima, who contrasted the sensitivity of input variations to relative prices in my formulation with Leontief's formulation[16] where they were invariant.

At Oxford, in the 1950s, I had many discussions with Peter Newman and Jim Ball about the form of macroeconomic models. In particular, these discussions led often to arguments about certain ratios and their stability in the actual economy. I conceived the idea of putting together a simple model of the economy as a whole, composed solely of ratio expressions. When I left Oxford and settled at Pennsylvania, I assigned each group of students to investigate the measurement and time series analysis of each main macroeconomic ratio. Afterwards, Richard Kosobud and I cleaned up all the data, and put together a complete model in terms of well-known ratios in the economy – savings rates, capital–output ratio, velocity ratio, wage share, participation rate.[17]

A later theoretical paper, in which I pulled together several strands of thought in my career, was prepared for the purpose of a presidential address for the American Economic Association in 1977. In that paper, I tried to recognize the change in the nature of contemporary economic problems that made them resistant to pure demand management policies of a Keynesian type. I felt the need to combine *demand and*

---

[16] 'On the interpretation of Professor Leontief's system,' *Review of Economic Studies*, **20** (1952–3), 131–6.

[17] 'Some econometrics of growth: Great ratios of economics,' *Quarterly Journal of Economics*, **75** (1961), 173–98.

supply management. In this connection, I found that the model that suited me best was a fusion of the macromodel of Keynes and the input–output model of Leontief.[18] That is an area of research that started with the group discussion, in 1961, concerned with building a composite model of the United States for a committee of the Social Science Research Council. It later became known as the Brookings Model. My former student and present colleague, Ross Preston, made significant advances in the implementation of the Keynes–Leontief system. Some fundamental contributions were made also by Bert Hickman and Lawrence Lau in extending the underlying production function from the Cobb-Douglas to the CES family.

ECONOMIC POLICY

Public policy analysis was always a goal that guided my interest in both econometric model building and macroeconomic theory. Towards the end of World War II there were many forecasts about how the economy would look after demobilization. The bulk of them predicted a return to the state of mass unemployment that existed just before the war, and an analysis about why that consensus view was incorrect was undertaken because a contrary conclusion was reached in our first exercise with the model that was built at the Cowles Commission.[19]

Through the years, any number of public policy studies were made, many of which were not published at all or were published in popular media. Many were prepared for oral presentation at meetings. The early policy analyses with the Klein–Goldberger Model, developed during 1951–3, were published in a book volume.

After the Wharton Econometric Forecasting Unit (later Associates, Inc.) was initiated in 1963, policy analyses were prepared at least quarterly, often more frequently. In a sense, this activity became routine. But one excursion into public policy analysis is worthy of note for inclusion in this *Collection*, because it dealt with one of the crises of our age, namely that precipitated by the oil embargo in 1973–4. This was an event that caused economic repercussions that were felt for a decade. Our econometric models were, in 1973, less than adequate to deal with the situation fully, but we had nothing better to use, and I prepared a lecture to a seminar at the University in Vienna, when I was

[18]'The supply side,' *American Economic Review*, **68,** March (1978), 1–7.

[19]'A post mortem on transition predictions of national product,' *Journal of Political Economy*, **54,** August (1946), 287–308.

visiting the Institute for Advanced Studies, just after having prepared the first forecast that incorporated the embargo conditions.[20] In that lecture, I showed how the Wharton Model was used for interpretation of the event – an enormous increase in the terms of trade for oil-exporting nations. Subsequently, elaborate energy sectors were introduced in Wharton Models and analyses of oil-price changes became routine, but it was a challenging problem in October and November 1973.

APPLIED ECONOMETRICS

In a sense, applied econometrics has been the theme of my life's professional work, with occasional forays into economic theory or econometric theory. A study in applied econometrics that had roots in my earliest works, was the problem of estimating equations for determination of wage and prices. As it was indicated in explaining my theoretical model of the Keynesian system, I formulated an expression for wage-rate determination that was the same thing as the Phillips Curve, back in the 1940s, when I was at the Cowles Commission. A statistical estimate was published in the Cowles Commission Monograph describing the first models. I got my idea about this equation from Tinbergen's works, but he formulated it in terms of wage level rather than wage change.

Jim Ball and I discussed the wage and price determination equations a good deal when we were putting together a model of the UK in Oxford. This was contemporaneous with Phillips' work at the London School of Economics. We made a significant distinction in our work of the difference between wage rate and earnings, accounted for by 'wage drift.' We published our results separately from the book on the UK model because the wage and price sector held together as a separate block of equations.[21] This work was completed in 1957, but we had many refereeing discussions with Roy Harrod, then editor of the *Economic Journal*, before it was finally published.

When I returned to America in 1958, after 4 years at Oxford, I started to rebuild models of the US economy, which initiated successive generations of the Wharton Model. On a trip to Japan in 1960, to renew my friendship with Michio Morishima and Shinichi Ichimura,

[20] 'Supply constraints in demand oriented systems: An interpretation of the oil crisis,' *Zeitschrift für Nationalökonomie*, **34** (1974), 45–56.

[21] 'Some econometrics of the determination of absolute prices and wages,' *Economic Journal*, **69**, September (1959), 465–82.

both of whom came to Oxford when I was there, I presented a seminar on the specification of the new versions of the US model. I was then taken up with the practical statistical aspects of measuring capacity output and the degree of capacity utilization. In the Osaka seminar, Morishima noted that a single production function contained two (and other) production points, one at actual levels of output and one at full capacity output. I saw then that the problem of production function measurement should be formulated in terms of determination of points on a production function. With my student (later a colleague), Ross Preston, I investigated individual sector Cobb-Douglas production functions for the generating of full capacity output levels and the degree of capacity utilization. We wrote a joint paper on this subject.[22]

Apart from the problem of estimating capacity utilization, the production function problem intrigued me for many years. The four-author specification (Solow, Minhas, Arrow, Chenery) of the CES function was a brilliant generalization of the Cobb-Douglas form, and I hastened to estimate it, using in part some of the new computer programs for nonlinear estimation. These programs were being used in joint efforts with econometricians at IBM to estimate likelihood functions for simultaneous equation models, a problem that was just being made tractable by the harnessing of the computer for econometrics in the early and mid 1960s. My student, and later colleague, Ronald Bodkin, wanted some challenging problems for sharpening his post-doctoral skills; so we collaborated on a paper to estimate CES production functions by nonlinear methods.[23]

From time to time, I prepared survey articles on econometrics or related subjects. The editors of the *Journal of the American Statistical Association* requested a survey on econometrics in the early 1970s. In addition to surveying what was being done at the time by way of econometric practice and knowledge, I tried to look ahead for the areas of new development.[24] As I reflect upon what I said about new directions of development in the subject in 1971, I feel satisfied that I was on a good track. As suggested in the review article, there have been developments in computer analysis of large data banks, enlarging the scope (completeness) of econometric systems, the development of control theory in econometrics, and the expansion of work in micro-

[22]'Some new results in the measurement of capacity utilization,' *American Economic Review*, **57**, March (1967), 34–58.

[23]'Nonlinear estimation of aggregate production functions,' *Review of Economics and Statistics*, **49**, February (1967), 28–44.

[24]'Whither Econometrics?' *Journal of the American Statistical Association*, **66**, June (1971) 415–21.

econometrics. I believe that I was also correct in noting that there would be stronger advances outside the United States and further work on lag distributions, the use of *a priori* information and pooling of diverse samples. All these areas are receiving attention, but I believe now that future work in econometrics will have to pay more attention to variable parameter models and observation errors.

The decade of the 1970s, just after the survey article was published opened a very expansive era of application of large-scale macromodels, based to a large extent on the greater use of the high-speed electronic computer. This was an important device that was being adapted to econometrics throughout the 1960s, and computer usage flowered in the 1970s. At that time a number of procedures and practices in the use of computer-based models was developing by means of oral tradition and the time was ripe for setting down procedures in a systematic way. A national seminar on use of large-scale macromodels under the aegis of a Conference on Econometrics and Mathematical Economics (supported by the National Science Foundation) met regularly, usually at Pennsylvania to compare model performance, among different primary research groups, under specified conditions. In connection with presentations of seminar research for the different national models, I prepared a paper with two colleagues, E. P. Howrey and M. D. McCarthy, on testing and using models for prediction.[25]

In this paper we examined the evaluation of *ex ante* forecast error in the light of data revisions, estimation efficiency, model specification and the use of *a priori* information. We were disturbed by some mechanistic testing procedures that failed to take into account the gains in efficiency that are realized by the various practices that are actually used in model applications. In a conference sponsored by the National Bureau of Economic Research at Harvard University in 1969, there were presentations that tested models without using them in the efficient way that they are actually applied. Our paper was a sytematic evaluation of that procedure against what we considered to be appropriate.

The role of money in macroeconometric model building has had a cyclical career. Tinbergen was strongly influenced by the stock and money-market movements of the 1920s, culminating in the 1929 Great Crash. The Keynesian models contained money and liquidity preference equations, but monetary analysis was not central. Keynes was personally involved in financial market activity, but the involvement was not fully reflected in his formal system of the *General Theory*, where the real multiplier relationship was predominant.

[25]'Notes on testing the predictive performance of econometric models,' *International Economic Review*, **15**, June (1974), 366–83.

In the postwar period, after reconstruction, money markets and interest rate movements became more active, with greater range of variation. Macroeconometric models became more and more involved with money-market analysis, and the monetarists started to use econometric models during the late 1960s and early 1970s. I accordingly became more interested in the role of money in the Wharton Models. At the invitation of an editor of a French journal, I prepared a paper on long-term simulations of the Wharton Annual Model with the objective of analyzing the role of money in this calculation. I found a long-run, steady-state tendency of money and nominal GNP to move proportionally.[26] In this paper, I tried to interpret the meaning of this result in terms of monetarism and the causal structure of econometric models.

For the *Journal of Money Credit and Banking*, I delivered a special lecture at the meetings of the Western Economic Association in June 1982.[27] The purpose of this research paper, written jointly with colleagues at Wharton Econometric Forecasting Associates, was to show how money and related magnitudes are actually handled in the Wharton Quarterly Model, a mainstream large-scale econometric model used extensively in contemporary forecasting of the US economy. As indicated above, money has come to play an increasingly important role in macroeconometric models, but it is far different from the role of money in monetarist models. In this paper, a great deal of attention is paid to the contrast between the mainstream and monetarist approaches in econometric model building or performance. The Wharton Quarterly model, at the time of development of the results for the special lecture, was closely integrated with a flow-of-funds model, which has long been one of my research goals.

It is not surprising that we find a great deal of significance for the role of money in the Wharton Quarterly Model and that it is very different from the monetarist interpretation of the functioning of the economy. In a spirited exchange, Robert Weintraub came to the defense of monetarism in a follow-on commentary in a subsequent issue of the *Journal of Money Credit and Banking*.

In a research study that builds on my interest in measuring capacity utilization and also in estimating it from production function analysis, I prepared a paper with my associate, Vincent Su, to show how capacity

---

[26]'Money in a general equilibrium system: Empirical aspects of the quantity theory,' *Economie Appliquée*, **31**, 1–2 (1978), 5–14.

[27]'Money in the Wharton Quarterly Model,' *Journal of Money, Credit and Banking*, **15**, May (1983), 237–59.

utilization is generated within the Wharton Model.[28] In many respects, this is a continuation of studies that I developed with Ross Preston in the early and middle 1960s. It also deals with another thorny problem in macromodel design, namely, whether to estimate unemployment as a residual in the identity

$$\text{labor force} - \text{employment} = \text{unemployment}$$

or to form a direct estimation equation for unemployment and derive labor force as a residual. Since there is great strategic interest in the unemployment estimates, by themselves, we may be well advised to estimate them directly because residual estimates tend to have large error variance.

With the help and objective judgment of Jaime Marquez, the selection of research papers for this volume provides a good cross-section of my scholarly activities over the past 40 years, but it must necessarily be selective. Some relevant things have appeared in book publications that are not represented fully, if at all, in the present volume. A number of popular articles on current affairs are also left out, but they tend to be of shorter run or transitory interest. If there is any single gap in the present volume, it concerns the published writings about project LINK which brings macroeconometric modeling into the international sphere. I have spent a large amount of my research effort on those problems during the past 10 or 15 years. That output is now building up to the point where it could occupy a volume by itself.

Of necessity, I shall have to be devoting a fair amount of my own research effort to the international economy in the context of project LINK. That research consists now of analyses of world recovery policies or scenarios (substantive), incorporation of developing country models into the system (methodological), explanation of capital flows and exchange rates (methodological). But where is research in quantitative economics leading?

The single researcher equipped with a microcomputer will do research of an older character on relatively smaller systems. This is not to say that large-scale macroeconometric models are out or are to receive diminished attention. Team efforts like those involved with models like the Wharton Models or project LINK will continue, and some of the most challenging problems will be examined with the help of the super computer. This will be with problems involving stochastic simulation, multiple model systems and optimal control – separately or in various combinations.

[28] 'Direct estimates of unemployment rate and capacity utilization in macroeconometric models,' *International Economic Review*, **20**, October (1979), 725–40.

But individuals will be able to take a fresh look at quantitative models, researching alone, assisted by a microcomputer and having access to data and software of large computer installations. Gradually, bigger problems will become manageable as the capacity of small computers enlarges, but there are management limits for the scope of the lone researcher; therefore, I do not expect these efforts to reach the scale of work with mainstream models of the present era.

From the methodological viewpoint of general econometric research, the frontiers will be pushed back on the treatment of dynamics, expectations, and variable parameters in macromodels. Significant advances have been made in dealing with microdata for individual consumers and producers or related distributions. Much more quantitative research will be devoted to the problems of microeconometrics. For my own part, I have not dealt, at first hand, with such issues since my days at the Survey Research Center, University of Michigan (1949–54) and the Oxford Institute of Statistics (1954–8).

Part I
ECONOMETRIC METHODOLOGY

1
Pitfalls in the Statistical Determination of the Investment Schedule

Numerous investigators have been interested in attempting to estimate future investment by means of a regression equation relating investment to income, a trend variable, and perhaps a variable which introduces a lagged income effect.[1] This procedure is especially important now, since many economists would like to be able to extrapolate their equations into the postwar period at the level of national income which is expected to occur then. Such a method of estimating future investment is valid only if one can obtain an approximation to the reversible, 'structural' investment-income relation rather than the savings-income relation. The question of whether one calculates a statistical savings schedule or a statistical investment schedule arises since we can look upon both schedules as different functions of income which intersect. The observable data on savings, investment, and income are then the co-ordinates of the intersection of these two curves. It will be argued below that an ordinary regression equation fitted to the time-series data on investment (= savings), national income, time, and a lagged income variable is probably a statistical savings equation and not a statistical investment equation. Hence when one estimates the future level of investment corresponding to an anticipated level of income, what one really obtains is not what investment will be, but what investment *would have to be* if it were to equal savings at that level of national income. A recent attempt by Dr Mordecai Ezekiel[2] to obtain both of the above schedules from the same set of data on income and investment (= savings) will be examined carefully as an example of the problem of estimating two intersecting schedules when one knows the

---

[1] Professor Paul A. Samuelson and Mr Joseph Ullman read the manuscript and made many helpful suggestions for which the writer is indebted. Dr Ezekiel has commented on the article, to which Mr Klein replied.

[2] 'Statistical investigations of savings, consumption, and investment,' *The American Economic Review*, **32,** March (1942), 22–50 and June (1942), 272–308.

coordinates of the two shifting sets of curves only at their points of intersection.

It is evident that the problem of calculating the empirical savings and investment relations is quite similar to that of obtaining statistical demand and supply schedules. This latter problem is much more familiar to economists, and it will be instructive to consider some general propositions in demand and supply analyses which also occur in the savings and investment studies. The first part of the paper will deal with statistical supply-demand equations and the second part will treat Ezekiel's data. The points that are to be made will be the following: Ezekiel did not in fact obtain both the statistical savings and investment schedules; his estimation of the investment equation (especially that part concerned with housing) is open to question, while the savings schedule is probably rather well approximated; and finally it is not thought by the present writer that the method employed by Ezekiel is of general validity.

THE GENERAL PROBLEM OF ESTIMATING ECONOMIC RELATIONS

Classical regression methods are being widely used by economists to estimate various parameters which occur in well-known economic relationships. One of the most troublesome questions is whether the calculated equations show reversible relations or merely irreversible time paths. In the study of supply and demand the investigator would like to be able to name the resulting equation as the statistical *demand* function or the statistical *supply* function. At least, he would like to be able to say this of the net regression of price on quantity sold or of sales on price when the other variables are assigned constant values. When the method of least squares is used for fitting an equation to the data, and this is often the case, what is actually obtained is an estimation equation; and if certain hypotheses are fulfilled by the observed variates or by deviations of the observed dependent variate from the calculated dependent variate (its expected value), then one can say that he has the 'best linear unbiased estimate' of the dependent variable, given the independent variables. But this method does not in general give a functional relation or a reversible economic schedule. The mere fact that the several elementary regressions are different shows that the end result is not the unique 'true' relation. Of course, 'true' relations are easily obscured by errors of observation, and if each variable is made up of a systematic element and an error term with a known distribution function, then we can tell under certain conditions whether any of the elementary regressions is the 'true' relationship.[3] But this technique requires additional *a priori* information. If we denote the observed variables by $X_1^* = X_1^*(X_1, \varepsilon_1)$; $X_2^* = X_2^*(X_2, \varepsilon_2)$; $X_3^* = X_3^*(X_3, \varepsilon_3); \ldots$ where $X_1^*, X_2^*, X_3^*, \ldots$ are the observed values of the variables; $X_1, X_2, X_3 \ldots$ are the 'true' values; and $\varepsilon_1, \varepsilon_2, \varepsilon_3, \ldots$ are the random elements; then in order to know whether our method of curve fitting will lead us to the true 'structural' relation, it will be necessary to know or assume *at least* two facts. First we must know the shape of the functions $X_i^* = X_i^*(X_i, \varepsilon_i)$. Often it is convenient to assume the relation $X_i^* = X_i + \varepsilon_i$; it may be valid to assume this provided that we know the distribution function of the ε_i. Secondly, it is necessary to know the general class of functions which show the relation between the 'true' variables, e.g.,

$$a_1 X_1 + a_2 X_2 + a_2 X_3 + \cdots = 0.$$

If the above facts are known, then we may be able to say whether or not the particular equation obtained by our method of fitting is the 'structural' relation.

STATISTICAL DEMAND AND SUPPLY SCHEDULES

Those who have studied the problem from the point of view of supply and demand equations have largely agreed on the conditions for obtaining a good approximation to one or both of the desired schedules.[4] It is by no means sufficient to say that because the slope of the net regression of price on quantity is negative we have an approximation to the demand curve, nor does a positive slope give conclusive proof that what was obtained represents supply. In either case it may represent neither demand nor supply.

Each observation in the price-quantity scatter is the result of the intersection of a demand and a supply curve at a given price and quantity, with other variables in the system at a given level:

---

[3] R. G. D. Allen has considered this problem for the case of additive error terms and linear regression between two variables. See 'The assumptions of linear regression,' *Economica*, New Series, **6**, May (1939), 191–201.

[4] See Ragnar Frisch, 'Pitfalls in the statistical construction of demand and supply curves,' *Veröffentlichungen der Frankfurter Gesellschaft für Konjunkturforschung*, Neue Folge, Heft 5, Leipzig (1933); L. Metzler, 'The Assumptions implied in least squares demand techniques,' *Review of Economics and Statistics*, **32**, August (1940), 138–49; H. Schultz, *The Theory and Measurement of Demand*, The University of Chicago Press (1938); E. J. Working, 'What do "statistical demand" curves show?', *Quarterly Journal of Economics*, **41** (1927), 212.

$$f_{(t)}(p, q: a'_t a''_t, \ldots, a_t^{m_t}) = 0$$
$$g_{(t)}(p, q: b'_t, b''_t, \ldots, b_t^{r_t}) = 0,$$
(1.1)

where $t = 1, 2, \ldots, n$.

The values of p (price) and q (quantity) which satisfy each pair of the n sets of equations are the values for which supply (f) is in equilibrium with demand (g). The $(a_t^{(j)})$ and $(b_t^{(i)})$ are the parameters at time t of the supply and demand functions respectively. It is self-evident that, in general, the price and quantity observations, in themselves, are insufficient to determine the parameters $(a_t^{(j)})$ and $(b_t^{(i)})$ except in the very unlikely case that $m = r = 1$ for all t and the forms of the functions $f_{(t)}$ and $g_{(t)}$ are known. All observations of price and quantity which are not coincident tell one that at least one of the curves has shifted in time. Obviously if one of the curves remains relatively stable while the other shifts very much, then a curve fitted to the observed coordinates traces out approximately the curve which has remained relatively stable. If both curves shift very much together, the resulting scatter of points may not be a good estimate of either schedule. In order to know which of the two schedules is represented by the fitted regression, we must have additional information on the shifts of the curves. On the assumption that the curves shift in a given regular manner, criteria have been developed on the basis of the variance of the parameters $(a_t^{(j)})$ and $(b_t^{(i)})$ to determine whether the calculated regression can be called the statistical demand or supply schedule. But in practice one rarely has enough information to know the required variances; in any case the observations alone will not supply the needed information no matter how long the period may be.

Under certain very special and restrictive conditions it may be possible to approximate both schedules from the same set of price-quantity data. The following consideration of the various situations under which it may be possible to derive *both* schedules is given merely to show the amount of outside information, in addition to the observed price-quantity data, that is needed.

The simplest case is that of the cobweb theorem in which the quantity demanded depends upon current prices and the quantity supplied depends upon the prices of the preceding period. Where this model is valid one merely needs to fit a demand equation of the type $q_t = f(p_t)$ and a supply equation of the type $q_t = g(p_{t-1})$. But this formulation assumes that the schedules have not shifted. The most general case is that in which both supply and demand schedules involve simultaneous price-quantity relationships, and in which both schedules have shifted over time. In this situation, one procedure would be to obtain the separate formulation of demand and of supply as equations in p and q, and some other variables in the system which are simultaneously determined with price and quantity. The empirical equations would be of the form $\phi(p, q, x_1, x_2, \ldots, x_n) = 0$ and $\psi(p, q, y_1, y_2, \ldots, y_m) = 0$, where the demand, ϕ, is taken to depend upon other variables in addition to the price and quantity sold, and similarly for supply, ψ. When the other variables $x_1, x_2, \ldots, x_n$ and $y_1, y_2, \ldots, y_m$ are assigned their values as of time, t, the two schedules ϕ and ψ should be good approximations to equations (1.1) at time, t. The additional variables (x_j) may involve the prices of other commodities, time, income, etc.; while (y_i) might include some of the same items, or production conditions such as climatic variables in the case of agricultural commodities. It is very possible that in some cases (y_i) and (x_j) may be exactly the same, and then the statistician will obtain identical results in his attempt to get the separate equations of supply and of demand by ordinary methods of fitting unless the separate effects of these other variables can be independently assessed to demand and to supply by an *a priori* weighting process. Thus there are two steps. First we must be able to choose all the variables which influence demand and all those which influence supply; then we must assign their relative contributions to the determination of the actual levels of demand and supply. Clearly the purpose of introducing these other variables is to show what happens to the demand and supply schedules when other things do not remain the same; hence (x_j) must account for all the shifts of the demand curve and (y_i) for the shifts of supply. Then the equations,

$$\phi(p, q, x_1^0, x_2^0, \ldots, x_n^0) = 0,$$
$$\psi(p, q, y_1^0, y_2^0, \ldots, y_m^0) = 0,$$

will be the familiar *ceteris paribus* demand and supply curves for a given level of the other variables. It is not necessary to assume that there is any great regularity or pattern of shift of the curves provided that the other variables can *adequately* account for these shifts. The net relation between price and quantity may be quite different when various constant levels are assigned to (x_j) and (y_i), but this is no problem as long as the additional variables are the correct ones which account for the shifts no matter how drastic they may be.

An alternative procedure for arriving at the same results would be first to adjust the original series of price and quantity observations to some preassigned level of the (x_j) and (y_i). This means that we have two new sets of adjusted observations which show what the original sets would have been if other things had remained constant at the given level. Separate regressions fitted to the two adjusted sets of data will approximate separately the *ceteris paribus* demand and supply schedules. In practice the adjustment is usually carried out by dividing the original observations by an index of each of the (x_j) and (y_i). This is the familiar method of deflation. At any rate, the results obtained by using adjusted data should agree closely with the net regressions between p and q in the multiple-correlation equations when the other variables (x_j) and (y_i) are assigned their values as of the adjustment period.

A much more elegant approach to the problem is that taken by Haavelmo.[5] He considers the variables in a stochastic scheme and estimates the parameters in the economic relations by estimating them as parameters in a joint probability distribution. In some cases, however, the assumptions needed in order to apply his methods may be quite arbitrary. In an economic scheme such as equations (1.1) (or in a more complicated model), the time series of price-quantity observations are regarded as functions of the parameters of the equations and some random elements. Then the probability distribution of the observed variables can be derived from the assumed distribution of the random elements. Obviously, the parameters of the original system of equations will be parameters of the joint probability distribution of the observed variables, and the estimation of these parameters is reduced to the straightforward statistical problem of estimating the parameters of the joint probability distribution. Both Haavelmo's method and the classical regression methods involve an *a priori* selection of the form of the equations in the economic model, but the former technique must also assume the probability distribution of the random elements of the observables. The latter assumption is not necessary to the validity of regression methods, for it has been shown that these methods need only the hypothesis that one is dealing with a set of independent random variables whose distribution function is not specified.[6]

EZEKIEL'S ANALYSIS OF SAVINGS AND INVESTMENT

General considerations of savings and investment

It is apparent that the problem of calculating statistical savings and investment schedules can be considered as analogous to that arising in

---

[5]See Trygve Haavelmo, *On the Theory and Measurement of Economic Relations*, Cambridge, Mass. (1941), and 'The statistical implications of a system of simultaneous equations,' *Econometrica*, **11**, January (1943), 1–12.

[6]See F. N. David and J. Neyman, 'Extension of the Markoff Theorem on least squares,' *Statistical Research Memoirs*, London, **2**, December (1938), 105–116.

supply and demand studies, for just as demand and supply were equal at a price, so savings and investment become equal at a level of national income. We have an intersection of the savings schedule and the investment schedule. In the remainder of this paper the following notation will be used: $I=$ total private investment; $S=$ savings; $Y=$ national income; $\Delta Y=$ the change in national income from the preceding year; $T=$ time, $I_1=$ permanent investment, $I_2=$ housing, $I_3=$ temporary investment, $I_4=$ quasi-investment.[7] All functional notation will use the same letter for the function and the dependent variable. For example, the investment function will be written $I = I(Y, \Delta Y^0, T^0)$ where ΔY^0 and T^0 are preassigned levels of ΔY and T. This gives the *ceteris paribus* relation between investment and income.

Economists have long indulged in the controversy over the equality of savings and investment. Ezekiel quite correctly assumes that $S(Y, \Delta Y^0, T^0) = I(Y, \Delta Y^0, T^0)$ for some unique value of $Y = Y_1$. Thus the equality between S and I is brought about at the existing level of national income, and $S(Y, \Delta Y^0, T^0) \neq I(Y, \Delta Y^0, T^0)$; i.e., S and I are not equal at all values of Y given $\Delta Y = \Delta Y^0$ and $T = T^0$. As observables, savings and investment have identical time series so that we might say $S_t \equiv I_t$ identically in time. But in the schedule sense, savings and investment are merely equal and not identical.[8] This clearly means that in any given year the observations of S, I, and Y are obtained as the simultaneous solution of two equations. We know then the coordinates of the point of intersection of the two curves; also it is reasonable to assume that both curves are positively inclined, the savings schedule intersecting the investment schedule from below. But this is invariably too little information in order to determine the location and shapes of the curves precisely.

What can we say *a priori* about a multiple-correlation equation fitted to data of the observed savings (or investment which is equal to the observed saving), income, change in income, and time? If we could establish likely hypotheses as to the shifts of the savings and of the investment schedules, then it might be possible to deduce which schedule the calculated equation approximates. The factors which determine the amount of savings are more institutional in character than those factors which determine the amount of investment. The amount of money that people are willing to save depends upon

---

[7]All the terms are defined in the sense in which Ezekiel used them. Permanent investment includes plant and equipment; temporary investment includes consumers' credit and inventories; quasi-investment is the net government contribution and the net foreign balance.

[8]That is, the savings schedule is not coincident with the investment schedule.

insurance premiums, pension-fund payments, trust-fund payments, spending habits, and other things which change only gradually and slightly over the short period of two decades. A. H. Hansen declares that 'the flow of savings is being canalized into institutional channels.'[9] But the same cannot be said about the motivations behind the amount that people are willing to invest. The level of investment is very volatile and subject to great change over the course of the business cycle. The important investment-determining forces are expected rates of return on capital outlays and these expectations vary widely with fluctuations in the level of business activity. Elsewhere Hansen says:

> Net investment, on the contrary, is a function of (a) economic progress, including new developments in the field of technology, discovery of new resources, the opening up of new territory, and the growth of population, and (b) changes in the rate of interest (brought about for example by monetary policy) independent of changes in thrift;[10] But in an expanding, dynamic economy, net investment is essentially spontaneous and independent of the current volume of consumption.[11]

Hence we should expect the savings schedule to remain relatively stable over the business cycle, and the changes that did occur in the position of the schedule should be rather well accounted for by a time variable and a change of income variable. On the other hand, the investment function is likely to undergo large and rapid shifts; therefore the results of empirical curve fitting should give a close approximation to the savings schedule. Only if the data were adjusted for those factors which cause investment to shift or if these factors were introduced as explicit variables, should we be able to calculate the statistical investment equation also.

Ezekiel's model

The points which are to be shown in the statistical arguments below are the following:

1 The method used by Ezekiel does not in itself enable one to approximate both the savings and the investment schedules. It is still necessary to make use of more outside information.

---

[9] A. H. Hansen, *Fiscal Policy and Business Cycles*, Norton, New York, (1941).
[10] Ibid., p. 328.
[11] Ibid., p. 303.

2 Ezekiel's regression of housing investment on income and time is not satisfactory because it contains two statistical pitfalls.

3 If the housing regression submitted by this paper is used instead, the results are entirely different.

Ezekiel's method is unable to distinguish the savings schedule from the investment schedule and he cannot have actually calculated both. In fact, the nature of his additional independent variables which account for the shifts of the schedules lead one to guess that his results give the statistical savings equation.

It should be very instructive to examine, critically, Ezekiel's problem and his proposed solution to see whether he actually did obtain both the savings and investment schedules. Ezekiel defines savings as $S = I_1 + I_2 + I_3 + I_4$. He obtained a least-squares regression equation $S = S(Y, \Delta Y, T)$ which he called the savings 'function.' The next step was to break up private investment into its several components and to calculate the separate regressions for each component on the relevant independent variables. $I_1 = I_1(Y, T)$; $I_2 = I_2(Y, T)$; $I_3 = I_3(\Delta Y)$; where $I_1 + I_2 + I_3 = I$. The remaining factor which brought investment up to the level of saving was I_4, which played the role of an autonomous variable in the proposed system. Under static conditions the savings 'function' is $S = S(Y, \Delta Y^0, T^0)$ and the investment 'function' is

$$I = I_1(Y, T^0) + I_2(Y, T^0) + I_3(\Delta Y^0),$$

where $\Delta Y^0 = 0$.

Apparently the rationale behind such a method of getting both schedules from the same set of observations is that if investment is split into its separate parts, each part will be an element of investment but not of savings and the sum of these separate investment component relations will be the total investment relation. But on purely statistical grounds, why can one expect to get more out of the data by breaking up the dependent variable into its various components and then adding the resulting regressions? There are two problems to be considered in this connection. First, under what circumstances will the sum of the separate regressions be statistically different from the original equation? Secondly, when the two results are significantly different, what are the conditions that one is the savings relation, while the other is the investment relation? Upon consideration of the first question it is immediately evident that this method of breaking up the dependent variable into its components cannot be of general validity, for it is a property of the method of least squares that if in each of the separate regressions of the several components all the variables that were significant in the total relation are significant, then the sum of the individual component equations is exactly the original total equation. It is only when some of the independent variables prove to be insignificant in several of the separate equations that the sum of these equations can be statistically different from the original equation. It is assumed that, when a regression coefficient proves to be not significant in an equation, a new equation is calculated which omits the insignificant variable entirely.

In answer to the second question, obviously, all the difficulties present in the original equation of knowing whether the over-all relation is a statistical investment or savings schedule, or neither, enter into each of the regressions of the separate investment components. For example, one must show that $I_i = I_i(Y, \Delta Y, T)$ is an approximation to the 'structural' relation between I_i and the independent variables involved. A close relation between I_i and Y, ΔY, T is not enough to warrant calling this a reversible economic relation. The components I_i of investment are also subject to the violent and irregular shifts over time that occur in total investment and it will usually be necessary to use more than T and ΔY to account for these shifts. Furthermore, one can hope at best to be able to get $I_1(Y, T)$; $I_2(Y, T)$; $I_3(\Delta Y)$, but the presence of the autonomous variable I_4 will always prevent one from obtaining the structural relationship of total investment and income.

The statistical findings

There is one obvious reason why different equations are obtained in each of Ezekiel's analyses, namely, that $S = I_1 + I_2 + I_3 + I_4$, while $I = I_1 + I_2 + I_3$. But for the period as a whole (1921–40), I_4 shows practically a zero scatter on income; and the shape of the net regression of S on Y is scarcely altered by the omission of I_4. Hence this omission should cause only a shift of the level of the net regression. Nonetheless, Ezekiel does get different shapes for $S = S(Y, \Delta Y^0, T^0)$ and $I = I(Y, \Delta Y^0, T^0)$ while we might well expect that the result should be the same, except for the constant term. The relation $S = S(Y, \Delta Y, T)$ is computed rather satisfactorily, but the regression $I_2 = I_2(Y, T)$ contains some questionable steps. There are two reasons why the calculation of this latter equation should be reconsidered. First the time variable which was used to represent the housing cycle is highly intercorrelated with income so that the regression equation may be only fictitiously determinate, and, in fact, Ezekiel recognizes this and mentions the fact, although he uses the two variables in the same equation anyway. He notes that the net regression of I_2 on Y could be drawn considerably

Table 1.1 Time variable of the housing cycle

1921	−4	1926	+35	1931	−15	1936	−21
1922	+10	1927	+31	1932	−27	1937	−18
1923	+23	1928	+24	1933	−31	1938	−14
1924	+32	1929	+13	1934	−30	1939	−11
1925	+35	1930	0	1935	−26	1940	−8

steeper (perhaps so much steeper that his net regressions of S on Y and of I on Y would not intersect?). Secondly, this time variable appears to have some very peculiar properties. It is nothing more than a curve which traces out the time series of housing. It traces out the time series so closely that the Pearson correlation coefficient between this variable and housing (I_2) is 0.999![12] Thus, so much of the variation in I_2 has been extracted through the time variable, that there is little left to be explained by Y. What is left to be explained will not be well explained by income anyway because a variable which is highly correlated with income has already accounted for all the variation in housing which could be related to income. The multiple-correlation analysis with I_2 as the dependent variable and Y and T (Ezekiel's time variable of the housing cycle; see table 1.1) as independent variables shows that the role of Y in the regression equation is not statistically significant. The ratio of the regression coefficient of Y to its standard error is only 1.812. This low value of the ratio means that we *cannot* reject the hypothesis that the true value of the regression coefficient is zero. Fifteen degrees of freedom were assumed in this application of the t-test, and this is generous considering the wiggles and assymetry in his periodic function which represented the housing cycle. On the basis of these two shortcomings in the calculation of $I_2 = I_2(Y, T)$, this study submits an alternative regression equation which is not open to such severe criticism. The equation now becomes:

$$I_2 = 0.095215 Y - 1.795925 T - 22.234040$$

where I_2 and Y are in 100 millions of dollars and T represents an ordered sequence of years, $0, 1, 2, \ldots, 19$, beginning with 1921. In this linear equation, all the regression coefficients meet the t-test, and the multiple-correlation coefficient is $R = 0.92$.[13] This regression does not fit

---

[12] The present writer obtained the data for the time variable by reading from the graph in Fig. 6, p. 287, of Ezekiel's article Part II. The figures on the accompanying table are centimeter readings of deviations of the curve from the 0 line in the above-mentioned chart.

[13] The adjusted value of R is $\bar{R} = 0.90$. However, the present writer considers the adjustment to be unsatisfactory on theoretical grounds.

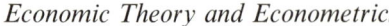

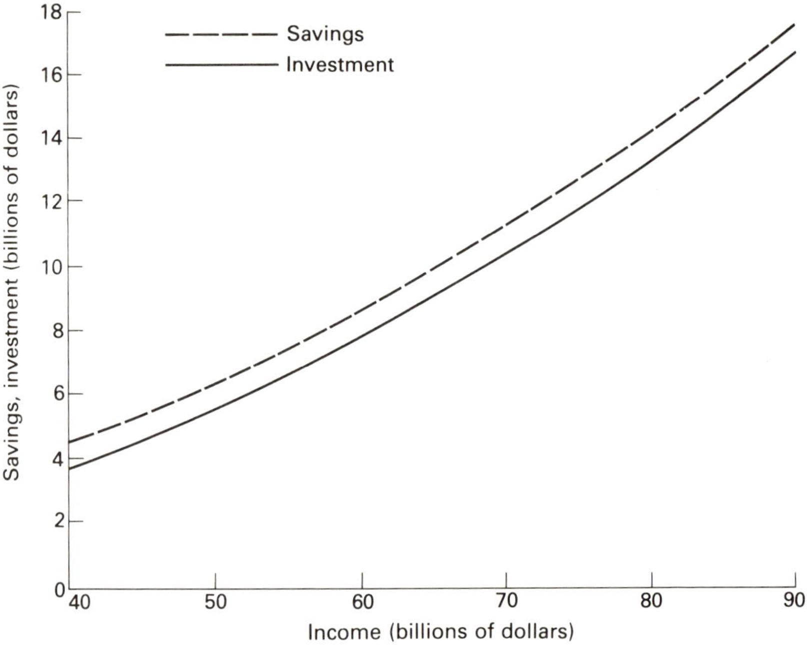

Figure 1.1 Relation between savings, investment, and income during the 1920s on the basis of the linear regression for I_2

the data poorly, and furthermore extremely high values of R are not by any means the sole criteria for the desirability of a particular regression equation. Ezekiel had an R of at least 0.999 but other criteria require his equation to be rejected. It might be mentioned in passing that he could also have extracted the trend effect from I_1 in the same way, as was done for I_2, but for some reason he chose to use only a linear trend in that case.

If we replace Ezekiel's equation for I_2 by the regression calculated above, $I_2 = 0.095215Y - 1.795925T - 22.234040$, the results of the analysis are entirely changed, for now we obtain what we should expect to get, namely, that the calculated investment 'function' at a static level differs from the savings 'function'[14] in only the level and not in shape. Figure 1.1 shows the savings schedule as calculated by Ezekiel for the 1920s at a static level. The investment schedule uses the same data as did Ezekiel for I_1 and I_3. I_2 is calculated by the linear equation obtained in this paper. Then $I = I_1 + I_2 + I_3$ in figure 1.1. Obviously the two curves are different aspects of the same thing and are separated by

[14] That obtained by Ezekiel in Part I of his article.

Pitfalls in the statistical determination of the investment schedule 37

Table 1.2 I_2 Calculated on the basis of the linear regression and the resulting values of I and S for the 1920s and the 1930s

1920s				1930s			
Y	I_2	S	I	Y	I_2	S	I
40	0.78	4.65	3.63	40	−1.02	3.70	1.13
50	1.73	6.50	5.68	50	−0.07	5.55	3.18
60	2.68	8.65	7.83	60	0.89	7.70	5.34
70	3.63	11.25	10.48	70	1.84	10.30	7.99
80	4.59	14.15	13.34	80	2.79	13.20	10.84
90	5.54	17.45	16.49	90	3.74	16.50	13.99

a constant. Table 1.2 gives the relevant calculations for figure 1.1 and also the data for the static level of the 1930s. If the argument is consistent, this difference in level should be explained by the omission of I_4 in the calculation of the investment equation, and then it would appear that Ezekiel should really have obtained the same thing by two different methods. At the static level of the 1920s set $\Delta Y^0 = 0$ and $T^0 =$ average value of T in the decade, 1921–30, then I_4 calculated from[15] $I_4 = 2.053383 T^0 + 0.542862$ or from $I_4 = 0.113521(T^0)^2 + 6.030156$ just makes up for this difference in the level of the two schedules in figure 1.1. When the calculations are carried out for I_4 at the average level of the 1930s, the result is not as close as in the previous case, but it is sufficiently close to the difference between the S and I curves to show that it accounts for the discrepancy. The conclusion to be drawn from these results is that the technique employed was not correct for determining both the savings and investment schedules, but that what was actually obtained was a statistical savings schedule.

If this system is carried to its logical conclusion, we should break down the components of investment still further, and we should have $\sum_{r=1}^{n} I_r = S$. In this situation, each of the I_r may be taken as such a small portion of S that the line of causation is fixed, i.e. from Y to I_r. This avoids in a sense the problem of choosing between two elementary regressions because I_r must clearly be taken as the predicting variable. The tail does not wag the dog! But this technique does not give the statistician any more confidence that the calculated least-squares regression such as $I_r = I_r(Y, \Delta Y, T)$ is the 'true' relation. The mere fact that

[15] Both T and T^2 are not statistically significant variables when used together in the same equation. The correlation between I_4 and T^2 is somewhat higher than that between I_4 and T. I_4 is in 100 millions of dollars.

the regression is unique, because our predicted and predicting variables are given, does not establish 'structural' relationship. Neither does this further subdivision of I into smaller parts contribute toward the problem of obtaining both schedules.

The small components of investment are probably no less volatile than the larger elements. It will still be difficult to get the proper independent variables that will account for the shifts of each of the I_r. Goodness of fit will not be a suitable criterion for determining whether or not the calculated equation for I_r is actually an investment relation since we should not be able to distinguish between an induced investment relationship and an autonomous relationship. Regressions of the latter type may very well show a close fitting but irreversible time path.

2

The Efficiency of Estimation in Econometric Models

At an early stage in the development of mathematical statistics and in its application to economics Professor Hotelling steered our thinking in the right direction towards the relationship between problems of parameter estimation from samples and problems of prediction outside the confines of the sample. The essence of the matter is contained in his 1929 paper written jointly with H. Working.[1] A more concise presentation was given later in Hotelling's appraisal of a research publication in psychology and sociology.[2] Hotelling's formulation of the prediction problem will long serve as a model in econometrics. In following up recent contributions on the efficiency of alternative methods of estimation in econometrics, it is found immediately useful to turn to Hotelling's basic formula for the standard error of forecast.

First I shall take up some problems in connection with the use of conventional least-squares methods of estimation in econometrics and then go on more specifically to the problems of prediction which rely so heavily on Hotelling's inspirational work.

A REVIVAL OF SUPPORT FOR LEAST-SQUARES ESTIMATES

Recent arguments in favor of reversion to conventional application of the method of least squares for estimating parameters in single equations in simultaneous systems dealt with in econometrics have stressed the comparative efficiency of this method. For example, in the discussions at the 1954 meetings of the Econometric Society in Uppsala, H. Theil outlined a theorem showing that the generalized variance of least-squares estimates of the parameters in a single equation is at least

---

[1] H. Hotelling and H. Working, 'Applications of the theory of error to the interpretation of trends,' *Journal of the American Statistical Association*, **24**, March Supplement (1929), 73–85.

[2] H. Hotelling, 'Problems of Prediction,' *The American Journal of Sociology*, XLVIII (1942), 61–76.

From *Essays in Economics and Econometrics*, **7** (1960), 216–32.

as small as that of limited-information-maximum-likelihood estimates.[3] It has long been suggested that it may be rewarding to gain some efficiency at the expense of bias by using the least-squares method, but the formal proof of the superior efficiency has only just been set out by Theil. Of course, we must know more about the 'utility function' of the users of estimated models before we can judge about the relative importance of bias and efficiency.

In this paper, I should like to suggest that Theil's results and, in fact, much of the discussion on the relative merits of different methods is misplaced. In systems of equations, with several parameters in each equation, it is misleading to look at individual parameters, one by one, or even restricted groups of them in reaching overall judgements about the importance of bias or efficiency. Users of econometric models are often not really interested in particular structural parameters by themselves. They are interested in the *solution* to the system, under alternative sets of conditions. In other, more technical words they are interested in the *reduced forms* of the estimated system.[4] It is the difference between *partial* and *general* analysis that is involved. It is conceivable that partial analysis is an end, in itself, for some problems – possibly those of a purely pedagogical nature – but most problems call for a more complete analysis of the system.

The transformation of a structural system to its reduced form can be associated with the process of *forecasting*. We shall use this term in a general sense in this paper, that is in the sense of making estimates of endogenous economic magnitudes outside the realm of past experience. In this sense, a wide variety of problems of empirical economic analysis are forecasting problems.

Propositions valid for partial systems may not carry over when complete systems are studied. Or even propositions valid for *structural* parameters may not be valid for *reduced form parameters*. A beautiful property of the maximum-likelihood method of estimation is that its characteristics are preserved under single-valued transformation of variables. Let Θ be an unknown parameter, $\hat{\Theta}$ its maximum-likelihood estimate, and $f(\Theta)$ a single-valued transformation function. Then it follows that the maximum-likelihood estimate of $f(\Theta)$ is given by $f(\hat{\Theta})$.

---

[3] 'Report of the Uppsala Meeting, August 2–4, 1954,' *Econometrica*, **23**, April (1955), 204–5. Limited information and other methods of estimation in econometric models are described in various publications. A good summary is found in Wm. C. Hood and T. C. Koopmans, 'The estimation of simultaneous linear economic relationships,' *Studies in Econometric Method*, John Wiley and Sons, New York (1953).

[4] Theil points out to me that for treatment of structural change and appraisal of the *a priori* 'reasonableness' of particular estimates one would be primarily interested in the individual structural estimates.

Efficiency of estimation in econometric models 41

As a result of this proposition, the desirable features of maximum likelihood estimates of structural parameters remain as desirable features when the parameters and estimates are transformed into reduced form coefficients. An analogous property does not hold for the method of least squares in general.

BIAS-STRUCTURAL EQUATIONS AND REDUCED FORMS

First, let us consider the question of bias. By comparing one-by-one the coefficients of a system estimated by the method of least squares with corresponding coefficients estimated by some unbiased method, investigators sometimes conclude superficially that the amounts of bias are unimportant. From studies of numerical methods of solving linear equation systems with parameters subject to error, we learn, however, that small errors in coefficients may lead to sizeable errors in the final solution.

Suppose that we have a linear equation system

$$By_t + \Gamma z_t = u_t, \quad y \text{ jointly dependent,} \quad z \text{ predetermined,} \tag{2.1}$$

with reduced form

$$y_t = -B^{-1}\Gamma z_t + B^{-1}u_t. \tag{2.2}$$

We shall denote a set of unbiased or consistent estimates as $\hat{B}$ and $\hat{\Gamma}$. Least-squares estimates will then be written as

$$\hat{B} + D(B), \quad \hat{\Gamma} + D(\Gamma).$$

$D(B)$ and $D(\Gamma)$ are discrepancy matrices showing how the least-squares estimates differ from the set $\hat{B}$, $\hat{\Gamma}$. For a given z_t-vector we shall then be interested in the effect of the discrepancies on the solution vector.

A first order approximation to the solution of

$$[\hat{B} + D(B)][\hat{y}_t + D(y_t)] + [\hat{\Gamma} + D(\Gamma)]z_t = 0$$

is given by

$$D(y_t) = -\hat{B}^{-1}[D(\Gamma)z_t + D(B)\hat{y}_t], \tag{2.3}$$

where

$$\hat{y}_t = -\hat{B}^{-1}\hat{\Gamma}z_t.$$

Except for the possibility that errors in the Γ-matrix, $D(\Gamma)$, compensate errors in the B-matrix, $D(B)$, these original errors will be reflected in errors in the vector, $D(y_t)$ after multiplication by $\hat{B}^{-1}$. In some problems $\hat{B}^{-1}$ can be a large factor, as will be illustrated below in a simple example.

Consider, for illustrative purposes, the simple multiplier model

$$C_t = \alpha Y_t + u_t, \tag{2.4}$$

$$Y_t = C_t + I_t. \tag{2.5}$$

where

C_t = consumption (endogenous)
Y_t = income (endogenous)
I_t = investment (exogenous)
u_t = random disturbance.

The unbiased estimate of the marginal propensity to consume is a, and the biased least-squares estimate is $a + e$.[5] The bias, when looked at from a partial point of view is simply e, but when considered from the more general point of view of the whole system it is $e/1 - a - e$, as can be seen from

$$C_t = (a+e)(C_t + I_t)$$

$$C_t = \frac{a+e}{1-a-e} I_t = \left[\frac{a}{1-a} + \frac{e}{(1-a)(1-a-e)}\right] I_t$$

$$= \left[a + \frac{e}{1-a-e}\right] \hat{Y}_t, \tag{2.6}$$

where

$$\hat{Y}_t = \frac{1}{1-a} I_t.$$

In the reduced form, or multiplier, equation the bias is magnified by the factor $1/1 - a - e$, which will be of the order of magnitude of the multiplier.[6] Another way of looking at the matter is to observe that the percentage bias is smaller in absolute value in the structural equation than in the reduced form equation.

$$\left|\frac{e}{a}\right| < \left|\frac{e}{a(1-a-e)}\right| \quad \text{as long as } |1-a-e| < 1.$$

---

[5]Haavelmo derives an explicit expression for the bias in this model and finds it positive under fairly general conditions. T. Haavelmo, 'Methods of measuring the marginal propensity to consume,' *Journal of the American Statistical Association*, **42** (1947), 105–22.

[6]Haavelmo, 'Methods of measuring,' shows numerically how a difference of 0.06 in the marginal propensity to consume becomes a difference of 0.68 in the multiplier.

Efficiency of estimation in econometric models 43

In this simple case, it is clearly seen that a discrepancy in the structural equation e, is magnified by the multiplier, $1/1-a-e$. The multiplier plays the role of $\hat{B}^{-1}$ in the more general formulation (2.3), showing the possibility of comparatively small discrepancies becoming comparatively large in the final result.

LEAST-SQUARES EFFICIENCY – STRUCTURAL EQUATION AND REDUCED FORM

This simple model of the multiplier process is useful in providing an example to show that Theil's proposition about the efficiency of least-squares methods cannot be extended to reduced form parameters. The efficiency properties of least-squares estimation of the parameter in the structural equation are not preserved under transformation to the reduced form, just as we know that the point values of least-squares estimates vary with the direction of minimization of squared residuals.

The variance of the direct least-squares estimate of the marginal propensity to consume is given by

$$\operatorname{var}(a+e) = \operatorname{var} \frac{\sum C_t Y_t}{\sum Y_t^2} = \operatorname{var} \frac{\sum (\alpha Y_t + u_t) Y_t}{\sum Y_t^2}$$

$$= \operatorname{var}\left(\alpha + \frac{\sum u_t Y_t}{\sum Y_t^2}\right) = \operatorname{var} \frac{\sum u_t Y_t}{\sum Y_t^2}.$$

Applying a first order approximation formula of a function of random variables to the right-hand expression we get the classical type result[7]

$$\operatorname{var}(a+e) = \frac{\operatorname{var}(u)}{\sum Y_t^2}, \qquad (2.7)$$

in the limit as the same size $\to \infty$. In deriving this result the standard independence assumptions are used about u_i and Y_t for unequal subscript values. Thus for large samples the classical formula is used even though u_t and Y_t are not independent (for equal subscript values).

In forecasting Y_t from estimates of the reduced form equation

$$Y_t = \frac{1}{1-\alpha} I_t + \frac{1}{1-\alpha} u_t,$$

---

[7]This is, of course, the same result that Theil derives by a different method in his comparison of the efficiency of least-squares and limited-information estimates. He deals with the *estimated* variance determined from the sample observations.

we are interested in the variance of the estimated multiplier

$$\text{est}\,\frac{1}{1-\alpha}.$$

The least-squares estimate of the structural equation leads to an estimate of the multiplier as

$$\text{ls est}\,\frac{1}{1-\alpha}=\frac{1}{1-a-e},$$

while the corresponding unbiased estimate will be written as

$$\text{ml est}\,\frac{1}{1-\alpha}=\frac{1}{1-a} \quad (\text{ml}=\text{maximum likelihood}).$$

We approximate the variance of the least-squares estimate as

$$\text{var}\,\frac{1}{1-a-e}=\frac{\text{var}(a+e)}{(1-a-e)^4}$$

$$=\frac{(1/1-a-e)^2\,\text{var}(u)}{(1-a-e)^2\sum Y_t^2} \tag{2.8}$$

$$=\frac{(1/1-a-e)^2\,\text{var}(u)(\sum Y_t^2)^2}{(\sum Y_t^2-\sum C_t Y_t)^2 \sum Y_t^2}$$

$$=\frac{\text{var}(u)}{(1-a-e)^2}\frac{\sum Y_t^2}{(\sum I_t Y_t)^2}.$$

The maximum-likelihood estimator is simply that multiplier value calculated from the least-squares regression of Y_t on I_t,

$$\text{var}\left(\frac{1}{1-a}\right)=\frac{(1/1-\alpha)^2\,\text{var}(u)}{\sum I_t^2}. \tag{2.9}$$

With a positive bias, $e>0$, we have the inequality

$$\frac{\text{var}\,u}{(1-\alpha)^2}\leqslant \text{plim}\,\frac{\text{var}(u)}{(1-a-e)^2}$$

since $\text{plim}\,a=\alpha$, and we assume $0<1-a-e<1$. Also

$$\frac{1}{\sum I_t^2}\leqslant\frac{\sum Y_t^2}{(\sum I_t Y_t)^2};$$

hence

$$\text{var}\left(\frac{1}{1-a}\right)\leqslant \text{plim var}\left(\frac{1}{1-a-e}\right).$$

Efficiency of estimation in econometric models 45

Thus our example shows clearly that the efficiency properties of least-squares structural estimates do not always carry over to the reduced form equations. This example is, of course, special as well as simple. The maximum-likelihood estimate of the reduced form equation is simultaneously, or can be transformed into, a least-squares estimate of the reduced form, a full-information maximum-likelihood estimate of the whole system, and a limited-information maximum-likelihood estimate of the consumption function. All three of these identical estimates are therefore superior to least-squares structural estimates, in a sense, for this model.

If a model is exactly identified, there exists a set of least-squares estimates that provide efficient estimates of the reduced forms. These are also maximum-likelihood estimates of the reduced form and can be transformed into maximum-likelihood estimates of the structural parameters. They are, however, very particular least-squares estimates and not those that are customarily obtained from the separate treatment of each structural equation. The least-squares estimates of the structural equation, in the form usually made, do not in general preserve their efficiency properties under transformation to reduced form parameters. To put this in concrete terms of the simple model considered in this section, we note that the least-squares estimate of the marginal propensity to consume does not provide an efficient estimate of the multiplier (although a least-squares estimate of the multiplier would, in fact, be efficient). In over-identified systems, the lack of invariance of the efficiency property under transformation proves to be more important.

In the next section, we shall compare efficiency of least-squares and full- and limited-information maximum-likelihood estimates of the reduced forms, in more general cases, including overidentification. In another section, however, we shall present some results of a sampling experiment with small samples and overidentification, which show clearly the failure of least-squares estimates to retain efficiency under transformation.

THE EFFICIENCY OF *A PRIORI* RESTRICTIONS

It has frequently been remarked that by imposing *a priori* restrictions on an economic model we gain efficiency of estimation because more information is brought to bear on the problem than is the case in the absence of such restrictions.[8] It is the purpose of this section to give a formal proof of this point of view and to interpret it.

[8]See e.g. T. C. Koopmans and Wm. C. Hood, 'Estimation of relationships,' esp. p. 176.

Liu has posed the seemingly paradoxical proposition: Least-squares estimates of the reduced form parameters in linear systems, ignoring all *a priori* restrictions, lead to a higher point on the likelihood function, assuming normally distributed disturbances, than do restricted maximum-likelihood estimates; therefore the unrestricted estimates are to be preferred.[9] Put in another way, he observes that squared discrepancies between predicted and actual values of endogenous variables in a linear model will be smaller over the sample period if calculated from (unrestricted) least-squares estimates of the reduced form equations than if calculated from any set of estimates of structural parameters using *a priori* restrictions.[10] If the least-squares values of the reduced forms give better 'predictions' over the sample period, should we not expect them to give better predictions outside the sample?

While the least-squares estimates of the reduced forms are *consistent* and while they lead to minimal squared residuals; they do not lead to *efficient* estimates of the reduced form parameters. We shall now turn to the proof of the proposition that the more one uses valid information in the form of *a priori* restrictions imposed on the system, the more efficient are the estimates.

Let us write a linear model as

$$By_t + \Gamma z_t = u_t, \qquad (2.1)$$

with reduced form

$$y_t = -B^{-1}\Gamma z_t + B^{-1}u_t. \qquad (2.2)$$

y_t, z_t and u_t are column vectors with n, m, and n components, respectively. B is a square, nonsingular, matrix of order $n \times n$, while Γ is rectangular of order $n \times m$.

We can also write the reduced form equation as

$$y_t = \Pi z_t + v_t, \qquad (2.10)$$

obscuring the relation between its coefficients and those of the structural equations. On multiplying both sides of this equation by B,

---

[9] T. C. Liu, 'A simple forecasting model for the U.S. economy,' *International Monetary Fund Staff Papers*, IV, August (1955), 464–6. Liu's argument is actually more in terms of a supposed inherent tendency towards underidentification in models of an economic system than in terms of the point reached on the likelihood function with and without restriction. He uses the latter point, however, in justification of his claim of lack of identifiability. His general conclusion is that we can do no better than to make unrestricted least-squares estimates of the reduced forms.

[10] In the case of exact identification, least squares estimates of the reduced form parameters will coincide with fully restricted maximum likelihood estimates.

however, we find

$$B\Pi = -\Gamma, \quad (2.11)$$

by equating coefficients of like variables in the reduced form and structural equations. Some elements of Γ are zero; therefore $B\Pi$ has the same zero elements. These are the restrictions. Let us write, symbolically,

$$(B\Pi)_r = 0 \quad (2.12)$$

to show that r elements of Γ are zero, and that corresponding elements of $B\Pi$ are zero.

The logarithm of the likelihood function of the entire system can be written as

$$L = \text{const} - \frac{T}{2}\log|\Omega_v| - \tfrac{1}{2}\sum_{t=1}^{T} v_t'\Omega_v^{-1}v_t + \lambda'(B\Pi)_r. \quad (2.13)$$

Ω_v = matrix of variances and covariance of elements of v_t. λ is a vector of Lagrange multipliers with r non-zero elements. If there were no restrictions on the system, variances and covariances of est Π are given by

$$\left\| -\frac{\partial^2 L}{\partial \pi_{ik}\partial \pi_{jl}} \right\|^{-1} = \left\| \sigma^{ij}M_{zz} \right\|^{-1} = \left\| \sigma_{ij}M_{zz}^{-1} \right\|. \quad (2.14)$$

where

σ^{ij} = typical element of Ω_v^{-1}.
σ_{ij} = typical element of Ω_v.
M_{zz} = moment matrix of predetermined variables, z_t.

The elements of this inverse matrix (2.14) are the variances and covariances of unrestricted least-squares estimates of Π. For any particular equation in this complete set of reduced forms, the appropriate variance-covariance matrix is $\sigma_{ii}M_{zz}^{-1}$. To determine the variance of forecast for any endogenous variable, outside the sample values, we have, by Hotelling's formulation of the problem of prediction error,

$$S_F^2 = \sigma_{ii}(1 + z_F'M_{zz}^{-1}z_F), \quad (2.15)$$

where z_F denotes a vector of values assigned to predetermined variables in the forecast period.

Suppose now that we have r restrictions on the maximization of the likelihood function, then the variances and covariances of est Π are given by the NW principal minor, $\hat{A}$, on the right-hand side of the following expression

$$\left\| \begin{array}{c:c} -\dfrac{\partial^2 L}{\partial \pi_{ik} \partial \pi_{jl}} & \Lambda \\ \hdashline \Lambda' & 0 \end{array} \right\|^{-1} = \left\| \begin{array}{c:c} \hat{A} & \hat{\Lambda} \\ \hdashline \hat{\Lambda}' & \Phi \end{array} \right\|. \tag{2.16}$$

The bordering matrix Λ consists of elements of λ obtained as $-\partial^2 L/\partial \pi_{ij} \partial b_{kl}$, where b_{kl} are the elements of B.

Theorem Consider an $m \times m$ principal minor of $\hat{A}$ corresponding to the ith reduced form equation. Denote this principal minor by $\hat{A}_{ip}$.
It follows that

$$z'_F \hat{A}_{ip} z_F \leqslant \sigma_{ii} z'_F M_{zz}^{-1} z_F.$$

Proof Denote a vector of mn elements by w.
Let

$$\det \left\| \begin{array}{c:c} -(\partial^2 L)/(\partial \pi_{ik} \partial \pi_{jl}) & \lambda \\ \hdashline \lambda' & 0 \end{array} \right\| = \Delta, \tag{2.17}$$

where λ is a vector.

Form the difference

$$\delta = \frac{\sum_{i,j=1}^{mn} \Delta_{00 \cdot ij} w_i w_j}{\Delta_{00}} - \frac{\sum_{i,j=1}^{mn} \Delta_{ij} w_i w_j}{\Delta}.$$

Δ_{00} is formed from Δ by deleting the last row and column. $\Delta_{00 \cdot ij}$ is formed from Δ_{00} by deleting the ith row and jth column.

$$\delta = \frac{\Delta \sum_{i,j=1}^{mn} \Delta_{00 \cdot ij} w_i w_j - \Delta_{00} \sum_{i,j=1}^{mn} \Delta_{ij} w_i w_j}{\Delta \Delta_{00}}.$$

By Jacobi's theorem on determinants[11] we have

$$\Delta \Delta_{00 \cdot ij} = \Delta_{00} \Delta_{ij} - \Delta_{0j} \Delta_{0i};$$

therefore

$$\delta = -\frac{\sum_{i,j=1}^{mn} \Delta_{0j} \Delta_{0i} w_i w_j}{\Delta \Delta_{00}} = -\frac{\left(\sum_{i=1}^{mn} \Delta_{0i} w_i \right)^2}{\Delta \Delta_{00}} \geqslant 0. \tag{2.18}$$

[11] See e.g. A. C. Aitken, *Determinants and Matrices*, London: Oliver and Boyd (1942), pp. 98–9.

The difference, δ, is positive since Δ_{00} is a positive definite quadratic form. Determinants of positive definite quadratic forms obtained by successive rows and columns of bordering alternate in sign; hence

$-\Delta\Delta_{00} > 0$.

Thus by bordering

$$\det\left\|-\frac{\partial^2 L}{\partial \pi_{ik}\partial \pi_{jl}}\right\| = \Delta_{00} \tag{2.19}$$

with one row and column, we find

$$w'(\Delta^{-1})_{00}w \leqslant w'(\Delta_{00})^{-1}w. \tag{2.20}$$

By bordering Δ with a row and column to form $(_{11}\Delta)$, we similarly find

$$w'[(_{11}\Delta)^{-1}]_{00.00}w \leqslant w'(\Delta^{-1})_{00}w, \tag{2.21}$$

and so on for successive borderings. By letting all elements of w vanish except the m elements in z_F corresponding to the $m \times m$ principal minor of $\hat{A}$ associated with ith reduced form equation, we have

$$z'_F \hat{A}_{ip} z_F \leqslant \sigma_{ii} z'_F M_{zz}^{-1} z_F, \tag{2.22}$$

as was to be proved.

The total variance of forecast from a system of structural equations is composed of two factors, the variance of disturbances σ_{ii} and a quadratic form (plus unity) in the assumed values of the predetermined variables. The matrix of this quadratic form when multiplied by σ_{ii} is the variance–covariance matrix of reduced form parameter estimates. By adding information to the system in the form of restrictions on the parameters, we decrease the magnitude of this quadratic form. The *estimated* value of forecast error will reflect differences in estimation procedure, the calculated variance of residuals being lowest when no restrictions are used. Nevertheless, the underlying or inherent error using the true value of σ_{ii} in the formula for prediction error will be smaller, the more one employs *a priori* restrictions in calculating the structural characteristics.

The succession of inequalities derived shows that full-information maximum-likelihood estimates will be more efficient than limited-information-maximum-likelihood estimates since more restrictions are used with the former than with the latter set. Both of these methods, in turn, will be more efficient than unrestricted least-squares estimates of the reduced forms.

In connection with limited-information estimates a word of explanation is in order. When any single equation in a system is being

50 Economic Theory and Econometrics

estimated, this method will produce a set of reduced form estimates, separately involving each of the endogenous variables in that equation. Insofar as a single endogenous variable appears in several different structural equations, there will be several possible reduced form equations that could serve as alternative forecasting equations. The best among these will be that set which yields the smallest quadratic form

$$z'_F \hat{A}_{ip} z_F.$$

This will be inferior to the full-information maximum-likelihood estimates. Another way of using limited-information estimates in practical forecasting, is by solving algebraically for reduced form equations in a structural system, each equation of which has been estimated by the method of limited information.[12]

The foregoing results on the efficiency of the use of *a priori* information follow closely a development by Samuelson called 'the generalized Le Chatelier principle.'[13] Samuelson shows that the sensitivity of an economic variable to a parameter change, e.g. price elasticity of demand, decreases as the number of restraints imposed upon the system increases. He proves this proposition by bordering a matrix of second derivatives of a function being maximized. In a sense, this paper extends his results from inequalities on diagonal elements of inverse bordered matrices to quadratic forms of principal minors.[14] If we were interested solely in variances of individual coefficients in the reduced form, his result would be directly applicable. Since the forecast error involves an entire quadratic form, his proposition must be extended. It may also be remarked that Samuelson's proposition is not a perfect analogue for ours. His bordered matrices are those familiar in establishing conditions for extremes, while ours would have to be bordered further to take that form.

SOME EXPERIMENTAL SAMPLING RESULTS

The argument so far has been based on asymptotic theory. In a constructed experiment with repeated small samples, G. W. Ladd has produced some extremely interesting findings relevant to the problems

---

[12]L. R. Klein and A. S. Goldberger, *An Econometric Model of the United States, 1929–1952*, Amsterdam: North-Holland Publishing Co. (1955).

[13]P. A. Samuelson, *Foundations of Economic Analysis*, Cambridge: Harvard University Press (1947), pp. 36–9.

[14]Samuelson's demonstration in the first printing contains some minor compensating errors, but the final results are quite correct.

of this paper.[15] His model consists of two overidentified (demand and supply) equations.

$$y_{1t} = \beta_{12} y_{2t} + \gamma_{11} z_{1t} + \gamma_{12} z_{2t} + u_{1t}$$
$$y_{1t} = \beta_{22} y_{2t} + \gamma_{23} z_{3t} + \gamma_{24} z_{4t} + u_{2t}.$$
(2.23)

He assigned specific population values to the structural coefficients and drew random numbers for the disturbances and the exogenous variables. The endogenous variables, y_{1t} and y_{2t}, were then computed from the structural equations in (2.23). Ladd was particularly interested in the effects of errors of observation; therefore he added to each of the endogenous and exogenous variables an error of observation.

Thirty samples of thirty observations each were obtained by drawing the six sets of observation errors repeatedly, while the disturbances u_{it}, are not changed from sample to sample. The errors in y_{1t} are, together with linear functions of u_{it}, values of reduced form disturbances; thus the model differs from that treated above by having observation errors in the other variables. For each sample, Ladd computed from the observations on the ys and zs, estimates of the structural parameters by the method of least squares and the method of limited information.[16] From each of these two types of estimates we can derive, algebraically, reduced form estimates in each sample.

If we denote least-squares estimates by a ~ sign and limited information estimates by a ^ sign, we can derive two possible reduced forms for each sample,

$$y_{1t} = \tilde{\gamma}_{11}\left(1 + \frac{\tilde{\beta}_{12}}{\tilde{\beta}_{22} - \tilde{\beta}_{12}}\right) z_{1t} + \tilde{\gamma}_{12}\left(1 + \frac{\tilde{\beta}_{12}}{\tilde{\beta}_{22} - \tilde{\beta}_{12}}\right) z_{2t}$$
$$- \tilde{\gamma}_{23} \frac{\tilde{\beta}_{12}}{\tilde{\beta}_{22} - \tilde{\beta}_{12}} z_{3t} - \tilde{\gamma}_{24} \frac{\tilde{\beta}_{12}}{\tilde{\beta}_{22} - \tilde{\beta}_{12}} z_{4t}$$
(2.24)
$$y_{2t} = \frac{\tilde{\gamma}_{11}}{\tilde{\beta}_{22} - \tilde{\beta}_{12}} z_{1t} + \frac{\tilde{\gamma}_{12}}{\tilde{\beta}_{22} - \tilde{\beta}_{12}} z_{2t} - \frac{\tilde{\gamma}_{23}}{\tilde{\beta}_{22} - \tilde{\beta}_{12}} z_{3t} - \frac{\tilde{\gamma}_{24}}{\tilde{\beta}_{22} - \tilde{\beta}_{12}} z_{4t}$$

or the same equations with $\tilde{\gamma}_{11}$ replaced by $\hat{\gamma}_{11}$, $\tilde{\gamma}_{12}$ by $\hat{\gamma}_{12}$, etc.

Alternatively, without taking any of the identifying restrictions into account, we can postulate general reduced form equations

$$y_{1t} = p_{11} z_{1t} + p_{12} z_{2t} + p_{13} z_{3t} + p_{14} z_{4t}$$
$$y_{2t} = p_{21} z_{1t} + p_{22} z_{2t} + p_{23} z_{3t} + p_{24} z_{4t}$$
(2.25)

[15] G. W. Ladd, 'Effects of shocks and errors in estimation: An empirical comparison,' *Journal of Farm Economics*, XXXVIII (1956), 485–95.
[16] In the least-squares regressions, y_{1t} is selected as the dependent variable.

52 Economic Theory and Econometrics

whose coefficients are estimated from the least-squares regressions of y_{1t} and y_{2t} on z_{1t}, z_{2t}, z_{3t} and z_{4t}. These regressions are obtained as a by-product of the limited-information estimates.

Table 2.1 gives the results of our computations from Ladd's data. For the three methods of estimating the reduced forms, I have calculated the mean and standard deviation of the thirty sample values of each parameter. The computations in the table assume, in effect, that there are thirty independent samples; however, the fact that the vectors $(u_{i1}, u_{i2}, \ldots u_{i,30})$ are unchanged in repeated samples, means that the

Table 2.1 Sample means and standard deviations of estimates of reduced form parameters obtained by three methods

	Population parameter	Sample mean	Sample standard deviation
1 Reduced form coefficients derived from least-squares estimates of structural parameters.			
p_{11}	0.05	0.011	0.017
p_{12}	0.27	0.094	0.083
p_{13}	0.06	0.116	0.040
p_{14}	0.11	0.127	0.036
p_{21}	−0.16	−0.295	0.280
p_{22}	−0.90	−2.054	0.360
p_{23}	0.30	0.670	0.224
p_{24}	0.56	0.770	0.323
2 Reduced form coefficients derived from limited-information estimates of structural parameters.			
p_{11}	0.05	0.045	0.046
p_{12}	0.27	0.254	0.042
p_{13}	0.06	0.037	0.026
p_{14}	0.11	0.123	0.046
p_{21}	−0.16	−0.127	0.118
p_{22}	−0.90	−0.957	0.132
p_{23}	0.30	0.175	0.089
p_{24}	0.56	0.559	0.129
3 Reduced form coefficients estimated directly from least-squares regressions of y_{1t} and y_{2t} on z_{1t}, z_{2t}, and z_{4t}.			
p_{11}	0.05	0.028	0.094
p_{12}	0.27	0.258	0.049
p_{13}	0.06	0.044	0.071
p_{14}	0.11	0.121	0.048
p_{21}	−0.16	−0.027	0.314
p_{22}	−0.90	−0.951	0.138
p_{23}	0.30	0.091	0.242
p_{24}	0.56	0.576	0.151

composite reduced form disturbance, consisting of a linear function of u_{it} and observation error, contains a common element in each sample. Since the variance of this linear function of u_{it} is not small relative to the variance of observation error there is significant correlation in the random terms from sample to sample. In comparing the different methods of estimation we do not have as much information as would be given by thirty independent samples.

In comparing the first two methods, least-squares and limited information structural estimates, the bias of the former is clearly shown.[17] In all cases, the mean of the limited-information estimate is closer than the mean of the least-squares estimate to the population value. In six of eight cases, the sample standard deviation of parameter estimates is lower for limited-information than for least-squares estimates. This is a reflection of the proposition that, in general, the optimal properties of least-squares estimates are not preserved under transformation.[18]

In comparing the last two methods, it can be seen that neither shows much bias, which is as expected, but that limited-information estimates have uniformly smaller variance. This is a small sample exposition of the results derived in the preceding section.

Ladd's results are extremely suggestive for our purposes though not conclusive. Of course, results from constructed experiments do not constitute general proof of investigated propositions, but Ladd's experiment is far less than perfectly designed for the particular objectives of this paper. It would be desirable to carry through similar experiments without the complication of observation error. Even within the framework of Ladd's experimental design, there are changes that could be made to strengthen the present inquiry. Both least-square structural regressions were made with y_{1t} as the dependent variable, but other choices deserve to be investigated in the present context. This is especially true since the population correlation between u_{2t} and y_{2t} is as high as 0.56. It is the correlation between disturbances and independent variables in regression analysis that introduces bias. The results in the table are also restrictive in that they deal only with variances and neglect covariance. A single statistic constructed along the lines of the standard error of forecast would be more adequate. In a future sampling inquiry some of these deficiencies can be remedied.

---

[17]Limited information estimates are consistent but not generally unbiased. In small samples of the type under consideration, bias may be revealed in them as well. Here the argument is simply that limited information estimates reveal, in the sampling experiment, a smaller degree of bias.

[18]The standard deviations are computed about sample means. If they were computed about population means, the least-squares results would compare even less favorably.

3

The Estimation of Distributed Lags

Koyck in his recent book proposes a particular lag scheme for the purpose of studying investment behavior and similar problems in econometrics.[1] A general distributed lag of the form

$$y_t = \sum_{i=0}^{\infty} \alpha_i x_{t-i} + u_t, \tag{3.1}$$

in which y_t and x_t are observable variables of interest to the economist and u_t is a random disturbance, is clumsy and presents inherent difficulties. In the first place, the right-hand sum must be truncated at a finite point allowing sufficient degrees of freedom in the statistical estimates of the parameters. Secondly, intercorrelation among the successive values of x_{t-i} often imparts a high degree of unreliability to the estimates of the individual parameters α_i. Sums or other functions of the parameters may be estimated with a fair degree of precision even though individual components are quite unreliable; nevertheless for some problems we may need to use estimates of specific parameters, not the more reliably estimated functions of them. Thirdly, a substantial amount of work may be involved in estimating all the individual coefficients α_i.

To get round these problems, Koyck proposes a more restrictive type of scheme

$$y_t = \alpha \sum_{i=0}^{\infty} \lambda^i x_{t-i} + u_t \qquad (0 \leqslant \lambda < 1) \tag{3.2}$$

In this system of lags the coefficients decrease geometrically. Irving Fisher put forward at one time a related scheme in which the coefficients decreased arithmetically.[2] Koyck's scheme has the apparent advantage that it is readily transformed into an equivalent relationship

---

[1] L. M. Koyck, *Distributed Lags and Investment Analysis*, Amsterdam: North-Holland Publishing Co. (1954).

[2] Irving Fisher, 'Note on a short-cut method for calculating distributed lags,' *Bulletin de L'Institut International de Statistique*, XXIX, 3, The Hague (1937), 323–7.

involving only three observable variables. Form the difference between the two equations:

$$y_t = \alpha x_t + \alpha\lambda x_{t-1} + \alpha\lambda^2 x_{t-2} + \cdots + u_t,$$

$$\lambda y_{t-1} = \alpha\lambda x_{t-1} + \alpha\lambda^2 x_{t-2} + \cdots + \lambda u_{t-1}$$

to get

$$y_t = \alpha x_t + \lambda y_{t-1} + u_t - \lambda u_{t-1}. \tag{3.3}$$

This is the simplified form that he uses in his study.

First I shall take up the statistical problem of estimating α and λ from a sample of observations on y_t and x_t. In a final section, I shall go on to a brief general discussion of the suitability of scheme (3.2) or its derivative (3.3), for the investigation of particular problems in econometrics. An obvious procedure leading to estimates of α and λ in (3.3), is the use of the ordinary method of least-squares regression of y_t on x_t and y_{t-1} with $(u_t - \lambda u_{t-1})$ treated as a composite disturbance term. Lagged values in small samples give rise to least-squares bias,[3] but even in large samples the straightforward least-squares treatment of (3.3) will, as Koyck has shown, lead to biased estimates. The bias occurs since u_{t-1}, part of the composite disturbance, is not independent of y_{t-1}, one of the 'independent' variables. In addition, the composite disturbance has an automatic serial correlation even if the u_t are serially independent, i.e. $u_t - \lambda u_{t-1}$ is correlated with $u_{t-1} - \lambda u_{t-2}$ because both expressions contain a mutual term in u_{t-1}.[4]

Koyck develops a method for estimating α and λ without bias but makes it depend on an assumed value for ξ in

$$u_t = \xi u_{t-1} + e_t. \tag{3.4}$$

In other words he assumes that the original series u_t may be autocorrelated, but does not give a method for estimating ξ from the sample data.

In this paper it is proposed to show that Koyck's consistent estimate is a type of maximum likelihood estimate in the case $\xi = 0$ (or some other known value) and to suggest a method for estimating α, λ, and ξ simultaneously from the sample data, when ξ is not assumed to be known. In addition, we shall show how the computational steps

[3]L. Hurwicz 'Least-squares bias in time series,' *Statistical Inference in Dynamic Economic Models*, ed. by T. Koopmans, John Wiley and Sons, New York (1950), pp. 365–83.

[4]Transformations of equations in dynamic systems may generally introduce serial correlation. See in this connection L. Hurwicz, 'Stochastic models of economic fluctuations,' *Econometrica*, 12 (1944), 114–24.

suggested by Koyck for obtaining a consistent estimate can be simplified.

NONAUTOCORRELATED DISTURBANCES ($\xi = 0$)

Koyck suggests that one first computes ordinary least-squares estimates of α and λ from the regression of y_t on x_t and y_{t-1}. Call these a and l. From this regression compute the sum of squared residuals

$$\sum_{t=1}^{T} z_t^2 = \sum_{t=1}^{T} (y_t - ax_t - ly_{t-1})^2.$$

For consistent estimates of α and λ, he proposes the two equations

$$\bar{\alpha}\sum x_t^2 + \bar{\lambda}\sum y_{t-1}x_t = \sum y_t x_t$$
$$\bar{\alpha}\sum x_t y_{t-1} + \bar{\lambda}\sum y_{t-1}^2 = \sum y_t y_{t-1} + \frac{\bar{\lambda}\sum z_t^2}{1+l\bar{\lambda}}. \tag{3.5}$$

If $\bar{\alpha}$ were eliminated from (3.5), we would have a quadratic in $\bar{\lambda}$.
Another way of looking at equation (3.3) is the following:

$$(y_t - u_t) = \alpha x_t + \lambda(y_{t-1} - u_{t-1}). \tag{3.3}$$

In this form, we have the classical equation of the linear relation with variables subject to observation error. Since u_t is, by assumption, a nonautocorrelated series, the two errors are independent. The 'true' values, or 'systematic' parts of the observed variables are each independent of the errors as required in the classical model as long as x_t is independent of the errors. This can be immediately seen from

$$Eu_t(y_t - u_t) = Eu_t \alpha \sum_{i=0}^{\infty} \lambda^i x_{t-i}.$$

In short, all the standard assumptions of the classical model are met in the case at hand. With that model it is well known that estimates of the coefficient parameters depend on the ratios of the error variances. In equation (3.3) this ratio is unity for a long series.

$$Eu_t^2 = Eu_{t-1}^2.$$

If only two variables are involved, a variance ratio of unity implies an orthogonal regression for estimation of the coefficients. In effect, we have a slight modification of that form of regression since two variables are assumed to be measured with the same error variance and a third with no error.

If the u_t follow the normal distribution, maximum likelihood estimates of α and λ from (3.3) are identical with a form of least-squares

Estimation of distributed lags 57

estimates.[5] Since the two error variances are equal, we can derive least-squares estimates as

$$\sum_{t=1}^{T} u_t^2 + \sum_{t=1}^{T} u_{t-1}^2 = \min$$

or

$$\sum_{t=1}^{T} (y_t - \alpha x_t - \lambda \eta_{t-1})^2 + \sum_{t=1}^{T} (y_{t-1} - \eta_{t-1})^2 = \min,$$

where

$$u_t + \eta_t = y_t.$$

The minimization is carried out with respect to each of the η_t (the 'systematic' part of the observed variable), α and λ. The first order conditions for minimization are

$$y_{t-1} - \eta_{t-1} + \lambda y_t - \lambda \alpha x_t - \lambda^2 \eta_{t-1} = 0 \quad (t=1,2,\ldots,T),$$

$$\sum_{t=1}^{T} y_t x_t - \alpha \sum_{t=1}^{T} x_t^2 - \lambda \sum_{t=1}^{T} x_t \eta_{t-1} = 0, \quad (3.6)$$

$$\sum_{t=1}^{T} y_t \eta_{t-1} - \alpha \sum_{t=1}^{T} x_t \eta_{t-1} - \lambda \sum_{t=1}^{T} \eta_{t-1}^2 = 0.$$

From the first of these three equations, we can express η_{t-1} in terms of y_t, x_t, y_{t-1}, and the parameters. Substitution of this expression into the other two equations and rearrangement of terms leads to

$$\lambda^2 \left(\frac{\sum x_t y_{t-1} \sum y_t x_t}{\sum x_t^2} - \sum y_t y_{t-1} \right)$$

$$+ \lambda \left[\sum y_t^2 - \sum y_{t-1}^2 + \frac{(\sum x_t y_{t-1})^2 - (\sum y_t x_t)^2}{\sum x_t^2} \right]$$

$$+ \left(\sum y_t y_{t-1} - \frac{\sum x_t y_{t-1} \sum y_t x_t}{\sum x_t^2} \right) = 0.$$

An estimate of λ is obtained directly by extraction of a root from this quadratic equation, and the other coefficient is estimated from

$$\text{est } \alpha = \frac{-\text{est } \lambda \sum x_t y_{t-1} + \sum x_t y_t}{\sum x_t^2}.$$

---
[5]See Appendix. The 'maximum likelihood' estimates discussed in the text are not *full* maximum likelihood estimates since some restrictions are ignored in the maximization process.

The advantage of this computing method over Koyck's is that one does not have to make estimates in two steps, but the values obtained will be exactly the same as his, computed from (3.5). Without going through the algebraic manipulations we may simply remark that the quadratic in $\bar{\lambda}$ implied by equation system (3.5) is exactly the same as that implied by (3.6).[6] Apart from the computational facility, we may interpret Koyck's consistent estimate as either a generalized least-squares or a maximum likelihood estimate. For given values of x_t, it can also be interpreted as the orthogonal regression of y_t on y_{t-1}.

Another way of looking at the problem, from a general point of view, is through the well-known determinantal equation associated with the estimation of the linear structural equation with observational errors. To estimate the coefficients of

$$\sum_{i=0}^{n} \alpha_i (y_{it} - u_{it}) = 0,$$

we form the equation

$$\det \left\| \sum y_{it} y_{jt} - \delta_{ij} \mu \sigma_{ij} \right\| = 0$$

where δ_{ij} is the Kronecker *delta* and σ_{ij} is the covariance between u_{it} and u_{jt}. The characteristic vector of this equation is the estimate of the coefficients α_i, but without knowing the ratios among the variances of the different u_{it}, we cannot find it. In the context of Koyck's equations, the appropriate determinant is

$$\begin{vmatrix} \sum y_t^2 - \mu \sigma^2 & \sum y_t x_t & \sum y_t y_{t-1} \\ \sum y_t x_t & \sum x_t^2 & \sum x_t y_{t-1} \\ \sum y_t y_{t-1} & \sum x_t y_{t-1} & \sum y_{t-1}^2 - \mu \sigma^2 \end{vmatrix} = 0.$$

This defines a quadratic equation in $\mu \sigma^2$, where σ^2 is the common variance of u_t and u_{t-1}, the root of this quadratic and the solution vector of the associated equation system.

$$\sum y_t^2 - \mu \sigma^2 - \alpha \sum y_t x_t - \lambda \sum y_t y_{t-1} = 0$$

$$\sum y_t x_t - \alpha \sum x_t^2 - \lambda \sum x_t y_{t-1} = 0$$

$$\sum y_t y_{t-1} - \alpha \sum x_t y_{t-1} - \lambda (\sum y_{t-1}^2 - \mu \sigma^2) = 0$$

yield the same estimates as those from either equations (3.5) or (3.6).

---

[6] To prove this, express $\bar{\alpha}$ in terms of $\bar{\lambda}$ in the first equation of (3.5); substitute into the second and collect terms. At the same time, the ordinary least-squares estimate of λ, written as l in (3.5), should be expressed in terms of the moments $\sum x_t^2, \sum x_t y_t, \sum x_t y_{t-1}, \sum y_{t-1}^2$, and $\sum y_t y_{t-1}$.

With this method of formulation, however, one can readily extend the principles to any number of variables.

AUTOCORRELATED DISTURBANCES ($\xi \neq 0$)

Koyck suggests that nonzero autocorrelation of disturbances is usual and assumes the more complicated model involving unknown ξ, although he gives no basis for estimating ξ from the data.

If we were not confronted with the additional difficulties concerned with distributed lags, we could readily develop a procedure for estimating a linear equation with autocorrelated disturbances.[7] In this case it is possible to derive a polynomial in the unknown autoregressive parameter, alone. For any given value of the autoregressive parameter, it is possible to estimate the other parameters from a linear system. Thus in two steps the nonlinear system of estimation equations can be solved.

The situation combining distributed lags and autocorrelated disturbances is similar but not quite so favorable. As in the simpler case mentioned above, the coefficient parameters can be directly estimated for any given value of the autoregressive parameter. We see this immediately by remarking that the equation to be estimated can be changed into one not involving autocorrelated errors by suitable transformations of variables. Thus if we have as an objective the estimation of (3.3) and if the disturbances follow the autoregressive law in (3.4), we find that (3.3) can be transformed to

$$y'_t = \alpha x'_t + \lambda y'_{t-1} + e_t - \lambda e_{t-1}. \qquad (3.7)$$

The transformations are

$$y'_t = y_t - \xi y_{t-1},$$
$$x'_t = x_t - \xi x_{t-1}.$$

If the variables are subjected to the same autoregressive transformation as that followed by the disturbances we can derive an equation that has the same form as (3.3). If ξ were known *a priori*, we could make the same computations with the transformed as with the original variables for the estimation of α and λ in the case treated previously with nonautocorrelated disturbances. The errors e_t are assumed to be nonautocorrelated.

---

[7]See L. R. Klein, *A Textbook of Econometrics*, Row, Peterson and Co., Evanston (1953), 85–9.

We can see from the substitution of (3.4) into (3.3),

$$y_t = \alpha x_t + \lambda y_{t-1} + \xi u_{t-1} + e_t - \lambda u_{t-1},$$

that the special case of $\xi = \lambda$ can be handled very simply. The least-squares regression of y_t on x_t and y_{t-1} would give consistent and efficient estimates.

The problem then is to estimate (3.7) for $\xi \neq \lambda$ and $\xi \neq 0$. Let us assume that e_t is normally distributed and nonautocorrelated. Maximum likelihood[8] or generalized least-squares estimates will be obtained from

$$\sum_{t=1}^{T} e_t^2 + \sum_{t=1}^{T} e_{t-1}^2 = \min$$

or

$$\sum_{t=1}^{T} (y_t' - \alpha x_t' - \lambda \eta_{t-1}')^2 + \sum_{t=1}^{T} (y_{t-1}' - \eta_{t-1}')^2 = \min,$$

where

$$e_t + \eta_t' = y_t'.$$

The minimization is carried out with respect to each of the η_t', α, λ, and ξ. Equations of the same form as those in (3.6) above will be obtained with the only alteration being that primes are placed on all the variables. Let us call such an equation system (3.6′). In addition there will be one more equation (minimization with respect to ξ).

$$\sum_{t=1}^{T} [y_t - \xi y_{t-1} - \alpha(x_t - \xi x_{t-1}) - \lambda \eta_{t-1}'](\alpha x_{t-1} - y_{t-1})$$

$$+ \sum_{t=1}^{T} (y_{t-1} - \xi y_{t-2} - \eta_{t-1}')(-y_{t-2}) = 0. \quad (3.8)$$

Equation (3.8) together with (3.6′) can be solved for all the unknown parameters jointly. From similar equations developed without taking up the question of distributed lags, it was possible to derive a single polynomial in the autoregressive parameter. The form of (3.8) and (3.6′) is not correspondingly simple, but a straightforward iteration process can be developed to obtain a solution. First assume a value for ξ and transform computed moments of the original variables into moments of the primed variables. Using the methods of the previous section ($\xi = 0$), one can solve equation system (3.6′) for estimates of α and λ. Next, with the first round estimates of α and λ, solve (3.8) for ξ. In doing this step

[8]See Appendix.

Estimation of distributed lags 61

η'_{t-1} will have to be eliminated from (3.8) by means of the first equation in (3.6'). Repeat the process using the first round estimate of ξ, and so on.

SOME COMMENTS ON THE INTERPRETATION AND SIGNIFICANCE
OF DISTRIBUTED LAGS

Koyck derives equation (3.3) from the original distributed lags form in equation (3.2). If the disturbances in (3.2) are nonautocorrelated, the disturbances in the equation (3.3) are autocorrelated. This approach may, however, be reversed. From an equation of the form

$$y_t = \alpha x_t + \lambda y_{t-1} + v_t,$$

with known initial value y_0, we can derive

$$y_t = \alpha \sum_{i=0}^{t-1} \lambda^i x_{t-i} + \sum_{i=0}^{t-1} \lambda^i v_{t-i} + \lambda^t y_0.$$

Thus if we start with the hypothesis that y_t is a linear function of x_t and y_{t-1}, subject to an additive nonautocorrelated disturbance, the derived equation of distributed lags will be autocorrelated. Between these extreme cases we have cases more general, but more difficult to handle, in which both u_t (of equation (3.2)) and v_t are autocorrelated.

It might be thought that if the whole history of explanatory variables, x_t, is taken into account there would not be autocorrelation in the residual variation. If this were the case, the simplest methods developed in this paper for $\xi = 0$ would be immediately applicable. In dealing with cross-section data, the techniques for $\xi = 0$ would seem to be appropriate. In a cross-section sample, we are concerned with mutual independence of all disturbances and lack of such independence is not, as in a time-series sample, represented by autocorrelation. The type of bias involved in Koyck's problem is, however, present if each unit in the sample is assumed to behave according to the distributed lag scheme of (3.2). When each individual's equation is transformed into (3.3), the sample estimate of the relationship should be made using the method developed here for $\xi = 0$. This type of model has been discussed by Prais in a study of corporate savings behavior from a sample of individual company records.[9] He follows Dobrovolsky[10] in making

---

[9] S. Prais, 'Some problems in the econometric analysis of company accounts.' Paper presented at the 1956 European meeting of the Econometric Society, Aix-en-Provence.

[10] S. P. Dobrovolsky, *Corporate Income Retention, 1915–43*, National Bureau of Economic Research, New York (1951).

lagged dividends a determinant of either current savings or dividend disbursements and shows how the latter's equation can be interpreted in terms of Koyck's distributed lags.

From an empirical point of view one is probably more likely to find low or negligible serial correlation in the computed residuals of the regression of y_t on x_t and y_{t-1}. The use of y_{t-1} as an explanatory variable will probably extract most of the serial dependence among the residuals. There is a measure of logical consistency in starting out with an equation of the form

$$y_t = \alpha x_t + \lambda y_{t-1} + v_t,$$

estimating the parameters by conventional methods on the assumption that v_t is nonautocorrelated, and then deriving the distributed lag scheme from this equation. Some authors have formulated their theories of behavior originally in terms of an equation of this type while others begin with the distributed lag of (3.2). Koyck, however, is alone in paying proper attention to the properties of disturbances when one passes from one form to the other.

In studies of the consumption function, Brown (with the present writer, Stone and Rowe following his lead) has used lagged consumption as an explanatory variable.[11] Stone and Rowe begin with the straightforward premise of lagged consumption behavior and derive Koyck's distributed lag model. They do not deal with the stochastic properties of the model and consequently do not go into the problems of bias in estimation. Friedman, in a recent attempt to construct a theory of the consumption function, has put forward a distributed lag scheme similar to Koyck's,[12] but as a continuous instead of a discrete distribution. Friedman obtains parameter estimates from a truncated distribution of lags without transforming to a simpler equation; however, his graphical residuals appear to be serially correlated. Brown's methods of estimation do not build on Koyck's premise, although his equation may be interpreted in this light. Brown estimates his equation, however, as though the disturbances are not serially correlated, and his residuals are not in fact serially correlated.

Intercorrelation among explanatory variables such as x_{t-1}, x_{t-2}, x_{t-3}, etc., is, as mentioned earlier, a reason advanced by Koyck for

[11] T. M. Brown, 'Habit persistence and lags in consumer behavior,' *Econometrica*, **20** (1952), 355–71. L. R. Klein and A. S. Goldberger, *An Econometric Model of the United States, 1929–52*, North-Holland Pub. Co., Amsterdam (1955). R. Stone and D. A. Rowe, 'Aggregate consumption and investment functions for the household sector considered in the light of British experience,' *National Økonomisk Tidskrift* (1956), 1–32.

[12] M. Friedman, *A Theory of the Consumption Function*, National Bureau of Economic Research, Princeton University Press, Princeton (1957).

making his distribution of lags depend on only two parameters, α and λ in

$$\alpha \sum_{i=0}^{\infty} \lambda^i x_{t-i}.$$

While it may frequently be the case that one finds high intercorrelation among different lagged values of the explanatory variable and consequent magnification of sampling errors in individual coefficients, this is perhaps not the best criterion to consider. An F-test which compares the ratio of variances with and without some entire particular lag scheme would seem to be more appropriate in choosing a system of lags than a separate test of each coefficient individually against some null hypothesis. Koyck's distributed lag has a very special time shape which cannot be justified on purely *a priori* grounds against other schemes, particularly those which allow more freedom to the estimation of the coefficients of the different values of x_{t-i}. An advantage, however, of Koyck's model is that it has an infinite time span historically and need not be cut off at an arbitrary finite lag.

For purposes of the present paper, I have tried to advance the understanding of Koyck's model by only one step. In doing so, his implicit assumption that x_t is an exogenous or predetermined variable has been retained. If there were a pure lag in equation (3.1), i.e. if this relation took the form

$$y_t = \sum_{i=1}^{\infty} \alpha_i x_{t-i} + u_t$$

by ruling out $i = 0$, large sample justification for the treatment in this paper could be made. Similarly if x_t is a purely exogenous variable (independent of u_t as Koyck assumes) the procedures developed follow quite readily. The estimation of the type of distributed lag considered for systems of simultaneous stochastic equations in which we do not have $Eu_t x_t = 0$ is a separate problem.

APPENDIX: MAXIMUM LIKELIHOOD ESTIMATES OF DISTRIBUTED LAGS[13]

In deriving maximum likelihood estimates of parameters in Koyck's distributed lag scheme

$$y_t = \alpha \sum_{i=0}^{\infty} \lambda^i x_{t-i} + u_t, \tag{3.2}$$

it would seem most natural to proceed directly without transforming the

---

[13] These remarks are the result of provocative queries by R. Radner.

equation to (3.3). Assuming $\xi=0$, the likelihood function is

$$e^L = p(u_1)p(u_2)\ldots p(u_T)$$

for a sample of T observations. If u_t is normally distributed with mean zero and variance σ^2, the maximization of e^L is equivalent to maximization of

$$L = -T[\log(2\pi)^{\frac{1}{2}} + \log \sigma] - \frac{1}{2\sigma^2} \sum_{t=1}^{T} u_t^2$$

with respect to α, λ, and σ. This, in turn, is equivalent to minimization of

$$S = \sum_{t=1}^{T} \left(y_t - \alpha \sum_{i=0}^{\infty} \lambda^i x_{t-i} \right)^2$$

with respect to α and λ. The first order conditions are

$$\sum_{t=1}^{T} \left(y_t - \alpha \sum_{i=0}^{\infty} \lambda^i x_{t-i} \right) \sum_{i=0}^{\infty} \lambda^i x_{t-i} = 0,$$

$$\sum_{t=1}^{T} \left(y_t - \alpha \sum_{i=0}^{\infty} \lambda^i x_{t-i} \right) \sum_{i=0}^{\infty} i\lambda^{i-1} x_{t-i} = 0. \tag{3.9}$$

Apart from involving infinite sums, these conditions are intractable nonlinear equations in α and λ.

In the definition of η_t as the 'true' or 'systematic' part of y_t,

$$y_t = \eta_t + u_t,$$

we see that η_t is also defined as

$$\eta_t = \alpha \sum_{i=0}^{\infty} \lambda^i x_{t-i}.$$

From this definition we can write

$$\alpha \sum_{i=0}^{\infty} \lambda^i x_{t-i} = \alpha \sum_{i=0}^{t-1} \lambda^i x_{t-i} + \lambda^t \eta_0.$$

Hence the sum of squares to be minimized is now written as

$$S = \sum_{t=1}^{T} \left(y_t - \alpha \sum_{i=0}^{t-1} \lambda^i x_{t-i} - \lambda^t \eta_0 \right)^2.$$

The first order conditions for minimization with respect to α, λ, and η_0 are

$$\sum_{t=1}^{T} \left(y_t - \alpha \sum_{0}^{t-1} \lambda^i x_{t-i} - \lambda^t \eta_0 \right) \sum_{0}^{t-1} \lambda^i x_{t-i} = 0,$$

$$\sum_{t=1}^{T} \left(y_t - \alpha \sum_{0}^{t-1} \lambda^i x_{t-i} - \lambda^t \eta_0 \right) \left(\alpha \sum_{0}^{t-1} i\lambda^{i-1} x_{t-i} + t\lambda^{t-1} \eta_0 \right) = 0,$$

$$\sum_{t=1}^{T} \left(y_t - \alpha \sum_{0}^{t-1} \lambda^i x_{t-i} - \lambda^t \eta_0 \right) \lambda^t = 0. \tag{3.10}$$

Estimation of distributed lags

These equations are in terms of finite sums but still remain highly nonlinear in the unknown parameters. It might be possible to solve them empirically by iteration although it may be a lengthy process. For an assumed value of λ, the first and third equations are linear in α and η_0. These two parameters can be estimated in the first round of approximations. With the first round estimates of α and η_0, λ can be estimated as a root of the remaining equation – a high order polynomial in λ. With a new estimate of λ, iterations of α and η_0 can proceed again, etc.

The estimates derived in the text by consideration of analogies from the theory of observation error are not maximum likelihood estimates in the sense of these implied by (3.10). In the first place, the double sum of squares

$$\sum_{t=1}^{T} u_t^2 + \sum_{t=1}^{T} u_{t-1}^2,$$

would be derived from the likelihood function (joint normal distribution)

$$p(u_1, u_0)p(u_2, u_1)\ldots p(u_T, u_{T-1}).$$

If we assume that $\xi = 0$, this expression becomes

$$p(u_0)[p(u_1)]^2[p(u_2)]^2 \ldots [p(u_{T-1})]^2 p(u_T);$$

if $p(u_0) = p(u_T)$ we have the square of the ordinary likelihood function

$$e^L = p(u_1)p(u_2)\ldots p(u_T).$$

The problem of end-effects in large samples is not serious; therefore this difference is not of major concern.

The straightforward procedure of minimizing

$$S = \sum_{t=1}^{T} \left(y_t - \alpha \sum_{i=0}^{t-1} \lambda^i x_{t-i} - \lambda^t \eta_0 \right)^2$$

can be derived from another formulation which is more closely connected with that used in the text. If we define

$$\eta_t = \alpha \sum_{i=0}^{\infty} \lambda^i x_{t-i},$$

the η_t must satisfy the recurrence formula

$$\eta_t = \alpha x_t + \lambda \eta_{t-1}.$$

The full maximum likelihood method is, therefore, equivalent to

$$S = \sum_{t=1}^{T} u_t^2 = \sum_{t=1}^{T} (y_t - \eta_t)^2 = \min$$

subject to

$$\eta_t = \alpha x_t + \lambda \eta_{t-1} \qquad (t = 1, 2, \ldots, T).$$

If instead of using Lagrange multipliers for minimization subject to restraint, we substitute all the constraints into S, term by term, we obtain

$$S=(y_1-\alpha x_1-\lambda\eta_0)^2+(y_2-\alpha x_2-\alpha\lambda x_1-\lambda^2\eta_0)+(y_3-\alpha x_3-\alpha\lambda x_2-\alpha\lambda^2 x_1-\lambda^3\eta_0)^2$$
$$+\cdots+(y_T-\alpha x_T-\alpha\lambda x_{T-1}-\alpha\lambda^2 x_{T-2}-\cdots-\alpha\lambda^{T-1}x_1-\lambda^T\eta_0)^2$$

or

$$S=\sum_{t=1}^{T}\left(y_t-\alpha\sum_{i=0}^{t-1}\lambda^i x_{t-i}-\lambda^t\eta_0\right)^2.$$

On the other hand, we did not fully substitute all the constraints when deriving the minimizing equation (3.6) in the text. There we substituted as follows:

$$\sum_{t=1}^{T}u_t^2+\sum_{t=1}^{T}u_{t-1}^2=\sum_{t=1}^{T}(y_t-\eta_t)^2+\sum_{t=1}^{T}(y_{t-1}-\eta_{t-1})^2$$
$$=\sum_{t=1}^{T}(y_t-\alpha x_t-\lambda\eta_{t-1})^2+\sum_{t=1}^{T}(y_{t-1}-\eta_{t-1})^2$$

since

$$\eta_t=\alpha x_t+\lambda\eta_{t-1}.$$

But this does not fully eliminate all the η_t except η_0.[14]

Two separate minimization problems may be formulated:

$$\sum_{t=1}^{T}(y_t-\alpha x_t-\lambda\eta_{t-1})^2+\sum_{t=1}^{T}(y_{t-1}-\eta_{t-1})^2=\min$$

subject to

$$\eta_t=\alpha x_t+\lambda\eta_{t-1} \quad (t=1,2,\ldots,T)$$

or

$$\sum_{t=1}^{T}(y_t-\alpha x_t-\lambda\eta_{t-1})^2+\sum_{t=1}^{T}(y_{t-1}-\eta_{t-1})^2=\min.$$

In the first, whether the method of Lagrange multipliers or direct substitution of restraints is used, the estimation equations are highly nonlinear. In the second, we have maximum likelihood equations not using all the constraints. We might call this a 'limited information maximum likelihood' method and it leads to nothing more complicated than a quadratic equation in the present model.

Two observations about the nature of the 'limited information maximum likelihood' estimates are revealing.

1 Although we do not have

$$\eta_t=\alpha x_t+\lambda\eta_{t-1}$$

for each time period, we do have

$$\lambda(\eta_t-\alpha x_t-\lambda\eta_{t-1})=-u_{t-1}-\lambda u_t;$$

therefore we can say that the restraint is satisfied, on the average.

---

[14] It may be remarked that if we had two separate 'systematic' variables, η_t and ζ_t, not related as are η_t and η_{t-1}, the simple elimination procedure would be valid.

2 The last two equations of (3.6) imply

$$\sum_{t=1}^{T}(u_t - \lambda u_{t-1})x_t = 0,$$

$$\sum_{t=1}^{T}(u_t - \lambda u_{t-1})\eta_{t-1} = 0.$$

By the assumption that x_t is an exogenous variable it is independent of both u_t and u_{t-1}. Since y_{t-1} is not independent of u_{t-1}, the method proposed in the text amounts to the definition of η_{t-1} in such a way that it is independent of $u_t - \lambda u_{t-1}$.[15] Koyck derives his correction for consistency of estimation from just this point of view.

[15] The first set of equations of (3.6) assigns values of η_{t-1} that will be independent of $u_t - \lambda u_{t-1}$.

4
Singularity in the Equation Systems of Econometrics: Some Aspects of the Problem of Multicollinearity

REVIEW

In estimating an equation of the form

$$y_t = \sum_{i=1}^{n} \alpha_i x_{it} + u_t \quad t = 1, \ldots, T,$$

it is well known that linear relationships among the 'explanatory' variables x_{it} give rise to singularities, indeterminancy, and nonfinite values of some parameter estimates.

We define

$$M = (m_{ij}) = \left(\frac{1}{T} \sum_{t=1}^{T} (x_{it} - \bar{x}_i)(x_{jt} - \bar{x}_j) \right),$$

$$M_{iy} = \begin{bmatrix} m_{11} & m_{12} & \cdots & m_{1,i-1} & m_{1y} & m_{1,i+1} & \cdots & m_{1n} \\ m_{21} & m_{22} & \cdots & m_{2,i-1} & m_{2y} & m_{2,i+1} & \cdots & m_{2n} \\ \vdots & \vdots & & \vdots & \vdots & \vdots & & \vdots \\ m_{n1} & m_{n2} & \cdots & m_{n,i-1} & m_{ny} & m_{n,i+1} & \cdots & m_{nn} \end{bmatrix},$$

$$m_{iy} = \frac{1}{T} \sum_{t=1}^{T} (x_{it} - \bar{x}_i)(y_t - \bar{y}).$$

Least-squares regression estimates of α_i have the form

$$\text{est } \alpha_i = a_i = \frac{|M_{iy}|}{|M|},$$

which becomes $0/0$ if x_{it} variables are linearly related.

The simplest case of such linear interrelationships among x_{it} is perfect correlation between two x_{it}s, say x_{kt} and x_{jt}. If these two variables were perfectly correlated, the kth and jth rows or columns of M would be proportional. Similarly, these two rows of M_{iy} would be

---

From *International Economic Review*, **3**, September (1962), 274–99; written jointly with Mitsugu Nakamura.

proportional since both x_{kt} and x_{jt} would have proportional moments (about mean values) with y_t. If rows of M and of M_{iy} are proportional, the respective determinants vanish, and we obtain indeterminate estimates of α_i, $i=1,\ldots,n$, in the sense that $0/0$ is indeterminate.

Sampling errors of a_i are given by the formulas

$$\text{var } a_i = \text{var}(u) m^{ii},$$

$$(m^{ij}) = M^{-1}.$$

If M is singular because of row proportionality, these sampling errors will be infinite. These results provide us with the justification for the intuitive, and now evident, notions that if explanatory variables move or vary together (more generally, in a linear relationship to one another) in a sample, we shall not be able to detect, from that sample, the separate contributions of the related variables towards the explanation of the 'dependent' variable. Moreover, whatever numbers we do compute in a regression calculation would be unreliable and subject to a high degree of sampling error. Thus the indeterminacy of coefficients and infinite size of sampling error in the extreme case of exact singularity are easily understood.

This problem arises, apart from the question of bias, in least-squares estimation within an interdependent system. It is worth reconsidering the problem of multicollinearity in the case when the x_{it} are all exogenous variables, i.e. independent of u_t. We shall, however, go on in subsequent sections to the new problems of multicollinearity in interdependent systems.

SOME NEW ASPECTS OF MULTICOLLINEARITY

Within the confines of single equation analysis, there are still some aspects of the multicollinearity problem that merit consideration. First, there is a *computing* problem. The expression for a_i can be written as

$$a = M^{-1} m_y,$$

where

$$a = \begin{bmatrix} a_1 \\ a_2 \\ \vdots \\ a_n \end{bmatrix},$$

$$m_y = \begin{bmatrix} m_{1y} \\ m_{2y} \\ \vdots \\ m_{ny} \end{bmatrix}.$$

It can be a serious numerical problem to find M^{-1} when M is *near* singular. In the limit, when we have a perfect linear relationship among the x_{it}, M is singular, and its inverse does not exist, but in practice the linear relationships among explanatory variables are only approximate. The higher becomes the correlation associated with such linear relationships, the more closely M approaches singularity, and the more difficult it becomes to compute elements of M^{-1}. If the 2×2 matrix

$$\begin{bmatrix} m_{11} & m_{12} \\ m_{12} & m_{22} \end{bmatrix}$$

is not singular, but if, say,

$$\begin{bmatrix} m_{11} & m_{12} \\ m_{12} & m_{22} \end{bmatrix} = 0.000000000\varepsilon,$$

we could evaluate the inverse by carrying enough digits at each stage of our computations. An accurate evaluation is considerably more difficult to obtain if the matrix is of a size 5×5 or higher. When a high degree of singularity is present, a computer working with an electric desk machine of the conventional sort may find substantial difficulty in getting accurate figures with moderate size matrices of 5×5 or higher. The problem is not solved if we point to the existence of powerful electronic computers, for the types of intercorrelations that we often encounter in economic time series have been found to give computing trouble with matrices no larger than 20×20. At the size of 30×30, difficulties have been found that proved to be almost insuperable with the most powerful machines.

In most estimates of single regression equations, it is unlikely that the number of explanatory variables will exceed 15, and it is quite possible that the most advanced computing machines will be able to provide accurate estimates of any single equation calculated by standard least-squares methods. However, the initial step in many equation-systems methods of estimation is the estimation of properties of a large set of regression equations. These equations are likely to include more than 20 explanatory variables, and the computing problem, as it arises when multicollinearity is present, might be formidable. This has been our sad experience.

Singularity in econometric systems

It must be emphasized that the question of accuracy in computation when multicollinearity is present has nothing to do with accuracy as measured by sampling error. We are here speaking of *arithmetic*. Even if the *arithmetic* is accurate we still have the problem of the preceding section of indeterminacy and tendency of sampling errors to go towards infinity.

A logical problem that arises in the analysis of multicollinearity for the estimation of the single regression equation is this: Is the limiting value of an estimated regression coefficient (limited as the relationship among explanatory variables approaches an exact relationship) determinate or indeterminate? The form 0/0 may or may not have a limiting value. This is an object of our present investigation.

To attack this problem, we introduce some simplifcations in notation. Let y_t and x_{it} be normalized over the sample observations. We shall measure them so that sample means are zero and sample standard deviations, unadjusted for degrees of freedom, unity. With original sample data, we subtract means and divide by standard deviations. The sample moments are then correlation coefficients

$$m_{ij} = r_{ij},$$

$$m_{iy} = r_{iy}.$$

Let us also assume that variables x_{1t} and x_{2t} are intercorrelated but that all other explanatory variables have zero correlations with each other and with x_{1t} and x_{2t}. We shall then have for our estimate of α_1

$$a_1 = \frac{\begin{bmatrix} r_{1y} & r_{12} & 0 & \cdots & 0 \\ r_{2y} & 1 & 0 & \cdots & 0 \\ \vdots & \vdots & \vdots & & \vdots \\ r_{ny} & 0 & 0 & \cdots & 1 \end{bmatrix}}{\begin{bmatrix} 1 & r_{12} & 0 & \cdots & 0 \\ r_{12} & 1 & 0 & \cdots & 0 \\ \vdots & \vdots & \vdots & & \vdots \\ 0 & 0 & 0 & \cdots & 1 \end{bmatrix}} = \frac{r_{1y} - r_{2y} r_{12}}{1 - r_{12}^2}.$$

This is the same estimate that we would obtain from the multiple regression of y_t on x_{1t} and x_{2t}, with all other x_{it} absent from the estimated equation. The intercorrelation is then the single one between x_{1t} and x_{2t}, giving rise to the same problems of collinearity as in the simplest possible case – that involving y_t and two correlated explanatory variables.

If there is perfect intercorrelation, we have

$$r_{12} = 1,$$

and

$$r_{1y} = r_{2y}.$$

The latter equality holds since if x_{1t} and x_{2t} have perfect correlation between them, they must each have the same correlation with y_t.

If we substitute these two equalities in the formula for a_1, we find

$$a_1 = 0/0.$$

We pose our question now as this: Does the limit

$$\lim_{r_{12} \to 1} a_1 = \lim_{r_{12} \to 1} \frac{r_{1y} - r_{2y}r_{12}}{1 - r_{12}^2}$$

exist? In most numerical studies, we shall find r_{12} not precisely unity, and a numerical value for a_1 may be obtained. If the arithmetic of calculation is accurate does the value obtained have any meaning as the limiting value defined above, or is it purely some accidental value?

In numerical studies of multicollinearity, Karl Fox and James Cooney found cases in which a limiting value was approached and also some in which it was not.[1] In some cases, they fixed $r_{1y} = r_{2y}$ to approach unity. The limiting values of a_1 and a_2 are

$$\lim_{r_{12} \to 1} a_1 = \frac{r_{1y}}{2},$$

$$\lim_{r_{12} \to 1} a_2 = \frac{r_{2y}}{2},$$

In cases where they fixed $r_{1y} \neq r_{2y}$ and allowed r_{12} to approach the highest possible value (consistent with the multiple correlation $R_{y \cdot 12}^2$ lying between zero and unity), there was no asymptotic limit value for a_1 or a_2.

We often find in estimating coefficients of distributed lags, the following results:

$$y_t = a_1 x_t,$$

$$y_t = a_2 x_{t-1},$$

[1] Karl A. Fox and James F. Cooney, Jr., 'Effects of intercorrelation upon multiple correlation and regression measures,' U.S. Dept. of Agriculture, Agricultural Marketing Service, Washington, April (1954).

Singularity in econometric systems

$$y_t = \frac{a_1}{2} x_t + \frac{a_2}{2} x_{t-1},$$

$$a_1 = a_2.$$

These empirical findings are only approximate. They say that the effects of the two variables are about evenly divided between the current and the lagged values. This is what Fox and Cooney find when $r_{1y} = r_{2y}$.

Let us rewrite the expression for a_1 as

$$a_1 = \frac{r_{1y} - r_{2y} r_{12}}{1 - r_{12}^2} = \frac{r_{1y} - r_{2y}}{1 - r_{12}^2} + \frac{r_{2y}}{1 + r_{12}}.$$

Let r_{12} approach unity in such a way that the vector $(x_{11}, x_{12}, \ldots, x_{1T})$ and the vector $(x_{21}, x_{22}, \ldots, x_{2T})$ approach each other. Then we have

$$\lim_{r_{12} \to 1} \frac{r_{1y} - r_{2y}}{1 - r_{12}^2} = 0,$$

as long as $r_{1y} = r_{2y}$, and

$$\lim_{r_{12} \to 1} a_1 = \frac{r_{2y}}{2} = \frac{r_{1y}}{2}.$$

This is the Fox–Cooney numerical result. More generally, we write

$$\lim_{r_{12} \to 1} a_1 = \lim_{r_{12} \to 1} \frac{r_{1y} - r_{2y}}{(1 - r_{12})(1 + r_{12})} + \lim_{r_{12} \to 1} \frac{r_{2y}}{1 + r_{12}}$$

$$= \lim_{r_{12} \to 1} \frac{r_{1y} - r_{2y}}{2(1 - r_{12})} + \frac{r_{2y}}{2}.$$

Divide the numerator and denominator of the first term on the right by

$$[\Sigma(x_{1t} - x_{2t})^2]^{\frac{1}{2}}.$$

We have

$$\lim_{r_{12} \to 1} a_1 = \lim_{r_{12} \to 1} \frac{[\Sigma y_t(x_{1t} - x_{2t})]/[\Sigma(x_{1t} - x_{2t})^2]^{\frac{1}{2}}}{[2\Sigma x_{1t}(x_{1t} - x_{2t})]/[\Sigma(x_{1t} - x_{2t})^2]^{\frac{1}{2}}} + \frac{r_{2y}}{2}$$

$$= \lim_{r_{12} \to 1} \frac{r_{y(1-2)}}{2 r_{1(1-2)}} + \frac{r_{2y}}{2}.$$

We use the obvious notation

$r_{y(1-2)} = $ correlation between y_t and $(x_{1t} - x_{2t})$,

$r_{1(1-2)} = $ correlation between x_{1t} and $(x_{1t} - x_{2t})$.

The denominator $2r_{1(1-2)}$ necessarily approaches zero as $r_{12} \to 1$. The numerator $r_{y(1-2)}$ may approach either zero or a nonzero value depending on the given vector $(y_1, \ldots, y_t)$ and the direction in which $(x_{11}, \ldots, x_{1T})$ approaches $(x_{21}, \ldots, x_{2T})$. Accordingly, a_1 has no limit, including explosive cases, in general, unless a particular approach of $(x_{11}, \ldots, x_{1T})$ to $(x_{21}, \ldots, x_{2T})$ is specified.[2]

Fox and Cooney show that the multiple correlation coefficient, in their special cases, has a finite limiting value as intercorrelation approaches unity. In the trivariate case (y as a function of x_1 and x_2), this limiting value is r_{y1} or r_{y2}, without adjustment for degrees of freedom lost, as $r_{12} \to 1$. Intuitively, we would guess that the multiple correlation coefficient or standard error of estimate, var(u), is invariant with respect to the degree of multicollinearity present.

Let us argue as follows: Suppose x_1 and x_2 to be intercorrelated as above. Form the multiple regression of y on $x_2, \ldots, x_n$.

$$y_t = a_2 x_{2t} + a_3 x_{3t} \ldots + a_n x_{nt} + (\text{res})_t,$$

$(\text{res})_t = $ residual for period t.

We know by the property of least-squares multiple correlation theory

---

[2] We demonstrate this by an example. We may write

$$\lim_{r_{12} \to 1} \frac{r_{y(1-2)}}{r_{1(1-2)}} = \lim_{\Delta x \to 0} \frac{(y \cdot \Delta x)}{(x_1 \cdot \Delta x)} = \lim_{\Delta x \to 0} \frac{(y \cdot \Delta x / |\Delta x|)}{(x_1 \cdot \Delta x / |\Delta x|)}.$$

Denote two unit vectors as e_0 and e_1; e_0 is orthogonal to e_1, x_2, and y; $(e_1 \cdot x_2) \neq 0$, and $(e_1 \cdot y) \neq 0$. Define x_1 by

$$x_1 \equiv x_2 + a_n(e_0 + b_n e_1)$$

or

$$\Delta x \equiv a_n(e_0 + b_n e_1),$$

where $a_n \to 0$, $b_n \to 0$, and $a_n/b_n \to 0$ as $n \to \infty$. We have

$$\frac{x_1 - x_2}{|\Delta x|} = \frac{e_0 + b_n e_1}{(1+b_n^2)^{\frac{1}{2}}};$$

therefore

$$\left(y \cdot \frac{\Delta x}{|\Delta x|}\right) = \frac{b_n(e_1 \cdot y)}{(1+b_n^2)^{\frac{1}{2}}},$$

$$\left(x_1 \cdot \frac{\Delta x}{|\Delta x|}\right) = \frac{b_n}{(1+b_n^2)^{\frac{1}{2}}}\left(\frac{a_n}{b_n} + (e_1 \cdot x_2) + a_n \cdot b_n\right),$$

$$\lim_{\Delta x \to 0} \frac{(y \cdot \Delta x/|\Delta x|)}{(x_1 \cdot \Delta x/|\Delta x|)} = \frac{(e_1 \cdot y)}{(e_1 \cdot x_2)} = \lim_{r_{12} \to 1} \frac{r_{y(1-2)}}{r_{1(1-2)}}.$$

that

$$\sum_{t=1}^{T} (\text{res})_t x_{it} = 0 \qquad i = 2, \ldots, n.$$

Consider the addition of x_{1t} to the correlation equation. If $r_{12} = 1$, we have

$$x_{1t} = a + b x_{2t}.$$

This relation has zero residuals since $r_{12} = 1$. By the rule of normalization, $a = 0$ and $b = 1$. Since x_1 is a linear function of x_2 over the sample values, we also find

$$\sum_{t=1}^{T} (\text{res})_t x_{1t} = 0.$$

Since x_1 is uncorrelated with the residuals, it will add nothing to the multiple correlation, and the variance of residuals will remain unchanged with the inclusion of the new variable that brings intercorrelation into the group of explanatory variables.

This point is of some significance in interpreting and appreciating the effects of multicollinearity in equation systems methods of estimation; therefore we shall prove it more generally, including limiting behavior, as well as for perfect intercorrelation.

$$T \text{var}(\text{res}) = TS_u^2 = \sum_{t=1}^{T} (y_t - \hat{y}_t)^2 = \sum_{t=1}^{T} (y_t^2 - \hat{y}_t^2),$$

$$\hat{y}_t = \sum_{i=1}^{n} a_i x_{it}.$$

In other words, $\hat{y}_t$ are the *computed* values of y_t, and have the property

$$\sum_{t=1}^{T} y_t \hat{y}_t = \sum_{t=1}^{T} \hat{y}_t^2,$$

since

$$\sum_{t=1}^{T} (\text{res})_t \hat{y}_t = 0.$$

The expression derived above for a_1 can be extended immediately to a_2. It is

$$a_2 = \frac{r_{2y} - r_{1y} r_{12}}{1 - r_{12}^2}.$$

For $i \geq 3$, we also have

$$a_i = r_{iy}.$$

Thus, we can write

$$TS_u^2 = \sum_{t=1}^{T} y_t^2 - \sum_{t=1}^{T}\left(\sum_{i=1}^{n} a_i x_{it}\right)^2$$

$$= T - \sum_{t=1}^{T}\left(\frac{r_{1y}-r_{2y}r_{12}}{1-r_{12}^2}x_{1t}+\frac{r_{2y}-r_{1y}r_{12}}{1-r_{12}^2}x_{2t}+\sum_{i=3}^{n}r_{iy}x_{it}\right)^2$$

$$= T - \sum_{t=1}^{T}\left(\frac{(r_{1y}-r_{2y})(x_{1t}-x_{2t})}{1-r_{12}^2}+\frac{(r_{2y}x_{1t}+r_{1y}x_{2t})}{1+r_{12}}\right.$$
$$\left.+\sum_{i=3}^{n}r_{iy}x_{it}\right)^2,$$

$$\lim_{r_{12}\to 1} TS_u^2 = T - \sum_{t=1}^{T}\left(\lim_{r_{12}\to 1}\frac{(r_{1y}-r_{2y})(x_{1t}-x_{2t})}{2(1-r_{12})}+\sum_{i=2}^{n}r_{iy}x_{it}\right)^2.$$

Rewrite

$$\lim_{r_{12}\to 1}\frac{(r_{1y}-r_{2y})(x_{1t}-x_{2t})}{2(1-r_{12})}$$

$$= \lim_{r_{12}\to 1}\frac{[\Sigma y_t(x_{1t}-x_{2t})]/[(\Sigma(x_{1t}-x_{2t})^2]^{\frac{1}{2}}}{[2\Sigma x_{1t}(x_{1t}-x_{2t})]/[\Sigma(x_{1t}-x_{2t})^2]^{\frac{1}{2}}}(x_{1t}-x_{2t}).$$

Denote the unit vector $(x_1-x_2)/[\Sigma(x_{1t}-x_{2t})^2]^{\frac{1}{2}}$ by e. We use the notation

$$x_1 - x_2 = (x_{11}-x_{21}, x_{12}-x_{22}, \ldots, x_{1T}-x_{2T}).$$

We have the relations

$$2|\cos(x_1 \cdot e)| = 2|(x_1 \cdot e)| = |x_1 - x_2|.$$

We take the norm

$$\left|\frac{(r_{1y}-r_{2y})(x_1-x_2)}{2(1-r_{12})}\right| = \frac{|(y \cdot e)| \cdot |x_1-x_2|}{2|(x_1 \cdot e)|} = |(y \cdot e)|.$$

We assume that x_1 approaches x_2 in such a way that the limit of $(x_1-x_2)/|x_1-x_2|$ exists. Call the limit $\bar{e}$.

$$\lim_{r_{12}\to 1} TS_u^2 = T - \lim_{r_{12}\to 1}|(y \cdot e)|^2 - \left|\sum_{i=2}^{n}r_{iy}x_i\right|^2$$

$$= T - |(y \cdot \bar{e})|^2 - \left|\sum_{i=2}^{n}r_{iy}x_i\right|^2.$$

Singularity in econometric systems

The multiple correlation $R_{y.12...n}$ is given by the expression

$$R_{y.12...n} = \frac{TS_u^2}{\sum_{t=1}^{T} y_t^2}.$$

Accordingly,

$$\lim_{r_{12} \to 1} R_{y.12...n} = \frac{T - |(y \cdot \bar{e})|^2 - \left|\sum_{i=2}^{n} r_{iy} x_i\right|^2}{T}$$

$$= 1 - r_{y.}^2 - \frac{1}{T}\left|\sum_{i=2}^{n} r_{iy} x_i\right|^2.$$

This means that as correlation between x_1 and x_2 approaches unity, the multiple correlation coefficient has a definite limit that does not depend on x_1, as long as x_1 approaches x_2 in such a way that the limit of $(x_1 - x_2)/|x_1 - x_2|$ exists. This assumption would seem to be satisfied in practical situations of near singularity.

SINGULARITY IN TWO-STAGE LEAST-SQUARES ESTIMATES

The equation to be estimated now has the form

$$y_{0t} = \sum_{i=1}^{n} \beta_i y_{it} + \sum_{i=1}^{m} \gamma_i x_{it} + u_t.$$

This equation is contained in a larger system with $N \geq n$ endogenous variables (and equations) and $M \geq m$ predetermined variables. We shall use the notation

$$x_t^* = (x_{1t}, \ldots, x_{mt}),$$
$$x_t^{**} = (x_{m+1,t}, \ldots, x_{Mt}),$$
$$x_t = (x_t^*, x_t^{**}),$$
$$y_t = (y_{1t}, \ldots, y_{nt}).$$

Two-stage least squares estimates are obtained by solving

$$\begin{bmatrix} \sum y_{0t} \hat{y}_t \\ \sum y_{0t} x_t^* \end{bmatrix} = \begin{bmatrix} M_{\hat{y}\hat{y}} & M_{yx^*} \\ M_{x^*y} & M_{x^*x^*} \end{bmatrix} \begin{bmatrix} \hat{\beta} \\ \hat{\gamma} \end{bmatrix}.$$

In contrast, the estimation equations for ordinary least-squares are

$$\begin{bmatrix} \sum y_{0t}y_t \\ \sum y_{0t}x_t^* \end{bmatrix} = \begin{bmatrix} M_{yy} & M_{yx^*} \\ M_{x^*y} & M_{x^*x^*} \end{bmatrix} \begin{bmatrix} b \\ c \end{bmatrix}.$$

The matrix notation is given by

$$M_{yy} = \left[\sum_{t=1}^{T} y_{it}y_{jt} \right] \quad i=1,\ldots,n, \, j=1,\ldots,n,$$

$$M_{yx^*} = \left[\sum_{t=1}^{T} y_{it}x_{jt} \right] \quad i=1,\ldots,n, \, j=1,\ldots,m,$$

$$M_{x^*y} = M'_{yx^*},$$

$$M_{x^*x^*} = \left[\sum_{t=1}^{T} x_{it}x_{jt} \right] \quad i=1,\ldots,m, \, j=1,\ldots,m,$$

$$y_{0t}y_t = \begin{bmatrix} y_{0t}y_{1t} \\ \vdots \\ y_{0t}y_{nt} \end{bmatrix},$$

$$y_{0t}x_t^* = \begin{bmatrix} y_{0t}x_{1t} \\ \vdots \\ y_{0t}x_{mt} \end{bmatrix},$$

$$b = \begin{bmatrix} b_1 \\ \vdots \\ b_n \end{bmatrix} \quad \hat{\beta} = \begin{bmatrix} \hat{\beta}_1 \\ \vdots \\ \hat{\beta}_n \end{bmatrix},$$

$$c = \begin{bmatrix} c_1 \\ \vdots \\ c_m \end{bmatrix} \quad \hat{\gamma} = \begin{bmatrix} \hat{\gamma}_1 \\ \vdots \\ \hat{\gamma}_m \end{bmatrix},$$

$$\hat{y}'_t = M_{yx}M_{xx}^{-1}x'_t,$$

$$M_{\hat{y}\hat{y}} = M_{yx}M_{xx}^{-1}M_{xy}.$$

In the last two formulas, M_{xx} is the moment matrix for all elements of x, including both x^* and x^{**}.

We are interested in the conditions under which the two matrices in the estimation equations tend towards singularity. They apparently differ only in that M_{yy} is substituted for $M_{\hat{y}\hat{y}}$.

$$\begin{bmatrix} M_{yy} & M_{yx^*} \\ M_{x^*y} & M_{x^*x^*} \end{bmatrix} \quad \text{or} \quad \begin{bmatrix} M_{\hat{y}\hat{y}} & M_{yx^*} \\ M_{x^*y} & M_{x^*x^*} \end{bmatrix}.$$

Singularity in econometric systems

We may put the matter this way. How does the existence of intercorrelation (or a linear relationship) among elements of y compare with the existence of intercorrelation among the elements of $\hat{y}$? In the one case we have a multiple regression of y_0 on $y_1,\ldots,y_n$, $x_1,\ldots,x_m$. In the other, we have a multiple regression of y_0 on $\hat{y}_1,\ldots,\hat{y}_n$, $x_1,\ldots,x_m$. Intercorrelation among elements of $(x_1,\ldots,x_m) = x^*$ appears in the entries of $M_{x^*x^*}$ which occupies the same position in both matrices. Similarly, intercorrelations between elements of $y_1,\ldots,y_n$ and $x_1,\ldots,x_m$ appear in the entries of M_{yx^*} or M_{x^*y}. These matrices occupy the same position in the above matrices of ordinary or two-state least-squares since

$$\sum_{t=1}^{T} y_{it}x_{jt} = \sum_{t=1}^{T} \hat{y}_{it}x_{jt}$$

or

$$M_{yx^*} = M_{\hat{y}x^*}.[3]$$

The crux of the matter lies in the comparison between intercorrelation among elements of y and among elements of $\hat{y}$. If y_{it} and y_{jt} are highly correlated, then $\hat{y}_{it}$ and $\hat{y}_{jt}$ will also tend to be highly correlated. In the limit, as $\sum_{t=1}^{T} y_{it}y_{jt} \to 1$, we also have

$$\sum_{t=1}^{T} \hat{y}_{it}\hat{y}_{jt} \to 1.$$

We explain this by observing that as y_{it} approaches y_{jt} (i.e. as these normalized variables have unit correlation), their respective regressions on $x_{it},\ldots,x_{Mt}$ must approach each other. The reverse does not hold, however, and this is the key to our principal conclusion. Even though $\sum_{t=1}^{T} \hat{y}_{it}\hat{y}_{jt} \to 1$, we need not have $\sum_{t=1}^{T} y_{it}y_{jt} \to 1$. Or even if y_{it} and y_{jt} have zero correlation, $\hat{y}_{it}$ and $\hat{y}_{jt}$ may have nonzero correlation.

The subject matter of the present paper arose in the context of our numerical calculation of large numbers of estimates, in an econometric model of substantial size, by the methods of ordinary least-squares, two-stage least-squares, and limited information. We detected great sensitivity of the latter two methods to what we suspected to be the presence of multicollinearity. The same findings had been noted in a long series of econometric model estimates over several years in different countries.

---

[3] We have here spoken only of simple intercorrelation between pairs in x^* or in y and x^*. The analysis can readily be generalized beyond simple correlation relationships to general linear relationships.

80   Economic Theory and Econometrics

We now put forward the proposition that two-stage least-squares estimates are more sensitive to the presence of multicollinearity than are ordinary least-squares estimates. In the next section we shall argue that limited information estimates are more sensitive than are two-stage least-squares estimates to the presence of multicollinearity.

If the correlation between y_{it} and y_{jt} is unity, sample values of y_{it} can be expressed as an exact linear function of sample values of y_{jt}. The regression of y_{it} on $x_{1t},\ldots,x_{Mt}$ must then be a linear function of the regression of y_{jt} on $x_{1t},\ldots,x_{Mt}$, and the correlations between $\hat{y}_{it}$ and $\hat{y}_{jt}$ will also be unity. Consider a trivial case in which $M=1$. We then have

$$\sum_{t=1}^{T} \hat{y}_{it}\hat{y}_{jt} = p_i p_j \sum_{t=1}^{T} x_{1t}^2 = p_i p_j = \sum_{t=1}^{T} y_{it} x_{1t} \cdot \sum_{t=1}^{T} y_{jt} x_{1t}.$$

The coefficients p_i and p_j are the regression coefficients of y_{it} and y_{jt}, respectively, on x_{1t}. Even if y_{it} and y_{jt} are completely uncorrelated with each other

$$\sum_{t=1}^{T} y_{it} y_{jt} = 0,$$

they each will generally have nonzero regressions on x_{1t}; therefore $p_i p_j$ is not zero, and

$$\sum_{t=1}^{T} \hat{y}_{it}\hat{y}_{jt}$$

does not vanish.

Generally, we may represent y_i and $\hat{y}_i$ as vectors related by

$$y_i = \hat{y}_i + r_i,$$

where the residual r_i is orthogonal to $\hat{y}_i$. We may also write

$$\hat{y}_i = A(x_1,\ldots,x_M) y_i.$$

The function A is a projection operator with respect to vectors $x_1,\ldots,x_M$ in T dimensional space. The number of independent vectors among a set of vectors $y_1,\ldots,y_n$ can never be increased through the operation of projection on these vectors, since a projection is a linear transformation. If $\hat{y}_1,\ldots,\hat{y}_n, x_1,\ldots,x_m$ are linearly independent, then $y_1,\ldots,y_n, x_1,\ldots,x_m$ must also be linearly independent.

The converse is not necessarily true. We can show this by a counter example. Let us assume that the vectors $\hat{y}_1,\ldots,\hat{y}_n, x_1,\ldots,x_m$ are linearly dependent with independence among $x_1,\ldots,x_m$. If we choose mutually linearly independent $r_1,\ldots,r_n$ orthogonal to $x_1,\ldots,x_M$, then $y_1,\ldots,y_n$,

Singularity in econometric systems

$x_1, \ldots, x_m$ are linearly independent. It is this general result that leads us to conclude that two-stage least-squares are more sensitive than are ordinary least-squares estimates to multicollinearity.

We may look at a comparison of the two methods from another viewpoint. Let us transform the estimation equations for two-stage least-squares.

$$\sum y_{0t} x_t^* = M_{x^*y} \hat{\beta} + M_{x^*x^*} \hat{\gamma}$$

$$\hat{\gamma} = M_{x^*x^*}^{-1} (\sum y_{0t} x_t^* - M_{x^*y} \hat{\beta})$$

$$\sum y_{0t} \hat{y}_t = M_{\hat{y}\hat{y}} \hat{\beta} + M_{yx^*} \hat{\gamma}$$

$$= M_{\hat{y}\hat{y}} \hat{\beta} + M_{yx^*} M_{x^*x^*}^{-1} (\sum y_{0t} x_t^* - M_{x^*y} \hat{\beta})$$

$$\sum y_0 \hat{y}_t - M_{yx^*} M_{x^*x^*}^{-1} \sum y_{0t} x_t^* = (M_{\hat{y}\hat{y}} - M_{yx^*} M_{x^*x^*}^{-1} M_{x^*y}) \hat{\beta}.$$

Consider the right-hand matrix expression

$$M_{\hat{y}\hat{y}} - M_{yx^*} M_{x^*x^*}^{-1} M_{x^*y}$$

or

$$M_{yx} M_{xx}^{-1} M_{xy} - M_{yx^*} M_{x^*x^*}^{-1} M_{x^*y}.$$

In order to compute $M_{\hat{y}\hat{y}}$ it is necessary to evaluate

$$M_{yx} M_{xx}^{-1} M_{xy}.$$

This is the first term in the above expression. There may be an important difference of degree here, as compared with ordinary least squares. The largest regression calculation that the authors have ever made for a single equation was one involving sixteen variables.[4] That is, however, exceptional, and rarely does one include as many as ten variables in a single equation in econometrics. The consequence of this observation is that there will rarely ever be a need to invert a least-squares regression matrix of order more than 10.

$$\begin{bmatrix} M_{yy} & M_{yx^*} \\ M_{x^*y} & M_{x^*x^*} \end{bmatrix}.$$

From the computational point of view it will usually be possible to obtain accurate estimates of an inverse of a matrix of order less than 10 considering the degree of intercorrelation or singularity found in typical series of economic data. On the other hand M_{xx} may very well be as large as (30×30), and we have found in practice that some of the most

---

[4] L. R. Klein and J. B. Lansing, 'Decisions to purchase consumer durable goods,' *The Journal of Marketing*, xx, October (1955), 109–32.

powerful computers available cannot obtain reliable inverses of M_{xx} when there is an ordinary amount of intercorrelation. As a rough statement, we have found that (30×30) matrices cannot be successfully inverted, while a 20×20 matrix with the most obvious intercorrelations deleted can be successfully inverted.[5]

In the previous section, we showed that the variance of residual error was almost unaffected in the limit by the presence of multicollinearity. If arithmetically accurate computations can be made, we can get good estimates of either

$$M_{\hat{y}\hat{y}} = M_{yx} M_{xx}^{-1} M_{xy}$$

or

$$W_{yy} = M_{yy} - M_{yx} M_{xx}^{-1} M_{xy}$$

even though there is multicollinearity present which makes the reliable computation of individual coefficients in

$$y_{it} = \sum_{j=1}^{M} \pi_{ij} x_{jt} + v_{it}$$

not possible. Thus we may not be able to compute useable estimates of reduced form coefficients, π_{ij}, but we may, nevertheless, be able to compute reliable estimates of $M_{\hat{y}\hat{y}}$ or W_{yy}. For either two-stage least-squares or limited information estimates we do not actually require precise knowledge of π_{ij}. We simply need estimates of $M_{\hat{y}\hat{y}}$ or W_{yy}. The problem of multicollinearity at this stage is, therefore, a computational problem, and it is a computational problem that does not arise in the same degree in ordinary least-squares estimation. It is, however, extremely common and has plagued many cases of equation system estimates known to the authors.

Apart from the computational problems, there are two possibilities of singularity in two-stage that never arose in the case of ordinary least-squares estimation. Both possibilities involve the x_t^{**} vector $(x_{m+1,t}, \ldots, x_{Mt})$, which is not used in ordinary single equation regression analysis.

The difference

$$M_{yx} M_{xx}^{-1} M_{xy} - M_{yx^*} M_{x^*x^*}^{-1} M_{x^*y}$$

---

[5]In the evaluation of $M_{yx} M_{xx}^{-1} M_{xy}$, we find it more efficient and accurate, from a computational point of view, to calculate $M_{xx}^{-1} M_{xy}$ (as the solution vectors of sets of simultaneous equations) and then premultiply by M_{yx}. Criteria for success are judged by the positive definiteness and symmetry of $M_{\hat{y}\hat{y}}$. Also inconsistencies in subsequent dependent calculations indicate arithmetic errors at this stage.

may be written as

$$M_{\hat{y}\hat{y}} - M^*_{\hat{y}\hat{y}}$$

or

$$W^*_{yy} - W_{yy},$$

where the * superscript denotes that only components of x_t^*, $(x_{1t},\ldots,x_{mt})$, are used in the evaluation of $\hat{y}_t$ or $y_t - \hat{y}_t$. The difference is, in words, the difference between moment matrices of computed values of y using all the predetermined variables and using the subset appearing in the equation being estimated. It is, correspondingly, the difference between the variance–covariance matrices of reduced form residuals using the subset of predetermined variables appearing in the equation and the whole set of predetermined variables.

In order for this difference matrix to be far from singular, there must be substantial additional 'explanatory' power among the elements of x_t^{**}. The endogenous variables must not be wholly or almost wholly explained by x_t^*. There must be predetermined variables in the system, but not in the equation being estimated, that are closely related to the y_{it}, $i=1,\ldots,n$. A form of multicollinearity could account for near singularity of this difference matrix. If all the elements of x_t^{**} are highly correlated with those of x_t^*, then we shall not get additional 'explanatory' power from using x_t^{**}, and the difference matrix will approach singularity. This will affect the estimates of the structural parameters. In a way, this situation reflects on identifiability. In a formal sense, an equation is identified by having coefficients set equal to zero (or having variables absent). The x_t^{**} vector consists of variables absent from the equation being estimated, and if they are highly correlated with elements of x_t^*, identifiability may be formally present but weak. It is interesting to note that Anderson and Rubin, in their basic article on the method of limited information, made x_t^* and x_t^{**} effectively independent by transforming variables.[6] They used only that part of x_t^{**} that was orthogonal to x_t^*. The other part was taken out by a regression of x_t^{**} on x_t^*.

We could find singularity in the difference matrix even though x_t^{**} and x_t^* were orthogonal. If y_{it} are unrelated to elements of x_t^{**} or almost wholly explained by elements of x_t^* alone, we may find

$$M_{yx}M_{xx}^{-1}M_{xy} - M_{yx^*}M_{x^*x^*}^{-1}M_{x^*y}$$

---

[6] T. W. Anderson and H. Rubin, 'Estimation of the parameters of a single equation in a complete system of stochastic equations,' *Annals of Mathematical Statistics*, XX, March (1949), 46–63, esp. 51.

close to being singular, and this will impair the estimates of β in the solution of the estimation equations.

SINGULARITY IN LIMITED INFORMATION ESTIMATES

Many investigators have noticed that limited information estimates sometimes appear to 'explode' in their hands. Ridiculous estimates are obtained, and reasons for this have not always been found. It may, in fact, be a consequence of multicollinearity – either of the form causing inaccurate arithmetic or of the form leading to indeterminate estimates.

For example, Carl Christ, in making a number of comparative least-squares and limited information estimates, found himself unable to account for the following results:[7]

least squares

$$W_1 = 2.08 + 0.480(pX - E) + 0.158(pX - E)_{-1} + 0.20t,$$
$$(0.04) \qquad\quad (0.04) \qquad\quad\ (0.05)$$

limited information

$$W_1 = 15.17 - 8.286(pX - E) + 8.949(pX - E)_{-1} + 3.49t,$$
$$(127) \qquad\quad (128) \qquad\quad (48)$$

where

$$W_1 = \text{private wage bill},$$
$$pX - E = \text{private output},$$
$$t = \text{time}.$$

The least-squares estimate looks fairly reasonable, and in other models has been estimated with similar coefficients by the limited information method. Christ's limited information estimates are, obviously, 'ridiculous.' While the marginal coefficients of output, by least-squares, conform to our *a priori* notions about movements of labor's share, it is hard to rationalize the limited information estimate. We observe, however, that the sum of the current and lagged output coefficients is 0.663, while the sum in the least-squares estimate is 0.638. This aspect of the estimates is not ridiculous, but the reference to the fact that the estimates 'exploded' means that the individual figures assume inordinately large values. The large sampling errors – written in parentheses below coefficients – suggest the presence of multicollinearity

[7] C. Christ, 'A test of an econometric model for the United States, 1921–1947,' *Proceedings of the Conference on Business Cycles*, National Bureau of Economic Research, New York (1951), 35–129.

and also that limited information estimates are more sensitive than are least-squares.

In a revised and updated version of the Klein-Goldberger model the following calculations provide another example of this explosive tendency of limited information estimates.[8]

least squares

$$L_2 - 0.25 W_1 = 2.20 - 0.85i - 0.042p + 0.49(L_2)_{-1},$$
$$\quad\quad\quad\quad\quad (0.43)\ (0.175)\ (0.03)$$

limited information

$$L_2 - 0.25 W_1 = 4.85 + 11.02i + 5.57p - 0.18(L_2)_{-1},$$
$$\quad\quad\quad\quad\quad (23.37)\ (11.01)\ (1.34)$$

L_2 = deflated business holdings of liquid assets,

W_1 = private real wage bill,

i = long-term bond yield,

p = index of general price level.

The coefficient of the wages bill (transactions coefficient) was fixed at 0.25 before estimation. The least-squares results are reasonable in size and sign; the limited information estimates make little economic sense.

Results like these have been found in numerous calculations. We notice that two-stage least-squares estimates 'explode' in this way less frequently than do limited information estimates. We were originally led to conjecture that two-stage least-squares estimates were more sensitive to multicollinearity than are ordinary least-squares estimates and that limited information estimates are more sensitive to multicollinearity than are two-stage least-squares estimates.

The Theil k-class of estimates can be written as[9]

$$\begin{bmatrix} \Sigma y_{0t} y_t - k \Sigma y_{0t} \hat{v}_t \\ \Sigma y_{0t} x_t^* \end{bmatrix} = \begin{bmatrix} M_{yy} - kW_{yy} & M_{yx^*} \\ M_{x^*y} & M_{x^*x^*} \end{bmatrix} \begin{bmatrix} \hat{\beta} \\ \hat{\gamma} \end{bmatrix}.$$

The only variables not previously defined are $\hat{v}_t$, which are vectors $(\hat{v}_{1t}, \hat{v}_{2t}, \ldots, \hat{v}_{nt})$ of residuals from the computed reduced form equations. When $k=0$ we have the formula for ordinary least-squares, and when $k=1$, we have the formula for two-stage least-squares. These are

[8] L. R. Klein and A. S. Goldberger, *An Econometric Model of the United States, 1929–1952*, North-Holland Publishing Co., Amsterdam (1955).

[9] H. Theil, *Economic Forecasts and Policy*, North-Holland Publishing Co., Amsterdam (1958).

nonstochastic values of k. For limited information estimates we choose a stochastic value for k. We let

$$k = 1 + \lambda$$

and choose λ as the smallest root of the determinantal equation

$$|B - \lambda W| = 0,$$

$$B = M_{yx} M_{xx}^{-1} M_{xy} - M_{yx^*} M_{x^*x^*}^{-1} M_{x^*y}.$$

B is the same difference matrix that we encountered in two-stage least-squares estimation. The same problems of singularity arise here as in the previous section. We have the additional complication that λ must also be estimated from the sample data and that multicollinearity may affect it and its use in obtaining final estimates.

Let us interpret limited information estimates geometrically. This may help to clarify relationships and differences with two-stage least-squares methods. Define the residuals of the regression of the elements of x_t^{**} on x_t^* as z_t.[10] Symbolically, we write

$$z_i = x_i^{**} - A(x_1, \ldots, x_m) x_i^{**}.$$

A, again, is a projection operator with respect to the vectors $x_1, \ldots, x_m$. Limited information estimates can be defined as the linear combination of projections of y into the space of z with the smallest Euclidian norm. We shall express $\tilde{y}$ as

$$\tilde{y}_i = A(z_{m+1}, \ldots, z_M) \hat{y}_i.$$

Our problem now is to find b_i, $i = 0, 1, \ldots, n$, which minimize

$$\left[\sum_{i=0}^{n} b_i \tilde{y}_i \right]^2$$

under the restriction

$$\sum_{i=0}^{n} \sum_{j=0}^{n} b_i b_j w_{ij} = \text{const}.$$

The terms w_{ij} are elements of the W_{yy} matrix defined above. The minimizing set of b_i is the characteristic vector corresponding to the smallest root of

$$|B - \lambda W| = 0.$$

The matrix B may also be expressed as the moment matrix of

---

[10] For the first m components of z_i, we have $z_i = x_i$, $i = 1, 2, \ldots, m$.

Singularity in econometric systems 87

$\tilde{y}_0, \tilde{y}_1, \ldots, \tilde{y}_n,$

$$B \equiv (\tilde{y}_0, \tilde{y}_1, \ldots, \tilde{y}_n)'(\tilde{y}_0, \tilde{y}_1, \ldots, \tilde{y}_n) = M_{\tilde{y}\tilde{y}},$$

while W_{yy} is the moment matrix of estimated residuals

$$\hat{v}_i \equiv y_i - \hat{y}_i \quad i = 0, 1, \ldots, n,$$

$$W \equiv (\hat{v}_0, \hat{v}_1, \ldots, \hat{v}_n)'(\hat{v}_0, \hat{v}_1, \ldots, \hat{v}_n).$$

Linear interdependence in the vectors is equivalent to singularity of the corresponding moment matrix. Suppose that $\hat{y}_1, \hat{y}_2, \ldots, \hat{y}_n, z_1, z_2, \ldots, z_m$ are linearly dependent; that is, there exists a set of real numbers $\mu_1, \mu_2, \ldots, \mu_n, v_1, v_2, \ldots, v_m$, of which at least one is nonzero, satisfying

$$\sum_{i=1}^{n} \mu_i \hat{y}_i + \sum_{j=1}^{m} v_j z_j = 0,$$

$$\sum_{i=1}^{n} \mu_i(\hat{y}_i - \tilde{y}_i) + \sum_{j=1}^{m} v_j z_j = -\sum_{i=1}^{n} \mu_i \tilde{y}_i.$$

In this expression, all the vectors on one side are orthogonal to those on the other side, so that both sides must vanish in order that the equality hold. Therefore, $\tilde{y}_1, \tilde{y}_2, \ldots, \tilde{y}_n$ must be linearly dependent as long as $z_1, z_2, \ldots, z_m$ are independent.

Conversely, if $\tilde{y}_1, \tilde{y}_2, \ldots, \tilde{y}_n$ are linearly dependent, then $\hat{y}_1, \hat{y}_2, \ldots, \hat{y}_n, z_1, z_2, \ldots, z_m$ will be dependent, since by assumption

$$\sum_{i=1}^{n} \mu_i \tilde{y}_i = 0,$$

and we must have

$$\sum_{i=1}^{n} \mu_i \hat{y}_i + \sum_{j=1}^{m} v_j z_j = \sum_{i=1}^{n} \mu_i(\hat{y}_i - \tilde{y}_i) + \sum_{j=1}^{m} v_j z_j = 0$$

by choosing $v_j, j = 1, 2, \ldots, m$, such that

$$\sum_{j=1}^{m} v_j z_j = -\sum_{i=1}^{n} \mu_i(\hat{y}_i - \tilde{y}_i),$$

for given $\mu_i, i = 1, 2, \ldots, n$, where at least one μ_i is nonzero. As a result, linear dependence of $\tilde{y}_1, \tilde{y}_2, \ldots, \tilde{y}_n$ turns out to be equivalent to that of $\hat{y}_1, \hat{y}_2, \ldots, \hat{y}_n, z_1, z_2, \ldots, z_m$, provided $z_1, z_2, \ldots, z_m$ are linearly independent.

In the case of singular B we have $\lambda = 0$ as the smallest characteristic root of the determinantal equation,

$$|B - \lambda W| = |B| = 0.$$

From the set of homogeneous equations, we may, in that situation, find a vanishing linear combination of $\tilde{y}_i$

$$\sum_{i=0}^{n} b_i \tilde{y}_i = 0.$$

By normalization $b_0 = 1$, we have

$$\tilde{y}_0 = -\sum_{i=1}^{n} b_i \tilde{y}_i,$$

We form scalar products with $\tilde{y}_i$, $i = 1, 2, \ldots, n$, to obtain

$$m_{0i} = -\sum_{j=1}^{n} b_j m_{ij}, \quad i = 1, 2, \ldots, n.$$

The coefficient matrix $B^* \equiv (m_{ij})$ is singular if and only if the set of vectors $\tilde{y}_1, \tilde{y}_2, \ldots, \tilde{y}_n$ is linearly dependent. We therefore come to exactly the same situation in determining the coefficients b_i as in the case of singular normal equations in the ordinary least-squares regressions discussed previously.

The same kind of singularity of B^* arises in the case of underidentified models by the order condition $n > M - m$, since the number of the independent vectors among $\hat{y}_1, \hat{y}_2, \ldots, \hat{y}_n, z_1, z_2, \ldots, z_m$ cannot exceed M. This implies linear interdependence of $\hat{y}_1, \hat{y}_2, \ldots, \hat{y}_n, z_1, z_2 \ldots, z_m$, and also of $\tilde{y}_1, \tilde{y}_2, \ldots, \tilde{y}_n$.

Two-stage least-squares estimation can be rewritten in terms of the $\tilde{y}_i$-vectors, $i = 0, 1, 2, \ldots, n$. Suppose that we are given the estimates b_i^*, c_j^* by the method of the two-stage least-squares estimation

$$y_0 = \sum_{i=1}^{n} b_i^* \hat{y}_i + \sum_{j=1}^{m} c_j^* z_j + \hat{u},$$

where $\hat{u}$ denotes the residual vector in the regression.

We form a projection $A(z_{m+1}, z_{m+2}, \ldots, z_M)$ on both sides of this equality, to get

$$\tilde{y}_0 = \sum_{i=1}^{n} b_i^* \tilde{y}_i + A(z_{m+1}, z_{m+2}, \ldots, z_M) \cdot \hat{u}.$$

We use the fact that z_j, $j = 1, 2, \ldots, m$; and z_k, $k = m+1, \ldots, M$, are orthogonal. Moreover, the vector which appears as the second term on the right-hand side must be orthogonal to $\tilde{y}_1, \tilde{y}_2, \ldots, \tilde{y}_n$, since the scalar products of $A(z_{m+1}, \ldots, z_M) \cdot \hat{u}$ and $\tilde{y}_i$, $i = 1, 2, \ldots, n$, can be transformed

Singularity in econometric systems 89

into sums or differences of orthogonal pairs.

$$[A(z^*_{m+1},\ldots,z^*_M)\cdot \hat{u}, \tilde{y}_i]$$
$$= [\hat{u} - \{\hat{u} - A(z^*_{m+1},\ldots,z^*_M)\cdot \hat{u}\}, \hat{y}_i - (\hat{y}_i - \tilde{y}_i)]$$
$$= (\hat{u}, \hat{y}_i) - (\hat{u}, \hat{y}_i - \tilde{y}_i) - [\hat{u} - A(z^*_{m+1},\ldots,z^*_M)\cdot \hat{u}, \tilde{y}_i]$$
$$= 0, \quad i = 1, 2, \ldots, n.$$

Accordingly, the two-stage least-squares coefficients b_i^*, $i = 1, 2, \ldots, n$, can be interpreted as the least-squares regression coefficients of $\tilde{y}_0$ on $\tilde{y}_1, \tilde{y}_2, \ldots, \tilde{y}_n$, and the relevant moment matrix in the normal equations will be B^*.

Thus we conclude that singularity of the B^*-matrix will occur in exactly the same way in two-stage least-squares estimation and in limited information estimation, as far as the effects of linear interdependence among $\hat{y}_1, \hat{y}_2, \ldots, \hat{y}_n, z_1, z_2, \ldots, z_m$ are concerned.

It may be worth while pointing out that we necessarily have singular B, but not necessarily singular B^*, in the just identified case ($n = M - m$), which means that we may find definite b_i, $i = 1, 2, \ldots, n$, together with the normalized value $b_0 = 1$, in spite of the fact that B is singular.

So far it has been shown that if any singularity occurs in two-stage least-squares estimation, it also occurs in limited information estimation. Conversely, if singularity occurs in B^*, *a fortiori* in B, in the limited information method, then singularity must occur in the moment matrix of $\hat{y}_1, \hat{y}_2, \ldots, \hat{y}_n, z_1, z_2, \ldots, z_m$ in two-stage least squares estimation.

Hence we conclude that if there exists any singularity proper to the limited information method apart from that occurring in two-stage least-squares estimation, it must be associated with nonsingular B.

We now assume that B is nonsingular, and, in addition, that the smallest root (λ_0) of the equation $|B - \lambda W| = 0$ is multiple.[11] According to an established theorem of algebra, we must also have $|B^* - \lambda_0 W^*| = 0$, where W^*, B^* stand for the $n \times n$ matrices formed from W, B, by dropping their first rows and columns. There must be two latent vectors r, p which are linearly independent with nonsingular W; i.e.

$$(B - \lambda_0 W)r = 0,$$
$$(B - \lambda_0 W)p = 0,$$
$$r'Wp = 0.$$

---

[11]This case has been discussed by Hood and Koopmans. See W. C. Hood and T. C. Koopmans, *Studies in Econometric Method*, John Wiley and Sons, New York (1953), pp. 112–99.

Suppose that r and p are normalized so that their first components are unity. Choose any real numbers a, b satisfying $a+b=1$; then the combined vector $ar+bp$ will satisfy

$$(B-\lambda_0 W)(ar+bp)=0,$$

and its first component will be unity according to our normalization rule. There exist an infinite number of pairs of (a, b), each of which gives the same value for $r'Br$ when it is adjusted by a scale change, keeping $r'Wr$ invariant in size. We have

$$\frac{k(ar+bp)'B(ar+bp)}{k(ar+bp)'W(ar+bp)} = \lambda_0,$$

where k denotes the scale factor.

In other words, our solution for the homogeneous equation has been shown to be indeterminate, regardless of normalization. In terms of statistical estimation, this situation may be interpreted as showing that we cannot find a unique set of estimates of the normalized latent vector which maximizes the value of likelihood function for the given observations.

This can also be seen from a consideration of

$$(B^* - \lambda_0 W^*)r = b_0^* - \lambda_0 w_0^*.$$

The characteristic vector has the value of 0/0 if λ_0 is a multiple root since the rank of $(B - \lambda_0 W)$ is then less than n.

How close must roots actually be, in practice, before they seriously affect limited information estimates? This is an important pragmatic question since they are hardly ever precisely multiple in empirical work. In the calculations cited above for the revised Klein–Goldberger model, sixteen equations were estimated. The two largest roots for the equation cited were 0.0355 and 0.0130.[12] These are close together, considering that in 13 of the 15 other equations the ratio of the largest to the next largest root was always greater than 8:1. In some cases it was 1000:1.

In a particular case, we find another possibility for there being no definite r satisfying the homogeneous equations $(B - \lambda_0 W)r = 0$, even though the root λ_0 is simple. If $(B^* - \lambda_0 W^*)$ happens to be singular, together with simplicity of the root λ_0, the solution of the homogeneous equations above would be explosive.[13] The rank of

---

[12] We transformed the calculations to estimate largest instead of smallest roots.

[13] Simplicity of λ_0 does not mean that every nth order determdinant of $(B - \lambda W)$ must be nonvanishing, only that one such determinant does not vanish.

$[(B^* - \lambda_0 W^*) \vdots b_0^* - \lambda_0 w_0^*]$ must be n due to the simplicity of λ_0, implying that $(B^* - \lambda W^*)$ should become nonsingular, as some column of it is replaced by $(b_0^* - \lambda_0 w_0^*)$.

The singular $(B^* - \lambda_0 W^*)$ with the simple root, λ_0, ought to be entirely compatible with nonsingular B, leading to the explosive solutions, or estimates, just as in singular cases of ordinary regressions.

In summary, we say that it is more plausible to expect that we will encounter singularity by the limited information method than by the two-stage least-squares method, because singularity of the former implies that of the latter ($|B|=0$), while the converse is not necessarily true since there may be cases in which limited information estimates happen to be indeterminate or explosive with nonsingular B.

SINGULARITY IN FULL INFORMATION ESTIMATES

The suggestion of the problem being investigated and the motivation behind our analysis came from applied work. Computation of two-stage least-squares and limited information estimates showed clearly the presence of near singularity and sensitivity of final results to this phenomenon. In the case of full information estimates, we have no such empirical guide lines. There has been very little computation of full information estimates, and that which has been done has been for small systems of two or three equations. We have not made a full analysis of full information techniques in terms of multicollinearity problems, but a few evident points are in order by way of rounding our presentation.

Since the full information methods give rise, in general, to nonlinear estimation equations, the solutions must be approximated by some iteration method. The iteration begins from some first approximations obtained possibly by the methods of two-stage least-squares or limited information, and requires inversion of the matrix of all variables in the system (endogenous and predetermined). At each iterative stage, this inverse matrix is used.

If the initial approximations are taken to be the two-stage least-squares or limited information estimates, then it is obvious that the sensitivity of these methods to multicollinearity is built into the full information estimates from the outset, and we would expect the latter method to be at least as sensitive as the other two. However, the matter is deeper than this trivial observation, and there is no reason why different initial approximations may not be used.

The important difference is that two-stage least-squares and limited information techniques are *single equation methods*. One can retain their consistency properties in incomplete systems. Not all predetermined variables need be used in the estimation of any single equation. A different subset; in particular, subsets with the most serious collinearities eliminated; may be used for the estimation of each equation. It may be possible to avoid problems of multicollinearity by the judicious choice of subsets of predetermined variables associated with the estimation of each single equation in the system. This cannot be done in full information calculations. The matrix of moments of all predetermined variables in the system must be inverted. Unless the specification of the model is changed, there are possibilities of unavoidable intercorrelations that may give rise to near singularity in full information but not necessarily present in the other methods. Moreover, the estimation of all equations in the systems will be affected by this singularity since it is not possible to use a different moment matrix for the estimation of each single equation.

The calculations by the full information method involve matrices of higher order than do the single equation methods; therefore, numerical precision in the face of singularity is more difficult to attain. The single equation methods are essentially linear computations. In the limited information method there is a small problem of extracting a characteristic root by an iterative process, but convergence is not difficult in this problem. The question of the convergence of the full information procedures is much more difficult. There are obviously possibilities for near singularity to interfere with convergence, and this would make the full information method more sensitive than the other two.

SOME PRACTICAL OBSERVATIONS ON THE INCIDENCE OF MULTICOLLINEARITY AND HOW TO DEAL WITH IT

It is the essence of equation systems that the endogenous (or jointly dependent) variables be interrelated. They are not joined to one another by exact relationships, but they are interrelated stochastically. We must accept these interrelationships as part of the systems that we are building.

The exogenous or predetermined variables are the 'explanatory' variables of the whole system, and it is intercorrelation among them that gives rise to much trouble in estimating the equations systems of econometrics. There may be a number of intercorrelations among elements of the x_t-vector $(x_1, \ldots, x_m, x_{m+1}, \ldots, x_M)$, and some problems caused by these intercorrelations can be avoided or minimized in empirical application. In the first instance, they may lead to inaccurate estimates of

$$W_{yy} = M_{yy} - M_{yx} M_{xx}^{-1} M_{xy}.$$

If two or more elements of x_t are related in a linear function, there will be no (or little) change in the calculation of W_{yy} if some of the related variables are omitted from the computation. We proved this in ordinary regression analysis for the case of a relationship between two elements of x_t. In the first stage of calculations of two-stage least-squares or limited information estimates we need evaluations of W_{yy} unadjusted for degrees of freedom; therefore we lose nothing if one of two *perfectly* correlated variables is omitted from the calculations.

Distribution of lags, alternative trends, and variables with similar cycles may give rise to the intercorrelations among elements of x_t. Nonspecific trends, the stock of capital, population, labor force and similar variables are not precisely equivalent or exactly related linearly. They are much alike and have high intercorrelations; yet they are just different enough so that an investigator may want to distinguish among them in particular structural equations. A nonspecific trend may be needed in a production function to represent technical change.[14] The stock of capital may be required in an equation of investment behavior; and population may be used in a consumption demand equation. Such intercorrelated trends as these are likely to be simultaneously present in a model of the economy as a whole, and care must be used to see that they are not included together in x_t^{**} for the estimation of any particular structural equation. In the full information method, however, we cannot avoid such cases of intercorrelated trends.

In the case of lag distributions, schemes with fixed relationships among coefficients of different lagged variables are now being widely used to overcome the complicating effects of multicollinearity. These, in effect, substitute a whole function of lags for each of the lags as separate variables. They require specification of the original model in terms of the lags used.

The method of principal components suggested by Kloek and Mennes may provide a solution to the problems of multicollinearity.[15] In place of the x_t vector, they recommend using a vector of principal components. These components are mutually orthogonal linear functions of the original components of x_t. They will not be intercorrelated. This is an alternative to the arbitrary dropping of some intercorrelated

[14]Trouble may arise if a technological trend and stock of capital variable are used together in a production function.

[15]T. Kloek and L. B. M. Mennes, 'Simultaneous equations based on principal components of predetermined variables,' *Econometrica*, XXVIII, January (1960), 45–61.

variables. It involves more computation, but brings more objectivity into the procedure of estimation.

We can form the regression of elements of x_t^{**} on x_t^*. Residual values from this regression will be orthogonal to x_t^* and this will reduce the possibility of multicollinearity. It will enhance the accuracy of estimation of W_{yy}, but it will not ensure that B_{yy} is nonsingular (or well conditioned). If the residuals are not significant and significantly related to elements of y_t, the difference matrix B_{yy} may approach singularity. The original system must always be specified so that it is strongly identified. The vector x_t^{**} must be important for each structural equation.

Finally, extreme care and precaution with accuracy of computation is not a fruitless and vain search for superfluous digits beyond the number significant in the original input. In spite of the fact that we have only two or three digits of significance in our original input variables and want only two- or three-digit coefficients as an end result, we may have to carry out intermediate calculations to a very large number of places. The intermediate stages of equations systems methods of estimation are quite intricate, and if we do not carry out all our results to many places and use the most accurate arithmetic procedures, we may find that our giant machines are spewing out masses of meaningless figures.

5
On the Interpretation of Theil's Method of Estimating Economic Relationships

Theil has proposed a new method for estimating the equation systems of linear econometric models.[1] He has established a formal mathematical relationship between his estimates and those obtained by either the method of least squares or limited information maximum likelihood. In this note I shall show how his method can be interpreted in terms of the method of instrumental variables, which has in fact been used or suggested previously although not on the systematic basis proposed by Theil. At the same time I shall be able to show, from another point of view, how his method is related to the method of limited information. Possibly the present development is more transparent than that of Theil in showing the nature of his methods of estimation.

AN OUTLINE OF THEIL'S THEORY

In a system of linear equations containing the N endogenous variables $y_{1t},\ldots,y_{Nt}$ and the R exogenous variables $z_{1t},\ldots,z_{Rt}$; let us write some particular equation as

$$x_t = \sum_{i=1}^{n} \alpha_i y_{it} + \sum_{i=1}^{r} \beta_i z_{it} + u_t \qquad n \leqslant N; r \leqslant R, \qquad (5.1)$$

in which one of the endogenous variables has been re-labeled as x_t, and the disturbance is denoted by u_t.

---

[1] H. Theil, Discussion, in Report of the Uppsala Meeting of the Econometric Society, *Econometrica* XXIII, April (1955) 204–5. See also *Estimation and Simultaneous Correlation in Complete Equation Systems*, Central Plan-Bureau, The Hague (1953) (mimeographed) and *Estimation of Parameters of Econometric Models*, in the Proceedings of the 28th Session of the International Statistical Institute, Rome (1953) XXXIV, 2nd edn., pp. 122–9.

From *Metroeconomica*, **7**, December (1955), 147–53.

The following matrix notation is introduced:

$$M_{zx} = \left\| \sum_{t=1}^{T} z_{it} x_t \right\|,$$

a column matrix $R \times 1$,

$$M_{zy} = \left\| \sum_{t=1}^{T} z_{it} y_{jt} \right\|,$$

a rectangular matrix $R \times n$,

$$M_{zz} = \left\| \sum_{t=1}^{T} z_{it} z_{jt} \right\|,$$

a square matrix $R \times R$.

Submatrices within each of these are formed by partitioning the z_t vector as

$$z_t' = (z_t^*, z_t^{**}),$$
$$z_t^{*'} = (z_{1t}, z_{2t}, \ldots, z_{rt})$$
$$z_t^{**'} = (z_{r+1,t}, z_{r+2,t}, \ldots, z_{Rt}).$$

All these matrices are the familiar moment matrices of linear regression.

Consider the set of linear equations in the unknown parameters α_i and β_i,

$$M_{zx} = [M_{zy} \quad M_{zz^*}] \begin{bmatrix} \alpha \\ \beta \end{bmatrix}. \tag{5.2}$$

A typical equation of (5.2),

$$\sum_{t=1}^{T} z_{it} x_t = \alpha_1 \sum_{t=1}^{T} z_{it} y_{1t} + \cdots + \alpha_n \sum_{t=1}^{T} z_{it} y_{nt}$$
$$+ \beta_1 \sum_{t=1}^{T} z_{it} z_{1t} + \cdots + \beta_r \sum_{t=1}^{T} z_{it} z_{rt},$$

is formed by multiplying both sides of (5.1) by z_{it} and summing over the sample observations making $\sum_{t=1}^{T} z_{it} u_t$ vanish by virtue of the assumption that z_{it} and u_t are independent. If the number of elements in z_t^{**} just equals n, the number of elements in y_t, there will, except in singular cases, be a unique solution to (5.2). This would be the case of exact identification and would provide the estimates for Theil's method as well as for limited information maximum likelihood.[2]

---

[2]Full information maximum likelihood estimates refer to an entire system and not to a single equation within the system. For an exactly identified system, the estimates of each structural equation are the same for either limited or full information maximum likelihood.

In the more usual case of overidentification, there will be more equations than unknowns in (5.2). Theil then proposes the following device. Regard a typical equation of the R equations in (5.2) as a regression of $\sum_{t=1}^{T} z_{it}x_t$ on the $\sum_{t=1}^{T} z_{it}y_{jt}$ and the $\sum_{t=1}^{T} z_{it}z_{jt}$ with a sample of R observations – one for each element of z_t. Theil derives the interesting result that his estimates, called *two-rounds estimates*, are obtained as the solution of

$$\begin{bmatrix} M_{yx} - kW_{yx} \\ M_{z*x} \end{bmatrix} = \begin{bmatrix} M_{yy} - kW_{yy} & M_{yz*} \\ M_{z*y} & M_{z*z*} \end{bmatrix} \begin{bmatrix} a \\ b \end{bmatrix} \quad (5.3)$$

when $k=1$. In this system of equations M_{yx} and M_{yy} are obviously moment matrices among elements of y and x and all pairs of elements of y, respectively. The matrix W is defined as

$$W_{yx} = M_{yx} - M_{yz}M_{zz}^{-1}M_{zx},$$
$$W_{yy} = M_{yy} - M_{yz}M_{zz}^{-1}M_{zy}.$$

W is the moment matrix of residuals from the least-squares regressions of the endogenous variables on all the elements of z_t. Limited information estimates are obtained from (5.3) if $k = 1 + v$, where v is the smallest root of the basic determinantal equation used in the method of limited information.[3] If $k = 0$, we have the least-squares regression of x_t on y_t and z_t^*.

AN INTERPRETATION OF THEIL'S THEORY – THE METHOD OF
INSTRUMENTAL VARIABLES

Equation system (5.2) suggests immediately the method of instrumental variables. By that method we choose enough exogenous variables, the instrumental set, so that when the equation to be estimated is multiplied by each and summed over the sample observations we have just enough equations to estimate all the unknown parameters. Except in the case of exact identification, and ignoring the case of underidentification, we have to select a subset of the instrumental set in order to obtain unique estimates. There is usually a certain amount of arbitrariness in this selection procedure.

---

[3] See T. W. Anderson and H. Rubin, Estimation of the parameters of a single equation in a complete system of stochastic equations, *Annals of Mathematical Statistics*, xx (1949), 53.

Geary,[4] in another context, has suggested that we may do better to choose some combination of instrumental variables rather than individual variables. I shall now prove that Theil's method of two-rounds estimation is the same thing as the method of instrumental variables, using a particular linear combination of instrumental variables and leaving no room for arbitrary selection.

Theorem Two-rounds estimates of the parameters in equation (5.1) are the same as estimates obtained by solving

$$\begin{bmatrix} M_{\hat{y}x} \\ M_{z^*x} \end{bmatrix} = \begin{bmatrix} M_{\hat{y}y} & M_{\hat{y}z^*} \\ M_{z^*y} & M_{z^*z^*} \end{bmatrix} \begin{bmatrix} a \\ b \end{bmatrix}$$

where $\hat{y}_{it}$ are the values of y_{it} calculated from the least-squares regression of y_{it} on all the elements of z_t.

Proof The least-squares regression of y_{it} on all the elements of z_t is given by the estimates of the π in

$$y_{it} = \sum_{j=1}^{R} \pi_{ij} z_{jt} + v_{it} \qquad (i = 1, 2, \ldots, n).$$

$$P = \text{est} \, \|\pi_{ij}\| = M_{yz} M_{zz}^{-1},$$

$$\hat{y}_t = P z_t.$$

Hence

$$M_{\hat{y}x} = P M_{zx} = M_{yz} M_{zz}^{-1} M_{zx},$$

$$M_{\hat{y}y} = M_{y\pi} M_{\pi\pi}^{-1} M_{\pi y},$$

$$M_{\hat{y}z^*} = M_{yz} M_{zz}^{-1} M_{zz^*} = M_{yz^*},$$

since M_{zz^*} is a submatrix of M_{zz}.

$$M_{zz}^{-1} M_{zz^*} = \begin{bmatrix} 1 & 0 & 0 & \ldots & 0 \\ 0 & 1 & 0 & \ldots & 0 \\ \vdots & & & & \\ 0 & 0 & 0 & \ldots & 1 \\ 0 & 0 & 0 & \ldots & 0 \\ \vdots & & & & \\ 0 & 0 & 0 & \ldots & 0 \end{bmatrix}$$

[4] R. C. Geary, Determination of linear relations between systematic parts of variables with errors of observation, the variances of which are unknown, *Econometrica*, XVII (1949), 30–58.

$$\begin{bmatrix} M_{\hat{y}x} \\ M_{z^*x} \end{bmatrix} = \begin{bmatrix} M_{yz}M_{zz}^{-1}M_{zx} \\ M_{z^*x} \end{bmatrix},$$

$$\begin{bmatrix} M_{\hat{y}y} & M_{\hat{y}z^*} \\ M_{z^*y} & M_{z^*z^*} \end{bmatrix} = \begin{bmatrix} M_{yz}M_{zz}^{-1}M_{zy} & M_{yz^*} \\ M_{z^*y} & M_{z^*z^*} \end{bmatrix}$$

If $k=1$,

$$M_{yx} - kW_{yx} = M_{yz}M_{zz}^{-1}M_{zx},$$
$$M_{yy} - kW_{yy} = M_{yz}M_{zz}^{-1}M_{zy},$$

and two-rounds estimates are given by the solution of

$$\begin{bmatrix} M_{yz}M_{zz}^{-1}M_{zx} \\ M_{z^*x} \end{bmatrix} = \begin{bmatrix} M_{yz}M_{zz}^{-1}M_{zy} & M_{yz^*} \\ M_{z^*y} & M_{z^*z^*} \end{bmatrix} \begin{bmatrix} a \\ b \end{bmatrix}.$$

This proves the theorem.

Geary remarks that instrumental variables should be chosen which are correlated as closely as possible with the endogenous variables of the equation to be estimated. By using $\hat{y}_t$ as instrumental variables, we choose those linear combinations of the exogenous variables in the entire system of equations which are correlated as closely as possible with the elements of y_t. Other linear combinations could be chosen, but the particular set given by the regressions of y_i on z_t is unique, saving one from arbitrary decisions. If the correlations between y_t and z_t are not significantly affected by the omission of some components of z_t in the calculation of $\hat{y}_t$, there will be little effect on the final result. In systems with large numbers of exogenous variables, one must watch the number of degrees of freedom used up in calculating the matrix P.

It remains to be shown, although it is quite straightforward and evident, that estimates given by

$$\begin{bmatrix} M_{\hat{y}x} \\ M_{z^*x} \end{bmatrix} = \begin{bmatrix} M_{\hat{y}y} & M_{\hat{y}z^*} \\ M_{z^*y} & M_{z^*z^*} \end{bmatrix} \begin{bmatrix} a \\ b \end{bmatrix} \tag{5.4}$$

are the same as

$$\begin{bmatrix} M_{z^{**}x} \\ M_{z^*x} \end{bmatrix} = \begin{bmatrix} M_{z^{**}y} & M_{z^{**}z^*} \\ M_{z^*y} & M_{z^*z^*} \end{bmatrix} \begin{bmatrix} a \\ b \end{bmatrix} \tag{5.5}$$

in the case of exact identification, i.e. n elements in z_t^{**}.

Premultiply both sides of equation system (5.2), which is the same thing as (5.5), by the $n \times R$ rectangular matrix P.

$$PM_{zx} = P[M_{zy} \quad M_{zz^*}]\begin{bmatrix} a \\ b \end{bmatrix}.$$

The result is

$$M_{yz}M_{zz}^{-1}M_{zx} = [M_{yz}M_{zz}^{-1}M_{zy} \quad M_{yz^*}]\begin{bmatrix}a\\b\end{bmatrix}$$

This in turn is equivalent to

$$M_{\hat{y}x} = [M_{\hat{y}y} \quad M_{yz^*}]\begin{bmatrix}a\\b\end{bmatrix}.$$

These n equations in $n+r$ variables, when combined with the r equations

$$M_{z^*x} = [M_{z^*y} \quad M_{z^*z^*}]\begin{bmatrix}a\\b\end{bmatrix},$$

form a complete system; thus (5.4) and (5.5) are equivalent.

COMPARISON OF TWO-ROUNDS AND LIMITED INFORMATION ESTIMATES

The method of limited information, for estimating the parameters of (5.1), maximizes the joint *normal* distribution of $(v_{x1}, \ldots, v_{xT}, v_{11}, \ldots, v_{1T}, \ldots, v_{n1}, \ldots, v_{nT})$ in

$$x_t = \sum_{j=1}^{R} \pi_{xj} z_{jt} + v_{xt},$$

$$y_{it} = \sum_{j=1}^{R} \pi_{ij} z_{jt} + v_{it} \quad (i=1,2,\ldots,n), \tag{5.6}$$

subject to

$$(1-\alpha_1-\alpha_2-\cdots-\alpha_n)\begin{bmatrix}\pi_{x,r+1} & \pi_{x,r+2} & \cdots & \pi_{xR}\\ \pi_{1,r+1} & \pi_{1,r+2} & \cdots & \pi_{1R}\\ \vdots & & & \\ \pi_{n,r+1} & \pi_{n,r+2} & \cdots & \pi_{nR}\end{bmatrix} = 0. \tag{5.7}$$

Equations (5.6) are the *reduced forms* and (5.7) are the *restrictions* associated with equation (5.1).

Another way of formulating this approach is to maximize the joint *normal* distribution of $(u_1, \ldots, u_T, v_{11}, \ldots, v_{1T}, \ldots, v_{n1}, \ldots, v_{nT})$ in

$$x_t = \sum_{j=1}^{n} \alpha_j y_{jt} + \sum_{j=1}^{r} \beta_j z_{jt} + u_t,$$

$$y_{it} = \sum_{j=1}^{R} \pi_{ij} z_{jt} + v_{it} \qquad (i = 1, 2, \ldots, n). \tag{5.8}$$

The $n+1$ equations in (5.8) represent an alternative way of writing (5.6) and (5.7) together. The restrictions have, so to speak, been substituted in the reduced forms and eliminated as separate equations.

Theil's two-rounds estimates, according to the theorem proved above, are derived by maximizing the joint *normal* distribution of $(v_{11}, \ldots, v_{1T}, \ldots, v_{n1}, \ldots, v_{nT})$. This step gives P as the least-squares estimate of $\|\pi_{ij}\|$. The final step is to solve

$$\begin{bmatrix} M_{\hat{y}x} \\ M_{z^*x} \end{bmatrix} = \begin{bmatrix} M_{\hat{y}y} & M_{\hat{y}z^*} \\ M_{z^*y} & M_{z^*z^*} \end{bmatrix} \begin{bmatrix} a \\ b \end{bmatrix}$$

by setting $\sum_{t=1}^{T} u_t \hat{y}_{it} = 0$, and $i = 1, 2, \ldots, n$.

REMARKS ON OTHER METHODS

The idea of using calculated values of endogenous variables from least-squares estimates of reduced form equations and treating them *statistically* as though they were exogenous variables is a procedure that was always mentioned as a possible approach in the 'oral traditions' developed at the Cowles Commission for Research in Economics during the days when limited information methods were first being developed.[5] In recursive systems, successively computed values of endogenous variables may be treated in a statistical way like exogenous variables, and have been so applied in particular empirical problems.[6]

In a more specialized model of recursion, Wold[7] has shown that least-squares estimates of each single equation in a system are full maximum likelihood estimates provided the disturbances in separate equations are independently and normally distributed. Equation system

---

[5] See L. R. Klein, *A Textbook of Econometrics*, Row, Peterson and Co., Evanston (1953), pp. 186–96 for some examples using this idea.

[6] See H. Barger and L. R. Klein, A quarterly model for the United States economy, *Journal of the American Statistical Association* (1954), IL 413–37.

[7] H. Wold (with L. Juréen), *Demand Analysis*, John Wiley and Sons, New York (1953).

(5.8) above is a recursive system, i.e. it has a triangular Jacobian

$$\frac{\partial(u, v_1, \ldots, v_n)}{\partial(x, y_1, \ldots, y_n)} = \begin{bmatrix} 1 & -\alpha_1 & -\alpha_2 & \cdots & -\alpha_n \\ 0 & 1 & 0 & \cdots & 0 \\ \vdots & & & & \\ 0 & 0 & 0 & \cdots & 1 \end{bmatrix} = 1.$$

However, if the reduced form equations for y_{it} in (5.8) are not *structural* equations, as such, we cannot assume that u_t is independent of v_{it}, since each v_{it} will generally be a linear combination of all the structural disturbances, including u_t.

6

Dynamic Properties of Nonlinear Econometric Models

INTRODUCTION

An investigation of the dynamic properties of an econometric model is frequently of considerable interest and an important source of information about the model. It may be useful, for example, to determine the extent to which the endogenous variables of a given model exhibit business-cycle variations of the type that are observed in the data. In addition to the cyclical response of particular endogenous variables, economists are often interested in timing relationships between endogenous variables in the system. System response characteristics can be used, for example, to test various propositions about the relationship between wages and prices, between investment expenditure and interest rates, and other pairs of variables. The dynamic properties of the model may also provide useful insights into the related problems of prediction and stabilization of the system that the model represents. For these reasons, the development of analytical techniques which can be used to determine the dynamic characteristics of a model is highly desirable.

Much of the hypothesis testing that has been carried out in recent years has been concerned with time-domain characteristics of econometric models; that is, the analysis has been concerned primarily with impact and dynamic multipliers, and with prediction or extrapolation in the time domain. More recently, however, spectrum analytic techniques have been used both in data analysis and in the investigation of the frequency response characteristics of econometric models. In connection with the study of stochastic systems, spectrum analysis has been used in two ways. First spectrum and cross-spectrum analysis has been used to analyze the results of stochastic simulations of

---

From *International Economic Review*, **13**, 3, October (1972), 599–618; written jointly with E. Philip Howrey.

econometric models [10]. Second, spectral methods have played an important role in the development of 'analytic' as opposed to stochastic simulation of econometric models [1,5]. Although these two uses of spectrum analysis convey the same type of information, analytic simulation has several advantages.

1 It is unnecessary to perform replications of stochastic solutions of the model.

2 Interpretation of the results of analytic simulation is simpler since the experimental error or sampling variability associated with spectrum estimates obtained from simulation runs is avoided.

3 Experimentation with alternative functional forms and coefficient estimates is simpler within the context of analytic simulation.

The major drawback of analytic simulation is that it has been applicable only to linear systems. In order to analyze nonlinear systems, a linear approximation must be obtained and for even moderately complex models this can be an extremely laborious process. Moreover, once a linear approximation is obtained, the usual procedure involves the inversion of complex-valued matrices of order n, the number of stochastic equations in the system. In addition, if the model contains important nonlinearities, the linear approximation may give a misleading impression of the dynamic characteristics of the model. The purpose of this paper is to describe a direct method that can be used to obtain the frequency response matrix of a nonlinear system. Using this method, an explicit linear approximation is not required nor is it necessary to invert complex-valued matrices. This method therefore appears to be a useful numerical procedure both from the point of view of computational efficiency and the ease of interpretation of the results.

In the next section, the computational procedure is described. As an illustration of this approach to the investigation of the dynamic properties of nonlinear models, results obtained for the Wharton Model are presented in the following section. For purposes of comparison, replicated stochastic simulations of the Wharton Model are analyzed using both spectral and regression models. The results are summarized in the final section of the paper.

ANALYTIC SIMULATION

In this section a method is proposed for the computation of the frequency response matrix of a system of stochastic equations. Although the theory is based on the analysis of linear systems for which the

Nonlinear models

results are asymptotically exact, the technique can be used to analyze a nonlinear system. However, no attempt is made at this point to justify this approach to the analysis of nonlinear systems beyond the analogy with linear systems.

Consider the linear system

$$A(L)Y(t) = B(L)X(t) + U(t) \tag{6.1}$$

where Y, X, and U are vectors and $A(L)$ and $B(L)$ are matrices of polynomials in the lag operator L. The moving-average representation of the system is

$$Y(t) = \Gamma(L)X(t) + \Delta(L)U(t) \tag{6.2}$$

where $\Delta(L)A(L) \equiv I$ and $\Gamma(L) \equiv \Delta(L)B(L)$. A control solution of this system, $Y^c(t)$, is defined by

$$Y^c(t) \equiv E[Y(t)|X(t)] = \Gamma(L)X(t) \tag{6.3}$$

and the deviations from this control solution corresponding to the disturbance process $U(t)$ is

$$D(t) = \Delta(L)U(t). \tag{6.4}$$

The problem now is to compute the spectral matrix of $D(t)$ to obtain a description of the stochastic deviations from the control solution. The straightforward solution is simply

$$S_y(\omega) = \Delta(e^{-i\omega})S_u(\omega)\Delta^*(e^{-i\omega}) \tag{6.5}$$

where Δ^* is the conjugate transpose of $\Delta(e^{-i\omega}) = [A(e^{-i\omega})]^{-1}$. Thus, given the spectrum matrix of $U(t)$, $S_u(\omega)$, and the coefficients of the operator matrix $A(L)$, the spectrum matrix of the deviation from the control solution can be computed directly from (6.5). It is clearly unnecessary to resort to stochastic simulation of (6.4) to obtain an estimate of the spectrum of the sequence deviations from the control path of the system.

The method proposed here involves a forward solution of the system to obtain the elements $\delta_{ij}(L) = \sum_{k=0}^{\infty} \delta_{ijk} L^k$ of the matrix $\Delta(L)$. Let $u_j(t)$, the jth element in the $U(t)$, be defined by

$$u_j(t) = \begin{cases} 0 & t < 0 \\ 1 & t = 0 \\ 0 & t > 0 \end{cases} \tag{6.6}$$

and let $u_i(t) = 0$ for $i \neq j$. Then the solution of (6.4) for $D(t)$ yields

$$d_i(t) = \begin{cases} 0 & t < 0 \\ \delta_{ijt} & t \geq 0. \end{cases} \tag{6.7}$$

The elements in the matrix of the frequency response functions are now approximated by

$$\delta_{ij}^n(e^{-i\omega}) = \sum_{k=0}^{n} \delta_{ijk} e^{-i\omega k}. \qquad (6.8)$$

Finally, the cross-spectrum matrix is approximated by

$$S_y^n(\omega) = \Delta_n(\omega) S_u(\omega) \Delta_n^*(\omega) \qquad (6.9)$$

where $\Delta_n(\omega)$ is the matrix with elements $\delta_{ij}^n(e^{-i\omega})$ defined in (6.8), $\Delta_n^*(\omega)$ is the conjugate transpose of $\Delta_n(\omega)$, and $S_u(\omega)$ is the spectral matrix of the disturbance process. The approximation to the cross-spectrum between y_i and y_j is therefore

$$\Sigma_{ij}^n(\omega) = \sum_k \sum_l \delta_{ik}^n(e^{-i\omega}) \bar{\delta}_{jl}^n(e^{-i\omega}) \sigma_{kl}(\omega) \qquad (6.9')$$

when Σ_{ij}^n are the elements of $S_y^n(\omega)$ and $\sigma_{kl}(\omega)$ are the elements of $S_u(\omega)$.

This procedure can be applied directly to nonlinear models as well as to linear models. Consider the nonlinear model

$$F[Y(t), Y(t-1), \ldots, Y(t-p); \; X(t), X(t-1), \ldots, X(t-q); \; U(t)] = 0. \qquad (6.10)$$

A deterministic control solution, $Y^c(t)$, corresponding to a given sequence of exogenous variables $X(t)$ is obtained by solving (6.10) with $U(t) = 0$. The sequence of coefficients δ_{ijt} is obtained by subtracting $Y^c(t)$ from $Y^s(t)$ where $Y^s(t)$ is the solution of (6.10) with $U(t)$ now defined by (6.6).[1] The spectrum matrix of the endogenous variables of the system is then obtained from (6.8) and (6.9).

Once the cross-spectrum matrix of the endogenous variables has been obtained, frequency-domain hypothesis testing is a relatively simple matter. For example, the power spectra $\Sigma_{ij}^n(\omega)$ can be used to determine the response of $y_i(t)$ to the disturbance process. Moreover, the coherence, gain, and phase relationships can be used to test propositions about pairs of endogenous variables.

By way of summarizing the analytic simulation approach to the study of nonlinear stochastic systems, we note that the following steps are involved in the computation of the spectral matrix of the endogenous variables of the model.

1. A control solution $y^c(t)$ is calculated for the system. If the deviations from a full-employment growth path are to be analyzed, for example,

[1] If the system possesses multiple equilibria, care must be exercised in the choice of the size of the shock administered to the system in order to ensure that $Y^c(t)$ and $Y^s(t)$ converge to the same limit point.

then the time path of the exogenous variables is chosen to yield a full-employment control solution.

2 The impulse response functions are then obtained by shocking the stochastic equations, one at a time, and solving for the corresponding time path of deviations of all endogenous variables from the control solution values of these variables.

3 The frequency response matrix of the system is then given by the finite Fourier transform of the impulse response functions.

4 An estimate of the cross-spectrum matrix of the disturbance process is obtained from the sample-period residuals.

5 The frequency response matrix and the disturbance cross-spectrum are combined to obtain the cross-spectrum matrix of the endogenous variables of the model.

DYNAMIC PROPERTIES OF THE WHARTON MODEL

As a test of the feasibility of the analytic simulation approach to the analysis of nonlinear models, the methods outlined in the preceding section have been used to analyze the Wharton Model. The version of the model that was used for both the analytic and stochastic simulation experiments reported here contains fifty-one stochastic equations which are described in [2]. The basic purpose of this set of exercises is to determine the extent to which the disturbance process introduces business-cycle variations about the full-employment growth path implied by the Wharton Model. Thus the analysis is confined to an examination of the power spectra of selected endogenous variables. The analytic simulation results are described first, followed by a discussion of the stochastic simulation experiments which were analyzed using both spectral and regression techniques.

Analytic simulation of the Wharton Model

In the application of the analytic procedure described in the preceding section, a number of decisions must be made. Since we are interested in lapses from full employment, a control solution which results in a 4 per cent unemployment rate was chosen as the time path from which to measure deviations. Response functions for $n=80$ periods were then computed using 5σ pulses, i.e. each equation, one at a time, was subjected to a disturbance that was five times as large as the sample standard deviation of residuals of the equation. The use of $k\sigma$ rather than unit pulses is motivated by two considerations. For some equations, unit pulses would result in deviations far beyond the realm of anything observed over the sample period which was used to estimate the model. The use of such large shocks would generate rather peculiar behavior of the system such as negative unemployment rates. On the other hand, unit pulses are too small for other equations and lead to such small values for the response function that numerical accuracy becomes a problem. Although the use of $k=5$ standard deviations is to a certain extent arbitrary, experimentation with alternative values of k led us to conclude that $k=5$ is consistent with considerations of numerical accuracy and the region in which the model can be expected to provide a reasonable description of reality.

The cross-spectrum matrix of the disturbance process was estimated in two different ways since the response to both correlated and uncorrelated disturbances is of interest. In order to determine if the model responds cyclically to uncorrelated disturbances, the contemporaneous variance–covariance matrix of the sample-period residuals was used as an estimate of the spectral matrix of the disturbance process. In view of the fact that the sample-period residuals from nearly all of the equations exhibit statistically significant serial correlation, the cross-spectrum matrix of the disturbance process was also estimated using the Parzen window with truncation point $m=20$. This estimate is then used to test the hypothesis that the model responds cyclically to disturbances which have the same serial correlation pattern as that found in the sample-period residuals.[2]

The spectrum of real GNP implied by the Wharton Model is shown in figures 6.1 and 6.2. The power at frequencies ranging from 48 quarters per cycle to 3 quarters per cycle are shown on these graphs. Several distinct impressions which emerge from an examination of these graphs can be summarized as follows.

1 There is a substantial concentration of power in the very low frequency end of the spectrum. This is not completely unexpected since characteristic root computations on a condensed, linearized version of the Wharton Model indicate that there are several roots close to unity [4]. Thus, this model tends to generate time paths of the endogenous variables that have the 'typical spectral shape' in which power decreases as the frequency of oscillation increases, at least at the low frequency end of the spectrum.

---

[2]Computational details are given in [6].

Nonlinear models

```
                         Power
  Period     Power    +-------------------------------+
  48.00      1817.0   *******************************
  44.00       708.4   *************
  40.00       192.3   ****
  36.00       560.5   *********
  32.00      1128.0   *********************
  28.00       390.5   ********
  24.00       459.7   ********
  20.00       142.9   ***
  19.00       154.7   ***
  18.00       370.7   *******
  17.00       368.6   *******
  16.00       129.4   ***
  15.00       188.6   ****
  14.00       288.3   *****
  13.00        95.2   **
  12.00       243.9   *****
  11.00       104.6   **
  10.00       128.7   ***
   9.00       167.3   ***
   8.00       142.5   ***
   7.00       118.9   ***
   6.00       105.0   **
   5.00       118.0   **
   4.00       660.3   ************
                     +-------------------------------+
```

Figure 6.1 Power spectrum of real GNP, analytic simulation with serially uncorrelated disturbances

```
                         Power
  Period     Power    +-------------------------------+
  48.00      1729.0   ******************************
  44.00       826.6   *************
  40.00       265.8   *****
  36.00       623.6   **********
  32.00      1322.0   **********************
  28.00       673.2   ***********
  24.00       540.0   *********
  20.00       408.2   *******
  19.00       195.8   ****
  18.00       512.7   ********
  17.00       848.7   ***************
  16.00       456.0   ********
  15.00       196.2   ****
  14.00       716.5   *************
  13.00       232.0   ****
  12.00       500.4   ********
  11.00       132.8   ***
  10.00       331.4   ******
   9.00       275.3   *****
   8.00       155.7   ***
   7.00        61.4   **
   6.00        36.2   *
   5.00        26.5   *
   4.00        22.4   *
                     +-------------------------------+
```

Figure 6.2 Power spectrum of real GNP, analytic simulation with serially correlated disturbances

2 For many of the variables, and GNP in particular, the slope of the power spectrum changes rapidly with frequency. That is, a substantial number of rather pronounced relative peaks appear in the power spectrum. This indicates that it would be impossible to construct a low-order autoregressive process that would have the same frequency response characteristics as those implied by the Wharton Model.

3 The power spectrum of real GNP implied by the Wharton Model indicates that there are relative concentrations of power at frequencies corresponding to 32, 24, 18, 14, 12 and 4 quarters per cycle in the response to uncorrelated disturbances; the peak frequencies are 32, 24, 17, 14, 12 and 4 for the response to correlated disturbances. For the serially correlated disturbances case, the two most important frequencies of oscillation are 32 quarters (8 years) and 17 quarters (4.25 years). This is somewhat reminiscent of the major – and minor – cycle variation found in previous studies of economic time series. However, in view of the additional spectral peaks that are found, this major–minor cycle scheme clearly does not characterize the process completely.

4 The use of serially correlated disturbances results in a more pronounced business-cycle variation than when uncorrelated disturbances are employed. This is not particularly surprising in view of the fact that nearly all the power spectra of the series of sample-period residuals exhibit a relative peak around the 16-quarter cycle. The model simply transmits with increased amplitude the business-cycle variation in the residuals to the endogenous variables.

Stochastic simulation of the Wharton Model

The analytic simulation results are particularly interesting, perhaps even rather surprising, when compared with the analysis of stochastic simulation experiments reported in [3]. The results reported in [3] are based on repeated stochastic simulations of the Wharton Model over 100 time periods using both uncorrelated and correlated disturbances.[3] The same full-employment control solution was used in both the stochastic and analytic simulations; so the two experiments are comparable in this respect. For each replication of the stochastic simulation, power spectra of selected endogenous variables were estimated. In each case, the first ten observations were deleted leaving $n=90$ data

---

[3]For a description of the method used to generate the disturbances for the simulations, the reader is referred to [3].

points for each replication. After control solution detrending,[4] spectrum densities were estimated using the Parzen window with truncation point $m = 80$. Finally, the spectrum estimates were averaged over 50 replications to obtain an average power spectrum.

The results for the simulations of real GNP with uncorrelated disturbances are shown in figure 6.3, and the GNP spectrum estimates obtained from the correlated disturbance simulations are shown in figure 6.4. The results can be summarized as follows.

1 With uncorrelated disturbances, the spectrum of GNP exhibits the so-called typical spectral shape of an economic variable in which power decreases smoothly as the frequency of oscillation increases. There is, however, a concentration of power of 4 quarters per cycle. It has been shown in [3] how this periodicity arises as a result of the use of several equations for wages and prices involving 4-quarter differences. It is not, therefore, the usual seasonal cycle. The absence of a pronounced business-cycle component is particularly noteworthy.

2 The spectrum estimates obtained from serially-correlated disturbance simulations indicates the presence of a business-cycle variation in these simulations. There is a pronounced peak in the spectrum at 16 quarters per cycle.

3 There is a substantial amount of variation in the spectrum estimates across replications. For example, the average power at the 16-quarter cycle is 239.59 for the uncorrelated-disturbance simulations and the standard deviation across runs is 137.8. However, this standard error is not substantially different from the expected result which states that the variance of the spectrum estimator using the Parzen window is $0.542 \, m s^2(\omega)/n$ where $s^2(\omega)$ is the true value of the spectrum at ω.

From a purely descriptive point of view these estimates indicate that the Wharton Model responds cyclically to disturbances which have the same pattern of correlation as that observed in the sample residuals, but the model does not respond cyclically to uncorrelated disturbances.

Since the results shown in figures 6.3 and 6.4 were obtained from stochastic simulation of the model, they are subject to experimental sampling error. It is therefore necessary to consider the stochastic properties of the spectrum estimates in order to determine the statistical significance of the peak in the spectrum of GNP obtained from serially correlated simulations. Using the standard χ^2 approximation, it follows

---

[4]The control solution is the disturbance-free solution of the model over the simulation period.

Period	Average power	Std error	Power
80.00	2897.0	3236.4	******************************
40.00	1009.7	833.4	***********
26.67	519.8	327.3	******
20.00	322.3	156.3	****
16.00	239.6	137.8	***
13.33	188.5	101.0	***
11.43	143.9	70.8	**
10.00	137.3	67.3	**
8.89	121.8	76.9	**
8.00	114.8	67.1	**
7.27	127.8	97.6	**
6.67	118.2	59.4	**
6.15	136.8	91.1	**
5.71	140.1	109.1	**
5.33	137.2	86.4	**
5.00	111.7	72.1	**
4.71	115.5	70.9	**
4.44	113.3	71.4	**
4.21	193.7	127.1	***
4.00	375.7	312.3	*****
3.81	222.4	178.6	***
3.64	111.5	75.2	**
3.48	89.4	63.1	**
3.33	88.4	49.4	**

Figure 6.3 Power spectrum of real GNP, stochastic simulation with serially uncorrelated disturbances

Period	Average power	Std error	Power
80.00	1328.0	1357.7	***************
40.00	538.8	327.7	******
26.67	355.2	182.1	*****
20.00	601.5	363.9	*******
16.00	849.1	490.6	**********
13.33	587.9	380.9	*******
11.43	258.0	163.3	****
10.00	88.9	45.9	**
8.89	58.9	37.3	*
8.00	60.2	35.3	*
7.27	53.1	29.6	*
6.67	43.5	27.8	*
6.15	47.2	34.5	*
5.71	38.0	25.6	*
5.33	31.0	19.1	*
5.00	25.6	15.6	*
4.71	14.2	8.1	*
4.44	16.0	8.4	*
4.21	50.4	31.1	*
4.00	110.6	83.2	**
3.81	70.7	39.8	**
3.64	48.8	28.2	*
3.48	28.2	17.3	*
3.33	16.8	13.5	*

Figure 6.4 Power spectrum of real GNP, stochastic simulation with serially correlated disturbances

that $v\hat{s}(\omega)/s(\omega)$ where $\hat{s}(\omega)$ is an estimate of the true spectrum $s(\omega)$ is a χ^2 variate with $v = 3.7\,n/m$ degrees of freedom. On the assumption that the $r = 50$ replications are independent, it follows that $rv\bar{s}(\omega)/s(\omega)$ where $\bar{s}(\omega) = r^{-1}\sum \hat{s}_i(\omega)$ is χ^2 with $rv = 3.7\,rn/m$ degrees of freedom. Thus, provided $\bar{s}(\omega_1)$ and $\bar{s}(\omega_2)$ are independent, the F ratio

$$F = \frac{\bar{s}(\omega_1)/s(\omega_1)}{\bar{s}(\omega_2)/s(\omega_2)} \qquad (6.11)$$

can be used to test hypotheses about $s(\omega)$. In particular, to test the hypothesis that $s(\omega_1) = s(\omega_2)$, the ratio of the spectrum estimates can be examined.

Using the F ratio defined in (6.11), the ratio most favorable to rejection of the hypothesis that the peak in the average spectrum is not significant is obtained by dividing the power at 16 quarters per cycle (849.1) by the power at 26.7 quarters (355.2). This yields an F ratio of 2.39. Which exceeds the critical value of $F\,(200, 200)$ at the 1 per cent level. It might be noted, however, that this comparison which is most favorable to rejection of the hypothesis may not be entirely valid since the estimate at 26.7 quarters is not completely independent of the estimate at 16 quarters per cycle. Using the Parzen window, the band width is $1/m$ cycles per quarter. Thus the estimate at one-sixteenth of a cycle per quarter is an average over the band $(1/16 \pm 1/m)$ or $(4/80, 6/80)$. Similarly, the estimate centered on $3/80$ is an average over $(2/80, 4/80)$. A more convincing test would require an increase in both m and n so that the resolution of the spectrum estimates is increased without reducing the number of degrees of freedom associated with each estimate.

An alternative approach to the determination of inherent cycle length of the series generated by the Wharton Model can be devised using regression techniques. This alternative approach derives from Slutsky's observation [13] that the tendency of a series to satisfy

$$\Delta^2 x(t) = x(t+2) - 2x(t+1) + x(t) = -\lambda x(t+1) \qquad (6.12)$$

implies that the series has approximately sinusoidal properties. This is so because the second derivative of a sine function is proportional to the negative of the sine function. The finite difference equation (6.12) has an undamped sinusoidal solution if

$$(2-\lambda)^2 < 4. \qquad (6.13)$$

This inequality implies that the roots of the characteristic equation

$$\rho^2 - (2-\lambda)\rho + 1 = 0 \qquad (6.14)$$

are complex, and the fact that the coefficient of $x(t)$ is unity means that the product of the roots will be unity. Thus, if inequality (6.13) is satisfied, together with an implied unit coefficient of $x(t)$ in (6.12), each root of (6.14) must have unit modulus and the solution will be an undamped sinusoid.

An estimate of $(2-\lambda)$ is obtained by regressing $x(t+2)+x(t)$ on $x(t+1)$:

$$\text{est}(2-\lambda) = \frac{\sum [x(t+2)+x(t)]x(t+1)}{\sum [x(t+1)]^2}. \tag{6.15}$$

It is useful to note that the estimate of $-\lambda$ is approximately

$$-\hat{\lambda} = 2\hat{\rho}(1) - 2 \tag{6.16}$$

where $\hat{\rho}(1)$ is an estimate of the first-order serial correlation coefficient of the series $x(t)$. It is easy to verify that the period of the sinusoid generated by (6.12) is

$$\hat{P} = 2\pi/\cos^{-1} \frac{(2-\hat{\lambda})}{2}, \tag{6.17}$$

or using the approximation (6.16),

$$\hat{P} \simeq 2\pi/\cos^{-1}[\hat{\rho}(1)]. \tag{6.18}$$

Now it is well known that the mean distance between upcrosses in a normal process is $2\pi/\cos^{-1}[\rho(1)]$ so that the period given by (6.17) can be interpreted as an estimate of the mean distance between upcrosses in the simulated series.

From the 50 replications of the stochastic simulation of the Wharton Model that were used for the spectral calculations plotted in figures 6.3 and 6.4, we obtained 50 estimates of $(2-\lambda)$ with

mean $\text{est}(2-\lambda) = 1.7945$.

In all 50 cases, the estimate of λ generated undamped sinusoids. For the mean estimate, we calculated

$$\cos \theta = \frac{1.7945}{2} = 0.89725$$

$$\theta = 26.17,$$

implying a period of 13.7 quarters, slightly below the value at the peak in figure 6.4.

Since the transformation from λ to θ or P is nonlinear, the mean period $\hat{P}$ transformed from the mean estimate of the autoregressive parameter $\hat{\lambda}$ in (6.17) is not necessarily the same as the mean of the periods estimated separately for each replication and then averaged. The average estimate of P is

$$\bar{P} = 16.8,$$

which is close to the standard 4-year cycle found in the spectral analysis.

The consistency of estimated autoregressive parameters is well known for the general case of any order finite difference equation provided all the roots lie within the unit circle, $|\rho| < 1$. The roots of (6.14) have unit modulus, however. Results on consistency for this case have been obtained only recently. Rubin [12] proved consistency for the first order case if $|\rho| \geq 1$, and Muench [9] extended this result to the general case of arbitrary finite order regardless of the multiplicity or location of roots. Actually, the autoregressive parameter of our constrained, second-order case is seen in (6.15) to be the sum of two first-order autoregressions, and does not involve the extension of Rubin's results to higher order cases.

Otsuki [11] has investigated an extension of Slutsky's suggestion to seek tendencies for the finite difference equation in (6.12) to be satisfied. Otsuki would extend the estimates of autoregressive equations to higher order. The fourth-order equation

$$x(t+4) + \lambda_1 x(t+3) + \lambda_2 x(t+2) + \lambda_1 x(t+1) + x(t) = 0 \qquad (6.19)$$

will have complex characteristic roots with unit modulus. It should be noted that the λ_i are constrained so that the coefficients of $x(t+3)$ and $x(t+1)$ are equal to each other, and the coefficient of $x(t)$ is unity. Otsuki's method is to fit autoregressive equations, appropriately restricted in order to obtain complex roots with unit modulus, of successively higher even order as long as the residual sum of squares decreases significantly. In the fourth-order case, the method is to regress $x(t+4) + x(t)$ on $x(t+3) + x(t+1)$ and $x(t+2)$. In the sixth-order case, the method is to regress $x(t+6) + x(t)$ on $x(t+5) + x(t+1)$, $x(t+4) + x(t+2)$ and $x(t+3)$.

Otsuki's approach is based on the consideration that solutions of stochastic finite difference equations may be governed by a sinusoidal limit theorem. As the order of the primary (econometric) system generating the x_t-series grows there is a tendency of the series to follow a sinusoidal limit if the characteristic roots are located in a certain portion of the unit circle. This consideration follows from the fact that solutions of linear stochastic difference equations may approximate the infinitely iterated moving averages of random series that Moran [8] showed to follow Slutsky's law of the sinusoidal limit. The fitting of autoregressive schemes with undamped nonexplosive sinusoidal solutions are simply statistical methods of *graduating* the harmonics that should be inherent in the x_t series, given that they are stochastic solutions of high order difference equations. Otsuki's results hold only for linear systems, and we have been using them by analogy in the same way that spectral methods are used in the nonlinear case.

The fifty replicated series for real GNP obtained from stochastic simulation of the Wharton Model were autoregressively estimated for the fourth- and sixth-order cases. The results in table 6.1 are obtained

Table 6.1 Restrained autoregressions of stochastic simulations, real GNP (means of fifty replications with serially correlated errors)

Order	Standard deviation of residuals ($ billion)	Periods estimated from coefficients averaged over replications (quarters)	Average of periods from each replication
2	7.9808	13.7	16.8
4	8.0234	3.3	3.3
		22.5	28.5
6	8.7261	2.6	2.6
		4.7	4.7
		27.2	36.2

from the means of autoregressive parameter estimates of each replicated case; i.e. the $\hat{\lambda}_i$ used in (6.19) and the corresponding sixth-order case are separately averaged from estimated λ_i values in each replication. The estimates were constrained to have conjugate complex roots with unit modulus. The sixth-order case provides a poorer fit than either the second- or fourth-order cases, which are close to each other. The spectral analysis shown in figure 6.4 suggests two periods, one of which is artificially generated by the 4-quarter change expressions in the wage and price equations. This suggests that the fourth-order case, which has marginally poorer fit than the second-order case may be the better choice, with two periods – one just under 4 quarters and one between 5 and 7 years in duration. The differences compared with the peaks in figure 6.4 do not seem to be large. In the second-order case we have a compromise single period estimate between a short and medium length cycle; in the fourth-order case we have two basic periods, one short and one of medium length.

Since the results shown in table 6.1 are mean estimates obtained from fifty stochastic simulations of the model, they are subject to

Nonlinear models

experimental error, the effect of which remains to be investigated. Returning to (6.18), it is clear that if $\hat{\rho}(1)$ is a consistent estimator of $\rho(1)$, then $\hat{P}$ is a consistent estimator of P. Approximate small-sample properties of $\hat{P}$ can be obtained in the following way. Let $\hat{\theta}$ be defined by

$$\hat{\theta} = \cos^{-1}(\hat{\rho}) \tag{6.20}$$

so that $\hat{P}$ is given by

$$\begin{aligned}\hat{P} &= 2\pi\hat{\theta}^{-1} \\ &= P - P^2(\hat{\theta} - \theta)/2\pi + P^3(\hat{\theta} - \theta)^2/(2\pi)^2 + \cdots. \\ &\doteq P - P^2(\hat{\theta} - \theta)/2\pi.\end{aligned} \tag{6.21}$$

This last expression is obtained by expanding $\hat{P}$ in a Taylor's series about the point $\hat{\theta} = \theta$ and retaining only the first two terms. Similarly, a linear approximation to (6.20) yields

$$\hat{\theta} \doteq \theta - (1 - \rho^2)^{-\frac{1}{2}}(\hat{\rho} - \rho). \tag{6.22}$$

Combining (6.21) and (6.22), we obtain

$$\hat{P} \doteq P + P^2(1 - \rho^2)^{-\frac{1}{2}}(\hat{\rho} - \rho)/2\pi \tag{6.23}$$

which can be used to examine the properties of the estimator $\hat{P}$.

The expected value of $\hat{P}$ is given by

$$E[\hat{P}] = P + P^2(1 - \rho^2)^{-\frac{1}{2}}E[\hat{\rho} - \rho]/2\pi, \tag{6.24}$$

and the variance of $\hat{P}$ is

$$V[\hat{P}] = P^4(1 - \rho^2)^{-1}V[\hat{\rho}]/4\pi^2. \tag{6.25}$$

Since both P and $(1 - \rho^2)^{-\frac{1}{2}}$ are increasing functions of ρ, it follows that for a given value of $V[\hat{\rho}]$, $V[\hat{P}]$ is an increasing function of ρ and hence the period P. Moreover, if the underlying process is either a Markov process or a first-order moving average process, $V[\hat{\rho}]$ is also an increasing function of ρ [7]. It therefore, follows that in these particular cases, the periodicity of a process with a short period can be estimated more precisely from a given sample than would be the case if the process had a long period.

The simulation results described above can be used to investigate the accuracy of the approximations on which (6.25) is based. The average value of $\hat{\rho}$ for the 50 simulation series is $\bar{\rho} = 0.89726$ implying an average period of $\bar{P} = 13.74050$ quarters per cycle. The variance of $\hat{\rho}$ over the 50 simulations is 0.00535. If the average values $(\bar{\rho}, \bar{P})$ are substituted for the (unknown) actual values (ρ, P) in (6.25), the formula yields 47.03329 for the variance of the estimate of the period. The variance of the 50 separate estimates of the period is 45.96339, which is remarkably close to the value given by the formula.

Although the estimate from each simulation is subject to rather large variation, the average over the simulations should be much more stable. Indeed, if there are r independent replications of the experiment, the variance of the mean period $r^{-1}\Sigma \hat{P}_i$ is $r^{-1}V[\hat{P}_i]$. With $r=50$ independent replications of the experiment, the variance of the mean period is only 0.9407. A two standard error confidence interval on the mean period $r^{-1}\Sigma \hat{P}_i = 16.81$ yields an interval estimate of 16.81 ± 1.94 or a range from 14.87 to 18.75 quarters per cycle.

Analytic and stochastic simulation: a comparison

The major difference between the results of the analytic and stochastic simulation experiments is that the analytic results indicate that the Wharton Model possesses extremely complicated dynamic properties, whereas the stochastic simulation results give the impression that the model has relatively simple frequency response characteristics. A possible explanation of these differences is that the linearization on which the analytic results are based is inadequate and therefore, the analytic results are misleading. Before attributing the disparities in the results obtained by the two methods to the nonlinearity of the model, it is necessary to examine the resolution of the spectral diagrams and the statistical properties of the spectral estimator that was used to analyze the stochastic simulations.

An obvious difference between the analytic results of figures 6.1 and 6.2 and the spectrum estimates in figures 6.3 and 6.4 is the spacing of the ordinates of the power spectrum. For purposes of comparison, the analytic results are shown in figures 6.5 and 6.6 for the same frequency points used in the analysis of the stochastic simulations of the model. The overall shape of these low-resolution results are remarkably similar to the spectrum estimates obtained from the simulation series. This comparison suggests that the resolution of the spectrum estimates is not high enough to reveal the complicated dynamics implicit in the Wharton Model. A more dense graph of the estimated spectrum is required in order to obtain an accurate description of the dynamic properties of the model.

A substantial increase in both the number of observations generated in each simulation run and the truncation point used in the estimator would be required to achieve the resolution that is obtained by analytic simulation. For example, with the Parzen window, the standard

Nonlinear models

```
                          Power
  Period    Power  +------------------------------+
  80.00     311.4  **************
  40.00     192.3  *********
  26.67     161.6  *******
  20.00     142.9  *******
  16.00     129.4  ******
  13.33     129.4  ******
  11.43     127.9  ******
  10.00     128.7  ******
   8.89     137.7  ******
   8.00     142.5  ******
   7.27     143.7  *******
   6.67     145.2  *******
   6.15     140.5  ******
   5.71     130.5  ******
   5.33     122.0  ******
   5.00     113.0  *****
   4.71     106.1  *****
   4.44     101.4  *****
   4.21     106.7  *****
   4.00     660.8  *******************************
   3.81     157.9  *******
   3.64     115.0  *****
   3.48      96.8  ****
   3.33      89.9  ****
                   +------------------------------+
```

Figure 6.5 Power spectrum of real GNP, analytic simulation with serially uncorrelated disturbances

```
                          Power
  Period    Power  +------------------------------+
  80.00     347.7  ***************
  40.00     265.8  ************
  26.67     328.8  ***************
  20.00     409.2  ******************
  16.00     456.0  ********************
  13.33     477.0  *********************
  11.43     427.6  *******************
  10.00     331.4  ***************
   8.89     242.1  **********
   8.00     155.7  *******
   7.27      92.8  ****
   6.67      64.2  ***
   6.15      50.9  **
   5.71      42.7  **
   5.33      32.9  *
   5.00      26.5  *
   4.71      27.2  *
   4.44      29.3  *
   4.21      35.7  *
   4.00     224.2  **********
   3.81      82.0  ****
   3.64      69.2  ***
   3.48      51.0  **
   3.33      34.4  *
                   +------------------------------+
```

Figure 6.6 Power spectrum of real GNP, analytic simulation with serially correlated disturbances

measure of bandwidth [6] is $2\pi/m$, where m is the truncation point of the lag window. In order to obtain independent estimates at 15, 16, and 17 quarters per cycle, a truncation point $m \geqslant 544$ would be required, for this is the minimum value of m which satisfies $1/17 + 1/m \leqslant 1/16 - 1/m$. Thus, the computational burden would be increased immensely if the same resolution were to be achieved for the stochastic and analytic simulation experiments.

The same considerations apply to the regression approach to the determination of the response characteristics of the Wharton Model. In particular, the spectrum computed by the analytic method suggests that a high-order difference equation is required to describe the system response adequately. In order to estimate the coefficients accurately, a rather long simulation would be required. With a short simulated series, statistically significant results for anything but a low-order equation would not be expected.

If the true spectrum were relatively smooth, it would be necessary to increase the resolution of the spectrum estimator to obtain an adequate representation of the dynamic properties of the system. Alternatively, the low resolution of the spectrum estimates shown in figures 6.3 and 6.4 may be adequate for some purposes. Even in this case, however, it is necessary to ask if the analytic results are consistent with the spectrum estimates based on the stochastic simulation. While the general shape of the spectrum is the same for both procedures, the actual values of the ordinates are quite different. In order to test the hypothesis that the estimates shown in figure 6.3 are consistent with the spectrum drawn in figure 6.5, it is necessary to consider both (experimental) sampling variability and the bias of the spectrum estimator.

The magnitude of the low-frequency bias due to mean detrending is shown in table 6.2. These entries are based on the approximation

$$E[\hat{s}(\omega)] \doteq (2N)^{-1} \sum_{j=-N+1}^{N} \Lambda(\omega - \omega_j) s(\omega_j) - (2N^{-1}\Lambda(\omega)s(0), \quad (6.26)$$

Table 6.2 Bias correction factors

Frequency $\omega_j = j\pi/40$	Period $80/j$	$(2N)^{-1}\Lambda(\omega_j)$	$(2N)^{-1}\Lambda(\omega_j)s(0)$
0	00	0.3333	16616.7
$\pi/40$	80.00	0.0548	2731.8
$2\pi/40$	40.00	0.0000	0.0
$3\pi/40$	26.67	0.0007	34.9
$4\pi/40$	20.00	0.0000	0.0
$5\pi/40$	16.00	0.0001	5.0

where $\hat{s}(\omega)$ is the estimator of $s(\omega)$ based on a sample of size N, $\Lambda(\theta)$ is the Fourier transform of the lag window used in the estimator, and $\omega_j = j\pi/N$.

The factor $(2N)^{-1}\Lambda(\omega_k)$ is shown for $\omega_k = k\pi/40$ ($k=0,1,\ldots,5$). In addition, $(2N)^{-1}\Lambda(\omega_k)s(0)$ for $s(0) = 49\,850$, which was obtained from the analytic simulation is also shown. It is apparent that the downward bias is substantial for the first several frequency points and becomes negligible as ω increases. The addition of the bias correction term to the estimates shown in figure 6.3 explains much of the difference between the low-frequency estimates obtained from the stochastic simulations and the analytic simulation results of figure 6.5.

An alternative procedure to determine the extent of the low-frequency bias in the spectrum estimates of figure 6.5 is to estimate the spectrum without first mean detrending. Since the stochastic simulation series are deviations from the control solution of the model, the expected value of each simulated value is zero. Hence mean detrending of each simulation series is unnecessary if the population mean (zero) is used instead of the sample mean. The spectrum average over the 50 replications with no mean correction is shown in figures 6.7 and 6.8 for the case of uncorrelated (correlated) disturbances. As expected from (6.26), a substantial increase in the power around zero frequency is observed. Other than this, however, the general shape of the estimated spectrum is unchanged.

With no mean correction, the expected value of the spectrum estimator reduces to

$$E[\hat{s}(\omega)] \doteq (2N)^{-1} \sum_{j=-N+1}^{N} \Lambda(\omega - \omega_j)s(\omega_j). \tag{6.27}$$

In order to determine the extent to which the analytic results are consistent with the spectrum estimates shown in figure 6.7, it is necessary to smooth the analytic results using the weighting function $(2N)^{-1}\Lambda(\omega - \omega_j)$. The results of this averaging are shown in table 6.3, together with the actual spectrum estimates. With the exception of the first two spectrum ordinates, the results are quite similar. Indeed, they are well within the standard confidence intervals for the spectrum estimates obtained from the simulation runs.

In summary, the differences between the stochastic and analytic simulation results appear to be due to three sources, (a) the bias of the spectrum estimator used to investigate the stochastic simulations, (b) experimental error of the spectrum estimator, and (c) the difference in resolution of the analytic spectrum and the experimental spectrum estimator. The fact that the analytically determined power spectrum is

Economic Theory and Econometrics

Period	Average power	Std error	Power
80.00	6371.9	7122.4	*******************************
40.00	1263.1	1011.1	*******
26.67	633.1	425.3	****
20.00	356.6	173.0	***
16.00	283.4	180.7	**
13.33	215.1	117.1	**
11.43	157.7	77.6	**
10.00	140.0	69.4	**
8.89	125.9	82.3	**
8.00	121.3	71.8	*
7.27	130.4	94.5	**
6.67	121.9	63.5	**
6.15	139.6	91.9	**
5.71	137.4	102.9	**
5.33	136.2	83.0	**
5.00	114.8	71.0	*
4.71	116.3	72.5	*
4.44	109.3	72.1	*
4.21	188.3	123.4	**
4.00	369.4	303.8	***
3.81	224.4	182.3	**
3.64	116.7	78.3	*
3.48	92.3	65.4	*
3.33	89.1	50.1	*

Figure 6.7 Power spectrum of real GNP, stochastic simulation with serially uncorrelated disturbances, no mean correction

Period	Average power	Std error	Power
80.00	3641.5	3598.2	*****************
40.00	623.5	416.2	****
26.67	391.1	227.7	***
20.00	615.4	388.6	****
16.00	853.1	475.4	*****
13.33	608.0	392.6	****
11.43	267.6	168.8	**
10.00	96.9	55.3	*
8.89	65.6	42.9	*
8.00	66.6	39.6	*
7.27	57.6	34.6	*
6.67	46.9	31.2	*
6.15	49.2	34.9	*
5.71	40.7	27.9	*
5.33	32.1	20.2	*
5.00	26.6	17.4	*
4.71	15.9	9.1	*
4.44	17.1	9.2	*
4.21	50.8	30.3	*
4.00	113.4	84.1	*
3.81	72.3	39.3	*
3.64	46.3	30.0	*
3.48	29.6	18.8	*
3.33	17.6	14.4	*

Figure 6.8 Power spectrum of real GNP, stochastic simulation with serially correlated disturbances, no mean correction

Nonlinear models

Table 6.3 Smoothed analytic spectrum and average simulation spectrum of real GNP, serially uncorrelated disturbances

Frequency	Smoothed analytic spectrum	Average simulation spectrum
0/80	29000	15773
1/80	9055	6372
2/80	1117	1263
3/80	573	633
4/80	334	357
5/80	244	283
6/80	192	215
7/80	165	158
8/80	149	140
9/80	143	125
10/80	134	121

highly variable over frequency is an interesting and perhaps even reassuring result. For if the power spectrum were smooth, it would suggest that the dynamic properties of the model could be explained by a lower-order autoregressive. On the other hand, the fact that the model implies a spectrum that exhibits a large number of relative maxima means that extremely long simulations would be required to discover these characteristics.

CONCLUDING REMARKS

This paper has been concerned primarily with the development of a technique that can be used to determine the dynamic properties of the endogenous variables of nonlinear econometric models. The procedure that is proposed is based on the theory of linear stochastic systems, but does not require an explicit linear approximation to the nonlinear model nor does it involve the inversion of large, complex valued matrices. It thus provides a computationally efficient scheme for computing the spectral matrix of the endogenous variables of a nonlinear system.

The procedure developed here has been applied to the Wharton Model to determine the frequency response characteristics of this system. It was found that the model exhibits rather complicated dynamic properties which would not be likely to be found in stochastic-simulation experiments unless extremely long simulations were analyzed. Thus, one of the important advantages of the analytic simulation procedure is that high resolution can be achieved while keeping the computational burden within reasonable limits.

Although this analysis has been concerned exclusively with univariate dynamic properties, the general approach can also be used to examine bivariate hypotheses. Relationships between pairs of endogenous variables in the model can be easily inferred from the cross-spectrum matrix of the system. This is potentially as interesting and important as the univariate analysis presented here. The experience that has been gained with the use of analytic simulation indicates that it is a feasible approach to the investigation of system dynamics.

REFERENCES

[1] G. C. Chow and R. C. Levitan, 'The nature of business cycles implicit in a linear economic model,' *Quarterly Journal of Economics*, LXXXIII, August (1969), 504–17.

[2] Michael K. Evans and Lawrence R. Klein, *The Wharton Econometric Forecasting Model*, 2nd enlarged edition, Economics Research Unit, University of Pennsylvania, (1968).

[3] Michael K. Evans and M. Saito, 'Short run predictions and long run simulation of the Wharton Model,' paper prepared for the Conference on Econometric Models of Cyclical Behavior, Cambridge, Mass., November, 1969.

[4] E. P. Howrey, 'Dynamic properties of a condensed version of the Wharton Model,' paper prepared for the Conference on Econometric Models of Cyclical Behavior, Cambridge, Mass., November 1969.

[5] E. P. Howrey, 'Stochastic properties of the Klein-Goldberger Model,' *Econometrica*, XXXIX (1971), 73–87.

[6] G. M. Jenkins, 'General considerations in the analysis of spectra,' *Technometrics*, III, May (1961), 133–66.

[7] M. G. Kendall and A. Stuart, *The Advanced Theory of Statistics*, III, London, Griffin (1966).

[8] P. A. P. Moran, 'Oscillatory behaviour of moving averages,' *Proceedings of the Cambridge Philosophical Society* (1950).

[9] T. J. Muench, 'Consistency of least squares estimators of coefficients in homogeneous stochastic difference equations,' paper presented at the meetings of the Econometric Society, December, 1969, (abstracts pp. 61–2).

[10] T. H. Naylor, K. Wertz and T. H. Wonnacott, 'Spectral analysis of data generated by simulation experiments with econometric models,' *Econometrica*, XXXVII, April (1969), 333–52.

[11] M. Otsuki, 'Oscillations in stochastic simulation of linear systems,' *Economic Studies Quarterly*, XXII (1971), 53–71.

[12] H. Rubin, 'Consistency of maximum likelihood estimators in the explosive case,' in *Statistical Inference in Dynamic Economic Model*, ed. T. C. Koopmans, John Wiley, New York (1950), pp. 356–64.

[13] E. Slutsky, 'The summation of random causes as the source of cyclic processes,' *Econometrica*, V, April (1937), 105–46.

7
Dynamic Analysis of Economic Systems

SUMMARY

Economists build dynamic models for studying cycles, forecasting, simulating alternative policies and generally understanding the structure of complicated systems. Mathematical, statistical and numerical methods are used for this kind of analysis and are described in this paper. This is just one aspect of the use of mathematical methods in economics, but it is one that is attracting increasing attention at the present time.

In theoretical dynamic economics, mathematical solutions for these problems have been worked out in full for linear systems and in special cases for non-linear systems. These solutions are generally for deterministic systems, but in econometrics, where we are trying to model the real world and estimate the models from actual data, it is necessary to consider stochastic systems. Some theoretical results can be worked out for stochastic systems, but empirical work with numerical simulations and calculations of spectral densities seem to be more fruitful. A survey is given of methods and some results in the mathematical study of empirical economic systems that are dynamic, non-linear and stochastic, using the methods of numerical simulation, autoregression and spectral analysis.

INTRODUCTION AND MOTIVATION

Mathematical models of an economic system – a nation or some major geographical aggregate – are, if they are to be realistic, dynamic, non-linear and stochastic. The methods of econometrics are designed to estimate the parametric structure of such systems on the basis of samples of economic data. Many such systems have, by now, been estimated in all parts of the world economy. For the purposes of the present paper, however, attention will be confined to a particular model with which the author is thoroughly familiar and for which many pertinent results have already been worked out.[1] This will be the Wharton Model.

Attention will not be devoted to the problems of numerical estimation of the Wharton Model and it will be assumed that such an estimated model is available so that attention can be devoted exclusively to the problems of dynamic analysis of the given system.

In order to motivate and perhaps understand better why econometricians try to make the particular kinds of measurement described in this paper, an attempt is made to summarize what is known in a general way about economic dynamics and what the principal objectives are in this kind of research.

One of the most intriguing problems of economics for more than 100 years has been to provide an explanation of the business cycle, an observed tendency towards periodic movement in various lines of economic activity and market prices. These cycles are known as alternating phases of prosperity (boom, expansion, inflation) and recession (depression, deflation). The typical cycle has often been classified in three components.

1 Long cycles of approximately 20 years' duration.

2 Classical business cycles of 8–10 years' duration.

3 Short inventory cycles of approximately 2 years' duration.

In the USA, detailed records of cyclical movements have been kept and these suggest that the average cycle is nearly 4 years in length. It may be an amalgamation of the long, classical and short cycle, but the evidence since World War II points towards the 4-year cycle as typical of a modern era in which the nature of the economy may have changed so that the classical cycle is no longer of central interest.

Within the post-war era alone, there is no justification for assuming that cycles are changing in amplitude or frequency, but they are probably different from those that existed earlier in this century, and it appears to be unlikely that the American economy faces another deep depression of near total collapse as in 1929–33.

The issue confronting a mathematical statistical analysis of this problem is to construct a dynamic model that is capable of producing an undamped oscillation of approximately 4 years' duration. A pure sine wave in which there is symmetry between upswing and downswing may not provide a satisfactory solution because it is generally observed that downswings are shorter than upswings.

Dynamic analysis of economic systems 127

A linear dynamic system is capable of producing linear combinations of trigonometric solutions. These may be satisfactory for combining cycles of different length, but they may not be able to show the kind of asymmetry between upswing and downswing that is typical, unless they are superimposed on a growing trend, which may make the upswing longer in an absolute sense.

Linear systems, however, are likely to be damped or antidamped, and the probability is small that statistical coefficients would turn out to be just right so that maintained cycles without increasing or decreasing amplitude would result. Mathematical economists have pursued two lines of thought to resolve this aspect of the problem. On the one hand, they have constructed nonlinear dynamic systems with limit cycles. These are maintained oscillations and they can exhibit the kind of asymmetry between expansion and contraction that is observed. On the other hand, they have constructed stochastic linear dynamic systems in which *damped* oscillations are kept alive by fresh random shocks that are occurring all the time. Cycles generated by a stochastic linear system with trend growth can appear to be highly realistic, in conformity with the patterns displayed by actual economic data. In the statistical construction of economic systems all these items are put together at once. The systems are stochastic, dynamic and nonlinear. It is the purpose of this paper to show how much systems are analyzed by mathematical methods in order to see whether they show frequency characteristics that conform to what is generally accepted as knowledge about business cycles.

Mathematical economic models have useful properties in both the *frequency* and *time* domains. The attempt to understand the mechanism of the business-cycle requires analysis in the frequency domain. Economists are also busily occupied with trying to predict the outcome of actual or hypothetical economic events. This is forecasting in the time domain. Mathematical–statistical systems are used to try to establish likely values for the main indicators of production, employment, prices, wage rates, interest rates and many other variables over future time spans ranging from 1–10 years, often in monthly or quarterly intervals.

In this paper, a brief survey is given of the techniques by which these dynamic analyses in the frequency and time domain are made.

THE LINEAR CASE

Although a linear model is not realistic or suitable for general economic analysis,[2] it serves as a convenient starting point for demonstrating techniques and problems. The reason for using the linear case for a start is that many important expressions can be derived in closed form. After the linear case is fully analyzed, an appropriate set of analogous procedures is indicated for the nonlinear case. Linearity will be the only simplification. Dynamic and stochastic properties are preserved.

The linear model will be

$$\mathbf{A}(L)\mathbf{y}(t) + \mathbf{B}\mathbf{x}(t) = \mathbf{e}(t). \tag{7.1}$$

$\mathbf{A}(L)$ is a matrix polynomial in the lag operator

$$L^j \mathbf{y}(t) = \mathbf{y}(t-j).$$

The matrix $\mathbf{A}(L)$ is square $(n \times n)$, and $\mathbf{y}(t)$ is a column vector

$$\begin{bmatrix} y_1(t) \\ y_2(t) \\ \vdots \\ y_n(t) \end{bmatrix}$$

of jointly dependent variables. The matrix $\mathbf{B}$ contains constant coefficients and is rectangular $(n \times m)$.

The column vector

$$\begin{bmatrix} x_1(t) \\ x_2(t) \\ \vdots \\ x_m(t) \end{bmatrix}$$

consists of m independent variables. Finally, the column vector

$$\begin{bmatrix} e_1(t) \\ e_2(t) \\ \vdots \\ e_n(t) \end{bmatrix}$$

is the n-element stochastic variable of the system. We shall assume that these random variables are distributed according to some unspecified joint probability distribution with a constant covariance matrix.

The elements of $\mathbf{A}(L)$ and $\mathbf{B}$ are not unrestricted. They have many zero and linearly related elements which identify the model as an economic system and not just any system of simultaneous equations.[3]

Dynamic analysis of economic systems

If we form the adjoint matrix $\mathbf{a}(L)$ and multiply both sides of equation (7.1), we obtain

$$\mathbf{a}(L)\mathbf{A}(L)\mathbf{y}(t) + \mathbf{a}(L)\mathbf{B}\mathbf{x}(t) = \mathbf{a}(L)\mathbf{e}(t). \tag{7.2}$$

This can be written as

$$\|\Delta(L)\|\mathbf{y}(t) + \mathbf{a}(L)\mathbf{B}\mathbf{x}(t) = \mathbf{a}(L)\mathbf{e}(t) \tag{7.3}$$

where $\Delta(L)$ is the determinantal polynomial $\det \mathbf{A}(L)$, and $\|\Delta(L)\|$ is a diagonal matrix with $\Delta(L)$ in each element of the main diagonal.

To solve the dynamic system (7.1), transformed to (7.3), we proceed in two steps. First we obtain the general solution of the homogeneous equation

$$\Delta(L)y_i(t) = 0 \tag{7.4}$$

which is the same for each variable in a linear system. Equation (7.4) is of order np if the polynomials in $\mathbf{A}(L)$ are of order p. There will thus be np roots, in general.

The solution of the homogeneous equation will be expressed as, $\mathbf{K}\lambda^t$, where $\mathbf{K}$ is an $n \times np$ matrix depending on initial conditions and λ^t is an np element vector of characteristic roots of equation (7.4), $(\lambda_1^t, \lambda_2^t, \ldots, \lambda_{np}^t)'$.

A particular solution of equation (7.1) is

$$\mathbf{y}(t) = -[\mathbf{A}(L)]^{-1}\mathbf{B}\mathbf{x}(t) + [\mathbf{A}(L)]^{-1}\mathbf{e}(t)$$

therefore we can express the complete solution as

$$\mathbf{y}(t) = \mathbf{K}\lambda^t - [\mathbf{A}(L)]^{-1}\mathbf{B}\mathbf{x}(t) + [\mathbf{A}(L)]^{-1}\mathbf{e}(t). \tag{7.5}$$

This is a convenient and informative closed form expression that brings out in display the principal components of cyclical variation in economics.

Traditionally, economists have concentrated on examination of λ, being mainly concerned with the existence of imaginary roots which give rise to cyclic processes. A pair of conjugate complex roots takes the form

$$\lambda = a \pm ib.$$

These can be expressed as

$$\lambda = r(\cos\theta \pm i\sin\theta)$$
$$\cos\theta = a/r$$
$$\sin\theta = b/r$$
$$r = (a^2 + b^2)^{\frac{1}{2}}.$$

An element of the first term in (5) is thus

$$K_1 \lambda_1^t + K_2 \lambda_2^t = K_1 r^t (\cos\theta + i\sin\theta)^t + K_2 r^t (\cos\theta - i\sin\theta)^t$$
$$= r^t [K_1 (\cos t\theta + i\sin t\theta) + K_2 (\cos t\theta - i\sin t\theta)]$$
$$= r^t [(K_1 + K_2) \cos t\theta + i(K_1 - K_2) \sin t\theta].$$

Since K_1 and K_2 are arbitrary, it is readily apparent that both terms in the last expression may be real. In this way, oscillatory properties, characteristic of the *business cycle*, may be implied by the conjugate complex roots of a dynamic economic model. The existence of complex roots and stability conditions such as $|r|<1$ were the concern of econometricians who first investigated dynamic properties of models.[4] Since the roots in λ depend on the coefficients in (7.4), it is evident that this contribution to the dynamic path of y_t is a function of economic structure which goes into the make-up of $\Delta(L)$.

The oscillatory description of an economic system is quite incomplete if one has only knowledge about the component $\mathbf{K}\lambda^t$, even though initial emphasis was on that term. For one thing, it would not be generally possible to account for the maintenance of the cyclic process through $\mathbf{K}\lambda^t$ alone. Except for highly special circumstances which produce values $|\lambda|=1$, we shall obtain either damped or anti-damped solutions

$$|\lambda|<1 \quad \text{or} \quad |\lambda|>1.$$

The explosive case is usually deemed to be unrealistic of established market economies, and, in fact, the numerical evaluation of elements of λ in cases where this has been possible suggest that this part of the solution is strongly damped, too strongly to be realistic in providing a description of a maintained cycle. It was mentioned in the first section that the business cycle is a maintained oscillation that should not fade out of existence. It is emphasized that possibly there has been some structural change in the economic system's structure, $\mathbf{A}(L)$, between major episodes as pre- and post-war that would reduce the average amplitude of cycles, but it is not felt that there has been a steady, gradual diminution of amplitude.[5]

Within the framework of the linear model, other cyclical elements must be investigated in order to supplement the contribution of $\mathbf{K}\lambda^t$. An alternative would be to consider a non-linear model, but this approach will be deferred to the next section below. Spectral analysis can be used to estimate the cyclical contribution of

$$-[\mathbf{A}(L)]^{-1}\mathbf{B}\mathbf{x}(t) + [\mathbf{A}(L)]^{-1}\mathbf{e}(t).$$

Dynamic analysis of economic systems

We can define a new composite variable v(t)

$$[A(L)]^{-1}Bx(t) + [A(L)]^{-1}e_t = A(L)^{-1}v(t)$$

and examine its spectrum. This is clearly proper for the second term in this expression, for this is a vector of random variables. It is less clear for the first term since x(t) may be simply a set of fixed variates and not admit of a stochastic interpretation. Spectral analyses have been done both ways, some analysing both parts[6] and some only the second part.[7]

The spectrum representation of v(t) is

$$v(t) = \int_{-\pi}^{\pi} e^{i\omega t} dV(\omega). \qquad (7.6)$$

It is assumed that v(t) is a stationary time series in the sense that its means, variances and lag covariances do not depend on t. It is this assumption that is dubious for x(t).

The definition of V(ω) is given by

$$dV(\omega) = \frac{1}{2\pi} \sum_{s=-\infty}^{\infty} e^{-i\omega s} v(s). \qquad (7.7)$$

The spectrum matrix is

$$f(\omega) = E[dV(\omega) dV^*(\omega)] = \frac{1}{2\pi} \sum_{s=-\infty}^{\infty} e^{-i\omega s} E[v(t)v^*(t-s)], \qquad (7.8)$$

where v* is the conjugate transpose of v. The spectrum matrix of v is

$$[A(L)]^{-1} \int_{-\pi}^{\pi} e^{i\omega t} dV(\omega) = \int_{-\pi}^{\pi} e^{i\omega t} T(\omega) dV(\omega). \qquad (7.9)$$

The transfer matrix T(ω) is defined as the matrix of rational functions in ω obtained by operating on $e^{i\omega t}$ by

$$\frac{a(L)}{\Delta(L)} = [A(L)]^{-1}.$$

The spectrum representation of the stochastic response of the system is

$$dY(\omega) = T(\omega) dV(\omega)$$

and the spectrum matrix is

$$E[T(\omega) dV(\omega) dV^*(\omega) T^*(\omega)] = T(\omega) f(\omega) T^*(\omega) \qquad (7.10)$$

This approach when implemented empirically for linear systems has indicated significant peaks in the spectral diagram that suggest the existence of a cycle of the usual length, approximately 5 years.[7]

The importance of adding $\mathbf{v}(t)$, especially the pure stochastic component, to the cyclical interpretation of the time path of $\mathbf{y}(t)$ is that this provides a way of explaining how the business cycle may be kept alive in spite of the fact that the characteristic roots in λ may be damped. The idea that time averages of random variables may be periodic derives from the work of Slutsky and Yule,[8,9] amplified by Frisch[10] who argued that random shocks repeatedly superimposed on a damped system may start up oscillations that are tending to die out and produce a resulting series that has an apparent maintained cycle.

Slutsky originally proved the *law of sinusoidal limit* which showed that moving averages and differences of a purely random series tend in the limit to a series that follow a pure sine wave.[8] This theory was generalized by Moran[11] who showed that an infinitely iterated moving average of a stationary random series has a spectral peak which indicates a dominant period of oscillation. The expression $[\mathbf{A}(L)]^{-1}\mathbf{e}_t$, is not strictly an infinitely iterated moving average, but it has many similarities. It can be expressed as

$$\sum_j \sum_i \frac{\lambda_j^{i+np-1}\mathbf{a}(L)}{\prod_{j \neq k}(\lambda_j - \lambda_k)} \mathbf{e}(t-i).$$

For large systems, the number of characteristic roots is likely to be sufficiently great so that asymptotic theory would be applicable in the same way, in the sense that this expression for $[\mathbf{A}(L)]^{-1}\mathbf{e}_t$ behaves like an infinitely iterated moving average.

The interpretation of the solution to a linear dynamic economic system in terms of characteristic roots for the deterministic and the stochastic components is quite informative in theory but has many practical limitations. The principal issue is that equation (7.4) is of such a high order that it is not usually possible to determine all the characteristic roots with a high degree of accuracy. In actual cases where the characteristic polynomial is of the order 45, it has not been possible to obtain a precise check on the computation of some strategic roots, particularly some imaginary ones that are of unusual importance for judging the cyclical properties of the associated model.[12,13]

The linear system written in operator notation in equation (7.1) can also be written as

$$\sum_{i=0}^{p} \mathbf{A}_i \mathbf{y}(t-i) + \mathbf{B}\mathbf{x}(t) = \mathbf{e}(t). \tag{7.11}$$

A single period's solution is

$$\mathbf{y}(t) = -\mathbf{A}_0^{-1}\left[\sum_{i=1}^{p} \mathbf{A}_i \mathbf{y}(t-i)\right] + \mathbf{A}_0^{-1}\mathbf{B}\mathbf{x}(t) + \mathbf{A}_0^{-1}\mathbf{e}(t) \tag{7.12}$$

Dynamic analysis of economic systems

At period $t=t_0$, the initial conditions $\mathbf{y}(t_0-1), \mathbf{y}(t_0-2),\ldots,\mathbf{y}(t_0-p)$ and independent variables $\mathbf{x}(t_0)$ can be substituted into equation (7.12) to obtain a solution $\mathbf{y}(t_0)$ for an expected value assigned to the error $\mathbf{e}(t)=0$. Given the computed value of $\mathbf{y}(t_0)$ together with $\mathbf{y}(t_0-1),\ldots, \mathbf{y}(t_0-p+1)$ and $\mathbf{x}(t_0+1)$, the same equation can be used to solve for $\mathbf{y}(t_0+1)$. By iterative steps a whole numerical solution (simulation) can be obtained

$$\mathbf{y}(t_0), \mathbf{y}(t_0+1), \mathbf{y}(t_0+2), \mathbf{y}(t_0+3),\ldots$$

The numerical simulation obtained with zero error and best judgement about values for $\mathbf{x}(t)$ over the simulation period will be called the *control* solution. Dynamic response properties of the system can be studied by computing *disturbed* solutions in which alternative inputs are used for $\mathbf{x}(t)$ or for parameter values in $\mathbf{A}_i$ or $\mathbf{B}$. If the disturbed solution is obtained by making a simple constant change in assumed values for $\mathbf{x}(t)$, we can calculate the *multiplier* of the system as

$$\frac{y_i^d(t) - y_i^c(t)}{x_j^d(t) - x_j^c(t)}, \quad i=1,2,\ldots,n, \; j=1,2,\ldots,m$$

where superscript d stands for *disturbed* solution and c for *control* solution. The multiplier values will depend on t; some will grow along a smooth trend, usually towards an asymptotic value, and some will oscillate. More elaborate changes in the disturbed solution will consist of non-uniform changes in $x_j(t)$, changes in several components of the vector $\mathbf{x}(t)$ and changes in parameter estimates. These will be typical economic policies of public authorities, who usually change many things at one time, and cannot be evaluated by simple multiplier formulas. It is only meaningful to construct two sets of simulation paths – one for $\mathbf{y}^d(t)$ and one for $\mathbf{y}^c(t)$.

A particular way of using dynamic solutions of economic systems is in forecasting. For economic policy consideration or multiplier calculations, it may be meaningful to substitute smooth or plausible paths for $\mathbf{x}(t)$ into equation (7.12), but for actual forecast exercises it is important to be as careful as possible about putting in values that are expected to be close to actual values when they are realized. It is also important to try to anticipate any parametric changes that may be introduced by public authorities over the prediction horizon. Forecasting, economic policy analysis and multiplier calculation are simply different ways of determining simulations of an empirical model.

The *control* simulation assigns a zero or some other fixed values to the random error vector $\mathbf{e}(t)$. A *stochastic* simulation is obtained by drawing random numbers in a specified way for each time period of the simulation. In the period of sample observation, $t = 1, 2, \ldots, T$, it is possible to compute the difference between values of $\mathbf{y}(t)$ determined from each separate equation of the system, normalized on one particular variable, assuming zero error and the actual values of $\mathbf{y}(t)$. This will provide a vector of equation residuals $\mathbf{r}(t)$. It is customary to make *stochastic* simulations by requiring that the random terms used in the calculation have the same variance–covariance matrix as the sample residuals.

The matrix of residuals is

$$\mathbf{R} = \begin{bmatrix} r_1(1) & r_2(1) & \ldots & r_n(1) \\ r_1(2) & r_2(2) & \ldots & r_n(2) \\ \vdots & \vdots & & \vdots \\ r_1(T) & r_2(T) & \ldots & r_n(T) \end{bmatrix}.$$

The covariance matrix is

$$\boldsymbol{\Sigma} = \frac{1}{T} \mathbf{R}'\mathbf{R}.$$

If we draw mutually independent numbers $n_i(t)$ from a normal distribution with zero mean and unit variance, the matrix

$$\frac{1}{T^{\frac{1}{2}}} \mathbf{NR}$$

where

$$\mathbf{N} = \begin{bmatrix} n_1(1) & n_1(2) & \ldots & n_1(T) \\ n_2(1) & n_2(2) & \ldots & n_2(T) \\ \vdots & \vdots & & \vdots \\ n_S(1) & n_S(2) & \ldots & n_S(T) \end{bmatrix}$$

will have expected variance covariance matrix $\boldsymbol{\Sigma}$. We use $(1/T^{\frac{1}{2}})\mathbf{NR}$ for the errors to be added to each separate equation in each simulation period $1, 2, \ldots, S$. It is also possible to restrict the error matrix further by requiring that it reproduce sample *serial* covariances as well as sample variances and covariances. This is done by defining $\mathbf{N}$ as

$$\mathbf{N} = \begin{bmatrix} n(1) & n(2) & \ldots & n(T) \\ n(T+1) & n(1) & \ldots & n(T-1) \\ n(T+2) & n(T+1) & \ldots & n(T-2) \\ & \vdots & & \\ & \text{etc.} & & \end{bmatrix}.$$

Dynamic analysis of economic systems

Stochastic simulations

$$\mathbf{y}^{(g)}(t_0), \mathbf{y}^{(g)}(t_0+1), \ldots, \mathbf{y}^{(g)}(t_0+S), \qquad g=1,2,\ldots,G$$

may be replicated G times. For each replication, cyclical analysis of the results can be made by alternative methods, the most direct of which is spectral analysis of the series $\mathbf{y}^{(g)}(t_0+S)$. The formula

$$f(\omega_j) = \tfrac{1}{2}\lambda_0 r_0 + \sum_{k=1}^{p} \lambda_k r_k \cos(\omega_j k) \tag{7.13}$$

gives a numerical estimate of the spectrum for a specific y-series. In this formula

$$\omega_j = \frac{\pi j}{n}, \quad j=0,1,2,\ldots,n$$

where

r_k = Autocorrelation coefficient of lag k.
λ_k = Weight of a filter.

$$\lambda_k = 1 - \frac{6k^2}{p^2}\left(1 - \frac{k}{p}\right) \qquad 0 \leqslant k \leqslant p/2.$$

$$\lambda_k = 2\left(1 - \frac{k}{p}\right)^3 \qquad p/2 \leqslant k \leqslant p.$$

p = Number of lags used.
n = Number of points at which the spectrum is evaluated.

The empirical evaluation of $f(\omega_j)$ from equation (7.13) provides an estimate of the expression in equation (7.8). For linear systems, the evaluation can be made directly as in equation (7.10) or by numerical simulation as indicated above.[14,15]

An example of the numerical simulation approach to evaluation of the spectrum for US GNP, generated by the Wharton Econometric Model is given in figure 7.1.

For each replication $g=1,2,\ldots,G$ a separate estimate of the spectrum may be obtained. A mean estimate, obtained by averaging the ordinates of the spectral density diagram over G replications, should provide a more stable estimate.

In a simulation of a growing economic system, which is the usual case dealt with, the solutions for many individual variables

$$\mathbf{y}^{(g)}(t_0), \mathbf{y}^{(g)}(t_0+1), \ldots, \mathbf{y}^{(g)}(t_0+S)$$

will have strong trends. Before spectral analysis is attempted, it is essential to extract trends. This may be done by some trend-fitting

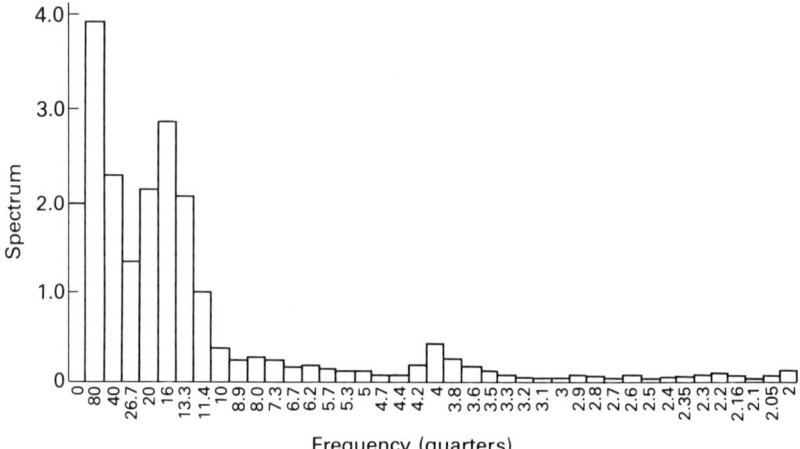

Figure 7.1 Spectral density of real GNP, USA (average of 50 replications)

process or by forming deviations from a trend solution. This would be either a non-stochastic simulation solution or the mean of the simulated solutions. Spectral analysis formulae, like equation (7.13), will then be used for

$$\mathbf{y}^{(g)}(t_0) - \mathbf{y}^{(0)}(t_0), \mathbf{y}^{(g)}(t_0+1) - \mathbf{y}^{(0)}(t_0+1), \ldots, \mathbf{y}^{(g)}(t_0+S) - \mathbf{y}^{(0)}(t_0+S)$$

which will be essentially trend free. In a linear system, the non stochastic simulation will be approximately the same as the mean of the replicated simulations.

There are advantages and disadvantages to these alternative approaches.

Analytic evaluation of the spectrum

This might be called 'simulation to infinity.' The method is not restricted by the length of the simulation, although it is implicitly limited by the length of the statistical sample on which the estimates of $[\mathbf{A}(L)]^{-1}$ in equation (7.9) are based. It is free of experimental error, but not free of sampling error in estimation of $\mathbf{A}(L)$. The theory is worked out for linear systems, to which the discussion is presently confined, but some analogous calculations can be made for nonlinear systems, as will be indicated below.

Evaluation of the spectrum by empirical simulation

This is a very flexible method, applicable to both linear and nonlinear systems. It permits replication of experiment so that sampling variability of the spectrum can be readily determined. The above formulas incorporate replication of simulation experiments for just one model, but analogous simulation methods can be used to estimate a whole sample of model structures, and each of these can be replicated; therefore the mean spectrum can be obtained by averaging over replicated estimates of the model and replicated simulations of each model. There is, however, experimental error in all these calculations. Every replication is associated with fresh drawing of random variables, and this introduces experimental error into the results. Also, there are limitations on the length, S, of simulation. For good estimates of the spectrum, S should be large, but the credibility of an empirical model is severely strained as it is simulated many periods – forwards or backwards.

A combination of numerical simulation and analytic evaluation of the spectrum can be used in yet another approach to cyclical analysis. Instead of shocking all the equations of a model simultaneously for repeated intervals by adding appropriate elements of $(1/T^{\frac{1}{2}})\mathbf{NR}$, we can make impulse shocks of given size for a single time period. To the system

$$\mathbf{A}(L)\mathbf{y}(t) + \mathbf{B}\mathbf{x}(t) = 0$$

which will provide a non-stochastic simulation solution, $\mathbf{y}^{(0)}(t)$, we add the vector

$$\begin{bmatrix} 0 \\ 0 \\ \vdots \\ \delta_i(t_0) \\ \vdots \\ 0 \end{bmatrix}$$

at $t = t_0$. For $t \neq t_0$, $\delta_i(t_0)$ is zero. This is done for each equation, one at a time, $i = 1, 2, \ldots, n$. From each of the n shocked solutions, we calculate deviations of the values for the jth variable,

$$y_j^{(i)}(t_0) - y_j^{(0)}(t_0), y_j^{(i)}(t_0+1) - y_j^{(0)}(t_0+1), \ldots, \qquad i = 1, 2, \ldots, n$$

for as long a period as we have numerically significant deviations. In a stable system, these deviations will dampen to zero. To get reasonable and uniform values for $\delta_i(t_0)$, we experimentally find a multiple of sample standard deviations of residual error

$$kS_i(r)$$

$$S_i(r) = \left\{ \frac{\sum_{t=1}^{T} [r_i(t)]^2}{T} \right\}^{\frac{1}{2}}$$

such that the system does not simulate outside plausible bounds and gives several periods of numerically significant deviations from the non-stochastic simulation. In the case of Wharton Model simulations, the value used was $k = 5.0$. The expression

$$\frac{\sum_s [y_j^{(i)}(t_0+s) - y_j^{(0)}(t_0+s)]}{\delta_i(t_0)}$$

is an alternative way of computing the dynamic multiplier for the system. This expression gives the multiplier for the response of the jth dependent variable with respect to a unit shift in the ith equation of the complete system.

Define

$$\delta_{ijs} = y_j^{(i)}(t_0+s) - y_j^{(0)}(t_0+s)$$

and form the sums

$$\delta_{ij}^n(e^{-i\omega}) = \sum_{s=0}^{n} \delta_{ijs} e^{-i\omega s}. \qquad (7.14)$$

The cross-spectrum matrix of the variables of the system is given by

$$\mathbf{S}_y^n(\omega) = \mathbf{\Delta}_n(\omega) \mathbf{S}_r(\omega) \mathbf{\Delta}_n^*(\omega) \qquad (7.15)$$

where $\mathbf{\Delta}_n(\omega)$ is the matrix with elements $\delta_{ij}^n(e^{-i\omega})$ given by equation (7.14); $\mathbf{\Delta}_n^*(\omega)$ is its conjugate transpose, and $\mathbf{S}_r(\omega)$ is the spectral matrix of the disturbances of the system (estimated from the computed residuals of each equation).

The estimated cross-spectrum between y_i and y_j is

$$\sum_{ij}(\omega) = \sum_s \sum_v \delta_{is}^n(e^{-i\omega}) \bar{\delta}_{jv}^n(e^{-i\omega}) \sigma_{sv}(\omega) \qquad (7.16)$$

where $\sum_{ij}^n$ are the elements of $\mathbf{S}_y^n(\omega)$ and $\sigma_{sv}(\omega)$ are the elements of $\mathbf{S}_r(\omega)$. This method has been used to estimate cyclical characteristics of the Wharton Model.[16]

The methods of cyclical analysis of an economic system described so far, except for the discussion dealing with the characteristic roots λ

Dynamic analysis of economic systems

from equation (7.4) have been concerned with measurement in the frequency domain. A revealing approach in the time domain has been suggested in a recent paper by Otsuki.[17] It turns out that his method follows from an implied suggestion of Slutsky.[8]

Let a simulated series from a stochastic solution of a model be denoted[18]

$$\mathbf{y}_i^{(g)}(t), \quad t = t_0 + 1, t_0 + 2, \ldots, t_0 + S$$

and its deviation be denoted

$$\mathbf{z}_i^{(g)}(t) = \mathbf{y}_i^{(g)}(t) - \mathbf{y}_i^{(0)}(t), \quad t = t_0 + 1, t_0 + 2, \ldots, t_0 + S.$$

For simplicity in exposition, we shall drop the super- and subscripts from $\mathbf{z}$ and simply discuss the estimation of cyclical characteristics of $\mathbf{z}(t)$.

Slutsky observed that the tendency of a series to satisfy the property

$$\Delta^2 \mathbf{z}(t) = -\mu \mathbf{z}(t+1) \tag{7.17}$$

indicated a tendency of $z(t)$ to be sinusoidal. We shall use an estimate of μ to obtain, by transformation, an estimate of periodicity of $\mathbf{z}(t)$. Heuristically we note

$$\mathbf{z}(t) = \sin(\mu)^{\frac{1}{2}}$$

$$d\mathbf{z}(t)/dt = (\mu)^{\frac{1}{2}} \cos(\mu)^{\frac{1}{2}} t$$

$$d^2\mathbf{z}(t)/dt^2 = -\mu \sin(\mu)^{\frac{1}{2}} t.$$

A sine function has the property that its second derivative is negatively proportional to itself.

The empirical series $\mathbf{z}(t)$ will not generally satisfy the second-order difference equation exactly, but it may do so approximately, and an estimate of μ may be obtained by finding the best fitting (least-squares) value. The equation may be written

$$\mathbf{z}(t+2) - 2\mathbf{z}(t+1) + \mathbf{z}(t) = -\mu \mathbf{z}(t+1) + \mathbf{r}(t)$$

where $\mathbf{r}(t)$ is approximation error. For

$$\sum_{t=1}^{T} [\mathbf{r}(t)]^2 = \min$$

we obtain

$$(2 - m) = \text{est}(2 - \mu) = \frac{\sum_{t=1}^{T} [\mathbf{z}(t+2) + \mathbf{z}(t)] \mathbf{z}(t+1)}{\sum_{t=1}^{T} [\mathbf{z}(t+1)]^2}. \tag{7.18}$$

This is the value obtained by regressing $z(t+2)+z(t)$ on $z(t+1)$. This is a restricted regression in the sense that the coefficient of $z(t)$ has not been determined from the sample data; it is fixed at 1.0. If the regression is so restricted and if

$$(2-m)^2 < 4$$

the non-stochastic solution of the estimated second-order difference equation will be an undamped sine function. The homogeneous equation will be

$$z(t+2) - (2-m)z(t+1) + z(t) = 0.$$

The characteristic equation will be

$$\rho^2 - (2-m)\rho + 1 = 0$$

giving

$$\rho = \frac{(2-m) \pm [(2-m)^2 - 4]^{\frac{1}{2}}}{2}.$$

It is thus evident that the roots will be conjugate complex if

$$(2-m)^2 < 4$$

and

$$|\rho| = 1.$$

In trigonometric terms

$$\frac{2-m}{2} = \cos \theta$$

and the angle of oscillation is

$$\theta = \cos^{-1}\left(\frac{2-m}{2}\right). \tag{7.19}$$

The average value of $2-m$ computed from 50 replications of the Wharton Model for GNP solutions is 1.7945, and this provides an estimated periodicity of 13.8 quarters per cycle, slightly less than the spectral estimate of 16 quarters. If the individual estimates of θ are averaged over 50 replications, the estimated period is 16.8 quarters.

The estimate of $(2-\mu)$ can be expressed in two parts

$$(2-m) = \frac{\sum_{t=1}^{T} z(t+2)z(t+1)}{\sum_{t=1}^{T} [z(t+1)]^2} + \frac{\sum_{t=1}^{T} z(t)z(t+1)}{\sum_{t=1}^{T} [z(t+1)]^2}$$

Dynamic analysis of economic systems 141

It is the sum of two estimates of the first-order serial correlation – between $z(t+1)$ and $z(t+2)$ and between $z(t)$ and $z(t+1)$. The first-order serial correlation of a series is known to be an estimate of the mean distance between up-crosses.[19]

Otsuki suggests the extension of this approach towards cyclical measurement in the time domain by examining the extent to which the fourth-order equation

$$z(t+4) + \mu_3 z(t+3) + \mu_2 z(t+2) + \mu_3 z(t+1) + z(t) = 0$$

is satisfied by the series $z(t)$. It should be noted that the coefficients of $z(t+1)$ and $z(t+3)$ are restricted to being equal. This restriction together with the unit restriction for the coefficient of $z(t)$ guarantees, for a wide range of values, that the characteristic roots will be in two conjugate complex pairs with unit modulus. The regression of $z(t+4) + z(t)$ on $[z(t+3) + z(t+1)]$ and $z(t+2)$ will provide at least-squares approximation to the fourth-order autoregressive equation and give estimates of two cyclical roots. The two periods corresponding to these two complex roots will indicate the superposition of one dominant cycle on another, a frequent characteristic of economic fluctuations in which different periodicities are compounded.

This procedure can be readily extended to sixth- and higher-order systems, at each time restricting the autoregressive coefficients so that all roots are conjugate complex with unit modulus. The combination of periods corresponding to this set of roots are estimates of the combination of periods in the economic cycle. The process of extending the order of the underlying autoregressive stops when there is no improvement in the degree of approximation. The GNP simulations of the Wharton Model appear to fit a second-or fourth-order process.

Table 7.1 Residual sum of squares and approximate periods. Autoregressive estimates of GNP simulations from the Wharton Model

		Period	
Order of autoregression	Standard deviation of residuals ($ billion)	Estimate from average coefficients (quarters)	Estimate from average of periods (quarters)
2	7.98	13.7	16.8
4	8.02	3.3	3.3
		22.5	28.5
6	8.73	2.6	2.6
		4.7	4.7
		27.2	36.2

There is a tendency of the Wharton Model dynamics to generate a 4-quarter cycle, which shows up in the high-frequency response for either the fourth- or sixth-order case. It is also evident in figure 7.1. This is an artificial aspect of the system's dynamics that comes about because of the use of four-quarter differences in some key equations for wage and price determination.[14]

Conventional measurement of postwar business cycles in the American economy suggests the prevalence of a 4- or 5-year cycle. That would be consistent with the second- or fourth-order autoregressive analysis, depending, of course, on whether we measure the average cycle from autoregressive coefficients averaged over sampling replications or periods averaged over replications.

THE NONLINEAR CASE

Many relevant expressions can be put in closed mathematical form in linear systems. Stochastic and nonstochastic components of solutions nicely form two additive parts. The statistical properties of the measures that are derived can more readily be ascertained and fully understood. It is not generally possible to do these things in the nonlinear case. For the most part it will be necessary to introduce some form of numerical analysis in order to study the frequency response characteristics of nonlinear systems.

There is an important philosophical difference between the two systems also. Nonstochastic linear systems cannot provide a general explanation of a *maintained* cycle – the business cycle as we have come to know it in dynamic economics. Maintained cycles can be obtained but only in systems with stochastic or exogenous shocks that keep alive damped oscillations which come from the complex roots. It is only with negligible probability that the roots of a general linear system would be such as to be conjugate complex with unit modulus. The idea of a stochastic system with roots inside the unit circle and maintained oscillations is a time-honoured position that received strong support from Frisch.[10] On the other hand, nonlinear models can produce nonstochastic limit cycles; thus many economists have been led to seek an *endogenous* explanation of the maintained cycle.[20–22] They have fully succeeded in producing theoretical nonlinear models with limit cycles, but empirical validation of such models has not been successful. The authors can prove the existence of limit cycles and can obtain graphical solutions, but they have not obtained solutions in closed mathematical form.

Little is known about the properties of nonlinear models under random shock. Stochastic stability properties have been obtained in a few cases.[23, 24] Nevertheless almost all empirical econometric models are nonlinear and contain error. It remains in this section to show how they can be realistically analyzed.

The most important step forward in making possible the extensive exploration of dynamic properties of large-scale dynamic nonlinear models in the stochastic case has been the computer programming of a fast algorithm for obtaining numerical solutions of such systems. In place of the general linear model (7.1), let us write

$$y_{it} = f_i(y_{1t}, \ldots, y_{nt}, y_{1t-1}, \ldots, y_{n,-p}, x_{1t}, \ldots, x_{mt}) + e_{it},$$
$$i = 1, 2, \ldots, n. \quad (7.20)$$

It may appear to be somewhat restrictive to assume that we can write the system so that one variable is isolated on the left-hand side, but this has always been possible in the hundreds of cases considered so far. It is *not* essential, however, that y_{it} be isolated on the left-hand side; it can also appear on the right-hand side. The Gauss–Seidel algorithm used for solving this system numerically is

$$y_{it}^{(r)} = f_i(y_{1t}^{(r)}, \ldots, y_{i-1,t}^{(r)},$$
$$y_{it}^{(r-1)}, y_{i+1,t}^{(r-1)}, \ldots, y_{nt}^{(r-1)}, y_{1,t-1}, \ldots, y_{n,t-p} x_{1t}, \ldots, x_{mt}). \quad (7.21)$$

It is assumed that e_{it} is assigned its mean value (zero) for the simulation path. Iteration stops when

$$\left| \frac{y_{it}^{(r)} - y_{it}^{(r-1)}}{y_{it}^{(r-1)}} \right| < \varepsilon, \quad i = 1, 2, \ldots, n. \quad (7.22)$$

In practice, we have been choosing $\varepsilon = 0.001$.

After a solution is obtained for some time period, given initial conditions for $y_{i,t-j}$ and values of x_{kt}, the solution values are used as initial conditions for the next period's solution, and the iteration process is repeated etc.

This numerical procedure has been found to work rapidly in practice and is much easier and cheaper to use than the Newton–Raphson method or other standard techniques. It does not, however, avoid a serious problem of multiple roots. We have no assurance that the solution is unique. In practice, we have varied the starting point widely, among admissible values, to discover if alternative solutions emerge. In complete system solutions, we have never encountered multiple roots on the basis of searching, but some multiple solutions of subsystems have been found.[25]

The speed of convergence and, indeed, the very existence of convergence, can be shown to depend, (a) on the rules for normalizing the system, i.e. the isolation of particular left hand side variables in each equation of (7.20), (b) the ordering of the equations in (7.20), and (c) the step size.[26] The last cited factor refers to the value chosen for h in

$$y_{it}^{(r)} = hf_i^{(r-1)} + (1-h)y_{it}^{(r-1)}. \tag{7.23}$$

In the previous statement of the Gauss–Seidel algorithm, it was assumed that $h = 1.0$, but in fact, the step size can be varied to try to speed up convergence. Econometric models of the USA and other countries can generally be solved in the nonlinear case in no more than approximately ten iterations. It takes less than one minute to generate numerical dynamic solutions over many (say, twenty) time periods on conventional large-scale computers.

Most of the methods of dynamic analysis worked out in the second section for linear models can be implemented by analogy in the nonlinear case. It is not possible to display formulas for the solution in closed form expressions but numerical simulations for control solutions, disturbed solutions and stochastic solutions can be obtained by using the Gauss–Seidel algorithm. Multipliers can be obtained as in the linear case.[1] Random shocks can be drawn according to the formulas cited in the second section and added to equation (7.20) for each period's solution by equation (7.21). Thus, a stochastic simulation can be obtained in the same way as for a linear system, and the spectral analysis can be done as in (7.13) for the simulated values.[14,15] Similarly the autoregressive approach to estimation of the period in equation (7.19) or higher order extensions implied by a set of simulated values of a nonlinear system can be applied as readily as in the linear case.

The analytic derivation of the spectrum matrix of a model in equation (7.10) holds only for the linear case. There is nothing to prevent, however, the use of the formulas developed in (7.14) and (7.16) for the unit impulse case to simulated values of a nonlinear system. All that is needed is a deterministic simulation and simulations obtained by making successive unit impulses for each stochastic equation of the system. The theoretical justification for this method of spectrum measurement can be given only in the linear case, but the same steps can be followed in the nonlinear case.[16] In actual applications, it appears to give quite reasonable results, as confirmed by other approaches to the measurement of frequency response characteristics. The problem is that the splitting of the solution (7.5) into a deterministic part $\mathbf{K}\lambda^t - [\mathbf{A}(L)]^{-1}\mathbf{B}x(t)$, and a stochastic part $[\mathbf{A}(L)]^{-1}\mathbf{e}(t)$, can be done in the linear case but does not generally hold for the nonlinear case. In that case, we do not even know the form of the solution. We know its approximate numerical valuation and that it has stochastic aspects, but we cannot isolate the stochastic component.

SOME SUBSTANTIVE RESULTS

What has extensive mathematical analysis of econometric systems by the methods described in this paper shown about dynamic characteristics?

Cycles

Evidence of cycles has been found in estimated spectra, and autoregressive analysis of simulated values. These estimates indicate the existence of a typical 4–5-year business cycle and show some evidence of a similar cycle in the rate of change of prices.[7,14,15,27] They confirm the earlier study[28] showing the extreme importance, even the necessity, of the stochastic component in generating a maintained cycle. Without the analysis of $[A(L)]^{-1}e(t)$ in the linear case, or corresponding contributions in the nonlinear case, the solutions would be strongly damped and cyclical fluctuations would die out. The existence of cycles is much more pronounced if generated errors are serially correlated than if they are independent. These findings have important philosophical implications for appreciating the nature of economic cycles and for understanding them in economic policy applications.

Multipliers

Various attempts at different methods of econometric model construction show widely varying estimates of multipliers. It is particularly apparent that many new attempts at modelling the monetary sector of the economy are producing comparatively high estimates of the multiplier effects of financial policy changes and low estimates of fiscal policy changes. These newer type models have not yet stood the test of time. Apart from their more unusual results, the majority of models show for the US that multipliers associated with changes in public expenditures are roughly 2.0,[1] sometimes smaller or larger in a range (1.5–3.0). The equilibrium value of a dynamic multiplier whether computed from a sustained change or the cumulation of effects of a unit impulse is reached after more than a year and oscillates. Multipliers associated with tax changes are slightly smaller than those associated with public expenditure changes and take longer to reach equilibrium values.

Multipliers associated with monetary expansion or contraction build up to equilibrium values even more slowly and ultimately reach values quite comparable with fiscal multipliers. The effect of monetary policy multipliers is not strongly felt for approximately 6 months and requires 3 or more years to reach equilibrium.

In more open economies where imports respond strongly to changes in economic activity, it has been found that multipliers are much smaller, more in the neighbourhood of 1.0 for countries like the UK and the Netherlands.

Stability

The tendency of the deterministic part of the cyclical mechanism to be damped introduces much stability into the economy. When the economy is disturbed it quickly returns to its long-run growth path. Simulations with unit impulse disturbances – as large as 5σ, where σ is the error variance – eventually converge to the deterministic simulation path.[16] This is evidence of stability. In attempts to recreate a simulation of the 1929 debacle, a model of the US economy showed great stability in the face of artificially generated shocks.[29]

Forecasting

In highly practical applications in forecasting the *future* time path of the economy over a horizon of 8 quarters, estimated mathematical models have shown independent contributions to our analytical powers to look ahead.[1,30,31] There is much room for improvement, but mathematical models definitely add something to our abilities in this difficult area.

FUTURE RESEARCH

There are many things for the professional economist or statistician to do by way of improving our theories of economic behaviour, understanding of economic organization or market structure and ability to measure economic magnitudes more accurately or more comprehensively. These will all lead to substantial improvement in economic dynamics, but the attention of this paper is focused on the mathematics of the problem. What are the promising and fruitful research areas for this aspect of dynamic economics?

Non-linear systems

As indicated in the third section, we can implement calculations for nonlinear systems and compute many of the properties that we study in linear systems. We do not, however, fully understand the theory of nonlinear systems. We do not understand why the numerical calculations with nonlinear systems apparently work in the sense that they provide reasonable results. There are questions of convergence, uniqueness and stability of solutions to problems in economic dynamics with nonlinear systems that need to be studied more deeply and displayed in more transparent form.

Cross spectral analysis

The spectrum of many economic variables has been evaluated for dynamic systems, but relatively little use has been made of results from cross spectral analysis. This kind of research deserves further emphasis. The expression in equation (7.16) gives the cross spectrum between any pair of dependent variables in a complete system. These spectral calculations can be used to show 'trade offs' between solutions for different variables in complete dynamic systems. An interesting example of much contemporary interest is the 'trade-off' between price changes ($p_{(t)} - p_{(t-1)}/p_{(t)}$) and unemployment rate (u_t) from a dynamic model, showing the dilemma between full employment and price stability in the modern industrial economy. Also lead–lag relationships between different pairs of dependent variables can be estimated from the cross-spectral analysis of dynamic solutions.

Continuous models

Dynamic economic systems are empirically formulated as finite difference equations, primarily because economic data on which the estimates of the systems' parameters are based are available only for discrete time intervals – decade, year, quarter, month, week or day. It is most usual to confine analysis to yearly or quarterly systems, but monthly systems may be used more in the near future. Mathematical analysis of the effect of changing the time unit on measurement of dynamic properties is an unsolved problem, but some preliminary studies have thrown some light on the issues.[32] Economic life is actually continuous, although our models of it are discrete. The relationship between dynamics of corresponding continuous and discrete systems is a mathematical problem of some interest to econometricians.

Probability structure

The error process e(t) is assumed to be multivariate normal, stationary and serially independent. Some of these assumptions can be relaxed for estimation of parameters in dynamic systems but is not done for the usual model. Implications of more general error structures for dynamic properties has not been examined. Errors may be autoregressive, moving averages, nonnormal, nonadditive (to the deterministic system) or nonstationary. The full dynamic implications of these various generalized assumptions calls for mathematical analysis.

REFERENCES

[1] M. K. Evans and L. R. Klein, *The Wharton Econometric Forecasting Model*, 2nd edn, Economic Research Unit, University of Pennsylvania (1968).

[2] D. Katzner and L. R. Klein, 'On the possibility of the general linear model,' in *Economic Models, Estimation, and Risk Programming* (Ed. K. A. Fox), Springer-Verlag, Berlin (1969).

[3] F. M. Fisher, *The Identification Problem in Econometrics*, McGraw-Hill, New York (1966).

[4] J. Tinbergen, *Statistical Testing of Business Cycle Theories: II, Business Cyles in the United States of America, 1919–1932*, League of Nations, Geneva (1939).

[5] M. Bronfenbrenner (Ed.), *Is the Business Cycle Obsolete?*, Wiley-Interscience, New York (1969).

[6] P. Dhyrmes, *Econometrics*, Harper and Row, New York (1970).

[7] E. P. Howrey, 'Stochastic properties of the Klein–Goldberger model,' *Econometrica*, **39**, 73–87 (1971).

[8] E. Slutsky, 'The summation of random causes as the source of cyclic processes,' *Econometrica*, **5**, 105–46 (1937).

[9] G. U. Yule, 'On a method of investigating periodicity in disturbed series, with special reference to Wolfer's sunspot numbers,' *Philosophical Transactions*, **226**, 267 (1927).

[10] R. Frisch, 'Propagation problems and impulse problems in dynamic economics,' in *Economic Essays in Honour of Gustav Cassel*, George Allen and Unwin, London (1933).

[11] P. A. P. Moran, 'The oscillatory behaviour of moving averages,' *Proceedings of the Cambridge Philosophical Society*, 272–80 (1950).

[12] E. P. Howrey, 'Dynamic properties of a condensed version of the Wharton Model,' *Econometric Models of Cyclical Behavior, Studies in Income and Wealth* (Ed. B. Hickman), Columbia, New York (1972), pp. 601–63.

[13] K. Mori, 'Generalized eigenvalue problem of an econometric model,' *Abstracts*, Second World Congress of the Econometric Society, Cambridge, England (1970).

[14] M. K. Evans, L. R. Klein and M. Saito, 'Short run prediction and long run simulation of the Wharton Model,' in *Econometric Models of Cyclical Behavior, Studies in Income and Wealth* (Ed. B. Hickman), Columbia, New York (1972), pp. 139–91.

[15] G. Green, 'Short- and long-term simulations with the OBE econometric model,' in *Econometric Models of Cyclical Behavior, Studies in Income and Wealth* (Ed. B. Hickman), Columbia, New York (1972), pp. 25–123.

[16] E. P. Howrey and L. R. Klein, 'Dynamic properties of nonlinear econometric models,' *International Economic Review*, **13**, 599–618 (1972).

[17] M. Otsuki, 'Oscillations in stochastic simulation of linear systems,' *Economic Studies Quarterly*, **22**, 54–71 (1971).

[18] Although the notation is similar to that used in the preceding case, the superscript (g) does not represent an impulse shock to the gth equation; it represents, in this case, the gth replication of a stochastic simulation in which all equations are simultaneously shocked for each time period.

[19] M. G. Kendall and A. Stuart, *The Advanced Theory of Statistics*, Vol. 3, Griffin, London (1966), pp. 378–9.

[20] R. M. Goodwin, 'A model of cyclical growth,' in *The Business Cycle in the Postwar World* (Ed. E. Lundberg), Macmillan, London (1955).

[21] J. R. Hicks, *A Contribution to the Theory of the Trade Cycle*, Clarendon Press, Oxford (1950).

[22] N. Kaldor, 'A model of the trade cycle,' *Economic Journal*, L, 78–92 (1940).

[23] L. R. Klein and R. C. Preston, 'Stochastic nonlinear models,' *Econometrica*, **37**, 95–106 (1969).

[24] R. Kosobud and W. O'Neill, 'Stochastic implications of orbital asymptotic stability of a nonlinear trade cycle model,' *Econometrica*, **40**, 69–86 (1972).

[25] B. Friedman, 'Econometric simulation difficulties: an illustration,' *Review of Economics and Statistics*, **53**, 381–84 (1971).

[26] G. Fromm and L. R. Klein, 'Solutions of the complete system,' in *The Brookings Model: Some Further Results* (Ed. J. Duesenberry), Rand-McNally, Chicago (1969).

[27] L. R. Klein, 'Price determination in the Wharton Model,' in *Conference on the Econometrics of Price Determination* (Ed. O. Eckstein), Federal Reserve, Washington (1972), pp. 221–36.

[28] I. Adelman and F. L. Adelman, 'The dynamic properties of the Klein–Goldberger model,' *Econometrica*, **27**, 596–625 (1959).

[29] L. R. Klein, 'On the possibility of another "29",' in *The Economic Outlook for 1967*, University of Michigan, Department of Economics, Ann Arbor (1967).

[30] F. G. Adams and M. K. Evans, 'Econometric forecasting with the Wharton Model,' *Business Economics*, **3**, 52–6 (1968).

[31] V. Zarnowitz, 'Forecasting economic conditions,' *National Bureau for Economic Research, Colloquium on Business Cycles*, New York (1970).

[32] R. F. Engle and T. C. Liu, 'Effects of aggregation over time on dynamic characteristics of an econometric model,' in *Econometric Models of Cyclical Behavior, Studies in Income and Wealth* (Ed. B. Hickman), Columbia, New York (1972), pp. 673–729.

8
Comments on Sargent and Sims' 'Business Cycle Modeling Without Pretending to Have Too Much *A Priori* Economic Theory'

It is fortunate that Tjalling Koopmans is present at these meetings to tell us what he really meant when he wrote 'Measurement Without Theory.' It seems to me that Sargent and Sims are misusing Koopmans' arguments for their own purposes. He criticized the National Bureau of Economic Research (NBER) for not using economic theory in their business cycle studies, and I would criticize Sargent and Sims for the same deficiency. Koopmans was also criticizing the National Bureau for not using statistical theory or stochastic specifications in their nonparametric approach to cycle measurement. Sargent and Sims very admirably use deep statistical theory with much stochastic structure in their analysis, but this is no substitute for economic theory. If they do not introduce some more aspects of system structure, both from economic theory and knowledge of economic institutions, for *restricting* the parametric specifications of their models, I am afraid that all is lost. All the problems of collinearity, shortage of degrees of freedom, and structural change will so confound the interpretation of their results that we shall not know what to make of them. In this respect, I find their approach to be disappointingly retrogressive and contrary to the main stream of econometric analysis today.

There are two bothersome misconceptions, either explicit or implied in the Sargent and Sims presentation, and I think that they are basic enough that it is worthwhile taking some time to consider them. One deals with the meaning and interpretation of the Phillips curve and the other, with the available or necessary degrees of freedom for econometric inference.

From *New Methods of Business Cycle Research: Proceedings from a Conference* (Ed. C. A. Sims), Minneapolis (1977).

THE PHILLIPS CURVE

The Phillips curve is not an optimizing relation that should be deduced from some principles of best behavior in either the micro or macro sphere. It is simply a market clearing relation. On the one hand, there are optimizing decisions of households (and trade unions) about labor supply and, on the other hand, optimizing decisions of firms about labor demand. When employee and employer representatives come to the bargaining table, with all the institutional apparatus that such a process entails, a wage bargain is struck on the basis of labor market and other economy-wide considerations. It is surely an accepted part of our subject's view of the working of markets that wages move in response to excess supply or demand in order to set up a tendency towards restoration of equilibrium. It is just a way of introducing dynamic adjustment processes into the reconciliation of two optimizing decisions, and it is fruitless to look about for some optimizing explanation of the Phillips curve.

Also, the Phillips curve is a structural relationship (or a whole set of them) within the context of a macro model. It is frequently confused with the 'trade-off' relationship between price change and unemployment level. But the 'trade-off' relation is not a structural relationship in the same sense; it is the 'parametric' relationship between two reduced form expressions – one for the rates of change of price and one for unemployment, each of which are endogenous variables in a complete system. We have, as part of the system solution

$(\Delta p/p)_t = f$ (initial conditions, exogenous history)

$U_t = g$ (initial conditions, exogenous history).

Since the arguments of f and g are the same, there is an implied relation between $(\Delta p/p)_t$ and U_t; this is the trade-off relation between price change and unemployment.

DEGREES OF FREEDOM

It is sometimes felt that the number of degrees of freedom are limited purely by the number of data points. A more revealing way of looking at the problem is to assume that one starts out a model investigation with nT degrees of freedom, where n is the number of equations in the system and T is the number of data points. The product nT gives the number of stochastic elements in the joint likelihood function. Against these nT degrees of freedom, the estimation of parameters uses many in the process of statistical inference. Some estimation methods are expensive; some are frugal. Requirements can be worked out for various methods from the most expensive

$$T > m + n \ (m = \text{number of predetermined variables})$$

in the case of *FIML*, to the most frugal

$$T > m_i + n_i - 1 \ (m_i = \text{number of coefficients of predetermined variables and } n_i = \text{number of coefficients of endogenous variables in the } i\text{th equation})$$

for *OLS* or *IV*. The point is that an appropriate method can almost always be found, even for the very large structural models now in use, and the full dynamic properties can be estimated. The standard approach to model building can always use more degrees of freedom to good advantage. Econometricians hardly ever have as much as they would like, but they do not have too few to make inferences. The situation is not as bad as Sargent and Sims imply. They use degrees of freedom wastefully because they are unwilling to let *a priori* economic analysis do some of their work. Their methods are much too gross and therefore need more observations.

Since Sargent and Sims draw upon the same data as do model builders, they should get broadly similar results. It would be most unusual if different reasonable analyses of the same data – by Sargent and Sims, the NBER, or model builders – came to radically different findings, except for the fact that nonstructural approaches may not be able to tackle certain types of hypothetical analyses. Model builders can do everything that Sargent and Sims do, and then some; with a model, we can analyze a rich variety of alternative policies or other simulations. I can agree with all the numbers and numerical calculations that Sargent and Sims come up with, and the same holds true of John Geweke's paper; but I cannot agree at all with their overly strong conclusions or interpretations. The causality lines that they claim to have established do not make sense to me.

Also, the Sargent and Sims results in the frequency domain should agree with similar results in the time domain. Much contemporary analysis using principal components, especially for data reduction in the case of the first stage of *TSLS*, show that the main economic indexes can be broken into major classes of trends and cycles of differing periodicities. This is all in line with the cumulative history of NBER findings. At a much earlier date, Stone[1] extracted the principal compo-

---

[1] J. R. W. Stone, 'On the independence of stock transactions', Supplement to the *Journal of the Royal Statistical Society*, **8**, I (1947), 1–32.

nents of the US national income accounts and found that their movement could be accounted for by a trend term, a GNP term, and a ΔGNP term. Time domain analysis of the cyclical content of the Wharton Model of the US economy shows the existence of two superimposed cycles after trend extraction, much in line with Stone's nonparametric investigation. At this level of analysis, I find no contradiction between the work of Sargent and Sims and either the model builders or time series studies in the time domain.

A point raised by several time series analysts, and also by Sargent and Sims, that estimation of economic relationships should pay more attention to the lag structure and the isolation of white noise residuals is well taken. I could find comfortable accommodation with the linear model specification

$$A(L)y_t + B(L)x_t = C(L)e_t$$

where y_t, x_t, e_t are n, m, n element vectors, respectively. Each equation of a complete system would thus be of the type used by Box-Jenkins in their *ARIMA* analysis. A good procedure might be to specify each equation individually on the basis of economic theory and other *a priori* information as a static equilibrium relation. It would then be cast in dynamic and stochastic form as a typical equation of the above system.

This specification for the structure of the system is convenient for demonstrating in closed form expressions the difficulties that arise in connection with Sargent and Sim's views about causality. The solution to the dynamic system, following E. P. Howrey's expressions, are given as

$$y_t = K\lambda^t - \{A(L)\}^{-1}B(L)x_t + \{A(L)\}^{-1}C(L)e_t$$

where K is a matrix depending on initial conditions and λ is a vector of characteristic roots of the system. The trade-off relation between $\Delta p/p$ and U is obtained by associating, in a two-dimensional graph, the solutions for these two elements of y_t obtained when the x_t vector is distributed in a particular way. I find, using the Wharton Model, that if x_t is disturbed through unusual rises in the fuel or food price components (internal or external) or in the exchange rate components that the associated changes in solution values $\Delta p/p$ and U are positively related. If, alternatively, the external stimulus comes from a domestic fiscal impact in taxing or public spending, I find an inverse relation between the changes in $\Delta p/p$ and U. The important point to be emphasized is that these two different trade-off relations were generated from the same model and that structural Phillips curves were included in the model. The structural analysis of behavior and implied causation is capable of generating quite different gross correlations that are really implied by trade-off relations. Gross correlations, no matter how many lead-lag combinations are analyzed by the Sargent and Sims approach, throw no light on underlying causal patterns or exogeneity. What I have done with respect to analysis of the trade-off relations in considering Phillips curve analysis could be done equally well for the analysis of the relationships between money and income. The Sargent and Sims approach, applied earlier to gross lead-lag correlations between money and nominal income by Sims, fails in the same way to reveal the causal pattern.

Finally, in commenting on the Sargent and Sims paper, I should like to direct attention to their system results in table 26.[2] These results are so implausible that I find it hard to see how they could have put them before this audience in a serious vein. Prices are not going to follow the course that they have projected. There must be something drastically wrong with their system or approach to have produced this result and many of the others in tables 26 and 27. The block structure discussed in this Appendix is not unlike the block recursiveness of the coefficient matrix and block diagonality of the covariance matrix introduced by Franklin Fisher to estimate large-scale models in mainstream econometric analysis.

In John Geweke's paper there are interesting numerical calculations whose arithmetic should not be criticized, but surely there is no basis for drawing such strong conclusions as

> a model ought to exhibit a reduced form equation in which the wholesale price index is the endogenous variable with factor prices (and not much else) explanatory. This property contradicts the frequent assumption that since wages and prices emerge from a complex set of interactions there is bound to be material feedback between these variables.

I find no evidence in his calculations that would lead to these rigid conclusions about two sets of endogenous variables – wages and factor prices. Also, there are many other variables, not considered at all, that should properly enter a reduced form equation for the wholesale price index.

At the outset of Geweke's paper there is a false distinction posed between nominal and real magnitudes. The proper procedure is to model structural behavior relationships, within the context of a complete system, taking variables as they should appear on the basis of

---

[2]T. Sargent and C. Sims, 'Business cycle without pretending to have too much *a priori* economic theory', in *New Methods of Business Cycle Research*, Proceedings from a Conference, Minneapolis (1977).

a priori considerations – in some cases using price relatives and deflated magnitudes and in others using absolute prices where speculative behavior is indicated. From this complete system, one can derive implied relationships among prices and wages in either real or nominal form. It is simply a case of setting up the appropriate calculations. Solutions for either form can readily be derived from dynamic simulations. One would have to be wedded to gross correlations or unstructured reduced forms to feel that a choice has to be made.

In the section of his paper dealing with prewar and postwar relationships, time series analysts are too prone to seduction, to the idea that structure has changed. Actually, there is more stability in basic economic behavior than unstructured time series analysis might suggest. It is important to sort out rather superficial changes of institutional conditions and input values of exogenous variables from parametric changes in fundamental behavior. The concept of *autonomy* of a relationship introduced at an early stage by Trygve Haavelmo is relevant in this respect. If, as suggested in other studies, the prewar UK consumption function remains basically stable after the interruption of World War II and postwar reconstruction, it is hard to think that basic household and firm reactions in less disturbed markets for determining wages and prices would not remain stable.

The complaint among time series analysts that either there is no suitable macro theory, or too many, for coming to a decision about model specification is not the right issue. We have good theories in economics, especially micro behavior and the functioning of markets. What is needed is a proper aggregation procedure for deriving the implied macro relations. Many specification restrictions are statutory; these are firm. Other restrictions based on institutional knowledge of the functioning of the economy must be used, too. Entirely too much emphasis has been placed, in today's discussion, on zero type restrictions. Other important restrictions from expenditure systems and optimal factor combinations for efficiency should also be used. These have been important in throwing light on investment incentive tax provisions through specification of investment functions. Such restrictions are likely to be important for cases of large step changes in prices where there has been relatively little sample variability. They also help immensely in getting around problems of identifiability, collinearity, and undersized samples. Generally speaking, they lead to nonlinear systems. The realism of the nonlinear aspects is an important advantage over the usual linear model of pure time series analysis. Without theory and other *a priori* information, we are lost. I wonder why Sargent, Sims and Geweke are trying to lead us away from the established path that was so long in being prepared?

9
Estimation of Distributed Lags

PRELIMINARIES

The use of distributed lags in econometric research is quite old. However, the current intensive interest in the subject dates back to the relatively recent work of Koyck [9]. Since then, a number of extensions have been made to the basic geometric lag distribution and the associated method of estimation taken up by Koyck. A number of such studies are summarized in Amemiya and Fuller [1]. More recently a search technique has been proposed by Dhrymes [2] for the case of a geometric lag distribution occurring in a relation characterized by a first order Markov process in its error term.

Jorgenson [7] has employed in empirical research rational distributed lags although he has not given a full treatment of the estimation problems of the parameters involved. Dhrymes [3] suggested a technique of estimating in a consistent and asymptotically efficient fashion the parameters of a rational distributed lag by the use of spectral techniques thus extending the results obtained by Hannan [5] in the case of the simple geometric lag structure.

At the same time, however, electrical engineers have been interested in much the same problems. In many instances they have produced the elements of a satisfactory solution to the problem of estimating the parameters of the rational distributed lag although their approach has not always been explicitly grounded on a statistical formulation and thus the properties of the resulting estimator were not clear. The present paper builds on an idea proposed by Steiglitz and McBride [13] in an engineering context.

Our purpose here is to give a rigorous formulation and solution to the problem of estimating, by maximum likelihood techniques, the parameters of a general lag structure, to point out the lines of research

The work of Kenneth Steiglitz was supported in part by Army Research Office-Durham under Contract DA-HCO4-69-C-0012. Some of the computer facilities used were supported in part by NSF grant GP-579.

From *International Economic Review*, **11**, June (1970), 235–250; written jointly with Phoebus J. Dhrymes and Kenneth Steiglitz.

and terminology followed in the literature of electrical engineering and thus to make available this literature to econometricians. We believe that such contact will prove quite fruitful.

ENGINEERING MOTIVATION AND SOME FORMAL ANALOGIES IN ENGINEERING AND ECONOMETRIC RESEARCH

The determination of the dynamic characteristics of an electrical or mechanical system from observation records has been of interest to engineers for some time, especially with regard to the construction of adaptive or learning control systems. Most of the work in electrical engineering has been concerned with the linear stationary case, since many physical systems are operated in a fixed environment with relatively small excursions from quiescence.

Thus, assume that the postulated linear stationary system can be described completely at any time t by an n-dimensional vector w_t, called *state vector* at time t. Assume also that the system is excited by a single scalar variable x_t, called the *input*, and that the system response is determined by the value of the scalar variable y_t, called the *output*.[1] We may associate x_t with an exogenous or explanatory variable and w_t, y_t with endogenous variables, the general point of view being that x_t is determined outside the system and affects (or determines) w_t and y_t in a *causal way*.

Finally it will be assumed that output is a *linear combination of the components of the state vector and a scalar random variable* u_t, which represents the effect on the system of nonmeasurable or unknown exogenous variables. We may thus write

$$w_t = A w_{t-1} + b x_t$$
$$y_t = c' w_t + u_t. \qquad (9.1)$$

In (9.1) A and b are respectively an $(n \times n)$ matrix and $n \times 1$ vector of constants, the assumption being that the transition from w_{t-1} to w_t is accomplished in a simple Markovian scheme, under the excitation induced by bx_t. For this reason the matrix A is called the *transition matrix* of the system, though it need not be a probability matrix.

---

[1] What follows can easily be extended to the multivariate case, i.e. we can easily deal with the case in which x_t and y_t are vectors of suitable dimensions.

Let z be complex, of unit modulus, and define

$$W(z) = \sum_{t=0}^{\infty} w_t z^{-t}, \ X(z) = \sum_{t=0}^{\infty} x_t z^{-t}, \ Y(z) = \sum_{t=0}^{\infty} y_t z^{-t}, \ U(z) = \sum_{t=0}^{\infty} u_t z^{-t}. \tag{9.2}$$

The first system equations in (9.1) may now be written as

$$W(z) = Az^{-1}W(z) + bX(z). \tag{9.2a}$$

Solving, we obtain

$$W(z) = (I - Az^{-1})^{-1} bX(z). \tag{9.2b}$$

Finally substituting in the last equation of (9.1) we have

$$Y(z) = c'(I - Az^{-1})^{-1} bX(z) + U(z). \tag{9.3}$$

Clearly $c'(I - Az^{-1})^{-1} b$ is a rational function of z^{-1} and as such it may be represented

$$c'(I - Az^{-1})^{-1} b = \frac{A(z^{-1})}{B(z^{-1})} \tag{9.3a}$$

where $A(z^{-1})$ and $B(z^{-1})$ are polynomials of suitable order. Clearly, the poles $(I - Az^{-1})^{-1}$ are the zeroes of $B(z^{-1})$. Indeed, if λ_i are the roots of A then it can be easily seen that

$$\frac{A(z^{-1})}{B(z^{-1})} = \sum_{i=1}^{n} \frac{c_i^*}{\left(1 - \frac{\lambda_i}{z}\right)}, \tag{9.4}$$

where c_i^* are suitable constants obtained through the process of expansion of the left hand side of (9.4) by partial fractions. Since the λ_i, $i = 1, 2, \ldots, n$ are less than unity in absolute value and z lies on the unit circle, we may expand

$$\frac{1}{1 - \frac{\lambda_i}{z}} = \sum_{k=0}^{\infty} \left(\frac{\lambda_i}{z}\right)^k. \tag{9.4a}$$

Thus the system in (9.3a) can be written as

$$\sum_{t=0}^{\infty} y_t z^{-t} = \sum_{i=1}^{n} c_i^* \sum_{t=0}^{\infty} z^{-t} \sum_{k=0}^{\infty} \lambda_i^k x_t z^{-k} + \sum_{t=0}^{\infty} u_t z^{-t}$$

$$= \sum_{\tau=0}^{\infty} \left(\sum_{i=1}^{n} c_i^* \left(\sum_{k=0}^{\infty} x_{\tau-k} \lambda_i^k \right) \right) z^{-\tau} + \sum_{t=0}^{\infty} u_t z^{-t},$$

where the last member of (9.4b) is obtained by putting $\tau = t + k$. Equating like powers of z^{-1} on both sides we find

$$y_t = \sum_{i=1}^{n} c_i^* \sum_{k=0}^{\infty} \lambda_i^k x_{t-k} + u_t \qquad t = 1, 2, \ldots, T, \qquad (9.4c)$$

which shows that the system in (9.3a) represents a lag distribution. Moreover, this is a weighted sum of n simple geometric lag distributions with parameters λ_i, $i = 1, 2, \ldots, n$. Further, from (9.4b) we note that z^{-1} plays exactly the same role in engineering literature as the lag operator L in econometric and statistical literature.

In what follows we shall therefore use the lag operator exclusively. By definition

$$L^k x_t = x_{t-k} \qquad L^0 = I \qquad I x_t = x_t \qquad k = 0, 1, 2, \ldots,; \qquad (9.4d)$$

therefore, in virtue of (9.4) and (9.4a) we can write (9.4c) as

$$y_t = \sum_{i=1}^{n} c_i^* \sum_{k=0}^{\infty} (\lambda_i L)^k x_t + u_t = \sum_{i=1}^{n} \frac{c_i^* I}{(I - \lambda_i L)} x_t + u_t = \frac{A(L)}{B(L)} x_t + u_t, \qquad (9.4e)$$

where $A(L)$ and $B(L)$ are polynomials of degree at most $n-1$ and n respectively. This is, of course, the notation of the standard rational distributed lag model discussed in the literature of econometrics. It is particularly striking, for example, that Jorgenson [7] and Steiglitz and McBride [13] use, in entirely different and unrelated contexts, exactly the same model (9.4e). This is an extreme instance of research convergence in econometrics and electrical engineering and should suggest to econometricians and electrical engineers the benefits to be derived from familiarity with certain aspects of the research in the two disciplines. We conclude this section by giving a table of equivalent terminology (table 9.1).

Table 9.1

Engineering	Econometrics
White-Gaussian error	Nonautocorrelated, normally distributed error
Colored-Gaussian	Autocorrelated, normally distributed error
Plant	Nonstochastic model
Record	Sample
Rational z transform	Rational lag distribution
Prefiltering	Exponential weighting
Identification	Specification and estimation of a model

ESTIMATION OF THE GENERAL RATIONAL LAG MODEL

Formulation

In this section we shall deal with the problem of estimating the parameters of

$$y_t = \frac{A(L)}{B(L)} x_t + u_t \qquad t=1,2,\ldots,T, \tag{9.5}$$

where L is the lag operator defined in (9.4d) and

$$A(L) = \sum_{i=0}^{\mu} a_i L^i \qquad B(L) = \sum_{j=0}^{\nu} b_j L^j \qquad b_0 = 1 \qquad \mu < \nu. \tag{9.5a}$$

The independent variable x is assumed to be nonstochastic or, if stochastic, uncorrelated with the random term u_t. The latter has the specification

$$u \sim N(0, \sigma^2 I), \; u = (u_1, u_2, \ldots, u_T)', \tag{9.5b}$$

and is assumed to be independent of x for all t. We shall employ maximum likelihood methods. Thus the (log) likelihood function of the observations in (9.5) is given by

$$L(a, b, \sigma^2; y, x) = -\frac{T}{2} \ln(2\pi) - \frac{T}{2} \ln \sigma^2$$
$$- \frac{1}{2\sigma^2} \left(y - \frac{A(L)}{B(L)} x \right)' \left(y - \frac{A(L)}{B(L)} x \right) \tag{9.6}$$

where

$y = (y_1, y_2, \ldots, y_T)'$,
$a = (a_0, a_1, \ldots, a_\mu)'$,
$x = (x_1, x_2, \ldots, x_T)'$,
$b = (b_1, b_2, \ldots, b_\nu)'$.

The first order conditions for a maximum are given by

$$\frac{\partial L}{\partial a_i} = \frac{1}{\sigma^2} \sum_{t=\mu+\nu+1}^{T} \left(y_t - \frac{A(L)}{B(L)} x_t \right) \frac{L^j}{B(L)} x_t = 0 \qquad j = 0, 1, 2, \ldots, \mu,$$

$$\frac{\partial L}{\partial b_j} = \frac{1}{2} \sum_{t=\mu+\nu+1}^{T} \left(y_t - \frac{A(L)}{B(L)} x_t \right) \frac{A(L)}{B(L)^2} L^s x_t = 0 \qquad s = 1, 2, \ldots, \nu, \tag{9.6a}$$

$$\frac{\partial L}{\partial \sigma^2} = -\frac{T}{2} \frac{1}{\sigma^2} + \frac{1}{\sigma^4} \sum_{t=\mu+\nu+1}^{T} \left(y_t - \frac{A(L)}{B(L)} x_t \right)' \left(y_t - \frac{A(L)}{B(L)} x_t \right) = 0,$$

We observe that while the equations in (9.6a) are highly nonlinear in the a_i and b_j, they are linear in a_i for given b_j and they are linear in σ^2. We can search the parameter space for estimates of a_i, given b_i or we can iterate for all parameter estimates simultaneously. Once we have estimates for a_i and b_j, however, an estimate for σ^2 will be easily obtained.

In what follows we shall concentrate our attention solely on the first two sets of equations which would correspond to the normal equations of least squares, although under the assumption of normality the resulting estimators would be maximum likelihood ones as well.

The strategy of our estimation procedure is to determine a consistent solution of the equations in (9.6a).

Since by a theorem of Huzurbazar [6], for large T there exists a unique consistent solution, and by a theorem of Wald [15] it corresponds to the global maximum of the likelihood function, we would then have found the maximum likelihood estimators of the parameters a_j, b_s, $j = 0, 1, 2, \ldots, \mu$, $s = 1, 2, \ldots, \nu$, which are asymptotically normal, unbiased, and efficient.

An iterative algorithm

Define

$$y_t^* = \frac{I}{B(L)} y_t \qquad x_t^* = \frac{I}{B(L)} x_t \qquad x_t^{**} = \frac{A(L)}{B(L)} x_t^* \qquad t = 1, 2, \ldots, T, \tag{9.7}$$

and note that the first two systems in (9.6a) may be written as

$$\sum_{t=\mu+\nu+1}^{T} [B(L) y_t^* - A(L) x_t^*] x_{t-j}^* = 0 \qquad j = 0, 1, 2, \ldots, \mu, \tag{9.7a}$$

$$\sum_{t=\mu+\nu+1}^{T} [B(L) y_t^* - A(L) x_t^*] x_{t-s}^{**} = 0 \qquad s = 1, 2, \ldots, \nu. \tag{9.7b}$$

The equations in (9.7a) and (9.7b) are linear in the parameters provided we deal in the transformed variables y^*, x^*, x^{**}. But this suggests how we can solve the system: it can be used to construct the variables y_t^*, x_t^*, x_t^{**}; then the system in (9.7a) and (9.7b) can be solved to provide another estimator $B^1(L)$, $A^1(L)$, etc., until the iteration converges, say at the kth step; this would mean that for prescribed $\varepsilon > 0$

$$\max_j |a_j^k - a_j^{k+1}| < \varepsilon \qquad \max_s |b_s^k - b_s^{k+1}| < \varepsilon. \tag{9.7c}$$

Let us see precisely what this algorithm entails. For computational convenience only, the various cross products involved will not contain the observations at times $r = 1, 2, \ldots, v$. To this effect, let

$$Y^* = \begin{bmatrix} y^*_{\mu+v} & y^*_{\mu+v-1} & \cdots & y^*_{\mu+1} \\ y^*_{\mu+v+1} & y^*_{\mu+v} & \cdots & y^*_{\mu+2} \\ \vdots & & & \vdots \\ y^*_{T-1} & y^*_{T-2} & \cdots & y^*_{T-v} \end{bmatrix}.$$

$$X^* = \begin{bmatrix} x^*_{\mu+v+1} & x^*_{\mu+v} & \cdots & x^*_{v+1} \\ x^*_{\mu+v+2} & x^*_{\mu+v+1} & \cdots & x^*_{v+2} \\ \vdots & & & \vdots \\ x^*_{T} & x^*_{T-1} & \cdots & x^*_{T-\mu} \end{bmatrix} \qquad (9.8)$$

$$X^{**} = \begin{bmatrix} x^{**}_{\mu+v} & x^{**}_{\mu+v-1} & \cdots & x^{**}_{\mu+1} \\ x^{**}_{\mu+v+1} & x^{**}_{\mu+v} & \cdots & x^{**}_{\mu+2} \\ \vdots & & & \vdots \\ x^{**}_{T-1} & x^{**}_{T-2} & \cdots & x^{**}_{T-v} \end{bmatrix}.$$

$$d = \begin{bmatrix} a \\ -b \end{bmatrix}$$

$$c^* = (c^*_j)$$

$$\begin{aligned} c^*_j &= \sum_{j=\mu+v+1}^{T} y^*_t x^*_{t-j} \qquad j = 0, 1, 2, \ldots, \mu \\ &= \sum_{t=\mu+v+1}^{T} y^*_t x^{**}_{t+\mu-j} \qquad j = \mu+1, \mu+2, \ldots, \mu+v \end{aligned} \qquad (9.8a)$$

$$W^* = \begin{bmatrix} X^{*\prime} X^* & X^{*\prime} Y^* \\ X^{**\prime} X^* & X^{**\prime} Y^* \end{bmatrix}. \qquad (9.8b)$$

With the aid of the notation in (9.8), (9.8a) and (9.8b), the system in (9.7a) and (9.7b) may be written compactly as

$$W^* d = c^*. \qquad (9.9)$$

Remark 1 We should observe that the definitions in (9.7), involving what engineers call prefiltering, are not as cumbersome as they appear. In particular, they need not involve power series expansions of the operators $I/B(L)$. To see this, note that by virtue of the convention in (9.5a), we can write

$$B(L) = I + \sum_{j=1}^{v} b_j L^j = I - B^*(L) \qquad B^*(L) = -\sum_{j=1}^{v} b_j L^j. \qquad (9.10)$$

Thus, the first equation in (9.7) implies

$$y_t^* = y_t + B^*(L)y_t^*. \tag{9.10a}$$

If initial conditions for y_t^* are specified, we see that y_t^* can be computed recursively, given b, for as many *values of the index* as y_t is available.

Similar comments apply to x_t^*. In the case of x_t^{**} we see that since x_t^* is defined over the same range of index values as x_t, then clearly x_t^{**} is defined for $t = \mu+1, \mu+2, \ldots$. Thus, y_t^*, x_t^*, x_t^{**} are all defined for $t = v, v+1, \ldots, T$ which is the range of index values appearing in the matrices Y^*, X^* and X^{**}. Finally, a convenient initial condition for y_t^* and x_t^* is

$$x_{-i}^* = y_{-i}^* = 0 \qquad i = 0, 1, 2, \ldots, v. \tag{9.10}$$

Since

$$y_{-i}^* = \frac{I}{B(L)} y_{-i}, \qquad x_{-i}^* = \frac{I}{B(L)} x_{-i} \qquad i = 0, 1, 2, \ldots, v, \tag{9.10c}$$

(10b) is equivalent to stating that

$$x_{-i} = y_{-i} = 0 \qquad i = 0, 1, 2, \ldots, v. \tag{9.10d}$$

This is not a serious handicap if the sample size T is large.

Remark 2 Observe that W^* and c^* are functions of d. In what follows we shall assume that for any admissible value of d, W^* is nonsingular. Now, it is clear from (9.9) that if an initial consistent estimator of d exists, say $\tilde{d}_0$, then W^* and c^* can be computed, say $\tilde{W}_0^*, \tilde{c}_0^*$, where the tilde is used to denote the fact that W^* is obtained on the basis of a consistent estimator of d and not on the basis of the true value of the parameter vector d.

In view of the above, we may iterate on d by solving, to obtain

$$\tilde{d}_1 = \tilde{W}_0^{*-1} \tilde{c}_0^*. \tag{9.11}$$

We may now evaluate W^* and c^* at $\tilde{d}_1$ and complete a second iteration

$$\tilde{d}_2 = \tilde{W}_1^{*-1} \tilde{c}_1^*. \tag{9.11a}$$

Two questions arise with respect to this procedure.

1 If $\tilde{d}_i$ is a consistent estimator of d, is it also the case that $\tilde{d}_{i+1}$ is a consistent estimator of d?

2 Does the iteration process converge, and, if so, under what circumstances?

164 Economic Theory and Econometrics

To this effect we prove

Lemma 1 Under the hypotheses of the model as exhibited in (9.5), (9.5a) and (9.5b), if $\tilde{d}_i$ is a consistent estimator of d then so is $\tilde{d}_{i+1}$, the latter being defined by

$$\tilde{d}_{i+1} = \tilde{W}_i^{*-1} \tilde{c}_i^*. \tag{9.12}$$

Proof We note that by definition

$$y_t^* = \frac{I}{B(L)} y_t = \frac{I}{B(L)} \left[\frac{A(L)}{B(L)} x_t + u_t \right] = x_t^{**} + u_t^* \tag{9.12a}$$

the starred quantities in (9.12a) having the obvious meaning. Thus

$$Y^* = X^{**} + U^* \tag{9.12b}$$

where U^* is constructed in exactly the same fashion as Y^*. Define

$$W^{**} = \begin{bmatrix} X^{*\prime} X^* & X^{*\prime} X^{**} \\ X^{**\prime} X^* & X^{**\prime} X^{**} \end{bmatrix}. \tag{9.12c}$$

Since

$$X^{*\prime} Y^* = X^{*\prime} X^{**} + X^{*\prime} U^*, \tag{9.12d}$$

then

$$\plim_{T \to \infty} \frac{X^{*\prime} Y^*}{T} = \plim_{T \to \infty} \frac{X^{*\prime} X^{**}}{T} \tag{9.12e}$$

since x_t is nonstochastic (or independent of u_t).

Since $\tilde{d}_i$ is a consistent estimate of d, it follows that

$$\plim_{T \to \infty} \frac{1}{T} \tilde{W}_1^* = \lim_{T \to \infty} \frac{1}{T} W^{**}. \tag{9.13}$$

We also note that, by the same argument,

$$\plim_{T \to \infty} \frac{1}{T} \tilde{c}_i^* = \lim_{T \to \infty} \frac{1}{T} c^{**} \tag{9.13a}$$

where

$$c^{**} = (c_j^{**}), \quad c_j^{**} = \sum_{j=v+1}^{T} x_t^{**} x_{t-j}^* \qquad j = 0, 1, 2, \ldots, \mu,$$

$$= \sum_{j=v+1}^{T} x_t^{**} x_{t+\mu-j}^{**} \qquad j = \mu+1, \mu+2, \ldots, \mu+v. \tag{9.13b}$$

Since

$$\tilde{d}_{i+1} = \left(\frac{\tilde{W}_i^*}{T}\right)^{-1} \frac{\tilde{c}_i^*}{T} \tag{9.14}$$

we conclude

$$\plim_{T\to\infty} \tilde{d}_{i+1} = \lim_{T\to\infty} \left[\left(\frac{W^{**}}{T}\right)^{-1} \frac{c^{**}}{T}\right]. \tag{9.14a}$$

The model obeys

$$B(L)y_t^* = A(L)x_t^* + u_t \qquad t = 1, 2, \ldots, T. \tag{9.15}$$

Putting

$$y^v = (y_{v+1}, y_{v+2}, \ldots, y_T)' \qquad u^v = (u_{v+1}, u_{v+2}, \ldots, u_T)', \tag{9.15a}$$

we can write (15) in the slightly altered form

$$(X^*, Y^*)d = y^v - u^v. \tag{9.15b}$$

Let

$$Z = (X^*, X^{**}) \tag{9.15c}$$

and consider

$$Z'(X^*, Y^*)d = Z'y^v - Z'u^v. \tag{9.15d}$$

We note

$$\lim_{T\to\infty} \frac{Z'(X^*, Y^*)}{T} = \lim_{T\to\infty} \frac{W^{**}}{T}, \tag{9.16}$$

$$\plim_{T\to\infty} \frac{Z'y^v}{T} = \lim_{T\to\infty} \frac{1}{T} c^{**}, \quad \plim_{T\to\infty} \frac{Z'u^v}{T} = 0 \tag{9.16a}$$

From (9.15d) we therefore obtain

$$\lim_{T\to\infty} \frac{W^{**}}{T} d = \lim_{T\to\infty} \frac{1}{T} c^{**}. \tag{9.16b}$$

Comparing (9.14a) and (9.16b) we conclude

$$\plim_{T\to\infty} d_{i+1} = d. \qquad \text{QED} \tag{9.16c}$$

The question of convergence for this procedure is rather difficult to settle definitively. Since asymptotically W^* converges to a positive definite matrix for every admissible d one would surmise that the iteration process will converge, at least for large T. Assuming that the process above is convergent, we are thus able to locate the consistent root of the maximum likelihood equations. By the theorem of Huzurbazar [6] we have therefore found, for large T, the global maximum of the likelihood function. Since the probability structure of the error term in (9.5) is regular, we conclude that such estimators are consistent, asymptotically efficient, and distributed as

$$T^{\frac{1}{2}}(\hat{d}-d) \sim N\left(0, \left[-\frac{1}{T} E \frac{\partial^2 L}{\partial d \partial d}\right]^{-1}\right). \tag{9.17}$$

One can handle rather easily the case of autocorrelated error terms provided the autocorrelation is first order Markov. Thus, if

$$u_t = \rho u_{t-1} + \varepsilon_t, t = 1, 2, \ldots, T, |\rho| < 1, \ \varepsilon \sim N(0, \sigma_\varepsilon^2 I) \tag{9.17a}$$

where

$$\varepsilon = (\varepsilon_1, \varepsilon_2, \ldots, \varepsilon_T)', \tag{9.17b}$$

then one can employ a scanning (search) technique. As shown by Dhrymes [2] in a slightly different but relevant context the resulting estimators of $[d \ \rho]'$, obtained by the procedure above coupled with a search on ρ, are consistent.

A MODEL WITH SEVERAL DISTINCT GEOMETRIC LAGS

It is interesting that the techniques of the previous discussion are easily applicable to the model

$$y_t = \sum_{i=1}^m \frac{\alpha_i I}{I - \lambda_i L} x_{ti} + u_t \qquad t = 1, 2, \ldots, T, \tag{9.18}$$

which has been found intractable in previous economic applications. When the number of lags is small, say two, then the search technique given in Dhrymes [2] can easily be extended to produce maximum likelihood estimators in a relatively simple manner. If, however, $m > 2$, then the search technique is, realistically, nonapplicable and should resort to the estimation scheme discussed above.

Let us see precisely what this entails. As before we shall assume

$$u \sim N(0, \sigma^2 I) \qquad u = (u_1, u_2, u_3, \ldots, u_T)' \tag{9.18a}$$

and that the x_i, $i = 1, 2, \ldots, m$ are either nonstochastic or eventually independent of the error terms of (9.18). The (log) likelihood function of the observations is

$$L(\alpha, \lambda, \sigma^2; y, X) = -\frac{T}{2}\ln(2\pi) - \frac{T}{2}\ln\sigma^2$$
$$-\frac{1}{2}\sum_{t=1}^{T}\left(y_t - \sum_{i=1}^{m}\frac{\alpha_i I}{I - \lambda_i L}x_{ti}\right)^2. \quad (9.18b)$$

The maximizing equations with respect to the α_i and λ_i are given by

$$\frac{\partial L}{\partial \alpha_k} = \sum_{t=1}^{T}\left(y_t - \sum_{i=1}^{m}\frac{\alpha_i I}{I - \lambda_i L}x_{ti}\right)\frac{I}{I - \lambda_k L}x_{tk} = 0$$

$$\frac{\partial L}{\partial \lambda_k} = \sum_{t=1}^{T}\left(y_t - \sum_{i=1}^{m}\frac{\alpha_k I}{I - \lambda_i L}x_{ti}\right)\frac{\alpha_i I}{(I - \lambda_k L)^2}x_{t-1,k} = 0$$

$$k = 1, 2, \ldots, m. \quad (9.19)$$

If we now define

$$x_{ti}^* = \frac{I}{I - \lambda_i L}x_{ti}, \quad x_{ti}^{**} = \frac{I}{I - \lambda_i L}x_{ti}^*, \quad y_{ti}^* = \frac{I}{I - \lambda_i L}y_t,$$
$$(9.19a)$$

the system in (9.19) may be written as

$$\sum_{i=1}^{m}\alpha_i\sum_{t=1}^{T}x_{ti}^*x_{tk}^* + \lambda_k\sum_{t=1}^{T}y_{t-1,k}^*x_{tk}^* = \sum_{t=1}^{T}y_{tk}^*x_{tk}^* \quad (9.19b)$$

$$\sum_{i=1}^{m}\alpha_i\sum_{t=1}^{T}x_{ti}^*x_{t-1,k}^{**} + \lambda_k\sum_{t=1}^{T}y_{t-1,k}^*x_{t-1,k}^{**} = \sum_{t=1}^{T}y_{tk}^*x_{t-1,k}^{**}.$$

Two aspects of (9.19b) should be pointed out: first as an identity we may write, for any k,

$$y_t = \frac{I - \lambda_k L}{I - \lambda_k L}y_t = (I - \lambda_k L)y_{tk}^* = y_{tk}^* - \lambda_k y_{t-1,k}^*. \quad (9.19c)$$

Second, although the summation over t has the range $(1, T)$ we take $y_{0k}^* = x_{0k}^* = 0$ all k so that no problem arises.

The estimation scheme here is exactly the same as in previous sections; thus if consistent initial estimators exist for the λ_i, $i = 1, 2, \ldots, m$, say $\tilde{\lambda}_i^0$, then the quantities $\tilde{x}_{ti}^*, \tilde{x}_{ti}^{**}, \tilde{y}_{tk}^*$ can be computed from the expressions in (9.19a) where in lieu of λ_i we make use of the $\tilde{\lambda}_i^0$. Hence from (9.19b) we shall obtain estimators, say, $\tilde{\alpha}_i^1, \tilde{\lambda}_i^1$; using the $\tilde{\lambda}_i^1$ we can recompute the quantities $\tilde{x}_{tk}, \tilde{x}_{tk}^{**}, \tilde{y}_{tk}^*$ from the expressions in (9.19a) and from (9.19b) obtain another set of estimators, say $\tilde{\alpha}_i^2, \tilde{\lambda}_i^2$ and so on until convergence is obtained, i.e. until at the sth step we find

$$\max\{|\tilde{\lambda}_i^s - \tilde{\lambda}_i^{s-1}|, \ |\tilde{\alpha}_i^s - \tilde{\alpha}_i^{s-1}|\} < \varepsilon \tag{9.19d}$$

where ε is a preassigned (small) positive constant.

AN ILLUSTRATION

Here we briefly examine the geometric lag distribution which has found extensive applications in econometrics. In this case

$$A(L) = \alpha I \qquad B(L) = I - \lambda L \qquad |\lambda| < 1. \tag{9.20}$$

The model in (9.5) becomes

$$y_t = \frac{\alpha I}{I - \lambda L} x_t + u_t \qquad t = 1, 2, \ldots, T. \tag{9.20a}$$

The equations in (9.7a) and (9.7b) become

$$\sum_{t=1}^{T} [(I - \lambda L)y_t^* - \alpha x_t^*]x_t^* = 0$$

$$\sum_{t=1}^{T} [(I - \lambda L)y_t^* - \alpha x_t^*]\alpha x_{t-1}^{**} = 0, \tag{9.20b}$$

where

$$y_t^* = \frac{I}{I - \lambda L} y_t \qquad x_t^* = \frac{I}{I - \lambda L} x_t \qquad x_t^{**} = \frac{\alpha I}{I - \lambda L} x_t^*. \tag{9.20c}$$

After some rearrangement we can rewrite (9.20b) as

$$\alpha \sum_{t=2}^{T} x_t^{*2} + \lambda \sum_{t=2}^{T} x_t^* y_{t-1}^* = \sum_{t=2}^{T} x_t^* y_t^*$$

$$\alpha \sum_{t=1}^{T} x_{t-1}^{**} x_t^* + \lambda \sum_{t=2}^{T} x_{t-1}^{**} y_{t-1}^* = \sum_{t=2}^{T} x_{t-1}^{**} y_t^*. \tag{9.21}$$

If we take an initial consistent estimator of λ and α, say $\tilde{\lambda}_0, \tilde{\alpha}_0$, then we can compute the prefiltered variables y_t^*, x_t^* and x_t^{**} recursively as follows:

$$y_t^* = y_t + \tilde{\lambda}_0 y_{t-1}^* \qquad x_t^* = x_t + \tilde{\lambda}_0 x_{t-1}^* \qquad x_t^{**} = \alpha x_t^* + \tilde{\lambda}_0 x_{t-1}^{**}. \tag{9.21a}$$

We can then solve the system in (9.21) to obtain another estimator, say $\tilde{\lambda}_1, \tilde{\alpha}_1$. We again compute the prefiltered variables in (9.20c) using the new estimators and continue until the iteration process converges, i.e.

Distributed lags

until

$$\max\{|\tilde{\lambda}_{i+1}-\tilde{\lambda}_i|, |\tilde{\alpha}_{i+1}-\tilde{\alpha}_i|\} < \varepsilon, \quad (9.21b)$$

where ε is some preassigned small quantity. An initial consistent estimator for α and λ can be obtained by instrumental variable techniques. In particular we can take the estimator proposed by Liviatan [10] which is obtained by solving

$$\tilde{\alpha}_0 \sum_{t=2}^{T} x_t^2 + \tilde{\lambda}_0 \sum_{t=2}^{T} x_t y_{t-1} = \sum_{t=2}^{T} x_t y_t$$

$$\tilde{\alpha}_0 \sum_{t=2}^{T} x_t x_{t-1} + \tilde{\lambda}_0 \sum_{t=2}^{T} x_{t-1} y_{t-1} = \sum_{t=2}^{T} x_{t-1} y_t. \quad (9.21c)$$

Efficient estimation of the geometric lag distribution has been the subject of extensive research; a part of this literature was referred to in the introduction. In this connection, it should be noted that a recent Monte Carlo study by Morrison [12] compares a number of proposed estimators of the parameters of the model (9.20a) where the error terms are assumed to have the classical properties. He finds that the estimator proposed by Liviatan [10] and Hannan [5], as interpreted in the time domain by Amemiya and Fuller [1], on the whole do not do very well. The estimators proposed by Steiglitz and McBride [13], a variant of which was discussed above, does extremely well for large samples (50 observations); that proposed by Dhrymes [4,2] performs relatively better than the Steiglitz and McBride estimator for smaller sample size, although for larger samples the two estimators perform equally well.

Finally, this is a convenient juncture to consider Malinvaud's comments [11] on the estimation of the geometric lag in the face of autocorrelated errors. Thus, suppose our model is

$$y_t = \frac{\alpha I}{I - \lambda L} x_t + u_t \qquad u_t = \sum_{i=1}^{k} \rho_i u_{t-i} + \varepsilon_t \qquad t = 1, 2, \ldots, T \quad (9.22)$$

where

$$\varepsilon \sim N(0, \sigma^2 I) \qquad \varepsilon = (\varepsilon_1, \varepsilon_2, \ldots, \varepsilon_T)'. \quad (9.22a)$$

We note that

$$y_t - \sum_{i=1}^{k} \rho_i y_{t-i} = \frac{\alpha I}{I - \lambda L}\left(x_t - \sum_{i=1}^{k} \rho_i x_{t-i}\right) + \varepsilon_t. \quad (9.22b)$$

We may then put

$$y_t' = \frac{\alpha I}{I - \lambda L} x_t' + \varepsilon_t \qquad y_t' = y_t - \sum_{i=1}^{k} \rho_i y_{t-i} \qquad x_t' = x_t - \sum_{i=1}^{k} \rho_i x_{t-i}.$$

$$(9.22c)$$

Malinvaud then claims that if we estimate α and λ by the method given in Klein [8] with y'_t, x'_t replacing y_t and x_t respectively, then the resulting estimators of α and λ are inconsistent. The iteration considered by Malinvaud begins with an inconsistent estimator of the paramters α, λ, ρ. It is simple enough to use Liviatan type or other consistent estimators to start the iterations.

Suppose that we have consistent estimators of the ρ_i, say $\hat{\rho}_{i0}$. Then we may define

$$y'_t = y_t - \sum_{i=1}^{k} \hat{\rho}_{i0} y_{t-i} \qquad x'_t = x_t - \sum_{i=1}^{k} \hat{\rho}_{i0} x_{t-i}. \tag{9.23}$$

If an initial consistent estimator of α and λ are also available, then we can apply the scheme of this section with $\tilde{y}'_t$ and $\tilde{x}'_t$ replacing y_t and x_t in (9.20a). Thus we obtain estimators $\tilde{\alpha}_1, \tilde{\lambda}_1$. Using these we can compute

$$\tilde{u}_t - \tilde{\lambda}_1 \tilde{u}_{t-1} = y_t - \tilde{\lambda}_1 y_{t-1} - \tilde{\alpha}_1 x_t. \tag{9.23a}$$

From the left hand side of (9.23a) we can obtain recursively the $\tilde{u}_t$, $t = 1, 2, \ldots, T$, on the assumption, say, that

$$\tilde{u}_0 = 0. \tag{9.23b}$$

The consequences of this assumption are minimal if the sample is at all large. Then we can regress $\tilde{u}_t$ on $\tilde{u}_{t-i}$, $i = 1, 2, \ldots, k$, to obtain another set ρ_{i1}, $i = 1, 2, \ldots, k$, and repeat the process. It is easily verified that this procedure will yield consistent estimators. Actually, in the empirically relevant case $k = 1$, one easily obtains a rather simply executed estimator which is consistent, asymptotically unbiased, and efficient. An alternative procedure if $k > 1$ may be as follows. Disregard the specification on u_t in (9.20) and obtain consistent estimators for α and λ by searching on λ. This may be done by using the form given in Klein [8]

$$y_t = \lambda^t \eta_0 + \alpha \sum_{i=1}^{t-1} \lambda^i x_{t-i} + u_t, \tag{9.24}$$

and employing ordinary least squares.

The resulting estimators of α, λ, say $\tilde{\alpha}_0, \tilde{\lambda}_0$, are consistent. Use the scheme of equations (9.23a) and (9.23b) to obtain the residuals $\tilde{u}_1, \tilde{u}_2, \ldots, \tilde{u}_T$. Then regress $\tilde{u}_t$ on $\tilde{u}_{t-i}$, $i = 1, 2, \ldots, k$, to obtain initial estimators of ρ_i say, $\hat{\rho}_{i0}$, $i = 1, 2, \ldots, k$. These are consistent estimators. Compute the quantities $\tilde{y}'_t, \tilde{x}'_t$ of (9.23) using the estimator $\hat{\rho}_{i0}$ above. Then consider

$$\tilde{y}'_t = \lambda^t \eta_0 + \alpha \sum_{i=1}^{t-1} \lambda^i \tilde{x}'_{t-1} + \tilde{\varepsilon}_t. \tag{9.24a}$$

This is asymptotically equivalent to

$$y_t - \sum_{i=1}^{t} \rho_i y_{t-i} = \lambda^t \eta_0 + \alpha \sum_{i=1}^{t-1} \lambda^i \left(x_t - \sum_{i=1}^{t-1} \rho_i x_{t-i} \right) + \varepsilon_t. \tag{9.24b}$$

Thus applying the search technique to (9.24a) in a least squares context yields asymptotically the maximum likelihood estimators of α and λ. One may, of course, iterate the procedure.

AN EXAMPLE

Here we shall apply the techniques developed in the previous sections to the problem of estimating the parameters of an investment function. Our purpose is not to give yet another theory of investment but rather to illustrate that the procedures developed have useful applications, and to indicate the extent of the variation in empirical results one might expect due to differences in estimation procedures. The example also demonstrates feasibility and convergence of the computational methods suggested. To this effect, we have chosen the investment function suggested by Jorgenson[2] with respect to the durable manufacturing sector. Our data are somewhat different from his, chiefly in that our sample period is 1948 (first quarter) to 1965 (fourth quarter) while his begin with 1948 and end with 1959. Aside from this both sets of data are comparable, and our results should be compared with the first row of Jorgenson's table 2.2 in the work cited above. In Table 9.2 I_t is Jorgenson's variable, investment at time $t - 0.0279$ times capital stock at time $t-1$, and X_t is Jorgenson's variable $\Delta[p_t x_t / c_t]$, i.e. the change in the value of output divided by user cost.

The point estimates of the parameters of the hypothesized model might appear from Table 9.2 to be quite close no matter how we estimate them. However, their implications in terms of meaningful economic theoretic constructs are rather substantially different. Before we explore this let us stress again that we do not advance our new estimates above as alternative empirical characterizations of investment behavior, rather as illustrations how alternative estimation techniques can lead to substantially differing conclusions.

First let us ask, What is the long run response of investment to the independent variable X_t? The answer is obtained by evaluating the

---

[2]D. W. Jorgenson, 'Anticipations and investment behavior' in *The Brookings Quarterly Econometric Model of the U.S.* (Eds J. S. Duesenberry, G. Fromm, L. R. Klein, E. Kuh), Rand McNally, Chicago (1965).

Table 9.2 Estimated investment function durable manufacturing, 1948.I–1965.IV

OLS	$I_{t+3} = \dfrac{0.007906 + 0.007944L + 0.0003197L^2}{1 - 1.541705L + 0.575882L^2} X_t$
Jorgenson*	$I_{t+3} = \dfrac{0.00096 + 0.00080L + 0.00034L^2}{1 - 1.29501L + 0.42764L^2} X_t$
Modified ML†§ (Instrumental variable) estimators	$I_{t+3} = \dfrac{0.0023863 - 0.0007789L - 0.0012922L^2}{1 - 1.965438L + 0.972074L^2} X_t$
Maximum likelihood§ estimators	$I_{t+3} = \dfrac{0.0018426 + 0.0001095L - 0.0015530L^2}{1 - 1.945464L + 0.952775L^2} X_t$

*Jorgenson's sample covers only 1948–1959.
†We shall explain the meaning of this below.
§The criterion of convergence employed in these computations has been the insensitivity of the residual sum of squares about its minimum.

rational functions of the table after replacing L by unity. The conclusions are: OLS: 0.05573, Jorgenson: 0.01583, Modified ML: 0.04749, ML: 0.05458. Without trying to explain the magnitude of these numbers – which in part reflect the units in which the variables are measured – we observe that simply by changing the sample period we obtain a more than threefold increase in this quantity. This is so since our OLS estimator is exactly like Jorgenson's estimator, the only difference being the sample period. On the other hand, OLS, modified ML and ML procedures yield roughly comparable quantities.

Now, if the denominator polynomial is written as

$$B(L) = I + b_1 L + b_2 L^2 = (I - \lambda_1 L)(I - \lambda_2 L) \qquad (9.25)$$

we have the identification

$$\lambda_1 + \lambda_2 = -b_1 \qquad \lambda_1 \lambda_2 = b_2. \qquad (9.25a)$$

The four sets of results given in table 9.2 imply the following estimators for λ_1, λ_2 respectively. OLS: 0.9043, 0.6347; Jorgenson: $0.6475 \pm 0.1825i$ ($|\lambda|^2 = 0.4525$); Modified ML: $0.9827 \pm 0.1234i$ ($|\lambda|^2 = 0.9809$); ML: $0.9727 \pm 0.1616i$ ($|\lambda|^2 = 0.9722$). These results indicate considerable variation in the conclusions to be derived from the four sets of estimators. First, by enlarging the period of the sample we do not have oscillations in the lag coefficients, i.e. OLS yields real roots while Jorgenson results yield complex roots. Second the modified ML and ML estimators yield complex roots; moreover their modulus is very close to unity. In addition to that, in the last two sets we may well obtain *negative lag coefficients* due to the negative point estimators in the numerator polynomials. Of course, we have not appraised the statistical significance of these results, nor have we experimented with the order of the numerator polynomial so as to obtain the 'best fitting' result as was the case with Jorgenson's study.

Finally, if we standardize the lag coefficients so that they add to unity we can obtain the implied mean lag as follows: Let

$$W(s) = \frac{\sum_{i=0}^{\mu} a_i s^i}{\sum_{j=0}^{\nu} b_j s^j} = \frac{A(s)}{B(s)} \qquad (9.26)$$

be the lag generating function; it is apparent that

$$W(1) = = \frac{A(1)}{B(1)} \qquad (9.26a)$$

represents the sum of the lag coefficients. If *all lag coefficients are positive*, as must be the case in Jorgenson's model, then it makes perfectly good sense to divide the lag coefficients by $W(1)$ so that they lie in the interval $[0, 1]$ and sum to unity. Thus, they have all the characteristics of a set of probabilities, and we may define the mean lag in the same way as we define the mean of a random variable. In this case we obtain

$$\text{Mean lag} = \frac{A'(1)}{A(1)} - \frac{B'(1)}{B(1)} \qquad (9.26b)$$

where $A'(1)$, $B'(1)$ indicate respectively the derivatives of $A(s)$, $B(s)$ evaluated at $s = 1$. This measure is not useful in the case of the modified ML and ML estimators – at least not in the present case.

The mean lag for OLS is 15.16 quarters; for Jorgenson it is 7.02 quarters. This is indeed a very substantial variation and one that we might not expect to materialize simply by the enlargement of the sample period. However, it is not our purpose here to comment on this substantive aspect.

To conclude our discussion let us elucidate two aspects. First, by modified ML estimators we mean the following. The maximum likelihood (ML) estimators are obtained by (iteratively) solving the equations (9.7a) and (9.7b). If, however, we replace the quantities x^{**}_{t-s} by

y_{t-s}^* then, in fact, we lighten the computational burden without losing consistency. Indeed, in view of the assumptions we make concerning the error term, the quantities y_{t-s}^* are not correlated with the error term and thus the estimators obtained (by iteration) from

$$\begin{bmatrix} X^{*\prime}X^* & X^{*\prime}Y^* \\ Y^{*\prime}X^* & Y^{*\prime}Y^* \end{bmatrix} d = \bar{c}^* \qquad (9.27)$$

where X^*, Y^* are as defined in (9.8) and

$$\bar{c}^* = (\bar{c}_j^*) \qquad \bar{c}_j^* = \sum_{t=\mu+\nu+1}^{T} y_t^* x_{t-j}^* \qquad j = 0, 1, 2, \ldots, \mu$$

$$= \sum_{t=\mu+\nu+1}^{T} y_t^* y_{t+\mu-j}^* \qquad j = \mu+1, \mu+2, \ldots, \mu+\nu,$$

(9.27a)

have an interpretation as instrumental variable estimators.[3] The advantage of making calculations with y_{t-s}^* instead of x_{t-s}^{**} is that the moment matrices of unknown coefficients (see equation (9.27)) are for each iteration symmetric and positive definite.

Second, we may obtain initial consistent estimators by an obvious extension of Liviatan-type methods or by using as initial instruments a suitable number of the principal components of *a set of lags in the independent variables*. This will have the effect of ameliorating the multicollinearity problems that are induced by using as instruments successive lags of the independent variable as Liviatan's method would suggest.

REFERENCES

[1] T. Amemiya and W. Fuller, 'A comparative study of alternative estimators in a distributed lag model,' *Econometrica*, XXXV, July–October (1967), 509–29.
[2] P. J. Dhrymes, 'Efficient estimation of distributed lags with autocorrelated error,' *International Economic Review*, X, February (1969), 41–67.
[3] P. J. Dhrymes, 'Estimation of the general rational lag structure by spectral techniques,' Discussion Paper No. 35, Department of Economics, University of Pennsylvania.
[4] P. J. Dhrymes, 'On the treatment of certain recurrent nonlinearities in regression analysis,' *Southern Economic Journal*, XXXII, October (1966), 187–96.
[5] E. J. Hannan, 'The estimation of relationships involving distributed lags,' *Econometrica*, XXXIII, January (1965), 206–24.
[6] V. S. Huzurbazar, 'The likelihood function, consistency and the maxima of the likelihood functions,' *Annals of Eugenics*, XIV (1948), 185.

[3] It should, of course, be noted that this is a less efficient estimator than the M.L. one.

- [7] D. W. Jorgenson, 'Rational distributed lag functions,' *Econometrica*, XXXIV, January (1966), 135–49.
- [8] L. R. Klein, 'The estimation of distributed lags,' *Econometrica*, XXVI, October (1958), 553–65.
- [9] L. M. Koyck, *Distributed Lags and Investment Analysis*, North-Holland Publishing Company, Amsterdam (1954).
- [10] N. Liviatan, 'Consistent estimation of distributed lags,' *International Economic Review*, IV, January (1963), 44–52.
- [11] E. Malinvaud, 'The estimation of distributed lags: A comment,' *Econometrica*, XXIX, July (1961), 430–3.
- [12] J. L. Morrison, 'Small sample properties of selected distributed lag estimators: A Monte Carlo experiment,' *International Economic Review*, IX, February (1970), 13–32.
- [13] K. Steiglitz and L. E. McBride, 'A technique for the identification of linear systems,' *IEEE Transactions on Automatic Control*, Vol. AC-10, No. 4, October (1965), 461–4.
- [14] K. Steiglitz and L. E. McBride, 'Iterative methods for systems identifcation,' Technical Report No. 15, June, 1966, Department of Electrical Engineering, Princeton University.
- [15] A. Wald, 'Note on the consistency of the maximum likelihood estimate,' *The Annals of Mathematical Statistics*, XX (1949), 595–601.

Part II
ECONOMIC THEORY

10

Macroeconomics and the Theory of Rational Behavior

THE PROBLEM

Many of the newly constructed mathematical models of economic systems, especially the business-cycle theories, are very loosely related to the behavior of individual households or firms which must form the basis of all theories of economic behavior. In these mathematical models, the demand equations for factors of production in the economy as a whole are derived from the assumption that entrepreneurs collectively attempt to maximize some aggregate profit; whereas the usually accepted assumption is that the individual firm attempts to maximize its own profit. For example Evans,[2] Keynes,[3] Hicks,[4] and Pigou[5] all have in their systems marginal-productivity (i.e. profit-maximizing) equations for the total economy or for some very large subsections such as the consumer-goods or producer-goods industries. These marginal-productivity equations are written, without justification, for the economy as a whole, in exactly the same form as the marginal-productivity equations for a single firm producing a single commodity. These aggregative theories have often been criticized on the grounds that they mislead us by taking attention away from basic individual behavior. The problem of bridging the gap between the traditional theories based on individual behavior and the theories based on community or class behavior is, to a large extent, a problem of proper measurement. This paper attempts to make a very modest contribution towards the formulation and solution of the problem.[1]

[1] Cowles Commission Papers, New Series, No. 14. Part of the work on this paper was done under a fellowship of the Social Science Research Council. The author is indebted to other members of the Cowles Commission staff for constructive criticism.
[2] 'Maximum production studies in a simplified economic system,' *Econometrica*, **2**, January (1934), 37–50.
[3] *The General Theory of Employment, Interest and Money*, Harcourt Brace, New York (1936).
[4] 'Mr. Keynes and the "Classics": A Suggested Interpretation,' *Econometrica*, **5**, April (1937), 147–59.
[5] *Employment and Equilibrium*, Macmillan, London (1941).

We have a body of theory which develops the economic behavior of individual households and firms. We also have many index numbers compiled according to definite formulas from individual observations. If we consider the index numbers as transformations of the variables that appear in the behavior equations of microeconomics, there possibly exists a definite set of relations among the index numbers which we may call our model of macroeconomics. But for most of the common index numbers, it is very difficult to determine whether a well-defined macrosystem follows from our theories of microeconomics. Consequently we may be forced to attempt to solve our problem in another way. Instead of assuming the theory of microeconomics and the index numbers, let us assume the theory of micro- and of macroeconomics, and then construct aggregates (usually in the form of index numbers) which are consistent with the two theories.

All too often, index-number theorists have devised arbitrary and even mutually inconsistent criteria which are imposed upon the construction of index numbers. We can well begin by setting down objective criteria of properly constructed economic aggregates which are consistent with the practices and aims of business-cycle theory. The general economic system is composed of equations relating to the behavior of households, firms, and interactions in the market between households and firms. We shall give detailed consideration in this paper only to those equations relating to the behavior of firms. Many of the propositions can be easily carried over to the equations of household behavior.

TWO CRITERIA FOR AGGREGATES

Our first criterion that an aggregate must satisfy is that: *If there exist functional relations that connect output and input (production functions) for the individual firm, there should also exist functional relations that connect aggregate output and aggregate input for the economy as a whole or an appropriate subsection.* For example, we have for the firm, in microeconomics,

$$F_\alpha(x_{1\alpha},\ldots,x_{m\alpha};n_{1\alpha},\ldots,n_{r\alpha};z_{1\alpha},\ldots,z_{s\alpha})=0 \qquad \alpha=1,2,\ldots,A. \quad (10.1)$$

This relation states that the αth firm produces the m commodities $\{x_{i\alpha}\}$ through the input of the services of r kinds of labor $\{n_{i\alpha}\}$ and of s kinds of capital $\{z_{i\alpha}\}$. We demand now that there exist a function, in macroeconomics,

$$F(X, N, Z) = 0 \qquad (10.2)$$

which states that the entire community of firms produces the aggregate output X through the input of the services of labor N and of capital Z.

A second criterion that we shall impose upon our aggregates is the following: *If profits are maximized by the individual firms so that the marginal-productivity equations,*

$$\frac{\partial x_{i\alpha}}{\partial n_{j\alpha}} = \frac{w_j}{p_i} \qquad i = 1, 2, \ldots, m;\ j = 1, 2, \ldots, r;\ \alpha = 1, 2, \ldots, A,$$

$$\frac{\partial x_{i\alpha}}{\partial z_{j\alpha}} = \frac{q_j}{p_i} \qquad i = 1, 2, \ldots, m;\ j = 1, 2, \ldots, s;\ \alpha = 1, 2, \ldots, A, \qquad (10.3)$$

hold under perfect competition, then the aggregative marginal-productivity equations,

$$\frac{\partial X}{\partial N} = \frac{W}{P},$$

$$\frac{\partial X}{\partial Z} = \frac{Q}{P}, \qquad (10.4)$$

must also hold,

where

w_j = the wage of the jth type of labor,
p_i = the price of the ith commodity,
q_j = the price of the jth type of capital service,
W = the wage aggregate,
P = the output-price aggregate and
Q = the capital-service-price aggregate.

Obviously the second criterion cannot be satisfied without the first.

These criteria imply that we derive our macrosystem of N commodities and M factors as though we were writing down the equations for a hypothetical microsystem of N commodities and M factors. Particular interest is attached to the case where $N = 1$ and $M = 2$.

A theory based on the second criterion alone has been studied extensively by Dresch[6] and has also been treated by Hicks[7] and

---

[6]'Index numbers and the general economic equilibrium,' *Bulletin of the American Mathematical Society*, **44**, February (1938), 134–41.

[7]*Value and Capital*, Clarendon Press, Oxford (1939), p. 312.

Lange.[8] Hicks has shown that the 'fundamental equation of value theory' (Slutsky equation) remains formally invariant if we lump together (treat as one good) any group of goods whose prices change all in the same proportion. This is clearly a sufficient condition for the solution of the aggregate problem, but it may not be the most satisfactory condition to impose because most prices do not change in the same proportion.

THE ATTEMPT OF FRANCIS DRESCH

Dresch,[9] in a suggestive article, has attempted to show that all the necessary conditions for maximum profits in the case of firm behavior hold in analogy for the economy as a whole if the macrovariables are properly defined in terms of the microvariables. Dresch's properly defined variables are Divisia[10] index numbers in every case. We shall show below that Dresch's aggregates do not satisfy our criteria.

We can best discuss the Dresch theory in a simple case of competitive firms making one product each. Let the production function for the αth good produced by the αth firm be

$$x_\alpha = f_\alpha(n_{1\alpha}, \ldots, n_{r\alpha}; z_{1\alpha}, \ldots, z_{s\alpha}) \qquad \alpha = 1, 2, \ldots, A. \tag{10.5}$$

Profit maximization under perfect competition leads to the necessary conditions

$$\frac{\partial x_\alpha}{\partial n_{i\alpha}} = \frac{w_i}{p_\alpha}, \qquad i = 1, 2, \ldots, r; \ \alpha = 1, 2, \ldots, A, \tag{10.6}$$

$$\frac{\partial x_\alpha}{\partial z_{i\alpha}} = \frac{q_i}{p_\alpha} \qquad i = 1, 2, \ldots, s; \ \alpha = 1, 2, \ldots, A, \tag{10.7}$$

where

w_i = the wage rate paid to the ith type of labor,
p_α = the price of the αth good,
q_i = the cost of the services of the ith type of capital.

The Divisia index of total output, X, is defined by the differential equation

$$dX = \frac{X}{V_x} \sum_{\alpha=1}^{A} p_\alpha dx_\alpha; \qquad V_x \equiv \sum_{\alpha=1}^{A} p_\alpha x_\alpha. \tag{10.8}$$

---

[8] *Price Flexibility and Employment*, Cowles Commission Monograph No. 8, Principia Press, Bloomington, Indiana (1944), pp. 103–6.

[9] F. W. Dresch, 'Index Numbers'.

[10] F. Divisia, *Economique Rationnelle*, Doin, Paris (1928), pp. 265–80.

But from the production function (10.5) we obtain

$$dx_\alpha = \sum_{i=1}^{r} \frac{\partial f_\alpha}{\partial n_{i\alpha}} dn_{i\alpha}, \tag{10.9}$$

if all $dz_{i\alpha}=0$, i.e. if we consider variations in output when labor alone varies and capital services of all types are held constant. Hence on substitution of (10.9) into (10.8) we get

$$(dX)_N = \frac{X}{V_x} \sum_{\alpha=1}^{A} \sum_{i=1}^{r} p_\alpha \frac{\partial f_\alpha}{\partial n_{i\alpha}} dn_{i\alpha}, \tag{10.10}$$

where $(dX)_N$ is defined as the change in total output when labor alone varies. Similarly the Divisia definition of the labor index is obtained from the differential equation

$$dN = \frac{N}{V_N} \sum_{\alpha=1}^{A} \sum_{i=1}^{r} w_i \, dn_{i\alpha}; \qquad V_N \equiv \sum_{\alpha=1}^{A} \sum_{i=1}^{r} w_i n_{i\alpha}. \tag{10.11}$$

The definition of marginal productivity is now taken to be the ratio $(dX)_N/dN$ or

$$\frac{(dX)_N}{dN} = \frac{(X/V_X) \sum_{\alpha=1}^{A} \sum_{i=1}^{r} p_\alpha (\partial f_\alpha/\partial n_{i\alpha}) \, dn_{i\alpha}}{(N/V_N) \sum_{\alpha=1}^{A} \sum_{i=1}^{r} w_i \, dn_{i\alpha}}. \tag{10.12}$$

But if we substitute the equilibrium conditions for profit maximization (10.6) we obtain

$$\frac{(dX)_N}{dN} = \frac{(X/V_X) \sum_{\alpha=1}^{A} \sum_{i=1}^{r} p_\alpha (w_i/p_\alpha) \, dn_{i\alpha}}{(N/V_N) \sum_{\alpha=1}^{A} \sum_{i=1}^{r} w_i \, dn_{i\alpha}} = \frac{V_N/N}{V_X/X}. \tag{10.13}$$

The ratio V_N/N represents the wage bill deflated by an employment index and can be called the average wage rate, an aggregate. Also V_X/X represents the value of output deflated by an output index, and can be called the price aggregate. Thus the proposition that the marginal productivity of labor equals the real wage rate in equilibrium holds in analogy for the macrosystem if the corresponding proposition holds for the microsystem. By a parallel procedure it follows that

$$\frac{(dX)_Z}{dZ} = \frac{V_Z/Z}{V_X/X}. \tag{10.14}$$

It is also true that this technique can be extended to the theory of consumer behavior except for the fact that the aggregations can only be taken over groups of commodities and not over individuals because of the difficulties of interpersonal comparisons of utility.

What is the meaning of the ratio $(dX)_N/dN$? Can this ratio properly be defined as marginal productivity, $\partial X/\partial N$? If such a partial derivative is to have meaning, then there must exist a differentiable aggregate production function, from which we can derive the marginal productivity for the economy as a whole or for some subsection of the economy.

This means that our first criterion must be satisfied. Formally, if there exists a set of production functions referring to the individual firms,

$$x_\alpha = f_\alpha(n_{1\alpha},\ldots,n_{r\alpha}; z_{1\alpha},\ldots,z_{s\alpha}) \qquad \alpha = 1, 2, \ldots, A, \tag{10.5}$$

with well-defined partial derivatives

$$\frac{\partial f_\alpha}{\partial n_{i\alpha}} \qquad i = 1, 2, \ldots, r;\ \alpha = 1, 2, \ldots, A,$$

$$\frac{\partial f_\alpha}{\partial z_{i\alpha}} \qquad i = 1, 2, \ldots, s;\ \alpha = 1, 2, \ldots, A,$$

then the criterion requires that there must also exist a function

$$X = f^*(N, Z) \tag{10.15}$$

with well-defined partial derivatives

$$\frac{\partial f^*}{\partial N},\quad \frac{\partial f^*}{\partial Z}.$$

It is by no means evident that an acceptable production function measured in terms of Divisia indexes exists; furthermore it is not evident that, if such a production function does exist, it has a partial derivative equal to $(dX)_N/dN$ as calculated above.

A precise statement of the conditions under which an aggregate production function exists can be made with the help of some propositions from the theory of functional dependence.[11] Let us write individual production functions, for the most general case, as

$$F_\alpha(x_{1\alpha},\ldots,x_{m\alpha}; n_{1\alpha},\ldots,n_{r\alpha}; z_{1\alpha},\ldots,z_{s\alpha}) = 0,$$

$$\alpha = 1, 2, \ldots, A. \tag{10.1}$$

---

[11] Leonid Hurwicz was very helpful in formulating the proposition to follow.

Macroeconomics and rational behavior

If these production functions are sufficiently well-behaved, as is generally assumed, we can rewrite them as

$$x_{1\alpha} = f_\alpha(x_{2\alpha},\ldots,x_{m\alpha}; n_{1\alpha},\ldots,n_{r\alpha}; z_{1\alpha},\ldots,z_{s\alpha}),$$

$$\alpha = 1, 2, \ldots, A. \quad (10.16)$$

We shall now define our aggregate as

$$X = G(x_{11},\ldots,x_{m1},\ldots,x_{1A},\ldots,x_{mA}), \quad (10.17)$$

$$N = H(n_{11},\ldots,n_{r1},\ldots,n_{1A},\ldots,n_{rA}), \quad (10.18)$$

$$Z = I(z_{11},\ldots,z_{s1},\ldots,z_{1A},\ldots,z_{sA}). \quad (10.19)$$

The definitions of the output, labor and capital aggregates define three transformation functions sending the variables $\{x_{i\alpha}\}$, $\{n_{i\alpha}\}$, and $\{z_{i\alpha}\}$ into X, N, Z, subject to the restraints of the production functions.

It is well known that the transformed variables are functionally related, uniquely, by a relation

$$\Phi(X, N, Z) = 0 \quad (10.20)$$

if the following rectangular matrix is of rank 2:

$$\left\| \begin{array}{ccc} \left[\dfrac{\partial G}{\partial x_{1\alpha}} \dfrac{\partial x_{1\alpha}}{\partial x_{i\alpha}} + \dfrac{\partial G}{\partial x_{i\alpha}}\right] & 0 & 0 \\[2ex] \left[\dfrac{\partial G}{\partial x_{1\alpha}} \dfrac{\partial x_{1\alpha}}{\partial n_{i\alpha}}\right] & \left[\dfrac{\partial H}{\partial n_{i\alpha}}\right] & 0 \\[2ex] \left[\dfrac{\partial G}{\partial x_{1\alpha}} \dfrac{\partial x_{1\alpha}}{\partial z_{i\alpha}}\right] & 0 & \left[\dfrac{\partial I}{\partial z_{i\alpha}}\right] \end{array} \right\|.$$

Each of the elements of this matrix are column vectors, the vectors of the first row having $(m-1)A$ elements ($i=2,3,\ldots,m$; $\alpha=1,2,\ldots,A$), the vectors of the second row having rA elements ($i=1,2,\ldots,r$; $\alpha=1,2,\ldots,A$), and the vectors of the third row having sA elements ($i=1,2,\ldots,s$; $\alpha=1,2,\ldots,A$).

The conditions that all third-order determinants vanish, *identically*, where $\partial H/\partial n_{i\alpha}$ and $\partial I/\partial z_{i\alpha}$ are not all zero, are

$$\frac{\partial x_{1\alpha}}{\partial x_{i\alpha}} \equiv -\frac{\partial G/\partial x_{i\alpha}}{\partial G/\partial x_{1\alpha}} \qquad i=2,\ldots,m;\ \alpha=1,2,\ldots,A, \quad (10.21)$$

$$\frac{\partial x_{1\alpha}/\partial n_{i\alpha}}{\partial x_{1\beta}/\partial n_{j\beta}} \equiv \left(\frac{\partial H/\partial n_{i\alpha}}{\partial H/\partial n_{j\beta}}\right)\left(\frac{\partial G/\partial x_{1\beta}}{\partial G/\partial x_{1\alpha}}\right)$$

$$i=1,2,\ldots,r;\ j=1,2,\ldots,r;\ \alpha=1,2,\ldots,A;\ \beta=1,2,\ldots,A, \quad (10.22)$$

$$\frac{\partial x_{1\alpha}/\partial z_{i\alpha}}{\partial x_{1\beta}/\partial z_{j\beta}} \equiv \left(\frac{\partial I/\partial z_{i\alpha}}{\partial I/\partial z_{j\beta}}\right)\left(\frac{\partial G/\partial x_{1\beta}}{\partial G/\partial x_{1\alpha}}\right)$$

$$i=1,2,\ldots,s;\ j=1,2,\ldots,s;\ \alpha=1,2,\ldots,A;\ \beta=1,2,\ldots,A. \qquad 10.23)$$

The choice of the aggregative functions G, H, and I must be such as to satisfy these identical relationships. The relationships state in a loose sense that marginal rates of substitution among variables of the aggregative functions must be the same as the marginal rates of substitution among the variables of the production function. It seems clear from these conditions that there must be some similarities in form between the basic production functions and the aggregative functions. It will be necessary to have some specifications, in any case, on the individual functions in order to know how to construct the aggregates so as to satisfy the theorem on functional dependence.

The conditions (10.21), (10.22) and (10.23) give us an exact judgment as to the desirability of any particular type of aggregation. For example, there may be considered the special case in which the different types of output and of factors are of the same dimensionality. Then we may be led to believe that simple summation is the natural type of aggregation. We would have

$$X = \sum_{\alpha=1}^{A}\sum_{i=1}^{m} x_{i\alpha}, \qquad (10.17a)$$

$$N = \sum_{\alpha=1}^{A}\sum_{i=1}^{r} n_{i\alpha}, \qquad (10.18a)$$

$$Z = \sum_{\alpha=1}^{A}\sum_{i=1}^{s} z_{i\alpha}, \qquad (10.19a)$$

and (10.21), (10.22) and (10.23) would become

$$\frac{\partial x_{1\alpha}}{\partial x_{i\alpha}} \equiv -1 \qquad i=1,2,\ldots,m;\ \alpha=1,2,\ldots,A,$$

$$\frac{\partial x_{1\alpha}}{\partial n_{i\alpha}} \equiv \frac{\partial x_{1\beta}}{\partial n_{j\beta}}, \qquad \begin{aligned}&i=1,2,\ldots,r;\ j=1,2,\ldots,r;\\ &\alpha=1,2,\ldots,A,\ \beta=1,2,\ldots,A,\end{aligned}$$

$$\frac{\partial x_{1\alpha}}{\partial z_{i\alpha}} \equiv \frac{\partial x_{1\beta}}{\partial z_{j\beta}}, \qquad \begin{aligned}&i=1,2,\ldots,s;\ j=1,2,\ldots,s;\\ &\alpha=1,2,\ldots,A;\ \beta=1,2,\ldots,A.\end{aligned}$$

This seemingly obvious type of aggregation would thus be suitable only if the marginal productivity of any type of labor (capital) in any firm were *identically* the same as the marginal productivity of any other type of labor (capital) in any firm. The restriction can be somewhat reshaped if the sums in (10.17a), (10.18a), and (10.19a) are changed to linear combinations. Then the marginal productivities need not be equal, but merely proportional.

It should be remarked that the functions G, H, I were made to depend only upon the physical quantities $\{x_{i\alpha}\}$, $\{n_{i\alpha}\}$, $\{z_{i\alpha}\}$. Most index numbers are constructed so that quantity indexes depend upon prices as weights, as well as upon quantities. We might construct our transformations as follows:

$$X = \frac{\sum_{\alpha=1}^{A} \sum_{i=1}^{m} p_i x_{i\alpha}}{\left(\sum_{\alpha=1}^{A} \sum_{i=1}^{m} p_i^0 x_{i\alpha}\right) / \left(\sum_{\alpha=1}^{A} \sum_{i=1}^{m} p_i^0 x_{i\alpha}^0\right)}, \tag{10.17b}$$

$$N = \frac{\sum_{\alpha=1}^{A} \sum_{i=1}^{r} w_i n_{i\alpha}}{\left(\sum_{\alpha=1}^{A} \sum_{i=1}^{r} w_i n_{i\alpha}^0\right) / \left(\sum_{\alpha=1}^{A} \sum_{i=1}^{r} w_i^0 n_{i\alpha}^0\right)}, \tag{10.18b}$$

$$Z = \frac{\sum_{\alpha=1}^{A} \sum_{i=1}^{s} q_i z_{i\alpha}}{\left(\sum_{\alpha=1}^{A} \sum_{i=1}^{s} q_i z_{i\alpha}^0\right) / \left(\sum_{\alpha=1}^{A} \sum_{i=1}^{s} q_i^0 z_{i\alpha}^0\right)}. \tag{10.19b}$$

The aggregates (10.17b), (10.18b) and (10.19b) are all value aggregates deflated by fixed-base price indexes.

By differentiating (10.17b), we find

$$-\frac{\partial X / \partial x_{i\alpha}}{\partial X / \partial x_{1\alpha}} \equiv -p_i / p_1. \tag{10.24}$$

This relation holds identically because of the definition of the aggregative function. It is also true that

$$\frac{\partial x_{1\alpha}}{\partial x_{i\alpha}} = -\frac{p_i}{p_1}, \tag{10.25}$$

but this relation does *not* hold identically; it holds only for the equilibrium conditions under profit maximization. It is not a relation that depends solely upon technological possibilities of substitution via the production function. Hence condition (10.21) is not *identically* satisfied for a very common type of index number. The same is true of (10.22) and (10.23).

It needs to be further pointed out that the inclusion of prices and wages as variables in the aggregation functions, G, H, and I complicates the functional matrix by the addition of more rows provided it is desired to find a relation

$$\Phi(X, N, Z) = 0 \tag{10.20}$$

that does not depend explicitly on the individual prices and wages. The simple addition of more rows, however, will have no influence on the previously stated conditions (10.21), (10.22), (10.23) that the matrix be of rank 2. These conditions become necessary but not sufficient in this case.

It can be seen from this discussion that the use of some very common types of index numbers is not justified on the basis of the criteria which have been stated at the outset.

The Divisia-type indexes which Dresch has employed are not covered by the functions G, H, and I above because these functions are ordinary point functions, while it is well known that the Divisia indexes are line integrals, i.e. functionals. They depend upon the entire paths of prices and quantities rather than merely upon point values. An investigation of the conditions under which a functional relation exists among X, N, Z when they are defined by functionals as opposed to point functions is more complicated. But it happens in that case also, that the appropriate determinants do not vanish identically. Dresch's theory has intuitive significance, but fails to satisfy both of the criteria put forth at the beginning of this paper.

A SUGGESTION

An alternative approach that retains the same goals can now be shown in an example. This approach is not general or unique but holds for a class of production functions that are very significant. By specifying, more closely, the shape of the production functions, we can derive a satisfactory explanation of the meaning of an aggregative production function.

Let

$$x_\alpha = B_\alpha f_\alpha(n_{1\alpha}, \ldots, n_{r\alpha}) g_\alpha(z_{1\alpha}, \ldots, z_{s\alpha}) \qquad \alpha = 1, 2, \ldots, A, \tag{10.26}$$

be the production function for the αth firm. A special case of this function is the logical extension of the Cobb-Douglas type function

$$x_\alpha = C_\alpha \prod_{i=1}^{r} n_{i\alpha}^{a_i} \prod_{i=1}^{s} z_{i\alpha}^{b_i}. \tag{10.26a}$$

Our requirement is that the production function partition into a product of a labor function and a capital function. We also attribute a single output variable to each but this is done for simplicity; it is not essential.

The transformations[12] will be defined according to

$$X = \left[\prod_{\alpha=1}^{A} x_\alpha \right]^{1/A}, \tag{10.27}$$

$$N^a = \left[\prod_{\alpha=1}^{A} f_\alpha(n_{1\alpha}, \ldots, n_{r\alpha}) \right]^{1/A}, \tag{10.28}$$

$$Z^b = \left[\prod_{\alpha=1}^{A} g_\alpha(z_{1\alpha}, \ldots, z_{s\alpha}) \right]^{1/A}, \tag{10.29}$$

$$X = DN^a Z^b. \tag{10.30}$$

The first criterion is satisfied because the aggregate production (10.30) does exist in explicit form. In order to apply the second criterion, we distinguish between two cases.

Case I: a and b, the elasticities of output, are constants. If p_α is the price of the αth good, w_i is the wage rate paid to the ith type of labor, and q_i is the cost of the ith type of capital services, then we define

$$P = \frac{\sum_{\alpha=1}^{A} p_\alpha x_\alpha}{AX}, \tag{10.31}$$

$$W = \frac{\sum_{\alpha=1}^{A} \sum_{i=1}^{r} w_i n_{i\alpha}}{AN}, \tag{10.32}$$

$$Q = \frac{\sum_{\alpha=1}^{A} \sum_{i=1}^{s} q_i z_{i\alpha}}{AZ}, \tag{10.33}$$

[12] In this discussion, the macrovariables are averages, but the entire analysis also follows if the averages are changed to aggregates. We use averages in order that the macrovariable be made less sensitive to variations in the output or input of a single firm. It should also be pointed out that firms with zero output are excluded; otherwise the entire aggregate would vanish if a single term vanished.

as the corresponding aggregates for average price of output, average wage, and average price of capital. These definitions lead by simple division to

$$\frac{W}{P} = \frac{X}{N} \frac{\sum_{\alpha=1}^{A} \sum_{i=1}^{r} w_i n_{i\alpha}}{\sum_{\alpha=1}^{A} p_\alpha x_\alpha}, \tag{10.34}$$

$$\frac{Q}{P} = \frac{X}{Z} \frac{\sum_{\alpha=1}^{A} \sum_{i=1}^{s} q_i z_{i\alpha}}{\sum_{\alpha=1}^{A} p_\alpha x_\alpha}. \tag{10.35}$$

Also by differentiation of the aggregate production functions, we get

$$\frac{\partial X}{\partial N} = a \frac{X}{N}, \tag{10.36}$$

$$\frac{\partial X}{\partial Z} = b \frac{X}{Z}. \tag{10.37}$$

Combining (10.34), (10.35), (10.36) and (10.37), we have

$$\frac{\partial X}{\partial N} = \frac{W}{P} \left\{ a \frac{\sum_{\alpha=1}^{A} p_\alpha x_\alpha}{\sum_{\alpha=1}^{A} \sum_{i=1}^{r} w_i n_{i\alpha}} \right\}, \tag{10.38}$$

$$\frac{\partial X}{\partial Z} = \frac{Q}{P} \left\{ b \frac{\sum_{\alpha=1}^{A} p_\alpha x_\alpha}{\sum_{\alpha=1}^{A} \sum_{i=1}^{s} q_i z_{i\alpha}} \right\}. \tag{10.39}$$

The aggregative marginal productivities are not in general equal to W/P or Q/P, but they will be when

$$a = \frac{\sum_{\alpha=1}^{A} \sum_{i=1}^{r} w_i n_{i\alpha}}{\sum_{\alpha=1}^{A} p_\alpha x_\alpha}, \tag{10.40}$$

$$b = \frac{\sum_{\alpha=1}^{A} \sum_{i=1}^{s} q_i z_{i\alpha}}{\sum_{\alpha=1}^{A} p_\alpha x_\alpha}. \tag{10.41}$$

Macroeconomics and rational behavior   191

Equations (10.40) and (10.41) are to be considered as equilibrium conditions for the macrosystem. The constant elasticities, a and b, are to be chosen as the average values over the time path of the *observed* ratios

$$\frac{\sum_{\alpha=1}^{A} \sum_{i=1}^{r} w_i n_{i\alpha}}{\sum_{\alpha=1}^{A} p_\alpha x_\alpha}$$

and

$$\frac{\sum_{\alpha=1}^{A} \sum_{i=1}^{s} q_i z_{i\alpha}}{\sum_{\alpha=1}^{A} p_\alpha x_\alpha}$$

respectively. The observed values of labor's share and capital's share will fluctuate about the average or equilibrium values and, therefore, cause $\partial X/\partial N$ and $\partial X/\partial Z$ in (10.38) and (10.39) to deviate from their equilibrium values W/P and Q/P. The macroequations for the firm will assume their equilibrium forms only when labor's share and capital's are at their equilibrium values.

Our equilibrium system, in abbreviated form, is then

$$X = DN^a Z^b, \qquad (10.30)$$

$$\frac{\partial X}{\partial N} = \frac{W}{P}, \qquad (10.42)$$

$$\frac{\partial X}{\partial Z} = \frac{Q}{P}. \qquad (10.43)$$

This is a complete analogue of the equilibrium system of microeconomics.

Case II: a and b, the output elasticities, are not constant.
Define

$$a_{i\alpha} = \frac{n_{i\alpha}}{x_\alpha} \frac{\partial x_\alpha}{\partial n_{i\alpha}}, \qquad i=1,2,\ldots,r;\ \alpha=1,2,\ldots,A,$$

$$b_{i\alpha} = \frac{z_{i\alpha}}{x_\alpha} \frac{\partial x_\alpha}{\partial z_{i\alpha}}, \qquad i=1,2,\ldots,s;\ \alpha=1,2,\ldots,A.$$

In addition to the transformation equations (10.27), (10.28) and (10.29), we also have

$$a = \frac{\sum_{\alpha=1}^{A} \sum_{i=1}^{r} a_{i\alpha} p_\alpha x_\alpha}{\sum_{\alpha=1}^{A} p_\alpha x_\alpha}, \tag{10.44}$$

$$b = \frac{\sum_{\alpha=1}^{A} \sum_{i=1}^{s} b_{i\alpha} p_\alpha x_\alpha}{\sum_{\alpha=1}^{A} p_\alpha x_\alpha}. \tag{10.45}$$

According to (10.44) and (10.45), the elasticities of output for the aggregative system are weighted averages of the elasticities of the individual firms. We retain the same definitions of P, W, Q given in (10.31), (10.32), and (10.33); consequently (10.38) and (10.39) still hold. We now propose to show that the equilibrium conditions (10.40) and (10.41) are true profit-maximizing conditions which hold whenever profits are at a maximum for each individual firm. In the microsystem, we have for equilibrium,

$$\frac{\partial x_\alpha}{\partial n_{i\alpha}} = \frac{w_i}{p_\alpha}, \qquad i = 1, 2, \ldots, r; \; \alpha = 1, 2, \ldots, A, \tag{10.6}$$

$$\frac{\partial x_\alpha}{\partial z_{i\alpha}} = \frac{q_i}{p_\alpha}, \qquad i = 1, 2, \ldots, s; \; \alpha = 1, 2, \ldots, A. \tag{10.7}$$

Then, on substituting the definitions of $a_{i\alpha}$ and $b_{i\alpha}$ into (10.6) and (10.7), we get

$$a_{i\alpha} = \frac{w_i n_{i\alpha}}{p_\alpha x_\alpha}, \tag{10.46}$$

$$b_{i\alpha} = \frac{q_i z_{i\alpha}}{p_\alpha x_\alpha}. \tag{10.47}$$

Summing over the i subscript in each case and then over the α subscript, we get

$$\sum_{\alpha=1}^{A} \sum_{i=1}^{r} a_{i\alpha} p_\alpha x_\alpha = \sum_{\alpha=1}^{A} \sum_{i=1}^{r} w_i n_{i\alpha}, \tag{10.48}$$

$$\sum_{\alpha=1}^{A} \sum_{i=1}^{s} b_{i\alpha} p_\alpha x_\alpha = \sum_{\alpha=1}^{A} \sum_{i=1}^{s} q_i z_{i\alpha}. \tag{10.49}$$

Macroeconomics and rational behavior 193

Divide both sides of (10.48) and (10.49) by $\sum_{\alpha=1}^{A} p_\alpha x_\alpha$ to get our previously stated equilibrium conditions,

$$a = \frac{\sum_{\alpha=1}^{A} \sum_{i=1}^{r} a_{i\alpha} p_\alpha x_\alpha}{\sum_{\alpha=1}^{A} p_\alpha x_\alpha} = \frac{\sum_{\alpha=1}^{A} \sum_{i=1}^{r} w_i n_{i\alpha}}{\sum_{\alpha=1}^{A} p_\alpha x_\alpha}, \qquad (10.40)$$

$$b = \frac{\sum_{\alpha=1}^{A} \sum_{i=1}^{r} b_{i\alpha} p_\alpha x_\alpha}{\sum_{\alpha=1}^{A} p_\alpha x_\alpha} = \frac{\sum_{\alpha=1}^{A} \sum_{i=1}^{s} q_i z_{i\alpha}}{\sum_{\alpha=1}^{A} p_\alpha x_\alpha}. \qquad (10.41)$$

The abbreviated equilibrium system, (10.30), (10.42) and (10.43), holds as before in Case I.

In the formulations above, a and b are like elasticities in that they are invariant under a change of units. But the quantity aggregates, X, N, Z, like any physical variable of economics, depend upon the choice of units.

If the functions f_α and g_α are known explicitly, then it is possible to show the precise manner in which the aggregates should be calculated. For example if

$$N^a = \left(\prod_{\alpha=1}^{A} f_\alpha \right)^{1/A} = \left(\prod_{\alpha=1}^{A} \prod_{i=1}^{r} n_{i\alpha}^{a_i} \right)^{1/A}, \qquad (10.28a)$$

$$Z^b = \left(\prod_{\alpha=1}^{A} g_\alpha \right)^{1/A} = \left(\prod_{\alpha=1}^{A} \prod_{i=1}^{s} z_{i\alpha}^{b_i} \right)^{1/A}, \qquad (10.29a)$$

then the logarithm of N is a linear combination of the logarithms of the various types of labor employed by the various firms, and similarly for capital.

As a practical method of procedure, we should calculate functions of the type (10.26a) for a large sample of cases. From the sample, calculate weighted geometric means of output, labor, and capital and weighted arithmetic means of the elasticities of output of labor and of capital. Knowing these averages and the numbers of firms, products, and factors, we can get good approximations of the proper aggregates. The problem of calculating the aggregates is mainly one of sampling.

The above demonstration has to be somewhat modified for the case of imperfect competition, but in any event the idea is clear for an important case. If we want to simplify mathematical models of general equilibrium into a small number of equations, it is useful to know that operationally significant concepts exist which justify such simplifications. It is only in models of macroeconomics that we can see through all the complex interrelationships of the economy in order to form intelligent judgments about such important magnitudes as aggregate employment, output, consumption, investment.

11

Remarks on the Theory of Aggregation

The contributions of Kenneth May and Shou Shan Pu,[1] presented elsewhere in this issue, raise some fundamental questions for the theory of macroeconomics. This theory is in a formative stage, and the basic objectives must be settled in order that a rigorous development may be forthcoming.

The aggregate equations of May and Pu have a very important common characteristic, namely, that they depend on the satisfaction of all the equilibrium conditions (profit maximization) in the systems. The same characteristic is found in the first formulation of index number theory in terms of rational behavior by Dresch.[2] In the theory of microeconomics, demand and supply equations are, of course, derived from these equilibrium conditions. We should expect that the aggregate demand and supply equations will also depend upon the fact that the equilibrium conditions hold. But there are certain equations in microeconomics that are independent of the equilibrium conditions and we should expect that the corresponding equations of macroeconomics will also be independent of the equilibrium conditions. The principal equations that have this independence property in microeconomics are the technological production functions. The aggregate production function should not depend upon profit maximization, but purely on technological factors.

Consider, for example, the αth individual firm producing goods $x_{1\alpha},\ldots,x_{m\alpha}$, at prices $p_1,\ldots,p_m$, using the labor input $n_{1\alpha},\ldots,n_{r\alpha}$, at wages $w_1,\ldots,w_r$, and using the capital input $z_{1\alpha},\ldots,z_{s\alpha}$ at prices

---

This paper was written during the tenure of a postdoctoral fellowship of the Social Science Research Council.

[1] Kenneth May, 'The aggregation problem for a one-industry model,' *Econometrica*, **14**, October (1946), 285–98; Shou Shan Pu, 'A note on macroeconomics,' *Econometrica*, **14**, October (1946), 299–302.

[2] Francis W. Dresch, 'Index numbers and the general economic equilibrium,' *Bulletin of the American Mathematical Society*, **44**, February (1938), 134–41.

$q_1, \ldots, q_s$. The model for this firm under perfect competition will be:

$$f_\alpha(x_{1\alpha}, \ldots, x_{m\alpha}, n_{1\alpha}, \ldots, n_{r\alpha}, z_{1\alpha}, \ldots, z_{s\alpha}) = 0$$

$$\alpha = 1, 2, \ldots, A;\ i = 1, 2, \ldots, m, \quad (11.1)$$

$$\frac{\partial x_{i\alpha}}{\partial n_{j\alpha}} = \frac{w_j}{p_i} \quad j = 1, 2, \ldots, r;\ \alpha = 1, 2, \ldots, A;\ i = 1, 2, \ldots, m, \quad (11.2)$$

$$\frac{\partial x_{i\alpha}}{\partial z_{j\alpha}} = \frac{q_j}{p_i} \quad j = 1, 2, \ldots, s;\ \alpha = 1, 2, \ldots, A. \quad (11.3)$$

Equation (11.1) is the production function and (11.2) and (11.3) are the marginal-productivity or profit-maximizing equations. In the system (11.1)–(11.3) there are $m + r + s$ independent equations for each firm,[3] involving $2(m + r + s)$ variables $\{x_{i\alpha}\}, \{n_{i\alpha}\}, \{z_{i\alpha}\}, \{p_i\}, \{w_i\}, \{q_i\}$. We can solve this system for each of the $x_{i\alpha}, n_{i\alpha}$, and $z_{i\alpha}$ in terms of the p_i, w_i, and q_i to get

$$x_{i\alpha} = x_{i\alpha}(p_1, \ldots, p_m, w_1, \ldots, w_r, q_1, \ldots, q_s)$$

$$i = 1, 2, \ldots, m;\ \alpha = 1, 2, \ldots, A, \quad (11.4)$$

$$n_{i\alpha} = n_{i\alpha}(p_1, \ldots, p_m, w_1, \ldots w_r, q_1, \ldots, q_s)$$

$$i = 1, 2, \ldots, r;\ \alpha = 1, 2, \ldots, A, \quad (11.5)$$

$$z_{i\alpha} = z_{i\alpha}(p_1, \ldots, p_m, w_1, \ldots, w_r, q_1, \ldots, q_s)$$

$$i = 1, 2, \ldots, s;\ \alpha = 1, 2, \ldots, A. \quad (11.6)$$

Equations (11.4), (11.5), (11.6) are the supply equations of output and the demand equations for input for the individual firm; they show how much of each commodity will be offered to the market and how much of each productive factor will be demanded corresponding to any price–wage situation. These equations depend upon the technological possi-

---

[3] The equations (11.2) and (11.3) can be written as

$$\lambda_\alpha \frac{\partial f_\alpha}{\partial x_{i\alpha}} + p_i = 0, \quad i = 1, 2, \ldots, m;\ \alpha = 1, 2, \ldots, A,$$

$$\lambda_\alpha \frac{\partial f_\alpha}{\partial n_{i\alpha}} - w_i = 0, \quad i = 1, 2, \ldots, r;\ \alpha = 1, 2, \ldots, A,$$

$$\lambda_\alpha \frac{\partial f_\alpha}{\partial z_{i\alpha}} - q_i = 0, \quad i = 1, 2, \ldots, s;\ \alpha = 1, 2, \ldots, A,$$

where λ_α is the Lagrange multiplier. The equations (11.2) and (11.3) of the text are obtained from these, which are $m + r + s$ in number, by eliminating the variable λ_α; hence (11.2) and (11.3) represent $m + r + s - 1$ independent equations.

Remarks on the theory of aggregation 197

bilities of production as given by (11.1) and upon economic decision as given by (11.2) and (11.3). The analogues for (11.4), (11.5), (11.6) in macroeconomics are

$$X = X(P, W, Q), \tag{11.7}$$

$$N = N(P, W, Q), \tag{11.8}$$

$$Z = Z(P, W, Q), \tag{11.9}$$

which state that aggregate supply, X, aggregate labor demanded, N, and aggregate capital demanded, Z, are functions of the price and wage aggregates P, W, Q. These equations too should depend upon economic decisions and upon technological possibilities.

But the equation (11.1) does not involve prices of products or factors. It is a purely technological phenomenon and not an economic decision.[4] The analogues of (11.1), (11.2), and (11.3) in macroeconomics are

$$F(X, N, Z) = 0, \tag{11.10}$$

$$\frac{\partial X}{\partial N} = \frac{W}{P}, \tag{11.11}$$

$$\frac{\partial X}{\partial Z} = \frac{Q}{P}. \tag{11.12}$$

If our system of macroeconomics is to be (11.10), (11.11), (11.12), the aggregates of (11.10) should be defined so that they do not depend on the equilibrium conditions in (11.2) and (11.3). On the other hand, if the business-firm side of the macroeconomic system is to be represented by (11.7), (11.8), (11.9), there is no reason to make the aggregates independent of the equilibrium conditions. The supply-demand equations are the result of a combination of technological and economic equations; consequently the aggregates should be constructed under the assumption that both types of equations hold. The decision as to what type of aggregate to construct (i.e. independent of or dependent upon the equilibrium conditions) can only be decided on the basis of the type of macroeconomic system that we want to develop. The latter decision can be made if we state our goals clearly. If our purpose is only to forecast aggregate output, we may dispense with the technological production function in the macrosystem and define our aggregates in

---

[4] It is an economic decision in the sense that less output than that shown by the production can always be obtained from any factor input. The rational entrepreneur operates with a production function that gives the maximum output corresponding to any input. However, market variables do not enter into this maximization decision. The engineer rather than the economist deals with this aspect of the production process.

terms of the supply-demand equations. An example of a system that is suitable for this purpose can easily be devised. Let us define the following variables:

X_1^S = supply of consumer goods,
X_2^S = supply of producer goods,
P_1 = price of consumer goods,
P_2 = price of producer goods,
N^S = supply of labor,
W = wage rate,
X_1^D = demand for consumer goods,
X_2^D = demand for producer goods,
N^D = demand for labor,
Y = income.

All variables are endogenous except N^S which is taken as given by demographic and other sociological forces. A model system is

$$X_1^S = X_1^S(P_1, P_2, W), \quad \text{supply of consumer goods,} \quad (11.13)$$

$$X_2^S = X_2^S(P_2, W), \quad \text{supply of producer goods,} \quad (11.14)$$

$$X_1^D = X_1^D(P_1, Y), \quad \text{demand for consumer goods,} \quad (11.15)$$

$$X_2^D = X_2^D(P_1, P_2, W), \quad \text{demand for producer goods,} \quad (11.16)$$

$$N^D = N^D(P_1, P_2, W), \quad \text{demand for labor,} \quad (11.17)$$

$$\dot{P}_1 = \dot{P}_1 \left[\int_{-\infty}^{t} \times (X_1^S - X_1^D) \, d\theta \right], \quad \text{price-adjustment equation for consumer-goods market,} \quad (11.18)$$

$$\dot{P}_2 = \dot{P}_2 \left[\int_{-\infty}^{t} \times (X_2^S - X_2^D) \, d\theta \right], \quad \text{price-adjustment equation for producer-goods market,} \quad (11.19)$$

$$\dot{W} = \dot{W}(N^S - N^D), \quad \text{wage-adjustment equation,} \quad (11.20)$$

$$Y = P_1 X_1^S + P_2 X_2^S, \quad \text{definition of income.} \quad (11.21)$$

The equation system (11.13)–(11.21) can be solved for Y, X_1^S, X_2^S, or N^D in terms of the exogenous variables and can thus be used for purposes of prediction of aggregate output or employment on the assumption that the parameters of these equations do not change. There are, however, no purely technological functions in this system; they have been, so to speak, solved out of the system. Every one of the equations in this simple system involves an economic decision or market behavior. Some are based on profit maximization, some on utility maximization, and some on market interactions. All the aggregates should account for these phenomena. The output aggregates should depend upon prices and wages via the profit-maximizing equations. The indexes of Dresch, May,[5] and Pu are appropriate for a model of this type. It should be remarked however, that the basis for the construction of their indexes must be extended to cover consumer and market behavior as well as firm behavior if they are to be used in a complete system like (11.13)–(11.21).

There is a very informative analogy in economic theory to the procedure of eliminating the production function from the equation systems. In the theory of consumer behavior, the usual practice is to start out with the utility function (or a monotonic transformation of the same), derive the utility-maximization equations, and finally solve for the demand equations in terms of prices and income. Utility never appears as a variable in the system because this variable, along with one equation, is eliminated in the process of solving for the consumer-demand equations. In a similar way the supply equations combine the production function and the profit-maximizing equations to obtain the supply equations as functions of wages and prices. The supply-demand equations hold only if the corresponding maximization equations hold; hence it is legitimate to construct the aggregates of supply and demand under the assumption that the maximization equations hold.

Let us now consider the conditions under which it is desirable to make some of the aggregates independent of the maximizing conditions. Suppose that we want to be able to forecast national product or total employment as a function of exogenous variables but also to forecast the effect upon the system of changes in fundamental parameters or controlled exogenous variables or of any other autonomous action. If the structural change in question is a change in parameters of the production function, we shall not be able to forecast the influence of the change without a knowledge of that function. To make the discussion concrete, suppose that marginal productivity of labor in the producer-goods industry changes by the amount ε. What is the influence of this change upon the system? To answer this question, we should need to work with a system like the following:

$$X_1^S = F_1(N_1^D, X_{2,1}^D, K_1, t), \quad \text{production of consumer goods,} \quad (11.22)$$

$$\frac{\partial X_1^S}{\partial N_1^D} = \frac{W}{P_1}, \quad \begin{array}{l}\text{marginal productivity of labor} \\ \text{in consumer-goods industry,}\end{array} \quad (11.23)$$

---

[5]May constructed his model so that all variables can be expressed in terms of N, aggregate employment. By similar methods, we can also express every variable in terms of price and wage aggregates like P_1, P_2, W. If we follow the latter procedure, May's macroeconomic system resembles (11.13)–(11.21) very closely.

$$\frac{\partial X_1^S}{\partial X_{2,1}^D} = \frac{P_2}{P_1},$$
marginal productivity of capital in consumer-goods industry, (11.24)

$$X_2^S = F_2(N_2^D, X_{2,2}^D, K_2, t),$$
production of producer goods, (11.25)

$$\frac{\partial X^S}{\partial N_2^D} = \frac{W}{P_2},$$
marginal productivity of labor in producer-goods industry, (11.26)

$$\frac{\partial X_2^S}{\partial X_{2,2}^D} = 1,$$
marginal productivity of capital in producer-goods industry, (11.27)

$$X_{2,1}^D + X_{2,2}^D = X_2^D,$$
definition of total demand for producer goods, (11.28)

$$N_1^D + N_2^D = N^D,$$
definition of total demand for labor, (11.29)

$$X_1^D = X_1^D(P_1, Y),$$
demand for consumer goods, (11.30)

$$\dot{P}_1 = \dot{P}_1[\int_{-\infty}^{t}(X_1^S - X_1^D)d\theta],$$
price-adjustment equation for consumer-goods market, (11.31)

$$\dot{P}_2 = \dot{P}_2[\int_{-\infty}^{t}(X_2^S - X_2^D)d\theta],$$
price-adjustment equation for producer-goods market, (11.32)

$$\dot{W} = \dot{W}(N^S - N^D),$$
wage-adjustment equation, (11.33)

$$Y = P_1 X_1^S + P_2 X_2^S,$$
definition of income, (11.34)

$$K_1 = \int_{-\infty}^{t}[X_{2,1}^D - D_1(X_{2,1}^D, K_1)]d\theta,$$
definition of stock of capital in consumer-goods industry, (11.35)

$$K_2 = \int_{-\infty}^{t}[X_{2,2}^D - D_2(X_{2,2}^D, K_2)]d\theta,$$
definition of stock of capital in producer-goods industry, (11.36)

where

N_1^D = demand for labor in consumer-goods industry,
$X_{2,1}^D$ = demand for new capital goods in consumer-goods industry,
K_1 = stock of existing capital in consumer-goods industry,
N_2^D = demand for labor in producer-goods industry,
$X_{2,2}^D$ = demand for new capital goods in producer-goods industry,
K_2 = stock of existing capital in producer-goods industry,

D_1 = depreciation of capital in consumer-goods industry,
D_2 = depreciation of capital in producer-goods industry,

and all other variables are as defined above.

If the marginal productivity of labor is to change by an amount ε through technological improvement in the producer-goods industry we should replace (11.25) and (11.26)[6] by

$$X_2^S = F_2^*(N_2^D, X_{2,2}^D, K_2, t), \qquad (11.25a)$$

such that

$$\frac{\partial F_2^*}{\partial N_2^D} = \frac{\partial F_2}{\partial N_2^D} + \varepsilon, \qquad (11.26a)$$

$$\frac{\partial F_2}{\partial N_2^D} + \varepsilon = \frac{W}{P_2}.$$

We can now compare the solutions to the equation systems under two hypotheses. One solution[7] will be for the system (11.22)–(11.36), given by

$$Y = Y(N^S, t); \qquad (11.37)$$

the other solution will be for the same system but with (11.25) and (11.26) replaced by (11.25a) and (11.26a). We shall have for this case, say,

$$Y = Y^*(N^S, t). \qquad (11.38)$$

A comparison between the properties of (11.37) and (11.38) will show the influence on the level of national income of a change in the marginal productivity of labor in the producer-goods industry.

The information about the change in productivity cannot, in general, be obtained from the system (11.13)–(11.21) where the production function has been solved out of the system and where only the supply and demand equations are used. From the system (11.22)–(11.36) we can derive the forecast equations like (11.37), and we can also appraise the results of technological changes.

The production functions of the system (11.22)–(11.36) are (11.22) and (11.25). These are meant to be purely technological functions which

---

[6] We are assuming that the marginal productivity of capital is unaffected by this change.
[7] We can solve the system for any of the endogenous variables.

show the relation between factor input and product output. When we speak of changes in productivity, as in the case above, we have in mind technological change which is independent of the economic calculations of profit maximization. These two aggregate production functions must show how much output can be obtained from any factor input whether this factor input satisfies the equilibrium conditions or not. If we construct our aggregates so that the aggregate production function exists only when the profit-maximizing equations exist, we do not obtain the technological relation between input and output; we obtain a relation between measures of input and output that satisfy certain economic criteria involving prices and wages.

If we want to develop systems like (11.13)–(11.21), the index numbers of Dresch and May can probably be adapted to such systems very elegantly. If we want to develop systems like (11.22)–(11.36), then we have to consider new types of indexes.[8]

There are some points made in Pu's paper that are not entirely well taken. These points are the following:

1 Distribution effects are not accounted for in the aggregates suggested in the present writer's earlier paper.
2 These aggregates have no economic significance.
3 The criteria put forth for the construction of these aggregates are too restrictive.

We shall now consider these points in order. If the production function for the αth firm can be written as

$$x_\alpha = C_\alpha \prod_{i=1}^{r} n_{i\alpha}^{a_{i\alpha}} \prod_{i=1}^{s} z_{i\alpha}^{b_{i\alpha}} \qquad \alpha = 1, 2, \ldots, A, \tag{11.39}$$

with the aggregates defined as

$$X = \left(\prod_{\alpha=1}^{A} x_\alpha \right)^{1/A}, \tag{11.40}$$

$$N^a = \left(\prod_{\alpha=1}^{A} \prod_{i=1}^{r} n_{i\alpha}^{a_{i\alpha}} \right)^{1/A}, \tag{11.41}$$

$$Z^b = \left(\prod_{\alpha=1}^{A} \prod_{i=1}^{s} z_{i\alpha}^{b_{i\alpha}} \right)^{1/A}, \tag{11.42}$$

---

[8] See L. R. Klein, 'Macroeconomics and the theory of rational behavior,' *Econometrica*, **14**, April (1946), 93–108.

then it has been shown[9] that a well-defined macroeconomic system can be established from a knowledge of the microeconomic system.

The aggregates X, N, Z defined in (11.40), (11.41), and (11.42) are weighted geometric means of individual x_α, $n_{i\alpha}$, and $z_{i\alpha}$, the weights being the individual production elasticities ($a_{i\alpha}$ and $b_{i\alpha}$) in the case of N and Z. Methods of calculating a and b, the exponents of N and Z respectively, have been given in the paper mentioned above. Pu claims to account for distributional effects by using the individual marginal productivities to derive his aggregates. Formulas (11.41) and (11.42) use the individual production elasticities to derive the aggregates. There is nothing to choose between using elasticities (logarithmic derivatives) and marginal productivities (ordinary derivatives) since they give approximately the same information. Elasticities are independent of units while marginal productivities are not; otherwise they are not essentially different. However, Pu is to be criticized for using equilibrium values of marginal productivities to obtain the aggregates which enter as variables in the production function. The objection to this method has already been discussed at length above. The elasticities used as weights in (11.41) and (11.42) are parameters of the individual production functions and do not depend upon the profit-maximizing equations. It is easy to see that if the distribution of the individual elasticities among firms is altered, the aggregates N and Z will be changed since the elasticities enter as weights in the calculation of N and Z. This is the sense in which these aggregates depend upon distributional characteristics.

What is the economic significance of aggregates? There is no reason to assume, as Pu does, that there is something sacred about a sum. It is true that the man in the street knows more about a sum than about many other types of aggregates, but in constructing scientific theory, we must look for useful results rather than things familiar to the layman. Any macroeconomic theory which will enable us to make people happier through an analysis of the interrelationship between aggregates of income, employment, output, etc., is a good theory regardless of the specific form of the aggregates. The economy is generally better off if the sum of all individual outputs[10] rises, and it is generally better off if the product of all outputs rises. A sum and product are often equally good for our purposes.

Pu's implied preference for his aggregates (sums) to (11.40), (11.41), and (11.42) (geometric means) brings to mind the lengthy discussion in

---

[9]L. R. Klein, 'Macroeconomics'.
[10]We assume a common unit of measurement.

the older books on statistical methods concerning the relative merits of arithmetic and geometric means. The right-hand sides of (11.41) and (11.42) are weighted geometric means of individual quantities and the exponents a and b of the left-hand side have a very simple economic interpretation; they are weighted averages of the individual elasticities in the production functions of the several firms.

There are at least two essentially different approaches to the problem of aggregation. We may accept the traditional theories of microeconomics and the commonly used aggregates such as the Federal Reserve Board production index, the Bureau of Labor Statistics price index, the Commerce Department national-income data etc., and try to determine the structure of a macroeconomic system that is implied by these two sets of information. Such a system may be very complicated or may not even exist, but if we could construct it, we could hope to make forecasts of these well-known aggregates. Alternatively we could proceed differently by assuming the theories of micro- and macroeconomics in advance and then discovering what aggregates are consistent with these assumptions. In this case, we cannot know in advance the form of the aggregates but must accept those forms which satisfy a mathematical requirement. In the latter approach we cannot in general claim to have models that help us to predict the Federal Reserve Board index or the Bureau of Labor Statistics price index. Instead we obtain models that attempt to forecast the particular aggregates that satisfy the criteria assumed. It will often be true that in practice the correlation between these aggregates obtained by the second method and the published indexes will be so high that one set can be substituted for the other.

The matter of whether or not the criteria imposed upon aggregates in the present writer's earlier paper are too restrictive may perhaps be settled by considering the assumptions made in (11.39) about the production functions for the individual firm. The rest of the model follows very readily if this assumption holds. In many particular firms, statisticians have found that the Cobb-Douglas function (or simple modifications of this function) fit the output-input data very well. If we can determine a large enough sample of these individual-firm production functions, it will not be difficult to construct the aggregates that satisfy the theory presented by the author. Thus far, there is no reason to believe that the logarithmic production function cannot be applied in general as a good approximation of the output–input relationship for the individual firm. However, if another universal form of the production function were found to approximate closely the data of individual firms, we could undoubtedly construct alternative aggregates which would also lead to simple macroeconomic systems.

In closing, it may be useful to outline some of the major unsolved problems in the theory of aggregation:

1 The aggregates must be constructed so that the macroeconomic models are complete, covering the rational behavior of households and market interactions between households and firms, as well as the rational behavior of firms.
2 The aggregates should be such that they can be readily constructed or approximated from available data.
3 The assumptions of perfect competition must be dropped.[11]
4 The entire theory of aggregation must be developed for stochastic models of micro- and macroeconomics.

[11]Dresch, 'Index numbers', has already made considerable progress in this direction.

12
Theories of Effective Demand and Employment

There is much talk about such matters as the downward rigidity of wage rates, the relationship of wages to employment and output, the influence of liquid assets on the level of economic activity, and the stage of maturity of the American economy. The various theories of employment must be examined in the light of these concepts in order to get some clear answers to important economic problems. The Keynesian theories[1] are often accused of being based on assumptions of rigid wage rates or interest-elastic liquidity preferences, but there may be much less truth in these assertions than is commonly thought to be the case. The purpose of this paper will be to study three theories of employment, – (a) the classical, (b) the Keynesian, and (c) the Marxian, – in order to attempt to clear up some confusions that still exist. One of the main objectives will be to try to show the distinctions between necessary and sufficient assumptions that underlie each theory.

THE CLASSICAL THEORY

Since the publication of the *General Theory*, there have been numerous discussions in the professional literature comparing Keynes and the Classics. As a result of these discussions, we now have a good idea as to the form of the classical model. The simplest version is as follows:

1 The supply of and demand for labor determine the real wage rate and the level of employment.
2 The technological input–output relationship determines the level of real output since the input of labor services has been determined by step 1. It is, of course, assumed that the stock of fixed capital is given.

[1] Some of the ideas on Keynesian economics contained in this article are more fully discussed in the author's book, *The Keynesian Revolution*, Macmillan, New York.

3 The equation of savings and investment determines the rate of interest.
4 Given output from step 2, the constant velocity of circulation and the given supply of cash determine the absolute price level (quantity theory).

The mathematical version of this system is

$$M = kpY, \quad \text{quantity equation,} \tag{12.1}$$

$$S(i) = I(i), \quad \text{savings-investment equation,} \tag{12.2}$$

$$Y = Y(N), \quad \text{production function,} \tag{12.3}$$

$$\frac{dY}{dN} = \frac{w}{p}, \quad \text{demand for labor,} \tag{12.4}$$

$$N = f\left(\frac{w}{p}\right), \quad \text{supply of labor,} \tag{12.5}$$

where

M = cash balances,
p = price,
Y = output,
i = interest rate,
N = employment,
w = wage rate.

Given the amount of money, there are five equations to determine p, Y, i, N, and w.

The classical economists not only counted relations and variables; they also assumed that the forms of their relations were such that a unique solution was possible. This solution will always be one of full employment because all who want to work at the going real wage rate can find a job; equation (12.5) tells us that. This equation shows how much employment will be offered at any real wage rate. If all the equations of the system are consistent, as was classically assumed, equation (12.5) must hold, i.e., all who offer their services at prevailing real wages can find employment. In this model, since all equations hold simultaneously, the solution must be on the supply curve of labor, which is what is meant by full employment.

It is easy to make a slight generalization of this model and still get the same results. Those defending the classical doctrine against Keynes's 1936 attack were quick to point out that the classical economists did not neglect the fact that the demand for money depends on the rate of interest or that savings and investment depend on income. The same results, so far as the level of employment is concerned, follow even if the quantity equation and the savings-investment equation are modified. Steps 1 and 2 of the process of solving the classical model remain as before. Steps 3 and 4 become:

3 Given the level of output from step 2, the equation of savings and investment determines the rate of interest.
4 Given the level of output from step 2 and the level of the interest rate from step 3, the given supply of cash determines the absolute price level.

Equations (12.1) and (12.2) are replaced by

$$\frac{M}{p} = L(i, Y), \qquad (12.1a)$$

$$S(i, Y) = I(i, Y). \qquad (12.2b)$$

The other equations remain as before.

As presented here, the classical system is static and should be looked upon as the equilibrium solution of a more general dynamical system. It is evident that the equilibrium will always be one of full employment. In the general case – when the system is not at its equilibrium position – there may be unemployment, but this unemployment will be only temporary if the dynamic movements are damped, as the classical economists implicitly assumed. When unemployment does occur in the state of disequilibrium, there is always an appropriate remedial policy available – namely, an increase in the amount of money or (its equivalent) a cut in prices or in wages. Every variable in the classical system can be expressed in terms of the autonomous supply of money as a parameter, and it is easy to calculate the effect upon the system of varying the quantity of money. The assumptions of the structure of the classical system are such that variations in the quantity of money tend to raise the level of output and employment when there is a deviation from the full-employment equilibrium.

THE KEYNESIAN THEORY

The Keynesian theory is quite different from the classical theory. The basic hypothesis of the Keynesian theory is that people make two kinds of decisions in our present type of economy. They decide, on the basis of their income, whether to spend or save; and they decide, on the basis

Effective demand and employment

of the rate of interest, the form in which they want to hold their accumulated savings – cash or securities. In the classical theory income is the strategic variable in the money equation (12.1), and interest is the strategic variable in the savings-investment equation (12.2). Exactly the reverse is true in the Keynesian system. Keynes's great contribution was to replace the classical savings-investment theory of interest with a savings-investment theory of the determination of income.

The simplest Keynesian theory is the following. Savings as a function of the level of income equals autonomous investment. This is one equation in one variable, namely, the level of income. Investment is considered to be autonomous because it depends upon such factors as the expectations of future market demand, innovations, fiscal policy, etc. It is obvious, however, that the validity of the Keynesian theory does not depend on the fact that investment is autonomous, for, if investment is also a function of income, the Keynesian theory of the savings-investment determination of the level of income still holds.

One pillar of support for the simplest Keynesian model is that it is not contradicted by the data. If the hypothesis is that savings as a function of income equals autonomous investment, there should be a close correlation between income and investment. The published data (USA) on disposable income (constant dollars, per capita) are very highly correlated with investment – defined as the difference between disposable income and consumer expenditures (constant dollars, per capita) – and lagged disposable income during the interwar period. There is nothing artificial in this high correlation, and statisticians have never found a similar confirmation of the alternative classical theories from the available data.

The Keynesian revision of the savings-investment theory is of profound importance. Since the Keynesian theory does not involve the introduction of any new variables and since it merely involves a change of form of some of the classical equations, it would seem natural that the system (12.1)–(12.5) could be re-written with the suggested revisions, so that we would again have a model of full-employment equilibrium. However, this supposition is not correct. The revised model would be

$$\frac{M}{p} = L(i), \quad \text{liquidity-preference equation}, \quad (12.6)$$

$$S(Y) = I(Y), \quad \text{savings-investment equation}, \quad (12.7)$$

$$Y = Y(N), \quad \text{production function}, \quad (12.8)$$

$$\frac{dY}{dN} = \frac{w}{p}, \quad \text{demand for labor}, \quad (12.9)$$

$$N = f\left(\frac{w}{p}\right), \quad \text{supply of labor.} \tag{12.10}$$

There is a basic contradiction and indeterminancy in this system. The supply of and demand for labor, plus the production function, determine the level of output. But the savings-investment equation also determines the level of output, and there is no obvious mechanism to insure that these two levels of output will be the same. Furthermore, the liquidity-preferrence equation cannot determine both the price level and the rate of interest.

There are various ways out of the difficulties that arise in the system (12.6)–(12.10). The liquidity-preference and savings-investment equations can be generalized; the supply-of-labor equation can be changed; or possibly other changes may be suggested. It should be pointed out, however, that there is little that can be done to either the production function or the demand for labor. The production function cannot be changed, because it is a technological phenomenon. The laws of nature cannot be tampered with, while the hypotheses of economic behavior can. Many empirical studies have shown that the aggregate production function can be closely approximated by a linear-logarithmic relation. From the theories of profit maximization it follows that a linear-logarithmic production function implies a demand equation for labor such that the wage bill is proportional to the aggregate value of output. This constancy of labor's share of the national product is precisely what the data show. In dynamic econometric models this relation can be improved by saying that the wage bill is a linear function of the value of current output, lagged output, and a time trend. A demand equation for labor, of this generalized dynamic type, can be easily derived from empirical production functions. In various econometric models that the author has constructed, there is no relation that is more stable than the demand for labor; hence it seems unwise to attempt to clear up the theoretical difficulties of the above model by altering (12.8) or (12.9). We must concentrate our attention on (12.6), (12.7), and (12.10). This is precisely the Keynesian approach.

If the generalized forms of the money equation and the savings-investment equation presented in the previous section – (12.1a) and (12.2a) – were substituted for (12.6) and (12.7), the Keynesian theory would appear to be coincident with the classical theory. But such a conclusion would be hasty. Suppose that (12.6) and (12.7) are replaced by (12.1a) and (12.2a). If there was formerly a contradiction between the level of output determined from one part of the model, (12.8)–(12.10), and from another part of the model, (12.7), a classical econo-

its full-employment equilibrium, competitive wage cuts during periods of unemployment solve the problem for Pigou.

Equation (12.7a) rests on an unconfirmed hypothesis, namely, that savings vary inversely with the real stock of cash balances. Just as the classical assumptions about the influence of interest rates on savings and investment have never been discovered to hold empirically, so has it never been discovered that consumption or savings patterns are significantly influenced by the stock of cash balances. The data of the interwar period show that cash balances, at best, had a very mild influence on consumption. If we adopt the following simple model for purposes of statistical investigation,[7]

$$S = \alpha_0 + \alpha_1 Y + \alpha_2 Y_{-1} + \alpha_3 \left(\frac{M}{P}\right)_{-1} = I = \text{autonomous} \qquad (12.12)$$

or

$$Y = \frac{-\alpha_0}{\alpha_1} - \frac{\alpha_2}{\alpha_1} Y_{-1} - \frac{\alpha_3}{\alpha_1}\left(\frac{M}{p}\right)_{-1} + \frac{1}{\alpha_1} I,$$

the least-squares estimates of the parameters are

$$Y = 186.53 + 0.30 Y_{-1} + 0.13 \left(\frac{M}{p}\right)_{-1} + 2.36 I.$$
$$(0.13)\phantom{Y_{-1} + }(0.10)\phantom{\left(\frac{M}{p}\right)_{-1} + }(0.34)$$

The standard error of the estimate of $1/\alpha_1$ is relatively small, 0.34. On the other hand, the standard error of the estimate of α_3/α_1 is relatively large. The coefficient of M/p could easily be close to zero, but since $1/\alpha_1$ is definitely not zero, it follows that α_3 could be zero. Pigou's hypothesis is not confirmed. Even if the true value of α_3 is not zero, it may not be very large. The main point, however, is that the size (and sign) of α_3 is very uncertain. There is no 'proof' of Pigou's hypothesis.

The size of the coefficient relating savings to cash balances is very important for Pigou's theory. Recall that the systems of this paper are regarded as equilibrium solutions of more complex dynamical systems. The classical theory implicitly assumes that the system returns rapidly to its equilibrium when it is displaced to a position of disequilibrium. This implies that the dynamical system is damped. But do wage and price cuts always lead to damped processes in time? In order to insure

---

[7] All variables are per capita in 1935–39 dollars. The time period is 1922–41. The figures in parentheses below the estimated parameters are standard errors of the estimates. Y = disposable income, S = personal savings, I = net investment, M = total cash balances (current dollars).

that the classical assumption of dampening is correct, it will be necessary to assume that a small cut in wages, for example, will tend to restore the system immediately to its position of equilibrium. Thus it is required that the multiplier effect of wage cuts (or increases in the real stock of cash) be very large. The statistical calculations of (12.12) do not show this. There exists the possibility, but not the necessity, that the increase may be practically zero. Instability may develop in a model like this. There is an initial position of unemployment. Wages fall, but employment and income increases little or not at all. Wages fall still further, but unemployment is still not eradicated. This is a perfect setting for expectations of further wage cuts, the very conditions that make the system unstable and make it likely that wage cuts will push the system away from rather than toward its full-employment equilibrium.

If there are expectations of falling wages, entrepreneurs will postpone production until a time when labor costs will be lower yet. Wage-earners will feel very insecure and spend as little as possible. Hyper-deflation will never cure unemployment. The only way that unstable situations of hyperdeflation can be stopped is by direct, autonomous action on the part of the state or some other authoritative agency, as was the case in the period 1929–33 in the USA. Admittedly, the process of hyperdeflation is the worst set of circumstances that can arise in Pigou's system yet – on the basis of the available data – an assumption of such unfavourable conditions is legitimate even though other assumptions can safely be made also. The problem, as yet, remains unsettled.

In the most general model – in which the savings-investment equation is (12.7a) and the liquidity-preference equation is (12.1a) – the expression for the rate of change of real income with respect to real cash balances is more complicated. Without going into the mathematics of this expression, it is possible to present certain results on an intuitive basis. If savings are insensitive to variations in i and M/p and if investment is insensitive to variations of i, then it will follow that real income will not be greatly stimulated by increases in real cash balances. These are the properties of the savings-investment equation that have already been discussed in the preceding pages. The conclusion about small variations in real income associated with variations in real balances is *reinforced* if we appeal to the Keynesian assumptions about the shape of the liquidity-preference equation. Keynes put forth the hypothesis that the demand for cash is infinitely elastic with respect to the interest rate in the neighborhood of low interest rates. Some economists have singled out this hypothesis of Keynes as his strategic

Effective demand and employment

assumption which is necessary for the validity of his theories. The truth of the matter is that high interest elasticity of liquidity preferences is sufficient in many cases but never necessary. The validity of the theory of employment does not depend on the validity of the assumption about the form of liquidity preferences. It is obvious that the simplest version of the Keynesian theory (savings as a function of income equals autonomous investment) has nothing to do with the theory of interest.

It is instructive to examine the empirical relationship between the interest rate and cash balances to see whether or not the Keynesian hypothesis is correct. If we identify active cash balances as circulating currency plus demand deposits, and idle cash balances as savings deposits, we find for the interwar period very strong linear correlations, (a) between active balances, net national product and trend, and (b) between idle balances, corporate-bond yield, lagged corporate-bond yield, lagged idle balances, and trend. The data also show that the corporate-bond yield is not a statistically significant variable in (a) and that net national product is not a statistically significant variable in (b). These latter findings imply that the empirical split between active and idle balances is not bad.

The fact that idle balances are linearly related to the interest rate in the interwar period implies that the Keynesian hypothesis of infinite elasticity cannot be correct. But the postwar data show something different. The current data are consistent with Keynes's hypothesis. While the interwar demand relation for active balances is close to the postwar facts, the interwar demand relation for idle balances gives a computed level of idle balances, for observed interest rates, much lower than the actual level. There are several explanations for the breakdown of this empirical function in the postwar years. One explanation is that the whole relation has shifted. Another explanation is that some variable, which was relatively unimportant in the past, is now important and accounts for the discrepancy. A third explanation, which is very appealing, is that the Keynesian hypothesis is correct. If the liquidity-preference function were approximately linear for interest rates above 3 per cent and asymptotic to the line, interest rate $=2.5$ per cent, it would fit the interwar data, the postwar data, and the Keynesian hypothesis. There are a variety of simple mathematical functions which have the required properties.

The intuitive significance of the various assumptions about interest elasticities can be summed up briefly. Assuming that the mechanism to maintain full employment equilibrium is a fluctuating stock of real balances, it follows that these fluctuations will have little influence on the interest rate if the liquidity preferences are highly elastic, and it follows further that they will have little influence on savings and investment if these schedules are interest inelastic. It may seem that much weight is attached to the interest rate, but the opposite is the case. The complex of elasticities assumed in the Keynesian theory makes the interest rate extremely unimportant. The same results can be obtained by altogether dropping interest as an independent variable from the system.

The other available alternative by which the contradictions of the system may be reconciled is the modification of the supply curve of labor. This is the alternative that Keynes chose for himself. Before discussing this alternative, however, several points should be made clear. We have been able to demonstrate a basic contradiction in the working of the capitalist system when the traditional supply curve of labor is used. The recognition of this contradiction represents a great step forward in economic theory, and this contribution has nothing to do with any special assumptions about wages. The truly important ideas of Keynes, contrary to much of popular belief, are independent of any special assumptions about the labor market. Keynesian theories of the savings-investment process superimposed on the classical theory of the labor market show that full employment is not automatic under capitalism.

Keynes recognized that full employment was not the equilibrium position for the real world, and he set about to develop a theory of an unemployment equilibrium by changing the classical supply curve of labor and by adopting a new definition of unemployment. It is this part of his theory that many of the modern Keynesians would like to give up while still retaining the savings-investment theory of income determination. The strict Keynesian approach amounts to replacing (12.10) by

$$N = F(w) \tag{12.13}$$

and adopting the well-known definition of involuntary unemployment found in the early pages of the *General Theory*. It is assumed that the new supply curve of labor has infinite wage elasticity up to the full-employment point. This system is rigged to get an unemployment equilibrium as much as the classical system is rigged to get a full-employment equilibrium. Neither approach is entirely acceptable.

There are at least two criticisms of the Keynesian solution. In the first place, Keynes's definition of unemployment has the unsavory implication that the cause of unemployment is a money-illusion on the part of workers; if workers would only bargain in terms of real wages instead of in terms of money wages, there would be no problem of

Effective demand and employment 217

unemployment, other than the frictional variety. Surely, a small thing like a money illusion cannot be responsible for the existence of unemployment. Second, the supply curve of labor given by (12.13) has never been tested against the facts and may not hold if it is tested. The behavior patterns of recent years (since the Little Steel Formula) give the impression that workers do not bargain exclusively in terms of money wages. They are very conscious of the relation between wages and the cost of living, and it does not seem correct to assume that they are fooled by any money illusion. Many of the parts of the Keynesian system have withstood the test of being consistent with observed data, but all that we can say about equation (12.13) is that we do not know about its validity. It must be re-emphasized, however, that the important parts of the Keynesian theory are independent of Keynes's own theories of wages and the labor market.

Joan Robinson has made a very important remark that holds the key to an answer to the problem. She said: 'Again, the orthodox conception of wages tending to equal the *marginal disutility* of labor, which has its origin in the picture of a peasant farmer leaning on his hoe in the evening and deciding whether the extra product of another hour's work will repay the extra backache, is projected into the modern labour market, where the individual worker has no opportunity to decide anything except whether it is better to work or to starve.'[8] The essence of capitalism is that there exists a definite legal respect for private ownership of the means of production. The owners of the means of production, the capitalists, make all the final decisions, with regard to the use of the means of production. The workers have nothing to say about the amount of employment that will be forthcoming at any point of time. Either the entire concept of the supply curve of labor must be dropped, or the supply curve of labor must become a curve of *virtual* points on which observations do not occur. The first alternative means that the demand for labor is given by profit maximization (marginal-productivity theory); the supply of labor is an exogenous variable represented by the labor force and determined by demographic factors; the wage rate is determined by a market adjustment between demand and supply (collective bargaining). The mathematical model would be

$$\frac{dY}{dN} = \frac{w}{p}, \quad \text{demand for labor,} \tag{12.9}$$

$$\bar{N} = \text{labor supply,} \tag{12.14}$$

[8] Joan Robinson, *An Essay on Marxian Economics*, Macmillan, London (1942), pp. 2–3.

$$\frac{d\left(\dfrac{w}{p}\right)}{dt} = g(\bar{N} - N). \tag{12.15}$$

Equation (12.15) could be replaced by

$$\frac{dw}{dt} = h(\bar{N} - N) \tag{12.15a}$$

if all the other equations of the system are used also. The same arguments about expectations and damping apply to the path by which this system approaches or diverges from equilibrium. If the system is damped and $g(0)=0$ or $h(0)=0$, we have a model of full-employment equilibrium.

It was pointed out above that equation (12.9) is based on sound empirical verification. Similarly, market adjustment equations like (12.15a) are also consistent with the data. First differences in the general wage rate (USA interwar period) are highly correlated (inversely) with unemployment and the lagged wage rate. The parameters of this empirical equation suggest that small wage cuts are not associated with large increases in employment and that $h(0) \neq 0$, from which we conclude that the system does not have a stable equilibrium of full employment.

If the concept of a supply curve of labor is to be retained, it must be interpreted in a new way. We can say that the supply curve of labor shows how much the people would *like* to work at any given real wage. It does not mean, as in the classical system, that people's desires become effective. In this situation the supply curve of labor exists as a set of virtual points which are never observed. However, it is known that the demand curve for labor represents a set of observed points. This means that we shall have an observed point on the demand curve and of the supply curve. If this point is such that supply exceeds demand (at the same wage) there is unemployment, and if this point is such that demand exceeds supply (at the same wage) there is overemployment. This concept of unemployment is not easily measurable, however, since it involves virtual, unobserved points. In order to measure unemployment in this model, we would have to sample the population, questioning them on the amount of employment that they would like to supply at prevailing wage rates.

Thus far we have attempted to point out the main differences between Keynesian and classical economics. But there is also an important aspect of similarity, namely, methodology. For both types of systems, macroeconomic models have been studied in this paper. The macroeconomic models are similar except for emphasis. A single model with one set of parameters yields the classical theory and with another set of parameters yields the Keynesian theory. However, the macroeconomic models are not the basic elements of either system. It is necessary to analyze the considerations that lie behind the macrosystem, i.e. the microsystem. It will be found here, too, that the methodologies of classical and Keynesian economics do not differ. There are two steps in the formation of the macroeconomic systems. First, it is necessary to formulate the behavior pattern of individuals. Both theories are based on household utility-maximization to get the demand for consumer goods and household cash-holdings, and on business-firm profit (or utility) maximization to get the demand for producer goods, labor, and business cash holdings. The second step is to show how to pass from a theory involving individual firms, households, factors, and commodities to a theory involving communities of individuals, composite factors, and composite commodities. This step involves the index-number problem. The discussion of both these subjects is important but lengthy. The reader is referred to other works for more extensive analysis.[9] The point to be emphasized at this stage is that the methodology is the same for classical and Keynesian economics at all steps in the process of deriving the macrosystems.

THE MARXIAN THEORY[10]

There are two important subsections of the modern theories of employment which need to be clarified. One subsection is the stagnation thesis, and the other is the relation between wages, profits and employment. The modern version of the stagnation thesis is an outgrowth of the Keynesian developments in American economic thinking. The opposite theory of the stationary state is a natural outgrowth of the classical system. But neither model, as usually stated,

---

[9]On the problem of the theories underlying the Keynesian and classical macroeconomic systems see Klein, *Keynesian Revolution*. On the problem of aggregation see Francis W. Dresch, 'Index numbers and the general economic equilibrium,' *Bulletin of the American Mathematical Society*, XL, February (1938), 134–41; Lawrence R. Klein, 'Macroeconomic systems see Klein, *Keynesian Revolution*. On the problem of aggregation see and 'Remarks on the Theory of Aggregation,' *Econometrica*, XIV, October (1946), 303–12; Kenneth May, 'The aggregation problem for a one-industry model,' *Econometrica*, XIV, October (1946), 285–98; Shou Shan Pu, 'A Note on macro economics,' *Econometrica*, XIV, October (1946), 299–302.

[10]The author is indebted to Professor Kenneth May for helpful criticisms in this section.

gives an adequate analysis of the theory of economic development. It is possible to modify these theories with the introduction of trend variables, the stock of capital etc., in order to get some information about the economic laws of motion of society; but it seems preferable to go to a theory which deals directly with this subject. From a historical point of view it is also fitting to use the theory which first tackled the problems related to the stagnation thesis. The Marxian theory of the falling rate of profit is one of the first, and probably one of the best, tools for analyzing the stagnation theory. Since Marxian theory comes to conclusions similar to those of the modern stagnationists, but for different reasons, it will also be instructive to study it in some detail.

The other problem, of the relation between wages, profits, and employment is of great current interest but also cannot be properly analyzed within the customary frameworks of Keynesian and classical economics. These theories can also be modified by distinguishing in the consumption function between wage income and profit income. But the Marxian theory is based fundamentally on the interrelationships between wages and profits. The Marxian theories of reproduction are well suited for the study of this problem.

Here it will be necessary to digress for a few pages in order to show explicitly the structure of the Marxian model. This model will then be compared with the Keynesian model and used for the analysis of the stagnation theory and the relationship between wages, profits, and employment.

The methodology of the Marxian approach is quite different from that of Keynes and the Classics: Instead of studying the behavior of individuals, Marx studied the behavior of classes directly. His theory is probably the origin of macroeconomics. But the Marxian system of macroeconomics differs essentially from the Keynesian and classical systems. The macrounits in the latter systems are producers and consumers, and this overlapping fails to bring out some essentials. The macrounits of the Marxian system are not only producers and consumers but also workers and capitalists. The latter two groups are, practically speaking, exclusive, and their basic conflict of interests can more easily be singled out as one of the moving forces in the system.

The economic writings of Marx were not presented in the form of systems of simultaneous equations. The equation-system approach to economics came at a later date. There are various equations throughout Marx's writings, but these equations are mainly definitions. They state, for example, that total output can be broken up into three components: constant capital, variable capital, and surplus value.

Effective demand and employment

Various manipulations are carried out with these components, but complete systems of equations are not formulated. However, imbedded in Marx's literary discussion and numerical examples, there are several hypotheses and assumptions that can be used to build a system of equations. The validity of the equation system depends upon the validity of the hypotheses made. It is the function of the empirical studies to test the validity of these equations.

The supply-demand equations of orthodox economics also are based upon some assumptions the validity of which cannot be assumed *a priori*. The systems of supply-demand equations are usually based on the assumptions that households maximize their individual utility functions subject to certain constraints. The assumptions produce the maximization equations which are essentially the supply-demand equations. In the same way, we shall have to introduce Marxian assumptions in order to construct an equation system out of *Capital*.

A concrete example will demonstrate clearly the relation between definitional equations and behavior equations (or refutable hypotheses). Suppose we write, as did Marx,

$$c + v + s = \text{total value}, \tag{12.16}$$

$$\frac{s}{v} = \text{rate of surplus value}, \tag{12.17}$$

$$\frac{c}{c+v} = \text{organic composition of capital}, \tag{12.18}$$

$$\frac{s}{c+v} = \text{rate of profit}, \tag{12.19}$$

where
c = constant capital,
v = variable capital,
s = surplus value.[11]

Equations (12.16)–(12.19) are definitions. They define four different terms and hold, regardless of any economic behavior patterns. We cannot test the validity of any of these equations because they must hold by definition. They are not refutable hypotheses.

According to the simplest rules of algebra the following equation,

$$\frac{s}{c+v} = \frac{s}{v}\left(1 - \frac{c}{c+v}\right), \tag{12.20}$$

---

[11] For the individual firm, c consists of depreciation and raw materials; v consists of wage payments; and s consists of profit, interest, and rent.

must hold[12] because

$$\frac{s}{v}\left(1-\frac{c}{c+v}\right) = \frac{s}{v}\left(\frac{c+v-c}{c+v}\right) = \frac{s}{c+v}.$$

Equation (12.20) is not a refutable hypothesis either. It, too, must hold, regardless of the actual values of the variables c, v, s. Equation (12.20) merely states the truism that

$$\frac{s}{c+v} = \frac{s}{c+v}.$$

In so far as Marxian economics is based on equations (12.16)–(12.20) no real progress can be made. None of these equations tells us anything about fundamental economic behavior. The extensive use by Marx and the Marxists of equations similar to (12.16)–(12.20) has undoubtedly led Oscar Lange to remark: 'This whole [Marxist] literature tries to solve the fundamental problems of economic equilibrium and disequilibrium without even attempting to make use of the mathematical concept of functional relationship.'[13]

But Marx was probably not so guilty as Lange's remark implies. In Volume III of *Capital*, when discussing the theory of the falling rate of profit, Marx[14] made specific assumptions in his numerical examples. He assumed that s/v in equation (12.20) is constant. Thus he was able to say that the rate of profit, $s/(c+v)$, varies inversely with the organic composition of capital, $c/(c+v)$. Here is a refutable hypothesis, namely, $s/v=$constant. This is an economic hypothesis that can be tested. We can examine data on wages, profits, interest, and rent to see whether or not s and v have a constant ratio. By making this assumption, Marx was able to develop the theory of the falling rate of profit which states that the rate of profit falls as the organic composition of capital rises. From equations (12.16)–(12.20) we can say nothing about the behavior of the economic system, but from equations (12.16)–(12.20) and the assumption $s/v=$constant we can say very much. However, the system is not yet complete even at this stage.

It is worth pointing out that this confusion is not peculiar to Marxian economics. It has arisen in non-Marxian economics in connection with the quantity theory of money. Let us define $M=$total stock of money; $V=$average number of times a monetary unit is spent in a

---

[12] For the use of such equations in Marxian economics see Paul M. Sweezy, *The Theory of Capitalist Development*, Oxford University Press, New York (1942), p. 68.

[13] Oscar Lange, 'Marxian economics and modern theory,' *Review of Economic Studies*, II, June (1935), 196.

[14] Karl Marx, *Capital*, Vol. III Charles H. Kerr, Chicago (1909), 247.

given period on newly produced goods and services; $p=$ average price of newly produced goods and services; $X=$ aggregate output of newly produced goods and services.[15] It follows by definition that

$$MV = pX. \tag{12.21}$$

Equation (12.21) tells us nothing about economic behavior. In its present form it is of the same nature as equation (12.20). There is no refutable hypothesis contained in either (12.20) or (12.21).

The classical economists did the same thing about (12.21) that Marx did about (12.20). They assumed that certain variables in (12.21) were known numbers. Specifically, they assumed $V=$ constant and $X=$ full-employment output. For them, V was determined by institutional and psychological phenomena such as the frequency of wage payments, attitudes toward holding cash, etc. With V and X known, the classical economists could say that the price level varies directly with the amount of money. The validity of this theory depends upon the validity of the assumptions about V and X.

These examples illustrate our method. We shall search through Marx's literary explanations and numerical examples for the strategic hypotheses that will produce a determinate system of equations.

First we must define the variables carefully. We shall retain Marx's notation of c, v, s. When referring to the individual firm, c consists of depreciation and purchases of raw materials, v consists of wage payments, and s consists of profit plus interest plus rent. The aggregate value of output for the individual firm is $c+v+s$. When referring to the economy as a whole, we must redefine constant capital in order to avoid double counting. For the entire system, constant capital, denoted by C, is defined as the value of depreciation charges. Constant capital does not include raw materials for the system as a whole because such an inclusion would lead to excessive double counting in determining the value of output. Variable capital for the entire system will be denoted by V and will include all wage payments. Surplus value for the entire system will be denoted by S and will include total profits, interest, and rents. In modern terminology, we have

$C+V+S=$ gross national income,

$V+S=$ net national income.

National income can be considered from two sides – production and factor payments. National income as the sum $V+S$ represents total

---

[15] The aggregates p and X are constructed so that their product, pX, is exactly equal to the total value of newly produced output.

factor payments.[16] From the side of production, national income can be considered as equal to the total production of two types of goods and services – consumption and investment (consumer goods and producer goods). Consumer goods are those that flow to households and producer goods those that flow to business firms. We shall denote consumption by R and net investment by I. Net national income will be denoted, as usual, by Y. We have, thus far, the two following definitional equations:

$$V + S = Y, \qquad (12.22)$$

$$R + I = Y. \qquad (12.23)$$

The variables V, S, Y, R, I are all measured in real terms, for example, constant dollars.

It is now necessary to develop behavior equations to show how these variables are determined. First consider R, consumption. Marx divided consumers into two strategic groups – workers and capitalists. He *assumed* that workers spend all their incomes on consumer goods and services. In fact, he wrote: 'the variable capital advanced in the payment of the labor-power of the laborers is mostly spent by them for articles of consumption.'[17] This assumption is also carried through in a purer form in his numerical examples of reproduction schemes in Part III, Volume II of *Capital*. In the numerical examples he always put workers' consumption exactly equal to wages (not approximately equal). In the quotation he said that wages are 'mostly spent' (but not entirely spent) on consumer goods and services. As a matter of fact, empirical data suggest that Marx's quoted assumption is the correct one. The marginal propensity to consume out of wages is not unity, although it is very close to unity.

It is less obvious how to determine the behavior pattern for capitalist consumption in the Marxian system. The main clue comes from a study of numerical examples that Marx used to analyze capitalist reproduction schemes. The theory of simple reproduction is not much of a clue, for in that scheme a steady state is assumed in which variable capital (wages) and surplus value are always exactly spent on consumer goods and capital is replaced without any net investment taking place. The schemes of accumulation and reproduction on an enlarged scale, found at the end of the Volume II of *Capital*, provide the basis for a theory of capitalist consumption.

[16] It is only in orthodox economics that S represents a factor payment. In Marxian terminology, S represents expropriation. The term 'factor payment' is used in the text only because it is customarily used today in discussions of national income statistics.

[17] Karl Marx *Capital*, Vol. II, 466.

Effective demand and employment 225

In his examples on accumulation, Marx divided the economic system into two departments – the department (I) producing producer goods and the department (II) producing consumer goods. In the first department, workers were assumed to spend all their wage income on consumer goods produced by the second department, while capitalists were assumed to spend only a part of their surplus-value income on consumer goods. The exact relation for capitalist behavior in Department I was

consumption $=\frac{1}{2}$ (surplus value).

This is the consumption function for capitalists in Department I. In a consistent theory it should be expected that capitalists in Department II would also behave in a similar fashion, their consumption being a function of their surplus value income. True, Marx assumed that the capitalists in Department II consumed out of their surplus-value income, but he did not assume that there existed an independent relation between consumption and surplus value for capitalists in Department II. The behavior of capitalists in the consumer-goods industry was entirely passive in the sense that their consumption was calculated as a residual. This residual consumption was taken to be the difference between total surplus value in Department II and that part of surplus value which was transferred to expenditure on constant and variable capital. The latter expenditure was calculated by Marx so that the reproduction scheme could work smoothly without a glut of the market. Marx did not assume, by any means, that capitalism works smoothly; but he set down in his reproduction schemes the conditions under which capitalism could work smoothly. He argued that if his conditions were not met a crash would occur. One step in a possible method of introducing fluctuations into the model, with recurring crises and recovery, is to make capitalist consumption in Department II also a function of surplus value. We can even simplify the entire system by doing away with the distinction between departments I and II. Let us assume instead that capitalists behave the same way in both departments. Identical behavior is assumed for workers in these two departments, and it seems reasonable to assume that capitalists should not have different consumption habits according as they produce consumer goods or producer goods. Hence we shall assume that the consumption of capitalists is a function of surplus value.

Denoting the consumption of workers by R_1 and the consumption of capitalists by R_2 we have the two consumption functions[18]

---

[18] As a first approximation, we shall assume a linear system.

$$R_1 = V, \tag{12.24}$$

$$R_2 = \alpha_0 + \alpha_1 S \qquad 0 < \alpha_1 < 1. \tag{12.25}$$

The total consumption function is given by

$$R_1 + R_2 = R = \alpha_0 + \alpha_1 S + V \tag{12.26}$$

In a more general formulation, where the workers' marginal propensity to consume is not unity, we have

$$R_1 = \alpha_2 + \alpha_3 V \qquad 0 < \alpha_3 < 1, \tag{12.24a}$$

$$R = (\alpha_0 + \alpha_2) + \alpha_1 S + \alpha_3 V, \qquad \alpha_3 > \alpha_1. \tag{12.26a}$$

The next step is to derive the demand for the other type of good in the system – investment or producer goods. We shall first derive the demand relation for constant capital (capital used up) according to Marx and then transform the demand for constant capital into investment. Workers buy only consumer goods in the Marxian system, for that is what distinguishes workers from capitalists. The demand for constant capital will be based entirely on the behavior of capitalists. Again, we rely on the examples of expanded reproduction in order to discover the variables influencing capitalists' demand for constant capital.

In Volume II, Marx assumed that capitalists in Department I (the producer-goods industry) spend from surplus value on constant capital. His relation was

$$\text{constant capital} = C_0 + k \text{ (surplus value)} \qquad 0 < k < 1,$$

where C_0 is the initial level of constant capital and k is a fraction which is the product of the fraction of surplus value to be accumulated in both variable and constant capital and the fraction of total capital represented by constant capital.

The expenditures on constant capital in Department II were like the expenditures by capitalists on consumer goods in that department in the sense that both expenditures were calculated as a residual. The capitalists in Department II did not decide, independently, to accumulate capital but based their decision entirely on the relationship between expenditures in both departments so that the process would run smoothly without a glut of the market. We can again do away with the assumption of a smooth-working capitalist system by supposing that capitalists behave the same way in both departments in so far as the demand for constant capital is concerned. We shall assume that capitalists in both departments demand constant capital as a fraction of surplus value.

Effective demand and employment

There is one condition, implicit in Marx's example, which must be avoided for our model. Marx assumed that whatever capitalists do not spend out of surplus value on consumer goods they spend on constant or variable capital. We shall assume, instead, an independence between the marginal propensity to consume and the marginal propensity to invest. We must point out, however, that Marx made this assumption only to obtain the conditions for a smooth-working system. He did not imply that these conditions held in the real world. Our alternative assumption is one way of achieving the conditions of the real world in the Marxian spirit.

We now have the equation

$$C = \beta_0 + \beta_1 S. \quad (12.27)$$

Since we are going to work with the variable I instead of C, it will be necessary to carry out a transformation of variables. The transformation involves common sense technological relations which are constructed by the present author and do not appear in *Capital*.[19]

The variable C represents the amount of fixed capital used up in the production process. The amount of capital used up (depreciation) will depend upon the stock of fixed capital in existence. The capital in existence will, in turn, be made up of the elements of durable capital, plant, and equipment – acquired at various stages of past history. Denoting the capital acquired during the pth preceding time period by x_{-p}, we have

$$C = C(x, x_{-1}, x_{-2}, x_{-3}, \ldots) \quad (12.28)$$

or in a linear approximation[20]

$$C = \delta_0 + \delta_1 x + \delta_2 x_{-1} + \delta_3 x_{-2} + \ldots. \quad (12.29)$$

In statistical work we cannot measure separately the capital purchased during every preceding time period, but we can approximate all these variables with a proxy variable which represents all the capital accumulated up to the time period under consideration. Instead of (12.29), let us write

$$C = \delta_0 + \delta_1 x + \delta_2' Z_{-1}. \quad (12.29a)$$

The stock of existing fixed capital, Z_{-1}, can be written in terms of the net investment of all preceding periods as

---

[19] These transformations are so obvious that it is assumed that anybody wishing to work with I instead of C would use approximately the same transformations.

[20] Since the linear function is an approximation, we shall not assume the constant term equal to zero, although logically there should be no constant term in this equation.

$$Z_{-1} = \sum_{t=-1}^{-\infty} I_t. \tag{12.30}$$

Equation (12.29a) at least makes the distinction between new and old capital, but it is not so complete as (12.29), which makes the distinction between capital of all different age groups. This distinction is useful because the capital in different age groups has different productivities, the newest capital being technologically superior.

It is net investment rather than gross investment which is of primary importance for the particular model of this paper. We can obviously write

$$x = I + C. \tag{12.31}$$

Substituting (12.31) into (12.29a) we get

$$C = \delta_0 + \delta_1(I+C) + \delta_2' Z_{-1} \tag{12.32}$$

or

$$C = \frac{\delta_0}{1-\delta_1} + \frac{\delta_1}{1-\delta_1} I + \frac{\delta_2'}{1-\delta_1} Z_{-1}.$$

We can now eliminate C between (12.27) and (12.32) to get

$$I = \beta_2 + \beta_3 S + \beta_4 Z_{-1}. \tag{12.32}$$

This is the final form of our investment function.

There is now lacking one more equation for the completion of the system. Capitalists demand commodities in the form not only of producer and consumer goods but also in the form of labor power. Our equation of the demand for labor power will appear in a disguised form. We shall develop an equation which serves to determine the aggregate amount of variable capital, V. But this variable represents the total remuneration paid out by capitalists for labor power. The equation which serves to determine V in our system is the same thing as the demand equation for labor power.

Those familiar with Marx will recall that he regarded the surplus value as transformed into variable and constant capital in his schemes of expanded reproduction. We could have made $C + V$ a function of S instead of making C alone a function of S. However, since Marx always assumed a definite relation between C and V, we were able to eliminate V in the above relation. He imposed the condition that variable and constant capital be used in the same proportions throughout the production process; hence we were able to develop a relation between C and S not involving V. While Marx assumed a definite relation between C and V, he also assumed a definite relation between S and V.

Effective demand and employment

It may appear that we are getting too many equations, but both these relations (that between C and V, and that between S and V) are not independent. Suppose that total capital is a function of surplus value

$$C + V = f(S) \tag{12.34}$$

and that variable capital is also a function of surplus value

$$C + V(S) = f(S) \tag{12.35}$$

or

$$C = f^*(S).$$

This forms the basis of equation (12.27). It is evident that there must also be a relation between C and V, since

$$S = V^{-1}(V) \tag{12.36}$$

and

$$C = f^*(V^{-1}[V]) = f^{**}(V).$$

This simple demonstration shows that a relation vetween C and S and a relation between V and S imply a relation between C and V. The latter relation is not independent of the other two; hence there are not too many equations.[21]

As was seen above in the brief discussion of the theory of the falling rate of profit, the assumption, $S/V = $ constant, led to very important conclusions, In the numerical examples of expanded reproduction, Marx maintained a constant ratio between S and V. This assumption implies that labor will receive a constant fraction of net national income. Economists have long been puzzled by the fact that national-income statistics have shown labor's share of total income to be nearly constant over a long time period. There has possibly been some trend in these data which show that labor's share has been gradually increasing. This trend term could be explained by the institutional phenomenon of a growing labor movement in the USA.

The next equation is thus

$$V = \gamma_1 S. \tag{12.37}$$

---

[21]The above demonstration is a method of keeping the system from becoming overdetermined. However, it is questionable whether Marx intended the relation between C and V to be dependent on other relations or whether he intended it to be an independent technological phenomenon. From a technological point of view, there is no reason why labor and capital should be used in a fixed relation during the entire production process; hence we have not made use of an independent technological relation between C and V.

We may introduce the trend by a modification to

$$V = \gamma_0 + \gamma_1 S + \gamma_2 t. \tag{12.37a}$$

Since $V + S = Y$, it is equivalent to say that V and S are proportional or that V and Y are proportional. In recent years the stability of labor's share has usually been discussed in terms of V and Y rather than V and S. As an alternative formulation, we could write

$$V = \gamma_3 + \gamma_4 Y + \gamma_5 t. \tag{12.38}$$

The Marxian system is now complete. The entire set of equations is[22]

$$R = \alpha_0 + \alpha_1 S + \alpha_2 V, \tag{12.39}$$
$$I = \beta_0 + \beta_1 S + \beta_2 Z_{-1}, \tag{12.40}$$
$$V = \gamma_0 + \gamma_1 Y + \gamma_2 t \tag{12.41}$$
$$Y = S + V, \tag{12.42}$$
$$Y = R + I, \tag{12.43}$$
$$\Delta Z = I. \tag{12.44}$$

Equation (12.39) follows from (12.26a), (12.40) from (12.33), (12.41) from (12.38), (12.42) from (12.22), (12.43) from (12.23), and (12.44) from (12.30). We have, in (12.39)–(12.44), six equations and six endogenous variables, R, V, S, I, Z, Y. All variables are measured in 'real' units, and we have been able to complete the system without introducing the quantity of money.

Several observations are called for before we go on to some problems of economic analysis based upon this model. While it is true that this version of the Marxian theory has been developed largely through an examination of Marx's writings and by a slight generalization of his own methods (i.e. a generalization of his numerical examples into functional relationships), the same model can readily be developed from other considerations. By assuming certain behavior patterns for workers and capitalists, like utility and profit maximization, we can obtain the same mathematical model. The reader will also notice that the model (12.39)–(12.44) is very similar to Kalecki's theories. Practically no model implies a unique theoretical basis. Furthermore, we have not utilized Marx's methods to their fullest extent. Only those aspects of Marx's theories are used that are necessary to build a complete system of equations. Many Marxian theories are unrelated to the principle of effective demand, but even some of those parts of his theory that are related to effective demand have been left out. It was necessary to make the latter omission in order to keep from getting an overdetermined

---

[22] We have renumbered all subscripts on the parameters for purely aesthetic reasons.

Effective demand and employment   231

model. For example, Marx assumed that the wage *rate* would be determined by the value of the means of subsistence of a worker, where the means of subsistence, in turn, depends upon the traditional standard of life in the particular region where the worker lives. But it is easy to show that the model cannot contain this theory of an autonomous wage rate as well as the theory underlying equation (12.41). Suppose that equation (12.41) is accepted as a correct theory. The model then enables us to determine the real wage bill and the level of output. Every system must contain a technological input–output relationship. In the Marxian system, input is given by the employment of labor power and the depreciation of fixed capital, C. From our discussion there are enough relations to determine output and C; hence the other type of input, employment of labor power, is uniquely determined. Since the real wage bill and employment are known, the real wage rate is also known. There is no room in this system for an autonomously determined wage rate. The strong empirical foundation behind equation (12.41) is an argument for using this Marxian hypothesis rather than the other hypothesis of a given wage rate. It is certain that both hypotheses cannot be used simultaneously within the framework of our model. This examples serves to show that the above model is not the only mathematization of *Capital*. There are a variety of models that can be developed from the Marxian theories, and we have chosen one that is plausible, simple, and useful for the analysis of specific problems.

It is interesting to make certain comparisons between the Keynesian and the Marxian models. A simple version of the Keynesian theory – in which the quantity of money and the interest rate do not appear as variables – is a special case of the Marxian model. By substitution from (12.41) and (12.42) into (12.39), it is possible to make consumption a function of income; and, by substitution from (12.46) and (12.42) into (12.40), it is possible to make investment a function of income and the stock of capital. For the short run theories, Keynes took the stock of capital as given; thus, such a reduced version of the Marxian model comes to the same thing as the simple Keynesian model. The primary advantage of the Marxian model is that it provides more information than does the Keynesian system. In the former model the complete solution always gives the demand for consumer goods, producer goods, and employment, while in some forms[23] of the latter model, complete solution gives only the demand for consumer goods and the demand for producer goods. The demand for factors of production (employment

[23]This is true in those forms of the Keynesian theory in which the savings–investment equation alone is used to determine the level of output.

and producer goods) determines supply; hence the Marxian model has the virtue of always giving the full conditions of demand and supply. This cannot be said, in general, of the Keynesian model.

It is not meant to imply that Marx fully anticipated the Keynesian theory of effective demand. Our model is intended as an extension of the Marxian analysis to a logical conclusion in terms of a theory of effective demand. Actually, Marx laid the groundwork for a complete equation system to determine the level of income (effective demand) but did not build the complete system. In his discussions of the reproduction schemes in Volume II of *Capital*, Marx set forth some conditions under which there would not be excessive savings in the system, conditions under which all savings are offset. He then showed that these conditions are very complex and that it is not reasonable to assume that they will always be met, hence the crisis. But he did not offer an exact theory to show the quantitative extent to which they will not be met. Keynes's theory also shows the conditions for full employment and argues that they will not always be met, but Keynes went one step further. He provided a general theory to determine the level of employment when it is not one of full employment. The Keynesian model shows how any level of employment is determined. Our procedure in this paper has been to introduce mathematical extensions of the Marxian theory to show how any level of income (or employment) is determined. In case the conditions for full employment – or for no glut of the market in Marx's sense – are not met, our mathematical model shows precisely what level of employment will ensue under the less-than-full-employment conditions.

It should be pointed out that the author has applied various methods of statistical estimation to the Marxian model and has found the estimated parameters to be very reasonable in size. Moreover, the model fits the observed data very closely, Except for small random error, workers and capitalists have, in fact, behaved as the Marxian model says they behave. Lags, government investment, taxes etc., were introduced in the statistical models in order to depict the real world more exactly. A discussion of the statistical results is too lengthy to be included in this paper, and the conclusions are mentioned only to inform the reader that the model is not purely hypothetical.

THE STAGNATION THESIS

It has become very popular of late to criticize the stagnation thesis severely and to assert that ours is still a young, vigorous, expanding

Effective demand and employment 233

economy. The critics have been quick to forget the lesson of the thirties and have misunderstood the thesis. Negative though most criticism has been, the spirit of this section is one of constructive criticism, by which some new ideas that support the thesis may be injected into the argument.

Despite the fact that the stagnation thesis grew out of the discussions of Keynesian economics of the past decade, the foundations of the theory are much older, going back to Marx's theory of the falling rate of profit. The critics would have had a much more difficult time finding evidence against a mature-economy doctrine based on the theory of the falling rate of profit than against the doctrine based on such factors as population growth, disappearance of the frontier, and growth of depreciation reserves. They were quick to point out that population growth slowed down and the frontier disappeared long before the decade of the thirties, yet stagnation did not then set in.

The Marxian theory states that, with a constant rate of surplus value (S/V), the rate of profit will vary inversely with capital accumulation. Equation (12.20) shows the rate of profit is the product of 'the rate of surplus value' and 'one minus the organic composition of capital.' Capital accumulation implies a rising organic composition of capital and, hence, a falling rate of profit from (12.20). The main hypothesis of this theory, the constancy of the rate of surplus value, is known to be valid, as shown by the available data. This theory can easily be applied to the interwar period. The application runs as follows: After World War I the profit outlook in manufacturing (especially automobile), utilities, and housing appeared to be good and persistent. Capitalists accumulated all during the twenties. They built so many plants and houses and so much equipment that the rate of return on the expanded volume began to fall. The rate of return on the greatly expanded capital structure was so small during the thirties that there was little capital investment and the system was depressed for a decade. It was the capital accumulation of the twenties which led to the fall in the rate of profit and the consequent stagnation of the thirties. The theory does not say that the stagnation or maturity is permanent. It is no contradiction of the theory to observe that housing capital, *relative to the population*, declined during World War II, thus generating a high rate of return on housing capital and a building boom again. Similarly, the present capital expansion in other industries is no contradiction of the theory. However, the theory indicates specifically that the capital expansion will not continue indefinitely. Once a large stock of capital has been accumulated again, the mature-economy doctrine should predict another stagnant period of a decade or more.

In the Marxian model, (12.39)–(12.44), it will be observed that the demand for investment goods depends upon two variables – profits and the stock of capital. The essence of the Marxian theory is that both variables must be in this relation. The dependence on profit is positive, and the dependence on capital is negative. The stock of capital becomes a very serious drag upon the system. Many of the present author's statistical investigations in separate industries, as well as for the economy as a whole, have shown that the stock of fixed capital is negatively related to investment. The more capital there is, other things unchanged, the less is the desire for new capital. The consequences of capital accumulation have never been fully explored. For example, if we drop the capital variable from the Marxian model or if we use the customary forms of the Keynesian model, the multiplier equation for the whole system usually takes the form:

$$Y + \alpha_1 Y_{-1} + \alpha_2 Y_{-2} + \ldots + \alpha_n Y_{-n} = \beta G, \qquad (12.45)$$

where

Y = real income
G = real exogenous investment.

If, on the other hand, the variable Z_{-1} = stock of fixed capital is introduced in the equation of demand for producer goods, the multiplier equation will have the form:

$$Y + \alpha_1 Y_{-1} + \alpha_2 Y_{-2} + \ldots + \alpha_n Y_{-n} = \beta_1 G + \beta_2 G_{-1}. \qquad (12.46)$$

The difference between (12.45) and (12.46) is significant. The values of β and β_1 will be positive, but if capital has a depressing influence on investment, the value of β_2 will be negative. Both the truncated and the untruncated multipliers from (12.46) will be smaller, the larger is the negative value of β_2. The depressing influence of capital accumulation operates not only partially in the demand equation for producer goods but also permeates the entire system with a depressing influence. The stimulative shocks given to the system by exogenous investment, such as new industries and government spending, will be cushioned by the depressing influence of capital accumulation.

The reason for introducing the stock of fixed capital in the investment-demand equation of the Marxian system is that in this form the equation fits in so well with the theory of the falling rate of profit. It is also possible to argue that an implied 'theory of the declining marginal efficiency of capital' in the Keynesian theory would call for the introduction of a variable representing capital accumulation in the Keynesian investment schedule. In the past, economists have modified

Effective demand and employment 235

the Keynesian investment function in this way, but only for the long-run theory in which investment is zero. The real world, however, is not one of long-run equilibrium in which investment is zero or one short-run equilibrium in which the stock of capital is taken as given. The real world falls between these extremes, and the Marxian model of this paper is a representation of the compromise.

REDISTRIBUTION OF INCOME

No theory has received more vulgarizations than has the theory of the effect on employment of the redistribution of income. The correct results need to be systematized with all assumptions stated explicitly. For simplicity, we shall consider redistribution between only two types of income, wages and nonwages (=profits). One type of vulgarization is to look at wages only as a demand factor and not at wages as a cost factor. The argument is that a redistribution from profits into wages will always increase income and employment.

Many old-fashioned trade-unionists argue that the only way to cure a condition of unemployment is to redistribute income from profits into wages. They see faulty distribution as the principal flaw in the economic system and regard its correction as a sufficient policy to insure smooth working of the social mechanism. Many economists who call themselves Keynesians have also relied very heavily on redistribution of income as a powerful antidepression policy. They have often overemphasized the demand aspects of wages to the neglect of the cost aspects.

There is another group of economists who look at wages purely as a cost factor and neglect the influence of wages as a demand factor. Most of the supporters of wage cuts as a policy for curing depressions are in this category. They argue that, if wages are cut, capitalists will have lower costs and hence will be able to expand their plants. This argument is wrong not only because it is based on an incorrect analysis of redistribution but also because it does not take into account the possibility that falling wages may generate adverse expectations.

Obviously, the most proper type of model for analyzing the effects of redistribution is one that gives full effect to wages as a cost factor and to wages as a demand factor. The Marxian model is very well suited for this purpose. The consumption function distinguishes between wages and profits as separate demand factors, while the investment function – an equation of capitalist behavior alone – depends on profits, which means that wages enter as a cost factor. If our analysis is limited to the instantaneous effect on output of redistribution of income *within a given period*, we can neglect the influence of capital accumulation as a variable in the investment function. The term $\beta_2 Z_{-1}$, in (12.40), can be incorporated with the constant term because $\beta_2 Z_{-1}$ is predetermined and thus given for any single time period.

The following result can be stated for our model: If the capitalists' marginal propensity to spend (consume and invest) is greater than the workers' marginal propensity to consume, redistribution from profits into wages will decrease income. If the two marginal propensities are the same, income will be unaffected by the redistribution, and if the latter marginal propensity is greater than the former, redistribution from profits into wages will increase the level of income. It is by no means certain, *a priori*, which propensity is greater. Capitalists like to accumulate, and workers like to consume. Only by making accurate quantitative measurements of the propensities can the final result be determined. The author has found that some methods of statistical estimation give one result, and some methods give another. By any method of estimation used thus far, the confidence intervals for the parameters are so large that no definite conclusion can be drawn.

The intuitive explanation of the foregoing propositions is very simple. If a dollar is taken away from a capitalist, he will cut expenditures by the amount of his marginal propensity to spend, and, if this dollar is given to a worker, he will increase expenditures by the amount of his marginal propensity to consume. The quantitative effect on income depends on the extent to which these marginal propensities diverge. The data upon which the statistical models are based show that the marginal propensities are, at least, close together. If we take into account the capitalists' marginal propensity to spend on producer goods as well as the marginal propensity to spend on consumer goods, we find that the total marginal propensity to spend is probably between 0.7 and 0.9. The workers' marginal propensity to spend is also in the same neighborhood, between 0.8 and 0.9. In the discussion of redistribution, economists often tend to consider only the two groups' marginal propensities to consume, which are, of course, much farther apart.

There are special cases in which unequivocal results can be obtained. Marx has been interpreted as having claimed that the workers spend all their income, i.e. have a marginal propensity to consume equal to unity. If, as seems reasonable, the capitalists have a marginal propensity to spend which is less than unity, it follows by assumption that redistribution from profits into wages will always stimulate production. It can be shown that, for this case in the Marxian model, the increase in

Effective demand and employment 237

income is always greater than twice the amount redistributed. This is not a realistic case, however, because time-series and family-budget data both show that the marginal propensity to consume out of wages is not so great as unity. The budget data show little or no aggregate savings in the low-income classes, but some investigators have wrongly interpreted this to mean that the marginal propensity to consume is unity. The thing to look at is not the aggregate savings in the low-income groups but the slope of the savings or consumption function in this income range. The slope is definitely not unity throughout the range $0–3000 income per year. In this income range there are both dissaving and saving, which cancel each other to a large extent and make the total appear small. But the dissaving can always be more or less than the observed amount, and it is not correct to infer that the existence of dissaving means that low-income families consume exactly 100 percent of every extra dollar of income that they receive.

Another special case in which the effects of redistribution can be more exactly assessed is that of exogenous investment. If it is believed that investment decisions of businessmen are unrelated to variables internal to the system – depending instead on innovations, psychological expectations, legislative decisions etc. – the only relevant parameters for the redistribution problem are the marginal propensities to consume of workers and capitalists. The data show definitely that the marginal propensity to consume of the former class is greater than that of the latter class; therefore, within the framework of the model of exogenous investment, redistribution from profits into wages will always stimulate income.

There are also special models where redistribution from profits into wages certainly decreases income. For example, there is a tendency on the part of many model-builders to assume that total income (wages plus profits) is the relevant variable in the consumption function. This assumption gives equal weight to wages and profits on the side of demand for consumer goods. If, to this assumption, is added the assumption that investment expenditures depend on profits, the marginal propensity to spend out of profits will be greater than the marginal propensity to consume out of wages, and redistribution will have the above-stated effect.

There is nothing in the uncertainty of the conclusions of this section to contradict either the Marxian or Keynesian theoretical systems. This point must be made clear because many supporters of these theories make more extravagant claims about redistribution than can be justified on the grounds of the theories of employment alone, convincing though these claims may be from the point of view of economic welfare, equity, and justice.

In the Marxian theory, to state matters mildly, there is no hint that redistribution of income is a sufficient policy to insure that capitalism will always provide uninterrupted full production and employment. This is consistent with the findings that the marginal propensity to spend out of profits is not very different from the marginal propensity to spend out of wages, so that the redistribution effect is minimized. If the system is such that the latter marginal propensity exceeds the former, one must conclude that workers are kept so close to physical subsistence that they are forced to spend practically all their income. This is the situation which calls for redistribution from profits into wages as an employment-creating policy. If the former marginal propensity exceeds the latter, the Marxian explanation is that capitalism generates such fears and uncertainties about the future in the minds of the workers that they are forced to save for the 'rainy day.' Precautionary saving of this type is enough to drive their marginal propensity to consume below the marginal propensity to spend out of profits. Under such circumstances, redistribution from profits into wages which does not alleviate the fear of the future[24] will not create employment. In the Marxian theory, redistribution policies which do not alter the mode of production are not adequate to solve the problem of the occurrence of crises.

---

[24]Social security planning is a type of redistribution which does alleviate the fear of the future.

13
Stock and Flow Analysis in Economics

It is not always irrelevant whether one deals with stock or flow variables in economic analysis. Some simple dynamic models are shown in which the choice between stock and flow variables becomes essential. It is also not true that the liquidity preference theory of interest is identical with the loanable funds theory of interest. This problem is intimately connected with the distinctions between stock and flow analysis. These two interest theories are shown to be different in simple dynamic models.

W. Fellner and H. M. Somers have overlooked[1] some of the important differences between the analysis of stocks and flows in monetary interest theory. It is correct but unenlightening to claim that, if the proper mathematical transformations are used, the relationships describing the economic system may be written either in terms of flows or of stocks. There are, however, some tricks involved, and it would be misleading simply to write off flow analysis and stock analysis as equivalent.

To fix ideas on a more precise footing, I shall proceed immediately to a simple mathematical model that contains the bare essentials of the matter at hand, I intend to show that there exist models in which the arguments of Fellner and Somers are incorrect, but I do not claim that there are no models in which they are correct, although I do consider the latter models trivial in some essential features.

Let us consider an aggregative economy in which the subjects can hold goods, perpetuities, or cash. Perpetuities are issued by the business firms and held by the households. The government controls the total issue of cash, which can be held by households or firms. Interest

---

Editor's Note In addition to the above reference, the reader's attention is invited to the following: W. Fellner and H. M. Somers, 'Alternative monetary approaches to interest theory,' *Review of Economics and Statistics*, **23**, February (1941), 43–8; and Lawrence R. Klein, *The Keynesian Revolution*, Macmillan, New York, pp. 117–23.

[1] W. Fellner and H. M. Somers, 'Notes on "stocks" and "flows" in monetary interest theory,' *Review of Economics and Statistics*, **31**, May (1949), 145–6.

payments are calculated on volume of securities held at the beginning of an accounting period. Accumulation of real capital will be ignored. The notation is as follows:

n_t = employment (flow during period t),
x_t = goods (flow during period t),
B_t = market value of perpetuities (stock at the end of period t),
M_{1t} = household cash (stock at end of period t),
M_{2t} = business cash (stock at end of period t),
w_t = wage rate (average during period t),
p_t = price of goods (average during period t),
r_t = interest rate (average during period t).

The equations of the system are

$$x_t^D = f_1(w_t/p_t, r_t), \quad \text{household demand for goods}, \quad (13.1)$$

$$x_t^S = f_2(w_t/p_t, r_t), \quad \text{business supply of goods}, \quad (13.2)$$

$$n_t^D = g_1(w_t/p_t, r_t), \quad \text{business demand for labor}, \quad (13.3)$$

$$n_t^S = g_2(w_t/p_t, r_t), \quad \text{household supply of labor}, \quad (13.4)$$

$$M_{1t}^D/p_t = h_1(w_t n_t^D/p_t, r_t), \quad \text{household demand for cash}, \quad (13.5)$$

$$M_{2t}^D/p_t = h_2(p_t x_t^D/p_t, r_t), \quad \text{business demand for cash}, \quad (13.6)$$

$$M_{1,t-1} + (1+r_t)B_{t-1} + w_t n_t^S - p_t x_t^D = M_{1t}^D + B_t^D,$$
$$\text{household budget restriction}, \quad (13.7)$$

$$M_{2,t-1} - (1+r_t)B_{t-1} - w_t n_t^D + p_t x_t^S = M_{2t}^D - B_t^S,$$
$$\text{business budget restriction}, \quad (13.8)$$

$$M_{1t}^D + M_{2t}^D = k = \text{constant, condition of stock equilibrium}, \quad (13.9)$$

$$x_t^D = x_t^S, \quad \text{condition of flow equilibrium}, \quad (13.10)$$

$$n_t^D = n_t^S, \quad \text{condition of flow equilibrium}. \quad (13.11)$$

In this system of eleven equations there are eleven variables as of time t: x_t^D, x_t^S, w_t, p_t, r_t, n_t^D, n_t^S, M_{1t}^D, M_{2t}^D, B_t^D, B_t^S. I shall assume that a unique, classical solution exists for this system, given the lagged values of M_1, M_2, and B. This procedure disregards, obviously, the possibilities of inconsistency which I look upon as the basis for the modern theory of employment and have discussed elsewhere. This accords also with my view of the de-emphasis of liquidity preference in the theory of employment.

This model is presented as a framework for analysis at the static level without further justification. It represents my version of classical economics except possibly for the fact that r_t appears as a variable in (13.5) and (13.6), but that is necessary in order to deal with the problem at hand. The question may legitimately be raised whether or not this classical model could be derived from the classical theories of utility and profit maximization in the household and business sectors of the economy. I shall only indicate an answer to this question without going into the formal details of derivation. Let us regard an individual consumer as maximizing a utility function depending upon a stream of goods, services, cash, and securities over a planning period and subject to a budget constraint. The budget constraint suitable for the maximization process will not be (13.7); it will instead be

$$\sum_{t=1}^{T} \frac{w_t n_t^S - p_t x_t^D}{(1+r_1)\dots(1+r_t)} = 0,$$

which is obtained by discounting the sum of (13.7) over the period $1, 2, \ldots, T$ and assuming that the capital value of the household plan is zero; i.e. that the discounted stream of first differences in each period's cash holdings and the difference between the initial stock of securities and the discounted final value are zero. Plans are laid anew for each accounting period so that the demand-supply equations for variables carrying a subscript $t=1$ become the effective demand-supply equations (13.1) and (13.4), and the effective budget restriction is (13.7). If the capital value of the plan is not zero, the equation system must be modified by allowing initial (lagged) stocks of wealth to appear as variables in (13.1)–(13.6). A similar scheme can be developed for the equations in the business sector of the economy.

From what I have presented thus far, it is not possible to say that the interest theory imbedded in (13.1)–(13.11) is based on the equation of supply and demand for cash or of supply and demand for securities. The demand equations for cash are (13.5) and (13.6); they are equated to the supply of cash in (13.9). The demand equation for securities is obtained by substituting (13.1), (13.4), and (13.5) into (13.7). The supply equation of securities is obtained by substituting (13.2), (13.3), and (13.6) into (13.8). If (13.9), (13.10), and (13.11) hold, then the demand for securities must equal the supply of securities. Hence a unique set of equilibrium market variables (w_t, p_t, r_t) is consistent with the two propositions that the supply and demand for the stock of cash are equated and that the supply and demand for the stock of securities are equated. I need not emphasize the emptiness of this proposition.[2]

[2]Since the interest and real wage rates can be obtained from (13.1)–(13.4) and (13.10)–(13.11), Hicks's time-honored demonstration of the equivalence of the liquidity preference and loanable funds theories makes little sense. The interest rate is determined in the real

The demand-supply equations for securities implied by (13.1)–(13.11) involve stock concepts. Since this model is a formalization of the Fellner-Somers model, I cannot understand why they insist that their supply-demand relation for securities (claims) is clearly a flow concept. Only if the derived demand-supply equations could be written with $B_t - B_{t-1}$ as a function of market variables alone is it reasonable to call them flow concepts.

I (and others) have really meant something more than is contained in the above model when I say that the determination of the interest rate is derived from the theory of liquidity preference. The static equilibrium model of (13.1)–(13.11) is only an abstraction (of high order) derived from a closer counterpart of the true economic process. I shall only invoke the classical 'law of supply and demand' to demonstrate what I mean by a liquidity-preference theory of interest. My version of a hypothesis, which can be tested against the facts, is the following: 'When the supply of cash exceeds the demand for cash the interest rate falls, and when the demand for cash exceeds the supply of cash the interest rate rises.' An additional specification of this nature is absolutely necessary in order to give some content to the idea that the interest rate is a variable which brings about an equation of the supply and demand for cash. In place of equilibrium condition (13.9), I shall write the dynamic equation

$$r_t - r_{t-1} = h_3(k_t - M^D_{1t} - M^D_{2t}), \tag{13.9a}$$

with the property $0 = h_3(0)$; therefore (13.9) is consistent with (13.9a). In the dynamic system k_t is an exogenous variable. It is not necessarily a constant. It should also be stressed that k_t includes the excess reserves of the banking system. With a precious-metal reserve of G_t and a reserve ratio of λ, one may look upon $(1/\lambda) G_t$ as the potential supply of cash.

The routine versions of the dynamic replacements for (13.10) and (13.11) are

$$p_t - p_{t-1} = f_3(x^S_t - x^D_t) \qquad 0 = f_3(0), \tag{13.10a}$$

$$w_t - w_{t-1} = g_3(n^S_t - n^D_t) \qquad 0 = g_3(0). \tag{13.11a}$$

---

sector of the economy, where cash and securities can *both be ignored, provided initial stocks of wealth are not included in* (13.1)–(13.4) as indicated above. This classical approach does not rule out the concept of liquidity preference; it merely shows that this concept fits in with conventional equilibrium theory as well as with the modern theory of employment.

Stock and flow analysis

In the dynamic model (13.1)–(13.8), (13.9a)–(13.11a), I have a liquidity-preference theory of interest, and I do not have a supply-demand-for-securities theory of interest. By this remark I mean that there is not, in the model, a unique relation between the excess demand for securities and fluctuations in the rate of interest. The algebra of the situation leads to an excess demand relation for securities of the form

$$B_t^D - B_t^S = h_3^{-1}(r_t - r_{t-1}) + (M_{1,t-1} + M_{2,t-1} - k_t)$$
$$+ w_t g_3^{-1}(w_t - w_{t-1}) + p_t f_3^{-1}(p_t - p_{t-1}) \qquad (13.12)$$

Unless the sum of terms of the right-hand member after the first vanish identically in t, the relation between excess demand for securities and interest fluctuations does not hold.

Should I suppress (13.9a) and use instead

$$r_t - r_{t-1} = h_4(B_t^S - B_t^D), \qquad (13.9b)$$

I should no longer claim that my model contains a liquidity-preference theory of interest.

I have followed the conventional treatment of the 'law of supply and demand,' but the more general possibility

$$h(k_t - M_{1t}^D - M_{2t}^D, p_t - p_{t-1}, w_t - w_{t-1}, r_t - r_{t-1}) = 0, \qquad (13.9c)$$
$$f(x_t^S - x_t^D, p_t - p_{t-1}, w_t - w_{t-1}, r_t - r_{t-1}) = 0, \qquad (13.10c)$$
$$g(n_t^S - n_t^D, p_t - p_{t-1}, w_t - w_{t-1}, r_t - r_{t-1}) = 0, \qquad (13.11c)$$

should not be overlooked. Instead of assuming that a single market price moves to wipe out a maladjustment between demand and supply, it seems preferable to assume that several market prices move to eradicate the maladjustment. Since many items are interrelated in demand or supply, it is not absolutely necessary that an item's own price must be called upon to perform the entire adjustment process. In a model consisting of (13.1)–(13.8) and (13.9c)–(13.11c), there is not enough information to characterize it as containing a liquidity-preference theory of interest rather than a supply-demand-for-securities theory.

The difference between flow analysis and stock analysis can be brought out clearly in this connection. Let the demand for any economic quantity during a period of time be denoted by y_t^D and the supply by y_t^S. The time dimension of these variables is such that they are flows. The average price at which they are traded during period t will be written as q_t. It is one theory to use the equation

$$q_t - q_{t-1} = F(y_t^S - y_t^D) \qquad F(0) = 0,$$

and quite another to use

$$q_t - q_{t-1} = F^* \left[\sum_{i=-\infty}^{t} (y_i^S - y_i^D) \right] \qquad F^*(0) = 0.$$

One relation assumes an adjustment to flow equilibrium and the other to stock equilibrium. In the continuous case it is well-known that these two theories lead to entirely different results.[3] It makes a good deal of difference in the Fellner-Somers theory whether the rate of interest is a fluctuating variable that tends to equilibrate the supply and demand for the outstanding stocks of securities or for the flow of securities during a period of time. For example, they must state unambiguously whether they view

$$r_t - r_{t-1} = G(B_t^S - B_{t-1}^S - B_t^D + B_{t-1}^D), \qquad G(0) = 0, \qquad (13.13)$$

or

$$r_t - r_{t-1} = G^*(B_t^S - B_t^D) \qquad G^*(0) = 0, \qquad (13.14)$$

as valid relationships, in case they support the supply-demand-for-securities theory of interest. This point they have failed to realize.

It is something of a generalization to go from static equilibrium to a dynamic model, but it is still unsatisfactory. In econometric work one is never permitted to disregard the fact that the model has a stochastic structure. The particular sort of stochastic structure that is almost always assumed is one that requires clear thinking on the matter of stocks vs. flows. The choice of a method of statistical estimation depends on whether one assumes that people behave so as to demand a *stock* of cash in relation to certain market variables and income plus a nonautocorrelated random error or whether behavior is such that people demand a *flow* of cash in relation to certain market variables and income (or differences of these variables) plus a nonautocorrelated random error.[4] One must first decide whether fundamental economic decisions are made in terms of stock or flow variables in each particular case.

A final remark concerns a statement of 'the obvious' by Fellner and Somers. They say:

> But it surely is evident without further argument that the value of a variable cannot equate the demand for anything with the supply

[3]See, for example, P. A. Samuelson, 'The stability of equilibrium: Comparative statics and dynamics,' *Econometrica*, **9**, April (1941), 107–8, 112–13.

[4]The choice between a stock or a flow formulation affects the autocorrelation properties of the random errors in an obvious way. It is, of course, possible that neither formulation leads to nonautocorrelation.

Stock and flow analysis

of that thing *over a period of time*, unless it also accomplishes the equality of the willingness to hold that thing and the existing stock of that thing at any point of time during that period!

Let the continuous variable $z(t)$ denote the flow of excess demand for z at instant t. Surely they would not claim that a price system securing $\int_T^{T+1} z(t)\,dt = 0$ automatically secures $\int_{-\infty}^{T+\theta} z(t)\,dt = 0$ for all θ, $0 \leqslant \theta \leqslant 1$. Even the stronger assumption of continuous market clearance of the flow over the whole interval $(T, T+1)$, i.e., $z(t) = 0$, $T \leqslant t \leqslant T+1$, does not imply the clearance of the market for stocks unless $\int_{-\infty}^T z(t)\,dt = 0$.

14
The Use of Econometric Models as a Guide to Economic Policy

It is desirable to provide tools of analysis suited for public economic policy that are, as much as possible, independent of the personal judgements of a particular investigator. Econometric models are put forth in this scientific spirit, because these models, if fully developed and properly used, eventually should lead all investigators to the same conclusions, independent of their personal whims. The usual experience in the field of economic policy is that there are about as many types of advice as there are advisors (sometimes even more!).

Statistical models of the working of the economy are not proposed as magic formulas which divulge all the secrets of the complex real world in a single equation. The statistical models attempt to provide as much information about future or other unknown phenomena as can be gleaned from the historical records of observable and measurable facts. To the extent to which people maintain their past behavior patterns in the future, the statistical models provide information about the quantitative properties of economic variables in the future. However, econometricians do not operate in a vacuum; their methods are not purely mechanical in the sense that they do nothing but substitute in formulas. Any information of a qualitative nature that is available should be used by the econometrician in drawing inferences about the real world from his models. For example, suppose that an econometrician is called upon to forecast next year's level of employment and suppose further that this econometrician knows that war will break out next year. Would the econometrician merely substitute into his equations of peacetime behavior patterns in order to forecast employment in a period during which there will be war? Obviously, any qualitative information (e.g. the outbreak of war next year) must be taken into account in order to make a proper forecast.

It must be emphasized that the forecasts for fiscal year 1947 in this paper were all made during the week of November 10, 1946.

This paper was presented at the meeting of the Econometric Society at Atlantic City, January 25, 1947. It was reprinted as Cowles Commission Papers, New Series, No. 23.

From *Econometrica*, **15**, April (1947), 111–51.

The nonstatistical economist has only qualitative information from which to make judgements. The statistical economist has this same qualitative information plus a thorough knowledge of historically developed behavior patterns; hence it may be said that the latter is better equipped.

TYPES OF POLICIES

The ideas that grew out of the discussion on the Full Employment Bill showed clearly the close relationship between forecasting and economic policy. As the Bill was originally drafted, it called for a periodic forecast of the deflationary or inflationary gap. A predicted deflationary gap would call for one type of policy and a predicted inflationary gap for another type of policy. Thus the first step in carrying out the provisions of the Bill is to make a forecast. The success of the public policy will depend vitally on the accuracy of the forecast. An important use of econometric models, as will be demonstrated below, is to make forecasts.

The second step in the implementation of a Full Employment Bill is to wipe out the forecasted deflationary or inflationary gap. This step will also have to be quantitative. How much employment will be created by an x per cent cut in taxes? By how much will prices be expected to rise if government expenditures rise by a known amount with constant tax rates? These are only a sample of the types of questions that must be answered in order to decide among alternative policies. It is evident that the answers to such questions depend upon consumer and business spending–saving habits. The statistical approach is to examine the spending–saving habits of past periods in order to get some idea of the pattern of future habits.

Suppose that the population's habits are going to change in a known way. We may want to know the effect of this change upon the entire system. If we have econometric models, we can often predict the results of such changes. An example can easily be given. If it is known that the introduction of a social security program will raise the marginal propensity to consume by y per cent because people will be more certain of the future, the quantitative effects of the program can be estimated in advance from statistical models. The estimate may very well have some influence on the decision whether or not to adopt the social-security scheme.

A similar use of models arises in the study of the effects of technological change. A change in the technique of production can often be translated into an exact quantitative change in some of the parameters of the production function that has been statistically determined from data which referred to the old process of production. It is possible to calculate the change in several relevant variables of the system such as employment, output, wages, prices etc., as a result of the technological change, provided we have an appropriate econometric model. On the basis of the limited number of observations available for testing different economic models from which to form policy decisions, it is not yet possible to select an unique model. More than one model are consistent with the observations. In this paper we shall present three plausible models, and methods of forming policy will be studied with each alternative. The reader is free to choose among the models, all of which rest on different hypotheses. Other models, in addition to those presented here, have also been studied by the author, but they are not demonstrated in order to avoid repetition.

MODEL I – EXOGENOUS INVESTMENT

A simple model in which there is little possibility of confusion is useful to demonstrate some very specific applications of econometric models in policy formation.

$\mathscr{C}$ = consumer expenditures measured in billions of current dollars.

$\mathscr{I}'$ = gross private capital formation measured in billions of current dollars.

$\mathscr{G}$ = government expenditures on goods and services measured in billions of current dollars.

$\mathscr{Y}$ = disposable income measured in billions of current dollars.

$\mathscr{GNP}$ = gross national product measured in billions of current dollars (expenditure concept).[1]

$\mathscr{T}$ = government payments + corporate savings + business reserves − transfer payments − inventory profits, all measured in billions of current dollars.

p = population of continental USA measured in billions of persons.

u = normally distributed random disturbance.

---

[1] Gross national product may be computed directly as the sum of consumer, business, and government spending (expenditure concept) or as the sum of income payments to factors of production and indirect taxes plus business reserves (income concept). The two measures should be equal but there is now a sizeable discrepancy of about $5 billion in the official estimates. The symbol $\mathscr{GNP}$ will refer everywhere in this paper to the expenditure concept.

The economic model connecting these variables is:

$$\frac{\mathscr{C}}{pN} = \alpha_0 + \alpha_1 \frac{\mathscr{Y}}{pN} + \alpha_2 \left(\frac{\mathscr{Y}}{pN}\right)_{-1} + u, \tag{14.1}$$

$$\mathscr{GNP} = \mathscr{C} + \mathscr{I}' + \mathscr{G}, \tag{14.2}$$

$$\mathscr{Y} + \mathscr{T} = \mathscr{GNP}. \tag{14.3}$$

Equation (14.1) is an economic-behavior equation which relates consumer spending to income, current and past. Since this is an equation of economic behavior, it is subject to random disturbance. Equations (14.2) and (14.3) are definitions. They hold exactly and are not subject to random disturbance.

The endogenous variables are $\mathscr{C}/pN$, $\mathscr{GNP}/pN$, and $\mathscr{Y}/pN$. The exogenous variables are $\mathscr{I}'/pN$, $\mathscr{G}/pN$, $\mathscr{T}/pN$. There is some question whether the truly exogenous variables of capital formation, government spending, and taxation, should be aggregates in current dollars or per capita variables in constant dollars. For the statistical estimation of the parameters of the system we shall proceed as though $\mathscr{I}'/pN$, $\mathscr{G}/pN$, and $\mathscr{T}/pN$ are the exogenous variables rather than $\mathscr{I}'$, $\mathscr{G}$, and $\mathscr{T}$, although the most correct solution is far from obvious.

Haavelmo[2] has shown that the system (14.1)–(14.3) may be solved to get

$$\frac{\mathscr{Y}}{pN} = \frac{\alpha_0}{1-\alpha_1} + \frac{\alpha_2}{1-\alpha_1}\left(\frac{\mathscr{Y}}{pN}\right)_{-1} + \frac{1}{1-\alpha_1}\left(\frac{\mathscr{I}'+\mathscr{G}-\mathscr{T}}{pN}\right) + \frac{1}{1-\alpha_1}u, \tag{14.4}$$

and that the parameters of this latter equation can be consistently estimated by the method of least squares if we make the assumptions that we have made about endogenous and exogenous variables. It will be observed that a knowledge of the estimates of the parameters of (14.4) leads to a knowledge of the estimates of the parameters of (14.1). Statistical estimates of (14.4) yield the results

$$\frac{\mathscr{Y}}{pN} = 202.54 + 0.37 \left(\frac{\mathscr{Y}}{pN}\right)_{-1} + 2.39 \frac{\mathscr{I}'+\mathscr{G}-\mathscr{T}}{pN}$$
$$\phantom{\frac{\mathscr{Y}}{pN} = 202.54 +\;} (0.12) \phantom{\left(\frac{\mathscr{Y}}{pN}\right)_{-1}\;} (0.28)$$

$$S = \$21.21; \quad \delta^2/S^2 = 1.14. \tag{14.5}$$

The numbers in parentheses below the coefficients are standard errors; S = square root of the estimate of the variance of $u/(1-\alpha_1)$; δ^2/S^2 = the ratio of the mean-square successive difference to the variance of the

---

[2] T. Haavelmo, 'Methods of measuring the marginal propensity to consume,' *Journal of the American Statistical Association*, **42**, March (1947) 105–22.

residuals. The distribution of this ratio has been tabulated,[3] and we conclude that the probability is slightly less than 3 per cent that we could get a sample value for δ^2/S^2 as small as 1.14 if the population values of the us were independent in time (i.e. nonautocorrelated). The sample value of δ^2/S^2 is slightly less than the size usually required (the value corresponding to the 5 per cent significance level) in order to be confident that the disturbances are random. The statistical methods assume that the disturbances are nonautocorrelated, and this assumption is not quite fulfilled in (14.5), although this is clearly a borderline case.

The numerical values of (14.5) imply the following numerical results for an estimate of (14.1):

$$\frac{\mathscr{C}}{pN} = 84.74 + 0.58 \frac{\mathscr{Y}}{pN} + 0.15 \left(\frac{\mathscr{Y}}{pN}\right)_{-1}. \qquad (14.6)$$

Provided the relevant information concerning the size of $\mathscr{I}', \mathscr{G}, \mathscr{T}$ is known in advance, equation (14.5) can be used to make forecasts. We generally know, in advance, the size of $\mathscr{G}$ and $\mathscr{T}$. Government expenditures are fixed by the budgets that are adopted by federal, state, and local governments; hence we can assign a definite value of $\mathscr{G}$. It is not possible to assign an unique value of $\mathscr{T}$ because the observed value of $\mathscr{T}$ depends upon the level of income. We estimated the parameters of (14.4) as though $\mathscr{T}$ were an exogenous variable but there is an error committed in this approach. $\mathscr{T}$, in fact, is a function of $\mathscr{Y}$ or $\mathscr{GNP}$, and the parameters of this function are the exogenous elements. One of the major elements of $\mathscr{T}$ is taxes. Taxes vary with income, but the government autonomously sets the tax rates. The parameters of the function connecting $\mathscr{T}$ and $\mathscr{GNP}$ are averages of these tax rates. In practice, we proceed as follows. We assume several hypothetical values of $\mathscr{GNP}$ and estimate according to existing laws on taxes, unemployment compensation etc., the corresponding values of $\mathscr{T}$. We then determine from these hypothetical values of $\mathscr{T}$ and $\mathscr{GNP}$ a relation of the form:

$$\mathscr{T} = \beta_0 + \beta_1(\mathscr{GNP}). \qquad (14.7)$$

This could also be written as:

$$\mathscr{GNP} - \mathscr{Y} = \beta_0 + \beta_1(\mathscr{GNP}),$$
$$\mathscr{Y} = -\beta_0 + (1 - \beta_1)(\mathscr{GNP}),$$

---

[3] J. von Neumann, 'Distribution of the ratio of the mean square successive difference to the variance,' *Annals of Mathematical Statistics*, **12**, 367–95; B. I. Hart and J. von Neumann, 'Tabulation of the probabilities for the ratio of the mean square successive difference to the variance,' *Annals of Mathematical Statistics*, **13**, 207–14.

or

$$\mathcal{T} = \beta_0 + \beta_1(\mathcal{Y} + \mathcal{T}),$$

$$\mathcal{T} = \frac{\beta_0}{1-\beta_1} + \frac{\beta_1}{1-\beta_1}\mathcal{Y},$$

since $\mathcal{GNP} = \mathcal{Y} + \mathcal{T}$. It is assumed that equation (14.7) is exact and not subject to a random disturbance.

Since population (N) changes very slowly, it is not difficult to assign a numerical value to this variable for a few months or a year in advance. The remaining variables that are necessary in order to forecast $\mathcal{Y}$ or $\mathcal{GNP}$ are $\mathcal{Y}_{-1}, p_{-1}, N_{-1}$, p, and $\mathcal{I}'$. The lagged variables are known from historically recorded observations, but the other two variables are not known in advance with the same certainty that we know $\mathcal{G}, \mathcal{T}$, or N in advance. Government agencies survey business firms in order to find out what the latter *intend* to spend on plant, equipment, and inventories. In this way, there is an attempt to assign a known value to $\mathcal{I}'$, but such attempts are not entirely satisfactory because businesmen are in no way committed to spend what they intend to spend. At best, we can solve the system of equations for $\mathcal{Y}$, given $\mathcal{G}, \beta_0, \beta_1, N, p_{-1}, \mathcal{Y}_{-1}, N_{-1}$, in terms of p and $\mathcal{I}'$. For the fiscal year 1947 we assign the values:

$\mathcal{G} = \$32.8$ billion,
$\mathcal{T} = -39.52 + 0.61\mathcal{Y}$,
$\mathcal{Y}_{-1} = \$138.7$ billion,
$p_{-1} = 1.30$,
$N_{-1} = 0.140$.

Substituting these numerical values into (14.5), we get:

$$\mathcal{Y} = 70.32 + 27.51p + 0.97\mathcal{I}'. \tag{14.8}$$

For any pair of values corresponding to p and $\mathcal{I}'$, there results a definite forecast of $\mathcal{Y}$. However, an error must be attached to this forecast. The quantity $u/(1-\alpha_1)$ in (14.4) fluctuates about its mean, zero, and thereby causes the observed value of $\mathcal{Y}/pN$ to deviate from the value calculated from (14.5). On top of this error caused by the disturbance $u/(1-\alpha_1)$, there is another error resulting from the fact that we do not know the exact values of the parameters, $\alpha_0, \alpha_1, \alpha_2$. The numerical (point) estimates given in (14.5) are subject to error, and only a range is known which encloses these parameters with a specified probability. A combination of the errors in the estimates of the parameters $\alpha_0, \alpha_1, \alpha_2$, and the disturbances u provides a range of error for any forecasts from this model.

Hotelling[4] has given a very clear exposition of the theory underlying errors in prediction. Hotelling's formula applied to our problem gives:

estimate of variance of forecast

$$= S^2 + S_{11}\left(\frac{\overset{*}{\mathscr{Y}}}{pN}\right)^2_{-1} + 2S_{12}\left(\frac{\overset{*}{\mathscr{Y}}}{pN}\right)_{-1}\frac{\mathscr{I}' + \overset{*}{\mathscr{G}} - \mathscr{T}}{pN}$$
$$+ S_{22}\left(\frac{\mathscr{I}' + \overset{*}{\mathscr{G}} - \mathscr{T}}{pN}\right)^2 + S^2\frac{1}{20}, \qquad (14.9)$$

where

S_{11} = estimate of the variance of $\alpha_2/(1-\alpha_1)$,
S_{12} = estimate of the covariance of $\alpha_2/(1-\alpha_1)$ with $1/(1-\alpha_1)$,
S_{22} = estimate of the variance of $1/(1-\alpha_1)$,

and the * sign denotes deviations from the sample mean. The numerical values of the estimated variance of forecast depend upon the values assigned to the predetermined and exogenous variables.

In carrying out the computations for (14.9), the value used for $\mathscr{T}$ was the value obtained by substituting the point estimate of $\mathscr{Y}$ into $\mathscr{T} = -39.52 + 0.61\mathscr{Y}$. However, since there is an interval of error to be attached to $\mathscr{Y}$, it is not obvious that the correct value of $\mathscr{T}$ for (14.9) can be estimated from the point estimates of $\mathscr{Y}$. But it happens that the error committed by this procedure is negligible. This can be seen as follows:

1. Solve for the forecast error as a function of $\mathscr{T}$.

2. Solve for $\mathscr{T}$ as a function of the point estimate of $\mathscr{Y}$ and the error attached to the point estimate of $\mathscr{Y}$.

3. Substitute $\mathscr{T}$ from step 2 into (14.9). This gives one equation in one unknown variable, namely, the error of forecast.

4. The error attached to $\mathscr{T}$ may be positive or negative. Choose that sign which gives the largest possible range of forecast error and solve the equation from step 3 for the error of forecast.

We find that the error of forecast obtained by computing $\mathscr{T}$ from the point estimate of $\mathscr{Y}$ alone is not different (in billions of dollars) from the worst possible error obtained by taking account of an error in $\mathscr{T}$.

[4] Harold Hotelling, 'Problems of Prediction,' *The American Journal of Sociology*, **48**, (1942), 61–76.

Econometric models as a guide to policy 253

We shall denote the expression in (14.9) by S_F^2. Probability theory tells us that there is somewhat less[5] than a 70 per cent chance that the true value of $\mathcal{Y}/pN$ will be in the range

$$\left[-S_F + \left(\frac{\mathcal{Y}}{pN}\right)^0, \left(\frac{\mathcal{Y}}{pN}\right)^0 + S_F \right],$$

where $(\mathcal{Y}/pN)^0$ is the value of $\mathcal{Y}/pN$ forecast from (14.5). If we want a larger probability of being correct, we must widen the range of forecast. In general, our forecast will be of the form:

$$\left(\frac{\mathcal{Y}}{pN}\right)^0 \pm t_\alpha S_F, \tag{14.10}$$

where t_α is taken from the table of the t-distribution at the αth significance level.

The ranges of error in table 14.1 refer to errors in the forecast of $\mathcal{Y}$ and $\mathcal{GNP}$ in current prices. Forecasts in constant dollars lead to much smaller ranges because the forecast equation (14.5) is in constant dollars, and when we multiply both sides of this equation by p to get forecasts in current prices, the forecast error is also multiplied by p, which is greater than unity during the present period. It is evident that the percentage error is the same for forecasts of disposable income in current or constant dollars. It should be pointed out, further, that the ranges of error are calculated from (14.10) under the condition that $t_\alpha = 1$.

Table 14.1 Forecasts for fiscal 1947: Model I

Price index p	Gross capital formation ($\mathcal{I}$)					
	30	32	34	36	38	40
Disposable income ($\mathcal{Y}$)						
1.35	137±6	139±6	140±6	142±6	144±6	146±6
1.40	138±7	140±7	142±7	144±6	146±6	148±6
1.45	139±7	141±7	143±7	145±7	147±7	149±7
1.50	141±8	143±7	145±7	147±7	148±7	150±7
Gross National Product ($\mathcal{GNP}$)						
1.35	181±10	184±10	187±10	190±10	193±10	196±10
1.40	183±11	186±11	189±11	192±10	195±10	198±10
1.45	185±11	188±11	191±11	194±11	198±11	201±11
1.50	187±13	190±11	194±11	197±11	200±11	203±11

[5]The value of t for the 30 per cent significance level and 17 degrees of freedom is 1.069. The significance level corresponding to $t=1$ is slightly larger than 30 per cent but is not given in all tables.

The forecasts presented thus far refer to fiscal year 1947, but, at this writing (November, 1946) part of this fiscal year has already elapsed. If we subtract what has already been observed for fiscal 1947 from the values in the tables, we have a forecast of the remainder of fiscal 1947, an unobserved period.

Table 14.1 tells us that the present price level (1.43–1.45) and volume of capital formation (32–34) imply a value of $\mathscr{GNP}$ for fiscal 1947 at about the present annual rate. If prices and private capital formation do not fall, the current rate of national product will be maintained, i.e. national product will not fall or rise appreciably in the first half of calendar 1947. If price and capital formation fall, $\mathscr{GNP}$ is likely to fall in calendar 1947 and if prices and capital formation rise, $\mathscr{GNP}$ is likely to rise in calendar 1947. Later we shall attempt to forecast the behavior of capital formation in a model where this variable is endogenous.

It is easy to see how other types of policy decisions could be made on the basis of this model. Various levels of government spending can be inserted into the numerical system. Each value of $\mathscr{G}$ will lead to a different set of values for $\mathscr{Y}$ and $\mathscr{GNP}$, hence we can judge the quantitative effects of government spending on income and national product. Similarly it is possible to calculate the effects of changes in tax rates by altering the numerical estimates of β_0 or β_1 depending upon the type of tax change under consideration. A different set of values for β_0 and β_1 will generate a different set of values of forecasted $\mathscr{Y}$ and $\mathscr{GNP}$. The change in the forecast as a consequence of the change in the tax laws, gives an evaluation of some of the important implications of the tax policies.

There are many steps involved in the computation of (14.7) and it is not entirely correct to assume that this equation is not subject to random error. The computation of the values of the parameters involves several approximations and the linear form of the equation is, in itself, an approximation; hence it would be desirable to attach an error to the estimate of (14.7), but this has not yet been done. We shall outline the steps involved in estimating the parameters of (14.7) in order that the various sources of error can be properly exposed:

1 Assume an arbitrary value of $\mathscr{GNP}$.

2 Subtract from $\mathscr{GNP}$, government interest and wage–salary payments, to get privately produced $\mathscr{GNP}$.

3 Estimate corporate profits before taxes as a function of private $\mathscr{GNP}$.

Econometric models as a guide to policy 255

4 Apply existing tax rates to the estimated corporate profits before taxes to get corporate taxes.

5 From corporate profits after taxes estimate the distribution between dividends and corporate savings.

6 For the hypothetical level of GNP and existing tax rates for other business taxes, estimate the volume of other business taxes (not corporate taxes).

7 For the hypothetical level of GNP, estimate the total business reserves (depreciation, depletion, capital outlays charged to current expense).

8 For the hypothetical level of GNP, estimate the profit or loss on inventory revaluation.

9 From GNP subtract corporate taxes, other business taxes, business reserves, and the negative of inventory profits. The result is a hypothetical level of national income corresponding to a hypothetical GNP.

10 Calculate transfer payments estimated at existing benefit rates for the assumed level of national income.

11 Compute the contributions to social insurance funds by applying existing rates to the hypothetical national income.

12 To national income add transfer payments and subtract the sum of corporate savings and contributions to social insurance funds. The result is income payments to individuals.

13 Apply existing personal tax rates to income payments to get personal tax and nontax payments to government.

14 Subtract personal tax and nontax payments from income payments to get disposable income.

It is obvious that all tax payments (personal, corporate, and other business) depend upon the distribution of income among taxpaying units as well as upon the sum of individual incomes. However, assuming little change in income distribution, it is possible to estimate approximately the tax revenues corresponding to any particular level of income. But it should be noted that this is an approximation and not an exact relation. However, there are other steps at which the approximations are less exact and subject to much wider errors. Steps 3 and 5 involve some estimates on which there undoubtedly could be improvement. Step 3 makes use of a behavior equation which should be part of the economic model and which should be subject to random disturbance. From past data, the regression of corporate profits on private $\mathcal{GNP}$ is obtained, and this regression is used to estimate corporate profits corresponding to the assumed hypothetical levels of total and private $\mathcal{GNP}$. The use of simple least-squares correlations between corporate profits and private $\mathcal{GNP}$ can fortunately be justified, although many investigators have been using this correlation in the steps outlined above without knowing why it is correct. The models which the author has constructed, have often contained the wage bill as a linear function of the value of private output. The best relation also makes use of a trend and lagged as well as current output. It has been found in several cases that the least-squares regression of wages on private output is practically the same as the relation obtained by the use of more satisfactory methods of statistical estimation that are known to be consistent (i.e. roughly unbiased in large samples). Since the sum of wages and profits is approximately equal to the value of private output, it is also true that the least-squares regression of profits on output will not differ appreciably from a consistent estimate of the true relation between these two variables. But no matter how correct we find the statistical estimates to be, the equation used in step 3 is an equation of economic behavior and is subject to random disturbance.

Step 5 also involves the use of an economic-behavior equation, and unfortunately this equation is not nearly as well established as that used in step 3. In step 5, it is necessary to split net corporate profits after taxes into two components, dividends and corporate savings. How do boards of directors decide upon their dividend policies? No simple economic theory seems to have been adequately developed to explain the behavior pattern of corporate directors. Tinbergen[6] has advanced a relation that is consistent with the observed data. He found that dividends are a linear function of net corporate income, current and lagged, and the accumulated surplus lagged. Until a theory of dividend distribution is more definitively established we shall have to work with Tinbergen's relation, but here, also, the relation is subject to error (probably a wide error) and consequently another inexactness is introduced into the model. In making up the table of the relationship between disposable income and assumed levels of $\mathcal{GNP}$, we should insert the latest observed figure of dividends corresponding to the observed levels of $\mathcal{GNP}$ and net corporate profits, and then from Tinbergen's formula calculate the change in the absolute level of

---

[6] J. Tinbergen, *Statistical Testing of Business Cycle Theories, Part II, Business Cycles in the United States of America, 1919–1932*, League of Nations, Geneva (1939), pp. 115–16.

dividends associated with any assumed change in the absolute level of net corporate profits. This procedure should be adopted because the lagged value of surplus (the other variable in Tinbergen's equation) is predetermined for our problem and does not vary with the different hypothetical levels of $\mathscr{GNP}$.

Finally, step 8 involves some very questionable relationships. Ordinarily, inventory revaluation might not be large, but in periods of rapidly changing prices, the capital gains (or losses) on stocks of goods are large and play an important role in determining the level of effective demand. Inventory profits are especially large now, and cannot be neglected. For any hypothetical level of $\mathscr{GNP}$, a figure for inventory revaluation must be estimated. Any estimates are subject to a large error. No systematic relationship has been used for the evaluation of this item other than some informed guesses as to future developments in the labor situation that will serve to determine wage rates and thus prices (assuming a fixed profit margin).

Forecasts from econometric models undoubtedly can be greatly improved, and one of the first points of attacks should be on the relationship between disposable income and $\mathscr{GNP}$. In the estimation of the parameters of the models, it has usually been assumed that the difference, $\mathscr{GNP} - \mathscr{Y} = \mathscr{T}$, is exogenous, but the above discussion has shown this to be an incorrect assumption. At best, we can assume that tax rates, unemployment compensation rates, pensions, government interest payments, and the like are exogenous. Further work is called for here.

MODEL II—EXOGENOUS INVESTMENT AND LIQUIDITY

Let us modify Model I by the addition of one new variable to the system, namely cash balances. One of the most frequently-heard explanations of the present boom is that private economic units have emerged from the War with large accumulations of liquid assets that cause people to spend at an abnormally high rate. This hypothesis can be tested from the data to see whether or not the total private holdings of liquid assets influenced spending habits in the past. Since we could not split total private holdings of cash balances for all past years into personal holdings and business holdings, we used the total private holdings of cash balances as the appropriate variable. For the prewar years in which total balances have been split into private and business categories, there is a close linear relationship between the two components;[7] so it seems that the total can be used as an index of either type in a linear system. The consumption function will now be written as

$$\frac{\mathscr{C}}{pN} = \alpha'_0 + \alpha'_1 \frac{\mathscr{Y}}{pN} + \alpha'_2 \left(\frac{\mathscr{Y}}{pN}\right)_{-1} + \alpha'_3 \left(\frac{\mathscr{M}}{pN}\right)_{-1} + u', \tag{14.11}$$

where

$\mathscr{M}_{-1}$ = currency outside banks + demand deposits adjusted + time deposits of the middle of the preceding year measured in billions of current dollars.

All the other equations of the system are unchanged. The forecast equation which is obtained by solving for $\mathscr{Y}/pN$ in terms of predetermined and exogenous variables is

$$\frac{\mathscr{Y}}{pN} = \frac{\alpha'_0}{1-\alpha'_1} + \frac{\alpha'_2}{1-\alpha'_1}\left(\frac{\mathscr{Y}}{pN}\right)_{-1} + \frac{1}{1-\alpha'_1} \frac{\mathscr{I}' + G - \mathscr{T}}{pN}$$

$$+ \frac{\alpha'_3}{1-\alpha'_1}\left(\frac{\mathscr{M}}{pN}\right)_{-1} + \frac{1}{1-\alpha'_1} u'. \tag{14.12}$$

The statistical estimate of (14.12) is

$$\frac{\mathscr{Y}}{pN} = 186.53 + 0.30 \left(\frac{\mathscr{Y}}{pN}\right)_{-1} + 2.36 \frac{\mathscr{I}' + \mathscr{G} - \mathscr{T}}{pN} + 0.13 \left(\frac{\mathscr{M}}{pN}\right)_{-1},$$
$$\phantom{\frac{\mathscr{Y}}{pN} = 186.53 + }(0.13)\phantom{\left(\frac{\mathscr{Y}}{pN}\right)_{-1} +}(0.34)\phantom{\frac{\mathscr{I}' + \mathscr{G} - \mathscr{T}}{pN}+}(0.10) \tag{14.13}$$

$$S = \$20.69; \quad \delta^2/S^2 = 1.28.$$

The statistic δ^2/S^2, in this model, is large enough so that we cannot reject the hypothesis that the us are nonautocorrelated at the 5 per cent level of significance.

From the estimates of the parameters of (14.12), we can derive estimates of the parameters of (14.11). They are

$$\frac{\mathscr{C}}{pN} = 79.04 + 0.58 \frac{\mathscr{Y}}{pN} + 0.13 \left(\frac{\mathscr{Y}}{pN}\right)_{-1} + 0.06 \left(\frac{\mathscr{M}}{pN}\right)_{-1}. \tag{14.14}$$

If to the estimates of the predetermined and exogenous variables used in Model I for fiscal 1947, we add the estimate $\mathscr{M}_{-1} = \$175.4$ billion,

---

[7] See S. Shapiro, 'The distribution of deposits and currency in the United States, 1929–1939,' *Journal of the American Statistical Association*, **38** (1943), 438–44.

the resulting forecast equation,

$$\mathcal{Y} = 69.96 + 31.13p + 0.97\mathcal{I}', \tag{14.15}$$

is obtained. Corresponding to table 14.1 used in conjunction with Model I, we now have table 14.2 which gives the forecasts obtained from Model II. In spite of the fact that the coefficient of $(\mathcal{M}/pN)_{-1}$ is small in (14.13), the value of this variable is so high now that the forecasted $\mathcal{GNP}$ is raised considerably as compared with Model I. But the standard error of the coefficient of $(\mathcal{M}/pN)_{-1}$ is very large. As a matter of fact, the standard error of the coefficient of $(\mathcal{M}/pN)_{-1}$ in (14.3) is sufficiently large that we cannot reject the hypothesis that the true value of the parameter is zero. The past data do not contradict the hypothesis that spending habits are not influenced by the holding of liquid assets. In estimating the error of forecast, however, it is not sufficient to look at the estimated standard error of the coefficient of $(\mathcal{M}/pN)_{-1}$ without taking into consideration the covariance of this coefficient and the other coefficients of the forecast equation. The application of Hotelling's formula for the estimate of the variance of the forecast explicitly takes into account the covariances as well as the variances of the parameters. The range of error attached to the forecasts of Model II is larger than the corresponding range for Model I, but the former range is not as much larger as one might hastily conclude from looking at the variance alone. A 70 per cent probability of being correct requires a range of $\pm\$13$–15 billion for forecasts of $\mathcal{GNP}$ in Model II; whereas the range for the same probability level in Model I is about $\pm\$11$ billion.

Table 14.2 Forecasts for fiscal 1947: Model II

Price index p	Gross capital formation ($\mathcal{I}'$)					
	30	32	34	36	38	40
Disposable income ($\mathcal{Y}$)						
1.35	141±7	143±7	145±7	147±7	149±6	151±6
1.40	143±8	145±7	147±7	148±7	150±7	152±7
1.45	144±9	146±9	148±8	150±8	152±8	154±8
1.50	146±10	148±9	150±9	152±9	154±9	155±8
Gross National Product ($\mathcal{GNP}$)						
1.35	188±11	191±11	194±11	197±11	200±11	203±10
1.40	190±13	193±11	196±11	199±11	203±11	206±11
1.45	193±15	196±15	199±13	202±13	205±13	208±13
1.50	195±16	198±15	201±15	204±15	208±15	211±13

Equation (14.1) might be used to answer another type of question that is important in policy formation. In the presence of unemployment what is the effect, on the level of income, of deficit spending with a constant real money supply, or of an increase in the real money supply with a constant deficit? To simplify the problem, let us try to answer these questions for the equilibrium situation, i.e. the situation in which all variables assume their equilibrium values. In equilibrium we have:

$$\frac{\mathcal{Y}}{pN} = \left(\frac{\mathcal{Y}}{pN}\right)_{-1} = \left(\frac{\mathcal{Y}}{pN}\right)^0, \frac{\mathcal{M}}{pN} = \left(\frac{\mathcal{M}}{pN}\right)_{-1} = \left(\frac{\mathcal{M}}{pN}\right)^0,$$

and

$$\frac{\mathcal{I}' + \mathcal{G} - \mathcal{T}}{pN} = \left(\frac{\mathcal{I}' + \mathcal{G} - \mathcal{T}}{pN}\right)_{-1} = \left(\frac{\mathcal{I}' + \mathcal{G} - \mathcal{T}}{pN}\right)^0.$$

The equilibrium solution for (14.13) becomes:

$$\left(\frac{\mathcal{Y}}{pN}\right)^0 = 266.87 + 3.37 \left(\frac{\mathcal{I}' + \mathcal{G} - \mathcal{T}}{pN}\right)^0 + 0.19 \left(\frac{\mathcal{M}}{pN}\right)^0,$$

(14.16)

assuming the point estimates for the parameters to be correct. From (14.16) we can calculate the following two multipliers:

1 An extra dollar of deficit spending (with a constant money supply) creates $3.37 additional disposable income.

2 An extra dollar of money supplied (with a constant deficit) creates $0.19 additional disposable income.

MODEL III – ENDOGENOUS INVESTMENT

The forecasts made from the first two models were, of course, contingent upon the correct choice of exogenous variables, of which some of the principal ones were government spending, government receipts and transfers, and private capital formation. There is little that can be done to improve upon the assumed levels of government variables for purposes of prediction, but we may be able to make considerable improvement in the estimation of private capital formation. If the latter variable is assumed to be exogenous, our only known method for the estimation of this variable is to survey businessmen and ask them what they *intend* to spend in the future on capital goods. However, if we assume that business decisions are endogenous variables, we can study the historical records to attempt to discover the laws of business

Econometric models as a guide to policy 261

behavior. Model III will be one in which definite behavior patterns are assumed for many more variables in the system than was the case for Models I and II. In this paper, we shall not attempt to present a theoretical justification for all the equations of Model III, but we shall write explicitly all the equations. In a subsequent publication, there will be a lengthy justification for the model on theoretical grounds. At present, we shall merely attempt to show how such models can be used in forecasting.

In forecasting, especially under the conditions of November, 1946, certain equations of the complete model are suppressed because of government controls or other reasons. The full set of equations will be presented and the suppressions will be pointed out for the applications.

The notation is as follows:

$I =$ net investment in private producers' plant and equipment, measured in billions of 1934 dollars.

$q =$ price index of private producer's plant and equipment, 1934: 1.00.

$p =$ price index of output as a whole, 1934:1.00.

$X =$ output of the private sector of the economy, exclusive of housing services, measured in billions of 1934 dollars.

$\mathscr{E} =$ excise taxes, measured in billions of current dollars.

$K =$ end-of-year stock of private producers' plant and equipment, measured in billions of 1934 dollars.

$H =$ end-of-year stock of inventories, measured in billions of 1934 dollars.

$\mathscr{W}_1 =$ private wage-salary bill, measured in billions of current dollars.

$Y =$ disposable income, measured in billions of 1934 dollars.

$C =$ consumer expenditures, measured in billions of 1934 dollars.

$D_1 =$ gross construction expenditures on owner-occupied, single-family, nonfarm residences, measured in billions of 1934 dollars.

$r =$ index of rents, 1934:1.00.

$q_1 =$ index of construction costs, 1934:1.00.

$\Delta F =$ thousands of new nonfarm families.[8]

$D_2 =$ gross construction expenditures on rented, nonfarm residences, measured in billions of 1934 dollars.

$i =$ average corporate-bound yield.

$v =$ percentage of nonfarm housing units occupied at the end of the year.

$N^s =$ millions of available nonfarm housing units at the end of the year.

$\mathscr{M}_1 =$ demand deposits adjusted and currency outside banks averaged during the year, measured in billions of current dollars.

[8]In what follows, we shall adopt the convention, $\Delta x = x - x_{-1}$ for any variable x.

$\mathcal{M}_2$ = time deposits, averaged during the year, measured in billions of current dollars.

$\mathcal{E}_r$ = excess reserves, averaged during the year, measured in millions of current dollars.

T = government revenues + corporate savings − transfer payments − government interest payments − inventory profits, all measured in billions of 1934 dollars.

G = government expenditures on goods and services − government interest payments + net exports + net investment of nonprofit institutions, all measured in billions of 1934 dollars.

D_3 = gross construction expenditures on farm residences, measured in billions of 1934 dollars.

D'' = depreciation of all residences (farm and nonfarm) measured in billions of 1934 dollars.

$\mathcal{W}_2$ = government wage-salary bill, measured in billions of current dollars.

$\mathcal{R}_1$ = nonfarm rentals, paid and imputed, measured in billions of current dollars.

$\mathcal{R}_2$ = farm rentals, paid and imputed, measured in billions of current dollars.

u_2 = estimate of the disturbances in the inventory-demand equation.

The equations are:

demand for private producers' plant and equipment

$$I = 2.18 + 0.13 \frac{pX - \mathcal{E}}{q} + 0.04 \left(\frac{pX - \mathcal{E}}{q}\right)_{-1} - 0.09 K_{-1}$$

$$S = 0.49,\ \delta^2/S^2 = 1.50; \quad (14.17)$$

demand for inventories

$$H = 0.79 + 4.17p + 0.11(X - \Delta H) + 0.50 H_{-1}$$

$$S = 0.61,\ \delta^2/S^2 = 2.17; \quad (14.18)$$

output adjustment equation

$$\Delta X = 2.99 - 4.25(u_2)_{-1} + 75.09 \Delta p \quad S = 5.98,\ \delta^2/S^2 = 1.69; \quad (14.19)$$

equation of the demand for labor

$$\mathcal{W}_1 = 5.03 + 0.42(pX - \mathcal{E}) + 0.17(pX - \mathcal{E})_{-1} + 0.17(t - 1931)$$

$$S = 1.00,\ \delta^2/S^2 = 1.86; \quad (14.20)$$

demand for new owner-occupied nonfarm residences

$$D_1 = -9.03 + 3.74\left(\frac{r}{q_1}\right) + 0.02(Y + Y_{-1} + Y_{-2}) + 0.0043\Delta F$$
$$S = 0.21, \ \delta^2/S^2 = 2.26 \quad (14.21)$$

demand for new rented nonfarm residences

$$D_2 = -2.14 + 2.81r_{-1} + 0.02(q_1)_{-1} - 0.44(q_1)_{-2} + 0.0016(\Delta F)_{-1} - 0.18i$$
$$S = 0.26, \ \delta^2/S^2 = 2.07; \quad (14.22)$$

demand for nonfarm dwelling space

$$v = 178.01 + 0.29Y - 2.62r + 1.42(t - 1931) - 3.76N^s$$
$$S = 0.79, \ \delta^2/S^2 = 1.52; \quad (14.23)$$

rent adjustment equation

$$\Delta r = -2.15 + 0.02v_{-1} + 0.00071Y + 0.17\frac{1}{r_{-1}}$$
$$S = 0.03, \ \delta^2/S^2 = 1.04; \quad (14.24)$$

demand for consumer goods

$$C = 11.87 + 0.73Y + 0.04(t - 1931) \quad S = 1.36, \ \delta^2/S^2 = 1.20; \quad (14.25)$$

demand for active cash balances

$$\mathcal{M}_1 = 8.45 + 0.24p(Y + T) + 0.03p(Y + T)(t - 1931) - 1.43(t - 1931)$$
$$S = 1.20, \ \delta^2/S^2 = 1.33; \quad (14.26)$$

demand for idle cash balances

$$\mathcal{M}_2 = 15.37 + 0.28i - 1.90i_{-1} + 0.74(\mathcal{M}_2)_{-1} - 0.18(t - 1931)$$
$$S = 0.67, \ \delta^2/S^2 = 1.49; \quad (14.27)$$

interest-rate adjustment equation

$$\Delta_i = 2.00 - 0.17\mathcal{E}_r - 0.37i_{-1} - 0.0052(t - 1931)$$
$$S = 0.47, \ \delta^2/S^2 = 1.77; \quad (14.28)$$

definition of net national product

$$Y + T = I + \Delta H + C + D_1 + D_2 + D_3 - D'' + G; \quad (14.29)$$

definition of privately produced output exclusive of housing services

$$X = \frac{p(Y + T) - \mathcal{W}_2 - \mathcal{R}_1 - \mathcal{R}_2}{p}; \quad (14.30)$$

definition of net investment

$$\Delta K = I; \tag{14.31}$$

definition of total nonfarm rent payments, paid and imputed

$$\mathscr{R}_1 = 0.278r\left(\frac{vN^s}{100} + \frac{v_{-1}N^s_{-1}}{100}\right)\frac{1}{2}. \tag{14.32}$$

All parameters have been estimated for the period 1922–41, except for (14.22), (14.26), (14.27), (14.28), when the period is 1921–41. The method of statistical estimation employed is called the 'method of reduced forms' and is one of the methods suited for obtaining consistent estimates of parameters in systems of simultaneous economic equations. This method has been developed by T. W. Anderson, Jr., M. A. Girshick and H. Rubin.[9]

It should be pointed out that the parameter 0.278 in equation (14.22) is known *a priori*. This equation is a definition and is not a behavior equation with unknown parameters to be estimated from the observed data. Since r is an index number while $\mathscr{R}_1$ is in billions of dollars, it is necessary to multiply the right-hand side of (14.22) by the base-year value of average rental payments.

The forecasts for fiscal 1947 will be made from equations (14.17), (14.18), (14.21), (14.22), (14.25), (14.29), and (14.30). Equation (14.19), if left in the system, would give us enough equations to determine the general level of prices, p, but this equation is not very well established as can be seen by the very large estimate of the variance of the disturbance. We can probably do best to assign a particular value to the price level which will be determined by other considerations, as will be explained later. Equation (14.20) is omitted because we have no direct need for the determination of W_1 in the system. However, if it were required to forecast W_1 as well as $p(Y+T)$, we should have to include (14.20). Implicitly, an equation like (14.20) will be used to determine the relation between T and Y for the step in which it is required to estimate corporate profits for each assumed level of $\mathscr{GNP}$. This estimate corresponds to step 3 on page 254 above. Equations (14.23) and (14.24) are suppressed for this calculation because the present level of rents is not determined in a free market as is assumed in these two equations. The specific assumptions pertaining to rent control will be stated below. Equations (14.26) and (14.27) are omitted

---

[9]A paper on the method of reduced forms was presented by Anderson at the August, 1946, meeting of the Institute of Mathematical Statistics, Ithaca, New York. See also M. A. Girshick and Trygve Haavelmo, 'Statistical analysis of the demand for food: Examples of simultaneous estimation of structural equations,' Econometrica, **15**, April (1947), 79–110.

because it is not desired to know the values of $\mathcal{M}_1$ and $\mathcal{M}_2$ for our forecasts. If we were interested in forecasting the demand for cash balances as well as the level of income and output we should need to make use of demand relations for cash, but for the present problem we can omit some of the equations referring to the money market. Equation (14.27), furthermore, does not fit the postwar data, and would be very poor for purposes of prediction. In the postwar situation, for observed values of i, i_{-1}, $(\mathcal{M}_2)_{-1}$, and t, the demand for idle balances, as estimated by (14.27), is much less than the observed value. There are several possible explanations for this phenomenon, but one tempting explanation is the following: The Keynesian hypothesis that the demand for idle balances has very large (practically infinite) interest-elasticity at low interest rates requires a highly nonlinear form for the liquidity-preference equation (14.27). In the prewar years, the linear equation fits the data well, but now we are getting so close to 'minimum' interest rates that the equation must be made very nonlinear in the region of present observations. There are several nonlinear functions that would fit the prewar data as well as (14.27) does and also fit the postwar observations very closely. Other explanations have to do with shifts (permanent or temporary) in the function, but, in any case, equation (14.27) is not satisfactory for prediction as it now stands. Fortunately, we are not attempting to estimate the demand for cash, so that (14.27) may be disregarded for the calculation in this paper. Finally, we shall also omit equation (14.28), which serves to determine the interest rate as a function of exogenous or predetermined variables. This equation also does not fit the postwar facts very closely and we can probably do better to assign the present rate of bond yields in equation (14.22), rather than attempt to estimate it from (14.28). During the war, the government and the central banking system made various manipulations in the money market to control the rate of interest, which may account for the fact that equation (14.28) appears not to hold very closely now.

Model III is an improvement over Models I and II in the sense that more variables that are not known accurately in advance are made endogenous and can be estimated from the model, but Model III is still far from being complete. The most glaring deficiency is in equations to determine the various price levels. To a certain extent, this deficiency is a result of the fact that there are not sufficiently detailed data available to construct, from past observations, a model that contains certain market adjustment equations necessary for the determination of price levels. Equation (14.24) is an example of the type of equation that is needed to determine a specific price level.

Instead of using behavior equations of the mathematical model to determine the levels of various prices, we have made use of certain information outside the model in order to assign specific values to p, q, q_1, r, etc. Our basic assumption in quantitative terms is that average prices (except rent) in fiscal 1947 will be about 10 per cent above those observed for fiscal 1946. Our reasoning is that prices will probably not fall by very much, if at all, in the latter part of the fiscal year because basic wage rates will not be permitted to fall. The latter observation follows from personal judgements (generally accepted) that collective bargaining in the early part of calendar 1947 will bring about some basic wage increases. Regardless of the level of prices assumed (within reason) the model leads to deflationary forecasts, i.e. falling production and employment, in the early part of calendar 1947; therefore we do not assume runaway price increases. However, the big increases of prices that occurred since the removal of OPA in the first half of fiscal 1947 will not be wiped out by the events of the second half of the fiscal year. There will probably be some price increase, on the average, for the fiscal year. In line with past experience since the end of the war when there have been similar rounds of wage and price increases, we assume a 10 per cent change. In tables 14.1 and 14.2, it can be seen by how much small variations in the price index lead to variations in the forecasts of national product. This method of assuming a side relation between prices and wages, where the latter are estimated by guesses as to the outcome of collective bargaining, is not satisfactory, and work must be done in order to improve the model by the introduction of more price-formation equations.

In table 14.3 are presented all the values assigned to predetermined or exogenous variables. In the appendix, the reader will find a detailed description of all the time series used in the estimation of the parameters of Model III and all the steps involved in the calculation of the values inserted in table 14.3. It is essential to study carefully the steps involved in the construction of the series in order to know how to calculate the values of table 14.3.

It is not possible to assign a specific value to the variable T because this variable will change with changing income. From our knowledge of existing tax rates, unemployment compensation rates etc., we obtain by the same methods that were used for (14.7):

$$T = -\frac{29.475}{p} + 0.385(Y+T). \tag{14.33}$$

A word of explanation is required about (14.33). The variable T is defined above as government revenues + corporate savings − transfer

Econometric models as a guide to policy

Table 14.3 Assumptions and initial conditions for Model III (fiscal years)

	Fiscal 1947	Fiscal 1946	Fiscal 1945
$\mathscr{E}$	5.5	7.3	
K_{-1}	114.3		
p	1.55	1.42	
H_{-1}	27.9		
r	1.20	1.15	
Y		100.0	103.0
q_1	2.00	1.825	1.69
i	2.8	2.765	
D_3	0.3		
D''	2.0		
G	21.4	36.3	
$\mathscr{W}_2$	16.2	24.75	
$\mathscr{R}_1 + \mathscr{R}_2$	12.4	11.8	
ΔF	500.0	800.0	
$p(Y+T)$		173.35	
q	1.50	1.36	

payments — government interest payments — inventory profits. Actually in the determination of the parameters from the data of the interwar period, inventory profits or losses were not subtracted from T, although, perhaps, they should have been. For the prediction in fiscal 1947 it does not seem correct to neglect inventory profits because they are so large. The consumption function (14.25) probably understates rather than overstates the consumption corresponding to a particular level of disposable income. The inclusion of inventory profits in Y (their exclusion in T) helps to explain the high levels of consumption; therefore Model III is interpreted as including inventory profits in Y, although this item was neglected in the past. Except for a couple of years in the interwar period, inventory profits were sufficiently small so that they would not have had an important influence on the numerical estimates of the parameters.[10]

Equations (14.17), (14.18), (14.21), (14.22), (14.25), (14.29), (14.30), (14.33) and the assumptions in table 14.3, lead to the following results:

---

[10]There is no error in this procedure if the marginal propensity to consume out of inventory profits is the same as the marginal propensity to consume out of other disposable income. If the two marginal propensities differ, the correct estimate for the model should be a weighted average of the two. The weight attached to inventory profits for the past observation will be small if inventory profits were a small percentage of disposable income, as was the case. The error is undoubtedly negligible.

$Y = \$83.3$ billion,

$Y + T = 104.5,$

$p(Y + T) = 162.0,$

$\mathscr{GNP} = 177.5.$[11,12]

The error to be attached to this forecast is not known exactly. In Models I and II, the statistical methods employed enabled us to determine the errors in forecasting that result from the variation of the disturbance and from the sampling fluctuations involved in the determination of the parameters of the forecasting equation, but we are not able to calculate both types of error in Model III. In the latter model we can calculate the error resulting from the variations in the disturbances but we do not have estimates of the other types of error, i.e. that type which results from the fact that we have only a finite sample to determine the parameters of the model. The size of the first type of error, however, gives a rough guide as to the accuracy of the results. The estimating square root of the variance of the disturbances involved in forecasting disposable income (constant dollars) is about $3 billion, the same as for Models I and II. If the sampling fluctuations lead to an error of the same relative size in all models, we can say that the estimates of $\mathscr{GNP}$ from Model III should lie in a range $\pm \$13$ billion with a 70 per cent probability.

It is instructive to examine the past record of Model III. In the spring of 1946, a list of exogenous and predetermined variables was prepared for the calendar year 1946 corresponding to the values given in table 14.3 for fiscal 1946. At the time of the actual forecast, 'reduced form' estimates of the parameters of Model III were not available; hence single-equation, least-squares estimates were used to make the forecasts. The estimated parameters obtained by the latter method are not appreciably different in this case from those obtained by the former method.

---

[11] There are definite correction factors that lead from the variable $p(Y+T)$ to the official government figures on $\mathscr{GNP}$. The exact series used for $p(Y+T)$ are given in the appendix so that the reader can determine exactly the relationship between this variable and the official figures of $\mathscr{GNP}$. If we add government interest + depreciation and depletion − net imputed rents on owner-occupied nonfarm residences to $p(Y+T)$ we get $\mathscr{GNP}$.

[12] It appears now (April, 1947) that the assumption of 10 per cent price increases is a low estimate. If the assumptions are modified by allowing a greater price increase, say 15 or 20 per cent, the forecasted level of $\mathscr{GNP}$ and the range of error will be raised.

Econometric models as a guide to policy

We shall now present a table of the assumptions actually used in the forecasts made in the spring of 1946 and substitute them into Model III. The comparison between actual and forecasted results will then show how well the prewar model fits the postwar data. The relation between T and Y that was used is given by

$$T = -\frac{42.4003}{p} + 0.440(Y+T). \tag{14.34}$$

The values in table 14.4 and (14.34) may not be the same as observed values.

Table 14.4 Assumptions and initial conditions for Model III (calendar years)

	Calendar 1946	Calendar 1945	Calendar 1944
$\mathscr{E}$	7.8	7.0	
K_{-1}	111.4		
p	1.53	1.38	
H_{-1}	27.4		
r	1.16	1.15	
Y		102.5	105.0
q_1	1.89	1.72	1.62
i	2.7	2.87	
D_3	0.3		
D''	2.0		
G	23.6		
W_2	19.5	30.6	
$\mathscr{R}_1 + \mathscr{R}_2$	12.0	12.0	
ΔF	821.0	691.0	
$p(Y+T)$		183.0	
q	1.46	1.33	

Equations (14.17), (14.18), (14.21), (14.22), (14.25), (14.29), (14.30), 14.34), and the assumptions lead to the following results

$$Y = \$95.8 \text{ billion},$$

$$Y + T = 121.6,$$

$$p(Y+T) = 186.0,$$

$$\mathscr{GNP} = 201.$$

If an error of $\pm\$13$ billion is attached to this forecast of $\mathscr{GNP}$, the range will certainly include the observed value.[13]

[13] *The Economic Report of the President to the Congress* (Jan. 8, 1947) estimates $\mathscr{GNP}$ at $194 billion for 1946.

Equation (14.34) was used in the spring of 1946 as the best available estimate, but it may not agree with observations. If we substitute (14.33), which was computed more recently for fiscal 1947, for (14.34), the forecasted point estimate of $\mathscr{GNP}$ is reduced to $191 billion.

THE FORECAST

What is the interpretation of these numerical results? Models I and III, the most reliable systems, state that $\mathscr{GNP}$ will, at best, maintain its present level and is likely to fall during the remainder of fiscal 1947. Model I states that the current rate of capital formation and price level will just maintain $\mathscr{GNP}$ during the rest of the fiscal year, but if we try to estimate capital formation from the structure of the system, as in Model III, we find that $\mathscr{GNP}$ is likely to fall. If there are any sizeable disturbances in these models, now, they are likely to be positive, i.e. on the side of abnormal spending. If our past estimates of the disturbances are used as a guide, we can say that $\mathscr{GNP}$ is likely to be in the range $177.5 billion to $190.5 billion[14] in the first half of 1947. The models point to a turning point for real income during fiscal 1947.

NEGLECT OF SUPPLY FACTORS?

Models like those of this paper have often been criticized for including only the demand side of the national market to the neglect of the supply side. This type of criticism has been especially prevalent in the recent months because it is often stated that demand is temporarily insatiable and the only limitation on the expansion of income during the postwar transition is the ability to supply goods. How can models composed exclusively of demand factors be useful in making predictions during such a period?

This criticism appears wrong, immediately, to those actively engaged in the construction of econometric models because we know that it is exhaustive to say that the economy can be decomposed into three groups, say, households, business firms, and government, and then to include the behavior pattern of these three groups in our models. What can we have neglected? The very simplest models, such as Model I, are deceptive because all the variables of this model are classified as demand variables. We have the demand by households for consumer

---

[14] Or in a corresponding higher range for assumed price increases greater than 10 per cent.

Econometric models as a guide to policy

goods, the demand by business firms for producer goods, and the demand by government for its goods and services. Where is supply? The difficulty lies in the fact that there are some equations that are imbedded within the business demand for producer goods and cover up the supply side even though it is nonetheless present. Business firms demand capital in order to produce goods that they supply to the market. Once we know the *demand* by business firms for factors of production, we know how much business firms will *supply* to the market because there is a technical relation connecting the output of business firms to their input of productive factors. The technical relationship, the production function, has been, so to speak, solved out of the system in constructing the models, but it has not been neglected.

A very simple example will make these points clear. Let us use Model I with the additional variable N_E = total number of employees, w = wage rate, and K_{-1} = total stock of fixed capital available at the beginning of the period. The complete set of equations is:

$$\frac{\mathscr{C}}{pN} = \alpha_0 + \alpha_1 \frac{\mathscr{Y}}{pN} + \alpha_2 \left(\frac{\mathscr{Y}}{pN}\right)_{-1} + u_1, \tag{14.35}$$

$$\mathscr{GNP} = \mathscr{C} + \mathscr{I}' + \mathscr{G}, \tag{14.36}$$

$$\mathscr{GNP} = \mathscr{Y} + \mathscr{T},$$

$$\frac{\mathscr{I}'}{pN} = \text{exogenous}, \tag{14.37}$$

$$\frac{\mathscr{G}}{pN} = \text{exogenous}, \tag{14.38}$$

$$\frac{\mathscr{T}}{pN} = \text{exogenous}, \tag{14.39}$$

$$\frac{\mathscr{GNP}}{p} = f\left(N_E, \frac{\mathscr{I}'}{p}, K_{-1}\right) + u_2, \tag{14.40}$$

$$\frac{wN_E}{p} = \gamma_0 + \gamma_1 \frac{\mathscr{GNP}}{p} + \gamma_2 \left(\frac{\mathscr{GNP}}{p}\right)_{-1} + u_3, \tag{14.41}$$

$$\Delta K = \frac{\mathscr{I}'}{p} - \text{depreciation}. \tag{14.42}$$

In this model, we can determine the demand for factors of production by business firms, their output or supply of goods, and real wages. This model might be called a model of effective demand, yet the production functions and demand for factors of production are part of the system. Equation (14.37) is the demand equation of business firms for producer goods; equation (14.40) is the technical input–output relation for business firms; and equation (14.41) is the demand equation of business firms for labor. It happens that the structure of the system is such that (14.35)–(14.39), as a unit, are sufficient to determine the level of output, but this does not mean that supply conditions are neglected.

There is a supply variable that is omitted from this model, namely, the supply of labor, or the labor force. The variable N_E represents the total demand for labor by business firms. Knowing N_E and the labor force, we can determine the amount of unemployment; however, the models have not been criticized for leaving the supply of labor out of account. The critics had the supply of commodities in mind rather than the supply of labor.

It is obvious that if the model forecast extraordinarily high levels of national product at present prices, say $\mathscr{GNP} = \$225$ billion, this forecast, in real terms, must be discarded because it exceeds our present capacity to supply goods. In the event that the exogenous and lagged variables are such that levels of national product exceeding our capacity are forecast, all that we can say is that real output will be at its maximum level and prices will rise. The exact rise in prices cannot be forecast with any confidence from the models of this paper, however. It is possible to construct models in which there are enough equations to determine prices as well as output, although satisfactory statistical estimates of such equations are still lacking.

THE USEFULNESS OF ECONOMETRIC MODELS

Those engaged in the construction of econometric models know only too well the limitations on these models. The ranges of error associated with forecasts at reasonable probability levels are larger than will be required for many problems. In several cases we shall find that the plus–minus bands of error include both inflation and deflation or yes and no. That part of the error associated with sampling fluctuations can be improved upon. We can get more data and better data, both of which give additional information and help to establish the parameters of the system with a greater degree of accuracy. For example, if we could get good quarterly observations for all series used in this paper over the entire interwar period we should have more information from which to estimate the parameters of the system. There would not be four times as much information, but there would be much more information.

It is, of course, important to know what we cannot do in order that we do not fool ourselves, but our results are not purely negative. They show clearly, in this paper, that the probability is high that national product will fall in the latter part of the present fiscal year. This forecast can be made in spite of the fact that the range of error is fairly wide, say $10 or $15 billion. From Model II, we deduce that deficit spending has a higher multiplier effect than is the case for an easy-money policy. This deduction follows in spite of the fact that the parameters of the model are subject to considerable error. In the recent past (fiscal 1946 and calendar 1946), Model III has shown that there would probably be an inflationary gap rather than a deflationary gap. Not only was this forecast definite, but it was also correct.

Even if a forecast from a model includes the joint possibilities of inflation and deflation, the forecast may be very useful in policy formation. Suppose that a particular value of $\mathcal{GNP}$, call it $(\mathcal{GNP})^0$, represents neither inflation or deflation. Suppose further that the forecast is that $\mathcal{GNP}$ will be in the range $[-\varepsilon_1+(\mathcal{GNP})^0, (\mathcal{GNP})^0+\varepsilon_2]$ with (high) probability, p^0. If $0<\varepsilon_1<\varepsilon_2$, there is a greater chance for inflation than for deflation. Government agencies that are prepared to combat inflation should be given greater powers than the agencies that are prepared to combat deflation, although both agencies should be given some powers because there is a possibility that either one may be needed. In the other case where $0<\varepsilon_2<\varepsilon_1$, the greater powers should be given to the anti-deflationary agency. In both examples, the amounts to be given each type of agency will depend upon the exact sizes of ε_1 and ε_2. But the principle of action is obvious.

The above type of policy is applicable only in the case in which the costs of preparing for inflation, or for deflation, or for both, are negligible. If there is a cost attached to the carrying out of policies, such as the cost of diverting resources to precautionary government activities, a different type of calculation must be made. If the cost of preparing for inflation when the true situation is deflation, the costs of preparing for deflation when the true situation is inflation, and the costs of preparing for the correct situation are known in advance, it is also possible to advise the government on a correct choice of alternative policies even though the forecast interval covers both inflation and deflation simultaneously.[15]

---

[15] The Appendix has been deleted because of its length.

15

A Constant-Utility Index of the Cost of Living

Attempts have been made to construct a true cost-of-living index by assuming knowledge of the Engel curves or by setting limits to the index in terms of Paasche and Laspeyres type indexes. The goal in all these attempts was to express the index of the cost of living in terms of measurable phenomena which are independent of the subjective concepts of utility. In this paper, we shall construct a cost of living index which depends only upon observable prices and properties of demand functions.

Let

u = utility index,
x_i = quantity of the ith commodity,
p_i = price of the ith commodity,
r = income.

We assume the following propositions from the theory of consumer behaviour:
Utility function

$$u = u(x_1, x_2, \ldots, x_n).$$

Budget constraint[1]

$$\sum_{i=1}^{n} p_i x_i = r.$$

Included in Cowles Commission Paper, New Series, No. 26.
[1] In some versions of the theory r = expenditures. In our formulation r = income. Some of the X_i may be future commodities (savings), and the corresponding p_i are the prices of the commodities properly discounted to the present.

From *Review of Economics Studies*, **15**, (1947–48), 84–7; written jointly with H. Rubin.

Conditions of utility maximization

$$\frac{\partial u/\partial x_1}{p_1} = \frac{\partial u/\partial x_2}{p_2} = \cdots = \frac{\partial u/\partial x_n}{p_n}.$$

Slutsky equation

$$\frac{\partial x_i}{\partial p_j} = -x_j \frac{\partial x_i}{\partial r} + s_{ij},$$

where

s_{ij} = the substitution term, which is symmetrical in i and j.

We may solve the budget constraint and the maximization equations for each of the x_i as functions of the p_i and r. These are the demand equations

$$x_i = x_i(p_1, p_2, \ldots, p_n, r) \qquad i = 1, 2, \ldots, n.$$

Substitute the demand equations into the utility index to get

$$u = u[x_1(p_1, p_2, \ldots, p_n, r), \ldots, x_n(p_1, p_2, \ldots, p_n, r)]. \tag{15.1}$$

The true cost of living index is defined as the ratio of two incomes. The denominator of this ratio is the actual base period income. The numerator is the smallest income required in order to buy, at current prices, that complex of goods which would leave one on the same level of utility as was experienced in the base period. This definition implies: u = constant, and $du = 0$.

In terms of equation (15.1) this definition leads to

$$du = \sum_i \sum_j \frac{\partial u}{\partial x_i} \frac{\partial x_i}{\partial p_j} dp_j + \sum_i \frac{\partial u}{\partial x_i} \frac{\partial x_i}{\partial r} dr = 0 \tag{15.2}$$

Everywhere along the constant level of utility we have

$$\frac{\partial u/\partial x_1}{p_1} = \cdots = \frac{\partial u/\partial x_n}{p_n} \tag{15.3}$$

These maximization conditions hold because we have defined the numerator of our index to be the *smallest* income which would leave the consumer at the constant level of utility.

On substituting (15.3) into (15.2), we get

$$\sum_i \sum_j p_i \frac{\partial x_i}{\partial p_j} dp_j + \sum_i p_i \frac{\partial x_i}{\partial r} dr = 0 \tag{15.4}$$

or

$$dr = -\frac{\sum_i \sum_j p_i (\partial x_i/\partial p_j) dp_j}{\sum_i p_i (\partial x_i/\partial r)}$$

This is a partial differential equation in r and the p_i, which is independent of the utility index.

Multiply both sides of the Slutsky equation by p_i and sum both sides over all i. The result is

$$\sum_i p_i \frac{\partial x_i}{\partial p_j} = -x_j \sum_i p_i \frac{\partial x_i}{\partial r} + \sum_i p_i s_{ij}.$$

It is a well established[2] theorem that

$$\sum_i p_i s_{ij} = 0;$$

therefore we get

$$\sum_i p_i \frac{\partial x_i}{\partial p_j} = -x_j \sum_i p_i \frac{\partial x_i}{\partial r}. \tag{15.5}$$

On substituting (15.5) into (15.4), our differential equation becomes

$$dr = \sum_i x_j(p_1, \ldots, p_n, r) dp_j \text{ along } u = \text{constant}. \tag{15.6}$$

If both sides of (15.6) are divided by $r = \sum_j p_j x_j$, the differential equation becomes the familiar Divisia-type price index. However, an index of the cost of living cannot be calculated from (15.6) by the usual methods[13] used to approximate Divisia-type indexes because the $x_j(p_1, \ldots, p_n, r)$ which appear as weights, must be taken along the constant level of utility, and these quantities are not, in general, directly observable.

First, we must examine the integrability conditions for the partial differential equation (15.6). If there is to exist a function

$$r = r(p_1, p_2, \ldots, p_n) \tag{15.7}$$

---

[2] See, for example, J. R. Hicks, *Value and Capital*, Oxford University Press (1939). pp. 310–11. This proposition can very easily be proved by using the Slutsky equation and the condition that the demand equations are homogeneous of order zero in prices and income.

[3] See G. C. Evans, *Mathematical Introduction to Economics*, McGraw Hill (1930), p. 103.

as an integral of (15.6), we must have

$$\left[\frac{\partial x_j(p_1,\ldots,p_n,r)}{\partial p_i}\right]_{u=\text{constant}} = \left[\frac{\partial x_i(p_1,\ldots,p_n,r)}{\partial p_j}\right]_{u=\text{constant}} \quad (15.8)$$

Equation (15.8) always holds as a consequence of the symmetry properties of the Slutsky equations. We have

$$\left[\frac{\partial x_j(p_1,p_2,\ldots,p_n,r)}{\partial p_i}\right]_{u=\text{constant}} = \frac{\partial x_j}{\partial p_i} + \frac{\partial x_j}{\partial r}\frac{\partial r}{\partial p_i} = \frac{\partial x_j}{\partial p_i} + x_i\frac{\partial x_j}{\partial r} = s_{ji}$$

since equation (15.6) requires that

$$\frac{\partial r}{\partial p_i} = x_i.$$

Similarly we have

$$\left[\frac{\partial x_i(p_1,\ldots,p_n,r)}{\partial p_j}\right]_{u=\text{constant}} = s_{ij}.$$

Thus the integrability conditions for (15.6) hold if the Slutsky equation holds, and equation (15.7) exists as the constant-utility level of income for the numerator of the cost of living index. If we know the demand functions, and if the Slutsky equation holds, we can always compute the true cost of living index by integrating (15.6). We shall next proceed to obtain an explicit form for (15.7) in a simple case.

Suppose that the demand equations are all of the form

$$x_i = \sum_j \alpha_{ij}\frac{p_j}{p_i} + \beta_i\frac{r}{p_i} \quad i=1,2,\ldots,n \quad (15.9)$$

The αs and βs in (15.9) are not unrestricted. If we multiply both sides of (15.9) by p_i and sum over all i, we get

$$\sum_i p_i x_i = \sum_i\sum_j \alpha_{ij}p_j + r\sum_i \beta_i = r.$$

Two sets of restrictions are

$$\sum_i \beta_i = 1 \quad \text{and} \quad \sum_i\sum_j \alpha_{ij}p_j = 0 \quad (15.10)$$

The symmetry properties of the Slutsky equation imply

$$\frac{\partial x_i}{\partial p_j} + x_j\frac{\partial x_i}{\partial r} = \frac{\partial x_j}{\partial p_i} + x_i\frac{\partial x_j}{\partial r} \quad (15.11)$$

or

$$\frac{\alpha_{ij}}{p_i}+x_j\frac{\beta_i}{p_i}=\frac{\alpha_{ji}}{p_j}+x_i\frac{\beta_j}{p_j} \quad i\neq j$$

On substituting (15.9) into (15.11), we obtain

$$p_j\alpha_{ij}+\beta_i\sum_k\alpha_{jk}p_k=p_i\alpha_{ji}+p_j\sum_k\alpha_{ik}p_k \quad i\neq j \quad (15.12)$$

If the coefficients of p_k on both sides of (15.12) are to be equal we must have

$$b_i\alpha_{jk}=\beta_j\alpha_{ik} \quad i\neq j\neq k \quad (15.13)$$

hence the coefficients of the price ratios in (15.9) must be of the form

$$\alpha_{ij}=\beta_i\gamma_j \quad i\neq j \quad (15.14)$$

For the more general case including $i=j$, we have

$$\alpha_{ij}=\beta_i\gamma_j+\delta_{ij}\varepsilon_i \quad (15.15)$$

where $\delta_{ij}=1$ for $i=j$, and 0 for $i\neq j$. From (15.10) we see that

$$\sum_i\sum_j\beta_i\gamma_jp_j+\sum_i\sum_j\delta_{ij}\varepsilon_ip_j=0$$

and

$$\sum_i\beta_i=1;$$

hence it follows that:

$$\varepsilon_i=-\gamma_i \quad (15.6)$$

If we substitute (15.14) and (15.16) into (15.9), we obtain

$$x_i=\sum_j\beta_i\gamma_j\frac{p_j}{p_i}-\gamma_i+\beta_i\frac{r}{p_i} \quad i=1,2,\ldots,n \quad (15.17)$$

The demand functions (15.17) are now constructed to satisfy the budget constraint and the Slutsky equation. If these functions are substituted into the differential equation (15.6), we find the integral for r to be

$$r=C\prod_i p_i\beta_i-\sum_i\gamma_ip_i \quad (15.18)$$

where C is a constant of integration. The cost of living index for this case is

$$\frac{r}{r_0}=\frac{C\prod_i p_i\beta_i-\sum_i\gamma_ip_i}{C\prod_i(p_i)_0\beta_i-\sum_i\gamma_i(p_i)_0} \quad (15.19)$$

In (15.19), the $(p_i)_0$ and r_0 are the observed prices and income of the base period.

The actual statistical estimates of r from (15.18) will not be exact. In the estimation of the βs and γs from samples of observations on prices, quantities and incomes, there will be sampling errors. At best, we shall be able to estimate confidence intervals for the βs and γs. The intervals for these parameters will imply, in turn, specific intervals for r. These intervals have one advantage over the intervals usually developed for the cost of living index from indexes of the Paasche and Laspeyres type. The latter intervals provided only an upper limit for the index on one base and a lower limit for the index on another base; they do not provide upper and lower bounds for a given index simultaneously. On the other hand, our intervals give upper and lower bounds for the index on any base; and, furthermore, it is possible to calculate the probability that the true value of the index will be covered by our interval in repeated samples.

It should be pointed out, however, that our index is subject to the restrictions that apply to all indexes based on the theory of consumer behavior. In addition to the fulfilment of the obvious restriction that the base period indifference map remains invariant in other periods, there are more subtle restrictions connected with the transformation from individual to market data. What the economic theory of the true cost of living index really gives is a cost of living index for an individual. This means that to use our method of calculating the index on the basis of parameters of the demand functions, we must have a knowledge of the properties of the demand equations of an individual. The demand equations that we customarily estimate statistically are demand curves based on market data that refer to an entire group of individuals.

The following interpretation of our results, and, for that matter, the results of other methods of calculating the true cost of living, seems to be the most satisfactory solution. Regard the indifference map as pertaining to an average individual, say, a family head earning an average wage in a typical urban area. This is specifically the situation that is claimed for many official cost of living indexes. Estimate the demand equations from per capita market data, and regard these statistical demand equations as pertaining to the average individual whose cost of living is being measured. This is the usual interpretation of per capita demand equations. Then use the estimated parameters of the per capita demand equation to calculate the cost of living index for the average individual whose utility level is to remain constant.

16
On the Interpretation of Professor Leontief's System

The widespread interest and development of input–output analysis introduced by Leontief and his followers raises basic questions of economic interpretation. Are the elements of input–output tables structural parameters of an economic system or are they merely ratios of two economic variables? If input–output coefficients are truly structural parameters, can they be identified with well-defined *technological* parameters or are they mixtures of several types of parameters including some that are not purely technological?

The standard assumptions of input–output analysis are that the coefficients of a *tableau économique* comprise a set of technological parameters in linear production functions with fixed proportions among the factors of production. In deriving a rationale for interpreting Leontief's system, the unrealistic assumption is made that each sector of the economy produced only a single type of output. Samuelson,[1] using this assumption and the additional assumption that the system has only one primary factor of production, has advanced our understanding of Leontief's system by showing that any set of input–output coefficients can be identified with two different underlying technological structures; one the system of linear production functions with fixed proportions among factors, and the other a system of production functions homogeneous of the first degree in all the input variables.

This paper will be reprinted as Cowles Commission Paper, New Series No. 69. The research was carried out as part of the program of the Research Seminar in Quantitative Economics, University of Michigan. Helpful suggestions have been made by H. S. Houthakker, T. C. Koopmans, J. Marschak, H. Rubin, P. A. Samuelson and D. B. Suits.

[1] P. A. Samuelson, 'Abstract of a theorem concerning substitutability in open Leontief models,' *Activity Analysis of Production and Allocation* Chapter VII (ed. T. C. Koopmans), John Wiley, New York (1951).

Particular interest attaches to the latter structure because, in contrast to the former, it permits substitution among factors of production.

The same assumptions have been used by Cameron[2] to establish a comparison between the systems of Leontief and classical general equilibrium. In these studies of the interpretation of Leontief's system it is assumed that conditions of market competition exist. The present paper is concerned with a more realistic interpretation of Leontief's system. In contrast with the other studies we shall try to adopt a theoretical model which corresponds to the practices of input–output analysis and which drops the assumption that each sector produces only a single output. We shall allow joint production in each producing sector. This is not to be regarded as a mere refinement since joint production is the rule and not the exception; moreover, it has a strong influence on the results we shall derive. An examination will also be made of the effects of dropping the assumption of market competition.

Let us classify our results into two groups.

1 Joint production and market competition. We are able to give a technological interpretation to input–output coefficients as structural parameters and extend Samuelson's findings on the possibility of substitution beyond the case in which each sector produces only one output.

2 Joint production and market imperfection. *In general*, input-output coefficients cannot be interpreted as purely technological parameters; they depend on the parameters of consumer demand and factor supply functions.

Let us now consider a formal development of these propositions. In the customary exposition of the Leontief system[3] we have

x_i = output of the ith sector,

x_{ik} = output of the kth sector used in the ith sector.

The technical coefficients are defined as:

$$a_{ik} = \frac{x_{ik}}{x_i}. \tag{16.1}$$

The a_{ik} are the elements, assumed constant, of the input–output table.

---

[2]Burgess Cameron, 'The construction of the Leontief system,' *The Review of Economic Studies*, XIX, (1) (1950–51), 19–27.

[3]See for example, W. Leontief, *Structure of the American Economy*, Oxford University Press, New York (1941).

One interpretation of (16.1) is that it defines a technological production function, with the condition that inputs are used in fixed proportions.

The actual expression for the production function would be:

$$x_i = \min\left(\frac{x_{i1}}{a_{i1}}, \frac{x_{i2}}{a_{i2}}, \ldots, \frac{x_{in}}{a_{in}}\right) \quad (16.12)$$

with (16.1) holding for all k as long as no inputs are free goods, thus insuring the equalities

$$\frac{x_{i1}}{a_{i1}} = \frac{x_{i2}}{a_{i2}} = \cdots = \frac{x_{in}}{a_{in}} \quad (16.3)$$

In order to measure input–output coefficients directly as in (16.1), it is necessary to assume that each sector produces only one type of output. However, even if input–output tables are refined to 1000×1000 classifications, the problem of joint production cannot be avoided. It is simply true, in most cases at least, that the a_{ik} are computed, not as the ratio of two physical quantities, but as the ratios of two values – the value of output of the kth sector used in the ith sector divided by the value of the output of the ith sector. Joint production is the rule and not a special case.

We shall now show that even in the case of joint production in a competitive economy, there may exist a production function permitting substitution among inputs and yielding a set of constant elements of an input–output table. The approach used here and the results obtained are not strictly parallel to those of Samuelson in the one commodity per industry case, but they do have a point in common, namely, to show that substitutability as an alternative to fixed proportions is consistent with Leontief's empirical findings and theoretical model.

Let

$x_i^{(s)} = s$th output of sector i,

$x_{ik}^{(r)} = r$th output of sector k used in i.

The elements of an input–output table are defined by:

$$a_{ik} = \frac{\sum_r p_k^{(r)} x_{ik}^{(r)}}{\sum_s p_i^{(s)} x_i^{(s)}}. \quad (16.4)$$

The problem is to determine the characteristics of a technological

Interpretation of Professor Leontief's system

relation, independent of market phenomena like prices

$$F_i(x_i^{(1)},\ldots,x_i^{(S)},x_{i1}^{(1)},\ldots,x_{i1}^{(R_1)},\ldots,x_{in}^{(1)},\ldots,x_{in}^{(R_n)})=0 \qquad i=1,2,\ldots,n, \tag{16.5}$$

such that the quantities (16.4) are constants. In order to solve this problem some assumptions must be made to connect the pricing system to the technology. In a competitive market

$$\frac{\partial F_i}{\partial x_i^{(s)}} = -\lambda_i p_i^{(s)}, \tag{16.6}$$

$$\frac{\partial F_i}{\partial x_{ik}^{(r)}} = \lambda_i p_k^{(r)}; \tag{16.7}$$

hence the ratio in (16.4) can be written as

$$\frac{\sum_r (\partial F_i/\partial x_{ik}^{(r)}) x_{ik}^{(r)}}{-\sum_s (\partial F_i/\partial x_i^{(s)}) x_i^{(s)}} = a_{ik} = \text{constant} \qquad k=1,2,\ldots,i-1,i+1,\ldots,n. \tag{16.8}$$

Equations (16.8) provide a set of partial differential equations of which the technological function in (16.5) is a solution.

H. Rubin suggests the transformation

$$y_i^{(s)} = [x_i^{(s)}]^{1/a_{ik}} \tag{16.9}$$

in order to put (16.8) in the form of Euler's equations for homogeneous functions

$$\sum_r \frac{\partial F_i}{\partial x_{ik}^{(r)}} x_{ik}^{(r)} = -\sum_s \frac{\partial F_i}{\partial y_i^{(s)}} y_i^{(s)} \qquad k=1,2,\ldots,i-1,i+1,\ldots,n. \tag{16.10}$$

Since Euler's equation is a necessary and sufficient condition for the homogeneity of the function in question, whether for all or a subset of variables in the argument, we see that F_i must be homogeneous of degree zero in each of the subsets

$$x_{i1}^{(1)},\ldots,x_{i1}^{(R_1)}, [x_i^{(1)}]^{1/a_{i1}},\ldots,[x_i^{(S)}]^{1/a_{i1}}$$

$$x_{in}^{(1)},\ldots,x_{in}^{(R_n)}, [x_i^{(1)}]^{1/a_{in}},\ldots,[x_i^{(S)}]^{1/a_{in}}.$$

An obvious example of a production function with these properties is

$$\sum_s \beta_i^{(s)} [x_i^{(s)}]^\beta - A \prod_k \prod_r [x_{ik}^{(r)}]^{\alpha_{ik}^{(r)}} = 0, \tag{16.11}$$

where the parameters (16.11) must be subject to:

$$\frac{\sum_r \alpha_{ik}^{(r)}}{\beta} = a_{ik} \tag{16.12}$$

in order that (16.8) be satisfied by (16.11). Other functions satisfying the system of partial differential equations can easily be constructed.

In studying a model of a competitive economy we have not assumed zero profits. Zero profits are not synonymous with the assumptions of competition in (16.6)–(16.7). It is sometimes argued that the existence of profits will lead to entry of new firms into a sector and indefinite expansion of production by all firms until profits vanish. A reverse process is assumed to take place when negative profits exist. The model of this paper implicitly rules out such arguments. By a competitive market, we mean simply one in which entrepreneurial decisions do not influence market prices viewed as parameters by them. Production will not necessarily be expanded indefinitely as a result of the existence of positive profits because entrepreneurs cannot vary fixed capital at will in a short period. The Leontief input–output tables we are considering in this paper do not have fixed-capital coefficients. The capital structure is taken as given and factors of production, in any particular sector, are purely current flows of output from other (inputting) sectors. We follow Leontief in assuming nonzero profits in each sector,[4] and do not view this as denying the applicability of equations (16.6)–(16.7) to our model.

In general the elements of Leontief's input output table may thus be interpreted as parameters of a class of production functions, all of which permit substitution among factors of production and types of output. Moreover, the a_{ik} can be interpreted as technological parameters.

This interpretation is applicable only if equations (16.4), (16.6) and (16.7) hold. Insofar as the a_{ik} are determined purely from engineering information *without any requirement that different products be weighted by relative prices*, equations (16.4) need not hold, and the above results about substitutability do not apply. In earlier publications of Leontief, equations of the type in (16.4) were used to determine the a_{ik}. Even engineering information, however, must make assumptions about the proportions in which different types of product or input are combined. In many or most cases, these proportions are current relative prices or time averages of them. For example, in studying railroad traffic in the

---

[4]W. Leontief, 'Wages, Profit and Prices,' *The Quarterly Journal of Economics*, LXI, November (1946) 26–39.

USA, one might use

Traffic unit = Freight ton miles + 2.4 passenger miles

as a composite output variable since it is not possible to make a complete separation of operations into those dealing exclusively with freight and exclusively with passenger service. The coefficient 2.4 is not a technological parameter; it is the mean price ratio of the two types of service averaged over many years.

The production function (16.5) and associated marginal productivity equations (16.6)–(16.7) are written as though there is only one entrepreneur in each sector. This would be strictly true only if a sector were a firm instead of a competitive industry. We shall now state, without proof, a result applicable to a model in which each sector contains several entrepreneurs. At the same time we retain our earlier assumptions of joint production under market competition.

Trivial results follow if we require that each entrepreneur within a sector has an identical production function or that the value of output be distributed in a known way among firms in the same sector. A less restrictive approach is to assume that the production function of each entrepreneur depends only on variables directly produced or used by his firm with no exchange of products among firms in the same sector. Under these conditions we can show the existence of a set of input–output coefficients as constants and parameters of production functions, the sum of which satisfy homogeneity conditions analogous to those derived above for individual functions. The homogeneity conditions can be extended to the individual production functions of each entrepreneur provided each function vanishes for zero values of all arguments. Essentially, our main conclusions of this paper are not dependent on the fact that we have simplified our models by treating them as though there were only one entrepreneur in each sector.

Returning to the model (16.4)–(16.7), we might consider the consequences of dropping the assumption of competitive markets. In this event, equations (16.6) and (16.7) do not hold. Corresponding equations for a non-competitive market can be written as:

$$\frac{\partial F_i}{\partial x_i^{(s)}} = -\lambda_i p_i^{(s)}(1+\eta_i^{(s)}), \tag{16.13}$$

$$\frac{\partial F_i}{\partial x_{ik}^{(r)}} = \lambda_i p_k^{(r)}(1+\varepsilon_{ik}^{(r)}), \tag{16.14}$$

in which $\eta_i^{(s)}$ and $\varepsilon_{ik}^{(r)}$ are entrepreneurs' estimates of parameters of demand and supply functions respectively.

In addition to equations (16.4), (16.3), and (16.14) we have in the system

$$p_i^{(s)} = g_i^{(s)}(x_i^{(1)}, \ldots, x_i^{(S)}), \tag{16.15}$$

$$p_k^{(r)} = h_{ik}^{(r)}(x_{i1}^{(1)}, \ldots, x_{in}^{(R_n)}), \tag{16.16}$$

the demand and supply functions, respectively, facing the ith sector. The parameters used in (16.13) and (16.14) are

$$\eta_i^{(s)} = \sum_u \frac{x_i^{(u)}}{p_i^{(s)}} \frac{\partial p_i^{(u)}}{\partial x_i^{(s)}}.$$

$$\varepsilon_{ik}^{(r)} = \sum_t \sum_v \frac{x_{it}^{(v)}}{p_k^{(r)}} \frac{\partial p_t^{(v)}}{\partial x_{ik}^{(r)}}.$$

In order to give a purely technological interpretation to the so-called technical coefficients, a_{ik}, we should be able to show that they depend exclusively on parameters of the production functions, F_i. This was the case in the corresponding competitive model as shown in equations (16.12) for a particular production function. Except under special circumstances, the a_{ik} will also depend on the parameters of $g_i^{(s)}$ and $h_{ik}^{(r)}$; therefore, they cannot strictly be regarded as technical coefficients.

This can be shown by reference to a particular solution of the present model. Let the production function be given by[5]

$$\prod_s [x_i^{(s)}]^{\beta_i^{(s)}} - A \prod_k \prod_s [x_{ik}^{(r)}]^{\alpha_{ik}^{(r)}} = 0, \tag{16.17}$$

and let the demand and supply equations be also of the constant elasticity type.

$$p_i^{(s)} = B[x_i^{(s)}]^{\eta_i^{(s)}} \tag{16.18}$$

$$p_k^{(r)} = C[x_{ik}^{(r)}]^{\varepsilon_{ik}^{(r)}}. \tag{16.19}$$

The technical coefficients must then satisfy

$$\frac{\sum_r (1/1 + \varepsilon_{ik}^{(r)}) \alpha_{ik}^{(r)}}{\sum_s (1/1 + \eta_i^{(s)}) \beta_i^{(s)}} = a_{ik} = \text{constant}. \tag{16.20}$$

The coefficients are thus defined in terms of constants in the production, demand and supply functions. Non-technological behavioral

---

[5] This production function is also apparently a particular solution of the earlier system of differential equations (16.8), yet it does not satisfy the second order conditions for profit maximization under competition. The same difficulty does not occur under conditions of imperfect markets.

changes in the economy; changes in tastes, for example; would cause the a_{ik} to change.

Leontief's model is estimated from data that are the complex result of many more economic interrelationships than are expressed by the *technical* relationships usually assumed to underlie input–output tables. Although a Walrasian type system is often cited in theoretical justification for input–output analysis, it is seldom recognised that numerous complex economic processes in addition to technological relations are involved in the interpretation of the a_{ik}. Perhaps the most realistic interpretation of Leontief's system is that of the imperfectly competitive economy in which the coefficients of input–output tables are not easily identified with any single set of basic structural parameters.

17

Some Econometrics of Growth: Great Ratios of Economics

Economists frequently base their reasoning on key ratios between variables. If these ratios are in the nature of fundamental parameters, simplifications of theory may result. If they are simply ratios of variables, it is questionable whether any theoretical advances can be made through the transformation from statements about a quotient to statements about numerator and denominator separately. Accountants often construct such key ratios from quick assets and liabilities, or inventories and sales, or earnings and fixed charges etc. By reducing measurements for firms in diverse size groups to a common order of magnitude these ratios may be of use, as they are, in international comparisons or historical growth comparisons. For theory construction, however, our standards must be high, and stability or plainly systematic variation in ratios must be found in order to enhance their usefulness.

Some celebrated ratios of economics are (a) the savings–income ratio (S/Y), (b) the capital–output ratio (K/Y), (c) labor's share of income (wN/pY), (d) income velocity of circulation (pY/M), and (e) the capital–labor ratio (K/N).

We are constructing a global model of growth and are therefore sliding over some fine points in the institutional structure of the economy. Until we come to the precise terms of actual measurement, we shall not distinguish between real output and real income; we shall not consider the government or foreign sectors explicitly; we shall use highly aggregative index concepts.

STATISTICAL ESTIMATION OF THE MODEL

With the abundance of long-run statistical series now available for the American economy, it may appear, *in prospect*, to be a fairly easy

---

From *The Quarterly Journal of Economics*, **75**, May (1961), 173–98; written jointly with R. F. Kosobud.

matter to collect the necessary series measuring each of the variables of the model in a mutually consistent fashion over a period as long as the first half of this century. It turns out, in fact, to be a substantial job of data collection and processing to prepare a consistent set of series for all the variables over this period.

The studies of Kuznets and Kendrick at the National Bureau of Economic Research are extremely helpful in providing series on national product, its components, and employment in a form that is readily adaptable to our uses.[1] The estimates of national product and capital formation by Kuznets are, in a sense, tailored to our needs by virtue of the fact that he provides series in both current and constant prices, that he revalues depreciation charges to replacement costs, and that he treats government capital formation like private capital formation. His estimates differ in one principal respect, however, from the official national accounting practices of the Department of Commerce. He does not classify total government expenditures on *current* goods and services as final purchases. He regards a large part of them (in recent years) as intermediate expenditures and excludes them from the total national product. He roughly allocates a small amount of them to personal consumption. In the postwar period of rapid expansion in the government sector, Kuznets' estimates are considerably lower than the official series. He gives a different statistical picture of the long-term growth of the American economy, and the estimates of our model reflect this fact.

Kuznets computes national product according to alternative variants. The one that we have selected shows no distinction between national income and net national product. It also allocates government expenditures, if they are not eliminated, to either consumption or investment spending. They are thus well suited to the global nature of our model in which our concepts and accounting relations make no explicit allowance for institutional features of the government sector. Although his allocations or adjustments may be rough, Kuznets makes them definite on the product side of the accounts. In certain extreme periods, such as wartime, this leads to some anomalous results for our calculations unless some compensating adjustments are made on the income side.

---

[1] S. Kuznets, *Capital in the American Economy: Its Formation and Financing*, National Bureau of Economic Research New York (1959) mimeographed. J. W. Kendrick, *Productivity Trends in the United States*, National Bureau of Economic Research, New York (1960).

THE SAVINGS-INCOME RATIO

Economists and statisticians have long been impressed with the findings of Kuznets that the percentage of income saved, by decades, has been fairly steady at about 10 per cent for the period since the Civil War.[2] Goldsmith in his more recent massive study of savings has confirmed this result for the relationship between personal savings and personal income.[3] Kuznets' decade averages iron out cyclical fluctuations, but Goldsmith's annual estimates for this century exhibit strong cyclical influences about a steady trend. In the short run, the ratio is clearly not constant. In the long run, considering only the trend development, there is evidence of constancy in the personal savings–income ratio.

Our figures in the present paper differ from those of both studies cited above. We examine the constancy of the ratio between consumption and net national product for the period 1900–53 as computed by Kuznets in his more recent study. Both series are expressed in 1929 prices. Since we deal with the consumption–income ratio directly for measurement purposes, the savings–income ratio is only indirectly measured as a residual. The implied concept of savings includes more than personal savings. It includes business and government savings as well. The income or product concept measures national income and not personal income.

Alternative probability structures underlying the estimates of the savings ratio, α, are plausible. They might be

$$C/Y = (1-\alpha) + u$$
$$C/Y = (1-\alpha)u$$
$$C = (1-\alpha)Y + u$$

where

C = consumption,
Y = national product,
u = random error.

In the first case, $(1-\alpha)$ would be estimated as the arithmetic mean of C/Y and in the second as the geometric mean. In the third case, some form of unbiased regression estimates would be needed. We have made both of the first two types of estimates. Our charts plot the ratios in

---

[2] S. Kuznets, *Uses of National Income in Peace and War*, National Bureau of Economic Research, New York (1942), p. 30.

[3] R. W. Goldsmith, *A Study of Savings in the United States*, Vols. I, III, Princeton University Press, Princeton (1955, 1956).

arithmetic units. Our computed equations are presented in logarithmic units, suited to the second case.[4]

The series are given in the accompanying table 17.1 and a chart of the consumption–income ratio together with the other great ratios is given in figure 17.1. The data show a consumption–income ratio just under 0.9 at the beginning of this century and a series of values above this level in recent years. A significant upward trend is suggested for this series. Our estimate is

$$\log C/Y = -0.03933 + 0.00054t$$

or

$$C/Y = 0.9134 \, (1.00129)^t.$$

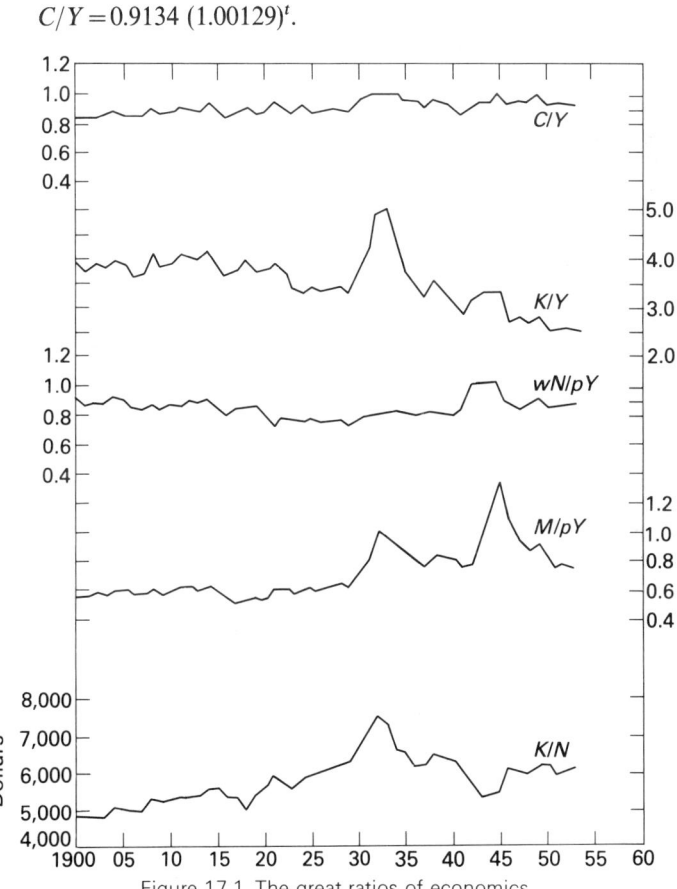

Figure 17.1 The great ratios of economics

[4]Both of the first two forms have been computed. The numerical results for the second are analysed in the text.

Time, t, is measured chronologically, centered at January 1, 1927, in terms of 6-months' units. At the midpoint of the sample span, the ratio is 0.9134 and increases at a compound interest rate of about 0.125 of 1 per cent semiannually. This trend is statistically significant. In the logarithmic formulation, the coefficient of t is more than five times as large as its sampling error.

Table 17.1 Consumption and net national product, United States (billions of 1929 dollars)

	Consumption	Net national product	Ratio C/Y
1900	27.8	33.0	0.842
1901	30.5	36.3	0.840
1902	30.9	36.8	0.840
1903	32.9	38.8	0.848
1904	33.3	38.1	0.874
1905	34.9	40.7	0.857
1906	38.3	45.4	0.844
1907	39.7	46.7	0.850
1908	38.1	42.6	0.894
1909	41.4	47.8	0.866
1910	42.1	48.2	0.873
1911	43.2	47.9	0.902
1912	42.8	48.5	0.882
1913	44.7	51.3	0.871
1914	47.1	49.8	0.946
1915	48.2	53.7	0.898
1916	49.4	58.8	0.840
1917	50.8	59.0	0.861
1918	49.6	55.4	0.895
1919	52.2	61.1	0.854
1920	54.2	62.2	0.871
1921	57.0	59.6	0.956
1922	59.2	63.9	0.926
1923	64.3	73.5	0.875
1924	69.0	75.6	0.913
1925	67.1	77.3	0.868
1926	72.5	82.8	0.876
1927	74.2	83.6	0.888
1928	76.3	84.9	0.899
1929	80.3	90.3	0.889
1930	75.9	80.5	0.943
1931	73.2	73.5	0.996
1932	66.4	60.3	1.101
1933	65.0	58.2	1.117
1934	68.6	64.4	1.065
1935	73.1	75.4	0.969

Some econometrics of growth 293

Table 17.1 (continued)

	Consumption	Net national product	Ratio C/Y
1936	80.8	85.0	0.951
1937	84.4	92.7	0.910
1938	83.0	85.4	0.972
1939	87.0	92.3	0.943
1940	91.7	101.2	0.906
1941	97.9	113.3	0.864
1942	96.2	107.8	0.892
1943	98.8	105.2	0.939
1944	102.2	107.1	0.954
1945	109.1	108.8	1.003
1946	122.3	131.4	0.931
1947	124.9	130.9	0.954
1948	127.5	134.7	0.947
1949	130.7	129.1	1.012
1950	138.7	147.8	0.938
1951	139.8	152.1	0.919
1952	143.9	154.3	0.933
1953	149.4	159.9	0.934

Source: Kuznets, *Capital in the American Economy*.

We conclude that the savings-income ratio is not a constant, but is on a *declining* trend (opposite trend to that of the consumption–income ratio).[5]

THE CAPITAL–OUTPUT RATIO

In the currently fashionable economics of growth, theorists do not rigidly assume constancy of the accelerator coefficient. In the short run, this ratio may be more constant if measured with capacity instead of actual output. In the long run, it is likely to fall in advanced industrial economies as a result of technical progress.

As in the case of the savings–income ratio, two of the principal investigators of the statistical capital–output ratio have been Kuznets and Goldsmith.[6] Kuznets' decade estimates rise from 2.83 to 3.19 between 1879 and 1944. There are great swings within this period, however. Goldsmith's annual estimates confirm this general pattern until World War II, after which his ratio shows a tendency to fall. Our

[5] Compare the observations of G. D. A. MacDougall, 'Does productivity rise faster in the United States?' *The Review of Economics and Statistics*, XXXVIII, May (1956), 173.

[6] S. Kuznets, 'Long term changes in the national product of the United States of America since 1870'; R. W. Goldsmith, 'The growth of reproducible wealth of the United States of America from 1805 to 1905,' *Income and Wealth*, Series II, Bowes and Bowes, Cambridge (1952).

estimate for this century, obtained by cumulating Kuznets' annual net investment figures from a starting figure for capital stock, shows a significant downward trend (table 17.2 and figure 17.1). Our equation is

$$\log K/Y = 0.54699 - 0.0015t$$

or

$$K/Y = 3.523 \, (1.0033)^{-t}.$$

Table 17.2 Capital stock and net national product, United States (billions of 1929 dollars)

	Capital Stock	Net national product	Ratio K/Y
1900	131.57	33.0	3.987
1901	136.71	36.3	3.766
1902	142.27	36.8	3.866
1903	147.72	38.8	3.807
1904	152.20	38.1	3.995
1905	157.65	40.7	3.873
1906	164.50	45.4	3.623
1907	171.25	46.7	3.667
1908	175.31	42.6	4.115
1909	182.05	47.8	3.809
1910	187.86	48.2	3.898
1911	192.45	47.9	4.108
1912	198.04	48.5	4.083
1913	204.38	51.3	3.984
1914	207.28	49.8	4.162
1915	210.36	53.7	3.917
1916	215.70	58.8	3.668
1917	220.26	59.0	3.733
1918	223.94	55.4	4.042
1919	229.37	61.1	3.754
1920	235.13	62.2	3.780
1921	236.19	59.6	3.963
1922	240.15	63.9	3.758
1923	248.87	73.5	3.386
1924	254.47	75.6	3.336
1925	264.08	77.3	3.416
1926	273.94	82.8	3.308
1927	282.61	83.6	3.381
1928	290.20	84.9	3.418
1929	299.42	90.3	3.316
1930	303.30	80.5	3.768
1931	303.42	73.5	4.128
1932	297.12	60.3	4.927
1933	290.12	58.2	4.985

Some econometrics of growth 295

Table 17.2 (continued)

	Capital Stock	Net national product	Ratio K/Y
1934	285.43	64.4	4.432
1935	287.78	75.4	3.817
1936	292.11	85.0	3.437
1937	300.33	92.7	3.240
1938	301.38	85.4	3.529
1939	305.58	92.3	3.311
1940	313.32	101.2	3.096
1941	327.41	113.3	2.890
1942	338.98	107.8	3.145
1943	347.08	105.2	3.299
1944	353.46	107.1	3.300
1945	354.13	108.8	3.255
1946	359.43	131.4	2.735
1947	359.30	130.9	2.745
1948	365.19	134.7	2.711
1949	363.21	129.1	2.813
1950	373.73	147.8	2.529
1951	385.95	152.1	2.537
1952	396.47	154.3	2.569
1953	408.01	159.9	2.552

Source: Kuznets, *Capital in the American Economy*.

This equation puts the rate of decline at about $\frac{1}{3}$ of 1 per cent semiannually. At the midpoint, $t=0$, we have a ratio of 3.523, and the coefficient of t in the logarithmic equation is seven times its estimated sampling error.

We did not estimate the accelerator form of this equation directly. To do so would require a different set of assumptions about the probability structure of the model and would involve the use of negative numbers, thus precluding the estimation of logarithmic trends.

LABOR'S SHARE

The wage share of national income has received at least as much measurement attention as any of the great ratios. In this case much more experimentation has been made with alternative numerators and denominators. Should payments to labor include salaries generally, salaries of company executives, income of small proprietors, or employer contributions to retirement? The denominator may be gross product, net product, national income, or personal income. Dunlop has charted labor's share for a great variety of these alternative concepts.[7] His graphs show no statistical grounds for choosing among alternative formulations. Over the long run, it appears, from his data, that the ratios are stable with considerable cyclical fluctuation. His findings are different for wages and for salaries. They also differ among industry groups, but exhibit no trend for the economy as a whole during the interwar period.

Johnson has imputed a wage to self-employed persons.[8] From the first decade of this century to the post World War II period he finds a growth in labor's share of about 5 percentage points. This longer period gives different results from Dunlop's interwar period. Were Johnson not to impute wages to self-employed persons, he would find nearly twice as large an increase in labor's share.

Kravis, in a study of Johnson's and later figures, adduces reasons for an increasing trend in labor's share.[9] He argues that demand for both labor and capital increased with output growth in an expanding economy. Capital supply was more responsive to the increased demand, and the comparative inelasticity of labor's response raised the wage share in national income.

The shift in population from rural to urban areas, and the increasing importance of the government sector may account for a large part of the increase in the share paid to labor since both phenomena represent a growth in sectors paying a larger share of output to labor. Social welfare legislation and growing strength of trade unions may also account for some of the increase.

If one confines calculations to what is purely wage income in official series, an increasing trend is likely to result. This will be true for the nonfarm private sector as well as for the whole economy; hence industry shifts will not fully explain the trend. Noticing, however, that the trend was reduced in Johnson's series of imputations of wage income to self-employed persons are made, and following a suggestion in Kuznets' work, we combine the whole of self-employed income with wage and salary income. The total of such income from active employment tends to be nearly a constant fraction of national income as far as trends are concerned. This wider scope of wage income is consistent with our scope for employment in the model, which is to

---

[7] J. T. Dunlop, *Wage Determination Under Trade Unions*, Kelley, New York (1950), chapter VIII.

[8] D. G. Johnson, 'The functional distribution of income in the United States, 1850–1952,' *Review of Economics and Statistics*, XXXVI, May (1954) 175–82.

[9] I. B. Kravis, 'Relative income shares in fact and theory,' *American Economic Review*, XLIX, December (1959), 917–49.

include all persons engaged, whether they be production workers, executives, managers, or self-employed. This wider scope of the payments and employment series is consistent also with the global character of our model.

Weintraub, in a recent study of price level phenomena, makes strong use of the constancy of labor's share. His numerator is the total of private wages and salaries. His denominator is the private gross national product. He argues in favor of constancy of this ratio from 1929 to recent years.[10]

Our data consist of the present official series published by the Department of Commerce on employee compensation and income from self-employment, extended back from 1929 to 1900 by splicing to Johnson's corresponding series. This series is expressed in current prices. The denominator of our ratio is the current price value of net national product estimated by Kuznets. From the graph and table, we can see the curious result that during World War II the earnings variable exceeded Kuznets' adjusted value of national product.[11]

A formal calculation of the trend in the ratio yields

$$\log \frac{wN}{pY} = -0.07369 + 0.000082t$$

or

$$wN/pY = 0.8439 \, (1.00019)^t.$$

The coefficient of t in the logarithmic form is less than half its sampling error. We suggest that there is no trend in this ratio. Without the trend we have

$$wN/pY = 0.8439.$$

---

[10]S. Weintraub, *A General Theory of the Price Level, Output, Income Distribution and Economic Growth*, Chilton, Philadelphia (1959).

[11]From 1941 an adjustment had to be made to the income side of the national accounts to correspond with Kuznet's adjustments to the product side. He subtracted personal tax and nontax payments from consumption (except for 3.6 per cent of consumption, which he treated as *final* government services to consumers). We subtracted this amount from the numerator of our ratio. There are obviously inaccuracies in this rough adjustment, but it brings us close to the Bowman–Easterlin treatment of the income side for Kuznet's concepts. They argue for factorial imputations of income after taxes. See R. Bowman and R. A. Easterlin, 'The income side: Some theoretical aspects,' in *A Critique of the U.S. Income and Product Accounts*, National Bureau of Economic Research, Princeton University Press, Princeton (1958), pp. 180–6.

Economic Theory and Econometrics

Table 17.3 Earned income and net national product, United States (billions of current dollars)

	Earned income	Net national product	Ratio wN/pY
1900	14.9	16.4	0.909
1901	15.8	18.0	0.878
1902	16.8	18.8	0.894
1903	17.9	20.0	0.895
1904	18.3	19.9	0.920
1905	19.5	21.7	0.899
1906	21.0	24.8	0.847
1907	22.1	26.5	0.834
1908	21.1	24.1	0.876
1909	23.6	28.1	0.840
1910	24.9	29.0	0.859
1911	24.7	28.6	0.864
1912	27.2	30.2	0.901
1913	27.9	32.1	0.869
1914	28.3	31.6	0.896
1915	30.1	35.2	0.855
1916	34.3	43.5	0.789
1917	44.5	53.9	0.826
1918	49.5	58.2	0.851
1919	56.5	65.2	0.867
1920	59.6	75.7	0.787
1921	44.4	61.8	0.718
1922	48.7	63.0	0.773
1923	57.0	74.1	0.769
1924	56.6	75.2	0.753
1925	60.8	78.6	0.774
1926	63.2	84.6	0.747
1927	63.0	83.1	0.758
1928	64.6	85.0	0.760
1929	65.9	90.3	0.730
1930	58.3	76.9	0.758
1931	48.4	61.7	0.784
1932	36.4	44.8	0.812
1933	35.1	42.6	0.824
1934	41.3	50.3	0.821
1935	47.7	58.2	0.820
1936	53.4	68.3	0.782
1937	60.6	75.1	0.807
1938	56.1	68.8	0.815
1939	59.7	73.8	0.809
1940	65.1	81.8	0.796
1941	82.2	99.0	0.826
1942	109.2	106.5	0.999
1943	137.8	113.2	1.092

Table 17.3 (continued)

	Earned income	Net national product	Ratio wN/pY
1944	150.9	118.7	1.146
1945	154.0	124.2	1.107
1946	154.3	160.5	0.877
1947	164.3	179.0	0.831
1948	181.2	192.8	0.863
1949	176.4	185.8	0.884
1950	191.7	215.0	0.827
1951	222.3	238.1	0.844
1952	237.2	245.6	0.858
1953	249.5	258.8	0.858

Source: Department of Commerce, and Kuznets, *Capital in the American Economy.* Johnson, 'The functional distribution of income in the United States, 1850–1952.'

VELOCITY OF CIRCULATION

It is an interesting property of the present system that the savings ratio, the accelerator coefficient, labor's share, and velocity can all be put together in a consistent framework, for separate investigators who have searched for economic insight in terms of any single one of these ratios have often been in heated dispute with one another. It is especially true that the velocity analysts have been set apart as students of monetary phenomena with entirely different views from those concerned with 'real' phenomena. The velocity ratio, by itself, has received great attention in a variety of forms, depending on the choice of numerator and denominator. Cash balances in the numerator may cover only checking accounts and circulating currency, or may be expanded to include time deposits, savings and loan shares, savings bonds, and other 'near' moneys. Balances may be segregated according as they are held by persons, business, or financial institutions. The denominator could be national expenditure, national income, personal income, disposable income, or some broad duplicative measure of transactions.

A recent authoritative summary of velocity statistics computed by many authors is given by Selden.[12] For his own calculations, Selden defines cash to include total deposits, currency outside banks, Treasury deposits with Federal Reserve banks, and money held in the Treasury. His denominator is measured as national income. He estimates velocity in a range between 0.75 and 1.76 for annual periods in this half-century. He finds both a trend and a cycle in these estimates.

[12] R. T. Selden, 'Monetary velocity in the United States,' *Studies in the Quantity Theory of Money* (ed. M. Friedman), University of Chicago Press, Chicago (1956), pp. 179–257.

300   *Economic Theory and Econometrics*

Our estimates are based on a money total that includes circulating currency, demand deposits, and time deposits of persons, business and government. The denominator of our ratio is the current dollar value of net national product, according to Kuznets' variant that does not differ from national income.

As the table and graph of our data show, there is a noticeable trend in this series. Our estimate is

$$\log M/pY = -0.15500 + 0.0025t$$

or

$$M/pY = 0.6998 \, (1.0057)^t.$$

At the midpoint of our series, the estimate of the reciprocal of velocity is 0.6998. This represents the well-known Cambridge k. In the semi-logarithmic form that was fitted to the data, the coefficient of t is more than ten times its sampling error.

Table 17.4 Cash balances and net national product, United States (billions of current dollars)

	Cash balances	Net national product	Ratio M/pY
1900	8.9	16.4	0.543
1901	10.0	18.0	0.556
1902	10.8	18.8	0.574
1903	11.5	20.0	0.575
1904	12.0	19.9	0.603
1905	13.2	21.7	0.608
1906	14.1	24.8	0.569
1907	15.1	26.5	0.570
1908	14.7	24.1	0.610
1909	15.8	28.1	0.562
1910	17.0	29.0	0.586
1911	17.8	28.6	0.622
1912	18.9	30.2	0.626
1913	19.4	32.1	0.604
1914	20.0	31.6	0.633
1915	20.7	35.2	0.588
1916	24.2	43.5	0.556
1917	28.2	53.9	0.523
1918	31.4	58.2	0.540
1919	35.6	65.2	0.546
1920	39.9	75.7	0.527
1921	37.8	61.8	0.612
1922	39.0	63.0	0.619
1923	42.7	74.1	0.576
1924	44.5	75.2	0.592

Table 17.4 (continued)

	Cash balances	Net national product	Ratio M/pY
1925	48.3	78.6	0.615
1926	50.6	84.6	0.598
1927	52.2	83.1	0.628
1928	54.7	85.0	0.644
1929	55.2	90.3	0.611
1930	54.4	76.9	0.707
1931	52.9	61.7	0.857
1932	45.4	44.8	1.013
1933	41.7	42.6	0.975
1934	46.0	50.3	0.915
1935	49.9	58.2	0.857
1936	55.1	68.3	0.807
1937	57.3	75.1	0.763
1938	56.6	68.8	0.823
1939	60.9	73.8	0.825
1940	67.0	81.8	0.819
1941	74.2	99.0	0.749
1942	82.0	106.5	0.770
1943	110.2	113.2	0.973
1944	136.2	118.7	1.147
1945	162.8	124.2	1.311
1946	171.2	160.5	1.067
1947	165.5	179.0	0.925
1948	167.9	192.8	0.871
1949	167.9	185.8	0.904
1950	173.8	215.0	0.808
1951	181.0	238.1	0.760
1952	191.0	245.6	0.778
1953	197.6	258.8	0.762

Source: Board of Governors of the Federal Reserve System, and Kuznets, *Capital in the American Economy.*

THE CAPITAL–LABOR RATIO

The capital–output ratio and the ratio of output to employment (productivity) have long been studied in great detail. Together they define the capital–labor ratio, but in this form the statistics have not so frequently been investigated. Kuznets has, however, analyzed this ratio in his long-run studies of the American economy.[13] He estimates that the capital–labor ratio has nearly tripled between 1879 and 1944. The most rapid growth occurred at the turn of the century.

[13]S. Kuznets, 'Long term changes in the national product of the United States of America Since 1870.'

Our series show a steady upward growth in this ratio from about $5000 per person engaged at about 1900 to about $6000 after World War II. This amounts to a compound interest rate of growth slightly under 0.25 of 1 per cent semiannually. Our trend formulas are

$$\log K/N = 3.76126 + 0.0010t$$

or

$$K/N = 5571\ (1.0023)^t.$$

The linear trend coefficient is statistically significant. It is more than six times its estimated sampling error. The series are given in table 17.5 and figure 17.1.

Table 17.5 Capital stock and persons engaged, United States
(billions of 1929 dollars and millions of persons)

	Capital stock	Persons engaged	Ratio K/N
1900	131.57	27.3	4820
1901	136.71	28.4	4814
1902	142.27	29.6	4806
1903	147.72	30.5	4843
1904	152.20	30.4	5007
1905	157.65	31.8	4958
1906	164.50	33.1	4970
1907	171.25	33.8	5067
1908	175.31	33.1	5296
1909	182.06	34.8	5231
1910	187.86	35.7	5262
1911	192.45	36.3	5302
1912	198.04	37.3	5309
1913	204.38	37.9	5393
1914	207.28	37.5	5527
1915	210.36	37.7	5580
1916	215.70	40.1	5379
1917	220.26	41.5	5307
1918	223.94	44.0	5090
1919	229.37	42.3	5422
1920	235.13	41.5	5666
1921	236.19	39.4	5995
1922	240.15	41.4	5801
1923	248.87	43.9	5669
1924	254.47	43.3	5877
1925	264.08	44.5	5934
1926	273.94	45.8	5981
1927	282.61	45.9	6157
1928	290.20	46.4	6254

Some econometrics of growth 303

Table 17.5 (continued)

	Capital stock	Persons engaged	Ratio K/N
1929	299.42	47.6	6290
1930	303.30	45.5	6666
1931	303.42	42.6	7123
1932	297.12	39.3	7560
1933	290.12	39.6	7326
1934	285.43	42.7	6685
1935	287.78	44.2	6511
1936	292.11	47.1	6202
1937	300.33	48.2	6231
1938	301.38	46.4	6495
1939	305.58	47.8	6393
1940	313.32	49.6	6317
1941	327.41	54.1	6052
1942	338.98	59.1	5736
1943	347.08	64.9	5348
1944	353.46	66.0	5355
1945	354.13	64.4	5499
1946	359.43	58.9	6102
1947	359.30	59.3	6059
1948	365.19	60.2	6066
1949	363.21	58.7	6188
1950	373.73	60.0	6228
1951	385.95	63.8	6049
1952	396.47	64.9	6109
1953	408.01	66.0	6182

Source: Kuznets, *Capital in the American Economy.* Kendrick, *Productivity Trends in the United States.*

THE MODEL AS A WHOLE

The variables in the ratios (or variables related to them) are:

S = savings,
Y = real income or output,
K = capital stock,
I = net investment,
w = wage rate,
p = price level,
N = employment,
M = cash balances.

An interesting point in connection with the use of these ratios defined in terms of the above eight variables is that they jointly comprise a closed system of aggregative economics. We write this system as,

$S/Y = \alpha$ savings–income ratio,
$K/Y = \beta$ capital–output ratio,
$wN/pY = \gamma$ labor's share,
$M/pY = \kappa$ reciprocal of income velocity,
$K/N = \delta$ capital–labor ratio,
$K - K_{-1} = I$ definition of net investment,
$S = I$ savings–investment equality.

These seven equations, together with an exogenously controlled money supply, constitute our model. The 'Greek' coefficients on the right-hand side of the first five equations imply an assumption of constancy of each of the great ratios.

A stepwise solution of this system is simple. The first two ratios and the last two equations may be condensed, through substitution, into the familiar multiplier-accelerator equation of growth theory

$$\alpha Y = \beta(Y - Y_{-1}).$$

This equation could be rewritten as

$$Y = \frac{\beta}{\beta - \alpha} Y_{-1},$$

and the future time path of Y obtained as the solution

$$Y_t = Y_0 \left(\frac{\beta}{\beta - \alpha}\right)^t$$

to this first order difference equation with a constant coefficient Y_0 is an initial value of Y. This time path is one of positive trend growth with ever increasing levels of activity in prospect, since it is reasonable to assume that $\beta/(\beta - \alpha)$ exceeds unity. The accelerator coefficient (or capital–output ratio), β, is likely to be a number substantially in excess of unity, while the savings–income ratio, α, is likely to be a small positive fraction.

We thus have a dynamic system of trend growth. From the real income level determined along this trend, we can, by using the velocity ratio and a given money supply, calculate the price level,

$$p = M/(\kappa Y).$$

In a similar way the capital stock can be determined from the capital-output ratio if the output level is known.

$$K = \beta Y.$$

Knowing this value of capital, we next determine the level of employment from the capital–labor ratio

$$N = K/\delta.$$

In the equation for labor's share, all variables except w are determined from previous steps. We can therefore determine the wage rate as

$$w = \gamma p Y/N.$$

The level of savings can be computed from the savings–income ratio relationship and the level of net investment from

$$\beta(Y - Y_{-1})$$

or from

$$K - K_{-1}.$$

The trend solution to this system takes the form

$$Y_t = Y_0[\beta/(\beta - \alpha)]^t$$

$$p_t = M_t/(\kappa Y_0)\left(\frac{\beta - \alpha}{\beta}\right)^t$$

$$K_t = \beta Y_0[\beta/(\beta - \alpha)]^t$$

$$N_t = (\beta/\delta) Y_0[\beta/(\beta - \alpha)]^t$$

$$w_t = \frac{\gamma \delta}{\kappa \beta} M_t/Y_0 \left(\frac{\beta - \alpha}{\beta}\right)^t.$$

On the assumption that

$$\beta/(\beta - \alpha) > 1,$$

output, capital, and employment all grow indefinitely at the common rate $\beta/(\beta - \alpha)$. For a constant money supply, the price and wage level tend towards a finite limit.[14] The rate of change of price and wage levels are given by

$$\frac{p_t}{p_{t-1}} = \frac{M_t}{M_{t-1}} \frac{\beta - \alpha}{\beta}$$

$$\frac{w_t}{w_{t-1}} = \frac{M_t}{M_{t-1}} \frac{\beta - \alpha}{\beta}.$$

Our empirical system is modified in comparison with our theoretical

---

[14]If the money supply is strictly constant, this limit is zero. After the elapse of infinite time, output is infinitely large and price would obviously have to be zero to clear the market.

model since only one of the great ratios actually appears to be stable. Moreover, we are writing the system with a consumption instead of a savings function. The actual economy is open with respect to external trade, although our original model assumed a closed economy. We denote the real trade balance by B.

The numerical system is

$$C/Y = 0.9134\,(1.0013)^t$$

$$K/Y = 3.523\,(1.0033)^{-t}$$

$$wN/pY = 0.8439$$

$$M/pY = 0.6998\,(1.0057)^t$$

$$K/N = 5571\,(1.0023)^t$$

$$Y - C = I + B$$

$$K - K_{-1} = I.$$

The first two and last two equations of the system (multiplier-accelerator system) lead to

$$Y_t = 0.9134\,(1.0013)^t Y_t + 3.523\,(1.0033)^{-t+1}[(1.0033)^{-1} Y_t - Y_{t-1}]$$

or

$$Y_t = \frac{3.523\,(1.0033)^{-t+1}}{0.9134\,(1.0013)^t + 3.523\,(1.0033)^{-t} - 1} Y_{t-1}.$$

A small foreign balance is neglected in this calculation.

If the trends were absent from all ratios, we would have had

$$Y_t = \frac{3.523}{0.9134 + 3.523 - 1} Y_{t-1} = 1.025\,Y_{t-1}.$$

The period-to-period rate of growth in real output would be 2.5 per cent. In the system where the ratios follow trends, the rate of growth varies over time. When $t=0$ (January 1, 1927), the ratio Y_t/Y_{t-1} is estimated at about 1.025, but when $t=60$ (January 1, 1957), this ratio is as low as 1.005.

The period-to-period rates of growth of other variables within the system can readily be deduced. We find

$$K_t/K_{t-1} = (1.0033)^{-1} Y_t/Y_{t-1}$$

$$N_t/N_{t-1} = (1.0023)^{-1} K_t/K_{t-1}$$

$$p_t/p_{t-1} = (M_t/M_{t-1})(1.0057)^{-1} Y_t/Y_{t-1}$$

$$w_t/w_{t-1} = (N_{t-1}/N_t)(p_t/p_{t-1})(Y_t/Y_{t-1}).$$

Some econometrics of growth

The decline in the semiannual growth rate of output from 2.5 to 0.5 per cent between 1927 and 1957 may seem to be too steep. A reason for this decline is the tendency for the consumption ratio to rise, providing a reduced supply of funds for investment, at a speed that is great compared with the rate of technical improvement. The latter phenomenon is represented by the declining capital–output ratio, giving a reduced need for capital funds.[15]

In our measurement, we shifted from the savings–income ratio to the consumption–income ratio. Ordinarily this change would have no significance, but we did it for a technical reason – to avoid negative numbers in our logarithmic calculations.[16] There are five sample observations (1932, 1933, 1934, 1945 and 1949) giving negative savings, measured as net national product minus consumption. If we exclude these from our sample and estimate the trend in the savings–income ratio, we obtain

$$\log S/Y = -2.08753 - 0.00502t$$

or

$$S/Y = 0.08175 (1.0116)^t.$$

The data used in computing this equation extend 2 years beyond the original sample since Kuznets' series were up-dated during the course of our calculations. This up-dating has no significant effect on any of our preceding calculations.

If this equation is used in place of the former equation for C/Y, together with the other equations of the model, we find the semi-annual rate of growth in output to be 2.7 per cent when $t=0$, but the decline is only to 1.8 per cent when $t=60$. In the previous calculations the consumption income ratio would have reached unity early in the present decade, but with the calculations based on positive savings values alone, the system reaches zero savings only asymptotically.

The negative trend in the savings ratio is statistically significant, the coefficient of t in the semi-logarithmic equation being five times its estimated sampling error.

---

[15]This line of reasoning is consistent with that suggested by MacDougall, 'Does productivity rise faster?'

[16]The reader should note that $S/Y = \alpha$ and $C/Y = 1 - \alpha$ are equivalent because of the identity $S + C = Y$. However, $S/Y = \alpha \rho^t$ and $C/Y = (1-\alpha)p^t$ are not equivalent. The equivalent expressions are $S/Y = \alpha \rho^t$ and $C/Y = 1 - \alpha \rho^t$.

SOME REMARKS ON THE RATE OF INTEREST

If our model were the static system without trends in any of the ratios, it would, as shown earlier, imply a common rate of growth for output, capital, and employment. This rate might be associated with the rate of interest. The association follows from von Neumann's interpretation of the rate of economic expansion in his celebrated article on general economic equilibrium. In a highly aggregative sense, we might call our model, like this, a balanced growth model.[17]

The results of von Neumann apply to a theoretical world in which workers only consume and capitalists only save. This is also the world of Mrs. Robinson, for her 'Golden Age' model is akin to the balanced growth model.[18] Morishima has generalized the results for such models to situations in which workers are permitted to save and capitalists are permitted to consume.[19] Instead of finding that the common rate of expansion in the real economy is the rate of interest, he finds that if workers consume *and* save, while capitalists *only* save *without* consuming then the rate of expansion exceeds the interest rate. In his second paper, he shows that if workers *only* consume without saving, while capitalists consume *and* save the growth rate falls short of the interest rate. In our model there is only one saving rate, which is presumably an average of both workers' and capitalists' saving rates. This case has not been considered generally. The computed growth rate of 0.027 semiannually (5.4 per cent annually) for $t=0$ in our model exceeds the long-term interest rate (corporate bond yield = 4.57 per cent in 1927).

Within our model we can develop an expression for the rate of return on capital. It is

$$\left(Y - \frac{w}{p}N\right) \bigg/ K = (Y/K)\left(1 - \frac{wN}{pY}\right).$$

For $t=0$, this expression becomes $0.156/3.523 = 0.0443$. This rate of 4.4 per cent comes close to the above figure for the interest rate. This correspondence will not hold for other periods, however, because Y/K rises on a trend, while $1 - wN/pY$ is constant.

---

[17] J. v. Neumann, 'A model of general economic equilibrium,' *The Review of Economic Studies*, XIII (1945–6), 1–9.

[18] J. Robinson, *The Accumulation of Capital*, Irwin, Homewood, Ill. (1956).

[19] M. Morishima, 'Some properties of a dynamic Leontief system with a spectrum of techniques,' *Econometrica*, **27**, October (1959), 626–37; 'Economic expansion and interest rate in a generalized von Neumann Model,' Discussion Paper No. 6, The Institute of Social and Economic Research, Osaka University, Japan.

For the period from 1900, it may be inferred that there is but a slight trend in the average rate of interest.[20] If the series is carried up to the present (through 1959), when interest rates have once again become high, it appears that there is little trend in the diagram. A least-squares trend line fitted to these data shows, however,

$$\log r = 0.56200 - 0.002373t.$$

The standard error of the trend coefficient is only 0.0007; therefore we cannot deny that there is a statistically significant trend. In arithmetic form this estimated equation is

$$r = 3.644(1.006)^{-t}.$$

In a 30-year period this estimated rate declines from 3.644 to 2.686, a considerably smaller decline than is found in our rate of growth of output if the consumption–income ratio is used. It is consistent with the falling rate of growth of our trend model if the saving–income ratio (for positive savings) is used. We deliberately extended our interest rate series beyond the sample span for the other variables in order to see whether the trend would be eliminated by the recent rise in interest rates. For the period 1900–53, the computed downward trend in rates would be steeper.

It is possible to extend the interest rate series back further in the nineteenth century. In a recent article, Goode and Birnbaum have charted interest series from 1866 to 1958.[21] Over this stretch of time, the downward trend in rates is even greater. Rates as high as 7–8 per cent were prevalent in the nineteenth century.

THE AGGREGATE PRODUCTION FUNCTION AND FACTOR SUBSTITUTION

The facts that the ratios K/Y and K/N have not been constant imply some substitution between labor and capital over time.[22] The only ratio that suggests the possibility of constancy is that for labor's share. This would be consistent with a Cobb-Douglas type production function. It turns out that our estimated ratios for K/Y and K/N can conveniently be cast into the Cobb-Douglas framework. Our logarith-

---

[20] Our representative rate is Moody's series on Aaa bonds, extrapolated back from 1918 to 1900 by a regression on railroad bond yields.

[21] Richard Goode and Eugene A. Birnbaum, 'The relation between long-term and short-term interest rates in the United States,' *International Monetary Fund Staff Papers*, VII (1959), 224–43.

[22] This discussion was stimulated by our colleague, S. Weintraub.

310   *Economic Theory and Econometrics*

Table 17.6   Corporate bond yield

Year	Yield	Year	Yield
1900	2.92	1931	4.58
1901	2.95	1932	5.01
1902	3.16	1933	4.49
1903	3.49	1934	4.00
1904	3.45	1935	3.60
1905	3.31	1936	3.24
1906	3.51	1937	3.26
1907	4.18	1938	3.19
1908	3.86	1939	3.01
1909	3.69	1940	2.84
1910	3.90	1941	2.77
1911	3.90	1942	2.83
1912	3.99	1943	2.73
1913	4.29	1944	2.72
1914	4.42	1945	2.62
1915	4.51	1946	2.53
1916	4.22	1947	2.61
1917	5.10	1948	2.82
1918	5.29	1949	2.66
1919	5.49	1950	2.62
1920	6.12	1951	2.86
1921	5.97	1952	2.96
1922	5.10	1953	3.20
1923	5.12	1954	2.90
1924	5.00	1955	3.06
1925	4.88	1956	3.30
1926	4.73	1957	3.89
1927	4.57	1958	3.79
1928	4.55	1959[a]	4.57
1929	4.73		
1930	4.55		

Source: Moody's Aaa series on corporate bonds as reported in the *Bulletin* and *Banking and Monetary Statistics* of the Federal Reserve System for the period 1919–59.

[a]1959 observation is the value for the week ending October 3, 1959.

mic estimate of K/N can be written as

$$\log K - \log N = 3.76126 + 0.0010t.$$

Multiply both sides by 0.8439.

$$0.8439 \log K - 0.8439 \log N = 3.17413 + 0.0008439t.$$

The estimate of $\log K/Y$ is

$$\log K - \log Y = 0.54699 - 0.0015t.$$

Subtraction of the preceding equation from this gives

$$0.1561 \log K + 0.8439 \log N - \log Y = -2.62714 - 0.0023439t$$

or

$$Y = 423.8 K^{0.16} N^{0.84} (1.0054)^t.$$

Had we multiplied through above by another common factor, we would have obtained a correspondingly different production function with homogeneity of the first degree. This particular multiplier is chosen for consistency with the equation of labor's share. This model implies imputation of wages according to the marginal productivity doctrine, but we cannot appeal to profit maximization since we have constant returns to scale.

Our model, therefore, which started out from factor proportions is found to be consistent with substitution in production according to the Cobb-Douglas function with first order homogeneity. It also implies a rate of technical progress of 0.54 of 1 per cent semiannually, but this technological trend is not apportioned to any one factor. It is a neutral factor compounded from the separate trends in K/Y and K/N. In this way, we avoid the embarrassing questions of attributing trends in K/Y or K/N (or Y/N) to variables left out of the respective ratios.

Our model, when cast into a form that includes the Cobb-Douglas production functions with allowance for technical progress, resembles Smithies' recently published growth model.[23] All the ingredients of our model are included in the general formulation of Smithies' model except for the appendage of the velocity ratio, which brings money and the absolute level of prices into the system. Smithies, in his theoretical analysis of alternatives, emphasizes more the interrelations between trends in productivity and real wages. Our empirical findings lead us to place more emphasis on the relationship between trends in the savings ratio and productivity (capital–output ratio). Smithies is willing to accept the view that there is 'no empirical evidence that the savings ratio has decreased,' although he does consider alternative possibilities. When the evidence is brought more up-to-date and when one takes a broader view of the process than is revealed in the *personal* savings–*personal* income ratio there does appear to be evidence of a falling savings ratio. It is the time rate of the fall in this ratio in relation to the rate of technical improvement that gives rise to America's growth problem. This conclusion may be accentuated by our use of Kuznets' series on national product, but a strong case can be made for preferring this concept when discussing America's growth problem.

[23] A. Smithies, 'Productivity, real wages, and economic growth,' *The Quarterly Journal of Economics*, LXXIV, May (1960), 189–205.

Economic Theory and Econometrics

Table 17.7 Persons engaged and population 15 years of age and over
(millions of persons)

Year	Persons engaged	Population 15 years of age and over	Ratio N/L
1900	27.295	49.948	0.5465
1901	28.425	51.088	0.5564
1902	29.647	52.301	0.5669
1903	30.525	53.463	0.5710
1904	30.419	54.679	0.5563
1905	31.814	55.988	0.5682
1906	33.071	57.281	0.5773
1907	33.848	58.543	0.5782
1908	33.086	59.905	0.5523
1909	34.785	61.315	0.5673
1910	35.708	62.787	0.5687
1911	36.274	63.859	0.5680
1912	37.341	64.912	0.5753
1913	37.896	66.243	0.5721
1914	37.475	67.556	0.5547
1915	37.669	68.544	0.5496
1916	40.126	69.514	0.5771
1917	41.531	70.517	0.5890
1918	43.998	71.213	0.6178
1919	42.313	71.677	0.5903
1920	41.497	72.677	0.5710
1921	39.361	74.146	0.5309
1922	41.383	75.233	0.5501
1923	43.938	76.743	0.5725
1024	43.315	78.486	0.5519
1925	44.512	79.906	0.5571
1926	45.795	81.302	0.5633
1927	45.900	82.775	0.5545
1928	46.382	84.207	0.5508
1929	47.611	85.565	0.5564
1930	45.465	87.738	0.5221
1931	42.607	88.231	0.4829
1932	39.274	89.323	0.4397
1933	39.615	90.435	0.4380
1934	42.739	91.641	0.4664
1935	44.224	92.867	0.4762
1936	47.078	94.067	0.5005
1937	48.233	95.252	0.5064
1938	46.379	96.503	0.4806
1939	47.769	97.761	0.4886
1940	49.606	99.017	0.5010
1941	54.097	100.194	0.5399
1942	59.056	101.384	0.5825
1943	64.864	102.508	0.6328

Some econometrics of growth

Table 17.7 (continued)

Year	Persons engaged	Population 15 years of age and over	Ratio N/L
1944	66.020	103.525	0.6377
1945	64.363	104.454	0.6162
1946	58.917	104.861	0.5619
1947	59.264	106.259	0.5577
1948	60.216	107.883	0.5582
1949	58.702	109.497	0.5361
1950	60.041	110.922	0.5413
1951	63.759	112.091	0.5688
1952	64.894	113.144	0.5735

Source: Kendrick, *Productivity Trends in the United States; Historical Statistics of the United States,* series B31–39.

Implied relationships between real wages and productivity or other magnitudes can be derived within the framework of our model as Smithies has done, but we have not attributed any initiating significance to real wages in the growth performance of our system. The period-to-period rate of growth in real wages *passively* equals the period-to-period rate of growth in labor productivity.

ANOTHER POSSIBLE GREAT RATIO

Our system of *great ratios* gives no information about labor supply or population. It assumes implicitly that all labor demanded will be forthcoming. Another ratio can be added to the system, without affecting any of the relations already derived, to show the relationship between persons engaged, N, and the potential labor force, L. The potential labor force is assumed to be the total population of persons 15 years of age and over. The ratio N/L is a version of a *participation rate*.

There is practically no trend in this measure of labor force participation. The ratio fluctuates above and below 0.55 during both the beginning and ending years of the sample 1900–52. The estimated equation is

$$\log N/L = -0.26030 - 0.000218t.$$

The trend coefficient is not statistically significant, and we write the constant ratio as

$$N/L = 0.5489.$$

At this level of the ratio, we conclude that labor supply should be ample to meet requirements of the growth values in the rest of the model.

Part III

APPLIED ECONOMETRICS

18

Some Econometrics of the Determination of Absolute Prices and Wages

INTRODUCTION

Much of the discussion of the current problem of inflation in the Western capitalist world is necessarily strongly coloured by awareness of the course of the leading statistical series on wages, prices, productivity, profits and unemployment during the last decade, when the general inflationary situation has caused many series to move together. It is rather difficult, but of the utmost importance, to try to unravel the chains of relationship among the several variables in order to delineate *structural* relations that have a high degree of *autonomy*.

The annual figures on wage-rates over the past 10 years are correlated with those on productivity, but they are as highly correlated with employment, unemployment or the price level. Many of the apparent correlations are derived relations obtained by combining more basic structural relations. Many such derived relations can be obtained from a given structure, and one must take great care in the conclusions drawn from empirical correlations. The problem is especially serious in this decade of annual observations when reversals of the broad trend give only delicate statistical movements that are not easily discerned with the use of blunt tools.

The present paper arises out of work being done by the authors on the construction of an econometric model of the UK economy as a whole.[1] This work involves the fitting together of autonomous struc-

---

[1]Our colleagues, A. Hazlewood and P. Vandome, of the Institute of Statistics, Oxford, have collaborated on the larger study, of which this paper is a part.

tural components, from which a partial subsystem of interest on the interrelations between wages and prices emerges. The findings we have obtained on this part of the model seem to be relevant in assisting an understanding and interpretation of the postwar inflation. We are thus moved to put forward some of our results at this stage. The entire investigation is based on quarterly series covering a wide variety of economic activities in the UK. It is hoped that by refining the sample data to this unit of observation we have a more sensitive and adequate body of information for discriminating among alternative explanations of the phenomena at hand. We cannot claim, however, to have found *the single* explanation of the inflationary process. That is hardly ever possible in our subject, and statistical analysis alone on the very best samples of economic data have never been able to prove that a particular relationship or explanation dominates the field to the exclusion of all others. We do, however, feel that our results are reasonable and carefully backed up by *a priori* considerations of autonomous patterns of behaviour. We can also bring evidence to bear against *some* alternative hypotheses.

In the discussion of postwar inflation, a number of economists have taken strong sides on the question of whether we have *demand* or *cost* inflation. Unfortunately, the great lesson of Walras has been forgotten in this debate. We have tried to keep a picture of the interrelated network of equations in the economy as a whole in front of us constantly, in building each component of the UK model, and feel that this may be advantageous in the interpretation of wage and price movements. In our system, and by our method of approach, it is possible for both demand and cost elements to show their respective strengths.

Some observers would base their characterisation of the type of inflation we have been having on the movements in such statistical series as the spread between wage rates and earnings, others on the share of profits in national income, others on the lead–lag relationship between price and wage indexes, and others on the relationship between productivity and earnings. We select no key series for our study of this problem but try to interrelate several series as part of a comprehensive model.

A MODEL OF THE WAGE–PRICE MECHANISM

The central equation of the model dealing with the determination of wages is based on the purely conventional assumption that market prices move in order to wipe out excess demand or supply. Economic theory has given us no reason to say whether dynamic movements of *relative* or *absolute* prices are associated with market clearing. We assume that money wage rates move over time in response to excess supply or demand in the labor market. This latter concept is given a statistical representation in the figures for unemployment, but such measures as unfilled vacancies may also be used.[2]

Actual bargaining over wage rates takes place in terms of monetary units, but this is not to say that a 'money illusion' is involved. Both sides are only too aware of the 'real' nature of economic affairs. Movements in the cost of living are prominent facts at the bargaining table. Instead of saying that dynamic movements in real wage rates are functionally related to unemployment, we take the somewhat more general and more realistic view that the time rate of change in money wage rates is a function of the level of unemployment and the time rate of change of the price level. A further reason for expressing the relationship in this way is that a time lag may exist between price and wage movements. The nature, extent and magnitude of this time lag is of key significance in the interpretation of inflation as being of either the demand or cost variety. With ten annual observations it is difficult to say anything very definite about the lag, but with quarterly data we may eventually hope to make a stronger inference, although not necessarily from the samples at hand.

Two other factors are frequently mentioned in connection with wage bargaining – profits and productivity. To some extent price movements and the level of unemployment already indicate the profit position, but in one of our experimental computations we explicitly introduce a profit variable into the relationship.

Productivity, we believe, is more properly entered at a different stage of the process, but we do not rule out the possibility that it can be a variable in its own right in the bargaining equation and similarly include it in an experimental computation.

If workers try to keep pace with the cost of living and find their bargaining power sensitive to the state of excess supply or demand in the labor market, we would be inclined to call the resulting movement in wages an expression of demand inflation. They simply follow the ordinary laws of the market. If, however, workers are able to push wages ahead of price movements or the level dictated by the state of the labor market, we have evidence of cost inflation spurred by

---

[2]Vacancy statistics are used by J. C. R. Dow and L. A. Dicks-Mireaux, 'The excess demand for labour,' *Oxford Economic Papers*, **10** (1958), 1–33.

deliberate trade union action. It is often said that trade unions cooperated with the postwar Labour Government and moderated their demands in accordance with a tacit understanding about general economic policy. It is further claimed that the trade unions became more aggressive or militant in pressing their claims after 1952 under the Conservative Government. To the extent to which trade unions can turn off or turn on steam in forcing the outcome of wage bargains in predetermined fashion we have cost inflation. In our equation we shall introduce a constructed statistical variable (sometimes called a 'dummy' variable) which assumes the value of zero before 1952 and unity thereafter, to take into account this dual character of the period under review. In this respect our model has some flexibility in describing events during the period 1948–57, but otherwise our system has the same structural coefficients at all times. We treat the whole group of quarterly periods since 1948 as homogeneous as far as the mechanism of inflation is concerned.

Another way of expressing the power of trade unions over and above their market-induced strength is to note that they force wage movements on an irreversible path upwards. Either a steady trend growth or some type of 'ratchet' variable could bring out this aspect of union strength on the side of cost-induced inflation. Our results do not have this irreversibility, and perhaps they are not typical of all business-cycle movements in this respect. In the framework of the postwar economy there are no adequate data for testing this hypothesis. The prewar data are unsatisfactory because many basic series are not available for that period. The power of trade unions is believed to have changed greatly since the war, and the structure of the economy as a whole has similarly changed. For these reasons, we are not pursuing the aspect of irreversibility in the present model.

We formulate a wage-rate equation, in which changes in wage rates appear as a function of previous price changes, and of the level of excess demand for labor as indicated by our proxy measure, the level of unemployment.

The particular form that we have given to this equation originates from a suggestion made to us by L. A. Dicks-Mireaux, who has pointed out the implications of discontinuity in wage bargaining. Broadly speaking, workers in any particular sector of the economy bargain for changes in wage rates once a year. The extent of the change will depend on the current level of excess demand, but also on the change in the price level that has occurred since the workers in that particular sector last had an increase in wage rates, i.e. the price change in the previous 12 months, assuming that workers receive wage increases at roughly the same time in each year. This assumption is, of course, not strictly true, since in some years the roles of leader and follower in wage demands may have been altered. Nevertheless, it is close to the now familiar concept of the annual round of wage-rate increases. It follows from this argument that wage-rate increases in any one quarter for workers having a change in that quarter will depend on the level of excess demand, and the price change over the previous 12 months.

For workers not subject to change in wage rates during that quarter, their wage rates will be related to excess demand and prices of previous quarters, i.e. the time of their last negotiations. If we follow through this scheme of discrete adjustment we find that the *average* wage change for all workers of any quarter over the same quarter of the preceding year is a function of a weighted average of past levels of excess demand and past changes in the price level. The weights in the average will depend upon the number of workers coming up for negotiation in each quarter, but we assume an even distribution of numbers among the quarters.

The equation to be estimated takes the form,

$$(w_r)_t - (w_r)_{t-4}$$
$$= \alpha_1 \left(\frac{U_t + U_{t-1} + U_{t-2} + U_{t-3}}{4} \right)$$
$$+ \alpha_2 \left(\frac{p_t - p_{t-4} + p_{t-1} - p_{t-5} + p_{t-2} - p_{t-6} + p_{t-3} - p_{t-7}}{4} \right)$$
$$+ \alpha_3 F_t + \alpha + \alpha_{s1} Q_{1t} + \alpha_{s2} Q_{2t} + \alpha_{s3} Q_{3t} + u_{1t} \qquad (18.1)$$

where

w_r = quarterly average of index of weekly wage rates,
U = index of unemployment,
p = quarterly average of index of consumers price level,
F = political factor, zero in quarters before 1952 and unity thereafter,
Q_i = seasonal factor, unity in the ith quarter and zero in any other quarter,
u_1 = disturbance.

It may be observed at once, from the form of (18.1), that the instititional character of wage bargaining has led to the formulation of an equation, in which there is, on the average, a 6-month lag between wage and price changes. But this lag does not carry any implications about what most people have in mind on the existence of demand or cost inflation. Nevertheless, it does introduce a lag of rates behind prices.

The political factor, F_t, needs no explanation beyond that already given. For every equation of the entire UK model the data used are completely unadjusted for seasonal variation. In each equation, however, we include explicit seasonal variables. Inspection of graphs has led us to posit a linear additive seasonal component throughout. In this equation with four quarter changes and moving averages there is little, if any, scope for seasonal influence. Indeed, the empirical results indicate this below, but every equation was treated for seasonal variation on the same basis, and we include the Q_{it} variables here for the sake of uniformity.

Equation (18.1) is a key equation in the UK model because it displaces, in a sense, the money balance equation for the absolute determination of prices and wages. It is difficult, again following the Walrasian idea, to say what determines what in a truly interrelated system, but the main function of equation (18.1) is to complete the system in respect of the determination of absolute wages or prices, while the cash-balance equation has the main function of completing the system in respect of the determination of the interest rate.[3] The state of the labor market displaces the state of the money market in determining the course of absolute prices or wages. 'It is hardly an exaggeration to say that instead of being on a Gold Standard we are now on a Labour Standard.'[4]

To be as realistic as possible we have carefully formulated the bargaining equation of our model in terms of a wage-rate variable. Earnings, however, not rates, are the important cost variables to an entrepreneur. We therefore seek to establish a relation between the two concepts of wage payment. The spread between earnings and rates has, as noted above, become an important statistical indicator in the view of many people who are trying to diagnose the inflationary process. Our measure of wage-rates used in this model is an index of weekly wages paid for a full-time standard work period. It is averaged to quarters for our purposes. The earnings variable is similarly an index of total wages paid for a week's work regardless of whether that week's hours consist

---

[3] These ideas are developed in connection with similar American models in L. R. Klein, 'The empirical foundations of Keynesian economics,' *Post Keynesian Economics* (Ed. K. Kurihara, Rutgers University Press, New Brunswick (1954); and L. R. Klein and A. S. Goldberger, *An Econometric Model of the United States: 1929-1952*, North-Holland Publishing Co., Amsterdam (1955).

[4] J. R. Hicks, 'Economic foundations of wage policy,' *Economic Journal*, LXV, September (1955), 391.

of short time, full time or overtime. It includes bonus or other premium payments as well. In some analyses an attempt is made to measure hourly earnings, in which case weekly earnings would have to be adjusted to a uniform number of hours worked, but we make no such adjustment.

If workers are paid, wholly or partially, on a piece basis, their earnings will rise with rising productivity; therefore the excess of the earnings index over the rate index is made to depend on the level of productivity. For those workers geared to a time rate of pay, their earnings will vary with hours worked. As they work more or fewer hours they will earn more or less per week. In addition, overtime work will provide a premium rate of pay. We make the spread between the two wage indexes a function of hours worked as well as of productivity. Hours worked are one of the most sensitive indicators of economic activity; therefore it is not necessary to introduce another variable into the relationship to indicate the level of demand pressure. The hours contribution to the earnings-rate spread seems to be a measure of demand pull, while the productivity contribution is perhaps more mixed in its cost and demand elements. Some writers, however, regard any positive movement in the spread as demand inflation. Our second equation takes the form

$$w_{et} - w_{rt} = \beta_1 h_t + \beta_2 (P/hE_p)_t + \beta + \beta_{s1} Q_{1t} + \beta_{s2} Q_{2t} + \beta_{s3} Q_{3t} + u_{2t}$$

(18.2)

where

w_e = quarterly average of index of weekly earnings,
h = quarterly average of index of hours worked per week,
(P/hE_p) = quarterly average of index of productivity (industrial production index divided by index of weekly man hours in corresponding production industries).

In contrast with the previous equation, there is a significant seasonal factor in the excess of earnings over rates, and the seasonal variables introduced in this equation are more important than in the previous one.

Hours are introduced as an explanatory variable in equation (18.2); hence we include an equation in our subsystem to show how hours worked are related to some of the other variables included in the same subsystem. Short of a presentation of our entire model consisting of more than a score of equations, we cannot show how industrial production is related to other variables of the system. For the purposes of the present paper we leave the system open at the production end. It is a partial and not a complete analysis.

When output is high hours worked are high. Hours are fairly closely tied to the general business cycle. They are also related to the pressure on facilities. When activity is slack, short time is introduced, and when labor is very scarce overtime comes back into operation. Our third equation thus relates the hours index to indexes of industrial production and of unemployment.

$$h_t = \gamma_1 P_t + \gamma_2 \left(\frac{U_t + U_{t-1} + U_{t-2} + U_{t-3}}{4} \right)$$
$$+ \gamma + \gamma_{1s} Q_{1t} + \gamma_{2s} Q_{2t} + \gamma_{3s} Q_{3t} + u_{3t}. \tag{18.3}$$

This equation shows that the hours variable in (18.2), accounting partially for the earnings-rate spread, is, in turn, related to the level of activity measured both by P_t and the average of unemployment.

The completion of our subsystem involves the construction of an equation giving a direct link between wages (earnings) and prices. It is, in effect, an equation of mark-up over prime costs. In the debates on the theory of the firm the adherents of full cost pricing as a pattern of behaviour would suggest an equation roughly similar to that which we propose below. An alternative approach, which we have not followed in this particular model, would be to construct equations proposed by the adherents of marginal analysis, i.e. marginal-cost or marginal-productivity equations. Such equations, transformed into equations of *labor's share* on the assumption of an exponential production function, have been estimated in the econometric models of the American economy.[5] The equation of entrepreneurial behavior introduced here is similar to that used in the model of the Dutch economy.[6] In our mark-up equation the index of price of final output is made a function of the earnings index, the import price index, and an index of indirect tax rates.

$$p_t = \delta_1 (w_e)_t + \delta_2 (p_i)_{t-2} + \delta_3 T_t + \delta + \delta_{1s} Q_{1t} + \delta_{2s} Q_{2t} + \delta_{3s} Q_{3t} + u_{4t}$$
(18.4)

where

p_i = index of import prices,
T = index of ratio of indirect taxes less subsidies to consumer expenditures.

---

[5] L. R. Klein and A. S. Goldberger, *An Econometric Model*.

[6] See *Scope and Methods of the Central Planning Bureau*, Central Planning Bureau, The Hague (1956), 70–3.

Determination of prices and wages

It is assumed that import prices affect final output prices with a time lag of two quarters, but a somewhat shorter lag, a somewhat larger lag or even no lag at all would not have greatly altered our statistical results or the conclusions based on them.

It may be thought that the mark-up over costs varies cyclically, and we have looked into this possibility by adding a productivity variable to the equation in an experimental calculation. Increasing productivity enables producers to moderate mark-ups over costs and yet retain levels of profits. We should expect to find a negative coefficient of a linear productivity variable if one is added to an equation like (18.4). Other cost variables may be considered as well, but we have restricted the analysis to prime costs covering wages, imports and taxes. To the extent to which fluctuations in import prices contribute to final price fluctuations we have a form of cost inflation (or deflation) but not one that is attributable in any sense to trade union power. In this equation and in our entire UK model import prices are treated as exogenous. While we attempt to close the system at many points in the trading accounts, we make no attempt to do so with respect to import prices.

STATISTICAL ESTIMATES OF THE MODEL

The four equations outlined in the preceding section have all been estimated from quarterly data of the period since 1948. The method of estimation used is known, in technical terms, as limited information maximum likelihood, a variant of the well-known method of maximum likelihood. This method has the desirable property of taking into account the structure of an interdependent model when estimating any particular part of it. For this reason it avoids the problems of bias (large sample theory) prevalent in application of what might be called single-equation methods such as the familiar methods of multiple-correlation theory applied to any particular equation without reference to the fact that it is imbedded in a larger inter-related system. Our method also has desirable properties in forecasting for the economy as a whole and is being used to estimate the entire UK model. The present estimates are a by-product of this effort.[7]

The estimated set of four structural equations in our partial model

---

[7]Substantive economic content and not econometric method occupies our main interest in this paper; therefore we shall not discuss the details of the estimation procedure. The method is explained and described in L. R. Klein, *A Textbook of Econometrics* (Row Peterson, Evanston (1953). An example of its application to similar problems is given in L. R. Klein and A. S. Goldberger, *An Econometric Model*.

with sampling errors noted in parentheses is

$$(w_r)_t - (w_r)_{t-4}$$

$$= -0.091 \left(\frac{U_t + U_{t-1} + U_{t-2} + U_{t-3}}{4} \right)$$
$$\ (0.013)$$

$$+ 0.854 \left(\frac{p_t - p_{t-4} + p_{t-1} - p_{t-5} + p_{t-2} - p_{t-6} + p_{t-3} - p_{t-7}}{4} \right)$$
$$(0.092)$$

$$+ 2.90 F_i + 10.26 + 0.10 Q_{1t} + 0.30 Q_{2t} + 0.19 Q_{3t} \qquad (18.1a)$$
$$\ (0.40) \quad\ \ (1.41)\ \ (0.57) \quad\ \ (0.57) \quad\ \ (0..57)$$

$$(w_e)_t - (w_r)_t = 2.06 h_t + 0.625(P/hE_p)_t - 272.72$$
$$(0.54) \quad\ (0.150) \qquad\qquad (45.80)$$
$$ + 0.001 Q_{1t} + 1.58 Q_{2t} + 5.54 Q_{3t} \qquad (18.2a)$$
$$\ (0.96) \qquad\ (0.98) \quad\ \ (1.36)$$

$$h_t = 0.089 P_t + 0.0068 \left(\frac{U_t + U_{t-1} + U_{t-2} + U_{t-3}}{4} \right)$$
$$(0.007) \quad\ (0.005)$$
$$ + 90.20 - 0.11 Q_{1t} + 0.15 Q_{2t} + 0.83 Q_{3t} \qquad (18.3a)$$
$$(1.13)\ \ (0.20) \qquad (0.20) \quad\ \ (0.22)$$

$$p_t = 0.421 (w_e)_t + 0.216 (p_i)_{t-2} + 0.013 T_t + 35.65$$
$$(0.013) \qquad\ (0.030) \qquad\ \ (0.161) \quad\ (13.03)$$
$$ + 0.94 Q_{1t} + 2.06 Q_{2t} + 1.18 Q_{3t} \qquad (18.4a)$$
$$(0.50) \quad\ \ (0.50) \quad\ \ (0.50)$$

All variables are measured as index numbers which average to 100 in the base period calendar year, 1948, except Q_{it} and F_t. These are constructed variables which take on the values of zero or unity in specified quarters.

The estimate of equation (18.1) gives a close correspondence between actual and computed four-quarter rates of change in wage rates. The degree of correlation, adjusted for degrees of freedom used up in estimation is 0.93 in our sample of 36 quarterly observations over the period 1948–56.[8] The residual variation appears to be slightly autocor-

---

[8] Although this is not an ordinary multiple-correlation estimate, we can compute an overall correlation coefficient defined as $(1 - S_u^2/S_y^2)^{\frac{1}{2}}$, where S_u^2 is the estimated variance of disturbances (determined from the variance of residuals) and S_y^2 is the variance of the normalised variable in the equation (the variable with a unit coefficient).

related, thus indicating that we have not isolated all the nonrandom factors. We measure autocorrelation in residuals by the statistic δ^2/s^2, known as the ratio of the mean square successive difference to the variance.[9] For values above 1.4 in samples of our size we accept the hypothesis of nonautocorrelation at the 5 per cent level of significance. In the present case our value is estimated at 1.02. By another test using a statistic which is smaller than δ^2/s^2 by the factor $(N-1)/N$ (N = sample size), we find an indecisive answer to the question whether or not there is significant autocorrelation.[10]

Our estimated equation suggests three positive conclusions.

1 Excess demand for labor as represented by a moving average of unemployment has been an important factor over the sample period.

2 Wage-rate adjustment to price changes has in effect roughly compensated for the effects of price increases between the times at which increases in wage rates have been obtained.

3 The behavior of wage-rate changes before 1952 is markedly different from that after 1952.

The latter point is illustrated by the magnitude and statistical significance of the coefficient of F_t in (18.1a). On the average, wage-rates moved up over a four-quarter interval by 2.90 more index points after 1952 than before, *ceteris paribus*. This might be taken as evidence of the strength of cost inflation.

Since the change in wage rates is measured over a period of four quarters, seasonal factors are effectively repressed. This is indicated by the small sizes and comparatively large sampling errors of the coefficients of the Q_{it} in (18.1a).

The main influence of demand inflation should be shown through the coefficient of $(U_t + U_{t-1} + U_{t-2} + U_{t-3})/4$, the index of unemployment averaged over the past four quarters. As would be expected from *a priori* considerations, this coefficient is negative and has a relatively small sampling error. In earlier work we estimated (18.1a) in the form.

$$(w_r)_t - (w_r)_{t-4} = \underset{(0.017)}{-0.021} \left(\frac{U_t + U_{t-1} + U_{t-2} + U_{t-3}}{4} \right)$$

---

[9] B. I. Hart and J. von Neumann, 'Tabulation of the probabilities for the ratio of the mean square successive difference to the variance,' *Annals of Mathematical Statistics*, XIII (1942), 207–14.

[10] J. Durbin and G. S. Watson, 'Testing for serial correlation in least squares regression, II,' *Biometrika*, **38** (1951), 159–78.

$$+0.975(p_t - p_{t-4}) + 3.88 F_t + 2.40$$
$$(0.115) \qquad\qquad (0.48) \quad (2.05)$$
$$-0.31 Q_{1t} - 0.25 Q_{2t} - 0.030 Q_{3t} \qquad (18.1a')$$
$$(0.67) \quad\;\; (0.67) \quad\;\; (0.67)$$

It will be noted that the principal difference between (18.1a') and (18.1a) is the size and significance of the coefficient of the moving average of unemployment. There seems a pronounced tendency for this coefficient to increase in absolute size and significance as we increase the lag in the price change. The estimate of (18.1a') was obtained using the method of limited information. We experimented, however, with an alternative form of (18.1a') using $(p_{t-1} - p_{t-5})$ as our price variable, and making use of the method of least squares. As we have observed, least-squares estimates of an equation of the form (18.1a) or (18.1a') will be biased estimates, but though they are biased, they probably give a good estimate of the change to be expected from introducing a new variable.[11] Using $(p_{t-1} - p_{t-5})$ as our price variable, the coefficient of $(U_t + U_{t-1} + U_{t-2} + U_{t-3})/4$ jumped to 0.06, and was significant as opposed to the estimate in (18.1a'), which is only just greater than its sampling error. Least-squares estimates of (18.1a') gave us a coefficient of 0.039, which suggests that 0.06 represents an upward biased estimate; nevertheless, the added importance given to the influence of demand as a result of the introduction of a price lag appears to be firmly established.

This result indicates that the magnitude of the coefficient of the moving average of unemployment in (18.1a) is not unexpected, since we have, in effect, an average lag of price changes of 6 months. The actual size of the coefficient in (18.1a) indicates that if the average price change were zero, and $F_t = 1$ for all t, the index of the moving average of unemployment would have to be about 150 before the change in wage rates would become negative. The rise in the coefficient of $(U_{t-1} + U_{t-2} + U_{t-3} + U_{t-4})/4$ in (18.1a) as compared to (18.1a') has been partially offset by the increase in the constant term from 2.40 to 10.26, which represents the trend increase in wage rates.

This raises the question to what extent equation (18.1a') can be considered reversible. It would undoubtedly be felt by some that even if the price level could be stabilized over the requisite period, a rise in the

---

[11] It may be observed that the least-squares estimates of the coefficients in (18.1a) are hardly distinguishable from those obtained using a consistent method of estimation. The coefficient of the moving average of unemployment is 0.089 as against 0.091, and that of the distributed lag in prices, 0.812, as against 0.854, with the sampling errors being virtually unchanged.

index of the moving average of unemployment to 150, representing an absolute level of unemployment of about 350,000, would not be sufficient to result in an actual decline in the wage-rate index. In the case of equation (18.1a'), unemployment would have to be about 520,000 before this eventually would take place, with perfectly stable prices. Even in this case, many would doubt this conclusion.

We prefer to reserve judgment on this point. The ever-continuing upward movement in money wage rates is only an assertion by some economists, who can read basic trends from something like a decade or two of experience. We believe that logically equation (18.1a) is more satisfactory than equation (18.1a'), since it reflects more closely the institutional character of wage bargaining, although it increases the possibility of a fall in the wage-rate index when the price level is stable. On the basis of our sample we are unable to reach any positive conclusion on this matter. Other economists have emphasized that the relation between changes in wage rates and excess demand for labor is nonlinear, so that a considerable rise in unemployment (say) may take place with the wage-rate index being unaffected.[12] We have seen no empirical evidence that justifies the fitting of a nonlinear rather than a linear function to the sample data, though to some this procedure is highly plausible on *a priori* grounds.

In assessing the responsibility for inflation it is important to be able to specify the lags involved, if any. As already pointed out, the particular form of the wage-rate equation (18.1a) has a built-in lag of 6 months between wage-rate and price changes. However, our sample does not permit a statistical discrimination of any other lag.

We have already mentioned the possibility that either the level of profits, changes in productivity or both should be included as variables in our wage-rate equation. Utilizing the method of least squares, we have experimented with their introduction into equation (18.1a').

Productivity change over four quarters when introduced into (18.1a') leaves the estimates of the other coefficients nearly the same and itself carries a negative coefficient. As a result of this finding we concluded that the inclusion of productivity change would not improve our basic model.

---

[12] In this connection we may mention a recent paper by A. W. Phillips 'The relation between unemployment and the rate of change of money wage rates in the United Kingdom, 1861–1957,' *Economica*, NS, xxv (1958), 283–300. Phillips explains wage-rate changes in terms of unemployment alone, except in periods of rapidly rising import prices. He estimates a non-linear (i.e. logarithmic) relation between wage-rate changes and unemployment.

The influence of profits was assessed by a similar least-squares computation, using as a variable the average of our index of company profits over the last four quarters. The result was that a positive coefficient larger than its sampling error was obtained on the profit variable. The coefficients of the other variable were, however, reduced, and strong autocorrelation was introduced into the residuals. This seems to lend weight to the idea put forward above that the influence of profits is largely reflected already in the other variables. Accordingly, we have not included the profit variable in our unbiased computations. We have conducted these experiments in an equation of the form (18.1a′). We believe, however, that the results obtained may be extended to an equation of the form (18.1a), and have therefore not included either the change of productivity or our profits variable in our basic equation.

Equation (18.2a) above represents the spread between earnings and wage rates. As it stands, this is in terms of the levels. The degree of correlation is estimated at 0.93, which indicates a fairly close agreement between the actual and computed value of the spread. Unlike the previous equation, however, its residual variation is decidedly not free of serial correlation. For this equation the measure δ^2/s^2 comes out as low as 0.73, which indicates a fairly high degree of autocorrelation in the residuals. The reason for this is not far to seek. Over the period covered by our sample, the spread has grown at a fairly steady trend rate. However, in explaining the spread we have used variables that are cyclical in character, the result being that we have introduced a cycle into the residuals which is inversely related to the cycle followed by the variables used.

In this case we have made an experimental calculation which removes the serial correlation of residuals, i.e. we have transformed all the variables to first differences.[13] With the first-difference transformations we have made a simple least-squares estimate of (18.2a) to compare with the same kind of estimate of the equation expressed in its original form. The two least-squares estimates are,

$$(w_e - w_r)_t = \underset{(0.67)}{1.55 h_t} + \underset{(0.118)}{0.538 (P/hE_p)_t} - \underset{(56.95)}{211.38} - \underset{(0.93)}{0.414 Q_{1t}}$$

$$+ \underset{(0.94)}{1.10 Q_{2t}} + \underset{(1.39)}{4.75 Q_{3t}} \tag{18.2a′}$$

---

[13] These differences are from quarter to adjacent quarter and not over four quarter periods as in equation (18.1a).

$$\Delta(w_e - w_r)_t = \underset{(0.365)}{1.737\Delta h_t} + \underset{(0.09)}{0.044\Delta(P/hE_p)_t} - \underset{(0.3275)}{0.00657\Delta Q_{1t}}$$
$$+ \underset{(0.377)}{0.346\Delta Q_{2t}} + \underset{(0.87)}{0.205\Delta Q_3} \quad (18.2a'')$$

The estimated equation (18.2a′) is roughly similar to that in (18.2a), and the degree of serial correlation in the residuals is equally high. On the other hand, (18.2a″), the estimate from transformed data, has no significant serial correlation in the residuals but gives a different figure for the relative importance of productivity in accounting for the spread. If anything, our estimates in (18.2a) are overgenerous in attributing fluctuations in the spread to those in productivity.

Our results are not inconsistent with the hypothesis that the spread is largely influenced by the level of demand. As pointed out above, hours worked constitute a very sensitive indicator of the level of demand. In one sense hours worked contribute to the spread in a purely accounting manner, as do, other things being equal, increases in output per man hour for pieceworkers.[14] We are unable, however, to separate out the relative importance of these two influences. No doubt, overtime, bonus payment, premium rates and changes in the length of the 'official' working week have all been important. On the demand side, it is often argued that a high level of demand has led to payments above the 'official' rates to bid labor away from some firms into others. Our results are consistent with either hypothesis alone or a combination of both.

It is interesting to compare our results with those obtained by the Swedish economists Bent Hansen and Gösta Rehn in their study of the Swedish economy.[15] They start from the assumption that wage rates are fixed institutionally, and that the influence of economic forces is reflected in the spread between earnings and wage rates, which they describe as the 'wage drift.' In our model we have not followed this assumption about rate fixing, putting forward instead the hypothesis that changes in wage rates are influenced by changes in the cost of living, by the demand for labor and by the political climate.

The procedure followed by Hansen and Rehn was to take a sample

---

[14] Among other things equal here, would be the timing of particular jobs. The effects of higher productivity on the spread may be to some extent offset by re-timing and re-estimating after the introduction of new capital equipment. We are unable to make any reliable estimate of the importance of this factor in cancelling out productivity changes.

[15] B. Hansen and G. Rehn, 'On wage drift, a problem of money wage dynamics,' *Economic Essays in Honour of Erik Lindahl*, Ekonomisk Tidskrift, Stockholm (1956) 87–139.

of annual data 1947-54, applied to eight main groupings within Swedish manufacturing industry. Briefly, their findings suggested that the main influence determining the 'wage drift' in Sweden over these years has been excess demand. They tested the further influence of 'excess profits,' and the hypothesis that increases in productivity have contributed substantially to the drift in the manner outlined above. Neither was found to be significant.

The relations estimated were between the rate of change of the 'wage drift,' the level of excess profit, the level of excess demand and the rate of change of productivity. It may be pointed out that while in our model productivity makes a significant contribution to the spread between earnings and wage rates, when all variables are expressed as levels, productivity ceases to be a significant factor in our least-squares computation, in which rates of change were introduced. It would appear, therefore, that our findings are not inconsistent with those of Hansen and Rehn. However, it must be re-emphasised that we have included an index of hours worked in our computation, which is an indicator of the direct influence of demand in the spread, but which also reflects other influences, and we have used weekly and not hourly earnings. Hansen and Rehn, on the other hand, construct an index of excess demand for labor, in some cases by taking the difference between unfilled vacancies and numbers unemployed, in others, where the numbers unemployed in the industry could not be ascertained, by using vacancy statistics alone.[16] We have included an explicit labor-demand variable, in the form of an average of the last year's unemployment, in the wage-rate equation (18.1a). This reflects our belief that the demand for labor can affect the wage bargain as well as the 'wage drift.'

We include the equation for hours worked in the subsystem to illustrate one of the ways in which demand enters the inflationary process. Our estimates in (18.3a) produce a correlation coefficient of 0.93 and a serial correlation measure of 1.23. Again we find evidence of slight serial correlation in residual variation.

It appears that the most important factor explaining the level of hours worked is the level of production. The coefficient of production is

---

[16]Hansen and Rehn attach significance to the use of vacancy statistics in addition to those on unemployment in order to measure excess demand during a period of sustained inflationary pressure. Following the suggestion of J. C. R. Dow, we have made experimental computations with a measure based on vacancy statistics (unemployment deflated by index of vacancies), and found the results on the basis of least-squares estimates not to be different in any essential way from those using ordinary unemployment figures. *Cf.* J. C. R. Dow and L. A. Dicks-Mireaux, 'The excess demand for labor,' for comparisons of vacancy and unemployment statistics.

Determination of prices and wages

small, but many times its sampling error. The small size of the coefficient is explained by the relative magnitudes of the range of the hours and production indices over the sample period. Hours worked are, on the whole, a fairly stable input into the productive process. Our estimates show that roughly a 10 per cent change in the industrial production index is required to produce a 1 per cent change in the hours index. The unemployment variable adds little to the computation. The coefficient is small, as one might have expected, but the sign differs from that anticipated, and the sampling error is sufficiently large to admit the hypothesis of either a positive or negative true value.

Thus it would be possible to substitute industrial production for hours worked in equation (18.2a), illustrating the relation of the spread between earnings and wage rates to the force of demand. Under the assumptions made in our model, this would, however, obscure the underlying chain of relationship.

Equation (18.4a) is the price or 'mark-up' equation. As pointed out above, the price index here used is that of the general price level of consumer goods. In the econometric model we also determine the price of investment goods, as a function of earnings and imported nonferrous metal prices. These two price indices can be weighted together to obtain an index of the general price level if so desired. The result established by the limited information estimate of (18.4a) is among one of the firmest in the model. The degree of correlation corrected for degrees of freedom is 0.996, which is very high. The measure of serial correlation δ^2/s^2 is 1.16, which indicates a moderate amount of serial correlation in the residuals.

It will be observed that the coefficients of $(w_e)_t$ and $(p_i)_{t-2}$ are many times their sampling errors. The coefficient of our measure of the influence of indirect taxes, however, is small, and very much smaller than its sampling error. As stated, we have expressed total indirect taxes paid, less subsidies, as a proportion of consumers' expenditure. Variations in this ratio have, on the whole, been small compared to the substantial changes in the indices of earnings and import prices, which are also included in the equation. Since the simple correlations between $(w_e)_t$ and p_t and between p_t and $(p_i)_{t-2}$ are so high, there is very little residual variation to be explained by the indirect tax variable. As changes in indirect tax rates are specifically directed, it might, perhaps, be argued that such changes tend to affect prices of, and expenditures on, particular goods, but will show little effect on the consumer price level as a whole, since the effects of the imposition of higher taxes on specific goods, may simply be to divert the expenditures elsewhere.

In the case of this equation there is remarkably close agreement between the results of the estimation by the method of limited information and by the method of least squares, which is largely a result of the high overall level of correlation. Applying the least-squares procedure to the equation in the form presented above, we obtain the result

$$p_t = 0.418(w_e)_t + 0.217(p_i)_{t-2} + 0.023(T)_t + 34.83 + 0.94Q_{1t}$$
$$\quad (0.013) \qquad (0.030) \qquad\quad (0.160) \qquad\quad (12.92) \;\; (0.50)$$
$$+ 2.06Q_{2t} + 1.18Q_{3t}$$
$$\;\;(0.50) \quad\;\; (0.49)$$

In a prototype model, based on a decade of annual data, this equation was estimated using Theil's two-rounds method,[17] in the form $p_t = \lambda + \lambda_1 (w_e)_t + \lambda_2(p_i)_t$. Using annual data, the seasonal variables and the lag in import prices disappear. We then obtained $\hat{\lambda}_1 = 0.48$ and $\hat{\lambda}_2 = 0.34$, where the $\hat{\lambda}_i$ are estimates of the λ_i. There is thus a very close relation between these three results, all obtained using different methods of estimation, and in the latter case using annual rather than quarterly data.

We experimented, using least-squares estimates, with the introduction of productivity into the equation. In formulating the 'mark-up' in their statistical study, Dow and Dicks-Mireaux introduced productivity as an alleviating factor on the influence of a rise in earnings on prices.[18] This follows the general custom of arguing that prices will be stabilized provided that earnings do not rise faster than productivity, or more generally that in times when productivity is rising fastest, prices will rise less fast than earnings. The least-squares estimate yielded a small coefficient of productivity with a positive sign contrary to expectations, and the sampling error was sufficiently large for the 'true' value to be assumed to be either positive or negative. We, therefore, concluded that our result afforded no evidence for the belief that the 'mark-up' varies in reponse to changes in productivity. Our results suggest that earnings have been roughly twice as important, at the margin, as import prices in determining the level of consumer prices over the period of our sample. It must not, however, be forgotten that in some sense we have established an average relationship, and this does not rule out the possibility that over certain periods within the sample, import prices

---

[17] H. Theil 'Estimation of parameters of econometric models' in the *Proceedings of the 28th Session of the International Statistical Institute* (Rome, 1953), XXXIV, Part 2, pp. 122-9.

[18] J. C. R. Dow and L. A. Dicks-Mireaux, 'The interrelationship between cost and price changes, 1946-1959; a study of inflation in post-war Britain,' *Oxford Economic Papers*, October (1961) **13**, 267-92.

may have contributed very much more than earnings to the rise in prices, as, for instance, at the time of the Korean war and shortly afterwards. How close we are to having established a basic structural relationship depends on the representative character of the sample, and as we have suggested elsewhere in this paper, there are reasons which give rise to doubt whether our sample is a representative one.

CONCLUSIONS

Our particular model of the inflationary process brings out points that have been raised by different authors and attempts to follow through some interrelated patterns of behavior in the sphere of wage and price determination. This model contains elements of both cost and demand inflation. Our model is not unique, as judged by its agreement with observed data, and it contains flaws; nevertheless, it appears to be reasonable, and the difficulties that it encounters are inherent in the nature of our basic economic information. We are not able to discriminate between certain competing key hypotheses, but it does not appear that other methods of analysis will be able to do so either.

The weaknesses of our results, such as serial correlation of residuals and some relatively large sampling errors, may perhaps be erased in a model of the same general type that specifies different relations among the variables or uses some more complex methods of parameter estimation, but we know of no such findings. Our model is aggregative, as is most of the analysis of the inflation problem, but one disaggregative type of analysis has been mentioned by several writers, namely, that changes in productivity in certain leading and rapidly advancing industries have been influential in securing favorable wage bargains in those industries in the first instance and that such awards have later spread, on equity grounds, to other sectors of the economy where productivity has advanced less rapidly. Phenomena like these are not adequately handled by our aggregative model, but they are not necessarily contradictory with what we find.

The model we have presented does not have irreversibilities that often are ascribed to the behavior of wage rates in modern society, but for the period under review a model with irreversibilities will probably not function much differently from ours. The test of the irreversibility hypothesis is yet to come, but we remain unconvinced of its correctness.

Our statistical analysis covers the postwar period as a whole. It gives a set of average relationships, which do not rule out dispersion. In the Korean period import prices were obviously of extraordinary significance. Some writers, such as Robbins, point to mainly demand inflation until the most recent months, when cost influences are considered to be dominant. Our only claim is that our model will tend to depict behavior on the average.

We cannot say whether there is a lag of a quarter or more in the adjustment of wage rates to price changes (see equation (18.1a)), but if there were definite evidence in favor of a lag we would lean more to the side of demand than to the side of cost inflation in the absence of substantial changes in import prices. The main element of demand inflation in this equation is through the effect of unemployment on wage rates. Our estimates of equation (18.1a) indicate the importance of the demand for labor, as represented by our variable on unemployment, on changes in wage rates.

Demand also enters the process through the strong influence of hours worked per week on the earnings-rate spread – the wage drift. Through the mark-up equation we have a measure of the influence of labor cost on price and import cost on price. These are both aspects of cost inflation, but the respective origins of cost must be kept firmly in mind when assessing the blame for inflation and formulating remedial policy action.

On the basis of our results we should be inclined to rule out the direct structural influence of productivity on wage-rate setting or on price mark-ups.[19] We similarly exclude profits from direct consideration in the rate equation. This is not to deny obvious chains of indirect influence of either variable throughout a larger and more complete interrelated system.

Our main point is that we should keep the interrelated structure of the economy more firmly in mind and not fall into the trap of ascribing our present difficulties with control of inflation to any single source in the economy.

As these pages are written, some countries in the Western world are experiencing a cyclical sag in output and accompanying growth in unemployment. Many people have been impressed by the fact that even during this cyclical phase, prices and wages have continued to rise, and they have taken this to be evidence that the prevailing structure should be described as cost, rather than demand, inflation.

Two points may be made in this connection. In the first place with regard to changes in the general consumer price level, it has been pointed out by Clague, that in the case of the US, rising prices during

---

[19] Subject to the above-cited influence of pace-setting industries.

the early stages have been a feature of previous recessions.[20] The American Consumer Price Index continued to rise for some time after the fall in production and employment and finally fell in the summer of 1958. The explanation of this is largely to be sought in the make up of the index (which closely resembles the price index used in our computation). The food component carries a large weight, and the comparative volatility of food prices is well known. Although, as Clague shows, durable goods prices respond fairly quickly to changes in the level of production, food prices are closely related to seasonal factors, and to the prevailing weather conditions. A poor harvest prior to the onset of a recession may keep food prices rising, the overall effect of which may offset falls in other prices to the extent that the total index rises rather than falls. The exceedingly great harvest of 1958 has been mainly responsible for the summer and autumn drop in American prices. In the longer run, it appears, food prices have adjusted themselves to the changed *general* economic conditions. Finally, a recession may get under way just before a normal seasonal pressure on food prices, so that the total index may still rise as output and employment fall. If the recession were sufficiently brief, it is possible that other prices may recover before the special factors keeping up the total index have worked themselves out, so that the impression is given that the recession has had no effect on prices. It follows that considerable care must be taken in interpreting movements in the consumer price level, when drawing conclusions about the character of current inflation. Wholesale prices, during the current American recession, did fall shortly after production turned down if food prices are excluded from the index.

Secondly, with regard to wage changes, it may be argued by those placing emphasis on demand that wage increases were much more difficult to obtain during the recession, and are much reduced in size. Bargaining power was distinctly impaired by unemployment. Both sides in the controversy have elements of truth in their arguments.

The dampening of demand had not fully checked inflation at the time of writing, and a simple theory leading to an equally simple policy proposal does not seem adequate to the situation. But neither would a 'deal' with the trade unions on a national wages policy, advocated by

---

[20]E. Clague 'The consumer price index in the business cycle,' *Monthly Labor Review*, **81** (1958), 616–20. G. H. Moore, in his work on statistical indicators of business cycles, confirms this laggard behavior of consumer prices at the upper turning point. See G. H. Moore, 'Measuring recessions,' *Journal of the American Statistical Association*, **53** (1958), 259–316.

some extremists on the side of cost inflation, do the trick.[21] It is a very simple solution based on a very simple theory. Just as we argue here for more tolerance for alternative points of view on the matter of a theoretical description of behavior, we feel that a broader approach to policy control based on both demand and cost aspects of the situation would lead to more fruitful results.

---

[21]B. C. Roberts, 'Lessons of a national wages policy,' *The Times Review of Industry*, May (1958), 36–7. Roberts remarks that even if a sensible agreement is worked out on a national scale among government, employers and trade unions, 'No trade unionist is able to stand silently by, as the Dutch have found out, when profits are rising rapidly.' We may prefer to cite another measure of activity besides *profits*, but the point of Roberts' observation remains well founded.

19

Some New Results in the Measurement of Capacity Utilization

STATEMENT OF THE PROBLEM

The concepts of capacity output and rate of capacity utilization have been prominent in recent discussions of US economic potential. These are important descriptive concepts for the economy as a whole and merit careful attention in statistical measurement. They are also very difficult concepts to measure and are not yet well established in our economic annals. Capacity variables have been significant ingredients in the econometric models constructed at the Wharton School, and a great deal of effort has been devoted to development of a measure which would reliably serve a wide range of uses in applied econometrics.[2,6]

The Wharton School Index of capacity utilization is constructed by a very simple procedure which enables us to provide quick and frequent estimates of this useful economic statistic. Briefly, the method involves marking off cyclical peaks for each of 30 component indices of the Federal Reserve Board's (FRB) Index of Industrial Production and then fitting linear segments between successive peaks. Between the present time period and the last established peak, the previous linear segment is extrapolated at its established slope unless the index in the present period exceeds the extrapolated trend line. In this case a new slope is computed by fitting a new linear segment from the last cyclical peak to the present value of the index. Revisions will be continuously made in the last linear segments until there is a cyclical downturn in the index of industrial production. This establishes a new peak, and the process thus begins again. The trend lines through peaks, we assume, represent an index of capacity output, on a base of actual output, namely the same base as that used in the FRB index.

In constructing the Wharton Series our basic data are quarterly series constructed from 3-month averages of the FRB seasonally

From *American Economic Review*, **57**, March (1967), 34–58; written jointly with R. S. Preston.

adjusted monthly industry indexes.[5] A monthly index is being constructed and tested, but we shall deal here with the quarterly index. Normally, peak values must exceed immediately preceding and following quarterly values, but we must deal with some special cases. When the index of output is unchanged for two or more successive peak quarters, we choose the first of the two as the capacity peak. When output declines from a peak and then rises again, with the decline no more than one quarter in duration, the greater of the two high values is selected as a single capacity peak.

The ratio of actual output to the trend line (linear segments) fitted through peaks is called capacity utilization. For each quarter, such ratios are computed for each of the 30 component industries and then averaged, using FRB index weights, to reach our economy-wide index of capacity utilization.

A principal objection to this method of estimating capacity utilization is that some peaks may be marked off as full capacity utilization peaks when in fact there may have been considerable underutilization of capacity. The objections have been summarized by A. Phillips[3] in his survey of various alternative capacity measures. To be practical and specific, the general presumption among economists is that the recovery from the 1957–9 recession was incomplete, and the subsequent peaks in many sectors represent points of substantial underutilization of capacity. The Wharton School Index of capacity utilization is therefore thought to be biased upwards since 1958–9.

It is the purpose of this study to develop an alternative measure of capacity and capacity utilization at the industry level from production functions. This is done for a sample of 11 of the 30 industries which make up the Wharton Index. We then compare the results from this newer method with those obtained by the method described above. An adjustment for those component Wharton Indexes which are found to be subject to bias drift is developed. Finally, a method is developed to adjust the aggregate Wharton Index for bias drift, based on our results of the sample of 11 industries studied.

THE ESTIMATION OF CAPACITY AND CAPACITY UTILIZATION FROM PRODUCTION FUNCTIONS

Another approach to the problem of capacity estimation is by estimation of cost or production functions by sector. In the case of cost functions, it has often been suggested that the point of minimum average cost may represent full capacity output (in a competitive

Measurements of capacity utilization

environment). The estimation of cost functions, by sectors, may be a fruitful step in capacity estimation, but there is a problem in obtaining a sharply defined minimum point for empirical average cost functions.

In this study we approach the problem through the use of production functions. For each sector we define actual output by the conventional production function relationship.

$$X_t = Ae^{\gamma t} L_{e_t}^\alpha K_{u_t}^\beta v_t, \qquad (19.1)$$

where

X_t = actual output at time t,
L_{e_t} = manhours employed at time t,
K_{u_t} = real capital utilized at time t,
$e^{\gamma t}$ = a proxy for technical change,
v_t = the disturbance at time t.

Full capacity output is defined as

$$X_{c_t} = Ae^{\hat{\gamma} t} L_t^{\hat{\alpha}} K_t^{\hat{\beta}}, \qquad (19.2)$$

where

X_{c_t} = full capacity real output at time t,
L_t = available manhours at time t (in practice, frictional unemployment is allowed for),
K_t = fully utilized real capital at time t,
$e^{\gamma t}$ = a proxy for technical change.

The function f is the same in (19.1) as in (19.2), apart from the fact that parameters in (19.1) have been replaced by their estimates in (19.2). The disturbance $\log v_t$ is given its expected value (zero) in (19.2). In our particular case, errors in estimating X_{c_t} will be caused by measurement error for L_t and K_t, by misspecification of the equation, or by biased parameter estimates of (19.1). Assuming that L_t and K_t are measured without error, that the relationship has not been misspecified, and that our estimating method produces unbiased estimates of the parameters, we may regard X_{c_t} as error free.

THE ESTIMATION OF SERIES ON UTILIZED CAPITAL STOCK AND CAPACITY MANHOUR INPUTS BY INDUSTRIAL SECTOR

Among the many time-honored problems in the estimation of production functions there are two particularly thorny ones involved in the present study. It is very difficult to determine K_{u_t} in (19.1) and L_t in

(19.2). If there were a large number of full capacity peak points for each industry, (19.2) could be estimated directly from a sample of peak observations on X_{c_t}, L_t, and K_t. Many difficulties would thus be overcome simultaneously. We considered the possibility of making direct estimates of (19.2) from the very small sample of post-war full-capacity, peak-point observations, but the smallness of the sample made the results too unstable for practical use. Equation (19.1) is the production function, whose statistical study was initiated by the great pioneering investigations of Paul Douglas. The problem in the present context is that capital is not fully utilized over the business cycle; therefore estimates of the stock of capital in existence (the only ones we have directly) do not furnish a suitable input variable during periods of under-capacity utilization. We do have direct estimates of X_t and L_{e_t}, the latter being expressed in manhours.

If we had estimates of (19.1), we could compute X_{c_t} as values on the production function surface corresponding to full capacity inputs of L_t and K_t. It is difficult to obtain estimates of the series K_{u_t} in estimating (19.1), and it is similarly difficult to obtain estimates of the series on L_t in estimating X_{c_t} from (19.2). Since we are estimating production functions and associated capacity values by industry, we have the difficult task of determining values of L_t for each industry.

We have an industrial distribution of actual manhour employment. From this we can aggregate and adjust this aggregate for induced labor force participation and the national rate of unemployment to arrive at an economy-wide supply of manhour series, but we do not know the supply of manhours to each sector. Such manhour data are not directly available.

Lacking estimates of capital utilization by industry, we are forced to use a proxy. Different measures have been used in previous studies, e.g. Carl Christ used the rate of new investment as such a proxy, on the assumption that new investment would be determined by the percentage of unutilized capital.[1] We have used a more direct proxy, namely the rate of manhour employment by industry. This, in concept, follows the procedure of Robert Solow.[4] It is apparent that the measurement of K_{u_t} cannot be completed until L_t is measured for each industry in our sample. Both measurement problems are tied together.

To relate capital utilization to manhour utilization, we assume, as Solow has done,

$$\frac{K_{u_t}}{K_t} = \frac{L_{e_t}}{L_t}. \tag{19.3}$$

Equation (19.3) is not an unreasonable assumption. It can be shown that this relationship in combination with the Cobb-Douglas form of the production function will enable us to relate the rate of unemployment directly to the rate of capacity utilization. In this case it can be shown that logarithms of estimated industry utilization rates are linear functions of logarithms of industry employment rates. The parameters in these relationships are those of the Cobb-Douglas production function and vary from industry to industry.

This can be seen very quickly. If we assume that the production function is Cobb-Douglas and that capacity output is defined as in (19.2), with K_{u_t} defined as in (19.3), then we find that

$$\frac{X_t}{X_{c_t}} = \left(\frac{L_{e_t}}{L_t}\right)^{\alpha+\beta} v_t.$$

For any given industry the degree of homogeneity of this function is the same as that of the production function for the industry. Increasing returns to scale in the production function would then be indirectly supported by the observation that proportional changes in unemployment rates result in more than proportional changes in the utilization of capacity.

Although we are limited to computing production functions for only 11 sectors, our restriction being availability of capital data, the construction of series on L_t, for each industrial sector, covers 31 sectors (both manufacturing and nonmanufacturing). These 31 sectors include all the industries included as component sectors of the Industrial Production Index plus all nonmanufacturing categories, except agriculture and the self-employed. As a result, the construction of series on L_t for each industrial sector involved a larger sample of sectors than the final computation of production functions. It is felt that, in the construction of L_t, as many sectors as possible should be taken into account in the aggregation to a national figure.

Our first step is to estimate full-employment (full capacity) manhours for the economy as a whole. We shall then allocate this total among sectors. Let us define (in terms of men – not manhours) L_t as total labor force at full capacity, L_{e_t} as employed labor force, L_{v_t} as involuntarily unemployed labor force, and L_{f_t} as frictionally unemployed labor force. We shall measure full-capacity labor force as the value of L_t which satisfies (19.4), given L_{e_t}, L_{v_t}, and L_{f_t}.

$$L_t = L_{e_t} + L_{v_t} + L_{f_t} + \delta(L_t - L_{e_t} - L_{f_t}). \tag{19.4}$$

where δ is the coefficient of response of labor supply to employment opportunities. This makes full-capacity labor force the sum of employed and unemployed persons plus an induced amount depending on the level of unemployment. We may solve (19.4) for L_t as follows.

$$(1-\delta)(L_t - L_{f_t}) = (1-\delta)L_{e_t} + L_{v_t}$$

$$L_t - L_{f_t} = L_{e_t}\left\{1 + \left(\frac{1}{1-\delta}\right)\left[\frac{L_{v_t}/(L_{e_t}+L_{v_t}+L_{f_t})}{L_{e_t}/(L_{e_t}+L_{v_t}+L_{f_t})}\right]\right\} \quad (19.4b)$$

so that

$$L_t - L_{f_t} = L_{e_t}\frac{1+(\mu_t - \mu_{f_t})}{(1-\delta)(1-\mu_t)}, \quad (19.4c)$$

where

$$\mu_t = \frac{L_{v_t} + L_{f_t}}{L_{e_t} + L_{v_t} + L_{f_t}} \quad (19.4d)$$

and

$$\mu_{f_t} = \frac{L_{f_t}}{L_{e_t} + L_{v_t} + L_{f_t}} \quad (19.4e)$$

We note that μ_t is equal to the total unemployment rate and μ_{f_t} is equal to the frictional unemployment rate. We shall measure full employment manhours, as actual manhours used (L_{e_t} expressed in hours) adjusted by

$$1.0 + (\mu_t - \mu_{f_t})/[(1-\mu_t)(1-\delta)]. \quad (19.5)$$

This gives us a measure of potential manhours less frictional manhours. The above adjustment factor is observable from published employment series provided we have estimates of μ_{f_t} and δ.

We choose μ_{f_t} as 2.67 percent, the low rate of unemployment observed in the record quarter of 1953. We place δ at 0.25, an estimate which is consistent with the labor supply equation estimated in econometric models developed at the Wharton School in which the capacity utilization indexes are intended to be used.[2]

The labor supply equation estimated in reference 2 is

$$L_{e_t} + L_{v_t} + L_{f_t} = 61.2 + 0.226t - 0.310(L_{v_t} + L_{f_t}). \quad (19.6)$$

We can see that the coefficient of 0.310 in this labor supply equation suggests a value of δ in (19.4) of 0.25. Write down the above expression (19.4) for L_t as

$$L_t = L_{e_t} + L_{v_t} + L_{f_t} + \delta(L_t - L_{e_t} - L_{v_t} - L_{f_t} + L_{v_t}). \quad (19.7a)$$

Rearranging terms, we find

$$L_{e_t}+L_{v_t}+L_{f_t}=L_t-\left(\frac{\delta}{1-\delta}\right)(L_{v_t}+L_{f_t})+\left(\frac{\delta}{1-\delta}\right)L_{f_t}. \qquad (19.7b)$$

We assume that the frictional unemployment rate is a constant proportion of fully employed labor force. Thus we can write

$$L_{f_t}=kL_t, \qquad (19.7c)$$

and we can rewrite (19.7b) as

$$L_{e_t}+L_{v_t}+L_{f_t}=\left[1+\left(\frac{\delta}{1-\delta}\right)k\right]L_t-\left(\frac{\delta}{1-\delta}\right)(L_{v_t}+L_{f_t}). \qquad (19.7d)$$

The coefficient of $(L_{v_t}+L_{f_t})$ in (19.6) is therefore equal to $-[\delta/(1-\delta)]$. This suggests an estimate of δ of about 0.25. We therefore evaluate

$$L_{v_t}-L_{f_t}=L_{e_t}\left[1.0+\frac{\mu_t-0.0267}{(1.0-\mu_t)(0.75)}\right] \qquad (19.8)$$

as our estimate of available manhours, where L_{e_t} results from the aggregation over our 31 industries in each time period.

It was found, after the series $L_t-L_{f_t}$ was computed from the series L_{e_t}, that this aggregate supply series still had cycles in it. This is in part due to the fact that our arguments in the previous section were carried out in terms of people and the final adjustment (19.8) was made to a manhour concept. We correct this in the following fashion. On *a priori* grounds the aggregate supply of manhours should have no cycle, but should be a smooth monotonic increasing function of time, reflecting additions to the labor force as the economy grows. The cycle in $L_t-L_{f_t}$ may be due to variations in overtime and short shift work which is not reflected in hiring and firing policy. At peaks of the series $L_t-L_{f_t}$ manhour employment resulting from overtime is at its peak; therefore, by fitting linear segments through peaks we approximate the smooth monotonic increasing trend of the aggregate supply of manhours for the 31 sectors as a whole.

These results are summarized in figure 19.1. In figure 19.1, series 1 is full employment aggregate manhours. This series has resulted from the linear interpolation of the peaks of $L_t-L_{f_t}$. Series 2 is actual manhours, in our notation L_{e_t}. Series 3 is, in our notation, $L_t-L_{f_t}$.

Our problem now is to redistribute series 1 in figure 19.1 over our 31 industries. In our sample of 31 industries, the distribution of employment changes over time due to changes in relative factor rewards (wage rates), caused by shifts in demand and changes in worker tastes. The

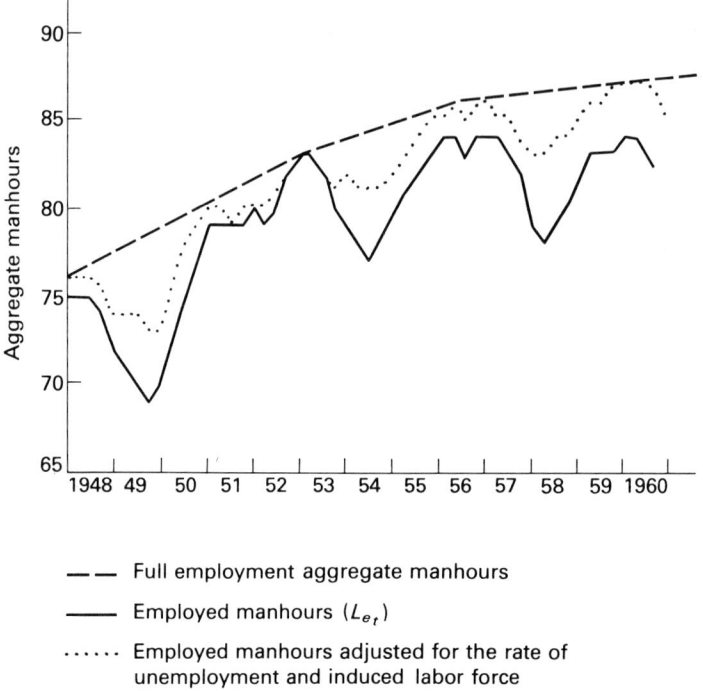

– – Full employment aggregate manhours
—— Employed manhours (L_{e_t})
······ Employed manhours adjusted for the rate of unemployment and induced labor force ($L_t - L_{f_t}$)

Figure 19.1 Aggregate manhours 1948-I–1960-IV

demand for a factor is a derived demand, derived from the demand for the product. With the aggregate supply function stable over time, the industry distribution of manhours is then determined by the relative importance of each sector in the production of aggregate output. We approximate the trend in *capacity input* of labor to each industry by first approximating the trend in the share each sector received of the aggregate at full-employment peaks. By fitting linear segments between these computed shares we can approximate the trend in the share of total manhours used by each sector at peak demand points.

It is important to understand that these linear segments were not fitted between peaks of the individual sector series, but between the benchmark manhour shares that each industry got at points where series 2 on figure 19.1 peaked. We now argue that these trend series represent the full capacity share for each of our 31 sectors at any point in time. We multiply these percentages into series 1 to arrive at the trend in capacity manhours for each of our individual sectors. Aggregate unemployment or induced labor force participation is distributed over industrial sectors in accordance with the trend in the *share* of each sector in the aggregate. As a result, those sectors whose share in the aggregate is increasing will also receive an increasing share of unemployment or induced labor-force participation. Furthermore, those industries that have larger shares in the aggregate will receive larger shares of aggregate unemployment or induced participation. This, of course, is a simplifying assumption.

THE ESTIMATION OF PRODUCTION FUNCTIONS

We do not assume constant returns to scale and thus place no restrictions on $\alpha+\beta$. There is much evidence in favor of this procedure in the case of the American economy, although there are some investigators who impose the restriction $\alpha+\beta=1$. If we assume cost minimization rather than profit maximization behavior, to allow for the presence of increasing returns to scale, it is possible to estimate the ratio β/α first from factor share data. Direct estimates of (19.1) lead to problems of multicollinearity and least squares bias. In the cost minimization equation

$$\frac{q_t K_{u_t}}{w_t L_{e_t}} = \frac{\beta}{\alpha} + z_t, \qquad (19.9)$$

where $q_t K_{u_t}$ is nonwage income originating in period t, $w_t L_{e_t}$ is wage income originating in period t, and z_t is a disturbance in period t, we have an estimate of β/α as

$$\left(\frac{\hat{\beta}}{\alpha}\right) = \frac{1}{T}\sum_{t=1}^{T}\frac{q_t K_{u_t}}{w_t L_{e_t}}. \qquad (19.10)$$

We then estimate A, α and γ from the regression

$$\mathrm{Log}_e(x_t) = \mathrm{Log}_e(A) + \gamma t + \alpha\left[\mathrm{Log}_e(L_{e_t}) + \left(\frac{\hat{\beta}}{\alpha}\right)\mathrm{Log}_e(K_{u_t})\right] + \mathrm{Log}_e v_t. \qquad (19.11)$$

With estimates $\hat{A}$, $\hat{\gamma}$, $\hat{\alpha}$ and $\hat{\beta}$, where $\hat{\beta}=\hat{\alpha}(\widehat{\beta/\alpha})$, we can now compute capacity output from (19.2), given K_t and L_t for each industry.

Using single equation least-squares regression methods to estimate (19.11), we shall obtain biased estimates of coefficients, as the error $\log_e v_t$ is not independent of $\log_e(L_{e_t}) + (\widehat{\beta/\alpha})\log_e(K_{u_t})$. We recognize the existence of this bias but do not take it into account in the capacity estimation procedure. The ratio of observed values of X_t to the computed values of X_{c_t} are our estimates of capacity utilization rates, R_t

$$R_t = \frac{X_t}{X_{c_t}}.$$

THE METHOD USED TO ADJUST THE COMPONENT WHARTON INDEXES

Denote the individual Wharton School Indexes by Wh_t. As will be seen below, p. 352, the time profile of the R_t and Wh_t series are remarkably similar. Both series deal with essentially the same phenomenon, but in some sectors the Wh_t series drifts higher than the R_t series, especially in recent years. This is the bias we are seeking to measure.

We correlate the two series to find

$$Wh_t = a + bR_t + ct. \tag{19.12}$$

Primarily, we are not interested in the difference in the level between Wh_t and R_t, for we think the Wh_t series establishes a reasonable level in the period before 1957. We are especially interested in the tendency of the Wh_t series to drift upwards in recent years. Therefore, where the estimated regression coefficient c is significant and positive, we assume that an element of bias has been found. The adjusted Wharton Index Wh_t^A is then for those industries where bias is found as

$$Wh_t^A = Wh_t - ct. \tag{19.13}$$

We make this adjustment to all sector Wh_t series where a significant and positive c coefficient is found.

THE METHOD USED TO ADJUST THE AGGREGATE WHARTON INDEX

As mentioned earlier our sample of industries studied deals only with a subgroup of those industries which make up the aggregate Wharton Index. We now develop a method which will enable us to draw a conclusion about the bias in the Aggregate Wharton Index on the basis of our sample subgroup. As mentioned earlier, this subgroup is composed of 11 industries.

Let r_i be the FRB weight for the ith industry. For the 11 industries in our sample, form (for $t = t_0$)

$$\frac{\sum_{i=1}^{11} r_i(Wh_i - c_i)}{\sum_{i=1}^{11} r_i} = \frac{\sum_{i=1}^{11} r_i Wh_i}{\sum_{i=1}^{11} r_i} - \frac{\sum_{i=1}^{11} r_i c_i}{\sum_{i=1}^{11} r_i}, \qquad (19.14)$$

$$= Wh^S - \bar{c}, \qquad (19.14a)$$

where S stands for sample subgroup. If we could do this for all industries in the index we would have

$$\sum_{i=1}^{11} r_i Wh_i - \sum_{i=1}^{11} r_i c_i + \sum_{i=12}^{30} r_i Wh_i - \sum_{i=12}^{30} r_i c_i = Wh^A, \qquad (19.15)$$

since

$$\sum_{i=1}^{30} r_i = 1.0.$$

We can combine the first and third terms to get

$$\sum_{i=1}^{30} r_i Wh_i - \sum_{i=1}^{11} r_i c_i - \sum_{i=12}^{30} r_i c_i = Wh^A. \qquad (19.16)$$

But we do not know the last term of the left-hand side

$$\sum_{i=12}^{30} r_i c_i.$$

If we assume that subgroups 1–11 and 12–30 would each give the same average correction term, we can write

$$\frac{\sum_{i=1}^{11} r_i c_i}{\sum_{i=1}^{11} r_i} = \bar{c} = \frac{\sum_{i=12}^{30} r_i c_i}{\sum_{i=12}^{30} r_i} \qquad (19.17)$$

or

$$\bar{c} \sum_{i=1}^{11} r_i = \sum_{i=1}^{11} r_i c_i,$$

and

$$\bar{c} \sum_{i=12}^{30} r_i = \sum_{i=12}^{30} r_i c_i.$$

As a result we can now write

$$Wh^A = \sum_{i=1}^{30} r_i Wh_i - \bar{c} \sum_{i=1}^{11} r_i - \bar{c} \sum_{i=12}^{30} r_i.$$

This reduces to $Wh^A = Wh - \bar{c}$, where Wh is the unadjusted 30 sector weighted average, Wh^A is the adjusted 30 sector weighted average, and $\bar{c}$ is defined above as the mean adjustment for the 11 sectors.

We assume that the bias accumulated in the Wh_t index by 1960 terminates a tendency of the Wharton School Index to drift upwards and make adjustment after that date by the fixed amount applied to 1960.

DESCRIPTION OF THE DATA

Our basic data series used in the present study are the FRB's monthly index of industrial production on a 1958 base, the FRB industry weights, a quarterly series on total manhours used by each sector, a quarterly series on GNP originating in 1954 dollars for each sector, a quarterly series on fixed capital in 1954 dollars for each sector, a yearly series on national income originating for each sector, and a yearly series on wages, salaries and supplements for each sector.

Three-month averages were constructed from the monthly series (seasonally adjusted) of the FRB index to yield a quarterly series of the industrial production index. For this series the sample period runs from 1947–1 to 1965–2. For all other series, the sample period runs from 1948 to 1960. The quarterly series on total manhour employment are aggregated from series on average weekly hours and average number of employees. The capital stock series is essentially a series on constant dollar net investment accumulated from an initial period estimate of the stock of capital. In the estimation of (β/α), income of nonlabor factors was computed by a residual method, namely as national income originating minus wages, salaries and supplements.

In two cases the Federal Reserve Board's classification did not agree with our production function breakdown. These were Food and Beverages and Gas and Electric Utilities. This was remedied by computing a weighted average of Food and Beverages of the Wharton Index using FRB weights and by computing a weighted average of Gas and Electric Utilities of the Wharton Index using FRB weights. In nine other FRB categories we have comparable data. For 17 other FRB categories we have no comparable production function data. The 11 groupings with which we finally ended included 62 per cent of the total FRB weight, including all the most important categories of the Wharton Aggregate Index.

THE ESTIMATED PRODUCTION FUNCTIONS

In table 19.1 we present the estimated production functions for the 11 sectors we are dealing with in this study. In all but two industries we find that the data suggest that increasing returns to scale is the proper assumption about the degree of homogeneity of the production function. Chemicals and food and beverages show decreasing returns to scale. Among all the industries studied, food and beverages yields the least reasonable estimate of α and β. Most of the variance of X_t is explained by a straight trend, our proxy for technical change. All the estimates of γ are positive and significant except for primary metals and paper and allied products, where the coefficient is not significant.

Table 19.1 Production function coefficients ($X_t = Ae^{\gamma t} L_{e_t}^{\alpha} K_{u_t}^{\beta} V_t$)

	$\widehat{\log A}$	$\hat{\alpha}$	$\hat{\beta}$	$\widehat{(\beta/\alpha)}$	$\hat{\gamma}$	$\bar{R}^2$
Primary metals	−3.848	1.141	0.371	0.325	0.0001	0.888
	(0.892)	(0.058)			(0.0005)	
Nonelectrical machinery	−0.291	0.953	0.240	0.252	0.0020	0.929
	(0.692)	(0.047)			(0.0004)	
Electrical machinery	0.122	0.924	0.228	0.247	0.0049	0.974
	(0.810)	(0.058)			(0.0008)	
Autos and equipment	1.935	0.699	0.387	0.553	0.0039	0.755
	(1.233)	(0.075)			(0.0009)	
Stone clay and glass	−0.941	0.988	0.273	0.276	0.0031	0.936
	(1.179)	(0.086)			(0.0006)	
Food and beverages	12.750	0.070	0.022	0.320	0.0059	0.972
	(1.177)	(0.075)			(0.0002)	
Textile mill products	0.111	0.898	0.192	0.214	0.0096	0.853
	(0.856)	(0.060)			(0.0006)	
Paper and allied products	−3.651	1.115	0.429	0.385	0.0006	0.985
	(1.052)	(0.072)			(0.0007)	
Chemicals	5.947	0.418	0.251	0.601	0.0130	0.971
	(1.701)	(0.099)			(0.0012)	
Rubber products	1.056	0.839	0.241	0.287	0.0043	0.939
	(0.813)	(0.063)			(0.0004)	
Public utilities	−3.791	0.763	0.763	1.000	0.0084	0.995
	(2.225)	(0.101)			(0.0016)	

THE TIME PROFILES OF THE Wh_t AND R_t SERIES AND THE ISOLATION OF THE BIAS DRIFT BY INDUSTRY

In table 19.2 we give the series R_t (column 1), the series Wh_t (column 2) and the difference $R_t - Wh_t$ (column 3). Although in the isolation of the bias drift primary emphasis will be placed on the regression results, in the final analysis both the inspection of table 19.2 and the regression results will play a part in determining whether a particular sector series is subject to drift.

For primary metals, both series agree on all turning points. The time path of the two series is similar until the 1959 steel strike. At this point the R_t series takes on higher peak and trough values. The computed regression result is

$$Wh_t = 12.682 + 0.917 R_t - 0.297t \qquad \bar{R}^2 = 0.9330.$$
$$\quad\;\;\;(3.613)\;\;(0.038)\;\;\;\;(0.033)$$

Although the coefficient of time is significant, its sign indicates a downward bias in the Wharton Index. This result is due to the extremely high peaks which the R_t series reached in the late fifties. As a result of the steel strike in 1959 and the associated production for inventories, it is felt that the Wh_t series is approximately correct, not subject to a bias drift, since the peak at 1959–2 was close to a full capacity peak on *a priori* grounds. The height of the R_t series in the 1958–60 range is due to a computed downturn in the level of capacity. This resulted in forcing the R_t series higher than the Wh_t series at this peak compared to other capacity peaks. This computed downturn in the R_t series begins in 1958. This may be seen by looking at table 19.2. Here we see the difference between R_t and Wh_t. This difference, until 1958, exhibits no clear trend; after 1958 there is a sharp increase in the difference. On the hypothesis that the 1959 peak was a capacity peak due to the steel strike and that the prediction of the R_t series after 1958 is false, we conclude that primary metals is not subject to a bias drift.

For nonelectrical machinery the time profile of the two series is quite similar. Both series agree on all major turning points except for the trough of the 1958 recession where there is one quarter difference. There is a bit of disagreement in the 1959–60 range. By looking at table 19.2 it is evident that there is no upward drift of the Wh_t series. Although there seems to be a systematic cycle, there is no evidence of a persistent upward drift in the Wh_t series. This is supported by the computed regression.

$$Wh_t = 9.217 + 0.906 R_t - 0.141t \qquad \bar{R}^2 = 0.8475,$$
$$\quad\;\;(4.904)\;(0.054)\;\;\;\;(0.034)$$

Table 19.2 Percentage utilization of capacity by industrial sector 1948–I to 1960–IV
($1 = R_t$; $2 = Wh_t$; $3 = R_t - Wh_t$)

Quarter	Primary metals			Nonelectrical machinery			Electrical machinery		
	1	2	3	1	2	3	1	2	3
48–1	93.44	95.99	−2.55	92.79	94.88	−2.09	88.24	93.96	−5.72
48–2	92.45	94.83	−2.38	90.75	93.60	−2.85	87.86	90.05	−2.19
48–3	96.52	98.89	−2.37	92.17	92.48	−0.31	85.80	88.53	−2.73
48–4	95.29	97.41	−2.12	88.48	89.67	−1.19	81.50	83.91	−2.41
49–1	91.72	93.39	−1.67	80.75	84.02	−3.27	75.76	76.14	−0.38
49–2	80.13	81.38	−1.25	72.91	75.76	−2.85	71.29	71.83	−0.54
49–3	76.18	76.95	−0.77	71.42	71.24	0.18	73.71	73.34	0.37
49–4	58.88	59.15	−0.27	67.56	66.54	1.02	72.67	73.91	−1.24
50–1	81.94	81.79	0.15	72.33	68.98	3.35	74.10	80.98	−6.88
50–2	94.62	94.05	0.57	78.93	75.87	3.06	79.96	89.86	−9.90
50–3	101.43	100.00	1.43	91.15	82.55	8.60	86.15	100.00	−13.85
50–4	100.66	98.78	1.88	92.37	87.12	5.25	90.38	94.44	−4.06
51–1	100.98	98.69	2.29	92.48	90.76	1.72	86.59	92.52	−5.93
51–2	102.61	100.00	2.61	96.88	93.91	2.97	86.14	87.48	−1.34
51–3	101.39	99.32	2.07	99.63	96.00	3.63	82.28	75.39	6.89
51–4	96.94	96.00	0.94	104.31	98.12	6.19	84.76	79.07	5.69
52–1	94.88	95.40	−0.52	102.04	98.86	3.18	89.57	82.85	6.72
52–2	72.51	73.86	−1.35	99.66	97.98	1.68	90.52	84.43	6.09
52–3	77.02	79.21	−2.19	97.10	95.07	2.03	95.11	88.74	6.37
52–4	96.82	100.00	−3.18	103.22	98.39	4.83	101.01	96.40	4.61
53–1	95.45	99.04	−3.59	105.66	100.00	5.66	99.96	100.00	−0.04
53–2	95.88	99.89	−4.01	105.31	99.70	5.61	103.21	100.00	3.21
53–3	95.44	99.12	−3.68	101.09	98.13	2.96	99.19	97.13	2.06
53–4	84.27	87.26	−2.99	92.14	91.70	0.44	87.93	87.14	0.79
54–1	74.20	76.40	−2.20	88.09	85.27	2.82	85.83	81.76	4.07
54–2	72.79	74.21	−1.42	84.31	82.92	1.39	83.37	82.08	1.29
54–3	73.55	74.54	−0.99	85.49	82.10	3.39	84.38	84.32	0.06
54–4	78.13	78.75	−0.62	80.84	80.39	0.45	88.91	86.72	2.19
55–1	88.46	88.71	−0.25	84.78	82.00	2.78	89.81	88.89	0.92
55–2	96.71	96.51	0.20	87.53	87.02	0.51	90.64	91.41	−0.77
55–3	100.31	99.27	1.04	91.70	90.42	1.28	93.72	93.70	0.02
55–4	102.16	100.00	2.16	94.74	94.52	0.22	92.87	94.49	−1.62
56–1	101.26	98.13	3.13	96.23	95.66	0.57	93.48	94.40	−0.92
56–2	100.67	96.84	3.83	97.96	97.07	0.89	101.94	99.19	2.75
56–3	78.49	75.34	3.15	99.21	100.00	−0.79	99.49	99.82	−0.33
56–4	100.46	96.75	3.71	97.38	98.96	−1.58	99.21	99.70	−0.49
57–1	96.60	93.67	2.93	92.85	97.07	−4.22	96.36	97.24	−0.88
57–2	93.25	89.99	3.26	93.73	93.33	0.40	96.13	94.45	1.68
57–3	93.37	89.70	3.67	92.19	91.29	0.90	98.04	94.09	3.95
57–4	80.86	77.37	3.49	83.40	83.64	−0.24	87.90	87.53	0.37
58–1	64.46	61.35	3.11	72.67	73.82	−1.15	78.71	80.17	−1.46
58–2	64.93	61.25	3.68	74.81	69.90	4.91	75.27	75.53	−0.26
58–3	75.06	69.67	5.39	77.10	71.95	5.15	80.65	81.29	−0.64
58–4	84.93	77.11	7.82	77.86	73.31	4.55	85.46	84.76	0.70
59–1	96.89	86.24	10.65	84.98	76.81	8.17	88.64	89.15	−0.51
59–2	114.86	100.00	14.86	94.08	84.28	9.80	94.71	94.25	0.46
59–3	56.70	48.78	7.92	93.35	87.36	5.99	94.04	97.90	−3.86
59–4	78.81	66.63	12.18	93.64	85.41	8.23	94.55	96.76	−2.21
60–1	111.07	92.74	18.33	99.21	84.57	14.64	96.43	100.00	−3.57
60–2	95.22	78.05	17.17	97.33	83.37	13.96	91.59	97.91	−6.32
60–3	84.74	68.89	15.85	94.13	83.55	10.58	89.40	94.29	−4.89
60–4	76.52	61.22	15.30	92.29	78.57	13.72	86.23	88.87	−2.64

Table 19.2 (continued)

	Primary metals			Nonelectrical machinery			Electrical machinery		
Quarter	1	2	3	1	2	3	1	2	3
48–1	91.81	90.73	1.08	96.21	94.29	1.92	101.51	94.28	7.23
48–2	91.48	87.74	3.74	95.66	95.64	0.02	101.68	94.53	7.15
48–3	95.03	89.52	5.51	95.97	95.36	0.61	99.82	92.63	7.19
48–4	97.24	89.15	8.09	93.09	93.03	0.06	100.43	93.20	7.23
49–1	91.49	81.92	9.57	85.98	87.72	−1.74	99.93	92.78	7.15
49–2	91.11	79.45	11.06	86.86	80.86	6.00	99.65	92.68	6.97
49–3	98.16	83.48	14.68	85.67	79.87	5.80	99.17	92.39	6.78
49–4	84.35	70.16	14.19	84.73	81.20	3.53	99.13	92.59	6.54
50–1	89.04	72.81	16.23	90.46	84.15	6.31	98.01	91.82	6.19
50–2	110.85	88.69	22.16	99.86	91.10	8.76	99.39	93.05	6.34
50–3	127.03	100.00	27.03	109.36	96.44	12.92	101.94	95.44	6.50
50–4	121.10	96.03	25.07	111.01	100.00	11.01	100.70	94.46	6.24
51–1	112.97	90.41	22.56	109.01	100.00	9.01	102.77	96.10	6.67
51–2	101.68	82.30	19.38	112.66	100.00	12.66	98.47	92.78	5.69
51–3	86.29	70.92	15.37	106.11	96.84	9.27	98.73	92.99	5.74
51–4	81.65	68.20	13.45	99.14	92.75	6.39	98.69	92.95	5.74
52–1	77.69	65.68	12.01	98.26	91.51	6.75	99.89	93.88	6.01
52–2	76.95	65.87	11.08	95.49	90.17	5.32	99.93	93.71	6.22
52–3	60.46	52.30	8.16	97.61	90.02	7.59	99.98	93.85	6.13
52–4	85.35	74.65	10.70	98.92	92.75	6.17	100.73	94.92	5.81
53–1	90.96	80.43	10.53	102.52	94.07	8.45	99.24	93.92	5.32
53–2	92.85	82.82	10.03	97.96	92.86	5.10	98.27	93.26	5.01
53–3	90.77	80.47	10.30	95.69	91.34	4.35	99.39	94.46	4.93
53–4	82.37	72.87	9.50	90.56	87.96	2.60	98.11	93.55	4.56
54–1	77.86	69.22	8.64	88.40	85.23	3.17	97.73	93.50	4.23
54–2	78.14	69.76	8.38	92.14	85.01	7.13	98.54	94.60	3.94
54–3	74.08	66.35	7.73	92.51	90.44	2.07	98.84	95.06	3.78
54–4	78.48	70.73	7.75	93.88	88.26	5.62	97.78	94.03	3.75
55–1	100.50	90.61	9.89	97.28	91.99	5.29	98.85	94.79	4.06
55–2	109.49	98.58	10.91	99.58	95.79	3.79	100.49	96.37	4.12
55–3	111.61	100.00	11.61	98.90	98.24	0.66	100.19	96.13	4.06
55–4	106.69	95.05	11.64	100.19	99.36	0.83	101.51	97.76	3.75
56–1	91.46	81.20	10.26	100.10	99.48	0.62	101.87	98.46	3.41
56–2	81.31	72.31	9.00	98.54	100.00	−1.46	101.56	98.38	3.18
56–3	78.02	69.73	8.29	97.12	97.64	−0.52	100.97	97.86	3.11
56–4	82.28	73.80	8.48	97.97	98.25	−0.28	100.94	97.90	3.04
57–1	89.84	80.45	9.39	97.87	96.34	1.53	99.61	96.50	3.11
57–2	87.85	78.00	9.85	94.92	95.12	−0.20	99.21	96.16	3.05
57–3	88.16	77.84	10.32	92.06	94.69	−2.63	99.46	96.15	3.31
57–4	80.82	70.49	10.33	85.57	90.76	−5.19	97.70	94.93	2.77
58–1	68.72	58.61	10.11	79.35	81.15	−1.80	97.41	94.81	2.60
58–2	62.84	52.81	10.03	83.56	83.16	0.40	98.82	96.27	2.55
58–3	62.50	52.16	10.34	90.80	91.26	−0.46	99.24	96.65	2.59
58–4	74.90	61.47	13.43	87.74	90.51	−2.77	98.93	96.75	2.18
59–1	90.31	72.00	18.31	92.30	93.32	−1.02	99.07	97.38	1.69
59–2	101.88	79.98	21.90	101.52	100.00	1.52	101.31	99.23	2.08
59–3	100.01	77.29	22.72	100.25	99.99	0.26	100.55	98.81	1.74
59–4	81.58	61.92	19.66	91.35	97.66	−6.31	99.97	97.78	2.19
60–1	117.01	87.79	29.22	95.24	96.88	−1.64	100.60	98.38	2.22
60–2	112.73	82.51	30.22	96.44	95.93	0.51	100.61	98.31	2.30
60–3	109.27	79.29	29.98	93.56	93.69	−0.13	100.96	97.80	3.16
60–4	101.76	72.60	29.16	88.29	90.62	−2.33	100.38	97.94	2.44

Table 19.2 (continued)

	Textile mill products			Paper and allied products			Chemicals		
Quarter	1	2	3	1	2	3	1	2	3
48–1	101.75	95.62	6.13	97.10	93.69	3.41	97.57	96.31	1.26
48–2	106.59	100.00	6.59	97.36	94.02	3.34	96.86	95.25	1.61
48–3	92.94	95.68	−2.74	94.71	91.51	3.20	96.45	94.26	2.19
48–4	92.28	88.21	4.07	90.83	87.69	3.14	93.51	90.70	2.81
49–1	87.98	85.35	2.63	85.67	82.35	3.32	89.88	86.56	3.32
49–2	79.79	78.33	1.46	81.06	77.60	3.46	84.71	81.10	3.61
49–3	86.64	85.53	1.11	85.56	81.48	4.08	85.26	81.12	4.14
49–4	94.50	93.04	1.46	90.18	85.37	4.81	88.85	84.21	4.64
50–1	93.73	91.93	1.80	92.11	86.83	5.28	92.64	87.68	4.96
50–2	94.55	92.33	2.22	96.16	90.26	5.90	98.32	92.89	5.43
50–3	100.04	97.80	2.24	102.07	95.32	6.75	103.65	97.70	5.95
50–4	101.18	99.25	1.93	104.81	97.17	7.64	105.95	99.49	6.46
51–1	101.52	100.00	1.52	107.54	98.73	8.81	106.63	99.75	6.88
51–2	99.01	98.32	0.69	106.33	100.00	6.33	106.77	100.00	6.77
51–3	88.37	87.94	0.43	96.54	88.48	8.06	104.24	98.15	6.09
51–4	84.81	84.46	0.35	90.11	83.34	6.77	101.43	95.91	5.52
52–1	87.31	87.12	0.19	91.02	85.01	6.01	101.20	96.45	4.75
52–2	86.89	86.86	0.03	88.12	82.97	5.15	98.82	94.75	4.07
52–3	93.85	93.56	0.29	89.37	84.39	4.98	99.49	96.01	3.48
52–4	96.77	95.79	0.98	94.18	88.85	5.33	100.46	97.81	2.65
53–1	96.40	94.45	1.95	94.73	89.53	5.20	99.92	98.14	1.78
53–2	99.83	96.76	3.07	96.66	91.42	5.24	101.08	100.00	1.08
53–3	95.40	92.17	3.23	96.69	91.63	5.06	98.92	97.96	0.96
53–4	85.30	82.76	2.54	92.81	88.09	4.72	94.27	94.13	0.14
54–1	83.46	81.38	2.08	91.32	86.79	4.53	90.92	91.23	−0.31
54–2	85.36	83.22	2.14	92.19	88.00	4.19	89.93	88.81	1.12
54–3	88.25	86.00	2.25	93.06	89.09	3.97	90.65	89.78	0.87
54–4	90.73	88.01	2.72	94.02	90.48	3.54	91.87	91.71	0.16
55–1	93.69	90.29	3.40	96.84	93.44	3.40	95.42	95.65	−0.23
55–2	96.06	92.09	3.97	99.72	96.57	3.15	98.72	98.26	0.46
55–3	97.40	92.85	4.55	101.43	98.29	3.14	100.61	99.71	0.90
55–4	99.35	94.44	4.91	102.63	100.00	2.63	101.71	100.00	1.71
56–1	99.92	94.64	5.28	101.59	99.42	2.17	100.12	99.51	0.61
56–2	98.62	92.98	5.64	100.66	98.85	1.81	100.66	99.86	0.80
56–3	98.13	92.16	5.97	99.61	98.50	1.11	100.85	100.00	0.85
56–4	97.44	91.25	6.19	97.27	96.95	0.32	98.91	98.89	0.02
57–1	95.38	89.07	6.31	95.19	95.62	−0.43	98.70	100.00	−1.30
57–2	95.56	89.82	5.74	93.08	94.12	−1.04	98.24	98.68	−0.44
57–3	95.12	89.93	5.19	92.64	94.40	−1.76	98.01	98.05	−0.04
57–4	88.42	83.86	4.56	90.99	93.33	−2.34	95.02	95.04	−0.02
58–1	83.68	79.45	4.23	86.66	89.38	−2.72	89.10	89.34	−0.24
58–2	86.56	82.31	4.25	86.22	89.22	−3.00	88.62	88.67	−0.05
58–3	93.55	89.29	4.26	90.97	94.36	−3.39	92.50	91.86	0.64
58–4	93.86	89.85	4.01	92.63	95.94	−3.31	93.61	92.18	1.43
59–1	97.88	94.99	2.89	92.33	96.01	−3.68	94.37	92.92	1.45
59–2	103.33	99.56	3.77	95.69	98.76	−3.07	98.88	96.01	2.87
59–3	104.08	100.00	4.08	96.68	100.00	−3.32	100.04	96.90	3.14
59–4	98.13	95.05	3.08	94.49	97.09	−2.60	98.30	95.41	2.89
60–1	98.18	94.58	3.60	94.95	97.11	−2.16	98.06	94.46	3.60
60–2	98.94	94.64	4.30	93.59	95.54	−1.95	100.44	95.09	5.35
60–3	95.96	91.58	4.38	92.15	94.27	−2.12	98.87	93.72	5.15
60–4	84.98	83.85	1.13	90.18	91.47	−1.29	95.44	90.98	4.46

Table 19.2 (continued)

	Rubber products			Public utilities		
Quarter	1	2	3	1	2	3
48–1	98.33	90.98	7.35	97.56	99.20	−1.64
48–2	95.32	88.39	6.93	96.86	97.40	−0.54
48–3	95.06	88.34	6.72	98.06	97.34	0.72
48–4	90.43	84.23	6.20	98.69	96.95	1.74
49–1	86.13	79.97	6.16	96.64	93.98	2.66
49–2	82.50	76.44	6.06	94.55	91.95	2.60
49–3	79.96	74.59	5.37	94.90	92.02	2.88
49–4	82.74	78.55	4.19	95.45	91.67	3.78
50–1	86.50	84.18	2.32	98.02	93.05	4.97
50–2	92.44	92.08	0.36	99.91	94.42	5.49
50–3	100.17	100.00	0.17	99.86	94.26	5.60
50–4	102.02	99.50	2.52	100.62	95.43	5.19
51–1	98.14	93.45	4.69	102.19	97.17	5.02
51–2	99.70	93.84	5.86	103.04	98.09	4.95
51–3	95.82	89.81	6.01	102.52	97.76	4.76
51–4	89.40	84.17	5.23	102.33	97.46	4.87
52–1	90.50	85.77	4.73	102.32	97.45	4.87
52–2	88.34	84.20	4.14	100.67	95.49	5.18
52–3	89.95	85.64	4.31	101.72	96.55	5.17
52–4	99.03	93.95	5.08	102.77	97.62	5.15
53–1	100.64	94.41	6.23	101.50	97.18	4.32
53–2	100.22	93.37	6.85	101.85	98.33	3.52
53–3	94.87	88.20	6.67	100.98	98.09	2.89
53–4	84.55	79.17	5.38	98.09	95.41	2.68
54–1	84.23	79.57	4.66	97.45	95.14	2.31
54–2	88.85	84.30	4.55	97.01	95.16	1.85
54–3	81.66	77.90	3.76	97.61	95.57	2.04
54–4	91.85	88.44	3.41	97.48	95.68	1.80
55–1	96.92	94.34	2.58	97.80	96.18	1.62
55–2	101.61	100.00	1.61	98.24	96.60	1.64
55–3	98.02	96.57	1.45	99.57	98.07	1.50
55–4	101.53	99.25	2.28	99.99	98.95	1.04
56–1	94.94	92.15	2.79	100.05	99.26	0.79
56–2	92.41	89.25	3.16	100.92	99.81	1.11
56–3	92.44	89.31	3.13	99.25	98.34	0.91
56–4	93.52	91.00	2.52	98.33	97.92	0.41
57–1	94.42	92.83	1.59	98.60	97.99	0.61
57–2	89.99	89.40	0.59	98.00	98.06	−0.06
57–3	92.18	91.76	0.42	99.12	99.12	0.00
57–4	87.10	86.06	1.04	96.98	97.26	−0.28
58–1	76.41	74.90	1.51	94.73	95.67	−0.94
58–2	77.98	76.10	1.88	93.09	94.30	−1.21
58–3	87.77	85.11	2.66	94.23	95.52	−1.29
58–4	94.21	90.60	3.61	93.95	95.76	−1.81
59–1	96.96	92.71	4.25	95.72	97.58	−1.86
59–2	94.34	89.84	4.50	95.95	98.42	−2.47
59–3	106.14	100.00	6.14	95.85	97.63	−1.78
59–4	99.08	92.03	7.05	95.49	98.24	−2.75
60–1	100.43	91.74	8.69	96.64	99.70	−3.06
60–2	101.17	91.22	9.95	96.16	99.06	−2.90
60–3	97.28	86.74	10.54	95.32	98.26	−2.94
60–4	91.51	80.42	11.09	94.22	96.47	−2.25

where the coefficient of time is of the wrong sign. We conclude that nonelectrical machinery is not subject to an upward drift.

By looking at the results for electrical machinery in table 19.2 we see an example of the bias we are looking for. For electrical machinery from 1951–3 onward, there is a persistent downward drift in the difference $R_t - Wh_t$. This means that the Wharton series has been drifting upwards relative to the R_t series. Computing the appropriate regression for the period 1951–3 to 1960–4 we have

$$Wh_t = -7.337 + 1.022R_t + 0.234t \quad \bar{R}^2 = 0.9316.$$
$$(4.416) \ (0.047) \quad (0.029)$$

The coefficient of time in this equation is significant and of the right sign. On this evidence we conclude in the case of electrical machinery that the Wh_t series is subject to drift since 1951–3.

In the case of autos and equipment the two series are extremely similar, with agreement at all turning points. By looking at table 19.2 it is apparent that there is no systematic drift on the Wh_t series. The regression results yield

$$Wh_t = 20.214 + 0.684R_t - 0.193t \quad \bar{R}^2 = 0.8418.$$
$$(4.338) \ (0.044) \quad (0.044)$$

Although the coefficient of time is significant, it is of the wrong sign. We conclude therefore that for autos and equipment the Wh_t series is subject to no bias drift.

For stone, clay and glass the time path of the two series is very similar. Table 19.2 reveals that there is a persistent upward drift in the Wh_t series. This drift begins in 1950–3 and continues through 1960–4. The regression for the period 1950–3 to 1960–4 yields

$$Wh_t = 8.690 + 0.821R_t + 0.286t \quad \bar{R}^2 = 0.8330.$$
$$(5.965) \ (0.057) \quad (0.033)$$

The coefficient of time is significant. For stone, clay and glass, an element of bias has been found.

Food and beverages reveal the most marked trend in the Wh_t series that we have noted thus far. The time profiles of the two series are extremely similar except for the persistent upward drift in the Wh_t series. This is revealed in table 19.2, where there is a marked downward drift in the difference $R_t - Wh_t$. Computing the appropriate regression for the period 1948–1 to 1960–4 we have

$$Wh_t = 3.980 + 0.885R_t + 0.114t \quad \bar{R}^2 = 0.9628.$$
$$(4.447) \ (0.045) \quad (0.004)$$

The coefficient of time is both significant and of the right sign. Food and beverages is subject to drift.

For textile mill products the time profile and agreement of turning points is remarkably similar. By looking at table 19.2 a slight downward drift in the difference $R_t - Wh_t$ is detected since 1957–1. This suggests that there has been a slight upward drift in the Wh_t series since 1957. Computing the appropriate regression for the period 1957–1 to 1960–4, we have the result

$$Wh_t = 0.490 + 0.933R_t + 0.204t \qquad \bar{R}^2 = 0.9847.$$
$$(3.019)\ (0.033) \quad (0.041)$$

Paper and allied products show a marked upward drift in the Wh_t series from 1951 to 1960. This upward drift is clearly shown in table 19.2. Apart from this drift, the time path of Wh_t is similar to that of the R_t series. Computing the regression for the period 1951–1 to 1960–4, we have

$$Wh_t = 0.176 + 0.916R_t + 0.298t \qquad \bar{R}^2 = 0.9530.$$
$$(3.618)\ (0.037) \quad (0.015)$$

Although chemicals and allied products have a tendency to drift upwards from the period 1951 to 1958, this upward drift does not continue, as seen in table 19.3. The regression for the entire period is,

$$Wh_t = 11.488 + 0.842R_t + 0.055t \qquad \bar{R}^2 = 0.8312.$$
$$(5.278)\ (0.054) \quad (0.018)$$

Although the coefficient of t is significant and has the right sign, we conclude that this series is not subject to bias drift. This result is based on the visual inspection of table 19.2 rather than the regression result. We feel that the table reveals the picture of a cycle rather than systematic drift. It is the long down swing in this cycle that yields the results of the regression, which we feel do not lead to correct judgement on trend drift.

For rubber products the time paths of the two series show agreement in all turning points as can be seen by inspection of table 19.2. Table 19.2 reveals no systematic drift in the difference between the Wharton series and R_t. Computing the appropriate regression for the period 1948–1 to 1960–4, we find

$$Wh_t = 3.068 + 0.919R_t + 0.001t \qquad \bar{R}^2 = 0.8549.$$
$$(4.919)\ (0.053) \quad (0.024)$$

It is apparent from table 19.2 that public utilities is subject to an upward drift. Table 19.2 suggests that this drift did not begin until

1950. Computing the appropriate regression for the period 1950–3 to 1960–4, we find

$$Wh_t = 7.307 + 0.869R_t + 0.199t \qquad \bar{R}^2 = 0.9163.$$
$$(4.408)\ (0.043)\ \ \ (0.010)$$

We have examined the 11 industries under study and found six of these subject to a bias drift. Electrical machinery has been drifting upward since 1951–3, food and beverages since 1948–1, stone, clay and glass since 1950–3, textile mill products since 1957–1, paper and allied products since 1951–1, and public utilities since 1950–3. We assume that the remaining industrial sectors in our sample are not subject to drift.

Let us stop here to make some observations. We have found in all eleven industrial sectors studied, only one, textile mill products, in which the bias drift conforms to previous suppositions about the nature and extent of the drift in the Aggregate Wharton Index. Only in textile mill products do we find a significant upward drift in the Wharton Index commencing in the period after 1957. In one other industry, this drift begins as far back as 1948 and seems to originate for the most part in the period around 1951 to 1953. This, of course, is the Korean war period. Our results suggest that peaks in the years subsequent to the Korean war period have not been full-capacity peaks. This result seems plausible; after 1951–3 the economy's rate of unemployment has never fallen to the level reached in 1951–3, even in the 1955–6 period.

THE ADJUSTMENT OF THE AGGREGATE INDEX

In table 19.3 we present the results of adjusting the Aggregate Wharton Index. Column one is the 30-sector weighted average (using FRB weights) of the original Wharton Component Sector Indexes. This is the series from which we wish to eliminate the bias drift. Column 2 is an 11-sector weighted average of the unadjusted Wharton Indexes under study. Column 3 is the 11-sector weighted average of the Wharton Sector Indexes with zero adjustment in five and adjustment by the amount $-ct$ over the period during which the other six were found to be subject to a biased drift.

On inspecting column 4, which is the empirical counterpart of expression (19.17), it is apparent that by 1953 the Wharton Index is one point too high, and by 1960 this drift has increased to 4.02 points. In terms of the Aggregate Index, the 1953 peak is now at 95 compared to

Table 19.3 The adjustment of the Aggregate Wharton Index

Quarter	Unadjusted Aggregate Wharton Index 1	Eleven sector-weighted average, no adjustment 2	Eleven sector-weighted average, six adjusted 3	2−3 4	1−4 5
1948–1	94.88	94.86	94.85	0.02	94.86
2	93.87	93.88	93.84	0.04	93.83
3	93.16	93.35	93.29	0.06	93.10
4	90.92	91.08	91.01	0.08	90.84
1949–1	86.62	86.79	86.69	0.10	86.53
2	82.33	81.70	81.59	0.12	82.22
3	81.22	81.45	81.32	0.13	81.09
4	79.21	78.97	78.81	0.15	79.06
1950–1	82.46	83.62	83.44	0.17	82.29
2	87.88	89.90	89.71	0.19	87.69
3	93.37	95.49	95.27	0.22	93.15
4	93.72	95.61	95.34	0.27	93.44
1951–1	94.09	95.88	95.54	0.34	93.75
2	93.14	94.83	94.43	0.41	92.73
3	90.16	91.25	90.75	0.50	89.66
4	89.56	90.19	89.60	0.60	88.97
1952–1	90.64	90.86	90.18	0.68	89.96
2	88.22	87.80	87.03	0.77	87.44
3	89.58	88.13	87.27	0.86	88.71
4	95.08	94.74	93.79	0.95	94.13
1953–1	95.79	95.62	94.57	1.04	94.75
2	96.19	96.15	95.01	1.14	95.06
3	95.22	94.84	93.61	1.23	93.99
4	89.79	88.99	87.67	1.32	88.47
1954–1	86.62	85.36	83.95	1.41	85.21
2	86.45	85.05	83.55	1.50	84.95
3	86.32	85.23	83.64	1.59	84.73
4	87.49	86.75	85.07	1.68	85.81
1955–1	90.91	91.18	89.41	1.77	89.14
2	93.74	94.90	93.04	1.86	91.88
3	95.17	96.44	94.49	1.95	93.21
4	96.43	97.62	95.58	2.04	94.38
1956–1	95.31	96.21	94.07	2.14	93.18
2	95.21	95.97	93.74	2.23	92.99
3	93.90	93.47	91.15	2.32	91.58
4	95.64	95.80	93.39	2.41	93.23
1957–1	95.27	95.14	92.63	2.51	92.76
2	94.10	93.29	90.67	2.61	91.49
3	93.32	93.01	90.30	2.71	90.61
4	88.49	87.82	85.01	2.81	85.68

Measurements of capacity utilization

Table 19.3 (continued)

Quarter	Unadjusted Aggregate Wharton Index 1	Eleven sector-weighted average, no adjustment 2	Eleven sector-weighted average, six adjusted 3	2−3 4	1−4 5
1958–1	82.02	80.81	77.90	2.91	79.11
2	80.92	79.64	76.62	3.01	77.90
3	85.09	83.32	80.20	3.11	81.97
4	87.32	85.77	82.55	3.21	84.10
1959–1	89.86	89.37	86.06	3.32	86.54
2	94.02	94.50	91.09	3.42	90.61
3	90.55	89.65	86.13	3.52	87.03
4	89.66	89.04	85.42	3.62	86.04
1960–1	93.13	94.27	90.55	3.72	89.41
2	91.35	91.66	87.84	3.82	87.53
3	89.52	89.22	85.30	3.92	85.60
4	86.12	85.21	81.19	4.02	82.10

96, the 1956 peak is now at 93 compared with 96 and the controversial 1960 peak is now at 89 compared with 93.

It is now clear that the Wharton bias may have been more the result of a long-term build up due to the fact that the 1956 and 1960 peaks were not as high as the 1951–3 peak, rather than the result of some short-term phenomenon associated with the lack of a full cyclical recovery in 1960. This phenomenon probably intensified the drift, but our results place the roots of the bias earlier in the 1950s.

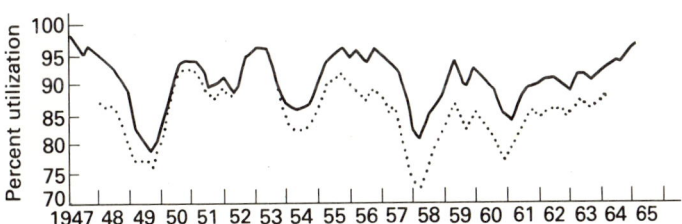

— FRB Series

······ Unadjusted Wharton Series

Figure 19.2 Percentage utilization of capacity 1947–65

COMPARISON OF THE ADJUSTED AND UNADJUSTED WHARTON SERIES WITH ANOTHER MEASURE OF CAPACITY UTILIZATION

Peter Gajewski and Frank de Leeuw have constructed a utilization of capacity series designed for comparison with the manufacturing components of the FRB industrial production index. For comparative purposes and contrast with the Wharton Index their series can be called the FRB series. Their series is based on three indicators, the Commerce Department's series measuring manufacturing capital stock in 1954 dollars, the McGraw-Hill index of manufacturing capacity, and the December–January averages of the Federal Reserve output index for manufacturing divided by McGraw-Hill estimates of the end-of-year 'rates of operation.' Details of the procedure used and a discussion of the results are given in reference 6. We will deal with a comparison of the Gajewski–de Leeuw series, denoted by I_t, with the adjusted and unadjusted Wharton series.

Figures 19.2 and 19.3 give a graphic display of the adjusted and unadjusted Wharton Index in comparison with the I_t series. In figures 19.2 and 19.3, series 1 is the I_t index. The unadjusted Wharton Index is found in figure 19.2 as series 2. The adjusted Wharton Index is series 2 in figure 19.3.

It is apparent by inspection of these two charts that the Wharton series, either adjusted or unadjusted, agrees in all turning points with the Gajewski–de Leeuw series. The cyclical pattern is extremely close. By comparing figure 19.2 with figure 19.3, the bias drift of the Wharton Index, in relation to the series I_t, is not only apparent, but also there is a clear indication that this drift has been reduced by our adjustment

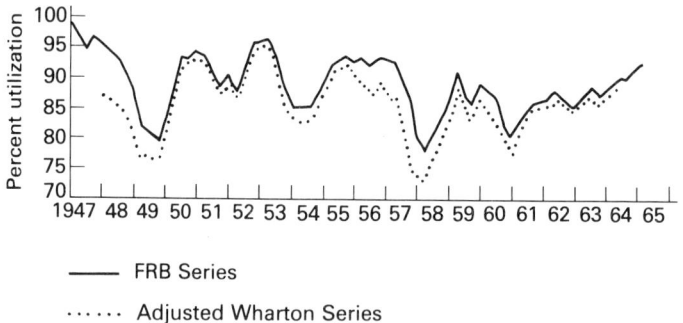

——— FRB Series

······ Adjusted Wharton Series

Figure 19.3 Percentage utilization of capacity 1947–65

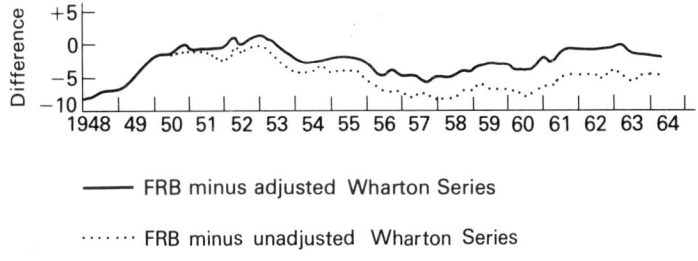

Figure 19.4 Drift in the difference 1948–64

method. Another view of this is also given figure 19.4. Here we see the difference $I_t - Wh_t^A$ and the difference $I_t - Wh_t$. The second difference is series 2. Series 2 has a clear negative trend in it. This suggests that the unadjusted Wharton series has been drifting away from the I_t series. This is supported by the regression result

$$Wh_t - I_t = 2.6798 + 0.0559t \qquad \bar{R}^2 = 0.1583.$$
$$(0.6375)\ (0.0156)$$

The coefficient of t is positive and significant. The difference which results after the adjustment of the Wharton index shows no clear trend. This is supported either by inspection of figure 4, series 1, or the regression result

$$Wh_t^A - I_t = 3.445 - 0.0243t \qquad \bar{R}^2 = 0.0254.$$
$$(0.558)\ (0.0149)$$

Here the coefficient of t is of the wrong sign and is barely significant suggesting that in relation to the series I_t the new Wharton Index is not subject to any bias drift.

CONCLUSIONS

We feel compelled to stress in bare form and all together the main bold assumptions that we have made in this paper. It is a strong assumption to claim that capital and labor are utilized, by industry, at the same rate; that our method of allocating labor force at full capacity among industries is correct; that firms minimize cost in a competitive factor market; that production follows the Cobb-Douglas law; and that our data properly measure the relevant economic concepts.

Some of these assumptions can be relaxed. Possibly other proxies for capital utilization can be tested, but it is unlikely that we shall actually be able to obtain direct estimates of capital utilization for most sectors. We do not contemplate testing alternative laws of production – certainly the CES function. At the same time it will be possible to eliminate some of the effects of least-squares bias in parameter estimation of production functions by estimating industry equations for cost minimization and production simultaneously. We can also introduce distributed lag adjustment processes that may improve our results generally, while enabling us to distinguish between short- and long-run capacity.

Data are continuously improving. In the future we should be able to make better industry estimates and to cover more industries.

In spite of these caveats and others that could be drawn, we feel that assumptions and procedures like ours must be followed if any results at all are to be obtained and that our results are plausible. We judge plausibility by the uses to which we have been able to put the measures. As general cyclical measures, our estimates have served well in investment and profit functions that are part of econometric models. It appears to be the case that our series give cyclical information in econometric equations that is not given by unemployment and other cyclically related series.

As to a more basic use of these series for gauging the long-run economic potential of the American economy. we are less definite that our series are the correct ones. Here we rely on arguments of intuitive plausibility. We feel that if the more extreme estimates that show utilization rates considerably below ours were to be raised to full capacity, the resulting targets would be incompatible and highly inflationary.

REFERENCES

[1] Carl Christ, 'A test of an econometric model for the United States, 1921–47,' *Conference on Business Cycles*, National Bureau of Economic Research, New York (1951).

[2] L. R. Klein, 'A post-war quarterly model: Description and application,' *Models of Income Determination*, Conference on Research in Income and Wealth, Princeton (1964).

[3] Almarin Phillips, 'An appraisal of measures of capacity,' *American Economic Review*, Proceedings, **53**, May (1963), 275–92.

[4] R. M. Solow, 'Technical change and the aggregate production function,' *Review of Economics and Statistics*, **39**, August (1957), 312–20.

[5] Board of Governors of the Federal Reserve System, *The Federal Reserve Bulletin*, current issues, and *Industrial Production, 1957–59 Base*, Washington, DC.

[6] *Measurement of Productive Capacity*, Hearings before the Subcommittee on Economic Statistics, Joint Economic Committee, 87th Congress, Second Session, Washington 1962.

20

Nonlinear Estimation of Aggregate Production Functions

1 INTRODUCTION

For nearly 40 years, the Cobb-Douglas form for the economy-wide production function has been popular, in both theoretical and empirical analyses. A good summary of much of the earlier work with aggregate Cobb-Douglas production functions appears in Paul Douglas' 1947 presidential address to the American Economic Association [11]. This function has been employed in more recent econometric studies of the American economy, such as the Brown-Popkin study of nonneutral technological change in the private domestic nonfarm sector [5] or Zvi Griliches' analysis of the role of research and extension expenditures and education in explaining the observed growth in agricultural productivity [16]. There have been many applications of the Cobb-Douglas production function to individual industries.[1] An interesting recent contribution, based almost completely upon engineering data in the metal machining industry, is a study by Mordecai Kurz and Alan Manne [23].

In recent years, a challenger to the long-reigning champion has appeared.[2] Arrow et al. [1] derived a family of production functions in which the elasticity of substitution is an unspecified constant. This family has both the Cobb-Douglas production function and a fixed-

---

The authors gratefully acknowledge their indebtedness to Harry Eisenpress for advice, to the IBM Corporation for computational assistance, and to Murray Brown, Romesh K. Diwan, Jan Kmenta, and Gian S. Sahota, for critical comments on earlier drafts of this paper. All of the above are absolved, however, from any responsibility for possible errors in this paper. This study was completed while Ronald Bodkin was a member of the research staff of the Cowles Foundation for Research in Economics, at Yale University.

[1] For a reasonably complete summary of these studies, see [34].
[2] The fixed-proportions or 'Leontief' production function, although it has not lacked adherents at the level of individual industries, has never been seriously suggested as an appropriate model for an aggregate production function, to the best of our knowledge.

proportions ('Leontief') production function as special cases.[3] The former is obtained when the elasticity of substitution is equal to unity and the latter emerges in the limit as the elasticity of substitution approaches zero. Thus the long-time champion was threatened, not merely with technological obsolescence, but with the indignity of being swallowed as a special case of a more general formulation. Arrow *et al.* [1] presented both cross-sectional (individual industries, observed across countries) and time-series (from the US economy) evidence that the elasticity of substitution was significantly different from both zero and unity. The conclusion from time-series data was corroborated by Murray Brown and John de Cani [3] and [4], whose alternative derivation of the Constant Elasticity of Substitution (CES) production function and empirical analyses allowed for nonconstant returns to scale. Romesh Diwan, analyzing data from the American manufacturing sector [8], came to a similar conclusion. That the CES production function could be useful at the industry level was shown by the recent Dhrymes-Kurz study of the electric power industry [7], in which a generalization of this form of the production function was used.

Data on factor shares and relative factor prices have always been an integral part of most studies of aggregate production functions. Sometimes these data have been used to check on the supposedly competitive nature of factor returns in the economy, as was done in the studies of Douglas *et al.* [11] and in some of the more recent contributions using the Cobb-Douglas (CD) form, e.g. [16] and [23]. Other studies, such as Robert Solow's pioneering 1957 study of technological change in the context of an aggregate production function [31], generally *assumed* competitive factor pricing (or some variant thereof, such as cost-minimization in competitive factor markets) and then employed the assumed optimality conditions to estimate the parameters of the aggregate production function. This has been true of the studies of the CES production function cited above. In this paper, we shall follow both approaches, providing direct (single equation) estimates of the two principal variants of an aggregate production function and, in addition, estimates obtained from a two-equation system requiring cost-minimization in competitive factor markets.

Our plan of attack, then, is as follows. In section 2, we present alternative specifications of the aggregate production function. Many of

---

[3]As a doctrinal note, we may comment that both popular parametric forms were discovered by others than those whose names are associated with the familiar formulas. It has long been known that wise old Knut Wicksell [37] predated Douglas and Cobb with the log-linear form, while J. K. Whitaker [36] has established H. D. Dickinson's priority of discovery for the CES function.

these specifications involve us in a nonlinear estimating problem if the parameters of the system are estimated simultaneously, rather than in a stepwise manner. In section 3, after a very brief description of the data employed, we present and interpret our results. In section 4, we present some qualifications of our work, a summary of our principal conclusions, and a statement of possible directions for future research.

Throughout this paper, we shall work with Hicks-neutral, disembodied technological change. Thus the output obtainable from a given combination of labor and capital is assumed to grow exponentially over time, in such a manner that the marginal rate of substitution between the unchanged amounts of these two factors remains constant. We thus make no allowance for technological change which can be utilized only if it is embodied in capital equipment of a current vintage and which has been studied in recent papers by Solow [32] and Edmund Phelps [28].[4] Nor do we allow for the possibility of non-neutral technological change over time, as was done to a limited extent (i.e. between 'technological epochs') by Brown and Popkin [5] and Brown and de Cani [3] and [4]. In terms of the CD and CES production functions which we examine, this amounts to the assumption that the parameters of these functions (except possibly the parameters directly representing neutral technological change) are stable over the period of estimation.

2 TWO PRODUCTION FUNCTION MODELS AND NONLINEAR ESTIMATION

Production functions and associated marginal productivity relations are essentially nonlinear relationships, but this aspect has been disguised or circumvented by transformation of variables and stepwise procedures of

---

[4]Benton Massell (in [26], section 4), presents some interesting evidence that investment may in fact serve as a carrier of technological change. In a cross-sectional analysis of individual industries, he finds a significant positive association between the terminal level of technology and the ratio of gross investment to capital stock, expressed as an average over his period of study.

Murray Brown has argued [2] that vintage effects are implicitly taken into account if, instead of gross capital stock, one uses a net series, with the associated depreciation concept including the effects of obsolescence in addition to wear-and-tear. Our text statement may be too pessimistic, that is, we may have implicitly taken some capital vintage effects into account, as we have used a net capital stock, which we took directly from Robert Solow's article [31]. The depreciation concept underlying this net series is based on an attempt to reconstruct book depreciation (in constant prices) and so it may indirectly reflect an obsolescence component.

estimation. With the help of new computer programs being developed, we intend to cut through these nonlinearities to obtain direct estimates of the parameters, through the use of nonlinear methods.[5]

The textbook form of the production function, in two dimensions, is an S-shaped curve passing through the stages of increasing marginal productivity, an inflection point, and decreasing marginal productivity. Eventually, production function specification must deal with multivariate parametric forms of this type. In most cases, investigators have confined themselves, in empirical research, to a single branch of this neoclassical production function – namely the branch of diminishing marginal productivity. Our investigation in this paper will also be confined to two specific parametric representations of single branches of the production function (with two factor inputs, 'labor' and 'capital'), namely the CD and CES representations. As noted above, the latter could imply the former, as a limiting case, but we can illustrate some methodological issues by considering the CD formulation explicitly.

The Cobb–Douglas case, with unconstrained returns to scale

The CD production function (with provision for disembodied neutral technical change at the rate of $10^\lambda - 1$) may be written as:

$$X_t = A 10^{\lambda t} L_t^\alpha K_t^\beta u_t, \tag{20.1}$$

where

X_t = real output,
L_t = the labor input,
K_t = the capital input,
u_t = a random disturbance,
A, λ, α, and β are parameters.

Equation (20.1) is nearly always treated as a linear relationship by making a logarithmic transformation, which yields:

$$\log X_t = \log A + \lambda t + \alpha \log L_t + \beta \log K_t + \log u_t, \tag{20.2}$$

where $\log u_t$ is treated as an additive random error with a zero mean. In this form the function is a single equation which is linear in the unknown parameters: $\log A$, λ, α, and β.

---

[5]The technical aspects of our nonlinear estimating procedures are given in much greater detail in [13]. We should also like to cite an earlier paper, which was called to our attention after this study was completed, by Clark Edwards [12]. Edward's study deals in a manner similar to ours with one of the cases of production function estimates taken up in the present study.

Aggregate production functions

There are two ways (at least) of obstructing this simple transformation to linearity in the unknown parameters.

1. We might specify the unknown, unobserved error term as being additive to the systematic (non-random) portion of output, instead of being multiplicative as in (20.1). In this case, the CD production function relationship is:

$$X_t = A 10^{\lambda t} L_t^{\alpha} K_t^{\beta} + u_t. \qquad (20.3)$$

The minimization of $\sum_t u_t^2$ is no longer a simple linear estimation problem. We shall consider this variant of the CD model.

2. Secondly, if we simultaneously introduce a marginal productivity condition representing cost minimization in competitive factor markets, we shall also have:

$$\frac{p_{K_t}}{w_t} = \left(\frac{\partial X_t^*/\partial K_t}{\partial X_t^*/\partial L_t}\right) v_t$$

$$= \left(\frac{\partial X_t/\partial K_t}{\partial X_t/\partial L_t}\right) v_t$$

$$= \frac{\beta}{\alpha} \frac{L_t}{K_t} v_t, \qquad (20.4)$$

where

X_t^* = the nonstochastic portion of total output (which might be interpreted as 'planned' output),
p_{K_t} = the price of capital services,
w_t = the wage rate,
v_t = a random disturbance reflecting incomplete cost minimization.[6]

As in equation (20.3), the disturbance to the cost minimization equation

[6]One might argue that, because actual output is a random variable, entrepreneurs attempt to minimize the costs of producing an expected level of output. The argument is similar to that of Zellner, Kmenta, and Dréze in [38], where the authors assert that, with a stochastic production function, the appropriate business objective is the maximization of expected, not actual, profits. In this case, equation (20.4) becomes:

$$\frac{p_{K_t}}{w_t} = \left(\frac{\partial X_t^{**}/\partial K_t}{\partial X_t^{**}/\partial L_t}\right) v_t, \qquad (20.5)$$

where X_t^{**} is the expected value (in the probability theory sense) of X_t. If we employ equation (20.1) as the production function and assume that u_t has a logarithmic-normal probability distribution, we shall have:

$$X_t^{**} = E(X_t) = A 10^{\lambda t} L_t^{\alpha} K_t^{\beta} \exp\left(\frac{\sigma^2 \log u}{2}\right)$$

may be written as an additive disturbance:[7]

$$\frac{p_{K_t}}{w_t} = \frac{\beta}{\alpha} \frac{L_t}{K_t} + v_t. \tag{20.6}$$

Equation (20.4), considered by itself, is a linear relationship in ratio variables with an unknown parameter β/α, which becomes evident when it is transformed to:

$$\log \frac{p_{K_t}}{w_t} = \log \frac{\beta}{\alpha} + \log \frac{L_t}{K_t} + \log v_t. \tag{20.7}$$

In the system (20.1)–(20.4), we have α and β as exponents in one equation and as the coefficients of a ratio variable in the other. If we form a joint likelihood function of all dependent or endogenous variables, this nonlinear role of α and β in the system (20.1)–(20.4) is evident. Let us suppose that L_t and K_t are jointly dependent variables and that X_t, p_{K_t}, and w_t are treated as exogenous. This would be a natural assumption to make in a cost-minimization model such as ours, where the expression:

$$w_t L_t + p_{K_t} K_t$$

is to be minimized subject to (20.1) or (20.3), (or to a simple expected value of these expressions), when X_t, w_t, and p_{K_t} are assumed to be given for the minimizing choice of L_t and K_t. The joint probability density function over the sample

$$\Pr(L_t, K_t; w_t, p_{K_t}; X_t; \alpha, \beta, \lambda, A; \sigma_u^2, \sigma_{uv}, \sigma_v^2),$$

where

σ_u^2 and $\sigma_v^2 =$ the population variances of u_t and v_t, respectively,

$\sigma_{uv} =$ the population covariance between these two random disturbances,

---

and

$$\frac{\partial X_t^{**}}{\partial K_t} = \frac{\beta}{K_t} A 10^{\lambda t} L_t^{\alpha} K_t^{\beta} \exp\left(\frac{\sigma^2 \log u}{2}\right),$$

with a similar expression for $\partial X_t^{**}/\partial L_t$: (Here, $\sigma^2 \log u$ is the variance of $\log u_t$.) Accordingly, equation (20.5) reduces to: $p_{K_t}/w_t = [(\beta/K_t)/(\alpha/L_t)]v_t$, which is the result obtained above in the text.

[7] If we use equation (20.3) in deriving (20.6), which would appear to be a natural choice, the error term in the production function, u_t, drops even more easily than it did in the multiplicative error case. Moreover, with an additive error in the production function, X_t^* can be interpreted either as the expected value of output *or* as the level of 'planned' output, provided only that $E(u_t) = 0$.

Aggregate production functions 371

defines the likelihood function to be maximized with respect to the parameter values. If the model is equations (20.1) and (20.4), α and β will enter the likelihood function in a complicated, nonlinear manner. If the error terms are further specified to allow us to consider the model as equations (20.2) and (20.7), the joint distribution of $\log L_t$ and $\log K_t$ will depend on α, β, $\log \alpha$ and $\log \beta$. Consideration of the reduced form equations for $\log L_t$ and $\log K_t$ is instructive.

Algebraic manipulation yields:

$$\log K_t = \left(\frac{\alpha}{\alpha+\beta} \log \frac{\beta}{\alpha} - \frac{1}{\alpha+\beta} \log A \right) - \frac{\lambda}{\alpha+\beta} t + \frac{1}{\alpha+\beta} \log X_t$$

$$- \frac{\alpha}{\alpha+\beta} \log \left(\frac{p_{K_t}}{w_t} \right) + \frac{\alpha}{\alpha+\beta} \log v_t - \frac{1}{\alpha+\beta} \log u_t, \qquad (20.8)$$

$$\log L_t = \left(-\frac{\beta}{\alpha+\beta} \log \frac{\beta}{\alpha} - \frac{1}{\alpha+\beta} \log A \right) - \frac{\lambda}{\alpha+\beta} t + \frac{1}{\alpha+\beta} \log X_t$$

$$+ \frac{\beta}{\alpha+\beta} \log \left(\frac{p_{K_t}}{w_t} \right) - \frac{\beta}{\alpha+\beta} \log v_t - \frac{1}{\alpha+\beta} \log u_t. \qquad (20.9)$$

These are seen to depend on the logarithms of α and β as well as on the ordinary (arithmetic) values of these parameters.[8]

Our CD estimation problems, in the unconstrained case, are thus well defined. We can estimate A, λ, α, β, σ_u^2, σ_{uv}, and σ_v^2 from the joint distribution of L_t and K_t (given p_{K_t}, w_t, and X_t), which is based upon the system (20.1) and (20.4) or the system (20.3) and (20.6). For comparison with earlier work, certainly going as far back as the original investigations of Cobb and Douglas, we shall also obtain ordinary multiple regression estimates (by requiring $\sum_t u_t^2$ to be at a minimum) of both equations (20.1) and (20.3).

A two-step procedure that avoids nonlinearity is to estimate β/α from equation (20.7) (by setting the sum of the logarithmic residuals equal to zero in the sample) and then to regress $\log X_t$ in equation (20.2) on t and $[\log L_t + (\widehat{\beta/\alpha}) \log K_t]$, where $\widehat{\beta/\alpha}$ is the previously obtained estimate of β/α.[9] The coefficient of the combined variables in the regression is an estimate of α. From the estimate of α and of β/α, we may obtain the

---

[8]The estimation problem need not be nonlinear in some cases where the parameters enter nonlinearly only in the constant terms of a regression. However, since the marginal productivity equations are specified, in the present model, without independent constant terms and slope parameters, there is an *essential* nonlinearity in equations (20.8) and (20.9).

[9]In keeping with our assumption of the exogeneity of X_t, we might better regress $[\log L_t \widehat{(\beta/\alpha)} \log K_t]$ on $\log X_t$ and t. The usual procedure is the reverse.

estimate of β as:

$$\hat{\beta} = \widehat{\left(\frac{\beta}{\alpha}\right)} \hat{\alpha}. \tag{20.10}$$

One of the objects of our study is to see whether simultaneous nonlinear estimation of the two equation system, (20.1) and (20.4), yields different results from this two-step linear procedure. To check on this, we shall examine r_{uv}, the sample coefficient of correlation between the disturbances of our two behavioral relationships. It would appear that efficient estimates of the production function parameters will be obtained through the use of this two-step procedure only when the stochastic terms in the two behavioral equations are independent or at least uncorrelated. In several specific instances, the estimates of the parameters based on this procedure will also be computed and compared with those obtained from the simultaneous nonlinear estimation.

The Cobb–Douglas case, with constant returns to scale

With constant returns to scale, the sum of α and β is equal to unity and the CD production function may be written as:

$$\frac{X_t}{L_t} = A 10^{\lambda t} \left(\frac{K_t}{L_t}\right)^{1-\alpha} u'_t, \tag{20.11}$$

or

$$\frac{X_t}{L_t} = A 10^{\lambda t} \left(\frac{K_t}{L_t}\right)^{1-\alpha} + u''_t. \tag{20.12}$$

With constant returns to scale, we may make the stronger assumption that each of the two factors of production will receive a factor price which is just equal to the value (in a competitive product market) of the respective factor's marginal product. As is well known, this assumption will, by virtue of Euler's Theorem, aside from stochastic disturbances, ensure that the total output is exhausted by both of these factor payments. Assuming that 'planned output' X_t^* is the relevant component in factor pricing, we have, for equation (20.11):

$$\frac{\partial X_t^*}{\partial L_t} = \alpha \frac{X_t^*}{L_t} = \alpha \frac{X_t}{L_t} \left(\frac{1}{u'_t}\right). \tag{20.13}$$

Next, we may insert this expression for the 'planned' level of labor's marginal productivity into a behavioral relationship which equates the real wage to this expression with allowance for a multiplicative disturbance. This gives:

$$\frac{w_t}{p_t} = \frac{\partial X_t^*}{\partial L_t} v_t, \tag{20.14}$$

where p_t is the price level of final product and so w_t/p_t represents the 'real' wage. By simple algebraic reduction, we obtain:[10]

$$\frac{X_t}{L_t} = \frac{1}{\alpha}\left(\frac{w_t}{p_t}\right) z_t,$$

where

$$z_t = \frac{u_t'}{v_t}. \tag{20.15}$$

Equations (20.11) and (20.15) are our complete system, as the return to capital is functionally dependent on the return to labor, by Euler's Theorem. Following the analogous model for the individual firm, which yields the profit maximizing output–labor and capital–labor ratios for a given real wage, we shall take the real wage w_t/p_t to be exogenous and the variables X_t/L_t and K_t/L_t to be endogenous, in this system.[11]

We may write down analogous expressions in the case in which the disturbances in the production function and the marginal productivity equation are additive. The corresponding equations are:

$$\frac{\partial X_t^*}{\partial L_t} = \alpha \frac{X_t^*}{L_t} = \alpha\left(\frac{X_t}{L_t} - u_t''\right) \tag{20.16}$$

---

[10]In this case (equality of the real wage to the marginal product of labor with a multiplicative disturbance in the linear homogenous production function), a different side condition will be obtained if one works with the mathematical expectation of output (X_t^{**}, in the notation of footnote 6), rather than with 'planned' output. In particular, $\sigma^2 \log u$ will no longer drop out of the side condition which is analogous to equation (20.15) and hence this new relationship, taken as a single equation, will no longer yield an unbiased estimator of $\log \alpha$. (All these assertions are demonstrated in the previously cited article by Zellner, Kmenta, and Drèze, [38].) However, we did not pursue these points further. It is perhaps worth pointing out that, if the constant-returns-to-scale production function has an additive disturbance, the 'planned' level of output and the mathematical expectation of actual output once more coincide (given that the fairly weak condition $E(u_t'')=0$ holds). Consequently, the argument leading to equation (20.18) below continues to be valid, even under this view of entrepreneurial behavior.

[11]Total profits will not, in fact, be maximized when returns to scale are constant, but our marginal productivity relations are those that would prevail in the case of the competitive individual firm under decreasing returns to scale. In the constant returns to scale case, the marginal productivity relations still yield the highest value of profits per unit of output, i.e. the levels of the capital–labor and hence output–labor ratios which correspond to maximum profit margins.

$$\frac{w_t}{p_t} = \frac{\partial X_t^*}{\partial L_t} + v_t, \qquad (20.17)$$

$$\frac{X_t}{L_t} = \frac{1}{\alpha}\left(\frac{w_t}{P_t}\right) + z_t', \qquad (20.18)$$

where

$$z_t' = u_t'' - \frac{1}{\alpha} v_t.$$

The simultaneous system with additive errors is, therefore, equations (20.12) and (20.18).

As in the CD case with unconstrained returns to scale, the parameters of the production function may be estimated by single-equation methods, by the stepwise procedure, or by nonlinear simultaneous estimation techniques. The earlier remarks on estimation are applicable also to this variant of the CD form, with only minor modifications. As before, we shall be interested in comparisons of these various types of parameter estimates.

The CES case

The CES production function may be written as:

$$X_t = A 10^{\lambda t} [\delta K_t^{-\rho} + (1-\delta) L_t^{-\rho}]^{-\mu/\rho} u_t, \qquad (20.19)$$

where δ, ρ, and μ are additional parameters which we introduce in connection with the CES production function. The elasticity of substitution, denoted as σ in conformity with previous notation used in [1], [3], and [8], is given by:[12]

$$\sigma = \frac{1}{1+\rho}. \qquad (20.20)$$

As in the CD case, the random disturbance may be either multiplicative or additive; thus we could also have:

$$X_t = A 10^{\lambda t} [\delta K_t^{-\rho} + (1-\delta) L_t^{-\rho}]^{-\mu/\rho} + u_t. \qquad (20.21)$$

With either formulation of the disturbance terms, this is a strongly nonlinear function of the parameters A, λ, δ, ρ, and μ, which cannot be

---

[12] Earlier, we used the symbol σ, with a subscript, to denote a population standard deviation or covariance. Here we are using the same symbol to denote the elasticity of substitution. This should engender no confusion because we shall use the symbol σ to represent the elasticity of substitution if and only if it appears without a subscript.

Aggregate production functions

made linear by a logarithmic or other simple transformation. The natural procedure in this case would seem to be to use nonlinear methods of estimation.

It should be noted that we do not assume constant returns to scale by restricting μ to unity. We allow this parameter to be determined from the sample. By not restricting (in the unconstrained case) the sum of the CD parameters, α and β to unity, we achieved the same flexibility in that case. However, as noted above, we do make some calculations for $\alpha + \beta = 1$ in the CD case for comparative purposes.

With the CES formulation, the marginal productivity relationship based upon cost minimization, may be written:[13]

$$\frac{p_{K_t}}{w_t} = \left(\frac{\partial X_t^*/\partial K_t}{\partial X_t^*/\partial L_t}\right) v_t = \frac{\delta}{1-\delta}\left(\frac{K_t}{L_t}\right)^{-(\rho+1)} v_t, \qquad (20.22)$$

$$\frac{p_{K_t}}{w_t} = \left(\frac{\partial X_t^*/\partial K_t}{\partial X_t^*/\partial L_t}\right) + v_t = \frac{\delta}{1-\delta}\left(\frac{K_t}{L_t}\right)^{-(\rho+1)} + v_t. \qquad (20.23)$$

The two-step procedure for estimation of CES functions would be to transform equation (20.22) logarithmically into:

$$\log \frac{p_{K_t}}{w_t} = \log \frac{\delta}{1-\delta} - (\rho+1)\log \frac{K_t}{L_t} + \log v_t \qquad (20.24)$$

and to compute estimates of $\delta/1-\delta$ and $(\rho+1)$ as regression coefficients. The regression of $\log(K_t/L_t)$ on $\log(p_{K_t}/w_t)$ would appear to be more appropriate than the reverse. With estimates of δ and ρ ($\hat{\delta}$ and $\hat{\rho}$, respectively) from this regression of logarithmic ratio variables, one can form:

$$\log X_t = \log A + \lambda t - \frac{\mu}{\hat{\rho}}\log[\hat{\delta} K_t^{-\hat{\rho}} + (1-\hat{\delta})L_t^{-\hat{\rho}}] + \log u_t. \qquad (20.25)$$

It is then possible to estimate A, λ, and μ from a second regression – either of $\log X_t$ and t and $\log[\hat{\delta} K_t^{-\hat{\rho}} + (1-\hat{\delta})L_t^{-\hat{\rho}}]$ or (preferably) of the constructed variable on the first two.[14]

---

[13] A result identical to equation (20.22) may be obtained if one works with the expected value of output from equation (20.19) instead of with 'planned' output. This is true because the expression involving the variance of the logarithm of u_t appears in both the numerator and the denominator of the ratio of the marginal products and, in consequence, it cancels out. (The mathematical details are very similar to those sketched in footnote 6 above). Equation (20.23) may be derived immediately under this approach; for additive errors in the production function, 'planned' output and expected output will generally coincide.

[14] Diwan has followed this estimating technique, in two papers [8] and [10] which have recently come to our attention. Brown and de Cani [3] and [4], also use a variant of this procedure to estimate parameters for their aggregate CES production function.

We did *not*, however, follow this stepwise procedure to get our preferred estimates of the parameters of the CES production function. Our technique, instead, is to form the likelihood function of L_t and K_t (with p_{K_t}, w_t, and X_t given) and find values of A, λ, δ, ρ, and μ that maximize this function. Both the system (20.19) and (20.22) and the system (20.21) and (20.23) are used as alternative sets of constraints. We also consider the ordinary least squares regression estimates of (20.19) and (20.21).

Nonlinear estimation

The unknown coefficients of the linear function:

$$\log X_t = \log A + \lambda t + \alpha \log L_t + \beta \log K_t + \log u_t \tag{20.2}$$

may be estimated in the traditional manner by minimizing:

$$S_1 = \sum_t (\log u_t)^2 = \sum_t (\log X_t - \log A - \lambda t - \alpha \log L_t - \beta \log K_t)^2 \tag{20.26}$$

with respect to $\log A$, λ, α, and β. It is evident that the resulting estimation equations will be linear in the unknown parameters. This is not true for:

$$S_2 = \sum_t (X_t - A 10^{\lambda t} L_t^\alpha K_t^\beta)^2 \tag{20.27}$$

or

$$S_3 = \sum_t (X_t - A 10^{\lambda t} [\delta K_t^{-\rho} + (1-\delta) L_t^{-\rho}]^{-\mu/\rho})^2 \tag{20.28}$$

or

$$S_4 = \sum_t \left(\log X_t - \log A - \lambda t - \frac{\mu}{\rho} \log[\delta K_t^{-\rho} + (1-\delta) L_t^{-\rho}] \right)^2. \tag{20.29}$$

A possible procedure for expression (20.28) is to select some initial values of the unknown parameters, A_0, λ_0, δ_0, ρ_0, and μ_0 and to form the following expression:

$$\begin{aligned} X_{0t} = {} & A_0 10^{\lambda_0 t} [\delta_0 K_t^{-\rho_0} + (1-\delta_0) L_t^{-\rho_0}]^{-\mu_0/\rho_0} \\ & + \left(\frac{\partial X_t}{\partial A}\right)_0 (A - A_0) + \left(\frac{\partial X_t}{\partial \lambda}\right)_0 (\lambda - \lambda_0) \\ & + \left(\frac{\partial X_t}{\partial \delta}\right)_0 (\delta - \delta_0) + \left(\frac{\partial X_t}{\partial \rho}\right)_0 (\rho - \rho_0) \\ & + \left(\frac{\partial X_t}{\partial \mu}\right)_0 (\mu - \mu_0). \end{aligned} \tag{20.30}$$

Aggregate production functions 377

The next step is to find the estimates of A, λ, δ, ρ, and μ which minimize the expression:

$$S'_3 = \sum_t (X_t - X_{0t})^2. \qquad (20.31)$$

Calling these computed parameter estimates A_1, λ_1, δ_1, ρ_1 and μ_1, one may again form a linearized expression:

$$\begin{aligned} X_{1t} = & A_1 10^{\lambda_1 t} [\delta_1 K_t^{-\rho_1} + (1-\delta_1) L_t^{-\rho_1}]^{-\mu_1/\rho_1} \\ & + \left(\frac{\partial X_t}{\partial A}\right)_1 (A - A_1) + \left(\frac{\partial X_t}{\partial \lambda}\right)_1 (\lambda - \lambda_1) \\ & + \left(\frac{\partial X_t}{\partial \delta}\right)_1 (\delta - \delta_1) + \left(\frac{\partial X_t}{\partial \rho}\right)_1 (\rho - \rho_1) \\ & + \left(\frac{\partial X_t}{\partial \mu}\right)_1 (\mu - \mu_1). \end{aligned} \qquad (20.32)$$

From the minimization of

$$S''_3 = \sum_t (X_t - X_{1t})^2, \qquad (20.33)$$

one can compute second-round parameter estimates, A_2, λ_2, δ_2, ρ_2, and μ_2. One can then continue this procedure iteratively until the parameter estimates appear to converge to a particular set of values.[15]

Another approach, which is in fact the one upon which our estimates in section 3 are based, is to form the system:

$$\frac{\partial S_3}{\partial A} = 0 \quad \frac{\partial S_3}{\partial \lambda} = 0 \quad \frac{\partial S_3}{\partial \delta} = 0 \quad \frac{\partial S_3}{\partial \rho} = 0 \quad \frac{\partial S_3}{\partial \mu} = 0. \qquad (20.34)$$

These are five simultaneous nonlinear equations in the five unknown parameters. Each of these equations can be expanded about assumed initial values of the parameters as follows:

$$\begin{aligned} \frac{\partial S_3}{\partial A} = & \left(\frac{\partial S_3}{\partial A}\right)_0 + \left(\frac{\partial^2 S_3}{\partial A^2}\right)_0 (A - A_0) \\ & + \left(\frac{\partial^2 S_3}{\partial A \, \partial \lambda}\right)_0 (\lambda - \lambda_0) + \left(\frac{\partial^2 S_3}{\partial A \, \partial \delta}\right)_0 (\delta - \delta_0) \\ & + \left(\frac{\partial^2 S_3}{\partial A \, \partial \rho}\right)_0 (\rho - \rho_0) + \left(\frac{\partial^2 S_3}{\partial A \, \partial \mu}\right)_0 (\mu - \mu_0) = 0. \end{aligned} \qquad (20.35)$$

[15]This is the method used by Clark Edwards [12] to estimate, by single equation methods, CD production functions in agriculture, with additive errors. Compare this with the use of gradient methods by Herman Chernoff and Nathan Divinsky [6].

Similar expression for $\partial S_3/\partial \lambda$, $\partial S_3/\partial \delta$, $\partial S_3/\partial \rho$, and $\partial S_3/\partial \mu$ about A_0, λ_0, δ_0, ρ_0, and μ_0 yield five linear equations in the five unknown parameters, which can then be solved for A_1, λ_1, δ_1, ρ_1, and μ_1. We then proceed iteratively. This technique, with modifications to approach the minimum S_3 efficiently, is the procedure followed by Eisenpress and Greenstadt in [13].[16] This procedure guarantees convergence to a local extremum, but we cannot be certain that we have found the global minimum. The number of iterations required will, of course, depend upon how accurate the initial guesses of the parameter values turn out to be, but it has been found that, with 'average luck', convergence is obtained after 10–15 iterations.[17]

Maximum likelihood estimation of parameters in a system of equations follows the same principles. Even if the equations to be estimated are linear, the joint likelihood function will generally lead to nonlinear estimation equations. Hence, essentially the same methods that have been used for solving the nonlinear estimation equations of maximum likelihood estimation for a system of linear structural equations can be employed in the treatment of a nonlinear structural system.

3 THE DATA AND SOME SUBSTANTIVE RESULTS

The data employed are those used in [1], which will facilitate comparisons with this original study of an aggregate CES production function. The immediate source of data used in Arrow et al. [1] was Solow's 1957 study of technological change in the context of an aggregate production function [31, p. 135]. The concept of real output is real private, nonfarm gross national product, i.e. both the government and the agricultural sectors have been excluded. The capital stock, which is a net concept and which includes land and mineral deposits, is measured in constant dollars, while the labor input is measured in manhours. Solow gives a series for the property share, the complement of which may be taken as the labor share. From these

---

[16]This method has previously been used in other nonlinear estimation problems. For an interesting application to the estimation of a particular type of single equation, see James Tobin's article on limited dependent variables [33]. This method is known as 'scoring' in statistical literature.

[17]The better one's initial guesses are, of course, the fewer the number of iterations which are required to obtain convergence. It seems likely that the initial guesses regarding these parameters could be improved by running a straight regression on a Taylor's series approximation to the CES production function (as developed by Jan Kmenta in [21]), which is linear in the combinations of the parameters to be estimated. First guesses of the estimates of the structural parameters can then be unscrambled from the estimated regression coefficients. However, we did not follow this approach here.

Aggregate production functions 379

share data, we can disentangle real factor prices through the use of accounting identities. The data refer to the US economy, over the period 1909 to 1949. Solow's more complete discussion indicates his sources and other details. There is, in general, no need to repeat that discussion here.

We may pause briefly to consider one problem, however, before passing to the statistical results. Capital data are most easily obtained as a series of *available* capital, while the notion most relevant to the concept of a production function is that of the flow of capital services. Solow's solution to this problem was to distinguish between available capital and capital actually employed. He assumed that capital and labor were equally underemployed during slack times so his estimate of employed capital for a particular year was that year's stock of available capital multiplied by the proportion of the labor force employed during the year.

One may criticize the assumption of such strong short-run complementarity between the two factors which this procedure entails, and Solow himself seemed to regard it as only a rough approximation that was better than no adjustment at all.[18] Thus, he pointed out that this procedure does not register a change in the capital input when the flow of capital services from a given amount of capital in use varies, as would occur if, for example, the length of the work-week changes. We believe that a somewhat better procedure is to obtain an independent measure of the degree of capacity utilization, constructed from series relating to individual industries at a detailed level of disaggregation, as was done for the aggregate production function estimated in [19].[19] But independent estimates of the degree of capacity utilization do not

[18] Actually, as Robert Solow has pointed out in conversation, a more fundamental problem arises. With either the CD or CES production function, the marginal productivity of capital is never zero (except for certain limiting values of the parameters in the case of the CES production function) for any finite amount of capital. Consequently, in the short run one might expect that the existing stock of capital would be fully used, since, once produced, it can be economically operated with even a zero quasi-rent, as long as it has positive marginal productivity. Nevertheless, for our empirical work some adjustment for underutilization of the capital stock would appear to be necessary, since we strongly believe that in the 'real world' plant and equipment, just like the labor force, can be less than fully employed. One might attempt to escape from this dilemma by bringing in the notion of the user cost of capital as an element of variable cost. However, it is not clear, in a deep recession, that the marginal user cost of the economy's stock of capital is positive. It may well be true that further utilization of the capital stock might prove beneficial to its longevity. In any case, one might just as well admit that the aggregate production function is a 'first approximation' which entails some amount of misspecification.

[19] A recent study of capacity utilization for selected two-digit manufacturing industries [20] has suggested, however, in a reassuring way that output measures of capacity utilization closely follow labor-input measures.

exist for the American economy prior to World War II, so this avenue is not open to us.[20] We have, therefore, decided to use Solow's series of employed capital for several reasons: first, it seems doubtful that one can do any better, for this historical period; secondly, the use of the Solow series will facilitate comparisons with the results of [1]; and thirdly, the data are readily available.

We may now turn to the substantive results of our investigation, which are presented in tables 20.1 to 20.3. (Rows (5) and (6) of table 20.3 should be ignored for the moment. They will be explained and discussed below.) Table 20.1 presents estimates of the parameters of the CD production function with unconstrained labor and capital elasticities, while table 20.2 gives estimates of the CD parameters with the labor and capital exponents constrained to add to unity. Table 20.3 presents parameter estimates for the CES production function. The symbols for parameter estimates or simple transformations of these parameter estimates, which are used as column headings, should be self-explanatory. We employ the same symbols in this section as in section 2. In the cells comprising these columns, the upper figure is the parameter estimate itself, while the figure below it, in parentheses, is (where given and/or appropriate) the associated standard error. The upper and lower figures $\bar{R}^2$ and $\bar{S}_u$, respectively, in the next to last column, are the coefficient of multiple determination and the estimated standard deviation of residuals from the production function relationship, both adjusted for degrees of freedom. The final column gives the von Neumann-Hart statistic (the ratio of the mean square successive difference of the residuals of the production function relation to the variance of these residuals). Finally, r_{uv} is the estimate from the sample of the correlation coefficient, under simultaneous estimation, between the residuals of the production function equation and those of the marginal productivity condition.

In all three tables, the first row is a straight (linear in the logarithms, except for table 20.3) regression of the production function relationship with a multiplicative error, while the second row is a straight (non-linear) regression of this relationship with an additive error. Thus, in tables 20.1 and 20.3, the dependent variable in the first two rows is total output, X_t, while in table 20.2 the dependent variable is X_t/L_t, the average productivity of labor. The third row in all cases presents the parameter estimates obtained by simultaneous estimation of the two-

[20]It is important to have an independent measure of the degree of capacity utilization. If one attempts to get this measure from the output series which serves as the variable to be 'explained' by the aggregate production function, this might induce spurious intercorrelation between capital input and the level of output, possibly biasing the estimated parameters. There are some capacity utilization series available for the 1920s and 1930s, but these are based directly on the movement of aggregate output.

Table 20.1 Estimates of the parameters of the Cobb-Douglas production function, with unconstrained returns to scale

	A or $\log A$ (1)	α (2)	β (3)	$\alpha+\beta$ (4)	λ (5)	10λ (6)	$\bar{R}^2$ S_u (7)	δ^2/S^2 (8)
Straight regression, multiplicative error (1)	1.9564 (0.0202)	1.167 (0.0505)	0.035 (0.054)	1.202 (0.048)	0.00696 (0.00033)	1.0162	0.9925 0.01353	1.38
Straight regression, additive error (2)	88.31 (5.66)	1.145 (0.0696)	0.062 (0.073)	1.207 (0.064)	0.00690 (0.00043)	1.0160	0.9899 2.807	1.07
Simultaneous estimation, multiplicative errors[a] (3)	1.7947 (0.0044)	0.960 (0.061)	0.496 (0.032)	1.456 (0.093)	0.00484 (0.00054)	1.0112	0.9795 0.02234	0.66
Simultaneous estimation, additive errors[b] (4)	61.87 (0.78)	0.964 (0.065)	0.501 (0.034)	1.465 (0.098)	0.00526 (0.00063)	1.0122	0.9811 3.839	0.64

Source: See text.
[a] $r_{uv} = -0.0101$.
[b] $r_{uv} = -0.0063$.

Table 20.2 Estimates of the parameters of the Cobb-Douglas production function, with constant returns to scale

	A or $\log A$ (1)	α (2)	β (3)	$\alpha + \beta$ (4)	λ (5)	10λ (6)	$\bar{R}^2$ S_u (7)	δ^2/S^2 (8)
Straight regression multiplicative error (1)	1.9803 (0.0232)	1.081 (0.055)	−0.081 (0.055)	1.00 (…)	0.00806 (0.00025)	1.0187	0.9712 0.01623	0.841
Straight regression additive error (2)	97.6 (5.90)	1.102 (0.062)	−0.102 (0.062)	1.00 (…)	0.00811 (0.00025)	1.0189	0.9658 3.725	0.762
Simultaneous estimation, multiplicative errors[a] (3)	1.8037 (0.00445)	0.658 (0.0028)	0.342 (0.0028)	1.00 (…)	0.00705 (0.00030)	1.0164	0.9322 0.02489	0.335
Simultaneous estimation additive errors[b] (4)	63.8 (0.73)	0.660 (0.0028)	0.340 (0.0028)	1.00 (…)	0.00745 (0.00035)	1.0173	0.9244 5.539	0.302

Source: See text.
[a] $r_{uv} = -0.377$.
[b] $r_{uv} = -0.394$.

Table 20.3 Estimates of the parameters of the CES production function

	A or $\log A$ (1)	ρ (2)	$\sigma = (1/1+\rho)$ (3)	δ (4)	μ (5)	λ (6)	10λ (7)	$\bar{R}^2$ S_u (8)	δ^2/S^2 (9)
Straight regression, multiplicative error (1)	1.6466 (0.1083)	9.593 (7.591)	0.0944	0.9975 (0.0160)	1.210 (0.0456)	0.00675 (0.00036)	1.0157	0.9926 0.01346	1.395
Straight regression, additive error (2)	40.46 (9.37)	10.18 (8.713)	0.0894	0.9992 (0.0061)	1.220 (0.0625)	0.00663 (0.00048)	1.0154	0.9900 2.731	1.085
Simultaneous estimation, multiplicative errors[a] (3)	1.7340 (0.0252)	1.130 (0.4169)	0.4694	0.6037 (0.0958)	1.238 (0.058)	0.00643 (0.00041)	1.0149	0.9804 0.02186	0.477
Simultaneous estimation, additive errors[b] (4)	58.39 (1.62)	0.4750 (0.1891)	0.6780	0.4471 (0.0434)	1.362 (0.0905)	0.00589 (0.00061)	1.0137	0.9834 3.591	0.618
Simultaneous estimation, less preferred specification of endogenous variables, multiplicative errors[c] (5)	1.7997 (0.00814)	−0.0065 (0.145)	1.0065	0.3391 (0.0312)	1.250 (0.0896)	0.00583 (0.00052)	1.0135	0.9817 0.02114	0.523
Simultaneous estimation, less preferred specification of endogenous variables, additive errors[d] (6)	63.13 (1.22)	−0.0590 (0.142)	1.063	0.3287 (0.0302)	1.255 (0.0907)	0.00648 (0.00056)	1.0150	0.9835 3.585	0.534

Source: See text.
[a] $r_{uv} = -0.72524$.
[b] $r_{uv} = -0.3575$.
[c] $r_{uv} = -0.1974$.
[d] $r_{uv} = -0.0983$.

equation system with multiplicative errors, while the fourth row gives similar estimates when the small system has additive errors. (In all cases, the parameter estimates in these rows are determined by non-linear estimation procedures.) In tables 20.1 and 20.3, the associated marginal productivity relationship is one of cost minimization, as outlined in section 2. The exogenous variables are t, X_t, and p_{K_t}/w_t, while the endogenous variables are the inputs, L_t and K_t. In table 20.2, the side condition is a stochastic equality between the marginal product of labor and the real wage. The exogenous variables are t and w_t/p_t, and the endogenous variables are X_t/L_t and K_t/L_t. In rows (1) and (3) of all three tables, the computations are performed on the logarithms of all the variables, while in rows (2) and (4), the arithmetic values are used instead. (This point explains the incomparability of the constant terms and the estimated standard deviations of residuals, between adjacent rows.)

The statistical picture which emerges is one of a very tight fit regardless of the variant of the production function which is selected. This is hardly surprising, in view of the strong trend in the output variable. We shall be more interested in the statistical significance of individual parameter estimates. In general, the residuals of the production function equation are significantly autocorrelated, as indicated by the generally low values of the von Neumann-Hart statistic.[21] Thus our statistical tests of significance, performed below, are somewhat vitiated by the presence of this phenomenon, although in many cases the t ratios are high enough that one might still be willing to place a fair amount of confidence in the statistical test under examination. In general, a very similar picture emerges whether the stochastic terms appear in multiplicative or additive form. The one exception to this generalization is the two sets of simultaneous estimates of the CES production functions (rows (3) and (4) of table 20.3).[22]

[21] For the number of observations employed (41), an approximate critical value of the von Neumann-Hart statistic, at the 5 per cent level, is 1.53 (see [17]). Since all of the observed values of this statistic are below this critical value, we may conclude that the residuals of the production function relationship are significantly autocorrelated, at this level of statistical significance. In fact, most of these production function equations, including all of those estimated by simultaneous equation methods, have significantly autocorrelated residuals at the 1 per cent level also.

[22] Our findings in this regard contrast with those of Edwards' study of agricultural production functions [12]. Using the CD form with cross-sectional data on individual farms, Edwards found, in two cases out of four, marked differences in the estimated structure depending upon whether the additive or multiplicative form of the error term was employed. The sum of the production function exponents (the elasticities of output with respect to the productive factors) was, however, quite insensitive to the specification of the error term.

We may now proceed to a discussion of the picture of the economic structure which emerges. The parameter estimates of the straight regressions are quite different from those generated by the simultaneous system. Before rejecting the existence of the marginal productivity equations under competitive conditions in the factor markets (and, for our constrained CD function, in the product market also), we should note that the picture of economic structure which emerges from these straight regressions is hardly believable. Thus both the constant returns and the unconstrained returns CD straight regressions show increasing returns to labor as a variable input, while the contribution of the capital input is not statistically significant. The view of economic structure which the straight CES regressions present, while not consistent with the straight CD regressions, is hardly more satisfactory. Here, it is the capital input which appears to do all the work, as indicated by a parameter estimate of δ insignificantly different from unity. Moreover, in the straight CES regressions, the sampling error of ρ is so large that one cannot estimate σ, the elasticity of substitution, with any degree of accuracy. Thus, although the point estimate of σ is very close to zero,[23] ρ is also not significantly different from zero, which would correspond to a unitary elasticity of substitution (the CD case). For these reasons, we are inclined to reject the straight regression estimates, rather than the existence of the marginal productivity side condition. One might explain these poor results, which diverge rather widely from the predictions of economic theory, in terms of single equation bias. Our results in rows (5) and (6) of table 20.3, which are discussed below, suggest that the parameter estimates are not insensitive to the specification of which variables are treated as endogenous and which are taken to be exogenous.

Next, we may turn to the question of returns to scale. For either the CD or CES formulation, we find evidence of increasing returns. Thus,

[23]One may estimate the standard error (denoted SE) of σ by applying the following approximation formula:

$$\text{SE}\,[f(x)] = |f'(x_0)|\text{SE}(x), \tag{20.i}$$

where $f(x)$ is a differentiable function of a random variable x, and x_0 is a fixed value of x. Applying this formula to the problem at hand, we shall have:

$$\text{SE}(\sigma) = \text{SE}\left(\frac{1}{1+\rho}\right) = \frac{1}{(1+\rho_0)^2}\text{SE}(\rho) \tag{20.ii}$$

Even if we chose ρ_0 to be 9.6 or 10.2 (its point estimates from the sample, depending upon whether one uses the formulation with multiplicative errors or additive errors), the sampling error of σ still turns out to be 0.068 or 0.070, respectively. Thus, even under these very generous assumptions, the estimates of σ, based upon the straight regressions, are not significantly different from zero.

for the CD function, the sum of the exponents in table 20.1 is significantly greater than unity, both t ratios for the simultaneous estimation results exceeding 4.5.[24] For our CES production function, we need merely examine the point estimates of μ and the significance of the difference of these estimates from unity. For our preferred results in rows (3) and (4), we have point estimates of returns to scale of 1.24 (with multiplicative errors) or 1.36 (with additive errors). In both cases, these point estimates are, by conventional criteria, significantly above the constant returns to scale value of unity, the t ratio in both cases being of the order of 4.0.

We may compare our results with those of some other studies of the aggregate production function. Using these same data, Walters [35] also found evidence of increasing returns to scale. Diwan [10] has examined data for the aggregate American economy and its manufacturing sector for several alternative specifications of the aggregate production function. His conclusion is that returns to scale are significantly greater than unity and quantitatively important in explaining the observed growth in output per head during the first half of the twentieth century.[25] Brown and Popkin [5] found evidence of increasing returns to scale in one of their three epochs, as did Brown and de Cani [4] in two of three epochs. At an industry level, Dhyrymes and Kurz [7] found, in the electric power industry, sharply increasing returns to scale with respect to the labor input, and mildly increasing returns to scale with regard to the fuel and capital inputs. Also, Gian S. Sahota [30] found evidence of increasing returns to scale for a group of firms in the US sulfur industry but no evidence against constant returns to scale in the US potassium industry. On the other hand, Paul Douglas' original research [11] gave very little support to the hypothesis of increasing returns to scale.[26]

---

[24]For the CD function, one might be tempted to compare $\bar{R}^2$s, the coefficients of multiple determination, between tables 20.1 and 20.2. This procedure, however, is not appropriate, because the dependent variable is not the same in the two tables. For the logarithmic variants in rows (1) and (3), $\bar{S}_u$, the estimated standard deviation of the residuals, is comparable between the two tables. This measure does indicate a tighter fit (after adjustment for degrees of freedom lost) with unconstrained returns to scale.

[25]Diwan [10] also cites evidence of increasing returns to scale in production functions fitted (by other investigators) to German and Australian data.

[26]Marvin Frankel [14] has examined the interrelationship between the aggregate production function and that of an individual firm in the economy. Frankel, who also finds some empirical evidence of increasing returns to scale in the aggregate production function, has an ingenious explanation of how the production function for the individual firm (or industry) can possess constant returns to scale and still give rise to increasing returns to scale in the aggregate.

Tentatively accepting the hypothesis of increasing returns to scale, we may compare tables 20.1 and 20.3 to see what support they provide for the hypothesis of a nonunitary elasticity of substitution. Looking at the simultaneous estimation results in rows (3) and (4), we see that the coefficients of multiple determination are slightly higher in table 20.3. Moreover, the point estimates of ρ (1.13 and 0.48) are both at least 2.5 times their respective standard errors and so are statistically significant, by conventional criteria. The corresponding point estimates of σ, the elasticity of substitution, are 0.47 (with multiplicative errors) and 0.68 (with additive errors). Using the procedure to calculate approximate standard errors of σ which has been outlined in footnote 23, we find that the standard error of our estimates of σ is roughly 0.10 in both cases. Thus, our estimates of the elasticity of substitution are significantly different from both the 'Leontief' special case of a zero value and the CD special case of a unitary value.

We may compare our estimates of σ with those of several other studies. Using these data with a procedure based on the assumption of constant returns to scale, Arrow et al. [1] estimated σ to be 0.61.[27] Brown and de Cani [3 and 4], employing a distributed lag variant of a cost-minimization relationship (which, as we showed in section 2, allows for nonconstant returns to scale) as the first step of a two-step procedure, estimated values of a long-term elasticity of substitution from 0.31 to 0.55, based on data on the US nonfarm private domestic sector, for the total period of 1890–1958. Using share data on the total US economy over the period 1900–57, Irving Kravis [22] estimated a value for the elasticity of substitution equal to 0.64. By a very similar technique, Kendrick and Sato [18] estimated σ as 0.58, for the private domestic economy over the period 1919–1960. Diwan [8] has estimated, for the US manufacturing sector over the period 1919–58, values of the elasticity of substitution equal to 0.54 or 0.68, depending upon which depression years are omitted. His technique is one of fitting a cost-minimization relationship as the first step of a two-step procedure. Thus our results are broadly consistent with those of a number of other studies of the aggregate production function, some of which used techniques quite different from those employed in this study.[28]

We may now examine the implied rates of disembodied, neutral

[27]Actually, the estimate of σ in [1] was 0.57, but one of us found himself unable to reproduce that estimate. Personal correspondence with Professor Arrow confirmed the existence of a small numerical error in the original calculations.

[28]The view that the CD value of a unitary elasticity of substitution is inaccurate has not been universally accepted, however, especially at the industry level. Thus Griliches [16] tests for a nonunitary elasticity of substitution for the agricultural sector and rejects this hypothesis in favor of the CD production function. In a like manner, Sahota tests the

technological progress (the column (6) value minus unity for tables 20.1 and 20.2, and the column (7) value minus unity for table 20.3). Our preferred point estimates of this growth rate come from the simultaneous estimation results of table 20.3. We take this rate to be 1.49 per cent per annum, using the multiplicative errors formulation of row (3) or 1.37 per cent per year, with additive errors. As Diwan [9] and Walters [35] have pointed out, allowing for increasing returns to scale reduces one's estimates of the pace of neutral technological progress of the disembodied type in a period such as this one during which factor inputs increased rapidly. This assertion can be confirmed by comparing column (6) of table 20.1 with the same column in table 20.2. The point is also valid for the CES formulation of the aggregate production function. Using those data, together with the assumption of constant returns to scale in their CES production function, Arrow et al. [1, p. 244] estimated a rate of neutral technological progress equal to 1.83 per cent per year, which is somewhat larger than the estimates of our table 20.3.[29]

In section 2, we raised the problem of comparing the results of a two-step estimation procedure (in which the parameters of the marginal productivity side condition are estimated first and then the remaining parameters are estimated from the production function relation) with those obtained by simultaneous estimation. It is time to return to this

---

elasticity of substitution against unity, between labor and capital at the firm level for United States fertilizer-mineral industries [30] and among labor, capital, and land at the village level for Indian agriculture [29]. In both cases, he rejects the hypothesis of a nonunitary elasticity of substitution in favor of the CD production function. Kurz and Manne [23] also test for a nonunitary elasticity of substitution with engineering data on the metal machining industry. Their conclusion is that the addition of another free parameter adds very little and that the CD formulation of the production function is quite adequate for this industry. In fact, Fuchs [15] has argued that the Arrow et al. cross-country data on individual industries support a CD function (after a correction is made for the level of economic development in the particular country) better than they support a CES production function with a nonunitary σ. (On the other hand, Leontief [24] has argued that these cross-country data on individual industries and similar data in [27] support a fixed-proportions or 'Leontief' production function better than they do a general CES formulation.) One industry study that provides some support to a general CES formulation of the production function is Dhrymes and Kurz's study of the electric power industry [7]. They found small but significant values for the elasticity of substitution between capital and fuel inputs (these values were in the range between 0.05 and 0.20), although there appeared to be virtually no substitutability between the labor input and the other two.

[29]The slight numerical error in the Arrow et al. published estimates of σ for their aggregate production function also affects to a very minor extent their estimate, from these data, of the pace of neutral disembodied technological progress. Employing the corresponding revised regression estimates, we have recomputed this rate to be 1.82 per cent per year.

question. For the CD variant, the two procedures would appear to yield very similar results. In table 20.1, we find that both coefficients of correlation, between the residuals in our two structural equations, are quite small and insignificant. In table 20.2, these correlation coefficients are somewhat larger and possess statistical significance by the usual tests. Nevertheless, the direct estimate of α, the only parameter that appears in the side condition, agrees (for both the variant with multiplicative errors and that with additive errors) to three decimal places with the corresponding estimates based on simultaneous estimation techniques.[30]

However, with the CES production function, the comparison yields different results. The large negative intercorrelation between the disturbances of the two structural equations, especially in the formulation with multiplicative errors, leads one to suspect that, in this case, the two-step procedure will yield different results from those based upon simultaneous estimation. This suspicion may be further checked by examining the variant of the cost-minimization equation with multiplicative errors, for the CES case. Since we take relative factor prices to be exogenous in our cost minimization model, we may rewrite equation (20.24), with the time subscript t omitted, as:

$$\log \frac{K}{L} = \frac{\log(\delta/1-\delta)}{1+\rho} + \frac{1}{1+\rho} \log \frac{w}{p_K} + z'', \qquad (20.36)$$

or

$$\log \frac{K}{L} = \frac{\log(\delta/1-\delta)}{1+\rho} + \sigma \log \frac{w}{p_K} + z'', \qquad (20.37)$$

where

$$z'' = \frac{1}{1+\rho} \log v.$$

Regressing $\log(K/L)$ on $\log(w/p_K)$, we obtain:

$$\log \frac{K}{L} = -\underset{(0.0581)}{0.115} + \underset{(0.0824)}{0.757} \log \frac{w}{p_K}. \qquad (20.38)$$

(As before, the numbers below the parameter estimates, in parentheses, are standard errors.) Consequently, we obtain another estimate (0.76) of

---

[30]Preliminary calculations (based on a less preferred specification of exogenous and endogenous variables) with the CD form permitting nonconstant returns to scale also indicated a substantial agreement between the estimates based on the two-step procedure and those based on the simultaneous estimation approach, although the agreement was not so close as with the constant-returns-to-scale CD production function.

the elasticity of substitution, also significantly different (by conventional standards) from either zero or unity. However, this estimate is appreciably different from 0.47, the corresponding parameter estimate of σ from row (3) of table 20.3, which is based upon simultaneous estimation techniques. Although we have not carried out the remainder of the two-step estimating procedure for the CES production function, it seems quite possible that some of these parameter estimates would differ somewhat from their corresponding numbers in row (3) of table 20.3.[31] (In any case, we are of course certain that the estimates of ρ and δ will be different.)

Finally, we may return to the issue raised above, namely the effect on the parameter estimates of the choice as to which variables should be exogenous and which should be endogenous. Rows (5) and (6) of table 20.3 present simultaneous equations estimates of the parameters of the aggregate CES production function, with the labor and capital inputs being exogenous and real output and relative factor prices being endogenous (just the opposite of our previous treatment). This would be an appropriate model if factors were always fully employed and if the growth of the labor and capital inputs over time were totally unresponsive to economic conditions. These results are quite different from those in rows (3) and (4) of table 20.3, although the conclusions of significant increasing returns to scale and the resulting lower estimates of the pace of neutral technological progress than the estimate presented in [1] continue to hold. The big difference, of course, is in the estimates of ρ and δ. The former is, with this specification, not significantly different from the CD value of zero, yielding values of the elasticity of substitution, in column (3), which are quite close to unity. The estimate of δ is also quite close to the corresponding CD measure, as one can verify by dividing the column (3) values of table 20.1, in rows (3) and (4), by the appropriate degree of homogeneity, which is represented by the corresponding column (4) value.[32] We do not

---

[31] Unscrambling the estimate of δ from equation (20.38), we find that this value is 0.413, which is somewhat different from the corresponding estimate of this parameter in row (3) of table 20.3.

[32] The small and insignificant coefficients of correlation between the residuals of the two structural equations suggest that, with this specification of exogenous and endogenous variables, the two-step procedure would yield estimates that are quite close to those of the simultaneous estimation method. To check this, we regressed the logarithm of K/L against that of p_K/w, thus obtaining estimates of ρ and δ which are comparable to those of row (5) of table 20.3, which were of course obtained by simultaneous estimation. (This regression was also performed by Arrow *et al.* and by Diwan [10], with these particular data.) The resulting estimates of ρ and δ were -0.096 (with a standard error of 0.098) and 0.32 (with a standard error of 0.02), respectively. The implied value of σ is 1.11. Thus, these parameter estimates are in substantial agreement with the corresponding estimates of row (5) of table 20.3, although the agreement is not extremely close.

accord much weight to these estimates of the CES production function because, in our view, the specification is an inferior one in light of the cost-minimization model which we have adopted. Nevertheless, these results are presented here because they are analogous to the procedure often followed and so would appear to be of some interest.[33]

4 QUALIFICATIONS OF THE RESULTS AND CONCLUSIONS

We have had a two-fold objective in this study. On the one hand, we wanted to have another look at substantive issues in the measurement of the aggregate production function for their bearing on the measurement of technical progress, the degree of returns to scale, and the magnitude of the elasticity of substitution. To add something to existing studies of these matters, we had to refine our model, especially to take economic-theoretic restrictions into account.[34] This immediately involved us in a nonlinear model, and we set as our second objective the testing in practice, of the new nonlinear methods of parameter estimation developed by Eisenpress and Greenstadt.

As to the second objective, we have found that it is feasible to apply these nonlinear methods and that the results may, in some cases, be quite different from those obtained by less general linear methods such as the two-step procedures which were outlined above. We are not absolutely certain, however, that our estimates are firm in the sense of representing the solution to the problem of finding the global maximum of the relevant likelihood function, rather than merely a local maximum. We have tried to guard against the latter possibility by trying other initial values in the appropriate parameter spaces, but we cannot be certain that we have succeeded.

Our conclusions concerning the first set of objectives are more qualified. We find evidence of increasing returns to scale and, associated with this phenomenon, somewhat lower rates of neutral technological progress than have been found by others who restrict returns to scale.

---

[33]The parameter estimates of the CD production function, with unrestricted returns to scale, when the labor and capital inputs are chosen as exogenous (not reproduced in this paper) also differ somewhat from those given in rows (3) and (4) of table 20.1. In particular, the estimates of the returns to scale are much lower, with homogeneity of degree 1.25, and the estimates of the pace of technological progress are correspondingly higher.

[34]Compare the present model with the approach taken in the pioneering study of production functions and associated marginal productivity equations by Marschak and Andrews [25]. They use a theoretical specification up to (but not including) the point of imposing restrictions on parameters occurring in more than one equation. By failing to impose these added restrictions they were able to deal with a completely linear model.

By using a cost-minimization model (instead of a profit-maximization model), we can still use factor share data and not force the sum of our CD exponents or μ to be restricted to their constant-returns-to-scale value of unity. It is our belief that the American economy does function under increasing returns to scale, and, as indicated in section 3, there are other studies to support this contention. The estimates of the elasticity of substitution from our CES model vary from approximately zero to approximately unity. In the most general, and preferred, case, the estimates are about 0.5 to 0.7 and significantly less than unity. At the top of a standard 95 per cent confidence interval band (bottom for our estimates of ρ), we would have estimates of σ less than unity but as high as 0.9. If we were to classify variables into endogenous and exogenous categories so that X_t is endogenous while K_t and L_t are predetermined, we could not reject the hypothesis that $\sigma = 1$.

To make our results comparable with other studies of empirical production functions, we restricted our data, sample period, degree of disaggregation, and scope of model. New series on GNP originating, capital stock, capacity utilization, and employees by type (production and overhead workers) are now becoming available, and one could potentially do a better job of production function estimation by using them. Our sample span, like Solow's (for comparison), includes wartime years and terminates in 1949. There would be no trouble in bringing the relevant series up to date, inclusive of 1964 or 1965 observations. Data are now available for several industrial sectors, and it seems to be highly desirable to carry out such studies, especially for technological progress, for more homogeneous subgroups.

One of the most serious limitations of our study is the incompleteness of our model. To use the new computer programs for maximum likelihood estimation in nonlinear systems, we had to classify variables into the endogenous and exogenous categories, and it is surely stretching one's imagination to claim that total output or relative factor prices are exogenous to the private nonagricultural sector of the economy as a whole. Thus, the rate of employment of the two factors of production will have a feedback influence on total output, through the well-known channels of aggregate demand influences. It is even doubtful whether output should be taken to be exogenous for a typical disaggregated industry, say at the two-digit manufacturing level. There is much scope for incorporating procedures like those used in this paper into a more adequate model of the whole economy. Computer programs for nonlinear systems are in their infancy, therefore, trials must first be made on simple, small models in which economic realism has to be sacrificed. In the future, we hope to be able to remedy this deficiency.

Possibly, if we could drop the assumptions of neutral technological progress and the equality of capital utilization with that of labor, we could obtain additional improvements over previous studies, besides those associated with generalization of the estimation procedures. Not only are the models employed too small, but they are static and as weakly specified as those models with which we were trying to gain comparison. Another step would appear to be to introduce the Solow-Phelps vintage measures of capital and other lag distributions to represent short-run output adjustments. The former would make allowance for embodied technological progress and would handle problems of measuring capital consumption in a superior way, that is, depreciation could include an obsolescence component in addition to one associated with ordinary wear-and-tear. Dynamic short-run production models may give a superior specification. Finally, and not unrelated to these points, is the recognition of substantial autocorrelation in the estimated residuals from the production function relationships of our models. Improvement of the sample, especially through a separate treatment of the wartime observations, and the introduction of short-run dynamic adjustments may considerably reduce such autocorrelation and otherwise improve upon our estimates.

REFERENCES

[1] Kenneth Arrow, Hollis B. Chenery, Bagicha Minhas, and Robert M. Solow, 'Capital-labor substitution and economic efficiency,' *Review of Economics and Statistics*, XLIII, 3, August (1961), 225–50.

[2] Murray Brown, 'An iconoclastic view of the new view of investment,' Econometric Institute Report 6402, Rotterdam (1964), mimeograph.

[3] Murray Brown, and John S. de Cani, 'Technological change and the distribution of income,' *International Economic Review*, **4**, 3, September (1963), 289–309.

[4] Murray Brown, and John S. de Cani, 'A measure of technological employment,' *Review of Economics and Statistics*, XLV, 4, November (1963), 386–94.

[5] Murray Brown, and Joel Popkin, 'A measure of technological change and returns to scale,' *Review of Economics and Statistics*, XLIV, 4, November (1962), 402–11.

[6] Herman Chernoff and Nathan Divinsky, 'The computation of maximum-likelihood estimates of linear structural equations,' in *Studies in Econometric Method* (eds William C. Hood and Tjalling C. Koopmans), John Wiley, 1953, New York, pp. 236–302.

[7] Phoebus J. Dhrymes and Mordecai Kurz, 'Technology and scale in electricity generation,' *Econometrica*, **32**, 3, July (1964), 287–315.

[8] Romesh K. Diwan, 'An empirical estimate of the constant elasticity of substitution production function,' University of Birmingham, UK, May (1963), mimeograph.

[9] Romesh K. Diwan, 'Technical change and aggregate production function: A comment,' (mimeograph).

[10] Romesh K. Diwan, 'Alternative specifications of economies of scale,' *Economica* (to be published).
[11] Paul H. Douglas, 'Are there laws of production?' *American Economic Review*, XXXVIII, 1, March (1948), 1–41.
[12] Clark Edwards, 'Non-linear programming and non-linear regression procedures,' *Journal of Farm Economics*, XLIV, 1, February (1962), 100–14.
[13] H. Eisenpress and J. L. Greenstadt, 'Non-linear full-information estimation' (paper presented at the December 28–30, 1964, meetings of the Econometric Society, Chicago, Illinois).
[14] Marvin Frankel, 'The production function in allocation and growth: A synthesis,' *American Economic Review*, LII, 5, December (1962), 995–1022.
[15] Victor R. Fuchs, 'Capital-labor substitution: A note,' *Review of Economics and Statistics*, XLV, 4, November (1963), 436–8.
[16] Zvi Griliches, 'Research expenditures, education, and the aggregate agricultural production function,' *American Economic Review*, LIV, 6, December (1964), 961–74.
[17] B. I. Hart and John von Neumann, 'Tabulation of the probabilities for the ratio of the mean square successive difference to the variance,' *Annals of Mathematical Statistics*, XIII, 2, June (1942), 207–14.
[18] John W. Kendrick and Ryuzo Sato, 'Factor prices, productivity, and economic growth,' *American Economic Review*, LIII, 5, December (1963), 974–1003.
[19] Lawrence R. Klein, 'A postwar quarterly model: Description and applications,' in National Bureau of Economic Research, Conference on Research in Income and Wealth, *Models of Income Determination*, Volume 28 of Studies in Income and Wealth, Princeton University Press, Princeton, N.J. (1964), 11–36.
[20] Lawrence R. Klein and Ross Preston, 'Some new results in the measurement of capacity utilization,' *American Economic Review*, **57,** 1, March (1967), 34–58.
[21] Jan Kmenta, 'On estimation of the CES production function,' *International Economic Review*, **8,** 2, June (1967), 180–9.
[22] Irving B. Kravis, 'Relative income shares in fact and theory,' *American Economic Review*, XLIX, 5, December (1959), 917–49.
[23] Mordecai Kurz and Alan S. Manne, 'Engineering estimates of capital-labor substitution in metal machining,' *American Economic Review*, LIII, 4, September (1963), 662–81.
[24] Wassily Leontief, 'An international comparison of factor costs and factor use: A review article,' *American Economic Review*, LIV, 4, June (1964), 335–45.
[25] Jacob Marschak and William H. Andrews, Jr., 'Random simultaneous equations and the theory of production,' *Econometrica*, **12,** 3–4, July–October (1944), 143–205.
[26] Benton F. Massell, 'Determinants of productivity change in United States manufacturing,' *Yale Economic Essays*, **2,** 2, Fall (1962), 302–48.
[27] Bagicha Singh Minhas, *An International Comparison of Factor Costs and Factor Use*, contributions to *Economic Analysis*, No. 31, North-Holland, Amsterdam (1963).
[28] Edmund S. Phelps, 'The new view of investment: A neoclassical analysis,' *Quarterly Journal of Economics*, LXXVI, 4, November (1962), 548–67.
[29] Gian S. Sahota, 'Land-labor-capital substitution and efficiency of resource allocation in Indian agriculture,' New York, paper presented at the December, 1965, meetings of the Econometric Society.
[30] Gian S. Sahota, 'The source of measured productivity growth: US fertilizer-mineral industries, 1936–1960,' *Review of Economics and Statistics*, XLVIII, 2, May (1966), 193–204.

[31] Robert M. Solow, 'Technical change and the aggregate production function,' *Review of Economics and Statistics*, XXXIX, 3, August (1957), 312–20.

[32] Robert M. Solow, 'Investment and technical progress,' in *Mathematical Methods in the Social Sciences 1959* (eds, Kenneth J. Arrow, Samuel Karlin, and Patrick Suppes), Stanford University Press, Stanford (1960), 89–104.

[33] James Tobin, 'Estimation of relationships for limited dependent variables,' *Econometrica*, **26**, 1, January (1958), 24–36.

[34] A. A. Walters, 'Production functions and cost functions: An econometric survey,' *Econometrica*, **31**, 1–2, January–April (1963), 1–66.

[35] A. A. Walters, 'A note on economies of scale,' *Review of Economics and Statistics*, XLV, 4, November (1963), 425–27.

[36] J. K. Whitaker, 'A note on the CES production function,' *The Review of Economic Studies*, XXXI (2), 86, April (1964), 166–7.

[37] Knut Wicksell, *Lectures on Political Economy*, George Routledge, London (1934).

[38] A. Zellner, J. Kmenta and J. Drèze, 'Specification and estimation of Cobb-Douglas production function models,' *Econometrica*, **34**, 4, October (1966), 784–95.

21
Whither Econometrics?

To try to chart the future of development in econometrics during the 1970s, it is useful to review the origins of the subject before World War II and the modern era in which our present body of knowledge flowered, 1940–1970. New developments should be made in computer analysis of large data banks, more complete systems, control systems, and microeconometric applications. It is likely that the future of the subject will be less tied to the US than in the past few decades. Problem areas where research developments should prove to be fruitful are in the treatment of nonlinearities, serial correlation of error, estimation of prediction reliability, small-sample distributions, pooling of diverse samples, lag distributions, and the use of *a priori* information.

REVIEW OF PROGRESS

Economics deals to a large extent with quantitative matters; therefore it is not at all surprising that economic analysis turns towards statistical description or verification of abstract theorizing. The physiocratic school apparently used quantitative methods in its tableaux as early as the eighteenth century, but in the nineteenth century beginnings of economic science the modest amount of reference that there was to statistical verification or description can be classified in today's language as 'casual empiricism.' An inverse variation of grain prices and quantities might have been loosely sighted as manifestation of a downward sloping demand function. The behavior of stated wages, prices, and general activity measures during the great disturbances of the nineteenth century (such as the Napoleonic Wars) may have been used as evidence in support of a macro theory, but there was after the physiocrats no systematic or scientific use of statistical data to give empirical content to economic theory.

Some important empirical regularities that are still used today were then discovered and generalized into 'laws.' The Malthusian population formulas and the Paretian distribution formula were discovered in this era of pre-econometrics. They were significant intellectual achievements, but were *ad hominum* in character and not produced by the scientific study of quantitative economics.

A higher stage of early econometrics, and indeed the founding era of the subject, came in the twentieth century as a result of the impetus of classical statistical theory. It was essentially a stage of the influence of Karl Pearson. Correlation theory provided the necessary tool to analyze statistical *relationships* in economics. Once economists learned multiple correlation analysis, they progressively became so enamored of this subject that they have never slowed down the generating of least-squares regression results.

In large part, econometrics became an application of multiple correlation theory. There is more to econometrics than the estimation of relationships, but that single aspect of the subject has swamped everything else. Now it is so easy to generate least-squares regression equations by the dozen that almost every practitioner's work, every professional journal, most dissertations, and even some legislative or judicial testimony contain the familiar sight of a linear multivariate statistical equation complete with standard errors, multiple correlation coefficient, and serial correlation statistics.

Correlation theory was the basic statistical tool for the pioneering work of Henry Moore [7], Henry Schultz [8], Paul Douglas [1] and Jan Tinbergen [10]. Ragnar Frisch [2] pushed the regression aspect of the subject much deeper and raised important conceptual issues as did Elmer Working [11]. The works of these men mark the beginnings of formal econometrics. Their analysis was systematic, based on the joint foundations of statistical and economic theory, and they were aiming at meaningful substantive goals – to measure demand elasticity, marginal productivity and the degree of macroeconomic stability.

The modern era of econometrics commenced in the early 1940s, just at the beginning of World War II. The turning point came in the work of T. Haavelmo [3,4] and A. Wald [6], who formulated the econometric problem in terms of the theory of statistical inference. From their contributions the subject of econometrics has actually become a special branch of mathematical statistics – the making of statistical inferences from nonexperimental data. It is given a special economics flavor by being tied to the equation systems that are derived from propositions of theoretical (mathematical) economics. The older approaches of econometrics developed in the prior decades of this century were not overturned; they were simply extended to be more specifically placed in the setting of quantitative economics. Also, some of the substantive problems and some of the techniques of analysis of estimated systems from the 1920s and 1930s are being taken up again. Recently, for example, econometricians have taken a renewed interest in problems of multicollinearity and cyclical measurement.

The results of Haavelmo and Wald were extended by Koopmans, Marschak, Hurwicz, Anderson and others at the Cowles Commission in a flurry of work during the late 1940s and early 1950s [5]. At this time econometrics and mathematical economics had to fight for academic recognition. In retrospect, it is evident that they were growing disciplines and becoming increasingly attractive to the new generation of economics students after World War II, but only a few of the largest and most advanced universities offered formal work in these subjects. The mathematization of economics was strongly resisted.

That resistance is completely a thing of the past now. At least, for the time being, the mathematical approach has been completely accepted and is now dominant. Having come out of the academic underground, it is now boldly assertive and aggressive. There is no doubt that econometrics received much encouragement from the widespread acceptance of the Keynesian theory of income determination and the associated development of national income accounting data on a broad scale. The Keynesian theory was simply 'asking' to be cast in an empirical mold. The materials, thanks to Kuznets, and the techniques, thanks to Tinbergen, were readily available. This became the proving ground for the modern theories of Haavelmo and Wald.

During the 1950s there was some consolidation of results. Applications to model building were made, but few new techniques were developed. Theil's work on two-stage, least-squares estimation [9] was an exception, but the decade was generally one of application with steady growth in the subject. The situation was reversed in the decade of the 1960s, possibly beginning with the late 1950s. New estimators were invented; new methods of lag distributions were explored; the methods of spectral analysis were introduced into econometrics; model building became more ambitious; estimated models were being used by many public and private bodies; old nagging problems of nonlinearities were overcome; and there was a general 'take-off' in econometric research.

WHERE DO WE STAND NOW?

The great flurry of activity that characterized the ending of the 1960s for econometrics has been due in large part to the computer. It is safe to say that this powerful instrument has now been harnessed for the needs of the subject. Methods of analysis that were formerly considered but dropped because of the enormity of computing burdens are now fully considered on their own merits. Nonlinear estimation equations have been successfully solved in many instances; nonlinear systems have been successfully solved in many instances; nonlinear systems have been estimated; nonlinear methods of analysis of estimated systems are commonplace; iteration procedures are no longer barriers; and exploration of alternatives is widespread. What formerly seemed out of reach is now accepted practice. The computer has radically changed the lives of econometricians and the bigger part of the change occurred in the latter part of the 1960s.

There are other important aspects of the present stance on the subject. There is now an attempt to bring input–output and more general programming methods into the mainstream of econometrics. I–O analysis stood apart for many years from the statistical inference approach of econometrics, but the full integration of I–O and macro-econometric analysis in the Brookings Model has demonstrated fully that the two are complementary rather than competing.

Econometrics flourished in the US, Canada and some countries of Western Europe. During the 1960s it fully caught hold in Japan and spread to other areas. Now we find that some laggard geographical areas in Europe including the socialist countries, Australia and other developed parts of the world are significantly expanding their scope of econometric research and application.

An equally significant development is the embracing of the econometric approach in many of the developing nations. It is now becoming an important tool in development planning for individual countries and for broader areas in supernational agencies. The geographical spread of econometrics is one of the most significant developments for the future growth of the subject. It was the 'newness' of the econometric approach that made it so attactive for application to the theory of employment in the 1930s and 1940s. Again, it is being taken up as a new tool for application to the emerging theories of planning and development in the socialist and developing nations.

It was noted above that econometrics received a major impetus from macroeconomic 'theory and its associated body of aggregative data. This helped to change direction from early work that had more of a microeconomic orientation. The emphasis is changing again. Macro-econometrics continues to flourish, but increasing attention is being paid to micro problems in demand analysis, theory of production, markets, and trading relationships. Some attention is being paid again to problems of income and wealth distribution.

The pioneering work of Henry Schultz was guided by the economic theory of consumer and market behavior, the work of Paul Douglas by the theory of marginal productivity pricing, and the work of Tinbergen by the theories of the business cycle. Economic theory was emphasized in the specification of the Cowles Commission models, just after World War II. A renaissance with stricter ties to neoclassical theory appeared in Dale Jorgenson's studies of investment behavior during the 1960s. The present generation of econometricians have turned increasingly to literal interpretations of standard economic theory for model specification. It is now a fashion in analysis of the unemployment-inflation trade-off and in the construction of more detailed monetary models. In this way, microeconomic theory is being used more in modern econometrics.

PREDICTING DEVELOPMENTS IN THE SCIENCE OF ECONOMIC PREDICTION

Econometrics had its origin in the recognition of empirical regularities and the systematic attempt to generalize these regularities into 'laws' of economics. In a broad sense, the use of such 'laws' is to make predictions – about what might have or what will come to pass. Econometrics should give a base for economic prediction beyond experience if it is to be useful. In this broad sense it may be called the science of economic prediction, and the main task of the present article is to try to foresee how this science of prediction will emerge in the 1970s and beyond.

It is a platitude to say that the computer will be used to a large extent in the future development of our subject. It has opened the way to the solution of seemingly intractable problems and will continue to do so in the next decade. It will also be used for the creation of new exercises and for the solution of entirely new problems in econometrics.

At the close of the last decade two significant developments were imminent, (a) the creation of large data banks of economic statistics, and (b) the use of remote access computer consoles. As usage of such systems develops, we can look forward to large public data files of consistently defined and completely updated socioeconomic statistics. These should be at least as complete as the *Survey of Current Business*, the supplement *Business Statistics*, the *Federal Reserve Bulletin*, the *Monthly Labor Review* and *Employment and Earnings*. There are, however, no foreseeable bounds to the bank's size. Nothing new is necessarily to be provided in this data system, but its accessibility and internal consistency should surpass what is now available.

The provision of a large public data bank is no panacea for econometric researchers. There will always be the need for specialized data not in the file. What is more significant, however, is the fact that a large public file cannot plausibly serve the specialized needs of econometrics in fine detail. It will always be necessary for the research econometrician to adjust, manipulate and rework public data in order to build statistical series that suit the concepts of economic analysis. Private data banks may be able to serve limited applications in econometrics without further working of the withdrawals, but the profession generally will have to look forward to a combination of the new method of withdrawing data from the bank and the traditional methods of combining various basic series into meaningful series with subtle economic content. It is surely to be expected that econometricians will always have to go outside data banks for some of their statistical information. They will not be able to send the computer to the library.

Central files of data, prior research results, existing economic models and programs for econometric analysis can all be stored in a limited number of locations that can be accessed from remote terminals. This means that information and analytic techniques will be available to a wider body of users. Further, since remote terminals are relatively inexpensive, computer power, existing research facilities, and existing research results can be made available to small schools, small research institutes, or research departments and will not be restricted to those who presently have access to large-scale systems.

In recent experience with the wider dissemination of technical facilities and results, we find that it is not an easy matter for people unfamiliar with all the details to use centrally provided materials. Although in principle, there is no reason why the remote user cannot employ technical econometric material as well as the original researcher who made the material available in the first place, this does not yet work smoothly in practice. The original researcher frequently has to intervene and may end up doing the work without benefit of remote access. Users must be educated in the techniques of econometrics to get remote access systems working smoothly, but we should be cautioned that good econometric research is not a 'push-button' affair. There will be large practical difficulties in reaching the high degree of automation implied by the widespread use of large data banks and remote access computer systems. In the long run, the highly automated system will undoubtedly prevail and should cross international boundaries so that researchers in different countries are all tuned into the same econometric system.

In the development of econometrics after World War II, the pervasive influence of the Keynesian theory of income determination led to great emphasis on *ex ante* forecasting and directed attention away from some earlier applications of econometrics pioneered by Tinbergen – measuring business cycles, and the testing of economic theory. As the subject has grown and produced a great deal of talent for *ex ante* forecasting applications, an increasing amount of attention has been drawn back to the earlier problems. The emergence of spectral analysis to replace the discredited forms of periodogram analysis and the facility of computer simulation of dynamic systems has led to renewed interest in cyclical analysis. We now have tools for attacking the cyclical aspects of nonlinear systems because numerical solutions can often be obtained with comparative ease and speed. While only a few graphical and qualitative explorations of solutions to small and nonlinear systems were formerly available, now the way is open for the solution of more realistic large nonlinear systems and for the inclusion of stochastic shocks.

On a few occasions, investigators have suggested the use of electro analog computers for the study of dynamic economic systems. These suggestions have been largely exploratory and were not pursued. They were usually confined to small expository systems. Such studies passed into oblivion with the rise of the digital computer. The power of the analog has enormously increased to be able to accommodate larger, more realistic systems, nonlinear systems and stochastic systems. The analog uses can also be made more flexible in a link with digital to form a hybrid computer system. There are some exploratory problems of parameter variation, both for estimating economic relationships and for investigating the properties of estimated systems, that make use of the analog seem attractive. The increasing attention of econometricians to the whole simulation path of an economic model system makes the analog useful because it can instantly display such paths. Indeed, instant display is a feature that should make analog devices useful for pedagogical purposes. In the past, mechanical or hydrological analogs never survived an initial interest because of their slowness, their cumbersomeness and their inability to deal with large systems. All these deficiencies can be overcome with the electro analog, and its revival should have a place in the new era of econometrics.

One of Tinbergen's original goals in building the first macroeconometric model of the US was to test alternative models of the business cycle. The testing of this and other bodies of theory should be a more active field of study now that so much effort is already being devoted to *ex ante* forecasting. During the 1960s (beginning in the late 1950s) there was extensive testing of Friedman's permanent income hypothesis. Work of this sort is likely to continue. Conclusions are rarely definitive in econometrics since the data are not sharp enough or plentiful enough to reject all the competing hypotheses for the explanation of a limited set of economic observations. The data situation, barring another global military conflict, should become better and better, making theory testing more conclusive and therefore more attractive to researchers. Also there are more competing models in existence and being repeatedly used in macroeconomics. These models have many nontrivial implications as to cyclical characteristics, growth characteristics, forecasting performance, information content, multiplier values and statistical inference methodology. There is much need for further comparative testing, both to find superior model characteristics and to test their different economic theoretic properties. It appears that major research efforts along these lines are already being planned as the decade opens.

At first econometricians were, quite properly, modest and hesitant about putting forward their findings for public and business use. Gradually, they were called on for applications and responded with their best efforts. Now that econometric methods have been widely accepted, the situation is different. Econometricians are becoming more boldly assertive and making positive proposals for model use. There will always be a need for their appraisal, in a passive sense, of what happened in the historical economy and what is likely to happen in the future. But econometricians are likely to come forward now with applications of their own design and objective from applications of control theory and public policy optimization. Instead of passive observation and prediction, there should be more searching for acceptable loss or gain functions that are to be optimized subject to restrictions of an estimated model. In this connection, a new problem must be faced soon, namely, an accounting for feedback influences of econometric results on economic performance. During the period when econometric methods have been experimentally and tentatively introduced, first confidentially, then publicly, we always replied when asked about the feedback effect that 'we would cross that bridge when we come to it.' The bridge is now in sight. There is no ready solution to this problem, but the feedback effect will have to be estimated and incorporated in econometric systems. This will be a fruitful area of future research.

With the passage of time, the subtle role of Tinbergen in shaping the development of econometrics emerges in more and more places. A return to his early ideas on cyclical measurement and theory testing has already been mentioned. His principal theoretical contribution in the postwar era has been in the formalization and quantification of the theory of economic policy, using models to show how instruments can be used to reach macroeconomic targets. This approach is now ready for expansion and implementation on a larger scale because we know enough about the properties of the frequently used larger systems and have the computer know-how to solve the technical problems. There has been much study of economic policy through model analysis, but much of this has been geared to provide a description of given policies or has been a cut-and-try search for desirable policy alternatives. The formal use of the Tinbergen approach is now possible for large-scale models and should undoubtedly be the focus of a significant amount of future econometric research.

As econometrics is used for comprehensive production and market analysis in the planned economy and as it is used in microeconomic studies for the free market economy, a new dimension in the use of control theory must be introduced. There must be a mathematical system for automatic decision-making on a whole range of prices and quantities. The macroeconomic welfare functions that play off such magnitudes as general inflation, total balance of payments, GNP growth rate etc., will not be suitable. Control theory for steering high dimensional vectors of prices and quantities toward equilibrium has to be developed. By order of magnitude this will become a whole new field of application for econometrics. We shall be called on to 'go' Walrasian.' This poses a whole new range of research objectives.

Macroeconometric systems, without becoming Walrasian in nature, have in fact been growing in size. This has been necessary to meet the needs of model users and to cope with the changing times. As monetary policy began to be more widely and effectively used in the 1950s, models had to expand to incorporate monetary sectors. As new monetary instruments were introduced, the monetary sectors had to expand – to accommodate certificates of deposit, Euro dollar balances, interest ceilings, and other institutional changes.

The original macroeconometric models were designed to go along with available statistical materials in the national income accounting (NIA) systems. Now, we recognize that full accounting for economic activity makes use of three systems, the NIA, the input–output (I–O) and the flow-of-funds (FF) systems. It has already been shown to be possible to build a model combining the NIA and I–O systems as accomplished in the Brookings Model and refined on a larger scale by Ross Preston in a new Wharton Model. In large part, the SSRC-FRB-MIT-Penn model has combined the NIA and the FF systems. These two kinds of mergers are presently being amplified in econometric research, but the ultimate step has not yet been taken. Macroeconometric model building is going in a direction, however, that is bound to culminate with a unified system combining NIA, I–O and FF all together. This will be in the neighborhood of the 1000 equation system. Work will still continue on the study of small models and their economic-statistical properties, but their output is so limited that research on the big system is bound to occur. Despite the fact that some limited aggregates, GNP and similar statistics, may be equally well predicted from large and small systems, research on the construction of large detailed systems will not be curtailed because interest in a whole variety of system outputs going far beyond the standard aggregates, is of overwhelming importance.

Econometrics had its roots in Europe and America jointly, but the greatest flowering occurred after World War II in the US. The period of American dominance is now probably drawing to a close. This is not to predict a decline in American econometric activity but rather an enormous increase abroad, in a way that will change relative proportions. In Norway and Holland, econometrics has always thrived under the leadership of Frisch and Tinbergen. There is a history of high-quality work in France, the UK, Sweden, Canada, Japan, India, Israel and other countries, but the magnitude of the effort has been less than in the US. That situation is rapidly changing. These centers of econometric research are paying increased attention to the subject, and entirely new centers are springing up all over the world in both developed and developing areas. There are dozens of macromodels, many partial investigations and theoretical research studies going on all over the world. The leading textbooks are not all from the US; basic theorems are coming from diverse geographical sources. The socialist countries are now taking up econometrics with great vigor and enlarging their interest beyond pure I–O systems or standard programming models. These countries are entering the mainstream of econometric analysis with a strong mathematics background and some reasonably good computer facilities. It seems appropriate to say that they are now at the stage where American and other Western world econometricians found themselves 10–20 years ago, but they have all our results at their fingertips and are likely to catch up during the 1970s. Significant new results should be forthcoming from non-American sources during the 1970s in such volume that pre-eminence will not be attributed to any single country. This development, which should bring a number of fresh, unsuspected new ideas into the subject, is surely welcome.

The existence of functioning macromodels in several countries motivated the sponsorship of project LINK by the Social Science Research Council's Committee on Economic Stability. In the first 2 years of LINK research, it has been found that international cooperation on world model building is feasible and fruitful. Separate country models can indeed be linked for consistent world trade projections. More sophisticated linkages are now being tried. This project provides a setting in which systems of international remote-access computer usage of econometric materials can be worked out. The international exchange of ideas within LINK has already been stimulating. The future for internationalization of our subject looks bright. This is bound to have a large impact on the nature of the research output.

As we enter the new decade there are several important unsolved problems that remain, and much future research effort needs to be allocated to them. Despite the recent advances in dealing with nonlinear systems, systems with serially correlated errors, the calculation of standard error of forecast, small sample distributions of estimators, pooling of different samples, the distinctive treatment of lagged variables and the use of *a priori* information, these problems are not fully under control. Much light has been cast on them in Monte Carlo studies, but only quite limited conclusions can be drawn from such investigations. Analytic methods should still be used to give more satisfying answers.

Nonlinear systems and nonlinear methods

Although we have come a long way in being able to estimate parameters in nonlinear models, to solve nonlinear estimation equations (for linear or nonlinear systems) and to find economic solutions to estimated nonlinear models, we do not fully know the stochastic properties of nonlinear systems. The fact that in linear systems, nonstochastic and stochastic components are additive greatly simplifies their analysis. In addition, closed form expressions exist for reduced forms, final forms, dynamic solutions and expected values of endogenous variables in linear systems. We cannot derive closed-form solutions in general for nonlinear systems, and this has curtailed our ability to give a full stochastic analysis of properties of estimates or system solutions. This is an important area for further research.

Serial correlation of error

Single linear equations with autoregressive error of finite order can now be fully estimated. We do not know all the small-sample properties of such estimates, but some headway has been made in dealing with this problem. In a practical sense the most general schemes of serial correlation, with cross-lagged correlation among equations, have not been handled in the actual estimation of simultaneous equation systems. On a theoretical level, more general schemes of serial dependence besides autoregression need much further investigation.

Lag distributions for single linear equations have been fairly fully studied, but as in the case of serial correlation of errors, there has not yet been a full extension to general lag distributions in a simultaneous equations framework. This is a problem for future study.

Standard error of forecast

The reliability of general predictive statements based on large systems of simultaneous equations is relatively unknown. There are some approximation formulas, and there are some Monte Carlo studies for small systems, but these seem to be unsatisfactory for the general case. They do not seem to be good indicators of revealed experience with repetitive predictive exercises. More accurate ways of measuring expected predictive accuracy are needed. Predictive statements based on econometric models can then be appropriately accompanied by regions of uncertainty and uncertainty coefficients.

Small-sample distribution

In some simple and specialized, cases, small-sample distributions have been obtained. These are all too infrequent and limited. This is one of the most challenging areas from a mathematical point of view. The fact that some results have been obtained should encourage much further research on this problem.

Pooling of samples

The combination of cross-section and time-series samples has been a time-honored technique in econometrics. It happily brings micro- and macroeconometrics together in many instances. In more recent years, we have become more critical of the procedures because of the different assumptions and underlying models for both sets of data. While this does not mean that pooling should be avoided, it should be done more carefully and according to a more satisfactory stochastic model.

Since econometric methods are now being taken up in several countries that have a weak data base, it is likely that there should be more reliance on supplementary samples of cross-section data. These can, in principle, be obtained to fill in some irreparable time-series gaps. Research on pooling will be needed in these cases, and also research on drawing econometric inferences from time sequences of cross sections should be further developed.

In macroeconometric models based largely on aggregative time series data, there is a role for obtaining supplementary information from sample survey cross-section data, especially for purposes of *ex ante* prediction. Much of this kind of analysis has already been undertaken in the postwar era, but it has not been carried through to ultimate refinements. There will be room for future research of this kind, but it is not clear that this line of investigation will hold as much promise for the period ahead as it did at the end of World War II.

Pooling of different samples will involve not only cross-section and time-series pooling. There is already a problem of pooling quarterly and annual time series information. A new dimension is on the horizon with the introduction of monthly models. There will probably be a separate research problem in the analysis of time disaggregation, but there will also be problems in the phasing-in of partial monthly or even weekly series to systems that are fundamentally based on data for longer intervals.

The treatment of lags

Apart from the problems of estimating serially correlated error processes and lag distributions, there is a further problem in the treatment of lagged dependent variables as though they were exogenous. There is large-sample justification of this in stable linear systems with additive normal disturbances. In less restrictive models and in small samples, it must be recognized that lags are endogenously generated within the process described by the equation system being estimated. We need to have more suitable estimation procedures for dealing with this situation.

The use of a priori *information*

It is narrow and surely wrong to think that quantitative numerical data available to us as econometricians contain the full secrets of the true undisclosed economic process. We are pitifully short of information and must make use of whatever we can put our hands on. There will, of course, be some part of behavior attributed to the random error terms, but it seems plausible to think that we can come by other pieces of information that are usable in combination with econometric models. New ways and systematic ways of using *a priori* information should be sought. Estimation under more *a priori* restrictions and solutions that incorporate *a priori* information have been studied in simple cases. Bayesian methods attempt to treat *a priori* information in a systematic way. As a pure and passive forecaster of econometric methodology I can see a great deal of future research effort being channeled in that direction. Systematic ways of introducing *a priori* information are to be desired. Techniques that rely on equal probability of the unknown or subjective probability, however, seem to me to be the wrong way of dealing with this problem.

The road ahead for econometrics is probably more technical, less glamorous and more one of building on past research efforts than was the case in the frontier years. New basic results will be harder to find, but the research army is bigger and better equipped. Progress should be solid but not necessarily spectacular.

REFERENCES

[1] C. W. Cobb and Paul H. Douglas, 'A theory of production,' *American Economic Review*, Supplement, **18** (1928), 139–65.

[2] Ragnar Frisch, *Statistical Confluence Analysis by Means of Complete Regression Systems*, Oslo: Universitets Økononiske Institutet (1934).

[3] Trygve Haavelmo, 'The statistical implications of a system of simultaneous equations,' *Econometrica*, **11** (1943), 1–12.

[4] Trygve Haavelmo, 'The probability approach in econometrics, *Econometrica*, Supplement, **12** (1944).

[5] Tjalling Koopmans (ed.), *Statistical Inference in Dynamic Economic Models*, John Wiley, New York (1950).

[6] Henry B. Mann and A. Wald, 'On the statistical treatment of linear stochastic difference equations,' *Econometrica*, **11** (1943), 173–220.

[7] Henry L. Moore, *Economic Cycles: Their Law and Cause*, Macmillan, New York (1914).

[8] Henry Schultz, *The Theory and Measurement of Demand*, University of Chicago Press, Chicago (1938).

[9] Henri Theil, *Economic Forecasts and Policy*, North-Holland, Amsterdam (1958).

[10] Jan Tinbergen, *Statistical Testing of Business Cycle Theories*, Vol. II: *Business Cycles in the USA, 1919–1932*, League of Nations, Geneva (1939).

[11] E. J. Working, 'What do statistical "demand curves" show? '*Quarterly Journal of Economics*, **41** (1927), 212–35.

[12] *International Encyclopedia of the Social Sciences*, references to 'Econometrics' and listed related subjects, Macmillan Free Press, New York (1968).
[13] Lawrence R. Klein, 'The scope and limitations of econometrics,' *Applied Statistics*, **6** (1957), 1–17.
[14] C. E. V. Leser, 'A survey of econometrics,' *Journal of the Royal Statistical Society*, Ser. A, **131** (1968), 530–66.
[15] Kenneth F. Wallis, 'Some recent developments in applied econometrics: Dynamic models and simultaneous equation systems,' *Journal of Economic Literature*, VII (1969), 771–96.
[16] A. A. Walters, 'Production and cost functions: An econometric survey,' *Econometrica*, **31** (1963), 1–66.

22
Notes on Testing the Predictive Performance of Econometric Models

INTRODUCTION

The past decade has seen the development of a number of large-scale econometric models.[1] It was the intention of the authors of these models that they be useful tools in the analysis of the economic impacts of a wide range of policy alternatives, thereby making possible more informed policy choices. Inevitably, models such as these were also used as economic forecasting tools. Attention was focused on the set of policy alternatives under serious consideration at the moment and on the future implications of these policies. Due to the policy orientation, the large-scale models are all stated as specific structural hypotheses. For example, the way that personal taxes are assumed to enter the demand equations for consumption goods is explicitly stated; the way that corporate taxes affect the various business relationships and the role of monetary controls in the money demand and supply relationships is also stated explicitly.

Inevitably and appropriately, questions were raised as to which of the various models (various competing hypotheses) was best, and a number of studies have recently been completed which purport to shed light on this question. One of these studies was conducted by Ronald L. Cooper [2] and a recent paper by R. J. Gordon [9] is also available. Papers by Zarnowitz, Boschan and Moore [18] and Evans, Haitovsky and Treyz [5] also deal with aspects of testing alternative models. The Cooper study merits special consideration because it attempts to construct a framework for general application based on an explicit testing methodology. Briefly, his study seeks to introduce uniformity among models by re-estimating each model (by an 'appropriate' method) using the same body of data. Tests of the competing models

---

[1] Some of the better known models that are currently operational are listed in Fromm and Klein [7].

From *International Economic Review*, **15**, June (1974), 366–83; written jointly with E. Philip Howrey and Michael D. McCarthy.

(hypotheses) were then performed. The models were also tested against autoregressive (naive) models. The naive models made the simple assumption that each economic variable depends only on lagged values of itself.

Two types of tests of the models were undertaken. First, the performance of the models over the sample used for estimation (1949–1960) was examined. Specifically, using the actual values of the exogenous variables, one-quarter forecasts were generated for the variables explained by the different models. Variable by variable, squared forecast errors were calculated, and compared, model by model. Second, a parallel set of one-quarter forecast tests were performed using data beyond the estimation sample period. These data were from the period 1961–5. The conclusion of the Cooper study was that, on the basis of his tests the simple autoregressive schemes seemed to perform at least as well from the viewpoint of squared-error considerations as the structural policy models.

The purpose of this paper is to consider what can reasonably be inferred from the Cooper study. More generally, our purpose is to explore alternative ways to assess the potential contribution of econometric models to prediction and public policy formation. Whether or not the Cooper study sheds light on this problem hinges crucially on the credibility of his conclusions. Credibility, in turn, depends on the evidence that his tests of hypotheses were in some sense good tests. If the Cooper study fails the credibility tests, we are still left with the very important issues associated with the design of tests of significance of econometric models.

The first part of this paper is devoted to a brief review of the Cooper study. Although the study is an admirable and heroic first effort, it raises a number of important questions since the test procedures employed deal with only limited aspects of model building. Model building consists of four interrelated activities (a) specification, (b) sample selection, (c) estimation, and (d) application, including prediction, simulation, and cyclical analysis. Cooper attempts to test specification mainly by single-period prediction analysis. The other dimensions of model building and analysis are left untouched. Even on the narrow issue of specification his approach is too restrictive. *A priori* information is not rich enough to provide us with complete specification. The precise nature of the lag structures, nonlinearities, the degree of aggregation, and the selection of exogenous variables are not fixed *a priori*. They can only be ascertained by experimental study of particular samples. The interaction of specification and estimation has certain implications for the tests that are proposed by Cooper. In the second section of this paper, some guidelines for tests of alternative models are presented.

THE COOPER STUDY: A REVIEW

In deciding on the credibility of Cooper's conclusions (or on the conclusions of any such study), we really focus on the issue whether the tests of different models were good tests. We seek evidence that, (a) taking the model structure as given, appropriate methods of estimation were used, (b) that adequate use was made of prior knowledge in specifying the model structures to be estimated, and (c) assuming (a) and (b) are satisfied, that the tests applied to the competing models seem to be good tests. We begin with an examination of the estimation procedure that was employed.

ESTIMATION METHOD

Structural econometric models are inevitably nonlinear in the endogenous and exogenous variables, yet feasible textbook estimation techniques are designed for linear systems. There is a presumption that estimation of nonlinear structural models by an appropriate method will give such models an advantage over the purely autoregressive schemes that they would not otherwise have had in a statistical horse race. The method Cooper used to estimate the different structural models is called repeated reduced-form estimation (RR). The method, attributed to Jorgenson, has been analyzed by Klein [12] within the context of a linear model.[2] Although the method has been shown to have certain desirable properties in the linear-model framework, it is not readily apparent that a straightforward extension of this method to nonlinear models is appropriate.

In order to investigate the applicability of the RR method of parameter estimation to a nonlinear model, assume that each dependent variable of the model can be written as a unique function of the exogenous variables and the other dependent variables in the system. For simplicity, suppose that the T observations on the variables in the ith equation can be expressed as

$$y_i = F_i(Y_i)\alpha_i + XB_i + \eta_i \qquad (22.1)$$

[2]Variations of this method were examined at an early stage by Houthakker, Theil and Nagar.

where $y_i' = [y_{1i}, y_{2i}, \ldots, y_{Ti}]$ is the vector of observations on the ith dependent variable, $Y_i' = [Y_{1i}, Y_{2i}, \ldots, Y_{Ti}]$ with Y_{ti} denoting the row vector of observations on the dependent variables (other than the ith) which appear in the ith equation, and

$$F_i(Y_i) = \begin{bmatrix} F_{i1}(Y_{1i}) & F_{i2}(Y_{1i}) & \ldots & F_{iG}(Y_{1i}) \\ \vdots & \vdots & & \vdots \\ F_{i1}(Y_{Ti}) & F_{i2}(T_{Ti}) & \ldots & F_{iG}(Y_{Ti}) \end{bmatrix}$$

where the $F_{ij}(.)$ are known functions of the rows of Y_i. The term α_i is an appropriately ordered vector of unknown coefficients and η_i is a vector of disturbances with the usual properties including nonautocorrelation.[3] The matrix X denotes the matrix of observations on all the exogenous variables in the model and B_i is the associated vector of coefficients. Generally, several of the elements in B_i will be zero in which case it is convenient to write

$$XB_i = x_i \beta_i \tag{22.2}$$

where β_i is a column vector of the nonzero elements of B_i and x_i is a matrix of the exogenous variables which appear in the ith equation. Thus equation (22.1) may also be written as

$$y_i = F_i(Y_i)\alpha_i + x_i\beta_i + \eta_i. \tag{22.3}$$

Writing $y = [y_1, y_2, \ldots, y_p]$, $F = [F_1, F_2, \ldots, F_p]$, $B = [B_1, B_2, \ldots, B_p]$, $\eta = [\eta_1, \eta_2, \ldots, \eta_p]$ and

$$A = \begin{bmatrix} \alpha_1 & 0 & \ldots & 0 \\ 0 & \alpha_2 & \ldots & 0 \\ \vdots & \vdots & & \vdots \\ 0 & 0 & & \alpha_p \end{bmatrix}$$

the entire system of $p \cdot T$ equations takes the form

$$y = F(Y)A + XB + \eta. \tag{22.4}$$

Note that this model, like the models estimated by Cooper, is nonlinear in the economic variables.

The RR method of estimation is a two-step procedure in which consistent estimates $\hat{\alpha}_i$ and $\hat{\beta}_i$ are first obtained for α_i and β_i ($i = 1, 2, \ldots, p$). We will assume that some such method exists. Given estimates $\hat{A}$ and $\hat{B}$ of A and B, an equation system of the form

$$y = F(Y)\hat{A} + X\hat{B} \tag{22.5}$$

[3] Problems created by autocorrelation will be treated below.

is then solved for y, yielding the solution[4]

$$\hat{y} = H(\hat{A}, \hat{B}, X). \tag{22.6}$$

Next, for each equation, estimates $\hat{F}_i$ of $F_i(Y)$ are computed as $\hat{F}_i = F_i(\hat{Y}_i)$, and second-stage estimates are then obtained by applying least squares to an equation of the form

$$y_i = F_i(\hat{Y}_i)\alpha_i + x_i\beta_i + v_i \tag{22.7}$$

where

$$v_i = \eta_i + [F_i(Y_i) - F_i(\hat{Y}_i)]\alpha_i$$
$$= \eta_i + f_i. \tag{22.8}$$

The estimates are calculated as

$$\begin{bmatrix} \hat{\alpha}_i \\ \hat{\beta}_i \end{bmatrix} = \begin{bmatrix} \hat{F}'_i\hat{F}_i & \hat{F}'_i x_i \\ x'_i\hat{F}_i & x'_i x_i \end{bmatrix}^{-1} \begin{bmatrix} \hat{F}'_i y_i \\ x'_i y_i \end{bmatrix}$$
$$= \begin{bmatrix} \alpha_i \\ \beta_i \end{bmatrix} + \begin{bmatrix} T^{-1}\hat{F}'_i\hat{F}_i & T^{-1}\hat{F}'_i x_i \\ T^{-1}x'_i\hat{F}_i & T^{-1}x'_i x_i \end{bmatrix}^{-1} \begin{bmatrix} T^{-1}\hat{F}'_i\eta_i + T^{-1}\hat{F}'_i f_i \\ T^{-1}x'_i\eta_i + T^{-1}x'_i f_i \end{bmatrix}. \tag{22.9}$$

The most obvious difficulty with this particular method of estimation is that due to the nonlinear nature of the functions in $F_i(Y_i)$, terms of the form $T^{-1}\hat{F}'_i f_i$ and $T^{-1}x'_i f_i$ will possess zero probability limits only under strong assumptions.[5] Hence this application of RR may not yield consistent estimates.

There are variants of the RR method which tend to alleviate this problem. In particular, an instrumental variable formulation would yield estimates of α_i and β_i of the form[6]

$$\begin{bmatrix} \hat{\alpha}_i \\ \hat{\beta}_i \end{bmatrix} = \begin{bmatrix} \hat{F}'_i F_i & \hat{F}'_i x_i \\ x'_i F & x'_i x_i \end{bmatrix}^{-1} \begin{bmatrix} \hat{F}'_i y_i \\ x'_i y_i \end{bmatrix}$$
$$= \begin{bmatrix} \alpha_i \\ \beta_i \end{bmatrix} + \begin{bmatrix} T^{-1}\hat{F}'_i F_i & T^{-1}\hat{F}'_i x_i \\ T^{-1}x'_i F_i & T^{-1}x'_i x_i \end{bmatrix}^{-1} \begin{bmatrix} T^{-1}\hat{F}'_i\eta_i \\ T^{-1}x'_i\eta_i \end{bmatrix}. \tag{22.10}$$

Consistency requires that the probability limits of both $T^{-1}\hat{F}'_i\eta_i$ and $T^{-1}x'_i\eta_i$ vanish.[7] The latter probability limit causes no difficulty under

---

[4]A fixed point in the neighborhood of Y_{t-1} appears to be typical for the class of models under consideration.

[5]This is essentially the point raised by Goldfeld [8] in connection with this version of the RR estimation procedure.

[6]The instrumental variable method is essentially the same (without iteration) as that proposed by Dutta and Lyttkens [4]. It was also taken up by Brundy and Jorgenson [1] modifying Jorgenson's original proposals cited above.

[7]It is assumed that the matrix $T^{-1}[\hat{F}_i x_i]'[F_i x_i]$ possesses a nonsingular probability limit.

the usual assumptions. In view of the way in which $\hat{F}'_i$ is defined, $T^{-1}\hat{F}'_i\eta_i$ can be written as $T^{-1}H_i(\hat{A},\hat{B},X)\eta_i$ where H_i is, in general, a nonlinear function in X. It appears likely that the probability limit of this term will be zero in any practical situation although there may be some pathological cases in which this is not true. In any event it is clear that instrumental variable estimators defined in (22.10) do not have the obvious problem exhibited by the two-stage least-squares estimator defined in (22.9).

It should be noted that due to nonlinearity, the consistency problems just discussed also arise in the first stage of the estimation procedure unless care is exercised at this stage. One device for circumventing the problem would be to calculate $\hat{F}_i$ as the predicted value from the regressions F_i on each of the columns of x_i and on appropriate linear and nonlinear functions of other exogenous variables.[8] That consistency is preserved is seen from a straightforward extension of arguments made by Fisher [6], Kloek and Mennes [13] and others.

This analysis indicates that the estimation procedure employed by Cooper does not in general yield consistent estimates of the parameters in nonlinear models. This certainly detracts from the prediction error tests that were performed with the re-estimated models. However, it should be noted that there is no guarantee that the small-sample mean squared prediction errors would have been smaller had a consistent estimator been used instead of the inconsistent estimator. Nor is it necessarily true that the prediction errors generated by the re-estimated models are larger than the errors generated by the original models. Indeed, the original models were frequently estimated by inconsistent methods, and the inappropriate estimators used in the original studies may have led to an acceptance of erroneous structural hypotheses.

USE OF PRIOR KNOWLEDGE IN SPECIFYING THE STRUCTURE

In testing competing hypotheses, it is desirable for the tests to be applied to comparable bodies of data. The Cooper study satisfies this requirement, but much more is required. In particular, in estimating a structural model, the sample data must be drawn from the same population. If samples are drawn from different populations, the estimates (and forecasts) can be expected to be biased. One thing that seems certain is that because of factors such as technical change, strikes,

---

[8]See Kelejian [11] for a further discussion of this point.

government economic policies, and wars, the structure of economic models shifts over time. An uncritical pooling of time series observations will surely involve sampling from different populations. Hence it is necessary to include known shifts in economic structure in the model.

The quarterly sample used in Cooper's study covered the period 1949 through 1960. Over this period a war occurred, and tax laws also changed. It is difficult to accept the single unchanging set of regression estimates for tax and transfer payment functions that was postulated. A minimal requirement in an econometric application is to change these functions as statutes change. This is of great importance. Moreover, it is likely that, due to strikes and technical progress, production functions, and hence investment-demand functions, as well as price mark-up relations, shift. These shifts need not be of a simple exponential sort. The shifts in the tax laws can also be expected to affect functions other than the equations for government tax receipts. Depreciation equations shift, and investment incentives are affected. This is only the beginning of a very long list of complications due to structural shifts.

It should be clear that building a good forecasting model involves a great deal of care. The economist begins by specifying an initial structural hypothesis; a prior or null hypothesis. This prior hypothesis involves a statement about the form of the structural equations, a statement of what knowledge is available concerning structural shifts, a statement of all prior knowledge about coefficient signs and magnitudes, and some statement about the error properties of the model. Finally, an explicit design of an appropriate sampling and estimation method is required. (Typically, the prior hypothesis implicitly involves a statement that some of the equations have stable structures.) The model is then estimated and some effort is then made to improve on it. This involves an examination of the initial estimates in the light of the prior hypotheses. If, for example, the original state of knowledge dictated that a coefficient was positive, and using an 'appropriate' estimator, a significantly negative estimate was obtained, there are grounds for rejecting (revising) some part of the prior hypothesis (or of the estimation and sampling procedure). If the prior hypothesis specified that the error of the structural equations were non-autocorrelated and the calculated residuals of the estimated equations show strong systematic behavior over time, this too would be justification for rejecting (revising) the prior hypothesis. Sometimes attention is focused on the form of the equations; variables may have been omitted or included in an inappropriate fashion. New knowledge (additional data and information) typically suggest an answer. In reconsidering the prior hypotheses attention is often focused on structural shifts not originally hypothesized. Here too, new knowledge (information not available in the initial data set) is required.[9]

Unfortunately, in the Cooper paper there is little evidence that anything was done other than to estimate mechanically the various models using a consistent body of data; this is of course no small task. In view of the fact that the body of data used for the study differed (because of data revision and because the author chose a different sample period) from the bodies of data used by the original authors, some attention to prior knowledge is certainly called for. What is lacking is evidence that in constructing the models the author gave the same tender loving care (TLC) to each one that the authors of the earlier studies gave in constructing their models. Suppose the sign of a particular coefficient was obviously wrong, or that due to pooling of data from periods in which there were different structures, the calculated residuals of some equations showed strong systematic behavior. No one would consider using equations with such difficulties in a forecasting exercise. At this point we merely note that if TLC is lacking there is a *presumption* that the models tested will yield seriously biased *ex post* and *ex ante* forecasts.

In view of the great amount of work involved in estimating a structural model, and in view of the large number of competing models that Cooper was testing, it is reasonable to infer that applications of TLC to all of them would have been too much for any one investigator (or several). Suppose, on the other hand, that it was feasible to apply TLC. It is just possible that none of the models would have made it to the final squared error tests in a form that would be recognized by the original authors. Some of them would have been rejected even after taking 'proper account' of strikes, wars and other structural shifts. The signs of many estimators may turn out wrong, and strong systematic behavior in the calculated residuals may lead to the conclusion that the earlier models were hopelessly misspecified. Even without the applications of TLC in the estimation process, some of the models might be rejected as being in obvious contradiction with the economic structure

---

[9]It is noted that the above discussion has a certain Bayesian flavor. However, the formal analytic Bayesian framework is not present. It will, in fact, probably never be present. From a Monte Carlo viewpoint, the situation is akin to that of the decision maker who, (a) has freedom to draw additional samples, but (b) who has only limited control over the characteristics of the sample, and (c) who has a certain amount of prior knowledge about the signs and magnitudes of the coefficients. Such a decision-maker could be expected to omit samples deemed to be outliers in terms of his prior knowledge. The investigator might well wish to examine the distribution of an estimator obtained by allowing for the exclusion of outliers. The statistical properties of such estimators would be close to the properties of the estimators used in a good forecasting model.

and institutions generating the data. Anyone who has carefully read *National Income 1954*, the volume which documents the construction of the NIA accounts (prior to revision), can cite numerous equation 'specifications' in existing models which are completely at odds with the procedures used by the agency generating much of the data. In a slightly different vein a casual review of the inventory 'theory' incorporated in many (perhaps all) of the models studied by Cooper will lead either to complete rejection or substantial revision of the inventory equations. The point is that had Cooper attempted to apply TLC he would possibly never have been content to race any of the old models against the autoregressive rabbit (our thanks to Goldfield [**8**]); he would have raced his own model or models fortified by TLC. (This is not to say that the old models do so badly in the race, when properly fortified.)

TESTS OF HYPOTHESES

As noted above the tests applied to the various models examined by Cooper were based on equation-by-equation comparisons of the mean squared error of one-quarter 'forecasts' over the sample period (1949–60) as well as mean squared errors calculated over the post-sample period (1961–5). Unfortunately, classical hypothesis-testing procedures cannot be employed since the small-sample properties of the mean squared error statistics are generally unknown. It is therefore necessary to resort to more or less straightforward descriptive comparisons. Three types of comparisons immediately suggest themselves. First, the sample mean squared errors can be compared across models to determine which of the models achieves the closest fit to the data. Second, the post-sample MSE cam be compared with the sample MSE in an attempt to ascertain the temporal stability of a given model. Finally, the post-sample MSE can be compared across models to determine which model has the smallest one-period forecast error. Of particular interest in all of these cases is a comparison of the MSE of a simple autoregressive model with the MSE of various structural models, the presumption being that the predictive accuracy of the structural model should at least equal if not surpass that of the autoregressive model in order to justify its use in forecasting. Each of these types of comparisons will now be considered in some detail in order to see what valid inferences can be drawn from such mean squared error comparisons.

Sample-period mean squared error comparisons

The major problems associated with the interpretation of sample-period mean squared error statistics become readily apparent in connection with a comparison of an autoregressive model with a structural model. Suppose that the null hypothesis is that the variable y_t is generated by an autoregressive process of order p; that is,

$$y_t = \sum_{i=1}^{p} b_i y_{t-i} + N_t. \tag{22.11}$$

For a sample of $T+1$ observations, the null hypothesis can be written as

$$y = Z_2 B_2 + N \tag{22.12}$$

where

$$y = \begin{bmatrix} y_t \\ y_{t-1} \\ \vdots \\ y_{t-T} \end{bmatrix}, \quad Z_2 = \begin{bmatrix} y_{t-1} & y_{t-2} & \cdots & y_{t-p} \\ y_{t-2} & y_{t-3} & \cdots & y_{t-p-1} \\ \vdots & & & \\ y_{t-T-1} & y_{t-T-2} & \cdots & y_{t-T-p} \end{bmatrix} \tag{22.13}$$

$$B_2 = \begin{bmatrix} b_1 \\ b_2 \\ \vdots \\ b_p \end{bmatrix}, \quad \text{and} \quad N = \begin{bmatrix} N_t \\ N_{t-1} \\ \vdots \\ N_{t-T} \end{bmatrix}.$$

The competing (structural) hypothesis is that y also depends on current and lagged exogenous variables and other lagged endogenous variables. In a linear framework, the alternative hypothesis is,

$$\begin{aligned} y &= Z_1 B_1 + Z_2 B_2 + \xi \\ &= ZB + \xi \end{aligned} \tag{22.14}$$

where Z_1 is a matrix of observations on exogenous and other lagged endogenous variables, B_1 is a vector of parameters, and ξ is a vector of disturbances.

Now the sum of squared errors obtained from the autoregressive model is,

$$\begin{aligned} S_1 &= [y - Z_2 \hat{B}_2]'[y - Z_2 \hat{B}_2] \\ &= y'[I - Z_2 [Z_2' Z_2]^{-1} Z_2'] y \end{aligned} \tag{22.15}$$

where $\hat{B}_2 = [Z_2'Z_2]^{-1}Z_2'y$ is the least squares estimate of B_2. Similarly, the sum of squared errors for the structural model is given by

$$S_2 = [y - Z\hat{B}]'[y - Z\hat{B}]$$
$$= [y - Z\hat{B}_L - Z(\hat{B} - \hat{B}_L)]'[y - Z\hat{B}_L - Z(\hat{B} - \hat{B}_L)] \quad (22.16)$$

where $\hat{B}_L = [Z'Z]^{-1}Z'y$ is the least squares estimate of B and $\hat{B}$ is a consistent simultaneous-equation estimate of B. It is not difficult to verify that

$$S_2 = S_1 - A + C \quad (22.17)$$

where

$$A = y'\hat{Z}_1[\hat{Z}_1'\hat{Z}_1]^{-1}\hat{Z}_1'y \quad (22.18)$$
$$C = (\hat{B} - \hat{B}_L)'Z'Z(\hat{B} - \hat{B}_L) \quad (22.19)$$
$$\hat{Z}_1 = [I - Z_2[Z_2'Z_2]^{-1}Z_2']Z_1. \quad (22.20)$$

We now note the following:

1 Both A and C are nonnegative.
2 Since $\hat{Z}_1$ is the matrix of residuals obtained from a regression of Z_1 on Z_2', it follows that if Z_1 and Z_2 are highly correlated within the sample, the calculated residuals will be small in absolute value and A will therefore be small relative to S_1. In other words, if Z_1 and Z_2 are highly correlated, the reduction in the sum of squares achieved by the introduction of the additional regressors Z_1 will be small and S_2 will not be significantly smaller than S_1 despite the fact that more regressors are used to obtain S_2.
3 The term C is larger the greater the deviation of $\hat{B}$ from $\hat{B}_L$. The effect of such deviation is to make S_2 larger than S_1. Since the structural model may involve restrictions on some of the elements of B, $\hat{B}$ and $\hat{B}_L$ will generally differ. For example, the structural model may impose zero restrictions on some of the elements of B_2. The effect on C of high order (nonsense) lags obtained by least-squares autoregression without regard to these restrictions is obvious. Another potentially important source of deviation of $\hat{B}$ from $\hat{B}_L$ is the case in which the error term exhibits serial correlation. In this case it is easy to show that the least-squares estimates are biased; the bias resulting from the fact that lagged values of the dependent variable explain to some extent the movement of the error term. The effect of this bias is to increase the value of C since the least-squares fit has the advantage of getting a lower MSE due to autocorrelated errors

whereas the restricted reduced form if estimated by consistent methods, can never expect this advantage (in large samples).

These observations lead to the conclusion that sample-period mean squared error comparisons of the autoregressive and structural models are not powerful tests for at least two reasons. First, because many exogenous variables exhibit autocorrelation and because of the joint dependency of lagged values of y and lagged values of the other dependent variables in the system, lagged values of y serve as good substitutes for Z_1 for purposes of one-quarter forecasts. This is true both within the sample used to estimate the parameters and outside the sample. Second, the squared errors of the structural model will be inflated due to the fact that the restricted reduced form estimate $\hat{B}$ will not be a least-squares estimate. One problem here is that by expanding the regressor matrix sufficiently, arbitrarily close least-squares fits to the data can be obtained. Unless some 'degrees of freedom' adjustment is made, it is extremely difficult to know what inferences to draw from the mean squared error comparisons. Unfortunately, the nature of an appropriate adjustment for degrees of freedom is not known. Even under the null hypothesis that the autoregressive model is true, the exact small-sample moments of the sample MSE are not known in general. The first order case could possibly be handled by an extension of the work of Takeuchi [17] or Richardson [16] on the exact small-sample moments of least-squares estimates of two-dependent variable econometric models; however, the general case appears to be intractable. Still some adjustment is appropriate, and the expectation is that the autoregressive one-quarter MSE is biased downward. The structural model MSE may also be similarly downward biased, though it seems unlikely that the structural MSE would be as seriously affected, since the structural estimation techniques do not lend themselves to error minimization in the same straightforward way that least-squares autoregression does.

It has been suggested by Goldfeld [8], McCarthy [14], BEA [10], and others that a more adequate test of structural estimation might be obtained if the models' MSE of forecasts with longer lead times were compared. The reason that multiperiod forecast comparisons might be more powerful is that in the case of long-term forecasts, the term Z_1 can be shown to contain variables from many periods beyond the periods represented in Z_2. In such a case Z_2 can be expected to do less well in explaining Z_1, and A can be expected to be larger. Moreover, the dependence of future errors on Z_2 is unlikely to be significantly less. This would be reflected in a smaller expected value for C. The longer-period forecasts take away the advantage that the autoregressive scheme has in the short run.

A striking example of how multiperiod forecast comparisons yield results that are at odds with those reported by Cooper can be found in an experiment recently conducted by the BEA staff [**10**] and summarized in table 22.1. It can be seen that the real GNP forecasts produced by the OBE model are more accurate than the autoregressive predictions even in the one-quarter case. But the advantage of the structural model is considerably more striking in the case of forecasts with longer lead times.

Table 22.1 Average absolute errors in real GNP over the 40 quarters 1955-I to 1966-IV (Billions of $)

	'Best' autoregressive equation	OBE model*
First-quarter forecasts	3.60	2.35
Second-quarter forecasts	6.93	3.58
Third-quarter forecasts	9.55	4.47
Fourth-quarter forecasts	11.39	4.92
Fifth-quarter forecasts	13.17	5.42
Sixth-quarter forecasts	14.43	5.82

*Adjusted for first order serial correlation of residuals.

Another way in which the power of forecast error comparisons might be increased is to place more weight on those periods during which the economy is undergoing unusual changes. The ability of a model to track turning points, for example, might be more important than the average error over the entire sample period. The potential increase in the power of turning-point comparisons again derives from the fact that when the economy is undergoing such adjustments, there is likely to be more independent variation in the exogenous variables and hence Z_2 will not provide as good a proxy for Z_1 as during periods of steady growth.

The following example illustrates this point. Using the time period 1949–64, roughly the period covered by Cooper's study, we found the 'best' autoregressive equation for real GNP to be,

$$x = 1.68 + 1.44 X_{-1} - 0.44 X_{-2}$$
$$(4.02)\ (0.11)\quad\ (0.11)$$

$$SE = \text{standard deviation} = 5.09. \tag{22.21}$$

(The numbers in parentheses are estimated standard errors.) This relationship may be rewritten as[10]

$$\Delta X = 1.68 + 0.44 \Delta X_{-1}. \tag{22.22}$$

In this form it is clear why this particular autoregressive scheme would not perform well around turning points. Such a model would forecast a decline in X only if the initial change (ΔX_{-1}) were negative and large enough in absolute value. If ΔX_{-1} were positive, the model would never forecast a downturn. In particular such an autoregressive model would have missed competely the recent downturn in economic activity (1969–70) as shown by the estimated forecast beginning in 1969–3 and extending to 1970–2 presented in table 22.2. For comparison, the Wharton Model post-release control forecasts made in August 1969 are also presented along with the actual figures.

Table 22.2 Forecasts of the recent recession (GNP, billions of 1958 dollars)

	69-3	69-4	70-1	70-2
Autoregression	730.0	733.1	736.2	739.2
Wharton	729.1	727.2	728.1	732.5
Actual	730.9	729.2	723.8	724.9

Source: Wharton-EFA, Inc., August 25, Post Release Control Solution.

Post-sample mean squared error comparisons

The difficulties associated with comparisons of mean squared error statistics within the sample period indicate that such comparisons must be interpreted with caution. The question we now consider is whether post-sample mean squared error comparisons are subject to similar difficulties. As mentioned previously, post-sample statistics can be used in two ways: to test for temporal stability of a given model and to evaluate the predictive performance of alternative models.

The post-sample tests performed by Cooper create the presumption that the models that were analyzed were subject to temporal instability since the post-sample MSE typically exceeded the sample-period MSE. This result should occasion no surprise among those who have used econometric models for economic forecasting.[11] Indeed, it is generally agreed that mechanistic extrapolation of an econometric model frequently yields unsatisfactory results. One interpretation of this is that the

---

[10] This equation is reminiscent of Orcutt's [15] single autoregressive equation used to represent all the dependent variables in Tinbergen's first US Model.

[11] A more careful procedure for evaluation of post-sample errors is discussed in Dhrymes, et al. [3].

sample-period mean squared error statistics are not good estimates of the variances of the residual process. This should simply serve to remind us of a point that is often lost sight of in model building; namely, the econometrician is attempting to estimate the variance–covariance matrix of the disturbance process as well as the coefficients of the model. The elements of the variance–covariance matrix are parameters of the model in the same sense that the coefficients of the model are parameters and the objective is to obtain a good estimate of this matrix and not necessarily to minimize its diagonal elements. A fact of life is that estimates of the variance–covariance matrix may leave us in the uncomfortable position that standard tolerance interval statements that should accompany simulations are very large. If one simply follows mechanical rules for model estimation and application, appropriate error and interval calculations may deprive the applied economist of any useful role whatsoever. The intervals are frequently so wide that almost anything from explosion to disaster can happen to the economy within their ranges.

We hasten to add, however, that this does not necessarily mean that it is impossible to derive from econometric models meaningful results for business or public policy use. It simply means that the contribution of econometric models to applied economics is increased substantially when it is used together with *a priori* information on error values to help reduce residual variance. And the intelligent user of econometric models would contend that there is a substantial amount of information that can be used to improve predictive performance. Many of the structural shifts that take place in the economy can be foreseen a quarter or more in advance; tax-law changes and important strikes are examples. In preparing forecasts, the intelligent model user would surely have included the effect of these shifts in the forecast. Even in the case of those shifts that were not foreseen, the model forecaster would surely have learned by experience: having observed that some of his structural equations had begun to exhibit large errors, he could be expected to take corrective measures. In such a case, the forecast MSE would be expected to be much lower than the beyond-sample errors calculated by simple extrapolation of the model. In short, the fact that the beyond-sample errors yielded evidence of structural shifts precludes their use as measures of forecasting ability unless we are to believe that the model builder will do nothing about such shifts. The significance of the evidence of structural change lies in the fact that in a realistic forecasting environment many structural shifts can not be foreseen. Structural change does erode forecasting performance, but to the extent that structural shifts are correctly anticipated or rapidly detected, the actual forecast error will not be as large as the MSE obtained by simple extrapolation of the model.

In summary, the following point emerges in connection with post-sample MSE comparison. If the post-sample MSE is significantly larger than the sample MSE for a given model, then the post-sample MSE may be a poor measure of the forecasting performance of the model. For in this case, a judicious use of prior and posterior (i.e. error analysis) information may well yield a measurable increase in forecast accuracy. It follows that in order to interpret the post-sample MSE correctly, it is necessary to isolate the way in which temporal instability manifests itself.

Remarks on ex ante forecasts

Fortunately, the economist is not forced to make a once and for all decision based on sample period statistics. These statistics dictate the model he uses for an initial forecast. However, after the results are in, the decisions may be reviewed. The new data may be pooled with the old, and new sample tests performed. (Some day, years from now, convergence in probability may actually take place to a degree that the small-sample problems discussed above may be ignored.) The major appeal of the *ex ante* forecast test is that it avoids the Monday Morning Quarterback aspects of the historical period tests. In this context, historical curve fitting buys the forecaster nothing. In a true *ex ante* forecast, models which have been 'forced' to a close-sample period fit may be expected to be poor performers. The autoregressive forecasters by choice make no use of exogenous variables, and hence are surely subject to error in an *ex ante* framework. The structural model forecaster must extrapolate the exogenous variables. On the other hand, in the near term, a good deal of intelligence is available on future values of these variables. For instance tax-law changes are often legislated years ahead. Also the structural models, if correctly specified, provide a framework within which good exogenous information might be used. In other respects the competing forecasting models seem to be on equal grounds in the *ex ante* forecasts. Their managers are free to make use of past errors in attempts to improve future forecasts.

SUMMARY: SOME GUIDELINES FOR FUTURE TESTING

In pointing out deficiencies in Cooper's testing procedures and conclusions, we do not intend to negate the possibility of testing models. We do firmly believe that if this form of analysis is properly done, it can shed light on model credibility, validation, and improvement. We shall try to outline in this section what we would regard as suitable model-testing procedures. Our recommended procedure will be far from the simple mechanistic approach followed by Cooper and will, in fact, be a more difficult, time-consuming process than that used in his study.

A guiding principle of our approach will be that the available information should be used efficiently – as efficiently as possible. Since economic samples are small and much less revealing than we would like, a great deal of TLC must be applied to all studies or nothing useful will be accomplished. The model tester should put himself in the position of the model builder and try to build the best possible structural model prior to testing; otherwise, he will be testing empty propositions.

Sample data

There is much to be said for choosing a fixed sample for fitting and extrapolation, common to all models being tested. It is not absolutely necessary to have the same sample for all models. In some cases it may not be possible, but for the most part homogeneity of sample appears to be desirable.

Within a fixed historical sample, the problem of data revision should not arise. It is not ruled out, however, because economic data are never 'true,' and measurement errors may affect different models in different ways. The best procedure, however, seems to be to choose a common sample period and fix the data for the whole set of test calculations.

Another caveat with respect to homogeneity of samples is the question of degrees of freedom. Alternative models and alternative methods of estimation have different requirements for degrees of freedom. This could be a factor in relaxation of the principle of sample homogeneity.

Specification

Economic theory and knowledge of the world around us can suggest a list of variables and some general parametric relationships. It cannot, however, set out in advance what the precise lag structure is nor all the departures from linearity. *That is a matter of sample experimentation and not purely a matter of specification.*

The model to be tested should be estimated, either by the tester or original model builder, with TLC to get as good a system as possible. We would have preferred that Cooper built his own structural models with TLC. This will be especially important for within-sample tests, for it is well known that sufficient work done on lag structure, a wide range of variable selection, or use of additional parameters can markedly improve the fit. An efficient search of the parameter space will not necessarily drive a complete system to close fit in simultaneous equation solution, but it often can improve the fit considerably. The autoregressive test equations are driven, equation by equation, towards close fit by experimenting with the lag structure and similar experimentation is needed for the structural model, subject of course, to *a priori* information about the nature of the overall relationship and the general shape of the lag distributions incorporated in the model.

Because we lack information on exact small-sample properties, historical period results are of limited value. Some thought should be given to designing tests of forecasting performance in a true *ex ante* framework.[12]

Estimation

Since different model structures have different degrees of freedom, within a given sample, and since methods of estimation are not equally sensitive to limitations of degrees of freedom it is not clear that all models to be tested should be estimated by the same technique. Each model should be estimated by a method that will give the best performance for that system. Best performance might be determined by simulation testing within the sample used for fitting. This is all part of TLC. Brookings-type models are so large that they cannot be estimated by maximum likelihood methods. Whether the other models likely to be considered can be so estimated or not is an open question, but this comparison illustrates that estimation methods must be tailored to the model.

Collinearity is as important as shortage of degrees of freedom in making estimation difficult or inefficient. Models differ as to degree of collinearity. Nonlinearity differences and identification differences provide additional reasons why estimation methods should not be made uniform.

Many models may, in fact, be well suited to the RR method used by Cooper, but if this method is to be used for each model to be tested, it should not be applied in the manner suggested by Cooper (or Jorgenson). The method consists of first estimating a model by some consistent method such as ordinary TSLS, indirect least squares,

---

[12]Cooper's extrapolation period tests should definitely not be viewed as *ex ante* tests, but as tests of structural stability with limited significance.

instrumental variables, or modified TSLS, where the first-stage regressors are some selected subset of instrumental variables in the whole system.[13] In the final stage of the RR method, regressors are constructed in each structural equation using computed values of dependent variables from the restricted reduced forms of the system (estimated at the earlier stage) and the included predetermined variables in each individual equation. As noted above, care must be taken at both stages of this process if consistency is to be preserved.

Since this process could be iterated, as in the work of Dutta and Lyttkens [4], but is usually stopped after the first or second iteration, the set of parameter estimates used will depend heavily on the value from the first round. It is, therefore, imperative to estimate the first round with much TLC and using an efficient selection procedure for obtaining instruments when there is a shortage of degrees of freedom. If there are enough degrees of freedom, the first round estimates to be used for getting the restricted reduced forms may well make use of all available instruments. If there are not enough degrees of freedom we recommend the data-reduction procedure of choosing appropriate principal components of predetermined variables or perhaps following the suggestions of Fisher [6]. Since system simulation performance depends on the choice of instruments, some experimentation may be called for.

Some parameter estimates may be manifestly unsatisfactory. The system should be respecified and re-estimated until the investigator is sure that all coefficients are satisfactory. This is estimation with TLC. Often only one or two poor equation estimates can be readily modified and change a poorly behaving system into a well-behaving system.

The final stage of the RR method should use an estimate of the first stage that a model builder would be willing to accept in deriving regressors for the second stage from system solutions of the first stage, i.e. from estimated restricted reduced forms if the system is linear. Again, however, TLC must be applied, for all estimates in the final-stage regressions will not necessarily turn out to be satisfactory. It is simply a fact of life that estimation or re-estimation of models in new or modified samples changes a few parameter estimates from being reasonable to being unreasonable. By respecifying and re-estimating, these changes can be effectively dealt with. In some cases, renormalization is all that is needed. Since the TSLS or RR method depends on units normalization and since the normalization rules are arbitrary,

---

[13]We have recently come to the view that the first-round estimator used need not be consistent, and OLS might be a good starting choice. Jorgenson and Brundy, in a later paper, suggest one extra iteration following an inconsistent (OLS) start.

such applications of TLC must be made. It has been found that iteration of the Wharton Model estimate (TSLS with principal components of predetermined variables) can produce within-sample simulations that reduce root-mean-squared error of GNP by $3–4 billion if one production function estimate is renormalized and restricted to have constant returns to scale. Otherwise there would be no improvement in simulation error. Why should a model tester throw away such valuable information simply because he wants to adhere to a strict mechanical rule?

Application

A rounded set of applications should be made in testing a model. Prediction performance should be tested, but both multi- as well as single-period predictions should be considered. Autoregressive or even more general autoregressive-moving average schemes are known to generate rapidly increasing prediction error as the time horizon of extrapolation lengthens; therefore, tests should not be biased by being confined to single-period prediction.

If major exogenous events occur in the extrapolation period that were not present in the sample period, and if these events could, in principle, have been known in advance of prediction, they should be quantified and introduced in the ex-post prediction tests. Statutory changes in tax, transfer, reserve, and other laws that form structural restrictions on the system must be introduced in the testing period as they occurred in actual economic life. This was not done in Cooper's tests. The *ex ante* prediction performance of models, in the hands of model builders using TLC, takes these events into account. That is an important reason why ex ante prediction records with models are so much better in terms of performance accuracy than mechanically applied *ex post* records. Although it takes painfully long to build up statistical samples of systematically applied *ex ante* forecast records, we feel that they are as revealing (perhaps even more so) in the validation of a model as are *ex post* prediction tests.

Some standards must be set on the variables to be tested. There is no unique way of writing a given model, for definitional identities can be added indefinitely. The generation of additional forecasts from a given solution has no bounds. There are actually only as many predictions of variables as there are stochastic equations of a system. Prediction tests often score points on accuracy of the GNP deflator, GNP in current prices, GNP in constant prices; yet these three variables are non-stochastically related in the identity

$pX = GNP.$

It may be of descriptive interest to see how well all three variables are predicted, but the error analysis does not constitute three independent pieces of test information. By judicious invention of additional identities, test scores may be drastically altered; therefore testing should be confined to as many dependent variables of a system as there are stochastic equations.

Prediction at turning points is of unusual importance, and these should be separately tested. The entire cyclical or frequency response characteristics of a model should be tested. The standard tests are in the time domain, but model performance in the frequency domain is of equal importance.

The growth characteristics of a model should also be tested. The short-run models may need amplification for this form of testing and the corresponding naive model may be different from the pure autoregressive, but this aspect of testing should not be overlooked.

In general policy simulation, the naive models have no content. If they are modified to include exogenous policy variables, they may cease to be naive alternatives. Without comparing models to the naive case, suitably built models may well be compared with one another in respect to response in alternative policy simulations. This could constitute another form of test and has been the procedure in the working seminar that gave rise to this symposium [7].

REFERENCES

[1] J. Brundy and D. Jorgenson, 'Efficient estimation of simultaneous equations by instrumental variables,' *Review of Economics and Statistics*, LIII, August (1971), 207–24.

[2] Ronald L. Cooper, 'The predictive performance of quarterly econometric models of the United States,' in *Econometric Models of Cyclical Behavior* (Ed. B. G. Hickman), Studies in Income and Wealth, No. 36, Columbia University Press for NBER, New York (1972).

[3] Phoebus J. Dhrymes *et al.*, 'Criteria for evaluation of econometric models,' *Annals of Economic and Social Measurement*, I, Summer (1972), 291–324.

[4] M. Dutta and E. Lyttkens, 'Iterative instrumental variables method and estimation of a large simultaneous system,' Discussion paper No. 7, Rutgers University, 1970.

[5] Michael K. Evans, Yoek Haitovsky and George Treyz, 'An analysis of the forecasting properties of U.S. econometric models,' in *Econometric Models of Cyclical Behavior* (Ed. B. G. Hickman), Studies in Income and Wealth, No. 36, Columbia University Press for NBER, New York (1972).

[6] Franklin M. Fisher, 'Dynamic structure and estimation in economy wide econometric models,' in *The Brookings Quarterly Econometric Model of the United States* (Eds J. Duesenberry, G. Fromm, L. R. Klein and E. Kuhn), Rand McNally-North Holland, Chicago and Amsterdam (1965).

[7] G. Fromm and L. R. Klein, 'A comparison of eleven econometric models of the United States,' *American Economic Review, Papers and Proceedings*, LXIII, May (1973), 385–93.

[8] Stephen M. Goldfeld, 'The predictive performance of quarterly econometric models of the United States: Comments,' in *Econometric Models of Cyclical Behavior* (Ed. B. G. Hickman), Studies in Income and Wealth, No. 36, Columbia University Press for NBER, New York (1972).

[9] R. J. Gordon, 'Large scale econometric models: An introduction and appraisal for non-econometricians,' February (1970), unpublished mimeograph.

[10] G. R. Green, M. Liebenberg and A. A. Hirsch, 'The predictive performance of quarterly econometric models of the United States: Comments,' in *Econometric Models of Cyclical Behavior* (Ed. B. G. Hickman), Studies in Income and Wealth, No. 36, Columbia University Press for NBER, New York (1972).

[11] Harry H. Kelejian, 'Two-stage least squares and econometric systems linear in parameters but nonlinear in the endogenous variables,' *Journal of the American Statistical Association*, LXVI, June (1971), 373–4.

[12] Lawrence R. Klein, *An Essay on the Theory of Economic Prediction*, Helsinki, 1968. Distributed by the Academic Bookstore, Helsinki. Enlarged US edition, Markham, Chicago (1971).

[13] T. Kloek and L. B. M. Mennes, 'Simultaneous equation estimation based on principal components of predetermined variables,' *Econometrica*, XXVIII, January (1960), 45–61.

[14] Michael D. McCarthy, 'The predictive performance of quarterly econometric models of the United States: Comments,' in *Econometric Models of Cyclical Behavior* (Ed. B. G. Hickman), Studies in Income and Wealth, No. 36, Columbia University Press for NBER, New York (1972).

[15] G. H. Orcutt, 'A study of the autoregressive nature of the time series used for Tinbergen's model of the economic system of the United States, 1919–1932,' *Journal of the Royal Statistical Society*, Series B, X (1948), 1–53.

[16] D. H. Richardson, 'The exact distribution of a structural coefficient estimate,' *Journal of the American Statistical Association*, LXIII, December (1968), 1214–26.

[17] K. Takeuchi, 'Exact sampling moments of the ordinary least squares, instrumental variable, and two stage least squares estimator,' *International Economic Review*, XI, February (1970), 1–12.

[18] Victor Zarnowitz, Charlotte Boschan and Geoffrey H. Moore, 'Business cycle analysis of econometric model simulations,' in *Econometric Models of Cyclical Behavior* (Ed. B. G. Hickman), Studies in Income and Wealth, No. 36, Columbia University Press for NBER, New York (1972).

23
Money in the Wharton Quarterly Model

THE MONETARIST DEBATE

Extremist positions usually have grains of truth, and it is natural to expect that the highly repetitive statements of the monetarist positions about the role of money in the economy, in particular its effects on inflation or in the determination of nominal income, would percolate through the thinking of nonmonetarists, leaving some traces of influence. While we would say that we are not persuaded by the monetarists' arguments, we can say that participation in the debate has been provocative and that model builders and operators are stimulated to thinking anew about how money and related variables enter macroeconometric models.

Over the years money has played an increasingly important role in the successive generations of Wharton models.[1] Interest rate levels and swings, deregulation, introduction of new credit instruments, and similar developments have made money markets more interesting from the viewpoint of economic analysis. They have also made credit changes more influential; therefore, it is no surprise that the monetary sectors are growing in importance and demanding more attention of model builders. A major step was taken in connection with the Wharton Model when a complete flow-of-funds model was introduced in 1977, work on this aspect having started as early as 1974.

The ongoing process of giving increasing importance to monetary phenomena in the model took on new significance with the advent of the adoption of new operating rules by the Federal Reserve System on

---

[1]Going back to a predecessor model, the Klein-Goldberger model, it can be remarked that Arthur Goldberger was originally encouraged to prepare a doctoral dissertation on a model of the money market for inclusion in the system. He, perhaps wisely, switched from that aspect to his important work on dynamic multipliers, but the idea of integrating money into the models of the macroeconomy predate present efforts, by more than two decades.

From *Journal of Money, Credit, and Banking*, **15**, May (1983), 237–59; written jointly with Edward Friedman and Stephen Able.

October 6, 1979. On that day, Chairman Paul Volcker announced that strict growth targets for M1 and M2 would henceforth be set. Previously, a great deal of weight was simultaneously given to interest-rate targets, and the targets for the money aggregates were adhered to with less steadfastness. It was a stated objective of President Carter's economic advisers for the monetary authorities to pay more attention to interest-rate fluctuations than to monetary growth. Doctrinaire monetarism had been popular early in the 1970s but was not vigorously promoted after the Nixon New Economic Policy period and the oil embargo of 1973–4.

Many nonmonetarists may have applauded or supported Federal Reserve decisions since October 1979, but they did not put as much confidence as monetarists in the success of the policies in restraining demand or reducing the rate of inflation. The linkages between money supply and behavior of nominal income or the general price level are viewed as being less tight by nonmonetarists than by monetarists.

HOW HAVE THINGS WORKED OUT?

In recent years, though not in every subperiod, the Federal Reserve did succeed in slowing the growth rate of M1 appreciably, but it was at the cost of driving up interest rates to unusual high points, both nominal and real. But the volatility and amplitude of changes, rather than levels, were the disturbing aspects of the new monetarist policies. Fluctuations in both M1 and Treasury bill rates were much greater after 1979 than before. These results can be seen quite clearly in time charts of quarterly averages of interest rates and of percentage changes in M1 (seasonally adjusted at annual rates). In the charts for M1 changes (Figures 23.1 and 23.2), it appears that the growth rate was held to a steady range for practically a decade, but as soon as the authorities turned monetarist, they immediately destabilized the movement in M1 (table 23.1).

To highlight the movements, we point out that the prime rate reached 20 per cent three times in the last 2 years, interspersed with swings of 600 basis points. These interest changes induced swings in loan demand and hence monetary growth. The Open Market Committee was forced to maintain sharper efforts in order to keep M1 in line. The pursuit of M1 targets may have actually destabilized M1 growth (Figure 23.3 and table 23.2).

On an annual basis, the amplitude of M1 movements does not appear to have been larger after 1979 than before that time, covering

Money in the Wharton Quarterly Model 435

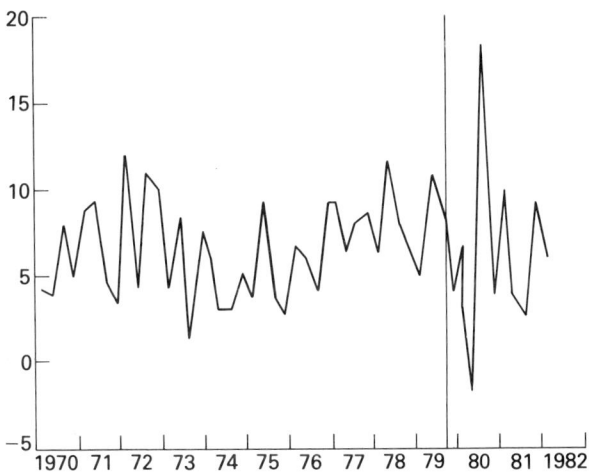

Figure 23.1 Percentage change in M1 by quarters, seasonally adjusted annual rates, 1970-I to 1982-I

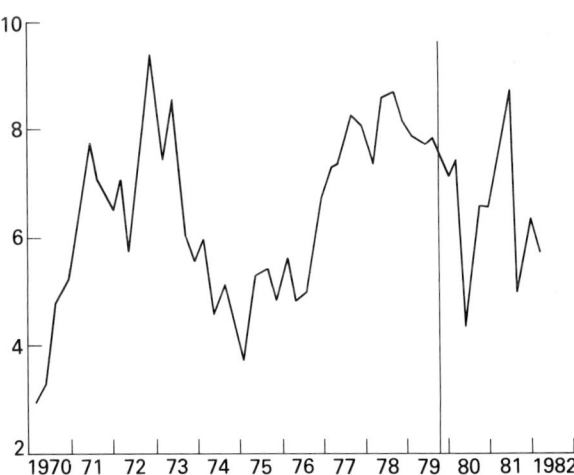

Figure 23.2 Percentage change in M1 from year ago, quarterly values, 1970-I to 1982-I

Table 23.1 Measures of growth variability (percentage change in M1, quarterly average basis. Seasonally adjusted annual rates)

	Mean	Standard deviation	Coefficient of variation
1970-1 to 1979-3	6.68	2.69	0.40
1979-4 to 1982-1	6.35	5.10	0.80

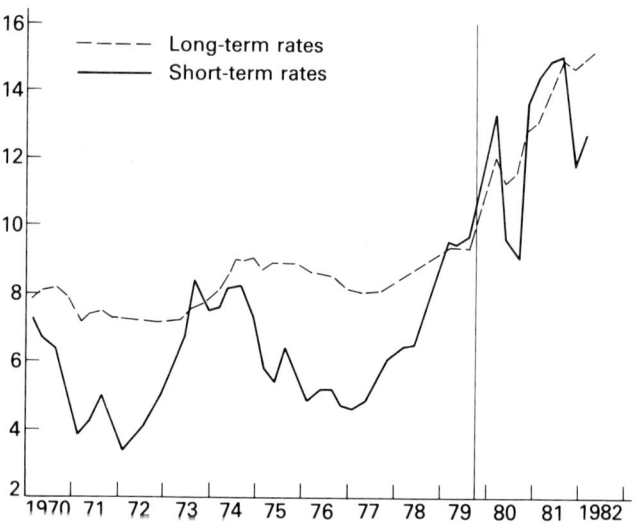

Figure 23.3 Long-term and short-term interest rates, quarterly averages, 1970-I to 1982-I

Table 23.2 Measures of interest rate variability (monthly average basis)

	Mean	Standard deviation	Coefficient of variation
Three-month treasury bills			
January 1970–September 1979	6.15	1.67	0.27
October 1979–May 1982	12.63	2.25	0.18
Moody's seasoned AAA bonds			
January 1970–September 1979	8.17	0.68	0.08
Octoober 1979–May 1982	13.08	1.58	0.12

all the years back to 1970. Nevertheless, the annual data do show much more frequent periodicity of swings in M1 growth after October 1979. These are related to the back-to-back recessions of 1980 and 1981.

At least two important voices within the Federal Reserve System have pointed out technical reasons why performance has been so unstable. President A. Solomon of New York (American Economic Association, December 1981) and President Frank Morris of Boston (Supply Side Conference of the Federal Reserve Bank of Atlanta, April 1982) have emphasized the technical changes taking place in banking and in money markets as being obstacles to the Fed's achieving the requisite degree of control needed in order to implement monetarism.

SOME MONETARIST PRINCIPLES

The operating rules of the monetary authority and their success, judged by monetarist standards, are one thing and monetarist theory is quite another thing. It is worthwhile to consider some leading points of monetarist theory in order to clarify some of the issues. Monetarist assertions are:

1 Money, alone, is the determinant of nominal economic activity in the aggregate (in other words, velocity is a *parameter* or, more generally, the money demand function is stable).
2 Money supply is either exogenous or a controllable target value.
3 Apart from transient redistribution of resources, caused by misperceptions of government policies, changes in money stock affect only price level changes and not real magnitudes in the economy.
4 Fiscal policies have no lasting impact on aggregate economic activity.

One-time increases in money supply should have no effect on interest rates because the demand for cash balances relative to interest-bearing claims is not affected by the level of interest rates. Increases in money are absorbed by proportional increases in nominal transactions requirements; thus velocity or money demand would be independent of interest rates, contrary to the assertions of the theory of liquidity preference. This is a key disagreement between the theory of the economy held by monetarists and by nonmonetarists.

Monetarists emphasize that money or liquid assets, in a broader sense, are key direct determinants of expenditure behavior. Increases in liquidity cause increases in total spending. By contrast, the life-cycle theory of consumer behavior holds, in a nonmonetarist view, that a measure of a lifetime income stream determines household spending.

This effect may be measured by total wealth (liquid and nonliquid). Current income provides needed liquidity for spending; therefore, it too should be a variable in an aggregate consumption function.

Only part of M1 should appear in total wealth because bank deposits are offset by private liabilities in the national balance sheet. Nonmonetarists also believe that all or part of the interest-bearing national debt is a component of national wealth. They believe that reaction to excess liquidity brings about a reshuffling of portfolio assets towards less-liquid, higher-earning assets. Asset prices and interest rates fall. The decline in borrowing costs stimulates fixed investment. Capital goods prices rise and interest rates fall. Eventually, total capital formation and total consumption are stimulated. Wealth would be marked up at the higher asset prices, and this too would stimulate spending.

Monetarists would say that the direct addition to wealth resulting from open market operations that increase money stock would promote spending even if interest rates were unchanged. Nonmonetarists would, contrariwise, say that changes in the money stock would affect spending only if interest rates and asset prices change.

A crude statement of the monetarist position would be that velocity, that is *some* measure of it, given the varieties of numerators and denominators that could be used, is a constant. It is not difficult to find contradictory data on this proposition. Velocity has moved both cyclically and secularly. To refute the constancy of velocity is much like the refutation of the crude accelerator hypothesis in investment analysis. Generalized accelerators and generalized investment functions fit the data much better than does the crude accelerator. Similarly, the dynamic extension of velocity to measure long-run concepts or the construction of generalized money-demand functions are preferable. A money-demand function may exist, but it has a large error component and recently has shown such instability that the operational technique for monetarism has been seriously doubted within the Federal Reserve System.

Another way of looking at this problem is to argue that not only is velocity a variable rather than a parameter, but that the velocity function, which is just a transformation of the money-demand function, depends on interest rates, inflation rates, and other variables of portfolio choice. From this point of view, conventional specifications of liquidity preference theory replace quantity theory, which is the point from which the whole debate began.

Positions have changed over the years, and monetarists now apparently agree with nonmonetarists that money-supply changes affect interest rates and that interest rates affect velocity, but on closer examination it turns out that that is because of the belief that money growth spurs inflation expectations, which become added premiums to real interest rates. Real rates, according to monetarists, are invariant with respect to changes in the quantity of money. The high nominal rates of the past few years imply to monetarists that expectations of future inflation have been rising, even though actual inflation rates have been falling for about 1 year. Prior to the resurgence of monetarism at the end of the 1960s, many of the differences between monetarist and nonmonetarist positions were empirical. Now there seem to be serious differences of opinion about the way the economy functions.

MONEY IN THE WHARTON MODEL

In the first generations of the Wharton Model, 1958-63, money and credit played a minor role. Increasing awareness of monetary effects and more intensive variation of monetary instruments by public authorities led to significant changes. Interest rates were more carefully integrated into expenditure equations; liquid assets were introduced into consumer-demand functions; the money markets were modeled in greater detail; and linkages were recognized between credit market variables and federal finance.

In the present version of the Wharton Model the money-interest rate connection is based on specifications used in the MIT–Pennsylvania–Social Science Research Council (MPS) model. On the demand side, the Treasury bill rate is principally a function of velocity and the ratio of privately held debt to private GNP, all variables with appropriate lag distributions. On the supply side, excess reserves at commercial banks are a function of the bill rate, the change in loan volume, change in unborrowed reserves, and the change in reserve requirements. After excess reserves are determined, M1 is estimated as the sum of currency holdings (from a behavioral equation) and checkable deposits. The latter come from the basic reserve identity.

From this money-interest rate nexus, come short-term rates, but the main variables influencing spending behavior and other nonfinancial magnitudes are long-term rates; they are generated from a term structure relationship. A summary of the main interest rate effects are:

1 Cost of borrowing or debt service effects on final demand items.
2 User-cost effects on sector producer prices.
3 Interest income effects on national income and thus final demand.

4 Interest cost effects on government outlays.

5 International capital flow effects on exchange rates and thus on exports, imports, and international price competition.

1 The best known of these effects is the impact of credit conditions on housing expenditures, construction activity, and consumer durable spending. Residential investment has closely followed interest and credit swings through one business cycle after another during the 1950s, 1960s, 1970s, and today.

The model has had to keep up with institutional changes affecting main actors in the mortgage and consumer credit sector. As we have shifted from disintermediation to costly competition for capital funds in new money-market instruments, the timing and severity of spending cycles have changed. As any forecaster knows, models must be restructured and retuned to deal with this changing environment.

2 The principal cost factor in price determination is unit labor cost. Producer price is often specified as a markup on this cost, but the concept has been extended to include user capital cost, as well as some intermediate costs. In electric utilities and other capital-intensive sectors with long planning horizons, the user-cost effect is quite important for pricing decisions.

3 Interest is both a receipt and a cost in the national economy. Interest income recipients must take account of money-market fluctuations in assessing their available income for spending. Counterbalancing the restrictive effects of high interest costs for spending on houses and durables, there is an offsetting income flow, in which many households and other economic units participate. The high interest rates generate high interest income for general spending.

4 On balance, the public sector borrows, although all units of government are not net borrowers. The end result of high interest rates is a contribution to debt servicing on the part of the public sector. In fact, the single most serious factor making for budget imbalance, prior to the onset of the recession, has been the high cost of public borrowing. It is very important to take this factor into account in the overall assessment of the effect of interest rates on the economy.

5 Relatively high rates attract foreign capital, both hot money at short term and longer-term investments too. There are many factors acting together to determine exchange rates, but interest rate differentials among countries are among the most important. High US rates have recently contributed to capital inflows into this country, thus strengthening the dollar. This has made imports less expensive and helped to

hold down inflation. There are numerous other effects of the exchange rate on trade flows and international payments balances. Overall, a strong dollar tends to make the US less competitive than otherwise in international commerce. The US is very much an open economy, and our interest rates have significant effects on both our own international position and on that of many of our international partners or borrowers.

The main financial effects in the nonfinancial sector of the present Wharton Model, as distinct from some earlier generations, is through interest rates, but there is another whole set of linkages that comes from the flow-of-funds submodel. As one step in a continuing tendency to introduce more financial content into the Wharton Model, we began some years ago to build a separate submodel based on the flow-of-funds accounts and to link it to the mainstream Wharton Model. A goal of our flow-of-funds research has been to generate the spectrum of interest rates from market clearing of different financial instruments. This goal has not yet been attained: the term structure approach is still being used to generate the spectrum of rates on the basis of the determination of the Treasury bill rate, but there are still very important linkages between the flow-of-funds submodel and the main system.

Money and interest rates affect the allocation of saving and existing portfolios in the flow-of-funds sectors. These feed back into nonfinancial variables because interest rates alone are not complete guides to credit availability. Interest differentials affect relative acquisition of assets and liabilities in five sectors of the model: commercial banks, thrift institutions, life insurance companies, households, and nonfinancial corporations. The feedbacks are from thrift deposit flows to housing starts, the level of corporate liabilities to business interest paid, the federal deficit to the level of the national debt to federal net interest paid, and international capital flow to the exchange rate.

The data base for the flow-of-funds model is the Federal Reserve's accounting statement for that area. It has the important features that sector balance sheets are in balance and that total acquisition of a particular claim equals the issuing sector's liability. The data base covers the whole economy in a 26-sector breakdown. In the Wharton Flow-of-Funds Model there are only five sectors, but these are the most important, measured by size.

Both the Federal Reserve data base and the Wharton Flow-of-Funds Model have additional features. The acquisition of deposits are directly related to savings determined from the National Income Accounts (NIAs), and corporate liabilities are related to the profit and investment figures from the same accounts. Forecasts of components of M2, or commercial loan volume, for example, are directly linked to ultimate sources of funds.

The involvement of the general population in money-market activities at high prevailing rates of interest together with the gradual removal of arbitrary ceilings have made interest rates more important than ever as guides to credit availability. At the same time, model building for the flow-of-funds proves to be useful in understanding macroeconomic activity, especially in showing the magnitudes of borrowing needs or lending capability of sectors who 'crowd' one another in supplying or using funds.

A schematic outline of explicit variables that are significantly and directly affected by interest rates in the Wharton Model follows:

Final demands
  Automobile purchases
  Expenditures on furniture and household equipment
  Nonresidential investment in structures
  Nonresidential investment in equipment
Intervening variables, related to final demands
  Owner-occupied housing units
  Renter-occupied housing units
  User cost of owner-occupied housing
  User cost of renter-occupied housing
  Single-family housing starts
  1–4 family housing starts
  5+ family housing starts
  User cost of fixed investment in eight production sectors, structures
  User cost of fixed investment in eight production sectors, equipment
  Present value of depreciation in eight production sectors
Sector prices
  Sector prices in eight production sectors
Interest payments and receipts
  Net interest in national income
  Federal net interest paid
  State and local net interest received
International
  Gross capital inflows
  Gross capital outflows

The eight production sectors are durable manufacturing, nondurable manufacturing, mining, communication, agriculture, utilities, transportation, wholesale and retail trade.

INTEREST RATE AND MONEY SUPPLY SENSITIVITIES IN THE WHARTON MODEL

Consider the economic situation of the US economy in the second quarter of 1982. A recession is still taking place, unemployment is rising to nearly unprecedented levels, inflation has just been brought down from above 10 per cent to almost a standstill, interest rates are at all-time high values, money supply has been restrained, and the dollar is uncommonly strong. Using these conditions, appropriately quantified, with many lags, we initialized the Wharton Model and projected it for twelve quarters (starting with 1982-2). Money supply (M1) was made exogenous and set at two growth rates, 5 per cent and 6 per cent, giving us two dynamic simulations – scenarios if you like. Between corresponding time indicators in each of the two scenarios, we computed the following four elasticity-multiplier ratios:

$$\frac{\text{Percentage change in } X}{\text{Percentage change in M1}} \qquad \frac{\text{Percentage change in } X}{\text{Percentage change in M2}}$$

$$\frac{\text{Percentage change in } X}{\text{Change in bond rate}} \qquad \frac{\text{Percentage change in } X}{\text{Change in bill rate}}$$

The changes are between the two scenario values at a given time point in the projection. The change in interest rates is figured in percentage points. It is not a percentage change of a percentage. The variable X ranges over a variety of interesting magnitudes extracted from a list of some 1000 different variables that are generated by the model in each of the 2 solutions.

It must be emphasized that these are not partial reaction coefficients; they are *total system changes*. In general, the directions of effect are intuitively plausible, but there are some special cases that need explanation. There is a key magnitude, namely, the percentage change in nominal GNP associated with a percentage change in either M1 or M2. According to the doctrines of monetarism, this elasticity should, in the long run, be unity. In our 3-year simulation exercises, we find ratios that are significantly less than unity. In this respect, the Wharton Model is not monetarist, although in a longer run it would be if the real growth rate, the interest rate, and the inflation rate were to settle down to an expansion path where the real interest rate and real growth rate were equated.[2]

---

[2] See Lawrence R. Klein, 'Money in a general equilibrium system: Empirical aspects of the quantity theory,' *Economie Appliquée*, **31** (1978), 5–14.

The elasticity–multiplier ratios are tabulated in table 23.3. Some features of the table deserve commentary. Real GNP changes by about 0.3 per cent for a change in M1 of 1.0 per cent after 3 years. The corresponding M2 ratio reaches 0.85 per cent. The nominal GNP ratios are 0.11 and 0.33 per cent, respectively. The latter two are significantly less than unity, but they are growing in a dynamic sense. Since the relationship between M1 or M2 and the bond or bill rate is inverse, we find that GNP rises as interest rates fall. Real GNP rises by 1.04 per cent corresponding to 1.0 percentage point drop in the bond rate. The corresponding figure is only 0.59 per cent for a full point drop in the bill rate. The nominal GNP ratios with respect to interest rate changes are much lower, being no more than about 0.40 and 0.23, respectively.

Price indexes, whether the GNP deflator or the Consumer Price Index (CPI), fall as money supply rises and fall as interest rates fall. These movements may seem to be counterintuitive, particularly in light of quantity theory teaching that the only way to lower the rate of inflation is to reduce the rate of growth of money supply. Basically, the quantity theory concerns a proportional relationship between money supply and the general price level, given full capacity output.

There are two reasons why price indexes are lower in the scenario with faster growth in money supply than in the other scenario. Interest is an important cost factor in price determination and also plays an unusually important role in the makeup of the CPI. As interest rates come down between the 5 per cent and the 6 per cent M1 scenarios, price indexes also are reduced. Also, more investment is stimulated and capital expansion eventually means higher productivity growth. That is why the price improvement is much greater after about 1 year. The improvement in the unemployment rate is quite modest, being no more than 0.12 per cent for the 1.0 per cent rise in M1 or 0.36 per cent for a 1.0 per cent rise in M2. That means that rekindling of inflationary pressure is unlikely for modest expansions in money supply growth.

In the case of the federal surplus (negative surplus is a deficit), we find that the increase in money supply leads to lower interest rates, which, in turn, lead to a lower deficit. By the same kind of reasoning, the change in interest rates is positively associated with a change in the size of the deficit – lower rates mean (*ceteris paribus*) a lower deficit and higher rates a higher deficit. This is why we find positive entries under interest-rate change.

The more favorable prices induced by the lower interest rates (cost reduction) lead to an improvement in the current-account balance. This results from a relative improvement in competitiveness, assuming that foreign monetary policy remains unchanged. The current account

Table 23.3 Wharton Model elasticities

Sec. 1	Change in GNP (1972 dollars) per change in			
	M1	M2	Bond rate	Bill rate
1982-2	0.017	0.061	−0.152	−0.038
1982-3	0.035	0.122	−0.266	−0.084
1982-4	0.059	0.201	−0.410	−0.145
1983-1	0.083	0.278	−0.536	−0.202
1983-2	0.107	0.349	−0.637	−0.253
1983-3	0.131	0.423	−0.722	−0.304
1983-4	0.157	0.499	−0.795	−0.356
1984-1	0.184	0.576	−0.856	−0.410
1984-2	0.212	0.651	−0.907	−0.462
1984-3	0.239	0.724	−0.961	−0.512
1984-4	0.265	0.795	−1.007	−0.556
1985-1	0.289	0.853	−1.042	−0.590

Sec. 2	Change in GNP (current dollars) per change in			
	M1	M2	Bond rate	Bill rate
1982-2	0.006	0.020	−0.050	−0.013
1982-3	0.012	0.043	−0.093	−0.029
1982-4	0.022	0.075	−0.152	−0.054
1983-1	0.029	0.098	−0.189	−0.071
1983-2	0.036	0.118	−0.216	−0.086
1983-3	0.044	0.143	−0.243	−0.102
1983-4	0.055	0.174	−0.276	−0.124
1984-1	0.066	0.206	−0.306	−0.147
1984-2	0.078	0.239	−0.333	−0.169
1984-3	0.090	0.271	−0.360	−0.192
1984-4	0.101	0.302	−0.383	−0.212
1985-1	0.112	0.329	−0.402	−0.228

Sec. 3	Change in bill rate per change in		Sec. 4	Change in bond rate per change in	
	M1	M2		M1	M2
1982-2	−3.550	−12.942	1982-2	−0.717	−2.612
1982-3	−3.588	−12.515	1982-3	−0.911	−3.179
1982-4	−3.278	−11.156	1982-4	−1.043	−3.548
1983-1	−3.239	−10.822	1983-1	−1.163	−3.887
1983-2	−3.481	−11.391	1983-2	−1.318	−4.314
1983-3	−3.467	−11.193	1983-3	−1.468	−4.739
1983-4	−3.742	−11.894	1983-4	−1.645	−5.228
1984-1	−4.024	−12.592	1984-1	−1.820	−5.695
1984-2	−4.350	−13.390	1984-2	−2.009	−6.184
1984-3	−4.690	−14.199	1984-3	−2.215	−6.706
1984-4	−4.742	−14.213	1984-4	−2.411	−7.226
1985-1	−5.277	−15.576	1985-1	−2.490	−7.350

Table 23.3 (continued)

Sec. 5	Change in GNP deflator (*level*) per change in			
	M1	M2	Bond rate	Bill rate
1982-2	−0.011	−0.041	0.101	0.025
1982-3	−0.023	−0.080	0.173	0.055
1982-4	−0.037	−0.127	0.258	0.091
1983-1	−0.054	−0.180	0.347	0.131
1983-2	−0.071	−0.231	0.422	0.168
1983-3	−0.087	−0.280	0.479	0.202
1983-4	−0.103	−0.327	0.520	0.233
1984-1	−0.119	−0.371	0.551	0.264
1984-2	−0.135	−0.414	0.577	0.293
1984-3	−0.150	−0.455	0.604	0.321
1984-4	−0.165	−0.495	0.628	0.347
1985-1	−0.179	−0.528	0.645	0.366

Sec. 6	Change in CPI (*level*) per change in			
	M1	M2	Bond rate	Bill rate
1982-2	−0.009	−0.034	0.084	0.021
1982-3	−0.019	−0.068	0.148	0.047
1982-4	−0.043	−0.147	0.299	0.106
1983-1	−0.069	−0.230	0.443	0.167
1983-2	−0.089	−0.290	0.530	0.210
1983-3	−0.107	−0.345	0.590	0.248
1983-4	−0.124	−0.393	0.626	0.281
1984-1	−0.140	−0.437	0.650	0.311
1984-2	−0.155	−0.476	0.663	0.337
1984-3	−0.168	−0.510	0.677	0.360
1984-4	−0.180	−0.540	0.685	0.378
1985-1	−0.191	−0.563	0.687	0.389

Sec. 7	Change in unemployment rate per change in			
	M1	M2	Bond rate	Bill rate
1982-2	−0.002	−0.006	0.015	0.004
1982-3	−0.006	−0.020	0.043	0.013
1982-4	−0.013	−0.044	0.089	0.032
1983-1	−0.022	−0.073	0.140	0.053
1983-2	−0.031	−0.103	0.188	0.075
1983-3	−0.042	−0.136	0.231	0.098
1983-4	−0.054	−0.170	0.271	0.121
1984-1	−0.066	−0.206	0.306	0.146
1984-2	−0.079	−0.243	0.339	0.172
1984-3	−0.093	−0.281	0.373	0.199
1984-4	−0.107	−0.321	0.407	0.224
1985-1	−0.121	−0.357	0.436	0.247

Note: The changes in unemployment rate are percentage point differences.

Table 23.3 (continued)

	Change in federal deficit (absolute value) per change in			
Sec. 8	M1	M2	Bond rate	Bill rate
1982-2	−0.316	−1.152	2.855	0.715
1982-3	−0.447	−1.560	3.392	1.069
1982-4	−0.664	−2.261	4.604	1.627
1983-1	−0.991	−3.312	6.384	2.408
1983-2	−1.351	−4.420	8.059	3.202
1983-3	−1.367	−4.412	7.526	3.168
1983-4	−1.630	−5.182	8.245	3.697
1984-1	−2.144	−6.709	9.962	4.774
1984-2	−2.637	−8.115	11.306	5.752
1984-3	−3.018	−9.137	12.130	6.458
1984-4	−3.580	−10.731	13.605	7.509
1985-1	−4.235	−12.502	15.271	8.651

	Change in current account per change in			
Sec. 9	M1	M2	Bond rate	Bill rate
1982-2	−0.658	−2.398	5.945	1.490
1982-3	−40.974	−142.910	310.790	97.915
1982-4	5.255	17.883	−36.413	−12.872
1983-1	4.581	15.306	−29.505	−11.130
1983-2	7.185	23.512	−42.870	−17.035
1983-3	8.939	28.859	−49.229	−20.772
1983-4	7.229	22.980	−36.566	−16.394
1984-1	7.453	23.325	−34.635	−16.599
1984-2	8.236	25.351	−35.318	−17.969
1984-3	9.479	28.698	−38.098	−20.285
1984-4	9.596	28.762	−36.464	−20.126
1985-1	12.615	37.237	−45.484	−25.766

	Change in residential investment (1972 dollars) per change in			
Sec. 10	M1	M2	Bond rate	Bill rate
1982-2	0.082	0.297	−0.737	−0.185
1982-3	0.213	0.744	−1.618	−0.510
1982-4	0.347	1.180	−2.403	−0.849
1983-1	0.445	1.487	−2.867	−1.081
1983-2	0.531	1.739	−3.170	−1.260
1983-3	0.648	2.092	−3.569	−1.502
1983-4	0.768	2.443	−3.887	−1.742
1984-1	0.874	2.735	−4.061	−1.946
1984-2	0.958	2.948	−4.107	−2.090
1984-3	1.011	3.062	−4.065	−2.164
1984-4	1.046	3.136	−3.976	−2.195
1985-1	1.069	3.155	−3.854	−2.183

Table 23.3 (continued)

Sec. 11	Change in residential investment (current dollars) per change in			
	M1	M2	Bond rate	Bill rate
1982-2	0.073	0.268	−0.663	−0.166
1982-3	0.197	0.688	−1.496	−0.471
1982-4	0.318	1.083	−2.204	−0.779
1983-1	0.398	1.330	−2.565	−0.968
1983-2	0.467	1.527	−2.784	−1.106
1983-3	0.566	1.827	−3.118	−1.313
1983-4	0.670	2.130	−3.389	−1.519
1984-1	0.758	2.373	−3.523	−1.689
1984-2	0.825	2.540	−3.538	−1.800
1984-3	0.863	2.612	−3.467	−1.846
1984-4	0.883	2.647	−3.356	−1.852
1985-1	0.893	2.637	−3.221	−1.824

Sec. 12	Change in nonresidential investment (1972 dollars) per change in			
	M1	M2	Bond rate	Bill rate
1982-2	0.021	0.078	−0.193	−0.048
1982-3	0.051	0.177	−0.385	−0.121
1982-4	0.113	0.384	−0.782	−0.277
1983-1	0.178	0.594	−1.145	−0.432
1983-2	0.243	0.796	−1.452	−0.577
1983-3	0.307	0.990	−1.689	−0.711
1983-4	0.375	1.191	−1.895	−0.850
1984-1	0.446	1.397	−2.073	−0.994
1984-2	0.523	1.611	−2.244	−1.142
1984-3	0.603	1.826	2.424	−1.291
1984-4	0.680	2.041	−2.587	−1.428
1985-1	0.754	2.225	−2.717	−1.539

Sec. 13	Change in nonresidential investment (current dollars) per change in			
	M1	M2	Bond rate	Bill rate
1982-2	0.035	0.049	−0.122	−0.031
1982-3	0.028	0.099	−0.215	−0.068
1982-4	0.075	0.257	−0.523	−0.185
1983-1	0.122	0.407	−0.784	−0.296
1983-2	0.170	0.555	−1.012	−0.402
1983-3	0.215	0.696	−1.187	−0.500
1983-4	0.267	0.850	−1.352	−0.606
1984-1	0.323	1.011	−1.501	−0.719
1984-2	0.386	1.187	−1.654	−0.841
1984-3	0.453	1.370	−1.819	−0.968
1984-4	0.520	1.557	−1.974	−1.090
1985-1	0.584	1.724	−2.105	−1.192

Table 23.3 (continued)

	Change in personal saving rate per change in			
Sec. 14	M1	M2	Bond rate	Bill rate
1982-2	−0.017	−0.063	0.156	−0.039
1982-3	−0.034	−0.117	0.255	−0.080
1982-4	−0.043	−0.146	0.297	0.105
1983-1	−0.049	−0.163	0.315	0.119
1983-2	−0.057	−0.186	0.340	0.135
1983-3	−0.065	−0.209	0.357	0.150
1983-4	−0.075	−0.238	0.379	0.170
1984-1	−0.086	−0.270	0.400	0.192
1984-2	−0.097	−0.300	0.418	0.213
1984-3	−0.110	−0.332	0.441	0.235
1984-4	−0.122	−0.366	0.464	0.256
1985-1	−0.135	−0.399	0.487	0.276

Note: The changes in saving rate are percentage point differences.

	Change in velocity per change in bill rate	
Sec. 15	M1 velocity	M2 velocity
1982-2	2.251	0.608
1982-3	2.360	0.656
1982-4	2.396	0.666
1983-1	2.358	0.656
1983-2	2.285	0.639
1983-3	2.216	0.616
1983-4	2.144	0.590
1984-1	2.080	0.565
1984-2	2.012	0.540
1984-3	1.948	0.515
1984-4	1.886	0.488
1985-1	1.815	0.464

Notes: The changes in M1 and M2 are percentage changes in dollar amounts. The changes in interest rates are percentage point differences, except for sections 3 and 4, where they are percentage changes in interest rates.

improvement results after an initial worsening, suggestive of a J-curve effect. The improved competitiveness is helped by a negative effect on the value of the dollar abroad (exchange depreciation), which results from a unilateral lowering of US interest rates.

The two interest-sensitive areas of the US economy are residential and nonresidential investment. Both respond inversely with movements of interest rates. Whereas total spending on the GNP shows an elasticity of much less than unity with respect to variations in money supply, the elasticities of nominal investment are much greater than unity for changes in M2. Their interest sensitivity shows clearly in this simulation.

Finally, two key ratios for the economy show an interesting response to changes in the money supply and the interest rate. The personal savings rate is positively associated with interest rate changes and negatively with money supply changes, just as we would expect. Velocity, based on both M1 and M2 measures, is positively associated with changes in interest rates.

Given this analysis of directions and magnitudes of impact of money in the Wharton Model, it is fair to ask whether it works better, in some sense, than the monetarist model. An objective of monetarism is surely to control inflation, but it cannot contribute to this end unless it can 'explain' or account for inflation. Accordingly we devised a statistical test to determine whether percentage changes in the money supply ($\Delta M1$) were more closely correlated with the inflation rate in the US, allowing suitably for time delays in this association, than the Wharton Model's interpretation of a whole group of exogenous variables including those associated with monetary policy. In other words, does the role of money, and several required instruments of policy, as interpreted by the Wharton Model, provide a more correct interpretation of inflation than does the central relationship of monetarism? The statistical test was designed according to suggestions provided by my colleague Albert Ando, who conducted a similar test with the MPS model.

We dynamically simulated the Wharton Model from fixed initial conditions over the period 1975–1 through 1982–2, by quarters, and generated estimates of the inflation rate. In this exercise, p refers to the GNP deflator and Δp to the actual inflation rate (the change in p divided by p). The corresponding estimate of the inflation rate is denoted by $\widehat{\Delta p}$.

A simple correlation of Δp on $\widehat{\Delta p}$ yields the estimated regression

$$\Delta p = 6.69 + 0.28 \widehat{\Delta p} \qquad \bar{R}^2 = 0.298;\ DW = 1.90;\ SEE = 1.89.$$
(16.19) (3.65)

This indicates that $\widehat{\Delta p}$ is significantly correlated with Δp. The explanatory variable depends, in a complicated nonlinear way, on the initial conditions of 1975–1 and the observed value of exogenous variables used to solve the Wharton Model during 1975–1–1982–2. It therefore depends on many variables, but implicitly includes a mainstream model interpretation of the role of money in this inflationary process.

Now, if we add the percentage change in M1 (denoted by $\Delta M1$) to the equation, we obtain the estimate

$$\Delta p = 6.88 + 0.29\widehat{\Delta p} - 0.032\Delta M1 \qquad \bar{R}^2 = 0.275; \text{DW} = 1.90; \text{SEE} = 1.92.$$
$$(9.17)\ (3.57) \qquad (0.324)$$

Thus, the percentage in money supply is not significant in this multiple-regression equation. Its effect is *crowded out* by $\widehat{\Delta p}$. At a pure bivariate level, the simple correlation (*r*) between Δp and $\Delta M1$ is only 0.23, while it is 0.57 between Δp and $\widehat{\Delta p}$. The relationship between Δp and $\widehat{\Delta p}$ is quite robust in the presence of $\Delta M1$, but the relationship between Δp and $\Delta M1$ is very 'fragile'. This same result obtains with lags of one to four quarters in $\Delta M1$, but some of the lag coefficients of $\Delta M1$ turn positive although *never* significant.

PERFORMANCE OF THE WHARTON MODEL IN FINANCIAL FORECASTING

The operation of the Wharton Model approaches the problem of forecasting many dimensions, about 1000 in all, of the US economy every quarter from a nonmonetarist point of view but relying very heavily on financial submodels and financial variables as outlined in the preceding sections of this paper. As strong believers in predictive testing and in the proposition that the real test of economic theory is its ability to predict, we place before you some statistics on forecast error. From the tabulations made by Stephen K. McNees and published from time to time in the *New England Economic Review*, the record of the Wharton Model is well known. Among McNees's tabulations, the most relevant financial variables examined for accuracy of prediction are M1 (level and growth rate) and the Treasury bill rate (level and change). Two related magnitudes are the inflation rate, measured by the GNP deflator, and real GNP (level and growth rate). Inflation and production are two good summary magnitudes that show overall forecast performance. The data in tables 23.4 and 23.5, taken from articles by McNees, tell the story quite well.

They show an error in M1 rising from $1.6 billion one quarter ahead to $6.2 billion six quarters ahead (table 23.4). The bill rate forecast error is only 20 basis points for short forecasts, one quarter ahead, but rises to 190 basis points six quarters ahead. It is not surprising that error grows as the horizon into the future lengthens. All these forecast errors are based on projections made *ex ante* – before the fact – and we

452 *Economic Theory and Econometrics*

Table 23.4 Forecast errors (mean absolute errors): 1970-2 to 1979-2. Wharton Model

	Horizon					
	1	2	3	4	5	6
Levels						
M1 ($billion)	1.6	2.9	4.2	5.0	5.7	6.2
Treasury bill rate*	0.2	0.7	1.2	1.5	1.7	1.9
Rate of change						
M1*	2.4	2.1	2.0	1.8	1.6	1.4
Change						
Treasury bill rate*	0.2	0.6	0.7	0.6	0.6	0.7

Source: Stephen K. McNee 'The forecasting record for the 1970s.' *New England Economic Review,* September/October (1979), 35–53.
*In percentage points.

Table 23.5 Forecast errors (mean absolute error): 1976-1 to 1980-2, Wharton Model

	Horizon							
	1	2	3	4	5	6	7	8
Levels								
Treasury bill rate*	0.7	1.0	1.2	1.5	1.8	1.9	2.2	2.5
Price deflator of GNP (index points)	0.4	0.7	1.1	1.4	2.1	3.0	4.0	4.6
Real GNP ($billion)	11.0	12.1	10.1	9.2	12.9	15.7	14.7	20.9
Growth rate: price deflator of GNP*	1.1	1.1	1.0	1.0	1.2	1.4	1.6	1.6
Real GNP*	5.1	2.8	2.0	1.5	1.4	1.3	1.1	1.2

Source: Stephen K. McNees, 'The recent record of thirteen forecasters,' *New England Economic Review* September/October (1981), 5–21.
*In percentage points.

were trying to look into the middle of next year, at the end point of McNees's horizon. In terms of change, measured as growth rate for M1 or as first difference for Treasury bill rates, the error reaches a plateau quickly.

In McNees's update of these error statistics for the second half of the decade, he presents the results for an eight-quarter horizon (table 23.5). The Wharton Quarterly Model, for example, is regularly projected for twelve quarters, and for some purposes even longer. The updated figures of McNees refer to the turbulent period that saw record high levels of interest rates. It is interesting to compare table 23.5 with table

23.4, which covers the whole of the 1970s, and to note that forecasts of the Treasury bill rate did not basically deteriorate in the period of the highest, most volatile rates. The very short-term forecast is worse, 70 compared with 20 basis points, but from the third through the sixth quarter ahead, the two error series are very close to one another. Errors in predicting the inflation rate are no worse than those in predicting nominal bill rates; in fact, the former are a bit better after the first two quarters. The real GNP growth rate is predicted in a fairly narrow range, from four to eight quarters ahead.

This is, in brief, the record associated with use of the Wharton Model. We need a standard of comparison in order to gain better perspective on our forecasting ability. In the financial sector, what better standard of comparison than the record of the central banking system itself?

Design of a test of the Fed versus Wharton begins with a consideration of the available data. Before the summer of 1980, the Fed would, once or twice a year, set a 'long term' target for growth of M1 over a 12-month horizon. Since 1979 it has done so only once yearly, in the autumn. Each month (the frequency of the Open Market Committee meetings at the time) it would also set a growth rate target for M1 for the current and succeeding month. The short-term target, which we shall designate as the Fed's forecast, was defined on monthly average data. The monthly average for the month preceding the forecast was used as the base. If the average level for that month for M1 were put at 100, and if a 12 per cent annualized growth rate for the interim (2-month) period were set, then the forecast for the current month would be 101 and that for the following month would be a little more than 102. The long-term forecast was to set the growth rate of M1 on a quarterly average basis that would prevail, on average, over the next four quarters. In all cases the Fed really specifies a band of tolerable growth rates; for comparison purposes, the average of the end points of the band is used in the comparison calculations. Wharton forecasts for M1 are available only on a quarterly average basis.

To make forecasts comparable is not difficult for the 'long-term' results. The Wharton postmeeting forecast, on about the first day of the middle month of each quarter, that is closest to the date at which the Fed first announced its annual target was selected. The Fed's implied level of M1 four quarters later and the Wharton forecast for the same period were each compared with *ex post* history.

For the short term, the Fed's close-in monthly forecast was converted to a quarterly series, as follows: the preceding month was accepted as history and averaged with the next 2 months' forecast, to obtain a quarterly figure. It was done only for the second month of each quarter's Open Market Committee meeting for comparison with Wharton's postmeeting forecast, usually about 2 weeks later. The Wharton forecasters would have an extra 2 weeks of data available, but the Fed would have inside information. Since summer 1980, the short-term target for a 3-month or 4-month period is announced. The comparison that is made is between the next full quarterly average forecast for M1 that is implied by the Fed's growth rate and the first forecast quarter of the nearest succeeding Wharton postmeeting forecast. The Fed's handicap is that it has less information at hand; its advantage is that it is trying so much harder now than before to hit an M1 target regardless of what happens to interest rates, as the much wider post-October 1979, federal funds nonintervention bands attest (table 23.6).

Table 23.6 FOMC-announced bands for nonintervention on the Federal funds rate

Meeting date	Announced bank (%)	Range in basis points
Pre-quantity-target years		
4-16-74	9.75–10.75	100
12-16-74	7.5– 9.0	150
12-16-75	4.5– 5.5	100
12-20-76	4.5– 5.0	50
4-19-77	4.5– 5.25	75
8-20-78	7.5– 8.0	50
9-18-79	11.25–11.75	50
Quantity-target years		
11-20-79	11.5–15.5	400
2-4-80	11.5–16.5	500
3-18-80	13.0–20.0	700
8-12-80	8.0–14.0	600
5-6-81	12.0–17.0	500
5-18-81	16.0–22.0	600
11-17-81	11.2–15.0	400

That there is a contest at all is due to, (a) the fact that there were apparently some heights and depths that the Fed would not tolerate in interest rates, and (b) the Fed had some concern about too much interest rate volatility, especially after the 1980 spring fiasco.

Our estimates of the implied forecasts of M1 by the Open Market Committee and our own Wharton forecast of the same magnitude reveal some interesting comparisons. Over the years and quarters since 1975 there have been three 'teams' at the Fed (Arthur Burns, G.

William Miller, Paul A. Volcker) and four at Wharton Econometric Forecasting Associates (David M. Rowe, Richard M. Young, R. Jeffrey Green, and Donald H. Straszheim). Changed perceptions of the economy and changed operating rules contribute to variations in ability to forecast the economy, the first and one of the most essential steps in understanding what is taking place in the system. The accuracy of the WEFA forecasts did not change significantly in this period; that is one of the features of Stephen McNees's periodic surveys of forecast error, but there is very significant change in the Fed's grasp of the situation since October 1979, the date of the change in operating rules (table 23.7).

Table 23.7 Comparison of short-term forecasting accuracy

	Actual	Fed	Fedmiss	Wharton	Wharmiss
1975-2	290.3	289.1	−1.2	288.0	−2.3
1975-3	294.2	294.9	0.7	295.5	1.3
1975-4	294.7	296.1	1.4	289.9	−4.8
1976-1	296.9	297.0	0.1	297.6	0.7
1976-2	302.7	303.1	0.4	303.8	1.1
1976-3	305.9	307.8	1.9	306.6	0.7
1976-4	310.9	311.1	0.2	310.7	−0.2
1977-1	315.0	314.9	−0.1	315.8	0.8
1977-2	321.1	321.0	−0.1	322.2	1.1
1977-3	328.5	327.5	−1.0	327.5	−1.0
1977-4	334.1	334.8	0.7	334.8	0.7
1978-1	339.5	340.4	0.9	340.2	0.7
1978-2	348.4	347.9	−0.5	347.4	−1.0
1978-3	357.3	356.0	−1.3	356.1	−1.2
1978-4	361.1	363.5	2.4	362.3	1.2
1979-1	359.2	361.4	2.2	361.7	2.5
1979-2	365.9	365.1	−0.8	362.2	−3.7
1979-3	374.3	374.0	−0.3	372.7	−1.6
1979-4	380.8	379.4	−1.4	379.9	−0.9
1980-1	374.8	390.8	16.0	386.9	12.1
1980-2	368.9	389.1	20.2	376.0	7.1
1980-3	379.0	395.0	16.0	379.0	0.0
1980-4	413.0	406.6	−6.4	388.1	−24.9
1981-1	419.3	423.5	4.2	417.1	−2.2
1981-2	431.2	427.9	−3.3	430.9	−0.3
1981-3	431.5	439.1	7.6	435.1	3.6
1981-4	436.7	436.9	0.2	435.1	−1.6
1982-1	447.9	448.6	0.7	447.5	−0.4
Root mean square error					
1975-2–1979-3			1.3		2.1
1975-4–1982-1			10.8		9.7

The monetarist Fed missed M1 projections by as much as $20 billion on occasion, and frequently had errors that were much larger than those of the nonmonetarist period. The largest miss before 1979-4 was less than $2.5 billion. In only two quarters since that date has the error been less. The Fed error was less than the WEFA error in two-thirds of the quarters prior to 1979-4. The root mean square error for the Fed before 1979-4 was $1.3 billion, while it was $2.1 billion for WEFA. In ten monetarist quarters since 1979-4, WEFA's error was less than the Fed's (by good-size margins) on eight occasions.

In examination of the long-term forecasts (four quarters after the setting of the target) WEFA's error is consistently less than that of the Fed. In the prior period (before 1979-4), the Fed error is occasionally less (table 23.8). Of course, the sample size is very small for the longer-term forecast error comparison.

Table 23.8 Comparison of long-term forecast accuracy

Forecast quarter	Ex post actual (quarterly average level four quarters after target was set)	Fed forecast	Error	Wharton forecast	Error
1976-3	305.9	312.6	6.7	319.8	13.9
1977-1	315.0	314.0	-1.0	317.0	2.0
1977-3	328.5	322.7	-5.8	333.0	4.5
1978-3	357.3	345.7	-11.6	347.8	-9.5
1979-3	374.3	371.6	-2.7	375.4	1.1
1979-4	380.8	371.9	-8.9	378.7	-2.1
1980-4	413.0	400.8	-12.2	403.5	9.5
1981-4	436.7	442.9	6.2	441.3	4.6

Allowing for the inadequacies of this comparative evaluation – the problem of estimating the Fed's forecast and the smallness of the sample – we still can say that the nonmonetarist Wharton Model, using financial behavioral relations as set out above, has done better in forecasting than the people who are ultimately responsible for creating M1. It appears that monetarism has its limits.

SOME COMMENTS ON RATIONAL EXPECTATIONS

There are many ways in which the thinking of monetarists and proponents of rational expectations are congruent. Monetarists, guided by their theory of the economy, believe that the only way to bring down the rate of inflation is to impose strict control over the money supply and to put its growth on a persistently lower path. The resolve of the Fed to pursue these policies will, according to rational expectations theorists, change people's expectations about future inflationary tendencies. It is also alleged that improperly anticipated monetary growth is the only way that money effects real magnitudes. It is further claimed that properly anticipated monetary growth only affects inflation expectations and so nominal but not real rates of interest.

Rational expectations theorists say that fiscal policy has no aggregate real effect because private sector decisions will occur to neutralize whatever public authorities do. They foresee 'crowding out' on a large, pervasive scale. Their view of the economy is not different in this respect from that of monetarists who find insignificant or negative coefficients of fiscal magnitudes in regressions of nominal income on money supply and public spending.

In the present policy environment, it becomes very important to sort out the contributions of real supply changes, the functioning of labor markets, monetary policy, and fiscal policy in making for lower inflation and the recession. A monetarist interpretation of events is that restrained growth of the money supply was instrumental in bringing down the rate of inflation and that people's lower inflation expectations convinced them that they should accept lower wage increases. There is also an opinion that monetary restraint caused the recession as a necessary precondition for lowering inflation.

The mainstream model interpretation from Wharton is quite different. We would attach a great deal of importance to weak oil prices, food prices, and other primary product prices in initiating the lowering of inflation rates. There were both supply and demand side contributions to price weakness in these commodity markets, worldwide. A very large fiscal deficit combined with a very restrictive monetary policy upset bond markets causing interest rates to be bid up to record high values. The interest rate effects on housing, consumer durables, investment, and other activities generated a recession. The associated rise in unemployment and prevalence of bankruptcy created job security fears in the minds of workers who were motivated to accept reduced wage gains or even decreases in some cases. In contrast to the quantity theory, we had the Phillips curve effects, as expected, in such mainstream models.

These are very different interpretations of the situation and call for quite different policies in order to bring the economy out of recession. For our part, we put our forecasts and models in the open for peer review and predictive testing. It is our opinion that mainstream models have performed well in these circumstances and need make no apologies for the forecast record.

CONCLUSION

Economic debate eventually sifts the valid from the invalid arguments about the way the economy functions. The debates about monetarism, supply side economics, and rational expectations eventually have impacts on model structure. Modern mainstream models have changed greatly since the earliest attempts to interpret the Keynesian revolution. The incorporation of financial magnitudes into models has been underway for some years and will continue.

There is increased detail in the financial sectors of models, together with a closer integration of the financial with the real sector. Without becoming monetarist, the Wharton Model has had increasing monetary content over the years. Ultimately, the direction of financial model building in the context of research on the Wharton Model will take the form of improving the linkages between the flow-of-funds sector and the NIA sector. Possibly, the spectrum of interest rates will eventually be generated in the flow-of-funds sector for use in the real sector.

24

Money in a General Equilibrium System: Empirical Aspects of the Quantity Theory

In his provocative paper of many years' standing, Don Patinkin investigated the determinancy properties of the classical model of general equilibrium.[1] There, he questioned an independent role for the quantity theory equation in determining the absolute price level, and argued that individuals cannot make decisions in the real sector that are independent of their decisions in the monetary sector. He clearly wrestled with the problem of money in a general equilibrium system.

In yet another paper, Patinkin examined the quantity theory from a general equilibrium viewpoint of the macro system of Keynes.[2] In this case, he derived properties of the quantity theory in the context of a model that had a liquidity preference basis for the holding of money. This might seem to be surprising in view of the fact that, at the behavioral level, the theory of liquidity preference is considered to be antithetical to the quantity theory. He argued that in a model with an equation of the form

$$M/p = L(r, Y)$$

where

M = nominal cash balances,
p = price level,
r = interest rate,
Y = real income.

---

[1] D. Patinkin, 'The indeterminacy of absolute prices in classical economic theory,' *Econometrica*, **17**, January (1949) 1–27.

[2] D. Patinkin, 'Keynesian economics and the quantity theory,' *Post Keynesian Economics* (Ed. K. K. Kurihara), Rutgers University Press, New Brunswick (1954), pp. 123–52.

if there is full employment and if all the equations of demand and supply (goods and labor services) are homogeneous of degree zero in prices, wages, and income, the covariation of M and p will be proportional. His is a comparative static analysis and introduces a real balance effect in the savings (consumption) function.

The quantity theory would assume.

$$M/p = kY,$$

where k is a given constant, but, contrariwise, a main feature of the Keynesian model was to make k a variable rather than a parameter.

$$k = k(r)$$

is one way of doing this;

$$M/p = L(r, Y)$$

is a more general way. Nevertheless, it is interesting to look at the total system property, as Patinkin does, apart from the structural equation property of the money–income relationship. It is important to bear in mind, however, that he makes his argument from the viewpoint of full employment equilibrium and comparative statics.

Motivated by Patinkin's reasoning, I plan, in this paper, to examine empirical aspects of the quantity theory in long-run equilibrium and find it important to distinguish between structural–behavioral relationships and implied system relationships.

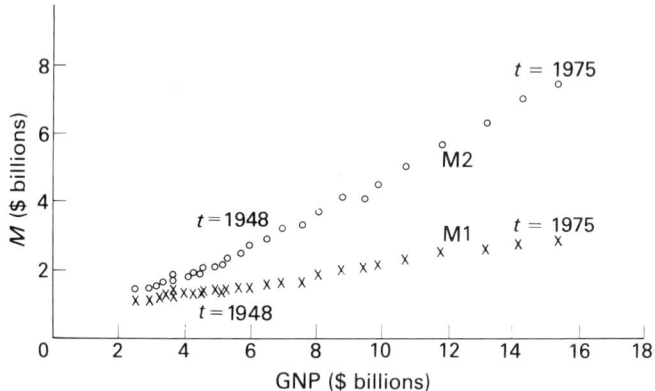

Figure 24.1 Historical values M1, M2: GNP
USA

If we try to get directly at the empirical quantity theory relationship by correlating money and income or by looking for the constancy of velocity over time, we would see immediately that the theory does not hold in the structural behavioral sense in either the short or the long run. This may, however, not be the best way to estimate the structural relationship. In our study of the velocity ratio, among other 'great ratios' of economics, R. Kosobud and I found a distinct trend in v.[3] It is evident from a time chart of v that it has a great deal of cyclical variability as well.

In *Business Conditions Digest* the definitive time series compendium published by the US Department of Commerce, both the M1 velocity series (ratio to GNP) and the M2 velocity series (ratio to personal income) exhibit distinct upward trends since 1953; it is especially strong for the velocity of M1. Cyclical variation is apparent in both series, but more pronounced for M2 than for M1. Both series are classified as generally coincident with the business cycle, but the M2 velocity series tends to lag at troughs.

An historical scatter diagram between M1 or M2 and GNP plotted in Chart 24.1 lends no supporting evidence for the strict quantity theory. The indicated relationships are neither linear nor proportional. This is a purely static plot, however, and does not rule out the possibility of the existence of a stable dynamic relationship with lag distributions. The long-run general equilibrium values, to be studied below, show a different picture in a similar scatter diagram.

In my opinion, one of the reasons why the St Louis Model of the US economy has failed as a forecasting tool is that velocity is a highly unstable parameter, expecially in the short run.[4] The pure quantity theory content of the fundamental St. Louis equation has been shown by B. Friedman to fail to withstand the tests of data revision and data extension.[5] Friedman shows that the reduced form expression for nominal GNP depends significantly, as a statistical correlation, on an exogenous fiscal variable as well as money supply. His results would

---

[3] L. R. Klein and R. F. Kosobud, 'Some econometrics of growth: Great ratios of economics,' *Quarterly Journal of Economics*, LXXV (1967), 173–98.

[4] See Leonall C. Andersen and Keith M. Carlson, 'St. Louis Model revisited,' *Econometric Model Performance: Comparative Simulation Studies of the US Economy*, (Eds L. R. Klein and E. Burmeister), University of Pennsylvania Press, Philadelphia (1976), esp. p. 47. See also, S. McNees, 'A comparison of the GNP forecasting accuracy of the Fair and St. Louis Economic Models,' *New England Economic Review*, September/October (1973), 29–34.

[5] B. Friedman, 'Even the St. Louis Model now believes in fiscal policy,' *The Journal of Money Credit and Banking*, IX, May (1977), 365–7.

suggest that the system properties of the quantity theory do not hold in the long run, when M1 is the intrumental variable.

It may be remarked that the original formulation of the St Louis Model contained both a liquidity preference equation and a long-run system (reduced form) equation in which the strict quantity theory was implied for the long run. In this respect, it appeared, before B. Friedman's re-examination that Patinkin's view was empirically validated.

I want, now, to turn to an alternative empirical view that is based on general equilibrium analysis and is system oriented. I propose to examine the co-variation of money supply and GNP in long-run simulations of the Wharton Annual and Industry Model. In this respect, attention will not be focused on the structural equations of the model for cash holding, but on the long-run solution of the model. System properties will be examined. Attention will not be placed on short-run cyclical variation but on long-term trends. First, I want to explain the nature of the system being used and secondly provide an interpretation of the kind of relationship being studied.

The Wharton Annual and Industry Model is particularly appropriate for this symposium because it is not a typical aggregative Keynesian model with excessive orientation on demand; it contains a complete 63×63 input–output table with a great deal of supply-side content.[6] It is, in a full sense, an integration of the Keynesian and Leontief Models. The Wharton Model does not contain a structural quantity-theory equation; it contains a liquidity-preference equation in which both interest rate and income variables influence the demand for cash. Money supply is generated by a reserve identity and central monetary authorities' control of reserve balances, discount rate, and reserve requirement rates. Behavioral equations of the system are homogeneous in the long run, but some institutional equations (taxes, transfers) are inhomogeneous, which is, of course, realistic and legalistic.

In addition to examining, testing, or estimating the structural equation for money holding, we may consider two other classes of relationships of a system – the *reduced form* (already considered above) and the *solution*. The reduced form is an expression that relates each dependent (endogenous) variable of a system to predetermined

---

[6]R. S. Preston, 'The Wharton Long Term Model: Input–output within the context of a macro forecasting model,' *Econometric Model Performance: Comparative Simulation Studies of the US Economy* (Eds L. R. Klein and E. Burmeister), University of Pennsylvania Press, Philadelphia (1976), pp. 271–87. The model described in this article is an earlier version of the one used for the simulations in this paper. The later version is based on revised data.

Money in a general equilibrium system

variables. The latter are lagged or independent (exogenous) variables. In a single-period sense, the reduced form is also a solution of a system.

In a linear system, a simple closed-form expression exists for the reduced form. In a nonlinear system, there is no general closed form expression for the reduced form. A parametric regression may be computed, as in the St Louis Model, for a reduced form, but such an equation has no obvious system basis and no related structural content. The derived reduced form in a linear system has structural content.

The solution to an econometric system is the integral of the (usual) stated finite difference equation system from fixed initial conditions. In the linear case, a closed-form expression can be obtained. It is a function of the initial conditions, the time path of independent (exogenous) variables and the characteristic roots.

Such an expression does not, in general, exist for a nonlinear system, but numerical simulations approximate the solution; therefore, time paths of dependent (endogenous) variables can be obtained over a given time span (horizon). In fact, even if a system such as the Wharton Annual and Industry Model were linear, it would not be practical to obtain calculated results from the closed-form solution. In a 1000-equation model, such as the one that we are dealing with, numerical simulation must be the method that is actually implemented for solution whether the system is linear or nonlinear. The Wharton Model is, in fact, nonlinear.

It is interesting to consider the sense in which a numerical simulation is a representation of general equilibrium. For 1, 2, or 3 years in advance (extrapolation), detailed input values for initial conditions and independent variables can be inferred from published data on the history of the economy, plans, budgets, commitments, and the like. In regular forward extrapolations of the Wharton Model, a great deal of contemporary business-cycle content is read into the simulation program, but beyond this short time period, smooth or normal input values are used. The normal growth of government budgets, existing tax laws, statutory rates for transfer payments (allowing for built-in changes), historical demographic trends, normal crop conditions, historical trends for world trade, and world peace are among the major input assumptions. A long-run solution to the year 2000 has been obtained under these normal or historical conditions. In addition to being guided by historical trends, we also make a systematic search over policy instruments in the fiscal, and monetary sphere for input values that would lead to balanced trend growth of the economy without excessive inflation, unemployment, external imbalance, domestic budgetary imbalance. Prior to the onset of the oil embargo and recognition of the energy problem, it was generally possible to find a balanced 4 per cent solution to the Model for the US economy; that is to say, there existed trend inputs for policy instruments that did not deviate much from normal experience and generated a solution with 4 per cent unemployment, 4 per cent inflation, 4 per cent real output growth, and 4 per cent real interest rate (nominal rate less inflation rate). These are time averages. It would be reasonable to call this solution a full employment equilibrium. The equality between the real growth rate and the real interest rate conforms to conditions for a von Neumann growth path of general equilibrium.[7]

After 1973, the 4 per cent rule has had to be relaxed. If the instruments were set for a full employment target at 4 per cent, higher inflation with significant trade imbalance was generated; therefore the long-run simulation to 2000 has undergone slippage to 3.0–3.5 per cent growth, 5 per cent unemployment and 5 per cent inflation. These are poorer targets, but under present circumstances will be considered to be characteristics of the dynamic general equilibrium solution.

History has been cyclical; so historical inputs for independent variables would not produce a general equilibrium path in simulation over past periods. We could, if so desired, solve the system historically with trend inputs, but much substantive interest is attached to the forward extrapolation, in any case.

Having a trend solution, in the general equilibrium sense, described above, what is the association between the generated time path of money supply and GNP, both measured in nominal terms? M2 consisting of currency, demand and time deposits, grows in this simulation at 9–10 per cent for the remainder of this decade, at a declining rate between 10 and 6 per cent for the 1980s, and fairly steadily between 4.5 and 6.0 per cent for the rest of the century.[8] In 1976, the initial condition is $805.9 billion, and in 2000 the extrapolated value is $4181.8 billion. This is roughly a five-fold increase.

Nominal GNP, on the other hand, grows at about 8–10 per cent until 1980, between 7 and 8 per cent during the 1980s, and between 4.5 and 6.0 per cent for the last decade of the century. The overall expansion is from an initial value of $1692.3 billion in 1976 to $8947.9 billion in 2000. This is also strikingly close to a five-fold increase.

If we consider M1 (currency plus demand deposits), the extrapolated

---

[7] J. V. Neumann, 'A model of general economic equilibrium,' *Review of Economic Studies*, XIII, 1 (1945–6), 1–9.

[8] The M2 concept used here includes all time deposits at commercial banks. In the official series, large certificates of deposits are excluded.

expansion is from $313.3 billion in 1976 to $1024.2 billion in 2000. This is only a bit more than a three-fold increase. We see, therefore, that quantity theory results prevail, in the long run, for M2 to a strikingly close degree, but not for M1. The velocity ratio for M1 is expected to rise markedly over the next 25 years. This is not surprising in view of technical and legal trends in methods of payment, clearing of checks, and in use of savings accounts.

There has, in fact, been recognition on the part of several monetary authorities that M2 is a more reliable and stable policy instrument in recent years than M1. The year-by-year relationships of both M1 and M2 to GNP in this simulation are presented in the accompanying chart.

The relationship between simulated M2 and GNP is practically proportional (straight line through the origin), while the relationship between M1 and GNP is linear but not proportional.

In many respects, this is a full general equilibrium manifestation, in the empirical domain, of Patinkin's original theorizing. It is a general equilibrium model with full-employment growth, in the sense stated above, with largely homogeneous functions for final demand and liquidity preference specifications of the demand for money.

This finding is not inconsistent with B. Friedman's results and evidence from the St Louis Model equation. In the first place, that equation is stated in terms of M1 and not M2. The fact that Friedman does not find a pure quantity theory interpretation of the St Louis reduced form equation with M1 as the instrument is consistent with the Wharton Model simulation result, in which the M1 velocity is not constant while the M2 velocity is approximately constant.

Secondly, the Wharton Model simulation results hold for particular time paths of all exogenous variables. They are not meant to hold for independent variation of all exogenous variables in the entire system, including fiscal variables. There is, nevertheless, special significance to the particular values of exogenous inputs chosen because they place the system, as a whole, on an empirical approximation of a general equilibrium growth path.

The statistical demonstration of the quantity theory or Patinkin's hypothesis is less than perfect because for this simulation the originally fitted equations for M1 and M2 had to be adjusted over the extrapolation horizon, 1977–2000, in order that free reserves of the banking system would move in a plausible, historical range. This meant that a linear function of time was added to estimated equations for the three components of liquidity preference:

1 Currency declining at a rate of $4.0 billion per annum,
2 Demand deposits declining at a rate of $22 billion per annum,
3 Time deposits rising at a rate of $40 billion per annum.

These were decided upon partly on the basis of residual variation from the equations during the decade preceding 1976. In each case the liquidity preference component took the form

$$\frac{M}{W} = L\left(r, \frac{Y}{W}\right) + bt,$$

where

W = nominal wealth proxy.

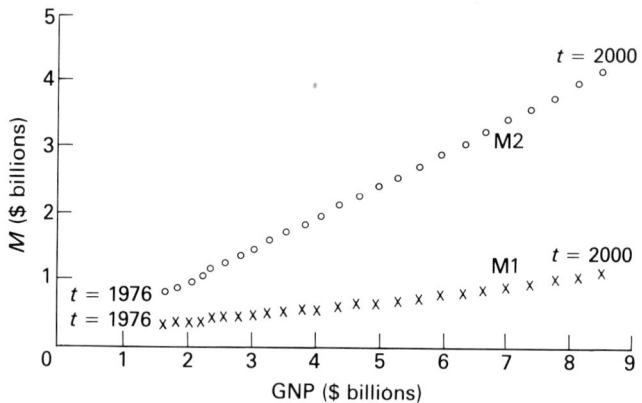

Figure 24.2 Simulated values M1, M2: GNP
Wharton Model

Lag distributions and alternative appropriate interest rates were used in the various component equations.

In order to gain a fuller insight into the methodology followed and results obtained, it is useful to consider a related problem that partially motivated and conditioned some of the findings in this paper. The related problem is one of energy consumption in a general equilibrium context.

A primary reason for econometric interest in long-run simulations, to 2000 and beyond, at the present time is to examine energy requirements for the long-run future. As in the case of the holding of cash balances, there are structural equations for energy input in the production process. These are implied in the intermediate deliveries from the energy sectors of the model (oil, coal, gas, electricity) to other producing sectors and also to final demand. These flows show up in the input–output module of the Wharton Model. The input–output coefficients are variable in this model, being sensitive to relative prices. This is much like the implied sensitivity of cash holdings to interest-rate changes in the liquidity preference theory as opposed to the constancy of v in the quantity theory variant.

Until 1973, there was remarkable constancy in the relationship between aggregate energy consumed, measured in BTUs, and real GNP. The ratio of total BTUs to GNP has been about 60 000 BTUs per dollar of GNP (1972 dollars). This ratio has fallen slightly during the recent periods of oil embargo and OPEC cartel pricing. The energy required for running the economy in this simulation to 2000 falls steadily to about 50 000 BTUs per dollar of GNP by 1990 and to 40–45 000 by 2000. This decline is induced in the general equilibrium solution because of substitution brought about by relatively high energy prices.

This solution corresponds to the case of M1 above. The growing economy is apparently capable of functioning with relatively less transactions money in a trend sense. It does, however, by contrast, require as much M2 as is presently required. By analogy with the energy case, we might conclude that relatively high interest rates, by historical standards, induce substitution between noninterest-bearing and interest-bearing bank deposits just as high energy prices induce substitution between energy and other goods or services.

25
Direct Estimates of Unemployment Rate and Capacity Utilization in Macroeconometric Models

1 MOTIVATING CONSIDERATIONS

The degree of resource utilization is an important and strategic economic concept in giving an overall measure of economic efficiency. The problem of measuring capacity utilization as an aggregative statistical indicator of resource utilization is an old one that has never been handled in a definitive way. In this paper, we do not claim to be definitive, but we do hope to have contributed to an understanding of some of the issues and offer a plausible, but tentative, solution.

At the same time, we try to clarify the role of the aggregate production function – or groups of them – in the specification and application of a macroeconometric model. As will be made clear in what follows, the aggregate production function will be seen to play a key role in estimating and defining capacity utilization.

Unemployment deals with utilization of a single production factor, while capacity utilization deals with all factors, in some sense; therefore we shall attempt to forge a link between these two separate measures – the unemployment rate and the rate of capacity utilization.

Capacity utilization has been estimated as a statistical series in a variety of ways and there are some highly significant differences among the various measures available.[1] From a theoretical viewpoint, full capacity output might be defined in terms of the cost function or the production function. In the former case, it is defined to be the point of minimum average cost. There can be alternative concepts in the short run and the long run, corresponding to minimum cost points on either the short-run or the long-run cost function. These are *economic*

---

[1] George Perry (1973).

Direct estimates of unemployment rates

concepts of capacity because they involve unit factor costs in determining macro cost functions. These are used to get at the output levels for minimum cost.

With the help of the macro production function, a *physical* measure of full capacity output can be designed. In the simplest case let us write

$$X = f(L, uK),$$

where

X = real output (value added),
L = employment,
K = the stock of capital,
u = the rate of capacity utilization.

L and uK are actual inputs of primary factors, and X is the output flow. Corresponding to this relationship among actual input and output flows, there is a specification showing *potential output* that is associated with potential inputs. The latter are measured by the available work force and capital stock. In place of L, we would use LF (labor force) as the input variable for the labor force in production, and in place of uK, we would use K as the input value for the capital factor in production. Implicitly, this assumes $u = 1.0$, or full utilization of capital,

$$X^c = f(LF, K)$$

where potential, or capacity, output is denoted by X^c. The ratio of X/X^c is an estimate of the degree of capacity utilization.

There are some features of this formulation of capacity measurement that merit emphasis. First, it should be noted that the same function, f, is used for both actual output and potential output determination. Capacity output is thus defined as a point on the production surface; actual output at any point in time is simply another point on the same production surface.

Second, labor force is not easy to define. It should indicate the potential work force available and not be subject to the cyclical swings that are often found in labor-force statistics. It should be a smooth trend in the long run. If the production function is completely economy wide, then there is a well-defined aggregate LF corresponding to an aggregate L. If, however, the production process is disaggregated by industries, as it undoubtedly should be for other reasons in macro-econometric model building, then the industrial or sector distribution of LF must be used to obtain separate arguments for separate sector production functions. This is a challenge to capacity measurement, but is capable of being estimated empirically by the distribution of employment at the most recent full-capacity point for the economy as a whole.

Finally, there is the problem of measuring utilized capital stock, as well as total capital stock. The rate of utilization is necessary for estimating f from actual input–output data. In the case of using potential output data, we could estimate f from observed series for X^c, LF and K, but there are likely to be few well defined periods of full capacity utilization from which to obtain observed data X^c. The problem is that X^c is difficult to measure directly from observed data – only limited points are available – and u is difficult to measure directly from observed data; so the more plentiful samples of data on X and L cannot be fully used until capital utilization can be directly measured. In a few unusual sectors, this may be possible, but generally speaking, u must be replaced by a surrogate series.

From a purely practical and empirical viewpoint, f is estimated from data on X, L, and uK, where the surrogate measure for u might be the unemployment rate. It is usually assumed that the capacity utilization rate is some simple linear function of the labor utilization rate, $u = a + b(U/LF)$. Production functions have occasionally been estimated from a limited sample of full utilization periods but there is a tendency not to rely on such small samples, and usually it is estimated from the mass of data on observed variations in X, L and uK.

The measure for X/X^c, so obtained, leaves out of consideration some basic economic costs of attaining potential output, but apart from the cost consideration, the use of the production function appears to be gaining in usage and acceptability.

The surrogate for capital utilization, u, is of great interest in its own right. It is one of the most sensitive (not in the sense of cyclical lead time) macro indicators for the economy as a whole. The rate of unemployment must satisfy the identity:

$$LF - L = U$$
$$1 - (L/LF) = U/LF.$$

There are three variables to be estimated, labor force, employment and unemployment. Any two can be estimated from statistical equations of the model system, but the third will be estimated from the identity and knowledge about the other two.

In the medium to long run, it is important to have strict imposition of accounting identities; otherwise simulation values for long periods of time are likely to drift away from consistent valuations. If U is estimated from the above identity on the basis of estimates of LF and

Direct estimates of unemployment rates

L, there may be even accumulation in the sense that errors in both LF and L will be present, in the absence of fortuitous compensatory cancellation. Experience shows that residual estimates of U do indeed suffer from joint errors in LF and L. Since U is such a key variable, it is important to have good estimates of it; therefore direct estimation equations for the unemployment rate are suggested as a means of reducing some error components.

The unemployment rate and the capacity utilization rate are, as indicated above, different measures of resource use in the economy; therefore they are related. We use the unemployment rate to estimate the coefficient, u, in the production function, and we shall use capacity utilization, X/X^c, as one of the explanatory variables in an equation for direct estimation of the unemployment rate.

In this study, first, the unemployment rate is related to the Wharton Index of Manufacturing Capacity Utilization and other relevant variables. Second, the Wharton Indexes are decomposed and explained by the ratio of actual output to capacity output in manufacturing industries. Third, capacity output in each component industry is determined by inserting capacity labor input and capital stock into an appropriate stationary-state production function. Capacity labor input is obtained after determining full-employment weekly hours and full-employment number of employees working in different industries. The latter involves the allocation of labor force among industries according to the full-employment level allocation and the determination of full-employment labor force participation rate.

Detailed discussion of the model will be presented in section 2 of this paper. Empirical findings will be reported in section 3. Evaluation and analysis, which include the complete model simulations and the comparison of our estimates with other utilization indexes, will be included in section 4. Section 5 provides a short conclusion.

2 THE MODEL

The unemployment rate equation

Labor and capital are jointly needed in industrial production. The capital–labor ratio in each industry is determined by the state of technology and level of economic activity, but it does not change significantly in the short run. Both capital and labor are limited resources in the economy in a given period of time and the extent of their utilization can in principle be measured. Usually, the degree of utilization of labor resources is measured by the unemployment rate and that of capital stock by the index of capacity utilization, in reality an output measure. Since the substitution between labor and capital in short run is rather inelastic, the idleness of one, for whatever reasons, affects utilization of the other. Therefore, a direct relationship can be established between the unemployment rate and the index of capacity utilization.

The utilization rate of existing capital stock cannot be directly measured except in limited sectors.[2] The Wharton index of capacity utilization is obtained by applying the trend-through-peaks technique to the series making up the Federal Reserve Board's industrial production indexes and then forming a weighted average of them. In the sample period, observations on variables designating capacity utilization to be used in the unemployment rate equation of the model are taken from direct readings of the Wharton index. This is one way of measuring capacity utilization, but it cannot be generated, in any structural way, for extrapolation into the future for forecast simulations. The definitions of capacity output as points of full input values associated with the stationary state production function provide an alternative measure. This alternative could also be used within the sample period, but the primary motivation for developing it is to have a measure for extrapolation as an endogenous variable. The ratio of actual output, also an endogenous variable from the model to capacity output from production function calculations gives the measure for the rate of utilization.

In our model, both indexes are used. The rate of unemployment (UR) is made a function of the *Wharton index* of capacity utilization in manufacturing industry ($WICUM$) and other relevant variables. The Wharton index for manufacturing is calculated as a weighted average of the component utilization rates in durables and nondurables. The utilization rates for durable and nondurable manufacturing are, in turn, regressed on the corresponding *alternative utilization index*, derived from a production function, in a simple regression. This procedure, in fact, uses the Wharton indexes as an *intervening variable* in the model. The impacts of capacity outputs derived from production functions are not passed into the unemployment rate equation without being filtered according to the empirical relationship between these two sets of indexes. This device provides the opportunity for off-setting any extreme observations in one of the two indexes since each is obtained

---

[2]Train hours in rails, seat capacity in airlines, and spindle hours in textiles are particular examples that are readily available.

Direct estimates of unemployment rates

from different sources. The estimates of these simple regressions can be considered as the *filtered utilization index*. The filtered index is more suitable than the straight mean or a weighted average of Wharton and alternative indexes because the empirical relationship between these two series has been incorporated in its formulation.

We use the index for manufacturing industries because the unemployment rate responds more sensitively to changes in the utilization rate in manufacturing industries than to changes in other industries. Furthermore, the capacity utilization rate in manufacturing industries reflects general economic conditions more promptly than do the rates in other industries.

In the equation for the unemployment rate, other relevant variables are included to reflect effects from other sources. The statistical series on average weekly hours (AWH) is often considered to be a leading indicator of general economic activity and is used as an explanatory variable to reflect cyclical movements in the equation for the unemployment rate.

The average productivity of labor (APL) is usually regarded as a determinant of the demand for labor. Given the level of output, the higher the level of productivity, the fewer workers will be hired and the more the unemployment rate will go up. Therefore, a positive relationship is expected between these two variables.

Total employment (TE) and the unemployment rate are, of course, inversely related. Given the size of labor force, higher employment means a lower unemployment rate. Therefore, the rate of unemployment can be made a function of total employment. The inclusion of an employment variable in the unemployment rate equation would also allow for some direct effects on the unemployment rate resulting from a government job program, when applicable.

In order to avoid statistical difficulties and to emphasize the importance of the *change* in unemployment rate, all variables used in this equation are expressed in either percentage changes or changes in per cent. This transformation scales all coefficients in the equation so that they approximately represent elasticities of change with respect to the explanatory variables. A direct comparison of the magnitudes of these coefficients would reveal their relative importance to the rate of unemployment. The final specification of this equation is as follows:

$$\Delta UR = b_{10} + b_{11} \times \Delta WICUM + b_{12} \times (\Delta AWH/AWH_{-1})$$
$$+ b_{13} \times (\Delta APL/APL_{-1}) + b_{14} \times (\Delta TE/TE_{-1}) + u_1 \quad (25.1)$$

where

UR = unemployment rate,
$WICUM$ = Wharton index of capacity utilization in manufacturing,
AWH = average hours worked per week,
APL = output per man hour,
TE = total employment.

The capacity utilization equations

The Wharton index of capacity utilization in manufacturing industries ($WICUM$) is calculated as the weighted average of its two major components:

$$WICUM = WICUMD \times (XMD/XM) + WICUMN \times (XMN/XM) \quad (25.21)$$

where XM, XMD and XMN denote actual outputs in total manufacturing, durables and nondurables, respectively. This average is slightly different from the Wharton index of capacity utilization of manufacturing industries in the data files. The index in the data files is directly calculated by taking a weighted average of 22 component industrial production series.

Each component index is, in turn, related to the ratio of actual output to capacity output, the alternative index, as below:

$$WICUMD = b_{20} + b_{21} \times (XMD/CXMD) \times 100 + u_2 \quad (25.2b)$$

$$WICUMN = b_{30} + b_{31} \times (XMN/CXMN) \times 100 + u_3 \quad (25.2c)$$

where $CXMD$ and $CXMN$ indicate capacity outputs in manufacturing durables and nondurables, derived from the corresponding production functions as shown in the next section.

In this way, we have, in fact, endogenized the Wharton indexes of manufacturing capacity utilization for use in model simulation outside the sample period. For the forecasting period in which observed values are not available, Wharton indexes used in the unemployment rate function will be estimated by these three equations.

Labour requirement functions

Assuming that the relationship between outputs and inputs in an industry follows a Cobb-Douglas type production function,

$$X = A \times L^{\alpha} \times K^{\beta} \times e^{\gamma t} \times u$$

Direct estimates of unemployment rates

where X, L and K are output, labor and capital inputs of this industry respectively, and t is a time trend which measures the impact of neutral technical progress. This relationship is, however, not independent of the level of utilization or the level of demand for output. Since nearly all the periods for which our model has been built are dominated by episodes of underutilization of both capital and labor resources, it is more realistic to assume that the real production function makes allowance for underutilization and represents a preferred version of the relationship between outputs and inputs. When the economy moves towards the full employment level, this relationship remains, but the degree of underutilization declines.

In econometric models, the production function is usually used in an inverted form for deriving labor requirements. The desired level of labor input (L^d) can be determined for given output, capital stock and the level of technology as follows:

$$\ln L^d = -\alpha^{-1} \times \ln A + \alpha^{-1} \times \ln X - \beta\alpha^{-1} \times \ln K - \alpha^{-1} \times \gamma \times t$$
$$- \alpha^{-1} \times \ln u.$$

Assume that the actual level of labor input in the short run is partially adjusted to the desired level. We can write:

$$\Delta \ln L = \lambda \times (\ln L^d - \ln L_{-1})$$

where λ is the short-run partial adjustment coefficient which indicates the speed of adjustment. Substituting this equation into the previous one, we obtain:

$$\Delta \ln L = -\lambda\alpha^{-1} \times \ln A + \lambda\alpha^{-1} \times \ln X - \lambda \times \{\ln L_{-1} + \beta\alpha^{-1} \times \ln K\}$$
$$- \lambda\alpha^{-1}\gamma \times t - \lambda\alpha^{-1} \times \ln u. \qquad (25.3)$$

This equation expresses the actual change in labor requirements, measured in manhours, as a log linear function of current level of output, a time trend and a compound variable which is the previous level of labor input plus the current capital stock multiplied by the ratio of capital–labor coefficients ($\beta\alpha^{-1}$). If the capital–labor coefficient can be extraneously estimated, ordinary least squares can be directly applied to this equation to obtain an estimate of λ and derive estimates of other parameters.

As indicated below, the statistical estimate of $\beta\alpha^{-1}$ is determined from factor-share data, averaged over the whole sample period. This implies, in the framework of our Cobb-Douglas production specification, that production is being carried out efficiently, on average. In the short run, there needs to be an adjustment process, but in the long run operations are efficient. Our production function specification for activity with a dynamic adjustment process to desired levels produces this result.

In terms of cost analysis, firms are producing along an implied cost function, although we use the actual equation for physical production and marginal productivity pricing for relative factor use. This does not imply that in the long run, firms are operating at minimum average cost. Free entry and full competition in product markets would be needed to establish that point. If the few occasions on which the economy touched discernibly full capacity were simultaneously periods of efficient use and pricing of factor inputs together with free entry (zero profits), we could claim that our full capacity output, X^c, coincided with the theoretical measure of the same. We cannot be sure of that, but we do have a physical interpretation of X^c.

After $\alpha, \beta, \gamma, \lambda$ and A are all estimated, capacity output at any point of time may be measured by inserting capacity labor input and capital stock into the estimated production function. In other words, as soon as the capacity labor is determined, the capacity output of the industry can be easily estimated by the following equation:

$$\ln CX = A + \alpha \times \ln CL + \beta \times \ln CK + \gamma \times t \tag{25.4}$$

where CX, CL, and CK denote capacity output, capacity labor and capacity capital, respectively.

The equation for capacity labor inputs

A simple way to derive capacity labor input in each industry is to estimate full-employment manhours for the economy as a whole, and then allocate the manhours at full employment to the different industries. However, this procedure assumes that different industries would reach their capacity simultaneously and that they would not compete with each other for productive factors.

Total labor input employed in an industry (L) is the product of average weekly hours (AWH) multiplied by the number of employees hired (E) and the number of weeks worked,

$$L = AWH \times E \times 52.$$

In order to obtain capacity labor inputs for an industry in a given period of time, it is necessary to determine the maximum number of weekly hours and the maximum number of employees the industry can hire. In order to maximize marginal productivity at the given wage rate and to minimize overtime costs, the management will usually not go over the maximum number of average hours set in the past peak periods. Consequently, the trend-through-peaks technique is applied to the historical data for this variable to obtain capacity weekly hours.

Unfortunately, the same approach cannot be applied to find the potential number of employees in an industry since the actual number of employees in most industries has been increasing even when demand is sluggish. This means there were no significant peaks in the past, which makes the determination of capacity labor inputs more difficult.

Furthermore, the potential maximum number of employees an industry can hire is also affected by other elements. First, workers may move from industry to industry when relative economic conditions change. Second, when the wage rate in one industry increases, it may draw additional workers from the unemployed labor force and may also encourage labor participation from the nonworking population.

Since we know that the distribution of total employment among industries, the level of employment, and the labor participation rate all influence the possible number of employees an industry can hire, the labor input identity can be modified to:

$$L = AWH \times (E/TE) \times (TE/LF) \times (LF/N) \times N \times 52$$

The item (E/TE) indicates the proportion of total employment which will be hired in this particular industry. This ratio varies as workers move in and out of the industry. If not all industries reach their peaks simultaneously, it is possible for one industry to bid workers away from others and the ratio will increase. In the long run, this ratio may also change with the level of technology and the elasticity of substitution between labor and capital. However, due to technical barriers such as required skills, geographical immobility of workers, limited information and competition among industries, the value of (E/TE) is always a fraction. The maximum value it can take is the percentage of allocation of total employment among industries at the full-employment level. Therefore, a trend-through-peaks technique is applied to this series in order to allocate total employment among various industries in the proportions in which they would be hired at full-employment.

By definition, the rate of employment (TE/LF) and the rate of unemployment add up to one. Even when the economy is considered to be at full employment, the actual value of the employment rate will be less than one because of frictional and voluntary unemployment. In the application of Okun's law, the full employment rate is defined to be 0.96. It would be more satisfactory if the level of full employment were derived from past experience. Therefore, the trend-through-peaks technique is applied to the historical value of this ratio to obtain the full employment level.

The labor participation rate (LF/N) varies with the state of the economy. When the economy is moving towards prosperity and the unemployment rate gets very low, people enter the labor force at an increasing rate. Usually, the highest labor participation rate is attained as the economy moves towards the full-employment level. Again, the trend-through-peaks technique is applied to obtain the maximum possible participation rate at the full employment level.

Finally, the capacity labor input in a particular industry is derived as:

$$L^c = AWH^c \times (E/TE)^c \times (TE/LF)^c \times (LF/N)^c \times N \times 52 \qquad (25.5)$$

The superscript c indicates either capacity value or a maximum ratio obtained by applying the trend-through-peaks method to historical data. As soon as the size of population (N) is known, we can derive an estimate of capacity labor input in a particular industry.

3 THE ESTIMATED MODEL AND ITS INTERPRETATION

The model was estimated with US quarterly data from 1953–3 to 1973–4. The method of ordinary least squares was used to estimate all parameters in each stochastic equation. The t-ratios are reported in parentheses under the estimated parameters

Unemployment rate equation

$$\begin{aligned}
UR - UR_{-1} = &\ 0.095661 - 0.087688 \times (WICUM - WICUM_{-1}) \\
& \ (2.05) \qquad (5.57) \\
& + 0.028965 \times (APL - APL_{-1})/APL_{-1} \\
& \quad (0.73) \\
& - 0.25696 \times (AWH - AWH_{-1})/AWH_{-1} \\
& \quad (3.04) \\
& - 0.25382 \times (TE - TE_{-1})/TE_{-1} + u_1 \\
& \quad (4.11)
\end{aligned}$$

$$R^2 = 0.714, \quad SEE = 0.223, \quad DW = 1.714. \qquad (25.6)$$

Capacity utilization, Wharton indexes

$$WICUM = WICUMD \times (XMD/XM) + WICUMN \times (XMN/XM) \tag{25.7a}$$

$$WICUMD = -4.8968 + 1.0684 \times (XMD/CXMD) \times 100 \tag{25.7b}$$
$$(1.42) \quad (26.14)$$

$$R^2 = 0.894, \quad SEE = 2.59, \quad DW = 0.317;$$

$$WICUMN = -6.9682 + 1.0774 \times (XMN/CXMN) \times 100 \tag{25.7c}$$
$$(1.06) \quad (14.79)$$

$$R^2 = 0.732, \quad SEE = 2.01, \quad DW = 0.215.$$

Employment functions

$$\Delta \ln LMD = \underset{(1.31)}{0.10664} + \underset{(12.46)}{0.35091} \times \ln XMD - \underset{(4.73)}{0.00094688} \times t$$
$$- \underset{(12.51)}{0.41516} \times \{\ln LMD_{-1} + 0.22472 \times \ln KMD\} \tag{25.8a}$$

$$R^2 = 0.691, \quad SEE = 0.014, \quad DW = 0.72;$$

$$\Delta \ln LMN = \underset{(2.07)}{0.25735} + \underset{(4.85)}{0.18763} \times \ln XMN - \underset{(2.37)}{0.000746} \times t$$
$$- \underset{(5.80)}{0.23936} \times \{\ln LMN_{-1} + 0.32954 \times \ln KMN\} \tag{25.8b}$$

$$R^2 = 0.301, \quad SEE = 0.0092, \quad DW = 0.891.$$

Capacity outputs in manufacturing industries

$$\ln CXMD = -0.303896 + 1.183 \times \ln CLMD + 0.265865 \times \ln KMD$$
$$+ 0.00269835 \times t \tag{25.9a}$$

$$\ln CXMN = -1.371583 + 1.2757 \times \ln CLMN + 0.420395 \times \ln KMN$$
$$+ 0.00397591 \times t \tag{25.9b}$$

Capacity labor inputs (in manhours)

$$CLMD = AHMD^c \times (EMD/TE)^c \times (TE/LF)^c \times (LF/N)^c \times N \tag{25.10a}$$

$$CLMN = AHMN^c \times (EMN/TE)^c \times (TE/LF)^c \times (LF/N)^c \times N \tag{25.10b}$$

Labor force identity

$$LF = TE + UR \times LF$$

The definitions of variables are:

- APL = output per manhour,
- $AHMD$ = average weekly hours in manufacturing durables,
- $AHMN$ = average weekly hours in manufacturing nondurables,
- AWH = average hours worked per week,
- $CLMD$ = capacity labor input (in manhours) in manufacturing durables,
- $CLMN$ = capacity labor input (in manhours) in manufacturing nondurables,
- $CXMD$ = capacity output in manufacturing durables,
- $CXMN$ = capacity output in manufacturing nondurables,
- EMD = employment (number of employees) in manufacturing durables,
- EMN = employment (number of employees) in manufacturing nondurables,
- KMD = capital stock in manufacturing durables,
- KMN = capital stock in manufacturing nondurables,
- LF = total labor force,
- LMD = actual labor input (in manhours) in manufacturing durables,
- LMN = actual labor input (in manhours) in manufacturing nondurables,
- N = population,
- TE = total employment,
- t = time trend,
- UR = unemployment rate,
- $WICUM$ = Wharton index of capacity utilization in manufacturing,
- $WICUMD$ = Wharton index of capacity utilization in durables,
- $WICUMN$ = Wharton index of capacity utilization in nondurables,
- XM = actual output in manufacturing,
- XMD = actual output in manufacturing durables,
- XMN = actual output in manufacturing nondurables.

Indeed, the relationship between the unemployment rate and the index of capacity utilization is most significant as indicated by the high t-ratio. Except for the percentage change in labor productivity, all explanatory variables in the unemployment rate equation are statistically significant. The R^2 (0.714) is also relatively high since the equation is measured in percentage changes.

In the capacity utilization equations, the Wharton indexes are solely related to the alternative indexes derived from the stationary state version of industrial production functions. Obviously, a perfect match between these two indexes would have a zero intercept and a unit slope. The t values in these two equations indicate that the slopes are not significantly different from unity at the 95 per cent confidence level. Obviously, when the two indexes are high, there is a definite tendency for the alternative index to overstate the Wharton index. When both of them are low, the tendency is reversed.

Since the utilization indexes are cyclical variables, the correlations of these two equations are expected to be low. The coefficients of determination (R^2) of the regressions for durables and nondurables are 0.89 and 0.73 respectively. These correlations are significantly higher than those found in a previous study.[3]

The capital–labor ratios ($\beta\alpha^{-1}$) in the employment functions are extraneously estimated. They are derived from sample data by the following formula:

$$\beta\alpha^{-1} = \sum_{1}^{T}(\text{income minus wage income})/\text{wage income}/T$$

where T indicates the number of sample periods. This formula assumes the marginal capital–labor ratio to be constant apart from random variation over the sample period. The estimated capital–labor ratios for durables and nondurables are 0.2247 and 0.3295, respectively. The employment functions are then estimated by applying the OLS technique.

The potential labor inputs in these two industries are derived from (25.5a) and (25.5b), respectively. The value of the first four items in each equation is determined by applying the trend-through-peaks techniques to the historical data. The peak-to-peak trends of average weekly hours in these two industries followed an increasing path in the 1950s and early 1960s. However, they started to decline after reaching a peak in 1966.

The trend-through-peaks path of the ratio of total employment to the labor force $(TE/LF)^e$ represents the full-employment level employment rate. This path is gradually declining, as many economists believe it should. According to our findings, it declines from 0.974 in 1953 to 0.964 in 1973. This is slightly higher than the level specified by Okun's law (0.96).

---

[3] Nerlove (1967, p. 230) found the simple correlation between the two measures of capacity utilization was only 0.64.

The only component in these two equations which is monotonically increasing is the potential labor participation rate $(LF/N)^c$. It rises from 0.583 in 1953 to 0.605 in 1973. This ratio is more affected by long-term structural changes than short-term elements in the economy. Dwindling family size and an increasing number of working wives are the main explanation for its drifting up.

The last element in (25.5a) and (25.5b) is the civilian population aged 16–64. This variable is of course growing with time.

The labor force identity (25.6) defines total labor force as the sum of employed and unemployed. This equation would make total labor force more sensitive to business cycles. When the economy is moving downward, total labor force diminishes due to the dropping out of the labor force of housewives, full-time students etc.

4 SIMULATIONS OF THE MODEL

The model presented in the previous section represents a recursive simultaneous-equations subsystem. As soon as the values of variables outside the subsystem are given, the endogenous variables can be determined in a recursive order. The subsystem can be simulated in two ways. It can be treated as an independent model and solved for all endogenous variables after exogenous variables have been assigned values. Or, the system can be treated as a recursive block and incorporated into a full-size econometric model for full model simulations. The former can be deemed as a partial model simulation and the latter a full-model simulation. There are two types of full-model simulations, (a) one-period or static simulations which are re-initialized every period, and (b) dynamic simulations which have fixed initial conditions. There is more possibility of error accumulation in the latter.

The full-size model used in this study in the Wharton Mark IV model which contains roughly 400 behavioral equations and identities. Owing to the deficiency of historical data of some variables which are not used in our system but appear elsewhere in Mark IV, the full model simulation cannot start before 1965.

Three sets of solutions are reported:

1 A partial model simulation: 1953-3–1974-4
2 A full model static simulation: 1965-1–1974-4
3 A full model dynamic simulation: 1965-1–1974-4.

The endogenous variables which will be studied here are the unemployment rate and the indexes of capacity utilization. In fact, two

Direct estimates of unemployment rates 483

sets of estimates of capacity utilization are endogenously produced. The alternative indexes are the intermediate and unrefined estimates, while the filtered indexes are the final and adjusted estimates.

The partial model simulation

In this simulation, our results show that both the Wharton and filtered indexes fluctuate closely with business cycles. Both series agree on all major turning points. The filtered index coincides with the Wharton index in the late 1950s. During the early 1960s, they are still coincident for durables, but the filtered index is consistently higher than the Wharton index for nondurables. Apparently, the Wharton index of nondurables has stronger lagged effects due to the recession in 1961.

However, these two series began to diverge in 1965 when the Wharton indexes started to drift upward with time rather rapidly. The divergence is more significant for nondurables. It seems that the Wharton indexes were more affected by the strong inflationary pressures of the Vietnam war and other fast-growing government outlays. This caused the filtered indexes to be consistently lower than the Wharton indexes until the alternative indexes also drifted upward in 1973 when the fast increase in output pushed the output–capacity ratio upwards.[4]

The cyclical profiles indicate that our model can predict better in the trend-dominated periods of upswing and downswing.[5] The partial model solution agrees with major turning points in the actual data. There appears to be a tendency of the estimates to lag behind by one quarter or so when the actual unemployment rate reaches a peak. On the other hand, when the unemployment rate hits a trough, the estimates capture it promptly. In other words, our model has an optimistic nature which responds to full employment at once but takes a longer time to catch up with a high unemployment rate. When the unemployment rate stabilizes at a low level the estimates oscillate about the actual data.

We were interested in finding out whether the predictive ability of our model was improved by the filter technique we used to estimate the capacity utilization rate. Since the alternative index is also an estimate

---
[4]Since we were interested in the tendency of the Wharton series to drift upwards with time in recent years, a time trend can be included in the filter equations. However, the time trend should not be used for long-run analysis or forecasting purposes, because the trend effect may build up so rapidly that it will overshadow the cyclical nature of the indexes.

[5]Time profiles of different simulations are available on request from the authors.

of the capacity utilization rate, it can be directly used in the equation for the unemployment rate to replace the Wharton index. This allowed us to bypass the two filter equations (25.2b and 25.2c) in our model. Such an equation was estimated and the error statistics were calculated. We find that the use of filter techniques improved the goodness of fit in the sample period significantly. In other words, the unemployment rate can be better explained by the Wharton index than by the alternative index.

The full model simulation solutions

Full model simulations were made with the Wharton Mark IV model in which all exogenous variables in our system were treated as endogenous variables except the six variables in (25.5a) and (25.5b) whose values were determined by the trend-through-peaks method.

The time profiles of the estimated capacity utilization rates show that the estimated utilization rates of durables and nondurables, generated by a static simulation, had difficulties in catching up with the Wharton indexes in the 1972–4 period because the actual outputs also had rapidly increased. In general, the estimated indexes are more oscillatory than the Wharton index.

The results of dynamic simulation are somehow reversed. The estimated indexes had overestimated the Wharton indexes in the late 1960s, but they were far below the Wharton index in 1973. This is because the new Mark IV model overestimated durables output in the period 1967–9 and underestimated nondurables output in the period 1972–4.

The dynamic simulation path and the actual path of the unemployment rate move, in general, in the same direction. However, the amplitude of the oscillation in dynamic simulation is significantly smaller than that in the actual data. The cyclical path especially has difficulties in reaching the high level of unemployment in the 1970s. It is apparent that the lag structure of Mark IV restrains the rate of unemployment from moving too high and too fast when the actual unemployment rate is shooting up rapidly.

5 CONCLUSION

The subsystem model derived in this study estimates capacity outputs from stationary-state production functions of different industries and generates a set of structural estimates of the rates of capacity utilization by using Wharton indexes as a filter. The filtered indexes of capacity utilization, as well as other relevant variables, are then used to produce direct estimates of the rate of unemployment.

The empirical results have justified, in our opinion, the validity of several important assumptions implied in this study. The implicit assumptions are: firms minimize cost in a competitive factor market; industrial production follows the Cobb-Douglas law; and capital and labor are utilized, by industries, at approximately the same rate in short run. In addition, the results have also indicated the plausibility of our method of allocating labor force at full capacity among industries and of filtering the estimates of capacity utilization with Wharton indexes.

In general, the rate of capacity utilization in durable goods industries is more sensitive and responsive to business cycles than in nondurable goods industries; i.e. the amplitudes of cyclical movements of the former are greater than those of the latter. This is because the durable goods industries are more capital intensive; their excess capacity will rapidly build up as the economy declines and vice versa. Our simulation results agree with this. In different types of simulation, it is evident that the amplitude of cyclical movements in the time path of durables is significantly larger than in nondurables. Our simulation paths of nondurables are smoother than the Wharton index, while our simulation paths of durables are as cyclical as the Wharton.

The overall unemployment rate in this study is made a function of the utilization rate of manufacturing industries. Since there are no reliable data on capital stocks of some industries, their production functions cannot be appropriately estimated. Thus, the capacity outputs in these industries cannot be derived from the stationary-state production functions. As data are continuously improving in the future, it is possible to expand the scope of this study by endogenizing the rates of capacity utilization in all industries and including them in the unemployment rate equation.

REFERENCES

R. M. Coen and B. G. Hickman, 'Aggregate utilization measures of performance,' memorandum No. 14, Center for Research in Economic Growth, Stanford University (1973).

B. M. Friedman and M. L. Wachter, 'Unemployment: Okun's Law, labor force, and productivity,' *Review of Economics and Statistics*, **56** May (1974), 167–76.

B. G. Hickman, R. M. Coen and M. D. Hurd, 'The Hickman-Coen annual growth model: Structural characteristics and policy response,' *International Economic Review*, **16** February (1975), 20–38.

L. R. Klein and V. Long, 'Capacity utilization: Concepts, measurement, and recent estimates,' *Brookings Papers on Economic Activity*, **3** (1973), 743–64.

L. R. Klein and R. S. Preston, 'Some new results in the measurement of capacity utilization,' *American Economic Review*, **57** March (1967), 34–58.

M. Nerlove, 'Notes on the production and derived demand relationships included in Macro-econometric Models,' *International Economic Review*, **8** June (1967), 223–42.

P. M. Norman and E. R. Moses, 'The role of capacity utilization in the REA 1/74 Model,' Research Discussion Paper 7502, Reserve Bank of Australia, March (1975).

A. M. Okun, 'Potential GNP: Its measurement and significance,' *Proceedings of the Business and Economic Statistics Section of the American Statistical Association* (1962).

G. L. Perry, 'Capacity in manufacturing,' *Brookings Papers on Economic Activity*, **3** (1973), 701–42.

Vincent Su and J. Su, 'An evaluation of ASA-NBER business outlook survey forecasts,' *Explorations in Economic Research*, **2** Fall (1975), 588–618.

J. Taylor and S. McKendrick, 'How should we measure the pressure of demand?' *Lloyds Bank Review* (1974), 13–26.

26

The Supply Side

THE MEANING OF SUPPLY AND DEMAND IN A MACROECONOMIC CONTEXT

It is worth considering whether a new basic model should guide our thinking about performance of the economy as a whole. It is not that the macromodels of the past 25 years or so have failed to serve us well. When we consider the state of our knowledge about the analytics of the economy at the end of World War II and the apprehensiveness with which we approached the modern era of expansion, it should be evident that we have come a long way professionally. Yet the economic problems of today seem to be intractable when studied through the medium of simplified macromodels. The new system should combine the Keynesian model of final demand and income determination with the Leontief model of interindustrial flows. This is the motivation for my focusing attention on the supply side of the economy.

It is frequently said, in almost an offhand manner, that the theories of aggregate employment and output determination are demand models, that economic policy for overall direction of the economy is a policy of *demand* management. I would generally agree with these remarks, but not in every last detail, once the meaning of demand in these contexts is carefully pulled apart and analyzed. The *demand* aspects are possibly overstated.

It is, of course, true that demand for the GNP built up as the sum of demands by consumers, business, government, and foreigners (consumption, investment, public spending, and net exports) covers total demand in the economy and is composed of demands by the constituent parts. But demand by firms, and, in many cases by government, are not ends in themselves. Business demand is largely for goods to produce goods. The capital formation that results from business demand goes into the increment of capital stock, after allowance for capital consumption, and the capital stock becomes a factor input in the production function. The accumulation of capital contributes to the

From *The American Economic Review*, **68**, March (1978), 1–7.

supply of goods and services. Indeed, investment *demand* now for new capital facilitates the implementation of the production process with the supply of factors of ever-increasing powers of productivity, thus making it possible to supply increasing amounts of goods and services with inputs that are increasing at a somewhat slower rate.

By focusing attention excessively on the 'short run,' in which the capital stock is timelessly held fixed by assumption only and not in reality, we have ignored the supply-side characteristics of investment demand. Students of today's business cycle commonly cite investment demand as the promising potential route to higher productivity in the relatively near future, thereby lessening inflationary pressure. In this respect, economic theoreticians have been myopic relative to the applied economic analysts in the world of affairs. Nevertheless, as we shall see, there is much more to the supply side than the transformation of investment into productive capital, and the basic characterization of contemporary macroeconomics as demand analysis has a point. A strong indication of the demand side orientation is given by the elaboration of the standard macromodel. In place of aggregate consumption, the more elaborate model gives separate treatment to consumer expenditures on durables, nondurables, and services. This is the first stage. At a higher stage, there is further disaggregation into types of durables, nondurables, and services such as food, cars, medical services etc. The detail that is introduced for consumption is repeated in business investment demand, housing demand, public expenditures, exports, and imports. Elaboration essentially means taking a closer look at demand side components by types of demand.

The *mainstream* model of macroeconomic thought has thus become a detailed system of demand analysis, but if it is to be a closed system, it will also have to include corresponding detail on the national income side of the social accounts. If this is done fully, there will have to be analyses of factor rewards, factor use, and pricing. The development of factor demand goes beyond capital formation, which appears as a demand for final goods in the GNP, and takes up an explanation of wage income. An adequate explanation of wage income cannot avoid the explicit treatment of physical production involving labor input as well as capital input. The demand for labor, like the demand for capital, is supply-side analysis. While the demand for capital enters directly as a component of total demand, the demand for labor, together with wage formation, enters national income, and only after expenditure does it enter final demand for GNP. To the extent that labor productivity affects wage determination and also price formation, we find supply-side factors influencing inflation and consequently the overall performance of the economy. Labor demand can also be associated with training. The training component is, in fact, investment – in human rather than fixed capital. Looked at in this way, factor demand for labor and factor demand for fixed capital are simply different, but related, aspects of total investment.

Behind the IS–LM diagram or other simplified renditions of the aggregate demand model lie many supply-side relationships. Not only is the supply side in the background, but it also plays a more essential role once it is recognized that the simplified model is actually incomplete. If we were to assume the existence of money illusion, it would be possible to consider the IS–LM system as a closed system of relationships depending on nominal income and nominal interest rates. I find this approach theoretically unsatisfactory. That simple system exists only as an aggregative approximation for a given price level. If we assume no money illusion and, more properly, I believe, the need to determine the aggregate price level, then the IS–LM diagram does not provide a closed-system analysis, and we must extend the system to include the whole supply-side apparatus of production relationships, factor demand, and factor supply.

It is well known that Keynes included the aggregate supply function in the General Theory, but it was introduced in his chapter on 'The principle of effective demand.' That part of his analysis dealing with supply has been largely played down by the profession at large – not by all students of macroeconomics.[1] Also, by way of side comment, Keynes probably confused the issues by making labor supply dependent on the nominal wage rate, assuming the existence of money illusion, and by not treating the stock of capital as an explicit variable.

If the demand relationships explaining the components of the GNP are disaggregated into a highly detailed set, it does not necessarily mean that the supply side must be equally disaggregated to a similar extent, as long as the total flow of income and purchasing power to be directed towards the expenditure flow can be generated. The detailed expenditure flow will, however, involve price relatives. That is a consequence of disaggregation. An aggregate supply-side explanation that generates only an average price level for output as a whole can be adequate, provided separate prices, needed for the price-relatives, can be explained in terms of a relationship to the overall price or wage level. This is much like the use of a term structure relationship in credit market analysis to explain the spectrum of interest rates, given one strategic rate.

---

[1] See Sidney Weintraub (1956, 1957).

It is, however, more satisfactory, and more revealing, to explain the whole set of prices, one by one, on the basis of costs in individual sectors. These sector prices, on the side of production, are then combined with input weights into the several final demand prices needed to account for variation in components of final expenditure. This brings us to a fundamental set of new considerations on the supply side.

THE TASK OF MODELING SUPPLY

If sector prices by line of production are to be explained in a fundamental way by sector costs, there will have to be an accompanying explanation of sector outputs and inputs. This brings us directly to the supply side of things. While the supply side is represented in the macro production function from an aggregative point of view, once we disaggregate the supply side by sector of production, we encounter a new dimension. The aggregate production function, in the spirit of Paul Douglas and Charles Cobb, expresses *value-added* as a function of primary factor inputs, namely, labor and capital. They were able to compress the technology as they did, because at a full macro level, one sector's output is someone else's input, and for the economy as a whole, only value-added is left in the output aggregation. Intermediate inputs or outputs may be neglected in the interests of avoiding double counting. This way of looking at things is strictly correct only for a closed economy. In an open system, intermediate imports must be treated like primary factor inputs.

At the sector level, however, there is no question about the need to consider intermediate inputs. Sector output (gross) is properly a function of intermediate inputs, labor input, and capital input – all sector designated. The presently fashionable way of summarizing this idea is to use the KLEM production function, whose inputs consist of capital, labor, energy, and materials.

The KLEM production function concept is useful in partial studies of separate industries or sectors, and has long been anticipated in aggregative production function studies. It has been routine in production function studies in agriculture to use feed, seed, fertilizer, and other intermediate inputs as explanatory variables. The dependent variable is generally a measure of gross output – gallons of milk, bushels of grain, or bales of cotton. In manufacturing, one of the earliest studies was by Ragnar Frisch. He expressed isoquants for the output of the Freia chocolate factory as a function of fat content and molding–cooling input. One of these is a pure material input and the other stands for some capital, labor, and general running cost input. In my own investigations of US railroad production functions, I included fuel consumption (in coal equivalents) as one of the factor inputs together with labor and capital. The gross output concept consisted of a log-linear combination of ton miles and passenger miles.[2]

These individual industry production functions with a small number of intermediate inputs are hardly substitutes for a detailed input–output analysis on a general system level. The role of input–output analysis is to explain *intermediate* flows in the economic system. The full system is needed in order to provide an adequate supply analysis because

1 There is much more to economic activity than can be summarized by the system of final goods production.
2 The explanation of types of final prices depends on highly specific types of intermediate, as well as final, goods/services prices.

The occurrence of bottlenecks – potential or realized – as in the oil embargo of 1973–4 or the diversion of large amounts of agricultural output to export markets as in 1973 and 1975 are striking examples of cases where there was a great deal of economic activity going on outside final GNP sectors. An economic understanding of those activities and an estimate of their macro impacts on the GNP could not be readily derived from demand analysis without consulting the table of intermediate flows in I–O analysis. These are only striking examples. Many more have arisen in the past, and more are bound to occur in the future; therefore, the concern of this presentation is not with singular events.

An adequate explanation of the price system, especially on the cost side, cannot stop at the KLEM level with separate consideration of energy, materials, wage, and capital costs. It must take account of prices of grains, ferrous metals, nonferrous metals, coal, crude oil, machinery, textiles, and the other component prices in an input–output system. The appropriate amount of detail is not a fixed matter. It depends on human capabilities of analysis, machine facilities, data bases, and other practical considerations, but it is, in any case, an order of magnitude greater than contemplated by mainstream macromodel analysis.

From an analytical point of view, what is being suggested is a full combination of two systems of thought, the Leontief Model and the Keynesian Model. That these two systems can be put back-to-back into

---

[2] See the author.

a single consistent model, with full feedback between each part, is now well known, having been implemented first with the Brookings Model and later with various generations of Wharton Models, and more recently by Dale Jorgenson in a translog mode. A principal feature of such combined systems is that they are not based on restrictive assumptions of the fixed coefficient input–output model, but are generalized to allow the coefficients of production to vary, according to the variation of relative prices.

The above expression, 'full feedback,' means that the macromodel of final demand and national income generation cannot be solved, by itself, without also solving the input–output system for generating sector production flows. Moreover sector prices cannot be solved without also solving the macromodel simultaneously.

Price formation in individual sectors is specified in terms of mark-up relations over unit labor costs. Thus, sector outputs and labor inputs are needed in order to explain sector prices. These prices are needed, in turn, in order to explain final demand prices. Similarly, sector investment depends on sector output as well as sector price. It is for these and similar reasons that final demand cannot be generated without making use of the input–output system in order to generate sector outputs.

At the same time, the input–output system is driven by final demand; therefore, the conventional macro demand model must be used in order to solve the input–output system. These are the specific senses in which full feedback is used in order to obtain simultaneous and consistent integration of the entire supply and demand sides of the economy.

In terms of the history of economic thought, the above approach means thinking in terms of the empirical implementation of the Walrasian system. Essentially, Tinbergen implemented the Keynesian system and Leontief implemented a part of the Walrasian system. By putting the two together, with due allowance to Kuznets for making the data bases of final demand and national income available, a complete synthesis of supply and demand in the economy as a whole can be put together. This gives the antecedents of what is meant by modeling supply, taking into account what is needed from demand models at the same time.

WHY MODEL SUPPLY?

At the time of the Keynesian Revolution, there was a pervasive deficiency of demand throughout most of the world. The Keynesian policy development, building on that model, did, in my opinion, much good for the economy of the Western world, enabling us to come through an expansive era of more than 25 years without a recurrence of a Great Depression. That does not mean that this system of thought and policy formation did its work for all time in putting the world economy on a stable footing. It carried the situation only so far, and undoubtedly underestimated inflation potentials, leaving us now at the point where new systems of thought, drawing more on the supply side, are needed in order to develop policies that will be able to deal with the world's contemporary economic problems; hopefully, policies that will have as much longevity as the demand-management policies of the last two to three decades. That should bring us nicely into the twenty-first century, which is about as far ahead as we might attempt to look at the present time.

The limits of demand management policies have become clearly visible in recent years. Let us look at the issues through the medium of specific problems, say the joint problems of too much unemployment and too much inflation. Policies of demand management alone have appeared to be adequate to deal with one or the other, but not both together. If demand is stimulated enough to bring down the unemployment rate to a full-employment minimum, there is danger of generating undue inflationary pressure as a side effect. Conversely, anti-inflationary policies of demand restriction run the danger of generating excessive unemployment while holding down the inflation rate.

How might supply-side policies be introduced to lower both the inflation and unemployment rates at the same time? It is conventionally thought that policies of aggregate demand stimulus through traditional fiscal and monetary policies might be able to bring down the US unemployment rate to about 5.5 per cent. This is not a firm point estimate, and is subject to error of at least one-half point above or below that figure, but it is not, in any case, a full-employment target figure.

One way, but not the only way, of getting to full employment without generating fresh inflationary pressure is to design a jobs program for about 1 million, long-term, hard-core unemployed. This jobs program cannot be described in full detail in the context of this presentation, but it is not to be viewed as an ordinary public jobs program. It is viewed as a job-training program aimed at people who show signs of receptivity to training and enlisting the participation of employers who provide really productive jobs with potential for upward mobility. The 1 million target, spread over 3 years, is not purely indicative. It is meant to be plausible and necessary if full employment is to be reached by 1980–2 in the US.

Apart from the fact that some public funds are to be spent on this program, it is not a typical demand-management policy. It is aimed at increasing the supply of goods, at raising labor productivity, at sectors of the economy where job training can be accommodated or needed, and at sectors of the labor force. It is basically a supply-side policy and needs for its implementation/assessment a full-scale analysis through the medium of a Leontief–Keynes system. In first approximations, such assessments have been made with the appropriate version of the Wharton Model.

In anticipation of criticism of this policy approach from the side of those who are strongly wedded to emphasis on demand management, I want to stress that a jobs program aimed at increasing productivity and reducing hard-core unemployment is not a futile exercise in pushing some subsidized workers into the ranks of the employed while pushing others out. The program is intended to have balance; i.e. to be part of a larger program with corresponding support from the demand side. Such support could not be justified from the point of view of inflation potential unless steps are being taken to complement the effect with a jobs program and eventual lifting of productivity. Undue preoccupation with demand policies is not going to be adequate to meet the problems of the day, nor is pure emphasis on supply. Both sides of the economy must be coordinated in policy formation.

It should also be emphasized that demand policies of federal expenditures for public-service employment appear to be inferior to private-sector jobs programs of the type being mentioned here. In the former case, there is no long-term opportunity for those taken into the program and there is no contribution to national productivity. As long as job expenditures are going to be made, they ought, preferably, to be directed to an effort that promises to have some lasting benefit.

This example of the jobs program is one that fits the contemporary American economic scene and has been investigated with a US model and data. The underlying idea, however, is meant to be much more general. It is that the whole industrial world is faced with a series of new supply-side economic problems. The problems of cyclical stabilization and reaching full employment without inflation will have to be dealt with as before, and the latter will require some degree of supply-side analysis in other economies as in the US case, but a whole new range of economic issues looms on the horizon. These are development of new, greater energy supplies, protection of the environment, controlling the exhaustion of resources, enhancing agricultural supplies, balancing population development, and others of like nature. The juggling of public budgets, the setting of tax rates, and the giving of a tone to money market conditions are not going to deal effectively with this new class of problems, from the viewpoints of influencing them in a favorable direction. Similarly, the demand oriented model is not going to provide much understanding of them.

The coming problems of the industrial economy are not going to be wholly dealt with or analyzed on the basis of the general purpose Leontief–Keynes system that is being advocated here. In many cases, the unforeseen problems that are bound to arise are going to be more specialized than can be conveniently anticipated. In such cases, the analysis must extend into partial system analysis giving more detailed and explicit treatment on the supply side. In terms of model building that means construction of many 'satellite' systems on the supply side, as the need arises. At the present time, many energy satellite systems are being developed to deal with new fuel processes, large energy-using sectors, and large energy-delivery sectors. These satellite systems are then all linked, in a technical and consistent way, with the input–output cum macromodel system. In any event, the intent is to move the discussion of macroeconomics and policy formation to a new plane of discourse.

The discussion, thus far, has focused on the modeling and related policy problems for the modern industrial economy. The analysis of the supply side, however, is not a new issue for the developing economy. A deficiency of demand analyzed within the framework of the Keynesian Model has not generally been thought to be the issue or approach for dealing with the problems of economic development. That is not to say that demand relations are nonexistent or unimportant for the developing economy. It is primarily a matter of emphasis. Availability of fixed capital treated as a limiting factor in production is central to understanding the problems facing many developing economies.

Energy problems of production and use are already apparent, as are population control and agricultural production. Where problems of environmental protection and resource exhaustion have not yet arisen, they are bound to occur in significant instances; therefore, it is wise for the development economist to be forearmed with a full model for analysis of both supply and demand sides.

The centrally planned economies are for the most part industrial economies and have the same needs for supply-side analysis. In their cases, the supply side has perhaps been excessively developed with inadequate attention paid to the demand side, not from the viewpoint of deficient demand but from the viewpoint of chronic excess demand, with latent inflationary pressure.

The present analysis attempts to look at a particular facet of the modern economy, namely the supply side. That does not imply, by any means, that monetary analysis and policy are unimportant. Most of the supply-side problems have monetary implications or aspects; therefore, monetary policy must be appropriate to insure the smooth working of the supply side of the economy.

In terms of the analytical apparatus needed to combine monetary analysis with the kind of supply–demand model that I have outlined above, it is a matter of integrating the flow-of-funds system together with the input–output and final demand national income system. It would also be in a full feedback mode. To complement the supply-side detail underlying the IS curve, we would turn to the complete flow-of-funds model to provide background for the LM curve.

It is my feeling that overall monetary and fiscal policies have been overworked, with expectations of results that are not justified. Without downgrading their very important role, the present message simply says that a full supply-side analysis must be developed into which an elaborated IS–LM system of thought can be fully integrated.

REFERENCES

R. Frisch, 'The principle of substitution: An example of its application in the chocolate industry,' *Nordisk Tidsskrift for Teknisk Økonomi*, **1**, September (1935), 21–7.

K. C. Hoffman and D. W. Jorgenson, 'Economic and technological models for evaluation of energy policy,' *Bell J. Econ.*, **8**, Autumn (1977), 444–66.

Lawrence R. Klein, *A Textbook of Econometrics*, Evanston (1953).

S. Weintraub, 'A macroeconomic approach to the theory of wages,' *Amer. Econ. Rev.*, **46**, December (1956), 833–56.

S. Weintraub, 'The micro-foundations of aggregate demand and supply,' *Econ. J.*, **67**, September (1957), 455–70.

27
Stochastic Nonlinear Models

The variance of solutions to stochastic linear dynamic systems tends to a finite limit if the system is damped. Limit cycles are possible in linear systems, but the corresponding solutions would have increasing variance in the stochastic case. On the other hand, nonlinear systems with limit cycles may have solutions with bounded variance in the stochastic case. A numerical example illustrating the limit cycles of Kaldor's nonlinear trade cycle model is shown to have solutions with bounded variance when the system is subjected to random shocks. The variance series is periodic with one-half the cyclical duration of the mean series. The amplitude of the mean series decreases over time. In a linear system, the mean series would have the same cyclical pattern as the nonstochastic solution.

1 STATEMENT OF THE PROBLEM

Trade cycle theorists have sought to construct nonlinear models because they are capable of producing maintained, endogenous cycles, while linear models do so only for very special parameter values, which might occur in real life with low or negligible probability. One of the uncommon linear models capable of producing a maintained cycle for a wide range of plausible parameter values was introduced by Francis Dresch, as an elegant achievement in cycle theory, and then rejected by Paul Samuelson, as being unstable in a probability sense when subjected to random shock.[1]

The authors are much indebted to M. Morishima and C. B. Winsten for helpful discussions on general aspects of the problem discussed here. Great assistance on the numerical work was provided by L. Fox and J. D. Donnelly of the Oxford University Computing Laboratory, where some of the calculations were made.

[1] P. A. Samuelson, *Foundations of Economic Analysis*, Harvard University Press, Cambridge (1947) p. 268.

From *Econometrica*, **37**, January (1969), 95–106; written jointly with R. S. Preston.

The Dresch model is very simple. It uses the law of supply and demand for a *stock* model

$$\dot{p} = \alpha \int_{-\infty}^{t} [D(p) - S(p)] d\tau \qquad \alpha > 0,$$

which becomes, for linear demand and supply functions,

$$\ddot{p} = \alpha(d_0 - s_0) + \alpha(d_1 - s_1)p.$$

For negatively sloped demand and positively sloped supply functions this model oscillates, in a pure sinusoidal manner, about equilibrium price. A wide range of parameter values produce these maintained oscillations.

Samuelson criticized this model on the grounds that if it were subjected to repeated random shocks, the variance of p would tend to grow with t. Samuelson's rejection of this linear oscillating model did not lead him to a nonlinear modification, but led him to introduce additional linear terms that might dampen the time movement of p. In a noncyclical context this is very much like Kalecki's modification of the process generating the lognormal law of income distribution.[2]

We shall develop our results for stochastic difference equations. In the linear cases, a general result is well known and can readily be found in two standard references (by H. Wold and by H. B. Mann and A. Wald) that are familiar to many economists.[3]

Consider the rth order linear difference equation,

$$x_t + \lambda_1 x_{t-1} + \lambda_2 x_{t-2} + \cdots + \lambda_r x_{t-r} = u_t,$$

where u_t is a random variable drawn from a population with constant variance. The solution to this equation can be expressed as

$$x_t = \sum_{i=1}^{r} C_i \rho_i^t + \sum_{i=0}^{t-r} B_i u_{t-i},$$

where the ρ_i are roots of the characteristic equation and C_i and B_i are constants depending on the initial conditions and λ_i. Since x_t is a linear function of random variables $u_r, u_{r+1}, \ldots, u_t$, it too is a random variable. The basic theorem states that $\text{var}(x_t) < M$, where M is some finite positive number, if all $|\rho_i| < 1$. This is both necessary and sufficient. A finite-difference version of the Dresch equation gives $|\rho_1| = |\rho_2| = 1$ and thus violates the condition of the theorem. The variance of price, p_t,

---

[2] M. Kalecki, 'On the Gibrat Distribution,' *Econometrica*, XIII, April (1945), 161–70.

[3] H. Wold, *A Study in the Analysis of Stationary Time Series*, Almqvist and Wiksells, Uppsala (1938). H. B. Mann and A. Wald, 'On the statistical treatment of linear stochastic difference equations,' *Econometrica*, XI, July–October (1943), 173–220.

derived from a stochastic form of his equation, is an increasing function of t, as Samuelson asserted.

It is instructive to review the solution to the general second-order linear difference equation:

$$p_t + \lambda_1 p_{t-1} + \lambda_2 p_{t-2} = u_t.$$

The solution can be expressed as[4]

$$p_t = C_1 \rho_1^t + C_2 \rho_2^t + \sum_{j=0}^{t-2} \frac{\rho_1^{j+1} - \rho_2^{j+1}}{\rho_1 - \rho_2} u_{t-j},$$

where C_1 and C_2 depend on the initial conditions, λ_1, and λ_2. The roots of the characteristic equation are ρ_1 and ρ_2. If λ_1 and λ_2 are such that the solution is an undamped sinusoid, as in the Dresch model, we have

$$\operatorname{var} p_t = \sigma_u^2 \sum_{j=0}^{t-2} \left(\frac{\rho_1^{j+1} - \rho_2^{j+1}}{\rho_1 - \rho_2} \right)^2$$

$$= \sigma_u^2 \sum_{j=0}^{t-2} \left[\frac{(\cos\theta + i\sin\theta)^{j+1} - (\cos\theta - i\sin\theta)^{j+1}}{(\cos\theta + i\sin\theta) - (\cos\theta - i\sin\theta)} \right]$$

$$= \frac{\sigma_u^2}{\sin^2\theta} \sum_{j=0}^{t-2} \sin^2(j+1)\theta.$$

This is clearly a monotonic function of t. Since $\sin^2(j+1)\theta = (1 - \cos(j+1)2\theta)/2$ we find that the periodicity of the time series of $\operatorname{var} p_t$ is one half that of the time series of p_t. This is a periodicity in the monotonic upward movement of $\operatorname{var} p_t$.

In the finite difference form of the Dresch theory, if the random error is added to the price adjustment equation, the final equation will be

$$p_{t+1} - [2 + \alpha(d_1 - s_1)]p_t + p_{t-1} = \alpha(d_0 - s_0) + u_{t+1} - u_t,$$

in which the disturbance is a first difference of independent random variables. These first-difference errors are not serially independent; therefore we must investigate the effect of this dependence on the variance of the solution.

The solution may be written as

$$p_t = C_1 \rho_1^t + C_2 \rho_2^t + \sum_{j=0}^{t-2} \frac{\rho_1^{j+1} - \rho_2^{j+1}}{\rho_1 - \rho_2} (u_{t-j} - u_{t-j-1})$$

[4] M. S. Bartlett, *An Introduction to Stochastic Processes*, Cambridge University Press, Cambridge (1955).

and the variance will be

$$\operatorname{var} p_t = 2\sigma_u^2 \sum_{j=0}^{t-2} \left(\frac{\rho_1^{j+1}-\rho_2^{j+1}}{\rho_1-\rho_2}\right)^2 - 2\sigma_u^2 \sum_{j=0}^{t-2} \left(\frac{\rho_1^{j+1}-\rho_2^{j+1}}{\rho_1-\rho_2}\right)\left(\frac{\rho_1^{j+2}-\rho_2^{j+2}}{\rho_1-\rho_2}\right)$$

$$= 2\sigma_u^2 \sum_{j=0}^{t-2} \left(\frac{\sin^2(j+1)\theta - \sin(j+1)\theta \sin(j+2)\theta}{\sin^2\theta}\right).$$

This series is not monotonic but will, in general, diverge. This can be seen as follows:

$$\operatorname{var} p_t = \frac{2\sigma_u^2}{\sin^2\theta} \sum_{j=0}^{t-2} \left(\frac{1-\cos 2(j+1)\theta}{2} - \frac{\cos(-\theta)-\cos(2j+3)\theta}{2}\right)$$

$$= \frac{\sigma_u^2}{\sin^2\theta} \left\{\sum_{j=0}^{t-2} (1-\cos\theta) + \sum_{j=0}^{t-2} [\cos(2j+3)\theta - \cos(2j+2)\theta]\right\}$$

The first term in brackets is an increasing function of t, while the second is bounded since

$$\sum_{j=0}^{t} \cos j\theta = \tfrac{1}{2}\left[1 + \frac{\cos(t-2)\theta - \cos(t-1)\theta}{1-\cos(\theta)}\right].$$

Since linear models with constant (nonstochastic) cycles have, when shocked, unbounded variance of solution over time and since dependence among errors does not stabilize variance, we now come to the main point to be investigated: What can we say about the finiteness of variance of solutions of *nonlinear* systems with limit cycles of constant amplitude?[5]

If we reject linear models with oscillations of constant amplitude, what alternative should we seek for the explanation of trade cycles? Should we seek damped (nonstochastic) linear models whose oscillations are kept alive by random shocks? We personally find such models attractive, but they have been rejected by some theorists who want a purely endogenous cycle mechanism. Or should we seek nonlinear models with limit cycles that do not die out? Nonlinearity may be basic to human economic behavior and should be incorporated where pertinent in our theories, but nonlinear models have been constructed nonstochastically, and little in a general sense is known about their behavior under random perturbation. We shall take up a special case in this paper.

---

[5] The serial dependence found in the errors $u_{t+1}-u_t$ is not of the general autoregressive type. If we add general autoregressive errors to the linear difference equation, we can show that the growth of variance occurs unless the roots of the characteristic equation for the deterministic case lie within the unit circle.

2 EXTENSION ON THE CONCEPT OF STABILITY

Samuelson injected a new dimension into the discussion of stability by bringing probability considerations to bear on the notion.[6] Let us assume that economic magnitudes generally are random variables. They may have some nonrandom components, but they also have random components and are, therefore, random variables. It is simplest, perhaps, to regard them as consisting of a systematic part plus a random part. We shall say that the solution to a dynamic system x_t is stable if $|E(x_t)| < M_1$, and $\sigma_x^2 = E(x_t - E(x_t))^2 < M_2$ for all t, where M_1 and M_2 are finite positive constants. In growth systems these can be modified by assuming that x_t are deviations from trend equilibrium.

3 A NUMERICAL CASE STUDY: A STOCHASTIC NONLINEAR TRADE-CYCLE MODEL

So much less is known about the behavior of nonlinear dynamic systems, even in the nonstochastic case, that we cannot aspire to the general theorems that have been established for the linear case. We can, however, use specific examples of nonlinear systems to demonstrate some general negative points. We saw, from the general theorem referred to above, that a linear system with cycles of constant amplitude (roots with absolute value of unity) will not have finite variance as $t \to \infty$. In a negative way we can say, from a specific example, that this is not generally so for nonlinear systems. It is possible for a nonlinear system with limit cycles of constant amplitude to have finite variance as $t \to \infty$. If we were to impose absolute (nonstochastic) floors and ceilings on total production as in the trade-cycle models of Goodwin and Hicks, or extensions of them, it is obvious that the variances must be finite because the probability of exceeding those finite, nonstochastic limits must be zero. Hyperinflation is not ruled out, but finite variance for the fluctuations in the real economy is assured.

The model we shall use for an example is somewhat different. It is the celebrated nonlinear model of the trade cycle proposed by Kaldor as early as 1940.[7] Professor Ichimura concluded his exhaustive mathematical analysis of Kaldor's model by observing that we need to know

---

[6] P. A. Samuelson, *Foundations*, 336 ff. See also 'Causality and teleology in economics,' *Cause and Effect* (ed. D. Lerner) Free Press, New York (1965), esp. pp. 121–3.

[7] N. Kaldor, 'A model of the trade cycle,' *Economic Journal*, L, March (1940), 78–92.

how it behaves under stochastic disturbances.[8] This is the line of argument that we now propose to follow.

We propose that the consumption function be an S-shaped curve – the logistic.[9] With a ceiling and floor to total consumption, we are assured that $mps \leq 1$. Some people may feel that Kaldor's theory is based on curves with very special 'wiggles,' but in fact it is a brilliant anticipation of the 'new theories of consumption' (and of investment) that are now readily accepted. Moreover, we would argue that there is good empirical evidence to support his ideas about saving behavior. From postwar UK data, the logistic curve depicted in figure 27.1,

$$Y - S = 12 + \frac{18}{3 + 17\exp[-\tfrac{5}{8}(Y-17)]},$$

was fitted by cut and try methods. In this formula, Y represents net

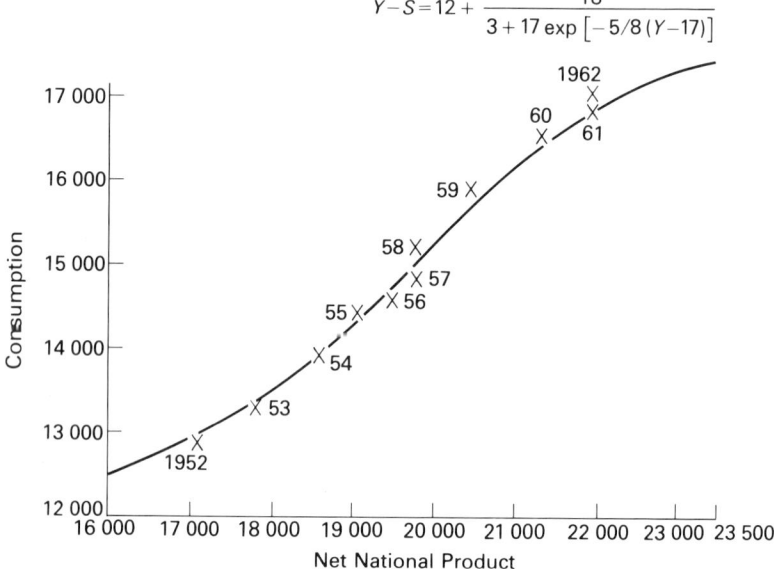

Figure 27.1 Logistic consumption function (UK data) (£ million, 1958 prices)

---

[8]S. Ichimura, 'Toward a general non-linear macro-dynamic theory of economic fluctuations,' *Post Keynesian Economics* (Ed. K. Kurihara) Rutgers University Press, New Brunswick (1954).

[9]Our present specifications of the Kaldor model differ in parametric structure from those introduced on an earlier occasion: L. R. Klein with the assistance of A. Buckberg, L. Gyorki, and H. Runyon, 'Quelques aspects empiriques du modèle du cycle économique de Kaldor,' *Les Modèles Dynamiques en Économétrie*, Centre National de la Recherche Scientifique, Paris (1956).

national product in 1958 prices, and S is net national product minus consumer expenditures in 1958 prices.

Total fixed capital formation (net) private and public, when fitted to postwar UK data in a linear relation, gives $I = -4.350 + 0.31Y - 0.0126 K_{-1}$.[10] This function, even if adjusted for exports minus imports, government current expenditures, and inventory investment, would not intersect the savings function property so as to produce a Kaldor limit cycle.

For numerical analysis, changes had to be made in these functions. First, the investment function was tilted so that it cut the savings function three times at reasonable levels. Then both the savings and investment functions had to be translated vertically so that zero savings (=investment) occurred between points where the savings function had slope 0.6, the new slope chosen for the investment function. The Kaldor Model does not oscillate unless the savings and investment functions are in proper relation to one another.

Thus the complete numerical model is

$$S = Y - 16.8 - \frac{18}{3 + 17\exp[-\tfrac{5}{8}(Y-17)]},$$

$$K - K_{-1} = -13 + 0.6Y - 0.1 K_{-1},$$

$$Y_{+1} - Y = 0.9(K - K_{-1} - S).$$

The third equation, the adjustment of aggregate output to discrepancies between savings and investment, was arbitrarily assigned an adjustment coefficient of 0.9.

This numerical model does, we believe, represent the nonlinear Kaldor theory, and it does have a limit cycle, but it does not faithfully represent the postwar UK economy. There is some realism, except for a translation constant, in the savings function. Investment may have the right variables, but not the right parameter values. Thus, we do not claim that the Kaldor theory faithfully describes UK cyclical fluctuations. It is probably better for a closed economy anyway, but it is an interesting vehicle for the study of nonlinear oscillations under stochastic disturbance.

It should be mentioned that the logistic consumption function has a ceiling and floor, but this does not impose a strict ceiling and floor on

---

[10] We prefer to emphasize the nonlinearity of savings together with a linear flexible accelerator. This is opposite to the emphasis in the Goodwin-Hicks models. The Kaldor theory is based on functions with both savings and investment nonlinear, or either one linear coupled with the other's being appropriately nonlinear.

total output because the investment function is linear. The depressing effect of capital accumulation (stimulating effect of capital depreciation) gives resistance to upward (downward) movements in the neighborhood of the cyclical peaks (troughs).

Let us now consider nonstochastic simulation of our numerical system of three equations. For given initial conditions ($Y=21$, $K_{-1}=0$ in the present case), the three equations can readily be solved. For the initial Y value, we obtain S from the first (nonlinear) equation. The initial Y and K_{-1} values are used in the second (linear) equation to obtain K. Having K, S, and the initial values, we obtain Y_{+1} from the third equation and then repeat the solution process. In figure 27.2, there are solutions for Y up to $t=500$. The first 65 values were listed for each integral value of t. From that point onward, only peaks and troughs were listed.

We find here a regular limit cycle that settles down to an amplitude in the Y scale between approximately 12.3 and 27.3. The full cycle runs its course in approximately 32 time periods. This is a numerical model of the working of the theory as Kaldor originally put it.

The next step was to simulate this model stochastically. To do this, independent normally distributed variables were added to the second and third equations. It was not necessary to add random shocks to the first equation since it is substituted without lags into the third equation; therefore the error in the third equation can be considered a linear

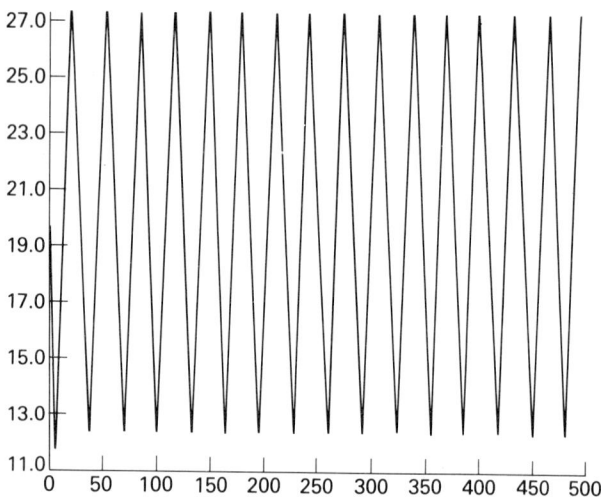

Figure 27.2 Nonstochastic simulations

combination of its own and that of the first equation. The normal variables chosen were uncorrelated and had zero means. In the investment equation (second) the random error was made to have standard deviation equal to 0.20 and in the adjustment (third) equation equal to 0.30. A solution under successive random shocks was obtained up to $t = 500$. This simulation process was repeated independently 100 times; thus we had results for 100 stochastic simulations of length $t = 500$.

In figure 27.3, there is a plotting of the mean and variance of these 100 stochastic simulations at successive time points. This is the main result of the present study. The means and variances were computed for each time period. They are means and variances across the 100 stochastic realizations.

In a linear stochastic model, the solution can be represented as the solution of the nonstochastic system plus a linear combination of error terms. We had previously expressed this as

$$p_t = C_1 \rho_1^t + C_2 \rho_2^t + \sum_{j=0}^{t-2} \frac{\rho_1^{j+1} - \rho_2^{j+1}}{\rho_1 - \rho_2} u_{t-j}$$

and

$$E(p_t) = C_1 \rho_1^t + C_2 \rho_2^t.$$

Thus the cyclical properties of the mean series are completely determined by those of the nonstochastic system. This is not the case in our

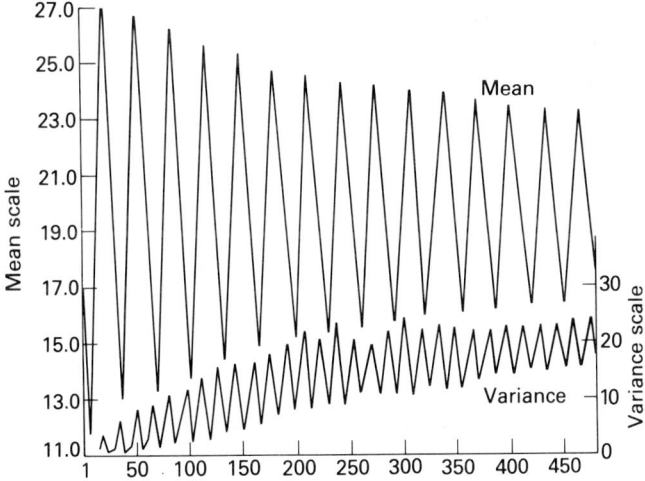

Figure 27.3 Mean stochastic simulations
($\sigma_1 = 0.2$, $\sigma_2 = 0.3$)

nonlinear model. The mean series is decidedly different from the solution to the nonstochastic system. It is clearly seen in figure 27.3 that the mean series is damped. If we were to predict the position of the system at time t in the future on the basis of initial conditions and the given nonstochastic structure, we would not know which particular random realization to choose and would have to base a prediction on the expected value. It is the series of these expected values that we find to be damped.

The effect then of introducing stochastic elements into our nonlinear theory of the cycle is to introduce dampening in this average sense. The actual stochastic cycle is not damped, but our judgement of where the cyclical system will be at future time points will be damped. A reason for this form of dampening is given below.

Consider now the variance series. It too is a period function, but its period is just one-half that of the mean series. This result is to be expected on the basis of the variance formula derived above for the linear case. When mean Y is at a peak or trough, the variance series is at a minimum point. In the middle of the Kaldor cycles, where there is instability, the variance series reaches a maximum. The variance series thus goes through two cycles while the mean series goes through just one. In addition, the variance series stabilizes and in 500 periods does not exceed a value of 24. We have, therefore, been able to construct a nonlinear model with fixed amplitudes, nonstochastic cycles, and bounded variance. The mean stochastic series is, however, damped. By contrast, in a linear model the expected value of the stochastic series would be the same as the nonstochastic series; therefore if the latter had constant amplitude, the mean series would not be damped, but the variance would grow indefinitely.

4 PIECEWISE LINEAR APPROXIMATION OF THE NONLINEAR MODEL

Another way of dealing with the nonlinear theory is to break it into separate, juxtaposed linear regimes. In place of the gradually curved savings function, we could have the piecewise linear approximation given in figure 27.4. The advantage of this type of formulation is that the solution can be written as a combination of solutions to linear problems, which can be generally represented as in section 1. Our piecewise approximation establishes three regimes. To the left of $Y=40$ the savings function is $S=-37+0.8Y$. In the middle range, $40<Y<60$, we have $S=-25+0.5Y$, and to the right of $Y=60$ we have

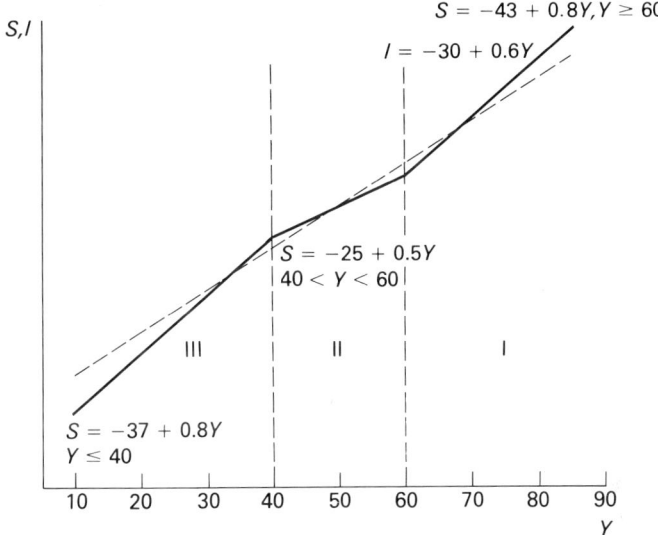

Figure 27.4 Linear approximation to Kaldor Model

$S = -43 + 0.8Y$. A symmetrical function approximating our transformed logistic has equal slopes for the left and right branches and a smaller slope (savings function) for the middle range. In the left- and right-hand regimes, the savings slopes exceed the investment slope, and the intersection points are stable in the comparative static sense. In the middle regime, the intersection is unstable and of the kind just analyzed for the linear, sinusoidal model.

Whenever values are to the right of 60, we can analyze the process by linear methods, as above, using the right hand branch of the savings function. When the investment function shifts downward as a result of capital accumulation and touches the corner of the savings function, we switch to a new linear model for the middle regime. When Y falls below 40 we shift to the left branch, still using explicit linear methods, etc.

This system, when simulated stochastically as in section 3, has a Kaldor-type limit cycle and a cyclical variance with a half-period.[11] This variance grows to an asymptotic value as does the variance of the stochastic nonlinear Kaldor model studied in the preceding section.

---

[11] The constants in the separate linear equations were chosen so as to produce a Kaldor limit cycle (nonstochastic) with the same (approximate) periodicity as the prior logistic model. The amplitude has been enlarged.

Within each of the three linear regimes, we can express the solution explicitly as

$$Y_{t_i} = C_{1i}\rho_{1i}^{t_i} + C_{2i}\rho_{2i}^{t_i} + \sum_{j=0}^{t_i-2} \frac{\rho_{1i}^{j+1} - \rho_{2i}^{j+1}}{\rho_{1i} - \rho_{2i}} u_{t_i - j} \qquad i = \text{I, II, III},$$

where t_i is measured from the point at which the system entered regime i. The roots ρ_{1i} and ρ_{2i} now vary, depending on whether the system is in regime I, II, or III.[12] Moreover C_{1i} and C_{2i} become stochastic. At the start of the system the initial conditions are fixed nonstochastically, and they change for each new regime as we switch over to a new linear solution. But this income level will be near the boundary values for the start of each regime. The initial values will have a random component at the start of each new linear regime. This gives a fundamental difference between the solution of linear and nonlinear systems. For the former, the initial conditions are fixed throughout. For the latter, we can look upon the solution as that appropriate to endogenous linear models with changing initial conditions.[13]

This throws useful light on an aspect of the stochastic simulation of the Kaldor model, namely, the tendency of the mean amplitude of the 100 stochastic solutions to fall with t. Even though a solution corresponding to a particular random sequence $u_{t_1}, u_{t_1+1}, u_{t_1+2}, \ldots$, i.e. a single realization, can be simply expressed by the above solution to a linear equation as long as Y stays within a given regime, there is nothing to guarantee that all member series of the simulation are at the same point or in the same regime at any instant of time. In fact, all the 100 simulations start out together and then get out of phase with one another. The mean series

$$\bar{Y}_t = \frac{1}{100} \sum_{i=1}^{100} Y_t^{(i)},$$

which averages the different stochastic terms of the simulation at a point of time, combines elements (in the resulting average) from different regimes.

The expected value of a stochastic solution will be

$$E(Y_t) = \sum_{i=\text{I}}^{\text{III}} w_i E(C_{1i}\rho_{1i}^{t_i} + C_{2i}\rho_{2i}^{t_i})$$

---

[12] By the symmetry of construction in the present numerical example, ρ_{1i} and ρ_{2i} are the same in regimes I and III.

[13] Cf. H. Minsky, 'A linear model of cyclical growth,' *Review of Economics and Statistics*, **41**, May (1959), 33–45.

where w_i is the probability that the solution will be in regime i at time t and t_i is the time that has elapsed at time t since the system entered regime i. The roots ρ_{1i}, ρ_{2i}, are nonstochastic, but the initial conditions and hence the constants C_{1i}, C_{2i} will have random elements depending on how near the boundary of the regime the solution starts up. In general, though, C_{1i} and C_{2i} have limited variation from re-entry to re-entry into a regime.

The expected value of Y_t is, therefore, an average of its values in each of the three regimes, where the average is weighted over the probabilities of being in each of the three regimes. We can estimate these probabilities from the empirical frequency distributions of Y_t at different values of t.

Consider the whole frequency distribution of Y values at $t=5$, $t=105$, and $t=495$ for the nonlinear Kaldor models in either the logistic or the piecewise linear form. At the beginning we have a unimodal distribution which gradually becomes dispersed. At $t=105$ there are possibly three peaks, but not less than two, and the spread at $t=495$ has definitely become trimodal. A crude frequency distribution is given in table 27.1 for the piecewise linear model. After the system settles into a pattern, the distribution shifts with a majority of cases staying in phase II and the number in phase I or III shifting as the average cyclical process changes. If we look at finer subdivisions within regimes, however, we find that the distributions eventually settle into an almost uniform distribution. In this event, the w_i in the above formula for $E(Y_t)$ are equal. This accounts for the time path of $E(Y_t)$ converging to a single value located in regime II.

Table 27.1 Standing of simulated series

Regime	Frequency		
	$t=5$	$t=105$	$t=495$
III	100	5	12
II	0	59	59
I	0	36	29

Part IV

PUBLIC POLICY

28

A Post Mortem on Transition Predictions of National Product

We all recall clearly the headlines in last autumn's press, declaring that 'Government economists predict 8 million unemployed by 1946.' At the same time, the newspapers were telling us of congressional action to lower corporate and personal income taxes, administrative action to relax ceiling prices on construction materials, lobbyists' pressure to weaken the strength of price controls, and many other inflationary policies. We now find ourselves in the first half of 1946 with about 3 million unemployed and facing one of the greatest inflationary pressures that we have ever experienced. The economists who were warning us of a deflationary danger during the early months of the postwar transition period should have been stressing precisely opposite economic policy.

There is no question that they made a mistake, but there are many questions concerning why they made the mistake. Was it a result of their methodology? Was it a result of their intuitive judgments? Was it a result of their theoretical economic systems? It is very important to answer these questions because many economists would discredit much more than the wrong estimates themselves. Some economists claim that the wrong predictions show that the entire theoretical economic model and the methodology of forecasting are wrong. We shall attempt to show that such claims are unfounded and that errors in forecasting may have nothing to do with the validity of many of the underlying theories. There are some economists who made more accurate predictions with other methods, but we shall also attempt to show that these more accurate predictions do not prove that their methods are superior to those that failed.

The current controversy contains several 'red herrings,' which should be disposed of before we can get at the truth of the matter. In the first

---

The author is indebted to Trygve Haavelmo, Leonid Hurwicz, Tjalling Koopmans, and Jacob Marschak for constructive criticism. This paper was written during the tenure of a postdoctoral fellowship of the Social Science Research Council.

From *The Journal of Political Economy*, **54**, August (1946), 289–308.

place, many of the estimates for the posttransition period are loosely quoted in reference to the transition period. The estimates of J. Mosak[1] for 1950 have frequently been mentioned, along with those pertaining to 1945, 1946, and 1947. While the estimates for the latter years are proving to be wrong, the former may still be correct, unfortunately. Second, the estimates of gross national product and of unemployment should be separated. It is possible for economists to predict output more closely than the difference between labor input and the labor force. Their models actually are intended to forecast gross national product, and their estimates of unemployment are a by-product. The validity of their models must be judged on the basis of the accuracy of their estimates of output rather than of unemployment.

It is not implied that unemployment estimates are unimportant. Our objective should be to forecast unemployment, but some of the steps in reaching that objective may be independent of others. A complete model and a good model will enable us to forecast both the level of output and the level of unemployment. In the abnormal conditions of the transition period, we may have to be satisfied with partial results.

THE METHOD

The customary model for prediction can be called the simplest Keynesian model: savings as a function of income equals autonomous investment.[2] This model has been slightly modified for the particular characteristics of the transition period, but the modifications are not basic. The model can be written as

$$GNP = C(GNP) + \bar{I},$$

where

GNP = gross national product,
$C(GNP)$ = the consumption schedule,
$\bar{I}$ = autonomous investment.

---

[1]'Forecasting Postwar Demand,' *Economic Reconstruction*, (Ed. S. Harris) McGraw-Hill, New York (1945).

[2]The terms 'autonomous' and 'exogenous,' and their respective opposites, 'induced' and 'endogenous,' will be used synonymously in this paper. They are all commonly found in the recent economic literature. Autonomous variables are those economic quantities that are determined outside the system of narrow economic forces. They are the result of political, sociological. institutional, technological, or natural forces only. Eventually we may hope to develop a complete social theory in which there are no autonomous variables except those like weather.

On the basis of *a priori* information, economists attempt to estimate $\bar{I}$, and from numerical data over a long-time period they attempt to get a statistical approximation of the function $C(GNP)$. For the transition estimates the common practice is to include in C only nondurables and services exclusive of paid rentals. Durable consumer goods and rents are classed with $\bar{I}$.

The function $C(GNP)$ is estimated in two steps. First, statisticians calculate the relation between consumption and disposable income, $C = C^*(Y)$. The difference between GNP and Y is governmental revenue plus business reserves[3] plus corporate savings minus transfer payments. The function $C = C^*(Y)$ is a structural behavior equation which can be derived, in a general form, from rational economic behavior patterns. The function $C(GNP)$ depends upon the relation between Y and GNP, a relation which is based, not on economic behavior patterns, but on autonomous governmental action with respect to the setting of tax rates, unemployment compensation rates, etc. From their knowledge of the autonomous parameters, such as tax rates, technicians of the Bureau of the Budget have very carefully computed $Y = Y$ (GNP) for different periods of the transition. For each tax system they obtain a different relation between Y and GNP. The statistician then substitutes the appropriate autonomous function $Y = Y$ (GNP) into the statistical behavior equation $C = C^*(Y)$ to get $C = C(GNP)$. The parameters of the Y-function, and hence of the C-function, will be different for each period of the transition, depending upon the autonomous factors.

Our Washington forecaster then computes, item by item, the components of $\bar{I}$. For example, he gets information from the Bureau of the Budget on governmental expenditures, from Commerce Department questionnaire surveys on capital formation etc. He makes allowances for production bottlenecks in supplying a virtually unlimited demand for some components, and he takes into account the quantity of surplus government property that will be used to satisfy some of the autonomous demand in the transition period. The latter correction should be subtracted from capital formation because no income is created by transferring ownership on already existing property.

This is the method. Let us see how it works.

ACCURACY OF THE ESTIMATES

Some of the better-known estimates among economists are those of E. E. Hagen, assisted by Nora Kirkpatrick, both of the Office of War

[3] Mainly depreciation charges.

Mobilization and Reconversion. These estimates were presented in a paper before the Conference on Research in Income and Wealth in November, 1945. The author saw them at an earlier date and hazards the guess that they had some influence on governmental policy declarations in the days just following the end of the war. In table 28.1 the Hagen–Kirkpatrick estimates are compared with the official observations for the fourth quarter of 1945, published in the *Survey of Current Business* (February, 1946, p. 7).

Table 28.1 Gross National Product: Seasonally adjusted annual rate

	Hagen–Kirkpatrick estimate (in billions)	US Department of Commerce, actual observations (in billions)
Gross National Product	$164.5	$182.8
Government expenditures	55.5	57.7
Federal war	39.7	43.3
Federal nonwar	8.0	6.5
State and local	7.8	8.0
Private gross capital formation	12.8	14.2
Construction	2.8	3.7
Producers' durable equipment	6.0	7.2
Net inventory change	4.0	1.6
Net exports	0.0	1.8
Consumer Expenditures	96.2	110.9
Durable goods	9.0	8.4
Nondurable goods	57.7	69.5
Services (excluding rent)	23.5	33.0
Rent	6.0	
Disposable income	119.9	137.3
	(in millions)	(in millions)
Civilian employment	46.1	51.7
Armed forces	10.8	9.2
Unemployment	6.3	1.8
Labor force	63.2	62.7

It is immediately obvious where this forecast failed – in the prediction of consumer expenditures, particularly expenditures on nondurable goods. The forecasts of most of the autonomous items of government expenditures or capital formation are only slightly below the observations, and these errors together do not contribute so much to the total error as does the error in consumption alone.

Post mortem on transition predictions   517

The order of magnitude of the error involved is great, and, what is more serious, it is great enough to lead to disastrous policy recommendations. The predicted *GNP* of $164.5 billion should call for an inflationary policy, but this is just the opposite of the policy that was needed.

The forecasts for the first quarter of 1946 are as wide of the mark as are those for the fourth quarter of 1945, and it is generally conceded that these forecasts will continue to be wrong for some time in the future. For example, Hagen and Kirkpatrick predicted *GNP* of $161.8 billion and unemployment of 8.1 million for the first quarter of 1946, while the *Sixth Report by the Director of War Mobilization and Reconversion* estimates *GNP* at approximately $180 billion and unemployment at approximately 3 million. A very recent (May, 1946) press release of the Commerce Department puts *GNP* at $183 billion for this period.

EXPLANATION OF THE FORECASTING ERROR

Errors may arise in the forecasting procedures of the Washington economists through three sources, (a) the autonomous variables may be set at wrong levels, (b) variables may be improperly classified, according as they are autonomous or induced, and (c) the estimates of the structural behavior equations involving the nonautonomous variables may be incorrect from an economic theoretical point of view and from a statistical point of view.

The first type of error does not appear to be serious from the data presented above. Furthermore, any method of forming economic policy judgements is subject to this error; consequently, the econometric method should not be discredited for wrong forecasts of autonomous variables. In any case, there is no serious problem in connection with this source of error.

Where induced variables were classified as autonomous in the transition forecasts, no serious harm resulted. It is often possible to obtain some of the correct results and yet commit the second type of error. If induced variables are set at autonomous levels that agree with the observed facts, this error will not, by itself, lead to an error in the estimate of *GNP*, but there will be an error in the evaluation of various multipliers in the system. The second source of error will lead us to estimate incorrectly the *increase* in *GNP* resulting from a given *change* in government spending. We may claim that the Hagen–Kirkpatrick estimate committed an error in classifying construction, inventories, and producers' equipment as autonomous variables; however, this error did not account principally for their low forecasts, since their autonomous variables were nearly equal to the observations.

Most critics will agree that the consumption function is incorrect,[4] i.e. that the third source of error is prominent. But the critics are strongly divided on the reasons why the consumption function is incorrect. The consumption function may be incorrect, because it was determined statistically in isolation from the rest of the system. The statistical parameters were calculated from least-squares regressions of nondurable consumption on disposable income and of service consumption on disposable income. No account was taken in these regressions of the interrelationships between these variables and other equations of the system.[5] It is not known whether this type of error will lead to an overestimate or an underestimate of consumption.[6] At least as important as the statistical errors, however, are the errors of economic theory. It is a real problem to construct a satisfactory economic model, and the pages immediately following will deal with this problem more carefully.

There are undoubtedly many arguments advanced to explain why the consumption of nondurable goods is high, relative to the prewar regression between this type of consumption and disposable income. We shall discuss arguments that are either plausible or commonly made.

THE FACTS

In order to make clear the various reasons advocated for changing the Hagen–Kirkpatrick Model, it will be illuminating to consider, in detail,

---

[4] Some, however, will claim that it was only temporarily incorrect during the special case of the postwar transition period and that it will be correct when we settle down again to a peacetime economy.

[5] For a popular exposition of the ideas underlying statistical estimation in economic systems, see the article by T. Koopmans, 'Statistical estimation of simultaneous economic relations,' *Journal of the American Statistical Association*, XL, December (1945), 448–66.

[6] The author's colleague, T. Haavelmo, has shown in a forthcoming article that the estimate of the marginal propensity to consume calculated as the least-squares regression of total consumption on disposable income is greater than the estimate obtained when all the equations of the simple Keynesian model used by the forecasters are taken into account simultaneously. The estimate of the constant term in the linear consumption function is greater by Haavelmo's method than by the customary least-squares method. He did not deal with the problem of estimating the parameters of the demand functions for nondurables, durables, and services separately. His results are very interesting, especially because the pessimistic forecasts of transition *GNP* have often been criticized for being based on a model with a marginal propensity to consume that is too low.

the reasons for the failure of their method. In the *Survey of Current Business* (February, 1945, p. 5) there are three graphs which shed much light on the mystery. These three diagrams show the scatter plots between disposable income and three types of consumer expenditures – durables, nondurables, and services. All the variables are aggregates measured in current dollars. It will be noticed that during the war years the observations for nondurable expenditures were on the 1929–40 regression, while the observations for durables and services were, for obvious reasons, far below the regression. The forecasters reasoned that nondurables, which had maintained their peacetime relation to income during the war, would maintain that relation during the postwar transition and that services would return to the peacetime relation for all categories except paid rentals, while durables would remain below the corresponding regression line. Thus they made durables plus paid rentals autonomous, and other services plus nondurables induced, according to the prewar regressions in relation to disposable income.

As matters developed, nondurable consumption expenditures were far above the regression for the fourth quarter of 1945, while services and durables were still below. These are the facts; the correct explanation of the error must show why the consumption of nondurables was so far above the prewar regression line.

DEMOBILIZATION

It must be remembered that consumer expenditures cover only civilian expenditures for consumer goods and services. We may have experienced a temporary deviation from established patterns by the sudden injection of demobilized servicemen into our civilian population over a very short period of time. While it may seem possible that the 8.5 million men restored to civilian life during the period between V-J Day and March 31, 1946, would have caused an abnormally high demand for nondurable consumer goods, the argument is not unambiguously established. It is true that a sudden increase of 8.5 million civilian mouths to feed and backs to clothe may very well have led to a temporary increase in the civilian consumption of nondurables, but their disappearance from civilian life during the prewar and the war years did not cause an abnormally low demand for nondurables. The demobilization process was strongly concentrated in a few months and thus may account for asymmetric behavior patterns, as compared with the period of induction.

Demobilization is a special factor. If it has accounted for a large underestimate of nondurable consumption, we should not be led to alter the statistical models for the post-transition period on account of their failures during the transition.

INSTABILITY OF THE CONSUMPTION FUNCTION

Some economists claim that the consumption function changes position radically in different economic situations, making it very difficult to forecast future consumption on the basis of past relationships between consumption and other economic variables. A recent exposition of this hypothesis is that of W. S. Woytinsky,[7] who claims that there is a different consumption function during depression and during prosperity. With our previous notation, this may be expressed, in a simple example:

$$C = a_0(Y) + a_1(Y)Y,$$

where

$$a_0 = b_0 + b_1 Y,$$
$$a_1 = c_0 + c_1 Y,$$

or

$$C = d_0 + d_1 Y + d_2 Y^2.$$

This function[8] has in simple form the properties stressed by Woytinsky, but there is so little curvature in the past relationship that there is very little gain in introducing the quadratic term. Either by the above simple scheme or by introducing additional variables (including time) into the consumption function, we can test the hypothesis that the consumption–income relation remains substantially valid over long periods of time. As yet, no econometrician has ever refuted the hypothesis. We find much evidence of this stability in both time series and family-budget data.

Woytinsky has another method of proving his claims. A complete discussion of his methods involves some digression, but the establishment of the true consumption function is so important in forecasting

[7]'Relationship between consumers' expenditures, savings, and disposable income,' *Review of Economics and Statistics*, XXVIII, February (1946), 1–12.

[8]In a more general case, $C = f[Y, a_0(Y), a_1(Y), \ldots, a_n(Y)]$, where $a_0, \ldots, a_n$ are certain parameters of the consumption function which fluctuate cyclically. If f, a_0, and a_1 are linear and all other a vanish, we get the simplest representation of this hypothesis, given in the text.

Post mortem on transition predictions

that we must rid the field of false alternatives. Woytinsky claims that we get one savings function if we use the data for years that he defines as 'depression years' and another savings function if we use the data for years that he defines as 'prosperity years.'[9] This is a scientifically unacceptable attitude because it makes the results depend entirely on personal judgement. If we define prosperity as high national income and depression as low national income, then national income should be a variable in the consumption function. If we think that the parameters vary over the business cycle, then we should make the parameters functions of income. But no econometrician is allowed to choose those observations which yield predetermined results. If the savings–income relationship has a *systematic* error when fitted to the data of the entire period covering both prosperity and depression (Woytinsky's point), then the residual variation not explained by the calculated savings function will have a systematic pattern which is not random. The duty of the econometrician is then to introduce other *objective* variables until the residual variation does become random. Woytinsky never examined his residual variation. It is possible to construct savings functions which have random residual variation over a period which covers all phases of the business cycle. These are the functions which must be considered as candidates for the true savings function and not those fitted to Woytinsky's personally selected points.

It should be pointed out that there are sometimes objective criteria for rejecting observations. We may agree beforehand that economic behavior patterns are distorted in wartime; hence we may cast out all observations pertaining to war years. There is, however, little room for personal judgement in this case because we usually know when we have a war economy and when we have a peacetime economy.

Woytinsky has another tool with which he tries to demonstrate the instability of the consumption or savings function. He correlates the ratio of savings to income with income and concludes that different regressions hold for different periods. If we write

$$\frac{S}{Y} = e_0 + e_1 Y,$$

then

$$S = e_0 Y + e_1 Y^2;$$

---

[9] It is completely trivial to distinguish between the consumption function and the savings function since the two are related by a simple definition. Some writers seem to think that they get more information from the savings–income data than from the consumption–income data.

thus we find that there is no constant term in the savings function. The extremely poor correlations that Woytinsky finds between S/Y and Y actually lead him to consider the alternative hypothesis that there is a constant term in the savings function instead of his conclusion that the savings function is not stable. He bases his argument on mechanical least-squares fitting to observations, which gives empirical equations that are not acceptable on any statistical grounds.

There is a good reason for believing that there is a significant constant term in the savings function. The aggregate savings function is obtained by summing all the individual savings functions. Suppose an individual has zero income. Will he consume anything? Of course, he will have positive consumption (negative savings), which represents his minimum subsistence level. Similarly, the community, as a whole, will show a positive expenditure for zero income. Woytinsky's saving-rate functions fail to show this constant term. A glance at family-budget data on consumption by income class shows very clearly that people spend more than their incomes in the low-income classes and that the consumption function has a positive intercept for zero income.

We must look further for a satisfactory explanation of the failure of the Hagen–Kirkpatrick consumption estimates.

LIQUIDITY

It has been suggested that the Keynesian models of macroeconomics be amended by introducing cash balances or, more generally, liquid assets as a variable into the savings (consumption) function.[10] The arguments about the relation of cash balances to savings are being revived again today, although for slightly different reasons than were put forth originally. Several economists claim that consumption is being maintained at an abnormally high level now because people have accumulated huge amounts of cash and liquid securities (in the form of war bonds). It is true that there is an observed correlation today between high levels of consumption and high levels of liquid assets, but it has not been proved that the structural savings function contains liquid assets as as an important variable.

The relationship between consumption and liquid assets is a hypothesis which must be tested from the available data. To test the existence of the consumption–income relationship, we examine the time-series data and the family-budget data. In the case at hand, we are

[10]See, e.g. A. C. Pigou, 'The classical stationary state,' *Economic Journal*, LIII, December (1943), 343–51.

very unfortunate in having no family-budget data and must rely on time-series data plus some recent surveys that have been conducted to discover what people intend to do with their war bonds and cash balances.

First, we must establish the theoretical principles from which we construct our consumption functions. A simple theory of consumer behavior is that the individual maximizes some preference function which depends on his consumption of all types of present and future goods, subject to the constraint that current spending and saving (spending on future goods) just exhaust individual income. It is well known that this maximization procedure leads to the individual demand equations for each commodity as a function of the prices of all goods and the budget constraint, which is income. The prices of future goods are related to present prices by the interest rate, so that the independent variables in the demand functions are present prices, the interest rate, and income. If these individual demand functions are approximately linear, we may aggregate them over all commodities and all individuals to find that total consumption of present goods depends upon the price level of consumer goods, the interest rate, and the level of the community's disposable income.

The consumption functions that are calculated today are based on this principle, except for the fact that they allow the income term to dominate the price level and the interest rate. They use only the expenditure–income correlation. In some cases prices are introduced as a deflator, i.e. they correlate real consumption and real income. This procedure is correct if the demand equations derived from the basic theory of consumer behavior are homogeneous of order zero in prices, as is commonly assumed.[11]

One obvious way to introduce liquid assets into the theory of the consumption function is to modify the budget constraint. Instead of maximizing satisfactions, subject to the condition that spending plus savings exhausts income, we can maximize satisfactions subject to the condition that spending plus savings exhausts some function of income and accumulated liquid assets. Alternatively, we may define the utility function to depend upon the consumption of present and future goods, the holding of securities, and the holding of cash. We may now proceed to maximize this function, subject to two constraints, (a) spending plus savings equals income, and (b) the value of securities plus cash equals historically accumulated savings plus current savings.

In these cases the maximization process leads to demand equations

---

[11]This homogeneity property means that, if prices and incomes are all changed in the same proportion, the demand for consumer goods will remain invariant.

with the new constraining factors as variables. In either case, both income and historically accumulated savings enter as independent variables.

This is the theoretical foundation of our hypothesis. Let us now examine the data to see whether or not it is true.

Correlations between consumption and cash balances from time-series data of the interwar period are nil, if the relationship between consumption, income, and time trend is taken into account. This same result was obtained independently by J. Mosak.[12] It is true that cash balances were much smaller in the interwar period, but so was the whole scale of operations in the economic system. We must admit, however, that liquid assets are extremely large today even in relation to the other variables of the system. It is also true that, in the past, assets were highly concentrated in a few hands. It is not known whether or not they are more democratically held today, but it is known that there is still much concentration. For example, governmental surveys[13] show that the upper 10 per cent of owners of liquid assets hold 60 per cent of the value of all liquid assets. The upper 20 per cent hold 77 per cent, and the lower 50 per cent hold only 3 per cent. It is also shown in these reports that the distribution of ownership of liquid assets was much less equitable than was the case for 1945 incomes, if we measure the degree of equitability by the area under the Lorenz curve. The people who own these assets are not those whose spending habits are likely to be influenced greatly by these holdings. When asked about their intentions with regard to the use of E bonds, only 5 per cent of all holders answered that they would use the proceeds for consumer expenditures. It is also estimated that these 5 per cent would spend only about $1.5 billion. Furthermore, only 5 per cent of all holders intend to use their E bonds for any purpose in 1946. Asset holders appear from these questions to be much more willing to spend bank deposits than E bonds in the near future. However, the anticipated expenditures of all types of assets on consumer goods should not be large enough to cause much of an error in the aggregate consumption function, relating consumption to income alone.[14] A future study of the influence of asset holdings on spending out of *current income* has been

---

[12]See his article, 'National budgets and national policy,' *American Economic Review*, March (1946), 20–43.

[13]Some of the results of the surveys are found in 'A national survey of liquid assets,' *Federal Reserve Bulletin*, June (1946), 574–80. The full report can be obtained from the Division of Program Surveys, Bureau of Agricultural Economics, US Department of Agriculture.

[14]The demand for residential housing (investment) may be very differently affected.

promised by those who conduct these surveys, and these results may be very important in testing the hypothesis that consumption depends upon the holding of assets as well as income. There is much more information in these reports, but it all points, thus far, to the same conclusion, namely, that the influence of liquid assets on consumption will be small. The hypothesis of the influence of liquidity is plausible and worthy of consideration, but it has not yet been shown to be correct.

SAVING VERSUS SPENDING

One of the simplest theories of consumer behavior is the following: individuals decide on the basis of their income how much they will spend and how much they will save (not spend). This behavior pattern means that, in a period when there are shortages of certain types of consumer goods, people will spend on available goods that which they are unable to spend on unavailable goods. Thus, today, according to this theory, we may argue that people spend on nondurables because they cannot buy durables or services. Furthermore, we say that the 'spillover' from unavailable goods to available goods is just enough to put total expenditures on the normal expenditure–income regression. During the war there were shortages, but civilians were not free to compensate by spending extra sums on available nondurables because of price control, rationing, and patriotic saving drives. Instead of arguing that the wartime experience of spending on nondurables according to the prewar regression between these expenditures and income gives us confidence in extrapolating this regression into the transition period (the method of Hagen and Kirkpatrick), we should argue that this wartime phenomenon was accidental. If there had not been artificial restraining factors, consumers would have been spending on nondurables above this regression, as was the case in the last quarter of 1945. In this latter period we find that consumers spent funds on nondurables above the regression line by just that amount which made total expenditures lie almost on the pre-war regression between total consumption and income.

It is one thing to say that there is a stable peacetime relationship between total consumption and income, and something else again to say that there is a stable relationship between each of several categories of expenditures and income. The forecasters adopted the latter formulation and ended up with poor forecasts. *If the Washington economists had used the total consumption function fitted to the data for 1929–41,* they would have been nearly correct in their forecasts for the fourth quarter of 1945.[15]

The saving-spending hypothesis of consumer behavior is plausible and is not refuted by the factual data, although we need more observations before we can be certain of its correctness. This hypothesis is certainly confirmed for the prewar data and also for the first transition observations, but this is not sufficient to establish its validity.

RELATIVE PRICES

There is yet another explanation of why expenditure–income relationships for various types of commodities cannot be used independently for projection into the future, i.e. why the regression between nondurable consumption expenditures and disposable income does not hold in the transition period when there are bottlenecks in the durable consumer-goods market.

The theory of consumer behavior tells us that the demand for each good in the system is a function of all relative prices, interest rates, disposable income, and possibly cash balances or general liquid wealth. Let us neglect, as a first approximation, the influence of interest rates and liquid assets. An aggregative approximation to our demand functions for durable goods, nondurable goods, and services is

$$\frac{C_1}{p_1} = a_{01} + a_{11}\frac{p_1}{p} + a_{21}\frac{Y}{p},$$

$$\frac{C_2}{p_2} = a_{02} + a_{12}\frac{p_2}{p} + a_{22}\frac{Y}{p},$$

$$\frac{C_3}{p_3} = a_{03} + a_{13}\frac{p_3}{p} + a_{23}\frac{Y}{p},$$

---

[15] Mosak's aggregate consumption function and Hagen's estimates of autonomous investment and governmental expenditures generate a *GNP* of $178 billion for the fourth quarter of 1945, very close to the observed figure. There are some compensating errors in this calculation, however, because the autonomous items are slightly below the observed figures, while Mosak's consumption function lies slightly above the observed point. If we use the correct values of the autonomous variables and Mosak's consumption function, the calculated value of *GNP* is above the observed value. The exact figure is not given here because it is necessary to know the *true* values of the autonomous *parameters* in the function $Y = Y(GNP)$, which have not yet been estimated. It is worth noting that Haavelmo's estimate of the consumption function, mentioned above, and the true values of the autonomous *variables* generate a *GNP* of $187 billion for the fourth quarter of 1945, which is closer than the results obtained by any other method yet tested.

where

C_1 = per capita expenditures on durables,
p_1 = price of durables,
C_2 = per capita expenditures on nondurables,
p_2 = price of nondurables,
C_3 = per capita expenditures on services,
p_3 = price of services,
p = price of consumption as a whole,
Y = per capita disposable income.

Suppose that there are shortages of durable goods so that we assign the value $(C_1/p_1) = \overline{(C_1/p_1)}$ to this category. The estimates of C_2/p_2 and C_3/p_3 from the last two equations cannot be made from the income term alone but must take into account p_2/p and p_3/p, the relative prices, which will, in turn, be influenced by the fact that durables are scarce. The coefficients of the relative-price terms are all negative. If, in the transition period, the prices of services and durables are extremely high relative to nondurables, there will tend to be an excess demand for nondurables above the consumption–income regression. We can hire domestic servants today, but only at a price. The durable goods which are almost nonexistent have virtually infinite prices. We should expect the relative-price term to favor the purchase of nondurables, as has been the case to date.

The general proposition that is to be made in this section is the following: we cannot estimate the consumption of a particular class of commodities from the relationship to the income variable alone but must consider relative prices as well. The Hagen–Kirkpatrick estimates are derived from the simple income regressions by type of commodity, which are not correct demand equations.

For the period 1919–39, there are time series[16] on all the variables in the preceding equations which enable us to estimate the coefficients numerically. The actual numerical size of the coefficients need not be taken too seriously, since they are known, in general, to be biased[17] estimates, calculated without a knowledge of the entire system. They are single-equation, least-squares estimates which have systematic bias no matter how large the sample used. However, they do show that there is a strong correlation between consumption and relative prices when the consumption-income correlation is taken into account. This is

---

[16]See the appendix below.

[17]An estimate of a parameter is biased if its mathematical expectation does not equal the parameter.

the main point. In the future we can hope to use methods which produce estimates that are unbiased for sufficiently large samples, but the present figures indicate roughly the orders of magnitude of the parameters involved.

The least-squares equations based on the observations 1919–39 are

$$\frac{C_1}{p_1} = 118.53 - 125.96 \frac{p_1}{p} + 0.1151 \frac{Y}{p} - 0.6468(t-1929),$$
$$(15.26) \quad (0.0236) \quad (0.1161)$$

$$\bar{R} = 0.98, \quad \bar{S} = \$2.97, \quad \frac{\delta^2}{S^2} = 2.08,$$

$$\frac{C_2}{p_2} = 204.43 - 96.70 \frac{p_2}{p} + 0.2843 \frac{Y}{p},$$
$$(14.50) \quad (0.0316)$$

$$\bar{R} = 0.94, \quad \bar{S} = \$6.60, \quad \frac{\delta^2}{S^2} = 1.87,$$

$$\frac{C_3}{p_3} = 68.32 - 46.35 \frac{p_3}{p} + 0.2551 \frac{Y}{p} + 0.8165(t-1929),$$
$$(19.30) \quad (0.0564) \quad (0.5243)$$

$$\bar{R} = 0.73, \quad \bar{S} = \$11.15, \quad \frac{\delta^2}{S^2} = 1.63.$$

Consumption and income are measured in dollars per capita per year. The prices are index numbers with the base-year values equal to unity for 1934. The statistics $\bar{R}$ and $\bar{S}$ are correct for degrees of freedom, and the statistic δ^2/S^2 is the ratio of the mean square successive difference to the variance of the residuals. The distribution of this ratio has been tabulated,[18] and we conclude from its size that we cannot reject the hypothesis that our residual variation is random.[19] The figures in parentheses below the regression coefficients are standard errors.

The principal thing to note is that a low relative price of nondurable goods in the transition period could easily account for the observed excess purchases above the consumption–income regression.

---

[18] J. von Neumann 'Distribution of the ratio of the mean square successive difference to the variance,' *Annals of Mathematical Statistics*, XII, 367–95; B. I. Hart and J. von Neumann, 'Tabulation of the probabilities for the ratio of the mean square successive difference to the variance,' *Annals of Mathematical Statistics*, XIII, 207–14.

[19] The statistic used to test the randomness of the residual variation is not entirely satisfactory, on theoretical grounds, for our purposes, but it is the best indicator known to the author.

Furthermore, the least-squares estimate of the marginal propensity to consume, obtained by adding a_{21}, a_{22}, and a_{23}, is much smaller than the estimate obtained from the simple correlation between total consumption and total income.

The relative-price theory of this section need not be inconsistent with the saving–spending theory of the preceding section. We may reconcile them as follows: The three equations

$$\frac{C_1}{p_1} = a_{01} + a_{11}\frac{p_1}{p} + a_{21}\frac{Y}{p},$$

$$\frac{C_2}{p_2} = a_{02} + a_{12}\frac{p_2}{p} + a_{22}\frac{Y}{p},$$

$$\frac{C_3}{p_3} = a_{03} + a_{13}\frac{p_3}{p} + a_{23}\frac{Y}{p},$$

can be written as

$$p\left(\frac{C_1}{p_1} + \frac{C_2}{p_2} + \frac{C_3}{p_3}\right) = (a_{01} + a_{02} + a_{03})p + a_{11}p_1 + a_{12}p_2 + a_{13}p_3 + (a_{21} + a_{22} + a_{23})Y.$$

Our method of construction of price and consumption aggregates leads to the following definition:

Total consumer expenditures $= C = p\left(\dfrac{C_1}{p_1} + \dfrac{C_2}{p_2} + \dfrac{C_3}{p_3}\right).$

Hence we have

$$\frac{C}{p} = a_0 + \frac{a_{11}p_1 + a_{12}p_2 + a_{13}p_3}{p} + a_2\frac{Y}{p}.$$

If the data show that

$$a_{11}p_1 + a_{12}p_2 + a_{13}p_3 = \lambda p$$

then our equation will be

$$\frac{C}{p} = a_1 + a_2\frac{Y}{p},$$

which is the usual form of the consumption function. The test of whether the general price index is approximately proportional to the above-specified linear combination can be carried out only after we have obtained unbiased estimates of the relevant parameters.[20] In any case, it is not evident that the saving–spending theory and the relative-price theory are contradictory.

Although the relative-price theory may indicate some of the reasons why the forecasts of national product were below the observed levels, it is hardly possible to make use of this theory for quantitative estimates. In order to estimate the different types of consumption during a period in which prices are autonomously fixed, we must have exact data on these fixed levels of prices, which are to be substituted into the demand equations. We must be able to estimate how much the consumption of nondurables will be increased as a result of the fact that the prices of nondurables are favorable, relative to other prices. Unfortunately, none of the published price indexes is satisfactory for this purpose at the present time. The published indexes were satisfactory in the prewar years in order to establish the regressions, but they are completely inadequate now. In the first place, the practice among those who construct index numbers is to drop scarce goods from the index in such a way that there will presumably be no effect on the index. It is, however, the scarce durable goods and services which are extremely costly today. Weights may be changed because the quantities are completely different from the base-year quantities, but there is a big difference between an index with high prices at a low weight and an index which ignores these prices. The relative-price theory, as an explanation of high nondurable consumption, depends on the changed price relationship between the goods that are now scarce and those that are now available – changes that are not reflected in the published data.

There are numerous other grounds on which the official indexes are an understatement of the actual price levels. The agencies which compute the index numbers admit the existence of quality deterioration but, at the same time, classify this phenomenon as unmeasurable; consequently, there is a serious downward bias in the price index.[21] Other events, such as uptrading, the growth of black markets, population redistribution etc., have led to an added bias in the price indexes.

The saving–spending approach is perhaps our best alternative at this time. It was shown above that the saving–spending theory, in constant dollars (real terms), may be equivalent to the relative-price theory for

[20]The least-squares estimates of a_{11}, a_{12}, a_{13}, when used as weights in the above formula for the price index, lead to a fairly stable ratio (λ) between the derived and the actual index. The annual figures for this ratio vary between -248 and -284, with a mean at -263.

[21]This was one of the major points stressed by the CIO in its criticism of the Bureau of Labor Statistics cost-of-living index.

estimates of total national product. But it is difficult to use the saving–spending theory in terms of constant dollars because the general price indexes are faulty. An empirical observation may be our salvation, namely, that statistical models couched in terms of constant dollars do not give very different results from models couched in terms of current dollars when there is no hyperinflation or hyperdeflation. If this empirical fact holds in the future, we can proceed, as was suggested above, by combining the aggregate consumption function in current dollars with the Hagen–Kirkpatrick estimates of the autonomous variables.

A TECHNICALITY

Recall that an important step in the Hagen–Kirkpatrick Model is the estimation of the autonomous function $Y = Y(GNP)$, which enables us to pass from disposable income (the relevant variable of the consumption function) to gross national product (the relevant variable for the estimation of employment). This function was constructed by the Bureau of the Budget from information based on tax rates, unemployment compensation rates, and guesses as to the level of depreciation and corporate savings. If the function were correct, the substitution of the observed GNP for the fourth quarter of 1945 should give the observed Y. But we get

$Y = 41.8 + 0.475\ (GNP)$,

$Y = 41.8 + 0.475\ (182.8)$,

$Y = 128.63$.

The observed disposable income was 137.3. This error led to a downward bias in the final result for the estimate of GNP, but this error was less serious than the error of the underestimate of the level of the consumption function.

Hagen, in private correspondence, has pointed out the reason for this technical error and shows that it is something that could not possibly have been avoided. According to his explanation, the function $Y = Y(GNP)$ is seasonally adjusted. Consequently, in the construction of the function, it was assumed that the quarterly installment on personal income taxes, due on December 15, should be subtracted from the fourth-quarter income payments. But Congress later postponed this quarterly installment to January 15. This fact, alone, accounts for most of the difference between the observed disposable income and the calculated disposable income.

There was also a smaller error in the autonomous function because demobilization of the armed forces proceeded at a much faster rate than had been anticipated and therefore led to an extraordinarily high rate of mustering-out pay.

A POSITIVE SUGGESTION

Two possible reactions to the recent failures are the following.

1 We may now discard these new-fangled and difficult econometric methods which have been proved wrong and relax again into armchair comments about the future course of economic events. This is certainly the line of least resistance.

2 We may tackle the forecasting problem with renewed vigor, making use of the valuable information that we have gained from this trial.

We shall dwell upon the second reaction exclusively.

A principal failure of the customary models is that they are not sufficiently detailed. There are too many variables which are classified as autonomous when they are actually induced, and there are no dynamic elements injected into the system. The surplus of autonomous variables results from a failure to discover all the appropriate relationships constituting the system. In addition to the consumption function, we should have the investment function, the inventory function, the housing function, the price-formation equations etc. There exist good theories from which these additional functions can be constructed, and one should not prematurely despair of determining these functions from the observed data. All the details of the construction of these functions must be the material of subsequent papers, but at this stage the statement can be made that many preliminary investigations[22] have shown these functions to exist.

The dynamical aspects of statistical models are also very important. While the consumption function has not been found to depend heavily upon lags or other dynamical elements, those functions which are erroneously assumed to be autonomous have been found to be very greatly influenced by such variables. For example, there are very strong correlations between current purchases of new plant, equipment, dwellings, and the holding of stocks of goods, on the one hand, and the past levels of prices, output, or income, on the other.

The existence of lags means that there are definite links between

[22] Presented by the author in a paper read before the Econometric Society in January, 1946. An abstract appears in *Econometrica*, April (1946), 159–62.

national income yesterday and today and tomorrow. Optimum forecasts of tomorrow's income should take into account the recently realized levels of income. Rather than make wild guesses, we should do better to forecast tomorrow's income as dependent on today's income. The extremely high wartime incomes made it unlikely (though not impossible) that the transition levels of income would be very low.

There are two ways of using the complicated dynamical systems for economic forecasting and policy recommendations. We may attempt to estimate all the relevant structural characteristics of the system, such as the various multipliers, elasticities, marginal propensities, marginal productivities etc. The other method of procedure is that of pure prediction, where we do not try to estimate all the structural characteristics of the system, but only those combinations that are necessary for prediction. The latter method cannot be used for all types of policy.

A simple example will make these ideas more specific. Suppose that we have a system of linear difference equations which describe the operation of the economy

$$L_i(y_{1t},\ldots,y_{nt}, y_{1,t-1},\ldots,y_{n,t-1},\ldots,y_{1,t-p},\ldots,y_{n,t-p}, z_1,\ldots,z_m) = u_{it} \ (i=1,2,\ldots,n),$$

where

L_i = linear operator,
$y_{j,t-k}$ = the jth endogenous variable of the kth preceding time period,
z_j = jth exogenous variable (current or lagged),
u_{it} = ith random disturbance.

If we know the initial conditions and the stochastic properties of the us, we may study the entire time path of the system of endogenous variables, in terms of the exogenous variables.

The statistical treatment of the above system of equations involves the computation of 'optimal' estimates of all the parameters of the L_i-functions, that is, estimates that have properties such as 'lack of bias,' 'consistency' etc.[23] We shall then be able to do two things.

1 We shall be able to forecast, for short periods in the future, the course of any endogenous variable in the system by assuming that the estimated parameters remain unchanged and solving the statistical equations in terms of the exogenous variables.

---

[23] An estimate of a parameter is said to be 'unbiased' if its mathematical expectation equals the parameter. A consistent estimate can be roughly defined as unbiased in large samples.

2 If the parameters are supposed to change in a known way because of government policy or for other reasons, we can estimate the effect of these changes upon the endogenous variables.

The alternative method of procedure is to solve the system of equations for any particular endogenous variable in terms of the exogenous variables and the lagged values of all the endogenous variables.

$$y_{it} = L_i^*(y_{1,t-1}, \ldots, y_{n,t-1}, \ldots, y_{1,t-p}, \ldots, y_{n,t-p},$$

$$z_1, \ldots, z_m) + v_i \qquad (i = 1, 2, \ldots, n),$$

where the vs are linear combinations of the us. If the us are nonautocorrelated random time series, then the vs will also be nonautocorrelated random time series. The L_i^* functions are called the 'reduced forms,' as distinct from the L_i functions, which are called 'structural behavior equations.' We may estimate the parameters of the reduced forms and then have enough information to forecast the time path of any single variable of the system, say GNP, in terms of the exogenous variables. There are great simplifying advantages in working with the L_i^* functions rather than the L_i functions because much more elementary statistical methods may be used to estimate the parameters of the former functions than may be used to estimate the parameters of the latter. In fact, the obvious procedure, in order to obtain the coefficients of the L_i^* functions, is to treat y_{it} as the dependent variable and to determine all the least-squares regression coefficients of this variable on the lagged variables and exogenous variables as independent variables. However, if we aim at estimating structural behavior equations, we cannot, in general, treat a single equation independently of the rest of the system and must use other methods of estimation. Obviously, it is preferable to work with the structural equations since we can do everything with them that we can do with the reduced forms, and, in addition, we can make certain types of policy judgments that we cannot make on the basis of the reduced forms.

A disadvantage of the reduced-form method of estimation is that there are usually not many degrees of freedom available for the estimation of the parameters, because of the short period of observation available in most economic series. There are usually so many exogenous and lagged endogenous variables in the system that 20 or 30 annual observations may be insufficient for statistical estimation.

Another type of reduced form is the following:

$$y_{it} = L_i^{**}(y_{i,t-1}, \ldots, y_{i,t-q}, z_1, \ldots, z_r) + w_i \qquad (i = 1, 2, \ldots, n),$$

where q and r depend upon the order of lags in the entire system. The L_i^{**} functions are obtained from the L_i functions by solving for any single endogenous variable in terms of its own lagged values and the exogenous variables. These reduced forms show the time path of any endogenous variable in the system in terms of exogenous variables and are very useful in studying the cyclical behavior of various endogenous variables. The primary disadvantage of this system is that the disturbances, the ws, will not, in general, be nonautocorrelated even though the us are nonautocorrelated in the original system. It can easily be shown that the process of reduction from the system involving the L_i functions to the system involving the L_i^{**} functions usually will introduce autocorrelation in the disturbances. We must have resort to more complicated statistical methods in the case when the disturbances are autocorrelated.

The author has attempted to get first approximations to the L_i functions by the single-equation, least-squares techniques, although it is known that the estimated values of the parameters might be changed considerably when the equation-system methods are applied. Bearing in mind the tentative nature of the conclusions, the author used these first approximations in September, 1945, to forecast the level of GNP for the fiscal year ending June, 1946. The usual assumptions were made about price control, government spending, tax receipts, etc. These autonomous variables in connection with the behavior equations of the system led to a forecast of GNP of about $190 billion for the fiscal year 1946. This forecast will be slightly above the true value, but it could have served as an intelligent guide to policy. It showed definitely that the danger for this fiscal year was one of inflation rather than of deflation.

There are some basic reasons why this model gave different results from the Hagen–Kirkpatrick model.

1. There were many lags in the system which tied the future levels of many economic variables to the past values, especially in capital formation.

2 The total consumption function, rather than the component regressions on disposable income alone, was used.

The total consumption function held true, while the individual regressions did not, as was discussed in previous sections.

AN APOLOGY?

Econometric models must necessarily be based on the long series of records that we have compiled from the workings of a normal peacetime economy. The models are meant to describe behavior patterns in a normal peacetime economy, not in a period of the aftermath of the world's greatest war, when there is a huge number of serious economic dislocations. We can look forward to much better results in the post-transition period, when there will be no production bottlenecks, European famine, price control, stocks of surplus war materials, readjustments to civilian life etc.

The alternatives to econometric methods of forecasting do not appear to be promising. We must form judgments in order to execute policies. Suppose these judgments are formed by the unsystematic methods of guessing which, in the period 1939–41, formed the basis of estimates of our capacity to produce or of the taxes necessary to prevent inflation. We cannot be very hopeful about solving our economic problems if we have to rely on such methods in the future. Most of the prewar guessers seriously underestimated the levels which national product would reach during the war, and they incorrectly predicted that, in an economy where the government spends nearly 50 per cent of the GNP on war goods, the mild tax rates voted by Congress in conjunction with direct price controls would not be able to prevent a disastrous inflation. Perhaps careful econometric studies of productivity and demand could have demonstrated, in advance, our potential level of output and the size of the inflationary gap to be closed by direct controls. Econometric methods certainly could not have been worse than any other methods that were used.

Economic policy during the 1930s was also based on incorrect judgements. We experimented with government deficits of $2–3 billion, but large-scale unemployment persisted. During the war the deficit grew manifold, and full employment followed immediately. We never realized the true size of our deflationary gap during the great depression because we did not have an accurate knowledge, then, of full-employment output. Again, econometric studies might have been able to show the necessary amount of government spending in order to generate a full-employment level of output. Certainly, alternative methods did not answer the appropriate questions of policy.

APPENDIX: The time series and their construction

Year	$C_1(\$)$	$C_2(\$)$	$C_3(\$)$	p_1	p_2	p_3	p	$Y(\$)$
1919	62.2	360.7	85.2	1.365	1.828	0.695	1.391	541.6
1920	66.7	377.6	138.1	1.602	2.042	0.936	1.559	619.0
1921	52.5	295.7	161.2	1.419	1.384	1.190	1.320	538.0
1922	59.1	297.1	154.5	1.151	1.330	1.149	1.248	532.5
1923	73.2	318.9	166.1	1.099	1.410	1.134	1.271	609.2
1924	69.2	304.1	186.7	1.102	1.346	1.210	1.262	594.1
1925	82.9	336.7	168.3	1.049	1.408	1.242	1.294	632.8
1926	81.8	340.7	185.7	1.003	1.382	1.313	1.296	654.2
1927	77.3	336.9	183.1	1.056	1.299	1.313	1.266	639.3
1928	77.2	330.3	195.8	1.070	1.301	1.311	1.269	626.6
1929	81.3	321.9	197.1	1.080	1.283	1.333	1.264	643.0
1930	65.8	293.3	186.9	1.059	1.185	1.361	1.221	596.4
1931	50.8	251.5	148.3	1.013	1.017	1.314	1.098	501.5
1932	33.6	196.3	125.0	0.995	0.866	1.191	0.972	382.9
1933	27.1	192.7	127.4	0.983	0.879	1.032	0.937	344.8
1934	38.0	225.5	121.9	1.000	1.000	1.000	1.000	398.8
1935	44.8	238.9	135.2	0.950	1.097	0.977	1.038	440.9
1936	52.3	264.7	152.1	0.922	1.102	1.000	1.044	517.8
1937	59.0	277.1	159.1	0.933	1.154	1.041	1.087	527.8
1938	46.2	261.9	153.3	0.968	1.044	1.064	1.042	483.0
1939	48.9	249.1	184.9	0.985	1.013	1.275	1.026	530.3

APPENDIX

C_1: Per capita expenditures on durable consumer goods.

$$C_1 = \frac{(1)[(2)+(3)]}{(4)(5)} \quad (1919\text{--}28),$$

$$C_1 = \frac{(6)}{(5)} \quad (1929\text{--}38),$$

$$C_1 = \frac{(7)}{(5)} \quad (1939).$$

(*1*) = Consumer expenditures on durable consumer goods (S. Kuznets, *National Income and Capital Formation, 1919–1935*, p. 85).

(*2*) = Total consumer expenditures, exclusive of net imputed rents on owner-occupied, nonfarm dwellings (Mary S. Painter, 'Estimates of gross national product, 1919–1928,' *Federal Reserve Bulletin*, September, 1945, pp. 872–3).

(*3*) = Net imputed rents on owner-occupied, nonfarm dwellings (S. Kuznets, *National Income and Its Composition, 1919–1938*, II, 735).

(*4*) = Total consumer expenditures (S. Kuznets, *National Income and Capital Formation, 1919–1935*, p. 85).

(*5*) = Population of continental US (*Statistical Abstract of the United States*, 1943, p. 3).

(*6*) = Consumer expenditures on durable goods (*Survey of Current Business*, April, 1942, p. 15).

(*7*) = Consumer expenditures on durable goods (*Survey of Current Business*, April, 1944, p. 13).

C_2: Per capita expenditures on nondurable consumer goods.

$$C_2 = \frac{(8)[(2)+(3)]}{(4)(5)} \quad (1919\text{--}28),$$

$$C_2 = \frac{(9)}{(5)} \quad (1929\text{--}38),$$

$$C_2 = \frac{(10)}{(5)} \quad (1939).$$

(*8*) = Consumer expenditures on perishable and semidurable commodities (S. Kuznets, *National Income and Capital Formation, 1919–1935*, p. 85).

(*9*) = Consumer expenditures on perishable and semidurable goods (*Survey of Current Business*, April, 1942, p. 15).

(*10*) = Consumer expenditures on nondurable goods (*Survey of Current Business*, April, 1944, p. 13).

C_3: Per capita expenditures on consumers' services.

$$C_3 = \frac{(11)[(2)+(3)]}{(4)(5)} \quad (1919\text{–}28),$$

$$C_3 = \frac{(12)-(9)+(3)}{(5)} \quad (1929\text{–}38)$$

$$C_3 = \frac{(13)+(14)}{(5)} \quad (1939).$$

(11) = Consumer expenditures on services not embodied in finished commodities (S. Kuznets, *National Income and Capital Formation, 1919–1935*, p. 85).

(12) = Consumer expenditures on nondurable goods and services (*Survey of Current Business*, May, 1942, p. 12).

(13) = Consumer expenditures on services (*Survey of Current Business*, April, 1944, p. 13).

(14) = Net imputed rents on owner-occupied, nonfarm dwellings, estimated by the present writer according to Kuznets' methods (see *National Income and Its Composition, 1919–1938*, II, p. 735). The figure for 1939 is $1.5 billion.

p_1: Price index of durable consumer goods.

$$p_1 = \frac{(15)}{98.5}$$

(15) = Price index of durable consumer goods, 1913: 100 (William H. Shaw, *Finished Commodities since 1879*, 'National Bureau of Economic Research, Occasional Papers,' No. 3, pp. 7–8). 98.5 = Price index of durable consumer goods for 1934, with 1913:100.

p_2: Price index of nondurable consumer goods.

$$p_2 = \frac{[(16)(17)+(18)(19)]/[(17)+(19)]}{110.8}$$

(16) = Price index of perishable consumer goods, 1913: 100 (*ibid.*).

(17) = Output of perishable consumer goods measured in 1913 prices (*ibid.*).

(18) = Price index of semidurable consumer goods, 1913:100 (*ibid.*).

(19) = Output of semidurable consumer goods measured in 1913 prices (*ibid.*).

$$110.8 = \left[\frac{(16)(17)+(18)(19)}{(17)+(18)}\right]_{1934},$$

where 1934 indicates the year for which the values are computed.

p: Price index of consumption as a whole.

$p = (20) \div 79.3 \quad (1919\text{–}38),$

$p = 1.026 \quad (1939).$

(20) = Price index implicit in the adjustment of total consumers' outlay, 1929:100 (S. Kuznets, *National Income and Its Composition, 1919–1938*, I, 145. table 4, col. 3).
79.3 = Price index for 1934.
1.026 = Weighted average of the Bureau of Labor Statistics cost-of-living index and the index of prices paid by farmers for subsistence. The weights are proportional to the nonfarm and farm populations, respectively, and the index is converted to 1934 as a base year.

p_3: Price index of consumers' services.

$$p_3 = \frac{C_3}{\frac{(2)+(3)}{p} - \frac{C_1}{p_1} - \frac{C_2}{p_2}} \quad (1919\text{–}38)$$

$$p_3 = \frac{C_3}{\frac{(2)+(14)}{p} - \frac{C_1}{p_1} - \frac{C_2}{p_2}} \quad (1939).$$

Y: Per capita disposable income.

$$Y = \frac{(21)}{(5)}.$$

(21) = Disposable income measured in billions of current dollars. This figure is built up from various component series and does not agree exactly with the published series of the Commerce Department. This particular series has been used because the consumption equations calculated here will become part of a more complete econometric study in which the author's own figures on disposable income will be used. Space here does not permit a detailed explanation of each of the steps used in the preparation of the series on disposable income; however, this series does not differ very much from the other available estimates of disposable income.

29

Supply Constraints in Demand-Oriented Systems: An Interpretation of the Oil Crisis

A thesis that appeals to me is that macroeconomic models, indeed other bodies of economic thought, too, are the products of their times. The Keynesian model that figures so importantly in our standard analysis of the Western industrial economy was fashioned particularly to deal with the problem of mass unemployment as it occurred in the period between the two wars.[1] Possibly, we have, in fact, been successful in eradicating mass unemployment. We cannot be sure of this in the industrial market economies, but there have not been discernible tendencies to return to the conditions of the 1920s or 1930s since the end of World War II. To be sure, a cycle problem persists, but this is likely to be a relatively short and mild cycle, together with a persistent inflation. The Keynesian model has been extended in various directions in order to deal with this situation (mild cycles, chronic inflation), but it remains demand oriented, as was the original system of *effective demand*, and gives us little help in dealing with an understanding of the allocation problems that must be faced, on the assumption that the mass unemployment problem has been settled.

P. Samuelson, writing on the economic outlook for 1974 has made the following comment.

> The usual macroeconomic model is not built in such a way that one can fit into it changing assumptions about a microeconomic availability of something like oil, or energy generally. Neither Keynes nor Irving Fisher gave us ways of handling an event of this type. Yet the forecaster must somehow adjust his system and

---

[1] At a later stage, I shall use the term 'model' in a more specific sense, referring to particular econometric models and their contemporary solutions. At this stage, I am using the term more loosely, as a way of thinking about the working of the economy. We may think about economic performance according to the Keynesian line of analysis without adhering to a particular system of equations with numerical coefficients.

From *Zeitschrift für Nationalökonomie*, **34** (1974), 45–56.

his thinking to allow for this new limitation on supply. What is he to do?

He may try to avail himself of Professor Leontief's input–output system. Nobel Prizes are deservedly awarded for breakthroughs like this. But the forecaster will learn that he must bring his own ingenuity to the task, since the Leontief analysis has been based on the pessimistic assumption that all production takes place with fixed and inflexible coefficients relating inputs to outputs. Clearly, all the substitutions and ingenuities in making the limited supply of energy stretch, and there will surely be many such, have to be guessed at by the analyst.[2]

It is precisely this stream of thought expressed by P. Samuelson that I want to address myself to in this presentation. His analysis of the current American outlook in the *Financial Times* makes reference to the econometric model projections put forward by me and my colleagues in the Wharton econometric group, and I want to try to explain how supply constraints were, in fact, treated in the context of the usual demand-oriented econometric model, which is, to a large extent, an empirical implementation of the Keynesian and post-Keynesian lines of thought.

Another relevant thought about the present situation, called the 'energy crisis' is that these troubled times with cloudy perspective may have some silver linings among the clouds. One may be optimistic in perceiving some hidden benefits from the sudden cut-off of oil supplies to the economies of the Western world. The present crisis may bring about constructive energy policies for the affected industrial nations. This already appears to be taking place in a few countries. In the intermediate or longer range, these new policies may give rise to significant stimuli for the economies involved, such stimuli analyzed through the multiplier process of the standard demand model. A second consideration, which is really Samuelson's point, is that the present crisis conditions should encourage us to look again at model structure in detail and think carefully about the kind of system that we shall want for the near term and the rest of the decade of the 1970s. I shall concentrate on the second of these two considerations, namely, to show how supply considerations can be introduced into contemporary models for immediate results and how these models might be extended so as to be prepared for other disturbing situations that might occur. First, let me point out that it is something of an overstatement to say that the standard Keynesian or neo-Keynesian model is purely a

[2]*Financial Times*, London, December 31, 1973.

demand model. It has some definite supply aspects, but not those that help very much in present circumstances. The demands for factors of production – labor and capital – are part of the supply process even though they are called demand relations. They are associated with the aggregate production function, which is purely a supply consideration. Also price and wage-rate determination in the context of the modern macromodel, if these processes are implemented properly, must involve supply and demand considerations jointly, for clearing supply/demand imbalances in the markets.

Nevertheless, in spite of these few supply considerations, there is a basic problem, manifested by the fact that the import multiplier is negative. Let us assume that imports depend on domestic activity and terms of trade

$$M = M\left(Y, \frac{PW}{PM}\right) + m$$

where

M = real imports,
Y = real output,
PW = world price level,
PM = import price level,
m = shift factor of the import function.

Standard multiplier calculation, using the accounting definition,

$$Y = C + I + G + X - M$$

where

C = real consumption,
I = real capital formation,
G = real government expenditures,
X = real exports,
M = real imports;

will show that

$$\frac{dY}{dm} < 0;$$

correspondingly, the export multiplier will be positive.

If oil imports are restricted, real output should rise according to this model, yet intuitive feeling throughout the world is that restriction of oil production by the Arab nations will lower imports into the industrialized economies of the West and lower output levels to the point of generating a small world recession or economic slowdown.

A second aspect of the model concerns exports. The typical macro-model export equation is

$$X = X\left(WT, \frac{PW}{PX}\right) + x$$

where

X = real exports,
WT = total volume of world trade,
PW = world price level,
PX = export price level,
x = shift parameter.

This relation says that real exports depend on the volume of trade and terms of trade. As world oil prices go to astronomical levels should the movement of the ratio PW/PX favor exports of the industrial countries? This, too, is a perverse result in the standard model.

The US models, which have been not only demand oriented, but also overly domestic in character have few provisions for indicating how high import prices (fuel in this case) contribute to domestic inflation. This is not a problem for European and UK model builders, however, because they have generally been alert to problems of imported inflation and allow for that factor in their domestic price formation equations

It is not only the oil crisis that brings home this deficiency in most US models, because dollar devaluation and high world prices for agricultural products of the past few years have shown dramatically how important it is to allow for imported inflation.

Looking at the pressure of events and trying to make predictions from formal models in disturbed circumstances of the oil shortage, I see three deficiences in the standard morel:

1 The productivity of imports is neglected. Some imports are for final consumption; some are in final form for use in the production process, and some are in the form of raw or intermediate materials. Consumer goods imports may well be treated as they now are in the standard model, and capital goods imports are reckoned, together with domestic capital goods, as part of the capital stock for production. There may be some gain in information, however, by separating domestic and imported capital as two distinct inputs in the production process. The crux of the matter, however, is in material imports. They should be

treated as a separate factor of production, on a par with original unproduced factors like labor and its capital transform. In conventional macroeconomic analysis, when we construct and use the aggregate production function, we assume that intermediate materials are simultaneously input and output. We, therefore, 'wash' them out of the analysis. Imported materials cannot be 'washed.'

2 The input–output structure showing the intermediate flow of materials from industry sector to industry sector must be introduced as an integral part of the model. I do not mean that I–O analysis should stand apart in a separate analysis as is usual among practitioners, but it must be formally and fully integrated with the macromodel of behavior in a joint feed-back solution of the complete supply and demand process. In our Wharton econometrics group, we have introduced an I–O sector in just that way.[3] It is coupled in a feed-back relationship with the macromodel. This system is necessarily large, consisting of several hundred equations, and is available only on an annual basis. It is used mainly for intermediate-range analysis, say a decade by yearly increments.

In concentrating attention on value added and other related macro concepts in a national income accounting framework, we have ignored intermediate flows, assuming that they cancel one another's effects nicely, and now find that intermediate deliveries of basic materials have almost supreme importance for understanding macro performance. Reliance will be heavy on I–O tabulations for what I have to say later about macroeconomic calculations of oil shortages in the USA.

3 Important as I–O coefficients are for getting some understanding of the supply-side problem, we must recognize that they have severe limitations. As fixed coefficients, they show only one way of doing things, from a technological view point, in the economy and do not take account of the substitutions and other modifications that P. Samuelson referred to in his *Financial Times* article. We are using the I–O method in a more flexible way that tries to take account of shifts in the coefficients over time. We may pick up some of the shifts induced by selective price changes, but not those resulting from large technological changes.[4]

---

[3] R. S. Preston: *The Wharton Annual and Industry Model*, Economics Research Unit, Philadelphia (1972).
[4] The actual I–O model used in the oil shortage calculations takes account of gradual trend and autoregressive drift in I–O coefficients. In a new version, not yet used for the oil crisis simulations, the coefficient changes are more systematically modelled on relative price changes.

These are the model changes that are ultimately needed, but only some aspects were available for the recent calculations, that had to be completed within a few weeks' time. Let me describe how the Wharton forecasts were modified in order to make those adjustments that P. Samuelson said every forecaster must make in the present circumstances.

The supply side of the large Wharton Annual Model was constrained by placing a ceiling on the production from two I–O industries – crude petroleum and natural gas mining (primary production) and petroleum and related industries (refining, distribution). US production had for some time been at full capacity in both of these sectors. Imports of crude and refined products pass through these two sectors as 'competitive imports' in our I–O table; therefore import restrictions, together with full domestic capacity, determine the output ceiling for each of these sectors. The magnitude of the restrictions needed to target the output ceilings were determined approximately according to the following calculations:

(Millions of barrels per day)
Normal consumption of petroleum products in the whole economy: approximately 18 million barrels per day
Domestic production: approximately 12 million barrels per day
Imports: approximately 6 million barrels per day
Expected shortfall: approximately 2 million barrels per day

A great statistical mystery of unusual proportions has been associated with such numbers since October, 1973; these are representative, but are, of course, subject to error. They are not seasonal extremes. Output of the two basic industries, primary production and refined production, total $12 billion and $6 billion per year, respectively, when measured in 1958 prices; therefore we simply constrained the model solution so that ceilings were reached at $11 billion and $5 billion, respectively. The limitation on daily physical consumption was thus translated into a limitation on annual dollar value of production. From the solution of the conventional I–O system

$$(I - A)X = F \tag{29.1}$$

$$X = (I - A)^{-1} F \tag{29.2}$$

where

$A =$ I–O matrix,
$X =$ output,
$F =$ final demand.

An interpretation of the oil crisis

We could have suppressed the rows of (29.2) corresponding to the two constrained production sectors. Instead we expressed these two equations in (29.2) as

$$X_i = \sum_{K=1}^{n} \alpha_{iK} F_K + \delta_i$$

$$X_j = \sum_{K=1}^{n} \alpha_{jK} F_K + \delta_j$$

where

α_{iK}, α_{jK} = elements of $(I-A)^{-1}$

and assigned negative values to δ_i, δ_j such that the complete system solutions for X_i and X_j were reduced to the pre-assigned ceiling levels. The required amounts for δ_i and δ_j were found by a succession of 'cut-and-try' calculations and turned out to be much less than the total shortfall of petroleum products.

Although the calculation starts from the supply side it would not be a realistic system solution if these were the only adjustments; we must look for a balanced adjustment by making simultaneous changes to the demand side. These were introduced as changes in the equations underlying F (final demand). They took the form of imposed exogenous shifts. Imports were reduced and consumer spending was simultaneously reduced. The former reductions reflected the boycott, while the latter represented efforts of authorities in prevailing upon the public to consume less gas and oil for motoring, less electric power, and less fuel for residential heating. Consumption functions for gas and oil and for household operations were correspondingly lowered by estimated amounts calculated by oil and electric industry economists on the expected reductions in use. As far as GNP and final demand determination are concerned, these are approximately offsetting adjustments. Import reductions tend to raise GNP in a pure demand situation, while negative shifts in consumption functions tend to lower GNP. Two additional demand-side corrections were made – one for higher import prices (exogenous) and one for inventory reduction in the nonmanufacturing sector.

The final system solution incorporated both these supply- and demand-side adjustments simultaneously. In addition, an adjustment was made for increased coal production, amounting to a fuel equivalent of 200,000 barrels per day, on the basis of direct mining-sector information. The end result was checked to make sure that production was held to the ceiling levels in the critical petroleum sectors. The whole adjustment process was scaled, on an annual basis, to be consistent with a shortfall of 2 million barrels per day for the first half of 1974, only, assuming that the boycott would be lifted by midyear.

Once the full calculation was made through the large-scale combined model, containing both I–O and final-demand sectors, a parallel calculation was made for the Wharton Quarterly Model, consisting of final-demand sectors alone. In this case, all the demand-side adjustments made in the Annual Model were immediately introduced (lower imports, lower consumption, higher import prices, lower non-manufacturing inventory change). In addition, manufacturing inventories were adjusted downwards by a further amount to give the same annual result (obtained by summing the quarters) obtained by the previous calculations. In a sense, negative inventory change becomes the channel by which supply limitations were introduced to the demand-oriented model. In this quarterly system, the adjustments were concentrated in the first two quarters and then gradually taken away. The quarterly solution was also checked by inspection, to see whether it was producing expected indirect effects of large magnitude in the form of decreased sales of motor cars and expenditure on some services.

The outcome of these calculations, keeping in mind the strong dependence on assumptions about the working of the Arab oil embargo and boycott show an unmistakable deflationary impact. In comparison with a simulation of the Wharton Model that assumes no oil shortfall, we find that the case of 2.0 million barrels per day shortfall cuts the expected real growth rate for the year 1974 from 2.1 to 0.6 per cent, raises the probable inflation rate from 5.8 to 7.2 per cent, and the unemployment rate from 5.2 to 5.5 per cent. At the end of 1974, the quarterly rate of unemployment is expected to be as high as 6.1 per cent. In looking at the projected quarterly pattern of output and employment, the calculations suggest that there will be a small recession in early 1974, with falling output and rising unemployment, in the midst of a strong inflation.

The growth rate has been declining in the US since last summer, and a growth recession was already predicted. The effect of the oil crisis is to create a disturbance that gives an added push to the economy to turn a growth recession into a regular recession. This is the kind of quantitative result that can be obtained from an adjusted demand-type model faced with supply shortages.

The point of making a simultaneously balanced adjustment between δ_i, and δ_j, on the one hand, to shift supply downwards, and similar shifts of imports, consumer expenditures, and inventories, on the other hand, is to divide the adjustment process between industrial effects from the I–O relationships and final-demand effects. The more consumers willingly adjust through restraint, the less disruption will there be on the supply side, enabling production to remain strong and prevent industrial bottlenecks from developing. In some separate calculations we made with the Wharton Model, we put the whole burden of adjustment on added consumer restraints and introduced no inventory restraints for the supply side. This case produced only a slightly worse outcome in terms of growth, unemployment rate, and inflation rate – further deteriorations of less than 25 basis points in each.

This shows that if the public would act responsibly and try to economize where energy use is concerned, there need be only a short-run adjustment with little rearrangement needed in the production structure. Dire consequences for the economy could be avoided.

The calculations with the Wharton Models concentrated on the US domestic effects. Some assumptions had to be made about world trade and prices, however, and these came from corresponding Project LINK calculations. Some interesting international repercussions were studied with the LINK world model, and it may be worthwhile to summarize them here.

Most participating LINK models for the industrial market economies of Western Europe, UK, North America, Japan and Australia belong to a common family, in which the same problem arises about incorporating supply constraints in a demand oriented system. It turned out that each LINK model proprietor was thinking along similar lines at the height of concern about oil shortages. They restrained consumption expenditures, imports, and inventory changes. A few exceptions occurred. In the case of Japan, the adjustment was in types of public expenditure instead of inventory change. Australia, Canada, Finland, France and some other LINK countries were not anticipating direct limitations of oil supplies. They were, however, fearful of *indirect* effects because of declines in activity in their trading-partner countries as a result of oil restrictions. Two kinds of LINK simulations have been made. The first is a hypothetical multiplier calculation, designed to show the sensitivity of the world economy to a uniform change simultaneously in several countries. The second is an attempt to model, selectively, the oil restrictions for each major country, together with markedly higher prices for crude. The first is hypothetical, though relevant to the current situation; the second tries to be realistic but cannot keep pace with the changing circumstances of the embargo and individual country adaptations. The hypothetical calculation simulated a decline of 100 basis points in real growth rate for the model of each separate major LINK participant (not in the regional models for

CMEA or developing countries). The choice of the uniform decline of 100 basis points was decided upon after it was seen that most individual models were showing declines of 100–200 basis points as a result of their own separate simulations, in first response to the perceived crisis, whether they were countries with direct or indirect effects. Since the simultaneous adjustments of reduced imports and reduced consumer expenditure tend to 'wash' out, we introduced a change in inventories alone for this simulation. This is the way most countries independently tried to model the oil crisis.

In a few cases, we changed an expenditure component other than inventory investment, but in almost all cases we lowered a country's inventory investment by an amount that would bring down the real GNP (GDP) growth rate by 100 basis points, where exports for each country were assumed to be exogenous and unchanged or to depend principally on world variables that could not change. The interesting result that emerged was that the declines of 100 basis points became amplified to approximately 150 basis points when all the declining economies were tied together in the LINK system via the trade matrix. It is in this sense of the main trading countries being linked together, following anti-inflationary policies at home and suddenly shocked by the oil embargo, that we could see the danger of a discernible world-wide recession developing, possibly like that in 1957–1958, in terms of severity.

This hypothetical simulation made no specific allowances for higher oil prices, for selectivity of oil deficiencies, or for adoption of specific national policies. We therefore made a second, more detailed simulation in which clear distinction was made between countries with direct and indirect effects, in which the magnitude of the short falls were quantitatively estimated by LINK participants, and in which exogenous shifts in final-demand components were tailored to the announced policies of each country. We were not able to include the special emergency measures for the UK resulting from domestic disputes with miners and railway workers.

The most important single result of this larger simulation is that the projected growth of world trade for 1974 would be reduced from about 6.3 per cent to only 4.8 per cent. The growth rate was partly held up by increased trade estimated for the socialist countries.[5] If they are excluded, real world trade would be expected to grow by little more than 1 per cent. These growth rates are accompanied by an estimated

---

[5] We tried to allow for expanded arms shipments from the USSR to the Middle East. This may be extended to other suppliers in the near future.

trade price inflation of 14 per cent in place of an earlier estimate of 7 per cent. Generally speaking, individual country growth rates were lowered by 100–200 basis points and inflation rates accelerated by 100–200 basis points. As expected, the Middle East regional group shows an enormous increment in an already favorable trade balance. Notable among the countries with deteriorating trade balances are the UK, France, Italy.

The overall dimensions of this simulation indicate a world economy thrown into a small recession. The calculations were made only for 1974, and with a temporary embargo expected, it is unlikely that the recession would be cumulative or lasting. The entire result is extreme and should be looked upon only as a simulation of what might have happened to the world economy had the boycott and crude production cut backs held firm. It is well known that there were many leaks in the embargo measures, and the cut backs with restrictive national policies that were programmed into this calculation were expressed reactions as of December 1973, that were strongly relaxed in January, 1974. This is not to say that there is no energy shortage or crisis; it is only a remark that the most severe reactions overemphasized the real shortages and difficulties.

What is the longer-run outlook as a result of a new attitude towards basic energy supply? To answer this question, we have simulated the large Wharton Annual Model for a whole decade, starting in 1973. Two principal policies were considered. One projected the future of the American economy with normal growth in oil consumption supplied from imports, at high and rising prices. The other attempted to interpret the President's request for implementation of a program in self sufficiency. We assumed, in line with contemporary thinking, that domestic production of crude oil could not increase enough to guarantee complete self sufficiency by the end of the decade, but could add about 8 million barrels per day by 1982. This goal would be reached by research, development, and capital formation to exploit shale, tar sands, offshore drilling, and nuclear power. It is also contained provision for expansion of refining capacity.

Both solutions go through a growth recession and then recover to a long-run expansion path at approximately a rate of 4 per cent for real GNP. The inflation rate in these simulations eventually comes down to about 4 per cent, while the unemployment rate settles at a rate between 4 and 5 per cent. In either case, the trade balance is eventually unfavorable, but if imports were to be relied on mainly, the deficit would become staggering. It ranges between $15 billion and $17 billion toward the end of the decade. With the partial move towards self sufficiency programmed here, the balance between imports and exports would be expected to converge to zero by 1982.

The self-sufficiency policy appears to be a viable and attractive alternative. Inflation should be eventually brought down to about 4 per cent and the increase in fixed capital formation associated with the program helps keep unemployment nearer to 4 than to 5 per cent along the real growth path of 4 per cent. The familiar Keynesian multiplier provides some help in this case without undue inflationary pressure.

Nevertheless, there will be some continuing strong inflation at the beginning of this simulation period. It is already evident. What should economic policy prescriptions be in a situation like this? There is need for counter cyclical stimulus at the present time, but there is simultaneous need to try to arrest inflation on both world and domestic fronts. I would argue for relaxed fiscal policies in the form of lower taxes and more generous transfer payments (unemployment benefits) to ease the short-term burden of adjustment that the oil shocks have already delivered to motor industry workers, airline employees, and other sectors immediately touched by the energy crisis. The expanded investment program appears to be strong enough to stimulate recovery to the longer-run growth path.

At the same time that fiscal measures are introduced to stimulate the economy, there should be continued monetary restraint as an anti-inflation measure. Some economists argue that the monetary authorities cannot use their standard policy parameters to fight one-shot world inflation factors like high oil prices. Last year, however, it was grain and beef. This year it is oil; what comes next? On the previous occasion, sharply rising food prices spread their influence in epidemic fashion to many other sectors of the economy in a series of inflation rounds. Fuel price rises could have the same spreading effect. I would argue, therefore, in favor of continued monetary restraint, offset by fiscal easing with a very strong energy investment program getting under way as soon as possible.

There is, therefore, no lack of analytical response, even to the point of policy analysis, in this new situation of supply-induced recessionary tendencies throughout the world, but especially in the US. Our present models are not as informative or useful as we want them to be (are they ever?), but they do contain a great deal of quantitative economic information if used properly. The kind of analysis that I have described in this presentation is not to be regarded as a desirable substitute for model reformulation and elaboration to cover both supply and demand aspects of the economy, but they do suggest, to me at least, that large detailed models can be used to much greater extent than many others might have realized. Some answers have to be reached in short order and the lines along which I have worked seem to me to be the best route to follow in these circumstances. Eventually, we should be better equipped.

30
Five-Year Experience of Linking National Econometric Models and of Forecasting International Trade

INTRODUCTION

Project LINK was conceived in 1968 and implemented over the past 5 years in an evolving process whereby the specification of the system crystallized, expanded, and improved, and the data and programs were refined.[1] In this paper I shall review the experience of using (not developing) the LINK system in forecasting and policy analysis in world trade.

The LINK system now consists of separate models for: (a) 13 countries, (b) regional models for four developing areas, (c) trade models for the CMEA group of socialist countries, and (d) some reduced form equations for 12 other developed countries. Finally, there is a residual group of rest-of-the-world countries that is not formally modeled and accounts for a small but not trivial volume of trade. The system has not always been structured as it is today. Simple GNP account models were used for France and Italy until fullfledged econometric models could be specially designed within the LINK group. The Australian model was entered in the computer program only in 1973; the Finnish model was made ready for entry in 1973 and is only being included in 1974. The models for the developing country regions and the CMEA trade models were added in 1971.

---

[1]LINK is a cooperative, international study group. The collective nature of the research project is exemplified in the first LINK volume (Ball, 1973). A series of reports, annual and general, in ITEMS of the Social Research Council, New York, gives a good sequential overview of the project's development. The system applications presented here draw upon the collaboration of Keith Johnson, Chikashi Moriguchi, Y. Nishino, Alain Van Peeterssen, M. Kurose, Louisa Sabater, and all participants from individual countries or regions.

From *Quantitative Studies of International Economic Relations* North-Holland, Amsterdam (1976).

National models

Australia, Reserve Bank of Australia model (RBA); Austria, Institute for Advanced Studies model; Belgium, Free University of Brussels (Ginsburgh model); Canada, University of Toronto (Trace model); Finland, Bank of Finland model; Germany, Bonn University (Bonner model); Italy, University of Bologna model; Japan, Kyoto University (Denken model); Netherlands, Central Planning Bureau model (CPB); Sweden, National Institute of Economic Research model; UK, London Business School model (LBS); US, University of Pennsylvania (Wharton Model); and France, Free University of Brussels (Guillaume's POM POM). These are mostly well-known models that have been explained elsewhere, but will be published together in a second LINK volume now in press.

Regional models (LDS)

Africa (excluding Libya and South Africa); South and East Asia; Middle East oil producers and Libya; and Latin America. These have all been constructed by UNCTAD.

CMEA model

USSR, Bulgaria, Czechoslovakia, East Germany, Hungary, Poland, and Rumania. These have been constructed by UNCTAD and specified as follows:

$$X_i^{ns} = b_{0i} + b_{1i}(TW)^{ns}, \tag{30.1}$$

$$X_i^s = X_i^T - X_i^{ns}, \tag{30.2}$$

$$X_i^s = \sum_{j=1}^{7} X_{ij}^s, \tag{30.3}$$

$$M_j^s = \sum_{i=1}^{7} X_{ij}^s, \tag{30.4}$$

$$M_i^T = c_{0i} + c_{1i} Y_i + c_{2i} X_i^T, \tag{30.5}$$

$$M_i^{ns} = M_i^T - M_i^s, \tag{30.6}$$

$$X_{ij}^s = d_{ij} X_j^T. \tag{30.7}$$

The first six equations hold for each CMEA country. The set of equations in (30.7) define elements of a trade shares matrix $D = \|d_{ij}\|$. According to the notation used here, X stands for exports, M for imports, superscript s for socialist, superscripts ns for non-socialist, superscript T for total world, TW for world trade, and Y for net material product of the socialist countries. While this is the system currently on the LINK computer file, it is being extended and modified with a view toward enhancing its realism and forecasting performance.

Rest-of-the-world models for developed countries

Denmark, Norway, Switzerland, Greece, Iceland, Ireland, Portugal, Spain, Turkey, Yugoslavia, New Zealand and South Africa. Estimates for these countries are all derived from the following equations:

$$M63\$ = \alpha_0 + \alpha_1(PX\$/PM\$) + \alpha_2 TW63\$ + \alpha_3(M63\$)_{-1}, \quad (30.8)$$

$$PX\$ = \beta_0 + \beta_1 PWX\$ + \beta_2(PX\$)_{-1}, \quad (30.9)$$

where

$M63\$$ = imports in 1963 US dollars,
$PX\$$ = the index of dollar denominated export prices,
$PM\$$ = the index of dollar denominated import prices,
$TW63\$$ = the total world trade measured in 1963 US dollars,
$PWX\$$ = the index of dollar denominated world export prices.

A pair of equations, such as these, is estimated for each listed country.

THE WORLD TRADE MODEL AND LINK ALGORITHM

For each country model we assume that export volume and import price are exogenous; while import volume and export price are endogenous. In the pair of reduced form equations (30.8) and (30.9), we see immediately that import volume and export price are explained by separate equations. The world trade model will be responsible for explaining export volume and import price.

For merchandise trade, in FOB valuation, by SITC groups 0, 1: food, beverages, tobacco; 2, 4: basic materials; 3: mineral fuels; and 5–9: manufactures; we have the following matrix equation:

$$X63\$ = (A)M63\$ \quad (30.10)$$

to compute exports, where $X63\$$ is the column vector of exports in 1963 US dollars, A is the trade shares matrix, $a_{ij} = X_{ij}/X_{.j}$. X_{ij} is the merchandise shipments from country i to country j, $X_{.j} = \Sigma_i X_{ij}$ is the imports of country j. $M63\$$ is the column vector of imports in 1963 US dollars. By construction, the columns of A sum to unity, i.e.

$$\sum_{i=1}^{n} a_{ij} = 1.$$

This property insures that

$$\sum_{i=1}^{n} (X63\$)_i = \sum_{i=1}^{n} (M63\$)_i \qquad (30.11)$$

(world exports FOB = world imports FOB).

This is an accounting identity or 'law of conservation.' It holds in both constant and current prices. Equation (30.11) is in constant prices; therefore the current price identity is

$$(PX\$)'X63\$ = (PM\$)'M63\$ \qquad (30.12)$$

or

$$(PX\$)'(A)M63\$ = (PM\$)'M63\$.$$

If we equate coefficients of $M63\$$ term by term in this last equation, we find

$$\sum_{i=1}^{n} (PX\$)_i a_{ij} = (PM\$)_j. \qquad (30.13)$$

Import prices are, therefore, explained as column weighted averages of other countries' export prices. This is 'dual' to the calculation of exports in (30.10) as row-weighted averages of other countries' imports.

These LINK equations are set out in terms of constant dollar trade matrices. If the matrices (A) are expressed in current dollars, the price conversion should be through column-weighted harmonic means rather than arithmetic means. The LINK algorithm works as follows.

1 Assume export volumes and import prices for each national model and solve, together with domestic exogenous inputs, for import volume and export price.
2 Use (30.10) and (30.13) to compute export volume and import price for each country. Volumes and prices must be converted from own-currency units to US dollar units for this calculation.
3 Re-solve each country model for new import volume and export price values, using as inputs the export volumes and import prices computed in step 2. This step requires reconversion from dollar to own-currency units. On each iteration, world trade is computed as the sum of world imports (FOB) and the process is assumed to have

converged when $TW\$$ does not change from iteration to iteration by more than a preassigned amount.

The main problem in using this approach is that matrix (A) does not remain stable over time. While we have an identity $(X63\$)_t = (A)_t(M63\$)_t$, we generate errors if we use

$$(X63\$)_t = (A)_0(M63\$)_t + (\text{error})_t. \tag{30.14}$$

With some reporting lag, we have yearly data on $(A)_t$. The latest year for which we have complete data is 1970, but some statistics on $(A)_t$ are available for 1971. Nothing later is available. In forecasting several years ahead, we are necessarily faced with the problem of generating $(A)_t$. This is a difficult problem, with almost complete analogy to the problem faced in input–output analysis subject to a changing technology. There are two general approaches to this problem – one is to try to project changes in individual cell elements of the variable matrices and the other is to try to project only the overall implied effects on marginal totals. At first, in the LINK project we attempted to use the second approach in a mechanical way, using trend and autoregressive corrections as these had been used for input–output analysis in the Brookings model project. This would amount, essentially to a trend-autoregressive model for $(\text{error})_t$ in (30.14). We have shifted from that technique to one that uses relative-price information in order to model $(\text{error})_t$. This is preferred because it has economic content. We replace (30.14) by

$$(X\$)_{it} = v_i(PX\$)_{it} + \delta_i(A_{i,69})(M\$)_t + \varepsilon_i(PCOM\$)_{it} + \xi_i t. \tag{30.14a}$$

Note that the *current-price* version of the trade matrix is presently being used. This refers to $A_{i,69}$, $M\$$, and $X\$$. $A_{i,69}$ is the ith row of A (in current dollars) for 1969; $PCOM\$$ is the index of dollar denominated export prices competitive with i's exports.

$$(PCOM\$)_i = \sum_{j=1}^n \lambda_{ij} \sum_{\substack{k=1 \\ k \neq j}}^n a_{kj}(PX\$)_k \qquad \lambda_{ij} = X_{ij}/X_i.$$

λ and a are both taken from trade matrix data of fixed periods.[2]

---

[2] The definition of competitive prices used here is taken from Hickman (1972). The base period for many index numbers in the LINK system is 1963; therefore the λ_{ij} are defined in terms of the 1963 matrix. The a_{kj} are taken from the 1969 matrix.

Equation (30.14a) has many analogies with the *linear expenditure system*, therefore we call it the LES version for projection of the trade matrix. If we were to restrict the coefficients in (30.14a) so that

$$\delta_i = 1 \quad \sum_i v_i(PX\$)_{it} = -\sum_i \varepsilon_i(PCOM\$)_{it} \quad \sum_i \xi_i = 0,$$

we would have formal analogy with the LES and an assurance of satisfaction of the world trade accounting identity in current prices. We have not, however, restricted our estimates, but the identity has held within \$1.0–2.0 billion in actual applications. If, however, we use $(A_{i,69})(M\$)_t$ to estimate bilateral flows in the ith row of the trade matrix, the results will not, in general, sum to $(X\$)_{it}$, the estimated marginal totals. We use a standard RAS adjustment technique to balance the table of bilateral flows to estimated marginal totals.

The LES method is robust for estimating trade flows, but not very powerful for estimating bilateral components.

A method that is more suited to estimation of bilateral flows in a system with changing trade shares matrices has been proposed by Moriguchi.[3] His basic equation for estimating all elements of A is

$$\log a_{ij} = \eta_i + \theta_i \log \frac{(PX\$)_i}{(PCOM\$)_i} + \iota_i \log \frac{(X63\$)_i}{(M63\$)_j} + \sum_{j=1}^{n} k_{ij} D_j. \quad (30.15)$$

In this formulation, a_{ij} from the current dollar matrix varies as relative prices and relative quantities vary. To simplify the work and enlarge the sample for estimating a_{ij}, Moriguchi has kept η_i, θ_i, and ι_i free of j subscripts. These coefficients are assumed to be the same along a given row, but the market of export destination is taken into account by the introduction of 'dummy' variables D_j for importing countries $-D_j = 1$ for country j, 0 otherwise.

A third method for projecting the trade matrix has been devised by Hickman and Lau (1973). They take the general trade model of Armington as a starting point, which assumes that an index of imports in country or region is a CES function of trade flows to that country or region (Armington, 1970). Armington worked out a complete set of trade equations based on this conception of imports. Hickman and Lau made a linear approximation of the Armington model, also using the trade shares matrix. They reduce their final equation for exports to the following form:

$$(X63\$)_{it} = (A_{i,63})(M63\$)_t - \bar{\sigma}_i(X63\$)_{i,63}[(PX\$)_{it} - (PCOM\$)_{it}]$$
$$+ \bar{\sigma}_i(X63\$)_{i,63} r_i t, \quad (30.16)$$

[3]Applications of the LINK system with this method of adjustment for changing the A matrix are given in Moriguchi (1973).

where

σ_i = elasticity of substitution between any pair of imports in the ith market,

$$\bar{\sigma}_i = \sum_{j=1}^{n} \sigma_j \lambda_{ij},$$

$$(PX\$)_i = \sum_{j=1}^{n} (\sigma_j/\bar{\sigma}_i)\lambda_{ij}(PX\$)_j; (PCOM\$)_i = \sum_{j=1}^{n} (\sigma_j/\bar{\sigma}_i)\lambda_{ij}(PM\$)_j,$$

$$r_i = \sum_{j=1}^{n} (\sigma_j/\bar{\sigma}_i)\lambda_{ij} r_{ij}.$$

The notation here is basically the same as in (30.14a) except that the base year of the index values and linearization should agree with the base year of trade-matrix coefficient computation. The analysis is made in terms of constant dollar trade flows, but could also be done in current dollar terms. Some additional weighting factors based on estimates of elasticities of substitution σ_j and $\bar{\sigma}_i$ are also used. This formulation is worked out so that the accounting identities necessarily hold for world exports and imports.

This equation system is designed to guarantee the adding-up property of world exports and imports. It gives not only the marginal totals for exports of each country in the trade matrix but also the bilateral flows derived on the basis of estimates of the elasticity of substitution between country pairs.

The Hickman–Lau method has been proposed and analyzed, but has not yet been incorporated in the LINK computer program for simulation solution of the whole world trade system. It will, however, be introduced as an empirical alternative in the near future.

These three methods are the principal ones being discussed for projection of the changing trade-shares matrices. Others may be considered in the future, some purely arithmetical such as the standard RAS method. The present systems, all of which rely on relative price movements, are, however, preferred within the LINK group. There is, however, another approach that bypasses use of the trade shares matrix. Instead of computing exports from (30.14) suitably adjusted for the changing A-matrix, we might estimate exports for each country from its tailored export equations. These are usually functions of activity or import levels in main partner countries, an index of price competitiveness, and special political or institutional factors. The trouble with this method is that countries tend to project – looking at their own economic situation in isolation – *larger* exports than other

LINK system experience

countries are willing to take as imports. In LINK we are considering some proportional scaling of exports to agree with world imports, This method has not been tried as a set of formal computations, but will also be carried out in the near future.

THE AIMS OF LINK PROJECTIONS

Within individual country models, the macroeconomic variable of greatest importance is GNP (GDP) in either current or constant prices, usually the latter. Associated macro variables or transformations of them are the real growth rate, inflation rate, unemployment rate, interest rate, and trade balance. These do not exhaust the list of interesting and important variables, but are central. In a world model, these same variables are of central interest for each country or region making up the model, but there is another key variable on which attention is focused, namely, world trade. The volume of world trade, its growth rate, and associated world export price inflation rate occupy the same role of strategic importance that real GNP, its growth rate, and price inflation rate occupy in a national model.

Total world production, industrial and agricultural, or world GNP could be singled out for *central concern*, but measurement and conceptual problems are probably great; therefore we shall primarily concern ourselves with total world trade. Many national export equations are expressed as functions of world trade and world price competitiveness, therefore once we have estimates of world exports and their inflation rate we are in a good position to judge external effects on a national economy.

In the course of studying LINK projections and judging their accuracy or usefulness, I shall first consider total world trade projections in terms of level and growth rates. At the same time the growth of the price index of world exports will also be considered. In order to compare trade-flow values across countries, a common *numéraire* unit will have to be adopted. This would be true for world GNP or world-trade measures, but currency unit conversions for traded goods appear to be more usual and natural, this being a basic reason why world trade is the main variable of interest. Possible *numéraires* are US dollar units, gold units or SDR units. So many world statistics are readily available in US dollar units that this will be the chosen *numéraire* for this study. At first, I shall study projections of total world trade and a world export price index, then I shall look at estimates of national or regional trade flows together with real growth rates. Gradually, we are standardizing summary tabulations for a wide number of variables across countries, but at the present time I shall confine my presentation to trade flows ($US) and real growth rates.

In the first and formative years of LINK, 1968–71, we were unsure of the structure of the system and were wrestling even more than today with massive programming problems. In this situation, many trial LINK projections were made at various times during the year. Some calculations were made *ex post*. Coverage was also in doubt. At first, we showed interest only in nonsocialist world trade, but socialist countries were eventually included on the basis outlined in the previous section. The first calculations were made one year at a time. These were gradually extended to two years and now computer capabilities exist for making calculations over indefinitely long horizons. It is not a purely computational problem: it is a case of assembling meaningful exogenous inputs for the separate models very far into the future and also a case of obtaining reasonable model solutions over multi year horizons.

Our procedures are now becoming more regular and comprehensive. In the autumn $(t-1)$ we solicit LINK model proprietors for input values for t, $t+1$, and $t+2$. Eventually these data will be obtained for $t+3$ and $t+4$.[4] Lagged values are also needed, and these must be estimated for $t-1$ in the autumn of the same year. After the beginning of year t, results come in from practically all countries, and the lagged values can be determined with more precision. By March, at the latest, preliminary estimates can be made for t, $t+1$, and $t+2$. It is now planned to review these estimates in a 2-day LINK meeting in April and revise them for an August or September meeting. This sequence will be repeated every year. Historical and policy simulation studies are also carried out frequently, but the procedures for regular projections must adhere to a fixed schedule.

SOME FORECAST EVALUATIONS

The period 1970–73 provides a first testing ground for gaining experience with the LINK system. As explained in the previous section, the system, the coverage, and the projection horizon were all undergoing development. Therefore the comparisons cannot yet be complete. It will take a few years of experience with the present systems before we can come to very definite conclusions, but the fragmentary evidence

---

[4] Some countries already have supplied 5-year extrapolations.

now available should be used for whatever light it can throw on system deficiencies.

At first, the world economy seemed to be presenting nothing more than chronic problems of surplus and deficit countries. In 1971, however, major developments occurred. There were devaluations, exogenous disturbances to trade, and world conferences on currency rates. The Smithsonian devaluation, followed by second waves in 1973, the large grain purchases by the USSR, and the energy shortfalls provided economic action to be interpreted with the system.

In broad outline, the LINK model projected a slowing down of the growth rate of world trade in 1970, immediately following a period of rapid expansion. In 1971 a continuation of moderate growth was foreseen. After the Smithsonian agreement, the LINK calculation was that the major imbalances (US, Japan, Germany) would not be changed. The system also estimated that developing countries would not be hurt by the currency realignments. In 1973, the system projections sighted a significant improvement in the US trade position, with moderate adjustments from Germany and smaller ones spread over a number of countries. A series of bad deficits was projected for the UK. The widening trade surplus for the Middle East, among regional models for developing countries, was recognizable in LINK simulations in 1972 and 1973. At new oil prices, it appears to be enormous in 1974. A worldwide slowdown caused by simultaneous anti-inflationary policies in several major countries was the central aspect of forecasts for 1974, as the second year $(t+1)$ of a 3-year projection made in 1973. This was enlarged into the dimension of a world recession as a result of synchronized shocks of the energy crisis.

It may be worthwhile to review some features of the post-Smithsonian calculation with LINK because that occasion exhibited a significant difference with other approaches to the estimation of realignment effects. At the time of the Smithsonian conference, and immediately afterwards, there were some notable estimates of expected strong effects. Indeed, President Nixon hailed the agreement as a landmark achievement in international finance. Then Mr Connally, the US Secretary of the Treasury, is reported to have projected a favorable swing of $80 billion in the US trade balance as a result of the realignment of exchange rates. This figure was scaled down from some larger estimates in the news media.

In a paper presented to the Brookings Panel on Economic Activity (April 1972), William Branson presented some trade model calculations and simulations that were generally accepted to be in support of the notion of a large favorable swing in the US balance. LINK results were presented by me as a contrast to the Branson estimates. It is difficult to make a very precise comparison between the Branson position and my interpretation of a LINK comparison because the time frames were not identical. LINK calculations were specifically for 1972, while Branson's were more in the spirit of comparative statics, giving a long-run or timeless effect. Also, Branson's were from a *partial* analysis (exchange rate changes *ceteris paribus*), while LINK results were from a *total* analysis (other things changing, including both activity levels and other policy changes associated with the US New Economic Policy).

Branson's results give larger swings to the US balance because his relevant price elasticities in trade were generally larger, his estimates cumulated all the delayed time effects, and he held activity effects constant. LINK estimates were based on continuing US recovery from the 1969–70 recession and the developing growth slowdown in Western Europe, the UK, and Japan. These aspects of international *Konjunktur* worked against improvements in the US balance on both the import and the export side. In addition, many LINK national models have low-parameter estimates of import price elasticities and distributed time lags.

It is not my purpose to argue here whether Branson's or the LINK estimates were more accurate because they are not strictly comparable on a scientific basis, but I do want to justify the reasonableness of the LINK results presented at the time of the beginning of large currency realignments. This was an early and large practical test of the LINK system. The system was not as ready as it is today to model such circumstances, but it did, I believe, provide some useful guidelines at the time.

LINK estimates were for an improvement in the constant dollar US balance and a deterioration in the current dollar balance for 1972. In table 30.5, computed some weeks after the Brookings meeting, the regular LINK estimates were for a US deficit of $4.0 billion, while the actual figure was more than $5.0 billion. There were few knowledgeable people in Washington or other circles who could foresee the disastrous trade figures for 1972 as early as the summer of that year.

The fact that the US position deteriorated at all during 1972 and even early in 1973, requiring a second double-barreled wave of dollar devaluation (February and March 1973), appears to vindicate the LINK position. It does not invalidate the comparative static, *ceteris paribus*, calculations of Branson, but it does question whether it would have been correct to examine his results and conclude from them that the outlook for the success of the Smithsonian was good and that one just had to be patient and await the favorable turn in the US balance.

LINK system experience

The 'elasticity pessimism' of the constituent LINK import functions is undoubtedly overdrawn, and work is progressing at various research centers to re-estimate the functions with longer time lags, but the short-run extrapolations are probably sound and the degree of pessimism may not turn out to be very large.[5] I think that import equations have some degree of price elasticity, but the figures are not high enough to warrant the inference that the Smithsonian changes were sufficiently large to restore international equilibrium. If the changes are large enough – Smithsonian devaluation plus double devaluation in 1973 – then the US balance can be expected to change by large amounts.

The situation was quite different in early 1973, after the new dollar devaluations. Some former optimists doubted that the US balance would quickly improve. The most prevalent notion expressed by knowledgeable people to me was that the new devaluations would do little good and that the US balance would remain in serious deficit. At this time, the basic LINK outlook changed as far as the US balance was concerned. The result suggested definite improvement in the US position for 1973 for the following reasons.

1 The time lags associated with the Smithsonian changes would accumulate more effect during 1973.
2 The total amount of devaluation was very large.
3 The US economy would slow down, while trading partners would be in a phase of cyclical upswing (opposite *Konjunktur* position to that of the Smithsonian).
4 Soviet grain purchases would be a net exogenous benefit to US exports.

The results in table 30.6 show that this optimistic projection for US exports in 1973 was justified, although the LINK system underestimated the magnitude of the improvement.

The preceding discussion in this section is highly impressionistic, subjective, and limited. Let us now turn to some statistical tabulations. In table 30.1 the observed data come from the UN *Monthly Bulletin of Statistics*. The estimated data for 1970 come from a paper, prepared for the annual LINK meeting, August 1970, in London. At that time, we were not including socialist countries in the LINK system. We were also using a constant dollar trade matrix and not computing directly the current dollar value of trade. We computed an estimate of change in world prices, but not an estimate of the index value.

---

[5]The arguments of Junz and Rhomberg (1963) are highly suggestive. Extension of lag lengths up to 5 years does indeed seem to improve US elasticity estimates.

Table 3C.1 World trade summary, 1970–2

	Observed	Estimated	Observed	Estimated	Observed	Estimated
Nonsocialist world trade (billion 1963 $)	247.9	250.6	264.2	257.5	286.2	277.9
Nonsocialist world trade (billion current $)	—	—	311.7	305.7	366.3	344.1
Nonsocialist world trade price index (1963: 100)	—	—	118.0	118.7	128.0	123.8
Total world trade (billion current $)	—	—	345.4	342.0	403.8	386.4

Two aspects are worth considering in a discussion of the results in table 30.1. In the first place, we must take up the accuracy of the 'observed' bench-mark data. Secondly, we must analyze the nature of the estimated errors. The observed data may be taken from two possible sources, either the UN *Monthly Bulletin* or the IMF *International Financial Statistics*. Alternatively, they could be taken directly from summations of individual country statistics, but we did not even consider that lengthy alternative. Depending on choice of exports or imports, on use of a quantum index or deflation of current dollar values, and on choice of source, it is possible to swing the observed numbers by as much as about 3 billion (or 1 percent). Import data tend to be reported CIF, while export data are FOB. The basic unit in the LINK is an FOB unit, therefore import totals have to be cut down by FOB/CIF ratios and this introduces an element of error. All the trade data in table 30.1 refer to commodity trade only. Services are excluded.

Given that we are unsure of our bench marks, how good are the total projections? Looking at the first row – for total real world trade – I would say that the estimate appears to be close for 1970; not as close as I would like to be for 1971 and 1972; good in estimating the increment from 1971 to 1972 but not so good in estimating the increment from 1970 to 1971. The slowdown from the high growth rates of the later 1960s was properly captured by LINK, but we overestimated the amount of slowdown during 1971. As for price estimates, we were close enough in 1971 but underestimated the substantial inflationary forces in 1972 trade. Estimated total world trade, including the socialist countries came out close in 1971, but too low in 1972, partly because of the underestimate of price level.

If we were to use the same standards in forecasting these aggregates – total world trade and the associated price level – that we use for projecting GNP and its deflator in major industrial countries, I would say that our performance is on the poor side. The error should be held to ± 5.0 billion on average before I would feel satisfied. The benchmark figure is shakier, the collection of models has some weak components, and experience in this exercise is limited. Progress is being made, but further gains remain to be realized.

The 1970–2 LINK projections were all made in the summer of the year being projected. Only partial results were known in each case by the summer, but the exercises were not true forecasts. In 1972, 2-year projections, and in 1973, 3-year projections were made. We shall probably adopt a 3-year standard, with some attempts to look ahead for 5 years, but greater efforts will be made to complete the first stages of forecasts in the spring of the first of the three years. In 1973 we began forecasting as early as March and kept revising projections until October, because it is a lengthy process to get revised data from all over the world when times are changing rapidly. By December 1973, we had completed LINK estimates of the effects of the world oil crises for 1974. This was a true *ex ante* forecast exercise.

In tables 30.2 and 30.3, there are various results for 1970 trade estimates by individual country. The first set includes the results published in the first LINK volume and are therefore separately discussed. They also include the so-called Mini-LINK estimates for import values alone.[6] These estimates force equality between total world trade and the sum of imports (FOB), but do not force equality between world exports and world imports. In this method, own-export equations are retained for each country.

In table 30.2 we see a troublesome LINK result that keeps turning up over and again in succeeding tables, but has finally been traced to a classification error and will now undoubtedly fall under statistical

Table 30.2 Trade projections, 1970 (billions of 1963 US $ FOB)

	Observed		Mini-LINK	LINK	
	Exports	Imports	Imports	Imports	Exports
Belgium/Luxemburg	10.7	10.3	7.2	10.2	9.8
Canada	10.9	13.7	13.4	11.8	12.5
France	16.5	15.8	12.4	13.2	15.6
Germany	25.4	30.0	24.6	23.5	29.7
Italy	12.9	12.0	10.5	10.8	12.6
Japan	14.3	17.4	16.6	21.8	15.5
Netherlands	12.6	10.9	10.4	10.7	10.2
Sweden	5.2	5.7	5.2	5.0	6.0
UK	17.8	17.3	14.9	15.9	17.7
US	32.7	35.2	31.1	30.8	36.8
Developing countries (LDC)	54.5	49.8	38.3	50.3	58.2
Other non socialist (ROW)	37.9	29.7	61.7	52.8	29.8
Total non socialist	251.7	247.9	246.4	256.7	253.8

[6] For an explanation of the Mini-LINK method and the tabulated data see Ball (1973, ch. 13).

LINK system experience

Table 30.3 Trade projections, 1970 (billions of 1963 US $ FOB)

	Observed		LINK	
	Imports	Exports	Imports	Exports
Belgium/Luxemburg	10.7	10.3	10.2	9.8
Canada	10.9	13.7	11.8	12.3
France	16.5	15.8	13.2	15.6
Germany	25.4	30.0	23.5	32.8
Italy	12.9	12.0	11.2	13.3
Japan	14.3	17.4	15.6	17.8
Netherlands	12.6	10.9	10.4	10.5
Sweden	5.2	5.7	4.9	6.3
UK	17.8	17.3	16.0	18.7
US	32.7	35.2	30.6	35.9
LDC	54.5	49.8	48.8	47.4
ROW	37.9	29.7	50.9	30.0
Total nonsocialist	251.7	247.9	250.6	250.6

control. We have a serious and regular underestimate of developing countries' imports, coupled with a corresponding overestimate of imports for the 'rest-of-the-world' group (nonsocialist). The total for the two residual groupings is more closely estimated than the components, but the total calculation is off by more than is desired. In the full LINK calculation, this kind of error leads to an overestimate of LDC exports because partner countries' imports are overstated.

The reason for the understatement of imports is that some areas were deleted from the regional models of developing countries but included in the trade matrix calculations. The 'rest-of-developing-America' was not included, e.g. in the Latin American regional model. Similar deletions in other LDC regional models were overlooked in the carrying out of this LINK exercise. Most of the error fell into the ROW category because its import trade was estimated as a simple proportion of world trade. In the latest LINK calculation, we have introduced the reduced form trade models for the ROW countries, and they seem, together with more careful accounting, to have reduced the projection errors considerably.

For the rest of the Mini-LINK estimates, the reader should note the relatively large errors for Italy and France. Hopefully, estimates for these two countries will improve in 1973 because new substantial models have been introduced in both cases. The UK and Belgian estimates are also low for 1970 by Mini-LINK, but there is no particular explanation for these faults. It should also be remembered that total non-socialist exports observed in constant dollars do not quite add to total imports. This is partly explained by the fact that the whole world is not covered and partly by data inaccuracies. On the whole, results are better for the full LINK estimates in table 30.2. The main exception is the case of Japan, where the import estimates are far too high. The same problems as in Mini-LINK exist in a diminished degree for the LDC and ROW imports.

Table 30.3 provides another look at 1970 estimates from the unpublished results reported at the LINK meeting in August 1970. These estimates have the usual problems with imports for LDC and ROW countries, but the export values are quite close. The German export and import estimates are not so bad individually, but imports are underestimated while exports are overestimated, and these amplify the error in the trade balance estimate. The French import figure is seriously underestimated, as in table 30.2.

Table 30.4 provides two estimates for 1971, one made prior to NEP by Mini-LINK only (published in the LINK volume) and the other made after NEP. The second estimate is in current prices, while the first is in constant prices. The standard deficiency in LDC imports shows up in table 30.4, together with overestimates of ROW imports by both methods. In addition, the persistent overestimation of Japanese imports shows up again for 1971. A corresponding underestimate of Japanese exports makes the trade surplus come out too low, UK imports are again underestimated. The other estimates of either exports or imports are not badly off, but some small errors on closely balanced accounts throw positive net figures into negative values and vice versa. The socialist countries (CMEA group) were introduced for the first time in 1971, and the initial set of trade projections are quite close in the aggregate.

In 1972 there are three sets of LINK forecasts to consider (table 30.5). Mini-LINK estimates were made, as usual, and the linear expenditure system method was introduced for correcting the static trade matrix calculations of exports. The other method of correcting the trade matrix through a system of equations for $\log a_{ijt}$ was also used. The LES method was reported to the annual LINK meeting in Vienna, August 1972, and the second set was reported by Moriguchi to the American Economic Association at its annual meeting in Toronto, December 1972. The LES system included some extensions that were not available to Moriguchi; nevertheless, the two sets of estimates are quite comparable.[7]

[7]The Austrian model was added to the LINK system for the first time in the LES method calculations for Vienna and were not separately in the system used by Moriguchi. Other system revisions were made for the Vienna paper as well.

Table 30.4 Trade projections, 1971 (billions of US $ FOB)

	Observed, 1963 prices		Current prices		Mini-LINK, 1963 prices		LINK, current prices	
	Imports	Exports	Imports	Exports	Imports	Exports	Imports	Exports
Belgium/Luxemburg	11.4	11.0	12.9	12.4	12.3		13.7	13.3
Canada	12.2	14.0	14.7	17.7	12.9		16.0	17.6
France	18.1	17.2	20.0	20.3	17.5		18.7	19.8
Germany	27.8	32.3	31.7	39.0	25.8		30.5	38.4
Italy	12.6	12.9	15.3	15.1	11.5		14.0	14.4
Japan	14.5	21.2	15.8	24.0	18.6		19.3	21.5
Netherlands	13.1	12.2	15.6	14.0	11.9		15.7	12.4
Sweden	5.3	6.0	6.6	7.4	5.7		6.6	8.0
UK	18.6	18.2	21.4	22.3	18.5		18.2	23.2
US	35.8	34.8	45.0	43.5	34.4		44.4	44.9
LDC	58.6	52.4	66.3	59.7	43.3		52.3	58.6
ROW	40.3	31.8	47.2	34.7	47.8		58.1	33.6
Total nonsocialist	268.4	264.1	312.5	310.2	260.1		307.6	305.7
Socialist CMEA	—	—	34.1	36.4	—		34.9	36.8
Total world trade	—	—	346.6	346.6	—		342.5	342.5

Table 30.5 Trade projections, 1972 (billions of US $ FOB)

	Observed, 1963 prices		Current prices		Mini-LINK, 1963 prices		LES system, current prices		Moriguchi system, current prices	
	Imports	Exports	Imports	Exports	Imports	Exports	Imports	Exports	Imports	Exports
Austria	4.1	3.3	5.1	3.9	—		4.5	3.4	—	—
Belgium/Luxemburg	12.7	12.8	15.6	16.1	13.6		15.4	15.3	14.9	15.6
Canada	14.4	15.9	18.0	21.0	13.6		17.3	19.9	18.0	20.5
France	21.0	20.0	25.3	26.4	19.0		23.1	21.6	23.7	23.7
Germany	16.2	34.9	37.2	46.7	29.0		36.6	45.3	38.2	44.7
Italy	14.0	14.7	18.5	18.5	12.9		15.8	16.7	17.5	17.7
Japan	15.8	22.9	18.8	28.6	19.4		21.3	26.1	20.8	27.0
Netherlands	10.4	13.4	17.6	16.8	12.3		17.9	16.0	16.4	15.2
Sweden	5.4	6.5	7.5	8.7	6.0		6.9	9.1	7.1	8.4
UK	20.0	18.1	25.0	24.4	19.1		22.4	22.8	25.5	23.9
US	31.1	38.3	54.9	49.8	35.7		54.1	50.0	55.6	49.0
LDC	—	64.9	74.1	70.2	45.2		51.7	64.2	61.4	65.8
ROW nonsocialist	—	30.0	47.6	39.3	50.8		57.0	33.7	—	—
Total nonsocialist	—	295.7	365.2	370.4	276.6		344.1	344.0	—	—
CMEA	—	—	39.1	37.6	—		42.3	42.4	—	—
Total world trade	—	—	404.3	409.8	—		386.4	386.4	—	—

LINK system experience 573

The Mini-LINK system strongly overestimates imports in both Japan and Germany. These do not lead to an overestimate of the total because there was probably a serious underestimate of LDC imports as a result of the usual classification and aggregation problems mentioned above, but LDC and ROW imports observed for 1972 have not yet been reported in constant dollars, FOB, because of time delays in preparing these figures.

For the two full-linkage estimates in current prices, the system of revision of cell coefficients of the A matrix proposed by Moriguchi appears to be slightly better; however, they have the benefit of later revision (December versus August) and are not good enough to warrant any definite conclusion at this time. The critical US balance is quite well estimated by both systems. Moriguchi's estimate of the Japanese balance is better, but his corresponding estimate for Germany is worse. The data appear to show a deficit for the CMEA countries (large Western purchases, especially grain), which is an unusual result. This swing was not anticipated in the summer of 1972.

It is too early at this time to make a full assessment of 1973 trade projections because data-reporting lags are substantial for many developing regions, the CMEA group, and some industrial countries. It is possible, however, to make some rough estimates for individual countries on the basis of partial information. On a very tentative basis, I include a table of results from the presentation to the annual LINK meeting in Stockholm in comparison with preliminary estimates for selected countries. The LINK estimates were completed in August (table 30.6). These estimates have since been updated with some improvements on the basis of newer inputs, yet these capture many aspects of 1973 properly. The small US surplus is not estimated although the deficit estimate represented a marked improvement over 1972. The dramatic restraint in US imports was missed. For Germany, LINK estimates of exports were much too low, while the Japanese surplus was lower than our predictions. The projections for Italy show the right deficit position but are too modest. The LINK figures for France appear to be low and underestimate the small trade surplus. Also the Australian export boom is underestimated by LINK in table 30.6.

The ROW nations are treated differently in LINK for the first time in 1973, using the reduced-form trade equations shown in the first section of this paper for individual countries. If we total the results for Denmark, Greece, Iceland, Ireland, Norway, Portugal, Spain, Switzerland, Turkey, Yugoslavia, New Zealand, and South Africa, we obtain the following provisional results for the 12 countries: observed imports

Table 30.6 Trade projections, 1973 (billions of US $ FOB)

	Observed, current prices		LINK, current prices	
	Imports	Exports	Imports	Exports
Australia	6.9	9.7	6.3	7.4
Austria	6.6	5.0	6.4	4.6
Belgium/Luxemburg	20.4	22.3	17.8	18.8
Canada	23.9	26.3	21.6	23.7
Finland	4.1	3.9	3.6	3.4
France	34.5	36.0	30.0	30.0
Germany	52.3	67.7	46.4	54.0
Italy	26.1	22.1	23.5	22.6
Japan	32.5	36.2	25.6	33.2
Netherlands	25.9	24.0	21.0	20.1
Sweden	9.8	12.1	8.6	9.4
UK	33.8	28.0	30.3	28.4
US	69.6	70.3	66.1	63.8
LDC	—	—	85.8	84.3
ROW	—	—	56.5	44.2
CMEA	—	—	51.1	52.9

48.6, exports 38.9; and LINK imports 47.8, exports 34.8. Although exports are underestimated, the new procedures show promise of bringing great improvement to the ROW group estimates. In later revisions, the export figure was brought even closer to the provisional observation value, leaving the import figure unchanged.

Although we do not have CMEA results yet, there has been some speculation that their trade balance may have been negative in 1973. There are two offsetting developments involved. Large imports from the West may have been a principal cause for thinking that the balance would be negative, but very large arms sales in the Middle East during the latter part of the year may have been substantial enough to reverse the figures. We must reserve judgment on this issue.

The LINK system is meant to be a trade model, but it does not deal with trade in economic isolation. It generates complete linked systems solutions for a wide variety of variables across countries. I have stressed the accuracy and interpretation of trade projections in this paper, but I might close with some figures on real output forecasts that provide the *Konjunktur* setting in which the trade values are realized (table 30.7). The most serious LINK error in table 30.7 is the underestimate for Germany. The observed data for the developing countries are highly tentative. Neither their overall accuracy nor the large overestimate for

LINK system experience

Table 30.7   Real GDP (GNP) estimates 1972

Country	Units	Observed	LINK
Austria	billion 1964 AS	336.4	332.7
Belgium	billion 1963 BF	1028.2	1010.9
Canada	billion 1961 C$	71.2	71.7
France	billion 1963 F	662.1	651.1
Germany	billion 1963 DM	418.3	396.0
Italy	trillion 1963 L	46.4	46.6
Japan	trillion 1965 ¥	65.3	66.6
Netherlands	billion 1963 Fl	88.3	87.9
Sweden	billion 1959 SK	107.4	107.4
UK	billion 1963 £	33.5	33.9
US	billion 1958 US$	789.5	788.1
Africa	billion 1960 US$	44.4	42.3
SE Asia	billion 1960 US$	128.4	132.2
Middle East	billion 1960 US$	31.3	42.2
Latin America	billion 1960 US$	136.4	138.9

the Middle East should be taken as seriously as the results for the other countries. The figures in table 30.7 are from the presentation at the LINK meeting, summer 1972.

Corresponding figures for 1973 are not yet available, but growth rates projected at Stockholm, summer 1973, can be compared with some very provisional figures for 1973 in a few cases (table 30.8). It will be some time before observed levels in different currency units can be assembled for comparison. These figures have the same provisional

Table 30.8   Real growth rate projections, 1973 (%)

	Observed	LINK
Australia	5.7	5.0
Austria	5.5	1.7
Belgium	5.7	4.3
Canada	7.1	7.0
France	6.1	4.1
Germany	5.3	4.5
Italy	5.4	6.1
Japan	10.6	9.9
Netherlands	4.7	5.3
Sweden	1.6	4.0
UK	5.4	6.8
US	5.9	6.6

status as those in table 30.6. Apart from the strange result for Austria, these are fairly good results. The Austrian result comes about partly because the model underestimated in 1972, and the base figure for computing the growth rate is the higher observed value. It would still be too low, however, even if based in the 1972 computed value. In a revised Austrian model with newer inputs, the 1973 growth rate was changed to 4.9 percent.

While these results, with the noted exception, look reasonably good as far as real growth is concerned, there was a LINK bias to underestimate inflation rates, As in the case of growth, these figures too, are provisional (table 30.9). Some of the LINK inflation rates are high, on past standards of performance or judgment. but with the exception of the US, observed rates are seriously underestimated in every major country. LINK models were not immune to the general mistake of the economics profession.

Table 30.9 Inflation rate projections, 1973 (%)

	Observed	LINK
Australia	12.5	8.4
Austria	9.1	7.3
Belgium	7.3	5.8
Canada	7.1	4.9
France	7.0	4.7
Germany	6.0	2.9
Italy	10.5	9.8
Japan	12.1	6.6
Netherlands	8.0	4.5
UK	9.0	3.7
US	5.4	5.6

CONCLUDING REMARKS

Only selected statistics on trade, real growth, and inflation have been withdrawn from the inventory of LINK system applications for this chapter. In the construction of large and complicated models in a new research area, there are necessarily many false starts, errors, and a tendency to discard many items from the build-up of working information. Many LINK model builders have found it virtually impossible to recover their sample data from a few years back because outdated series were discarded as revisions became available. Similarly, it is difficult to recover all the old trial forecasts from the earliest experimental stages of the project. We have concentrated on getting usable programs, a working system, and a more comprehensive system. In this concentration, I have buried in research files many older results; therefore only a sampling is given here. From this point onward, more convenient summary tables are being prepared, and it will be possible to maintain better records for future study. Thousands of variables are generated in each simulation, and it is a problem to decide which to concentrate attention on, Also, during the course of a year's projection round, the system is simulated almost every month with slight changes and fresh inputs. I have tried to emphasize those particular simulations that were presented publicly or in annual LINK meetings. The tabular presentations in this paper emphasized extrapolation accuracy of LINK, but this is only one aspect of the experience gained during the 5-year history of the project.

There are many interesting issues about data preparation, data reliability, data inconsistency, system specification, and policy application. The exciting events associated with currency crises of 1971-3 naturally tempted us to try to study implications in the light of the LINK system, and this brought us directly into the rough arena of forecasting. Many of the component LINK models are regularly used for national economic forecasting; so it is not unusual to try to use them all together in international forecasting. The contemporary energy crisis provided another instance of immediate LINK application to forecasting.

Forecast validation is important in establishing credibility in a model, and credibility is essential for usefulness in other important directions, namely, studies of the international transmission mechanism and policy analysis. LINK has been used to estimate some international multipliers, to study effects of alternative national policies, and to simulate various exchange rate configurations.

It is possible that errors involved in comparing alternative simulations are smaller than forecast errors. This would suggest using the system apart from its forecast reliability. But the forecast analysis must go forward, and the more accurate they become, the more faith users can have in the policy simulations.

Considering the errors and surprises in recent analysis of the world economy, I do not believe that the numerical performance record of LINK, as detailed above, is bad. It provides useful additional information, in my opinion, but it also indicates that we have a long way to go. The problems are incredibly difficult, so I am pleased to pick up even tiny increments in information. LINK forecasts have not been misleading on the main effects of the currency realignments and have pointed out trouble spots in the world economy – the failure of the US balance to improve during 1972, serious deterioration of the UK balance in 1973 (and afterwards), the build-up of a massive surplus in the Middle East, and others of lesser moment. The system was quick to foresee a possible world recession and slow growth of trade as a result of simultaneous anti-inflation policies in 1973 and the pending US slowdown. In the latest energy crisis simulations, when additional shocks are imposed on a world economy that was already slowing down, LINK projects a deepening recessionary movement, and a year or two later a proper post-mortem of this forecast can be made.

REFERENCES

P. Armington, 'A many-country model of equilibrating adjustments in prices and spending.' Appendix in: R.R. Rhomberg, 'Possible approaches to a model of world trade and payments,' *IMF Staff Papers*, March (1970).

R.J. Ball, (Ed.) *International Linkage of National Economic Models*, North-Holland, Amsterdam (1973).

B.G. Hickman, 'Prices and quantities in a world trade system,' LINK working paper No. 1, (1972).

B.G. Hickman, and L. Lau, 'Elasticities of substitution and export demands in a world trade model,' LINK working paper No. 4, *European Economic Review*, 4 (1973), 347–80.

H. Junz and R. Rhomberg, 'Price competitiveness in export trade among industrial countries,' *American Economic Review, Papers and Proceedings*, LXIII, May (1963), 412–18.

C. Moriguchi, 'International linkage of econometric models and its application for measuring the effect of the 1971 currency realignments,' *American Economic Review, Papers and Proceedings*, LXIII, May (1973).

Index

accelerator coefficient, 299
aggregate income, 5
aggregation
  problems of, 204
  and rational behavior, 205
  theory of, 205
anti-inflationary policy, 550
a priori information, 19, 27, 63, 84,
  152, 153, 155, 318, 327, 396, 406,
  408, 409, 412, 425, 428, 515
a priori restrictions, 45, 46, 49
a priori selection, 30
ARIMA, 153
autocorrelation, 327
  in residuals, 330–1, 333, 335, 407
autonomous relationship, 155
autoregressive model, 125, 412, 419,
  420
  sample period mean square error
    of, 422

business cycle, 4, 10, 11, 32, 103, 107,
  110, 111, 126, 130, 132, 142, 145,
  150, 179, 320, 324, 342, 400, 402,
  403, 461, 463, 482, 485, 488
  classical, 126
  inventory, 126
  long, 126
  maintained, 142
  theory, 180

capacity output, 347
  full, 341
  long-run, 364
  short-run, 364
capacity peak points, full, 342
capacity utilization, 4, 20, 342, 343,
  379, 468, 472, 484, 485

economy wide index of, 340
filter index of, 473, 483, 484
rate of, 339
Wharton School index of, 339, 340,
  344, 348, 350, 352, 359, 362, 472,
  474, 484, 485
capital, organic composition of, 221,
  222, 233
capital–labor ratio, 301, 470
capital–output ratio, 293, 301
cash balance equation, 322
CES production function, 18, 364,
  374, 376, 380, 386, 388, 389, 390,
  391, 559
  maximum likelihood estimator of,
    378
  two step estimation of, 375, 390,
    391
characteristic vector, 86
circulation, velocity of, 206, 299
classical model, 206, 208, 212
Cobb–Douglas
  law, 363
  production function, 12, 371, 372,
    380, 389, 474, 475
  utility function, 15
cobweb theorem, 28
conservation, law of, 557
cost function, 468
consumer behavior, 184
consumption function, 502, 518, 520,
  522, 523, 532, 535
  logistic, 503
control solution, 133
cost minimization, 347, 370, 387, 389,
  391, 392
cost of living index, 274, 275, 279,
  319

Cowles Commission, 7, 8, 9, 11, 12, 13, 14, 15, 16, 17
cross spectral matrix, 106, 107, 108, 138
cross spectrum analysis, 103, 147
currency realignment, 578

demand management policy, 494
demand model, 548
determinantal equation, 86
distributed lags, 10, 72, 93, 156
 and autocorrelated disturbances, 59
 and investment behavior, 9
 general, 156
 geometric, 156, 166, 168, 169
 rational, 156, 160
disturbed solution, 133
Divisia index, 182, 188, 276
dollar devaluation, 544

econometric model
 linear stochastic, 123
 nonlinear, 123
effective demand, principle of, 230, 232, 541
elasticity of substitution, 385, 387, 390, 391, 392
 of capital and labor, 477
employment
 full, 478, 494
 total, 473
energy crisis, 542, 548, 550, 552
energy supply, 551
Engel curves, 274
envelope aggregation, 3
estimation efficiency, 19, 45
Euclidian norm, 86
Euler's equation, 283, 372, 373
ex ante forecast error, 19

fiscal policies, 552
flow analysis, 239
flow equilibrium, 244
flow of fund system, 404, 441, 442
forecast
 error of, 252, 412, 451
 ex ante, 402, 403, 418, 426, 430, 568
 ex post, 418
 mean square error of one quarter, 419
 multiperiod comparison, 423
 standard error of, 407
 of turning points, 423, 431
 validation, 577
 variance of, 49, 252
forecasting, 40, 146
Fourier transform, 107, 121
frequency domain, 106, 127
frequency response function, 106
frequency response matrix, 104, 107
full information maximum likelihood, 2, 7, 50, 91, 93, 152
functional dependence, theory of, 184, 186
functional matrix, 188

Gauss–Seidel algorithm, 143, 144
general analysis, 40
generalized least squares, 58, 59
gradient methods, 377

Hotelling forecast variance formula, 259

identification problem, 2, 5, 6, 7
 exact, 45, 96
 over, 45, 97
implied system relationship, 460
import multiplier, 543
impulse response function, 107
indirect least squares, 428
inflation
 cost, 318, 319, 320, 321, 322, 325, 327, 335, 336
 demand, 318, 319, 321, 322, 325, 327, 335, 336
input–output
 analysis of, 280, 287, 399, 491, 545, 558
 coefficients, 280, 281, 282, 285
 system, 3, 15, 404, 492, 542, 545, 546
 tables, 280, 281, 282, 284, 287
instrumental variable estimator, 7, 8, 95, 97, 98, 152, 429
integrability conditions, 276, 277

Index

interest rate
  determination, 322
  liquidity preference theory of, 239, 242, 243
  loanable funds theory of, 239
inventory function, 532
investment, 25
  behavior, 54
  function, 6, 30, 31, 32, 504, 532

Kaldor model, 507, 509
k-class estimators, 7
Keynesian model, 5, 13, 14, 19, 206, 208, 209, 216, 220, 234, 460, 487, 491, 514, 522, 541, 542
  comparison to Marxian model, 231
Keynesian multiplier, 552
Koyck's distributed lag, 54, 63

labor
  average productivity of, 473
  force, 469, 473
  share, 295, 299, 311, 324
  supply equation, 344, 345
lag structure, 427
Lagrange multiplier, 66
Laspeyres index, 274
Le Chatelier principle, 2, 8, 50
Leontief model, 491
likelihood function, 8, 65
  joint, 151
limited information maximum
  likelihood, 2, 7, 40, 50, 51, 66, 79, 80, 84, 85, 86, 89, 91, 93, 95, 96, 101, 325, 328, 333, 334
linear expenditure system, 3, 14, 15, 559, 570
linear system
  dynamic, 127
  stochastic, 127
  stochastic, dynamic, 497
LINK, 4, 21, 406, 549, 550, 554, 558, 562, 563, 574, 576
  mini, 568, 569, 570, 573
  projections, 561, 570
liquidity preference, 19, 214, 462

macroeconometric
  analysis, 399
  model, 402, 404, 405, 408

macroeconomic
  targets, 404
  welfare function, 404
macroeconomics, 180, 195
marginal productivity
  aggregate, 179
  pricing, 400
marginal propensity
  to consume, 3, 42, 43, 45, 227, 236, 518, 529
  and social security program, 247
  to invest, 227
markup, 324, 325, 333, 334, 336
Marxian model, 206, 219, 220, 222, 224, 226, 230, 233, 234, 235
  comparison to Keynesian model, 231
maximum likelihood estimator, 40, 44, 55, 58, 59, 66, 156, 325
microeconomics, 180
model specification, 19
monetary instruments, 439
money illusion, 319
money–income relationship, 460
moving averages, 11
  infinitely iterated ... of random series, 115, 132
  representation, 105
multicollinearity, 2, 10, 69, 71, 72, 74, 75, 80, 81, 82, 84, 85, 91, 93
multiple correlation coefficient, 74
multiplier, 42, 43, 133, 144, 145
  dynamic, 103, 138, 144, 145
  fiscal, 146
  impact, 103
  international, 577
  Lagrange, 66
  monetary policy, 146
  process, 542
  response, 11

National Bureau of Economic
  Research, 11
national income accounting, 404, 441, 545
net regression, 27
Newton–Raphson method, 143
nonlinear estimation, 399, 406
  simultaneous, 372
nonlinear system, 402, 406, 413
  dynamic, 127, 501
  stochastic, 127

observation errors, 19
oil
  consumption, 551
  crisis, 544
  embargo, 550
  imports, 543
Open Market Committee, 453
ordinary least squares, 79, 80, 81, 82, 85, 88, 152
output, potential, 469, 470
overidentification, 45, 97

Paasche index, 274
partial analysis, 40
participation rate, 313
Parzen window, 111, 113, 118
periodogram, 402
permanent income hypothesis, 403
Phillips curve, 17, 151, 154, 457
Pigou's hypothesis, 213
power spectra, 106, 107, 110
  average, 111
price formation equation, 532
principal components, 93, 152, 429
production function, 183, 184, 417
  aggregate, 180, 184, 188, 189, 190, 195, 202, 365, 380, 387, 388, 391, 468, 469, 490, 543, 545
  and technological change, 378
  CES, see CES production function
  Cobb–Douglas, see Cobb–Douglas production function
  KLEM, 490
  stationary state of, 484
productivity, 323
  of labor, 494
  marginal, 324, 380
profit
  maximization, 347
  theory of falling rate of, 229, 233
projection operator, 80, 86

quantity theory, 460, 461, 462

railroad traffic, 284
RAS adjustment, 559, 560
ratchet variable, 320
rational expectations, 456
real balance effects, 460
recursive systems, 482

reduced form, 7
  parameters, 40, 43
  least-squares estimation of, 46
  unrestricted least-squares estimation of, 47
  variance-covariance matrix of, 49
  relations, 534
repeated estimation, 413
returns to scale, 385, 386, 388, 390, 391
  constant, 372, 387
reversible relations, 26

sample experimentation, 427
sample pooling, 407
satellite systems, 495
savings function, 6, 30, 31
  aggregate, 522
savings–income ratio, 290, 299
seasonal components, 327
  linear additive, 322
simulations
  analytic, 104, 110, 118, 120, 121
  dynamic, 482
  nonstochastic, 504
  static, 482
  stochastic, 103, 110, 116, 118, 120, 121, 133, 134
single equation
  bias, 385
  estimator, 7, 91, 325
sinusoidal limit theorem, 115, 116, 132
Slutsky equation, 182, 276, 277
small sample distribution, 407
Smithsonian devaluation, 563
social security program, and marginal propensity to consume, 247
spectrum
  analysis, 103, 116, 125, 136, 399, 402
  average, 137
  densities, 111, 125
  estimator, 118, 120
  matrix, 105, 106, 131, 138
stability conditions, 130
stabilization policy, theory of, 1
stagnation theory, 220
state vector, 157

Index

stochastic
  cycle, 506
  difference equation, 498
stock
  analysis, 239
  equilibrium, 244
structural
  change, 130
  models, 2, 416, 419, 420, 421, 422, 423, 427, 428
    sample period mean square error of, 422
  parameters, 40
    efficiency properties of least squares estimates of, 45
    maximum likelihood estimates of, 41
  policy model, 412
  relations, 27, 154, 317, 335
  shift, 417, 425
  system, 49
structural behavioral equation, 460, 534
supply
  constraints, 542, 549
  function
    aggregate, 346
  side, 270, 487, 547, 549
  policies, 493, 494
surplus value, rate of, 221, 233

technological change
  disembodied, neutral, 387
  embodied, 393
  neutral, 390, 393
  temporal stability, 424
  term structure, 439, 441

time
  domain, 127
  series, 11
    cross section pooling, 408
trade matrix, 550, 560
trade unions, 320
transfer matrix, 131
transition matrix, 157
trend through peaks technique, 477, 478, 481, 484
two-stage least squares, 2, 7, 77, 79, 80, 81, 82, 85, 86, 88, 89, 91, 93, 152, 334, 398, 428

unemployment, 319, 324
  moving average of, 328
  rate, 472, 473
utility theory, 8

variable parameter models, 19
vector autoregressive model, 2
velocity
  of circulation, 461
Von Neumann–Hart statistic, 380, 384

wage
  bargaining, 320, 321, 329
    institutional aspects of, 329
  drift, 331, 332, 336
  rate equation, 320
Walrasian system, 287
Wharton Model, 17, 104, 107, 108, 110, 111, 113, 114, 118, 120, 123, 126, 138, 140, 141, 153, 430, 433, 452, 463, 482, 484, 492, 546, 548